INTERNATIONAL MOBILITY AND MOVEMENT OF CAPITAL

NATIONAL BUREAU OF ECONOMIC RESEARCH

UNIVERSITIES—NATIONAL BUREAU CONFERENCE SERIES

1. Problems in the Study of Economic Growth (in mimeograph)
2. Conference on Business Cycles
3. Conference on Research in Business Finance
4. Regularization of Business Investment
5. Business Concentration and Price Policy
6. Capital Formation and Economic Growth
7. Policies to Combat Depression
8. The Measurement and Behavior of Unemployment
9. Problems in International Economics
10. The Quality and Economic Significance of Anticipations Data
11. Demographic and Economic Change in Developed Countries
12. Public Finances: Needs, Sources, and Utilization
13. The Rate and Direction of Inventive Activity: Economic and Social Factors
14. Aspects of Labor Economics
15. Investment in Human Beings
16. The State of Monetary Economics
17. Transportation Economics
18. Determinants of Investment Behavior
19. National Economic Planning
20. Issues in Defense Economics
21. The Role of Agriculture in Economic Development
22. The Technology Factor in International Trade
23. The Analysis of Public Output
24. International Mobility and Movement of Capital

INTERNATIONAL MOBILITY AND MOVEMENT OF CAPITAL

EDITED BY

FRITZ MACHLUP
WALTER S. SALANT
LORIE TARSHIS

A Conference of the Universities – National Bureau
Committee for Economic Research

NATIONAL BUREAU OF ECONOMIC RESEARCH

New York 1972

Distributed by
Columbia University Press
New York and London

RELATION OF THE NATIONAL BUREAU DIRECTORS TO
PUBLICATIONS REPORTING CONFERENCE PROCEEDINGS

Since the present volume is a record of conference proceedings,
it has been exempted from the rules governing submission of
manuscripts to, and critical review by, the Board of Directors
of the National Bureau.

*(Resolution adopted July 6, 1948,
as revised November 21, 1949,
and April 20, 1968)*

Funds for the economic research conference program of the National Bureau of Economic Research are supplied by the National Science Foundation.

CONTENTS

INTRODUCTION

FRITZ MACHLUP   Princeton University and
New York University

THIS volume collects all papers and comments that were prepared for the conference on "International Mobility and Movement of Capital." The conference was held in the auditorium of the Brookings Institution in Washington, D.C., on January 30 and 31, and February 1, 1970. It was sponsored by the Universities—National Bureau Committee of Economic Research. The exploratory committee, as well as the program committee for the conference, consisted of Richard N. Cooper, Yale University, Ilse Mintz, National Bureau of Economic Research, Walter S. Salant, Brookings Institution, David W. Slater, Queen's University (Canada), and Fritz Machlup, Princeton University (Chairman). The task of editing this volume was shared by Fritz Machlup, Walter Salant, and Lorie Tarshis of Stanford University. The volume was prepared for the printer by Ruth Ridler of the National Bureau of Economic Research. H. Irving Forman, also of the Bureau, made the charts.

MOBILITY AND MOVEMENT

IN CHOOSING the title for the conference and for this volume, the committee deliberately included both "mobility" and "movement" of capital in order to stress the difference between the two. For there may be great mobility without any movement—when there is no inducement to movement. And there may be much movement despite little mobility —when the stimuli are very strong. Thus, measurements of actual movement without measurements, or estimates, of all relevant stimuli tell us nothing about mobility.

It is possible to treat certain obstacles to movement, that is, certain factors reducing the mobility of capital, as negative stimuli. For example, the cost of transactions may well be included as a variable in an equation that is designed to explain movements of capital as a func-

1

tion of variables expressing various incentives and disincentives. Negative signs would then differentiate the factors that have reduced movement from those that have increased it, provided we can find acceptable statistical proxies for all theoretical variables. This, however, is unlikely. It is especially unlikely with respect to some of the factors which we know impede the movement of capital but which cannot be quantified. Moreover, as will be shown later, a deliberately imposed restriction may at times actually increase capital movements instead of reducing them. The positive sign in the numerically estimated equation would then characterize as a stimulus what the government intended as an obstacle. It would not be helpful to present an inefficient, perversely working restriction as an encouragement of capital movements just because the figures and, perhaps, also the facts in a particular situation at certain times and places resulted in a positive instead of a negative sign.

Even the briefest conceptual reflection about the meanings of mobility and immobility makes us realize that several of the theoretically relevant variables resist statistical treatment or even casual empirical observation. We may attempt to distinguish several types of causes of immobility: ignorance, vague or specific fears, general reluctance, prohibitions and other impediments imposed by government, and real costs of services required for transactions. Some of these distinctions may be rejected as not being backed by genuine differences. For example, both ignorance about existing opportunities (of obtaining attractive yields) and fears about particular risks may be the consequence of an absence of reliable information, as well as of great uncertainty regarding particular kinds of information; or reluctance concerning lending and investing abroad may be caused by the kind of information available, as well as by attitudes created by public pronouncements; and transactions costs may partially reflect the need for overcoming artificial institutional impediments and partly the need for making use of technologically required services. Still, the proposed distinctions are suggestive of a variety of causes of immobility. Some of these causes change over time. The availability of good information sometimes changes quite abruptly, as do some kinds of fear created by hints or rumors. Prohibitions, controls, and other restrictions imposed by governments are, of course, subject to sudden change, either through new laws and decrees, or through altered administrative procedures.

We may note that the causes of limited mobility may be either environmental or psychological in origin. Environmental causes may be institutional (such as governmental controls and private cartel arrangements) or technological (such as indispensable inputs of services like banking and communication). Psychological causes may relate to expectations (say, concerning risks and uncertainty) or to tastes and preferences (like aversion to risk, dislike of uncertainty, propensity to gamble). It is possible, without undue strain, to fit the theory of limited mobility into the Walrasian frame of *les goûts* (tastes) and *les obstacles* (costs). It is especially the role of tastes in the theory of mobility that accounts for the fact that we cannot hope for a complete econometric model where all variables must allow operational definition and quantitative analysis. We recall Frank Knight's remark that "we cannot measure, but we measure anyhow"; it means that we should be aware of a fact of life — whatever we measure is never quite the thing that represents, or closely corresponds to, the theoretical concept of our theories.

If mobility means sensitivity to stimuli, one has to realize that responses to different stimuli may be very different: how are they to be weighted in an evaluation of "sensitivity"? If several types of stimuli are selected — say, interest differentials, expectation of currency appreciation, and so on — one has to bear in mind that capitalists in different countries may react with different alertness and alacrity; in country i they may be more sensitive than elsewhere to stimulus j but less sensitive to stimulus k. If mobility is explained in part by an absence of impediments, one should not forget that the same objectively defined obstacles may impede capitalists in different countries in different degrees. If mobility is measured by elasticities — by the ratio of relative changes in quantities to relative changes in some "price term" (such as a rate of interest or a rate of return) — the question is whether the quantity of capital moved from, or to, a country should also be related to the stock of capital accumulated, the stock of liquid funds held, the flows of gross or net saving generated per year, or to other magnitudes considered relevant in the context.

Little of this sort is discussed in the papers collected in this volume. This is somewhat disappointing to me, because it indicates that too often researchers do not question the meanings of the terms with which they work; they are diving into piles of third-rate statistical data which they believe, or assume, to be suitable proxies for the vague or ambiguous theoretical concepts with which their supposedly first-rate models are furnished. This grumble of mine is meant not as a criticism of the papers collected in this volume, but rather of the scientific attitude of a generation of economists contemptuous of "philosophical" reflection and impatient to get on with the business of measuring.

RESTRICTIONS IMPOSED BY GOVERNMENT

OF THE papers collected in this volume, a large proportion deal explicitly with limitations which governments have imposed on international mobility of capital. One paper does so in a largely historical and institutional mode (Gillespie), others attempt to obtain quantitative impressions, or even econometric estimates, of the effectiveness of government restrictions (Branson and Willett, Stevens, Severn, Prachowny), again others express doubts about the econometric techniques employed and the results obtained (Leamer and Stern, Bryant and Hendershott), and one paper offers a comparison of the social costs of restrictions on capital movements with the costs of restrictions on trade and on monetary and fiscal expansion (Cohen). The references are to different countries: United Kingdom (Cohen, Gillespie), France and Germany (Gillespie), the members of the European Economic Community (Hawkins), Japan (Bryant and Hendershott), and the United States (Branson and Willett, Stevens, Severn, Prachowny). The governmental restrictions in question are on short-term lending (Bryant and Hendershott, Branson and Willett) and on direct investment (Stevens, Severn, Prachowny).

Some of the econometric estimates of the effectiveness of controls are surprising, at least to those expecting that restrictions would restrict. Yet, one paper reports that estimates of short-term movements which ignored the existence of controls were not much different from estimates which explicitly took account of the controls (Bryant and

Hendershott); and another reports that the impact of the restraint program on bank lending which the United States instituted in 1965 did not show up strongly in the estimates, although the restraints "probably reduced the sensitivity of short-term capital to changes in interest rates" (Branson and Willett). As to the voluntary and mandatory restraints upon direct foreign investment by American corporations, one study finds no effects (Stevens); another, using in its model a dummy variable for the restraint program, obtains a positive sign for its influence, indicating that the controls resulted in larger, not smaller, direct investments abroad (Severn); and a third finds direct investment increased in some years but reduced in other years as an effect of the governmental restraints (Prachowny). The last cited explains its result by larger anticipatory investments, that is, investments above currently desired magnitudes, undertaken to beat the controls that would in later years hinder American corporations in transferring funds abroad when they might really want to do so.

INTERNATIONALIZATION OF CAPITAL MARKETS

THAT certain impediments to the international mobility of capital have in recent years been weakened or offset is implied by the "increasing internationalization of capital markets, especially the development of the Eurodollar market." This quotation comes not from the papers in this volume but from the Annual Report of the Council of Economic Advisers, who go on to say that the "increasing mobility of capital is a reflection of the growing flexibility and responsiveness of capital markets. . . ." (See *Economic Report of the President*, 1971, p. 143.)

This assertion probably conforms to the facts, and readers of the papers in this volume may find support for it in some of the attempts at measurement. Unfortunately, no study included in this volume treats of the effects the Eurodollar market and the Eurobond market have on international mobility and movements of capital. There is a natural time lag of economic analysis behind new economic developments, which explains the absence of scholarly investigations of money markets and capital markets in Eurocurrencies. Although the program committee for the conference had some forty papers to choose from, none was offered on this increasingly important phenomenon, perhaps because the call for papers was issued in the summer of 1968, when these markets were of far less importance, and the responses to that call were presumably dominated by topics that the respondents had chosen to work on even earlier.

CAPITAL MOVEMENTS AND BALANCE OF PAYMENTS

MUCH economic discussion in recent years has dealt with the effects of capital flows upon the balance of payments; with the possibility and desirability of trade flows adjusting themselves promptly to changes in capital flows; and with attempts to prevent or obviate such adjustments by influencing the direction and size of capital movements in such a way as to have them match the existing balance of transactions on current account. Relatively little of that discussion appears in this volume — not because of any shortage of supply of papers, but because of a deliberate choice by the program committee.

The primary concern of the program committee was to explain international movements of capital and their changes; that is, to find what causes them, or influences them, not to analyze their consequences. Thus only a few papers in this volume address themselves to the question of the effects of changes in capital movements upon the current account and upon net monetary movements; and even these few do so only collaterally. Two papers have titles that may give the impression that they deal chiefly with the problems arising for the balance of payments from the change or state of the capital balance (Howle, Prachowny). In fact, however, these papers are cast differently and the approaches employed are not those of the usual discourses on the international adjustment problem.

Two other papers come within the compass of balance-of-payments problems, but they do not interpret the enduring deficits of the United States as a failure of the adjustment process to work or of adjustment policies to be adopted. One of these papers interprets the supposed imbalance as a failure to understand that the statistical "deficits" (or some part of the deficits) may represent "equilibrium" in a world in which the United States provides financial intermediation for other countries (Laffer). The other critically examines the arguments presented to refute this hypothesis and finds them deficient or inconclusive (Salant).

ASSEMBLAGE WITHOUT VISIBLE ORGANIZATION

FROM what has been said thus far, one would think that the papers collected in this volume fall into recognizable groups which can be arranged under various headings. Yet, the Table of Contents shows no division of themes into separate parts, and readers may well complain about being offered an unstructured assemblage of papers, strung together without any attempt at organization according to some inherent order or systematic arrangement.

Let me say that we intended to present a well-structured collection of papers and have worked hard to find a system of headings under which the papers could be grouped. Our first plan was to divide the volume into four parts: I. Recent Developments in Capital Markets. II. Mobility and Movements of Capital: Theoretical Studies. III. International Capital Flows: Empirical Studies. IV. Policy Implications. This organization proved unworkable. Several months before the conference, when the contributors were shown in which group their papers would be placed, many of them argued that they regarded their product as belonging in some other group.

In a second attempt to group the papers, I proposed the following four headings:

Part I. Historical-Institutional. The major emphasis is on observed changes in capital markets of particular countries or groups of countries.

Part II. Analytical-Theoretical. The major emphasis is on recent developments in the theory of mobility and movements of capital, especially new or controversial hypotheses.

Part III. Numerical-Empirical. The major emphasis is on the use of numerical data in testing or illustrating particular hypotheses concerning mobility and movements of capital.

Part IV. Pragmatic-Instrumental. The major emphasis is on policy implications concerning mobility and movements of capital.

These headings did not, however, provide any better way of arranging the papers than the previous ones had. Alternative groupings — for example, according to the type of capital movement investigated or according to the major variables chosen to explain them — struck me as too artificial, and I finally decided against building Procrustean beds into which the contributions to the conference might be forced. The sequence in which the papers are presented and their arrangement in pairs for comments by discussants should give enough order to the contents of this volume. Incidentally, the assignment of papers to commentators on the basis of titles before the actual contents were known became a constraint in rearranging the order in which the material is presented in this volume.

There was a good reason for departing from the more usual pattern of assigning only one commentator to each paper. By selecting two commentators we hoped to reduce the risk that a contributor might find his paper appraised by a particularly unsympathetic critic who failed to understand the contribution and did it injustice. On the other hand, to have two comments for each paper would have required 34 commentators had we not assigned two papers to each pair of commentators. The total number of commentators is thus still equal to the number of papers, though there are two comments on each paper. If both of them contain severe criticisms, it is quite likely that the paper truly deserves them. Moreover, joint comments on two papers afford the commentator an opportunity of comparing methods and findings of two different inquiries into related subjects.

ABSTRACTS OF THE PAPERS

THE reader of this volume may find it helpful to have brief abstracts of all 17 papers. Needless to say, abstracts are not supposed to be substitutes for the papers themselves, but they may guide the reader much better than the mere titles could to the papers in which he is especially interested. In the preparation of these abstracts I had the help of the contributors. I wish to thank them for their cooperation and to ask their forgiveness for my making abstracts of the abstracts that they provided. It should go without saying that these sketches cannot attempt to tell what will be found in the papers; only a small fraction of their contents can be alluded to.

Benjamin J. Cohen. "The United Kingdom as an Exporter of Capital."

Britain, once the most important international investor and originator of investible funds, has become an international investment banker, a middleman of funds. When Britain for several years refused to treat the imbalance in its foreign accounts with adjustment of the exchange rate, it chose to treat it by restrictions on capital movement in preference to restrictions on trade or to retrenchments of domestic expenditures. This choice was less costly than unemployment or trade restrictions would have been.

Robert G. Hawkins. "Intra-EEC Capital Movements and Domestic Financial Markets."

It is conceivable that the proposed European monetary coordination, together with the continuing integration of commodity markets and labor markets, will eventually provide for more mobility of capital among member countries of the European Community than between these and other countries. The experience of recent years, however, has been otherwise. Capital movements among EEC countries were not becoming more important than between these countries and the rest of the world, and there was no strong tendency for interest differentials to become narrower within the EEC than between these and other countries. Integrating forces within the Community seem to have been less significant than the internationalization of capital markets by facilities such as the Eurodollar system and Eurobond markets.

John E. Floyd. "Portfolio Equilibrium and the Theory of Capital Movements."

A general-equilibrium model of a small, fully employed economy in a large trading world is constructed. In the model, international movements of capital tend to bring about portfolio balance by stock adjustments, as well as by changes in the national ownership of the continuous additions to the stock of capital through time. A small country maintaining a fixed exchange rate for its currency has little control over its internal price level. An increase in the domestic stock of money will result, not in a proportional rise in the price level, but in a portfolio disequilibrium that is resolved by purchases of assets abroad. Where the exchange rate is flexible, the resulting reduction first in the external, and then in the internal, value of the currency will reverse all of the once-for-all and steady state effects of the increase in the nominal money stock, driving the real money stock back to its initial level.

Edward S. Howle. "Capital Mobility and Payments Equilibrium."
Perfect mobility of capital makes the specie-flow mechanism inoperative. In the long run, a region can grow or inflate no faster than is warranted by the world's demand for the region's goods. This "demand constraint" (rather than a "liquidity constraint") tends to produce a dynamic payments equilibrium in which the region's imbalance of payments and foreign indebtedness grow at the same rate as its capacity to produce. The analysis attempts, among other things, to explore the nature of the ultimate limits of fiscal policy that are imposed by fixed exchange rates.

Edward E. Leamer and Robert M. Stern. "Problems in the Theory and Empirical Estimation of International Capital Movements."
A distinction is made between models using type of activity and those using type of transactor to classify influences explaining capital movements. Portfolio-adjustment theory uses transactor models not relevant to transactors of all kinds of transactions. In the choice of explanatory variables, most models of capital movements use an "activities framework." The choice and measurement of appropriate variables for wealth, yields, and trade finance are particularly problematic. While a portfolio approach is appropriate for decisions on portfolio investment, it is not suitable for decisions on direct investment. Foremost among the problems of empirical estimation is the choice of representative information on expected returns and risks,

on speculation, capital controls, and credit rationing, but there are also purely statistical matters regarding disaggregation, lag structures, and simultaneity. Empirical work is likely to be more effective when meaningful alternative hypotheses are more carefully constructed.

Ralph C. Bryant and Patric H. Hendershott. "Empirical Analysis of Capital Flows: Some Consequences of Alternative Specifications."

Useful empirical knowledge of the behavior relationships determining capital flows cannot be acquired rapidly and at small cost. Needed are a judicious selection of the particular flows to be studied, well thought-out theoretical specifications appropriate in the particular circumstances, and careful collection of reliable and relevant data. The researcher is frequently unable to discriminate clearly, in purely statistical terms, among alternative imperfect specifications; he can easily find specifications that will give a good statistical fit. Much more reliable criteria of success are needed than the customary tests of statistical significance. One well-researched relationship based on prior development of a sound theoretical framework, and on careful matching of empirical counterparts to theoretical constructs, will usually prove more useful and interesting than scores of equations with good fits but weak theoretical underpinnings.

Norman C. Miller and Marina v. N. Whitman. "The Outflow of Short-Term Funds from the United States: Adjustments of Stocks and Flows."

A model for the explanation of movements of short-term funds is constructed with both a supply function of foreign I.O.U.'s to American lenders and a demand function for foreign I.O.U.'s by American lenders. Both these functions are based on postulated optimization by debtors and creditors who take account of interest rates and risk conditions. This theory is tested against quarterly data on flows of American capital from 1959 through 1967. The flows are interpreted as the result of stock adjustment—as Americans alter the proportion of foreign assets in their portfolios; and of flow adjustment—as investors increase the size of their portfolios through new saving. The desired proportions are estimated first and then used for the separation of the two components of the movement of funds. Deviations of the

GNP of the United States from its time trend were used as a proxy for risk conditions. These deviations, together with levels of domestic and foreign interest rates, emerge as the essential influences on flows of capital. Government policy affecting these two variables is quickly reflected in the total flow of capital, but chiefly by way of stock adjustments and only very little by adjustments of the permanent flow.

William H. Branson and Thomas D. Willett. "Policy Toward Short-Term Capital Movements: Some Implications of the Portfolio Approach."

Interest rates and trade flows show up as the most significant variables explaining changes in the flow of short-term funds. If interest rates rise abroad, there will be a one-time outflow of funds due to a stock switch, which will be followed by a rise in the continuing outflow as portfolios grow in size. The ratio of the effect on the continuing flow to the initial effect on the stock tends to be equal to the growth rate of the total portfolio. The increase in interest income earned abroad — because the rates are higher and because more foreign assets were acquired in the stock switch — may offset, or more than offset, the continuing-flow effect. As a result, if we look at the effects on capital and income accounts together, we may find net financial inflows, rather than outflows, after the stock switch is completed. An illustrative estimation of the flows of American short-term funds shows their sensitivity to changes in interest rates, which was slightly reduced by the restraint program imposed by the government. The role of stock-adjustment implies that a crawling peg for exchange rates need not constrain national interest-rate policies as much as it appears to do when that role is not considered. Flows of short-term funds induced by expectations of a crawl will be only temporary and easily handled by official financing; the funds that move in the stock switch will return when the exchange rate reaches its new equilibrium level.

Guy V. G. Stevens. "Capital Mobility and the International Firm."

The capital movements resulting from the decision of firms to make direct investments abroad, and their choice of whether to finance these expenditures at home or abroad, are depicted in a model that includes among its variables the firms' expenditures for plant and equipment, the changes in their current assets abroad, the profits from their foreign activities, and the repatriation of foreign dividends. Previous studies have not yielded econometrically defensible estimates concerning the effectiveness of the restraint program of the United States; the firms may have borrowed more abroad but they did not reduce direct investments. There is a distinct possibility that financial flows are indeterminate if the conditions for the Miller-Modigliani theorems hold.

Alan K. Severn. "Investment and Financial Behavior of American Direct Investors in Manufacturing."

The firms' decisions to invest abroad and to raise funds abroad are interrelated with their domestic activities. Net outflows of funds (net of repatriated profits) are expected to be positively related to their domestic incomes and foreign investment, and negatively to their foreign income, domestic investment, and payments of dividends. Simulation indicates that macroeconomic policies can have only small net effects on the balance of payments through their influence upon direct investment: the effect of changes in the outlays of firms for domestic investment and dividend payments is offset by the opposite effect of changes in their domestic incomes. The results suggest that foreign and domestic investment are interrelated primarily through financing mechanisms, chiefly the firms' decisions to allocate their internally generated funds in optimal ways.

Robert W. Gillespie. "The Policies of England, France, and Germany as Recipients of Foreign Direct Investment."

Since the end of World War II, the three major West European countries have followed different policies with regard to direct investment and take-overs by foreign firms. Their policy actions, however, have often been inconsistent with their official statements of the reasons for their policies. The announced objectives have stressed the state of the balance of payments, the implementation of economic planning, the existence of a technology gap, and various political considerations. Economic nationalism was obviously a dominant element in the direct restrictions imposed in France. To some extent this holds also for the United Kingdom, where, however, an effort to change the structure of domestic industry was at the bottom of the defenses against foreign take-overs. This seems to apply as well to the policies now being formulated by the European Economic Community.

Martin F. J. Prachowny. "Direct Investment and the Balance of Payments of the United States: A Portfolio Approach."

Demand equations for foreign assets are developed both for American firms making direct investments abroad and for foreign firms investing in the United States. The main explanatory variables are relative rates of expected returns and risks, the latter divided into those due to internal causes and those due to external ones, such as devaluation and expropriation. The empirical results indicate that, at least in 1966, the restraint program of the United States had perverse effects on the balance of payments, probably because of anticipatory investment abroad in excess of what would have been optimal had not demand been restrained by controls. Monetary and fiscal policies have only short-run effects on the balance of payments as long as wealth is a constraint and risk is considered.

Grant L. Reuber and Frank Roseman. "International Capital Flows and the Take-Over of Domestic Companies by Foreign Firms: Canada 1945–61."

Foreign take-overs are part of the general phenomenon of business mergers in most countries. In order to evaluate the importance and characteristics of foreign take-overs, mergers of domestic firms are taken as a control group. Variations over time in the number and pattern of foreign take-overs in Canada are largely explained by the level and pattern of mergers in the United States. In addition, variables such as tariff policy, corporate cash flows (as influenced by governmental financial policies), and the level of business activity (also influenced by macroeconomic policies) are significant in explaining variations in take-overs. Little or no influence is attributed to such variables as aggregate economic growth, economies of scale, research and development, and changes in antitrust laws and their enforcement in the United States. Only very little of the foreign control of Canadian industry in 1962 resulted from take-overs between 1944 and 1961, and the number of such take-overs has been small relative to the total number of firms in Canada.

Alan R. Dobell and Thomas A. Wilson. "The Impact of Taxation on Capital Flows and the Balance of Payments in Canada."

The hypothetical effects of major tax reforms in Canada (as proposed, but not adopted, in 1967 and 1969) upon international movements of capital and the balance of payments are analyzed on the assumption that the foreign-exchange rate is kept unchanged. The analysis includes portfolio capital, as well as direct investment, and takes account of induced changes in saving and investment, interest rates and rates of return, government revenues and expenditures, various components of the balance of payments, and other endogenous variables. After certain short-run adjustments to the change in taxation are completed the equilibrium effects on investment yields and capital flows are modest enough to be readily accommodated by the use of normal macroeconomic policy instruments. None of the proposed reforms would have had devastating effects on the balance of payments.

George H. Borts and Kenneth J. Kopecky. "Capital Movements and Economic Growth in Developed Countries."

On the assumption that a balance on current account is offset by an equal and opposite balance on capital account, a model that provides solutions for saving and domestic investment explains also international movements of capital. A growth model is constructed to generate a country's equilibrium pattern of these aggregative variables, including the return flows of interest and dividends earned abroad. The main feature of this model is that international capital movements are independent of national differentials in interest rates and continue in a given direction with a uniform worldwide interest rate. In general, a country will lend more the higher its ratio of saving to income, the lower its rate of growth, the smaller the share of capital income in GDP, the higher the rate of depreciation on its fixed capital, the larger the share of taxes, and the smaller the share of government spending in GNP. Multiple-regression analysis applied to statistical data on these variables for thirteen countries leads the authors to conclude that capital movements can be explained by means of a growth model without any reference to differential yields or to any monetary factors.

Walter S. Salant. "Financial Intermediation as an Explanation of Enduring 'Deficits' in the Balance of Payments."

Provision of financial intermediary services by one country to others could be explained by any of three phenomena: (1) lower liquidity preference of residents (including financial intermediaries) in the country providing the services than in foreign countries; (2) greater competitiveness of that country's financial-intermediary industry than in those of foreign countries; or (3) lower costs of intermediating. International financial intermediation by the United States satisfies the growth in foreign private and official demand for liquid dollar assets in a growing world economy, and can cause deficits in this country's balance of payments on both the liquidity and official-settlements definitions. Deficits limited to satisfying growth in that demand are not only consistent with equilibrium but necessary for it. This hypothesis does not assert or imply that continuing financial intermediation by the United States would be compatible with the present international monetary system, or that it will continue indefinitely. The available empirical evidence is also consistent with other explanations of the enduring deficits, but none of the evidence or theoretical arguments adduced thus far has eroded the thesis that financial intermediation by the United States accounted for a good part of its liquidity deficits in the 1950's and 1960's.

Arthur B. Laffer. "International Financial Intermediation: Interpretation and Empirical Analysis."

The demand for money in each country is assumed to be a function of real income, price level, the cost of money, and the demand elasticity with respect to the cost of money. The supply of money is assumed to be determined exogenously by the monetary authorities of the United States, since they create the primary monetary asset used in the world. Equilibrium between the world's demand for money and, the supply of it, is achieved by a change in the world price level. The essential parts of the model are then the net capital account of the banking nation, the increase in the total supply of money, real income, and other exogenous variables that influence the demand for money. An empirical counterpart of this theoretical model is constructed and regression coefficients are provided from quarterly data for 1958–67.

A one-to-one relationship is found between capital outflow and trade surplus, a positive relationship between capital outflow and increases in the American money supply, and a negative relationship between capital outflows and real growth, increases in exports, and the velocity of money in the United States. There is no empirical evidence that American deficits imply overvaluation of the dollar. Policy, unless extreme, appears to have had little, if any, effect on the balance of payments.

A TABULAR CHARACTERIZATION OF THE PAPERS

NO ONE will be surprised to find that the papers in this volume, though addressing themselves to the same theme, differ considerably in many respects. After all, people, tastes, talents, interests, and techniques differ widely; such differences are reflected in the papers presented. I thought it might be interesting to compare some of their main characteristics. (See the table beginning on the next page.)

The comparison provided here is in tabular form to allow the reader to compare at a glance the modes of exposition, theoretical models and variables used, quantitative data, econometric techniques, and policy implications — to the extent that these rubrics apply. No value judgments are implied — at least, not by me. For example, whether second-hand statistical data used by a contributor are, or are not, reproduced in his paper is neither good nor bad. To have them reproduced is a waste of space but may save some readers the time of looking them up in the original sources. Or, to give another example, use or nonuse of econometric techniques is neither good nor bad on principle. But it may be of interest to note that only five of the 17 papers are without econometrics. Similarly, only four contributions are without policy implications; apparently, scholars these days do not want to be open to the charge that their work lacks political relevance. On the other hand, the subject of this volume is so timely that any findings of research in this field may be significant for policy-making even if the researcher is quite unaware of such significance.

Authors and Titles of Papers	Mode of Exposition	Theoretical Model and Variables
Cohen The United Kingdom as an Exporter of Capital	Verbal	Alternative costs of measures to cope with imbalance of payments
Hawkins Intra-EEC Capital Movements and Domestic Financial Markets	Verbal	International integration of capital markets
Floyd Portfolio Equilibrium and the Theory of Capital Movements	Algebraic and geometric	Portfolio balance. Variables: real-money stock, permanent income, price level, fixed exchange rate, contrasted with flexible rates
Howle Capital Mobility and Payments Equilibrium	Algebraic and geometric	Adjustment processes with perfect mobility of capital. Demand constraint versus liquidity constraint
Leamer and Stern Problems in the Theory and Empirical Estimation of International Capital Movements	Verbal	Activity models versus transactor models of portfolio adjustment
Bryant and Hendershott Empirical Analysis of Capital Flows: Some Consequences of Alternative Specifications	Algebraic	Portfolio balance. Lagged responses are incorporated with and without controls of capital movements
Miller and Whitman The Outflow of Short-term Funds from the United States: Adjustments of Stocks and Flows	Algebraic and geometric	Portfolio balance with stock- and flow-adjustments. Supply and demand as functions of returns and risks

Use of Numerical Data	Data Repro-duced	Econometric Techniques	Policy Implications
Long-term capital movements, U.K., annual, 1952–68	Yes	None	Restrictions on capital are less costly than trade restrictions or demand cuts in coping with imbalance of payments
(1) Inflows and outflows of capital for direct and portfolio investment, EEC countries, annual, 1960 or 1963 to 1967	Yes	Simple correlation	None
(2) Relative shares of intra-EEC and total flows	Yes		
(3) Interest rates, 1960–69	Yes		
None	No	None	The conflict between internal and external balance inherent in fixed exchange rates and adjustable pegs is more serious than commonly realized
None	No	None	Fixed exchange rates impose limits on fiscal employment policy
(1) Forward exchange rates of French franc, DM, and £, 1960–69	Yes	Discussion of choice of variables	Existing empirical evidence may not be sufficiently reliable for purposes of balance-of-payments policy
(2) Effects of change in interest rates on capital flows, U.S. and Canada	No		
Borrowings by Japanese banks from American banks, annual, 1959–67 and 1964–68	No	Multiple regression	None
Short-term capital flows, U.S., quarterly, 1959–67	No	Multiple regression	Government policies changing interest rates and GNP have quick effects on capital flows by way of stock adjustment; effects via permanent flows are miniscule

Authors and Titles of Papers	Mode of Exposition	Theoretical Model and Variables
Branson and Willett Policy Toward Short-term Capital Movements: Some Implications of the Portfolio Approach	Algebraic	Portfolio balance. Portfolio distribution is a function of returns and risks. Stock- and flow-adjustments are separated
Stevens Capital Mobility and the International Firm	Algebraic	Decisions of manufacturing firm: flexible accelerator model for plant and equipment. Internal and external financing at home and abroad
Severn Investment and Financial Behavior of American Direct Investors in Manufacturing	Algebraic and geometric	Marginal efficiency of investment by American firms in manufacturing, domestic and foreign outlays. Variables include dividend payments and net outflows, depending on income, investment, and dividends
Gillespie The Policies of England, France, and Germany as Recipients of Foreign Direct Investment	Verbal	None
Prachowny Direct Investment and the Balance of Payments of the United States: A Portfolio Approach	Algebraic	Portfolio balance of assets at home and abroad. Investments abroad by Americans and in the United States by foreigners as functions of relative returns and of internal and external risks
Reuber and Roseman International Capital Flows and the Take-over of Domestic Companies by Foreign Firms: Canada, 1945–61	Verbal and algebraic	Variations in foreign take-overs as functions of tariffs, government financial policies, total business activity, and internally generated funds of the firms
Dobell and Wilson The Impact of Taxation on Capital Flows and the Balance of Payments in Canada	Algebraic	Effects of changes in taxes on balance of payments, chiefly through government revenues, business investment, capital requirements, and dividends

Use of Numerical Data	Data Repro- duced	Econometric Techniques	Policy Implications
Short-term capital flows, U.S., quarterly, 1960–64 and 1965–68	No	Multiple regression	Interest constraint of gliding parity changes is not so strong as to eliminate freedom of monetary policy
Current assets, financial flows, sales, and investments, foreign manufacturing affili- ates of U.S. corporations, annual aggregates, 1957–65 or 1968	Yes	Multiple regression	Direct foreign investment is not affected by controls, but foreign borrowing by parent firm probably is
Domestic and foreign activi- ties of individual manufactur- ing firms, U.S., annual, 1961– 66	No	Multiple regression	Domestic macropolicy has small effects on direct-invest- ment component of balance of payments: positive effects are offset by negative ones
None	No	None	None
Foreign direct investment by U.S. firms and foreign firms, annual, 1963–64	No	Multiple regression	Monetary and fiscal policies affect balance of payments only in short run, apart from wealth effects
Domestic and foreign merg- ers in Canada, annual, 1954– 61	No	Multiple regression	Foreign control of Canadian industry has not been seri- ously affected by take-overs since 1945
Estimated changes in taxes with estimates of variables used in model	No	Simulation in econometric model	Effects of changes in taxation on capital flows and payments balance are too small to con- stitute a serious constraint on reform plans

Authors and Titles of Papers	Mode of Exposition	Theoretical Model and Variables
Borts and Kopecky Capital Movements and Economic Growth in Developed Countries	Algebraic	International capital flows as functions of growth, the ratios of saving to income, capital to GDP, and government expenditures to GDP, also of taxes and depreciation, but independent of differences in monetary policy or interest rates
Salant Financial Intermediation as an Explanation of Enduring "Deficits" in the Balance of Payments	Verbal	International intermediation due to national differences in liquidity preferences and in cost and competitiveness of banking
Laffer International Financial Intermediation: Interpretation and Empirical Analysis	Algebraic	International money flows, instantaneously adjusted to demand for money as a function of real income, the world price level, and the world interest rate

Use of Numerical Data	Data Repro- duced	Econometric Techniques	Policy Implications
Ratios of net factor income earned abroad to GNP, 13 countries, annual, 1956–65	Yes	Multiple regression	None
None	No	None	Better understanding would lead to acceptance of endur- ing U.S. deficits as condition of international equilibrium
Current account, capital ac- count, money supply, index of industrial production, U.S., quarterly, 1958–67	Yes	Multiple regression	Policy acting directly on the U.S. balance of payments may be futile; U.S. deficits need not imply that dollar is overvalued but may reflect ability of private capital to supply external as well as in- ternal liquidity. Lack of con- fidence may represent failure to recognize this function

THE COMMENTATORS

EVERY one of the 17 papers is subject to two comments by official commentators, that is, by specialists appointed to this task before the conference. At the conference itself, lively discussion from the floor followed the formal comments, but (with one exception) only the formal comments are reproduced here.

A few of the comments are rather colorless, being confined to polite commendation and needless paraphrase of the paper under discussion. Most of them, however, provide good criticism, or amplification, of the contents of the papers. Perhaps I ought to remain an impartial *conférencier,* but I cannot resist recommending to readers who merely "sample" this volume that they peruse the comments by Bloomfield, Lanyi, Black, Yudin, Flanders, Rhomberg, Lipsey, McKinnon, Tarshis, Balassa, and Modigliani.

THE EDITORS

THE three editors of this volume have given unusually large amounts of time to their task. Every paper was carefully read by each editor, first by Tarshis, then Salant, and finally Machlup. The authors received critical comments and suggestions in all three phases as their manuscripts went through the three stages of purgatory (or was it hell?). Each editor "sat" on the manuscripts for roughly three months; each engaged in considerable correspondence with the authors; and each found the authors responsive to, and appreciative of, critical suggestions. We would not now be willing to take responsibility for either substance or form of the papers as they are presented in this volume, but perhaps we may claim a little credit for having shortened some of the papers and removed a few flaws of exposition or style.

It has been a pleasure to be associated with Lorie Tarshis and Walter Salant in this enterprise. I want to thank them for a labor of love. They have assuredly earned the gratitude of every reader.

THE UNITED KINGDOM AS AN EXPORTER OF CAPITAL

BENJAMIN J. COHEN · Fletcher School of Law
and Diplomacy

THE United Kingdom has traditionally been a substantial exporter of long-term capital. In the nineteenth century no other country loaned nearly so much abroad to so many for so long. And even into the 1920's the London capital market was still a prime source of external finance. In the decades since the Great Depression, however, dramatic changes have occurred in Britain's position as a capital exporter. The purpose of this paper is to review some of these more recent developments.

The paper will concentrate on the period since 1952, and in particular on the years since 1958.[1] Admittedly, this is a short focus; a longer perspective might have been preferable. But unfortunately we are constrained by data inadequacies. Unitl 1952 no separate statistics exist for private long-term movements, these being lumped together with miscellaneous official long-term capital, nonreserve short-term movements, and the so-called "balancing item" (errors and omissions). Moreover, even though separate estimates of private capital flows have been published since 1952, those published before 1958 are not necessarily very accurate or complete. Only since 1958 are there comprehensive, detailed, and reliable data on both official and private long-term capital movements.

The paper will be divided into two parts. Part 1 will consider changes in the magnitude, direction, and composition of British capital exports since 1952. Here I shall argue that the main impact of these

---

NOTE: The author was affiliated with Princeton University at the time of the conference.

[1] The period prior to 1952 is already covered by an extensive literature, including in particular A. K. Cairncross, *Home and Foreign Investment, 1870–1913,* Cambridge, Mass., 1953; A. H. Imlah, *Economic Elements in the Pax Britannica,* Cambridge, Mass., 1958; E. V. Morgan, *Studies in British Financial Policy, 1914–25,* London, 1952; and United Nations, *International Capital Movements During the Inter-War Period,* Lake Success, N.Y., 1949.

25

developments has been to begin a transformation of the United Kingdom from its role as an originator of funds to essentially that of entrepôt. Part 2 will then take up some aspects of the recent history of official British capital controls. Here I shall argue that so far as Britain is concerned, capital restriction is a cheaper means of adjusting the balance of payments than either trade restriction or domestic demand management (expenditure reduction), which in the short term (given a decision to maintain a fixed rate of exchange) are the other policy alternatives commonly relied upon by the British authorities.

1

AN ENTREPÔT

Since 1952 Britain has exported capital regularly and in fairly substantial volume. But as compared with earlier periods of sizable British net investment abroad—specifically, the gold-standard era and the 1920's—significant changes have occurred. First, in relative terms the scale of capital exports has been much reduced. Secondly, the geographic pattern of lending has become much more concentrated than previously, outflows now being directed primarily toward the sterling area; vis-à-vis nonsterling areas, capital is now imported on balance. And finally, the composition of lending has altered radically. Portfolio investment, traditionally the commonest form of lending abroad, has declined in favor. Today it is subordinated to official capital flows (including grants as well as loans), and to direct investment, where British residents have a controlling interest in the foreign operation.

The implication of all these changes is that the United Kingdom is ceasing to be of much importance as a *source* of net capital exports. Today it is much less a provider of funds than it is a processor. Essentially, it is becoming an *intermediary*—an entrepôt for long-term investments. Britain has long functioned as a clearing bank at the short-term end of the market. Now, increasingly, at the long-term end, it is functioning as an investment bank as well.

Although short-term financial markets are not the subject of this paper, it would not be inapposite at this point to remind the reader briefly of what recently has been happening there. Basically, over the last decade or so, Britain has developed almost exclusively into the role of middleman. The role is formalized institutionally in the Euro-dollar market which, although extraterritorial and international, happens to be centered functionally in the City of London, where the largest part of its business is done. The City does not provide its own funds in the Eurodollar market; what it does provide is the flexibility and expertise of its financial institutions. It processes and adapts other people's money to be used by other people. It is a fixer—a clearing bank in the classic sense, taking deposits and lending, but venturing little of its own capital.

In a similar fashion, this seems to be happening in the long-term sphere as well, albeit rather less formally and rather more slowly. The major theme of this paper is that the United Kingdom is developing almost exclusively into a middleman in capital markets, too. Once the country was an international investor; now, primarily, it is becoming an international investment banker. The change may be seen in the comparatively narrow margin between gross long-term outflows and gross long-term inflows, especially in recent years. It may be seen as well in the increasing dependence of long-term outflows on short-term inflows (net): little of Britain's net capital export today is transferred in the form of real goods and services; the country, more and more, must borrow short in order to lend long. The change may also be seen in the geographic pattern of net outflows to sterling-area countries offset to a considerable extent by net inflows from nonsterling areas. And, most obviously, it may be seen in the thriving international bond (Eurobond) market, where for long-term portfolio investors the City now performs precisely the same function it does for short-term depositors and borrowers in the Eurodollar market—namely, the function of fixer. All of these developments appear to point in the same direction, toward the conclusion that I have suggested.

TABLE 1

Summary of British Long-Term Capital Movements, 1952–68
(£ million)

	Official Movements			Private Movements			Over-all Movements		
	Grants & Loans by U.K.[a]	Grants & Loans to U.K.[b]	Net Out-ward Move-ment	Invest-ment Abroad	Invest-ment in U.K.	Net Invest-ment Abroad	Out-flow	In-flow	Net Cap-ital Ex-ports
1952	66	104	−38	127	13	114	193	117	76
1953	53	65	−12	173	28	145	226	93	133
1954	39	−3	42	238	75	163	277	72	205
1955	84	−1	85	182	122	60	266	121	145
1956	71	−44	115	258	139	119	329	95	234
1957	68	80	−12	298	126	172	366	206	160
1958	67	−57	124	310	164	146	377	107	270
1959	60	−146	206	303	172	131	363	26	337
1960	125	−72	197	322	233	89	447	161	286
1961	99	−64	163	313	426	−113	412	362	50
1962	181	−44	225	242	248	−6	423	204	219
1963	192	−45	237	320	276	44	512	231	281
1964	243	−36	279	399	152	247	642	116	526
1965	246	−16	262	354	237	117	600	221	379
1966	263	3	260	304	272	32	567	275	292
1967	267	22	245	457	380	77	724	402	322
1968	211	54	157	736	573	163	947	627	320

SOURCE: *United Kingdom Balance of Payments,* selected issues.
  [a] Loans net of repayments; also includes British government subscriptions and contributions to international organizations, and other British official long-term capital (net).
  [b] Loans net of repayments.

MAGNITUDE

British capital movements since 1952 are summarized in Table 1. Official movements differ from the published statistics in that they include grants as well as intergovernment loans (net of repayment) and other official long-term capital. In most years, repayments by the government of the United Kingdom on previous loans from abroad have exceeded new loans received. Private movements include net overseas investment by British residents (direct plus portfolio) less net investment by foreigners in the United Kingdom. Over-all movements are recorded in the final three columns of the table.

On balance, Britain exported capital in every year between 1952 and 1968, at an average over-all rate of some £250 million per annum. In certain years net capital exports were diminished because of unusual inflows of funds — as in 1952 and 1953, for instance, when more than £220 million of defense aid was received from the United States government. Likewise, in 1957 and again in 1966–68 there were large special credits totalling some £325 million from the United States Export-Import Bank for the purchase of American military aircraft and missiles, and in 1961 there was a £132 million increase in the foreign private-investment figure for the United Kingdom, reflecting the Ford Motor Company purchase of locally held shares in its British subsidiary. If these extraordinary inflows are excluded, the average over-all rate of British capital exports was really in the vicinity of some £290 million per annum.

Figures like these are impressive. The scale of British grants and investment abroad certainly has been substantial — indeed, in absolute terms, more substantial than either under the gold standard or during the 1920's. But we must keep such numbers in perspective. In relative terms British foreign lending is much less important than it ever was before the Great Depression. Prior to 1930 net capital exports, as a proportion of national income, tended as a rule to fluctuate in a fairly regular cyclical fashion, between 1 per cent of the gross national product at the bottom of the cycle and 6–7 per cent at the peak.[2] Since 1952, by contrast, net capital exports have accounted for hardly more than 1 per cent of the gross national product of the United Kingdom.

To be sure, net capital exports did accelerate rapidly over the period in review. During the 1950's the average rate of outflow was only £195 million a year (£235 million if extraordinary inflows are excluded), whereas during the 1960's it was higher, at £300 million a year (£340 million if extraordinary inflows are excluded). This reflected a substantial increase in the average rate of gross outflows of capital, from £300 million a year in the 1950's to £585 million in the

[2] Alexander G. Kemp, "Long-Term Capital Movements," in D. J. Robertson and L. C. Hunter, eds., *The British Balance of Payments,* London, 1966, p. 137.

1960's. But this increase was not out of line with the growth of the British economy in general or of its total foreign trade: in relation to the gross national product and visible trade, capital exports did not rise significantly. On the other hand, there did happen to be a large rise in gross long-term inflows between 1952 and 1968. Consequently, over the period as a whole, net capital exports as a percentage of gross capital exports actually fell—from roughly two-thirds in the 1950's to only about one-half in the 1960's. This emphasizes the evolving transformation of Britain's capital function from investor to investment banker: today, half of the country's gross investment abroad is based on someone else's money.

Why is there now such a narrow margin between gross outflows of long-term funds from the United Kingdom and gross inflows? Why has the country ceased to be of much importance as a source of net capital exports? One is tempted to suggest that it is because of the stringency of exchange-control regulations: relax the restrictions and lending is sure to increase. But such an answer obviously would be naive, confusing cause and effect. Certainly British exchange controls are tight, but they are tight precisely because, given its present economic behavior, the country cannot increase its net foreign lending. Britain presently absorbs far too large a proportion of its current income for its own purposes—for private and public consumption and for home investment. Not enough is left to invest abroad. In brief, there is no *exportable surplus*. The only way to increase net capital exports is to increase the exportable surplus—that is, to reduce real domestic absorption relative to real national income—but so far no postwar British government has been able to figure out how to do this.

For evidence of the narrowness of the capacity for foreign lending, we may consider net capital exports specifically in relation to the other major categories of the balance of payments—the balance of current transactions and the balance of monetary movements. These are shown in Table 2.[3] The former balance (assuming it is in surplus) is an indication of the extent to which the net export of financial capital

[3] In the table, the balance of current transactions as recorded in British statistics is adjusted to exclude net official transfers, which for our purposes are included in net capital exports. The balance of monetary movements is adjusted to include the "balancing item" (errors and omissions), on the grounds that this item reflects mainly unrecorded flows of short-term funds.

TABLE 2

Long-Term Capital Exports, Current Balance, and Monetary Movements
in the British Balance of Payments, 1952–68
(£ million)

	Net Long-Term Capital Exports	Balance of Current Transactions (deficit −)	Balance of Monetary Movements plus "Balancing Item" (deficit −) [a]
1952	76	112	36
1953	133	90	−43
1954	205	135	−70
1955	145	−132	−277
1956	234	255	21
1957	160	287	127
1958	270	418	148
1959	337	225	−112
1960	286	−171	−457
1961	50	114	64
1962	219	233	14
1963	281	246	−35
1964	526	−218	−744
1965	379	127	−252
1966	292	244	−48
1967	322	−95	−417
1968	320	−87	−407

SOURCE: *United Kingdom Balance of Payments,* selected issues.
[a] Represents the excess (net) of the second column over the first column.

is translated into a genuine transfer of capital—a movement of real goods and services. The latter is an indication of the extent to which, in a macroeconomic sense, the net outflow represents merely an exchange of one type of asset or liability for another—short-term borrowing (net) for long-term lending. It can be seen from the table that throughout the 1950's, and even as late as 1963, British capital exports, though small, were at least generally transferred successfully. Except for 1955 and 1961, the current account was continuously in surplus, often by considerable amounts. Over the period as a whole the cumulative net outflow of real goods and services accounted for more than two-thirds of the net export of financial capital. After 1963, by contrast, the balance of payments was in almost continuous crisis, and the current account recorded a cumulative deficit of near-record proportions (for peacetime). Net long-term foreign lending was thus based entirely on net short-term borrowing from abroad—in other words, once again, on someone else's money. Overseas short-term borrowing mainly took the form of accumulation of liquid liabilities rather than liquidation of short-term assets.[4]

DIRECTION

Britain's developing role as an intermediary in capital markets is emphasized too by the geographic pattern of long-term inflows and outflows. Detailed statistics on the direction of capital movements were not available before 1958. However, since then a clear pattern has been evident: net outflows to sterling-area countries are offset to a considerable extent by net inflows from nonsterling areas (Table 3). This is a pattern reinforced and encouraged by British exchange-control regulations, which make a sharp distinction between sterling-area countries (the so-called "scheduled territories") and others. Restrictions on capital exports have been in operation since 1939. But traditionally restrictions have not been applied to the bloc of countries which (in addition to maintaining a portion of their reserves in London) enforce a system of controls similar to Britain's. In effect, exchange regulation operates around the whole group of sterling-associated countries rather than around the United Kingdom alone; within the group, relative freedom of investment prevails.[5] It should

---

[4] Between 1962 (the first year for which such data are available) and 1968, while Britain's total long-term assets rose by £5 billion, liquid liabilities increased by more than £9 billion, from roughly 70 per cent of the sum of long-term assets to over 100 per cent. Short-term assets meanwhile rose by just over £7 billion, and long-term liabilities by a little more than £2 billion. "An Inventory of U.K. External Assets and Liabilities: End-1968," *Bank of England Quarterly Bulletin*, December, 1969, pp. 444–445.

[5] This is what first defined the sterling area formally as a legal entity. During the 1930's it had not been much more than an arrangement de convenance, an informal

TABLE 3

Direction of Long-Term Capital Exports, 1958–68
(£ million)

	All Areas			Overseas Sterling Area			Nonsterling Areas		
	Official	Private	Total	Official	Private	Total	Official	Private	Total
1958	124	146	270	94	200	294	30	−54	−24
1959	206	131	337	120	135	255	86	−4	82
1960	197	89	286	125	175	300	72	−86	−14
1961	163	−113	50	166	134	300	−3	−247	−250
1962	225	−6	219	145	130	275	80	−136	−56
1963	237	44	281	150	149	299	87	−105	−18
1964	279	247	526	192	218	410	87	29	116
1965	262	117	379	174	254	428	88	−137	−49
1966	260	32	292	182	174	356	78	−142	−64
1967	245	77	322	186	223	409	59	−146	−87
1968	157	163	320	181	324	505	−24	−161	−185

SOURCE: *United Kingdom Balance of Payments*, selected issues.

not be surprising, therefore, that British capital outflows over the years have tended to be mainly concentrated within the sterling area itself.

In fact, outflows to the sterling area have been sizable, averaging almost £290 million a year in 1958–63, and rising to more than £410 million a year thereafter. The rise reflects principally an increase of private investment outflows; United Kingdom government grants and loans (net of repayments) in the sterling bloc have held relatively steady since about 1964. But at the same time inflows from nonsterling areas have also been sizable, reflecting a high rate of both portfolio and

grouping of countries with close commercial and financial connections. But from 1939 on, it became a formal monetary region defined technically by British exchange-control regulations. In recent years some restriction has been imposed on capital transfers even within the sterling area. See below. For a valuable survey of British exchange controls over the years, see "The U.K. Exchange Control: A Short History," *Bank of England Quarterly Bulletin*, September, 1967, pp. 245–260.

direct investment in the United Kingdom, particularly from the United States. (Net inflows would have been even larger but for the British government's need to meet the annual installments on Canadian and American postwar loans.) It is evident that British capital exports over-all would be much smaller were it not for this steady net inflow of funds from nonsterling sources.

COMPOSITION

Regarding the composition of inflows and outflows, the most striking development recently is the rise to prominence of *official capital movements*. Except during the two world wars, the British government did not take much hand directly in the import or export of capital; that was the province of private borrowers and lenders. Traditions change, however, and in the postwar period the government itself has become a prime mover of long-term funds. While private capital exports have been held down by exchange restrictions, public capital exports have burgeoned. In fact, the change has been swift. As late as just a decade ago, official outflows still accounted for only about one-third of Britain's net capital exports, and private outflows for two-thirds. But in the last decade positions have been rapidly reversed; today, official outflows account for 80 per cent or more of the net total, private outflows for under 20 per cent (Table 1).

The details of official capital movements are summarized in Table 4. The role played by grants is outstanding. In the early 1950's, inward transfers were large enough to produce over-all net inflows of public funds; in the 1960's, outward transfers have been sufficient to explain the sharp rise of over-all outflows. Grants received by the British government between 1952 and 1958 consisted almost entirely of defense aid from the United States. Grants by the United Kingdom government, on the other hand, have been largely for economic rather than military purposes: for bilateral economic assistance plus subscriptions and contributions to international aid organizations. United Kingdom government loans likewise have been largely in connection with the British foreign-aid program. Loans to the United Kingdom government have been unimportant, apart from the Export-Import

TABLE 4

Official Long-Term Capital Movements, 1952–68
(£ *million*)

| | Outflows | | | | Inflows | | | Net Out- ward Move- ment |
	Grants	Loans (net of repay- ments)	Other (net)[a]	Total	Grants	Loans (net of repay- ments)	Total	
1952	62	−16	20	66	120	−16	104	−38
1953	61	−27	19	53	122	−57	65	−12
1954	65	−34	8	39	51	−54	−3	42
1955	70	4	10	84	47	−48	−1	85
1956	73	−20	18	71	26	−70	−44	115
1957	75	−16	9	68	21	59	80	−12
1958	77	−16	6	67	3	−60	−57	124
1959	82	−28	6	60	–	−146	−146	206
1960	94	20	11	125	–	−72	−72	197
1961	118	−48	29	99	–	−64	−64	163
1962	121	47	13	181	–	−44	−44	225
1963	132	52	8	192	–	−45	−45	237
1964	163	65	15	243	–	−36	−36	279
1965	177	50	19	246	–	−16	−16	262
1966	180	64	19	263	–	3	3	260
1967	188	61	18	267	–	22	22	245
1968	178	60	−27	211	–	54	54	157

SOURCE: *United Kingdom Balance of Payments,* selected issues.
[a] Includes subscription and contributions to international organizations, and other United Kingdom official long-term capital (net).

Bank credits for military purchases in 1957 and 1966–68; in all other years since 1952 repayments on previous loans have exceeded new loans received.

After stagnating throughout most of the 1950's, the British foreign-aid program accelerated rapidly following the 1958 Commonwealth Economic Conference in Ottawa. In response to pressures from less developed Commonwealth members, the United Kingdom pledged to expand its aid effort—and expand it did. Between 1959 and 1964 development grants and loans each were approximately doubled in volume.[6] However, after 1964 a new stagnation set in, albeit on a higher plateau than previously, owing to the crisis of the balance of payments. There has been little further increase in the program, despite the fact that virtually all aid today is tied to the purchase of British goods and services, either customarily (as in the case of dependent territories) or by regulation. According to one estimate, taking "switching" into account, the "flowback" to British exports amounted to nearly three-fifths of Britain's bilateral aid (net of repayments) in 1963.[7] For political reasons practically all of Britain's bilateral aid goes to sterling-area countries. The main recipients include India and Pakistan (which between them get about one-quarter of all British economic assistance) and the former colonies of East and Central Africa.

Private capital movements in recent years have been dominated by direct investment flows. Detailed statistics on the composition of private capital movements were not available before 1958. The data since then are summarized in Table 5. They show that direct investments accounted for almost two-thirds of the total of net private investment in either direction between 1958 and 1968. And indeed, the actual fraction was probably even higher than that—perhaps as high as three-quarters, possibly even as high as four-fifths—since "other" investments in the British statistics include investments by the oil companies. These are known to be large, and are thought to be mainly direct investments rather than portfolio.

The reasons for the relative dominance of direct investment in private capital movements are not difficult to discover. As far as outward movements are concerned, the principal explanation seems to lie in the differential severity of Britain's exchange-control regulations.

[6] The apparent increase of loans in Table 4 is exaggerated owing to substantial loan repayments by Germany and France (averaging £65 million a year in 1959–61), which terminated after 1961. The increase of gross loans between 1959 and 1964 was from £48 million to £85 million. The figures in the table are not adjusted for interest payments on Britain's development loans, which averaged nearly £25 million a year in 1963–65. Ministry of Overseas Development, *British Aid: Statistics of Official Economic Aid to Developing Countries,* London, 1967.

[7] Andrzej Krassowski, "Aid and the British Balance of Payments." *Moorgate and Wall Street,* Spring, 1965, p. 32.

TABLE 5

Private Long-Term Capital Movements, 1958–68
(£ million)

	Investments Abroad				Investments in U.K.				Net Out-ward Move-ment
	Di-rect[a]	Port-folio	Other (oil & misc.)	Total	Di-rect[a]	Port-folio	Other (oil & misc.)	Total	
1958	144	166	[b]	310	87	77	[b]	164	146
1959	196	107	[b]	303	146	26	[b]	172	131
1960	250	−37	109	322	135	43	55	233	89
1961	226	−28	115	313	236	115	75	426	−113
1962	209	−39	72	242	130	61	57	248	−6
1963	236	5	79	320	160	19	97	276	44
1964	263	3	133	399	162	−39	29	152	247
1965	308	−94	140	354	197	−46	86	237	117
1966	276	−82	110	304	195	−59	136	272	32
1967	281	52	124	457	170	11	199	380	77
1968	429	218	89	736	245	87	241	573	163

SOURCE: *United Kingdom Balance of Payments,* selected issues.
[a] Excluding oil and, before 1963, insurance.
[b] Included in portfolio investment.

Portfolio outflows have traditionally been restricted more tightly than direct-investment outflows (even though the latter, unlike the former, are subject to administrative control). As far as inward movements are concerned, the principal explanation seems to lie in the uncertainty regarding the sterling exchange rate. Portfolio investors are discouraged by the risk of potential devaluation or a floating rate. Direct investors, meanwhile, are encouraged by the general expansion of the British economy, and also, it has been suggested, by "the relative inefficiency of British entrepreneurs either in discovering investment opportunities or in translating them in practice."[8]

Between 1958 and 1968 the rate of direct investment in the United

[8] A. G. Kemp, *op. cit.,* p. 149.

Kingdom as well as of direct investment abroad (both excluding the oil industry) virtually tripled. However, it is interesting to note that the increases of investment have not been matched by correspondingly large increases of funds actually flowing into or out of the country. British statistics (unlike those of the United States) define "direct investment" in either direction to include the parent company's share of the unremitted profits of overseas subsidiaries that are retained for reinvestment (a contra item being entered additionally in the current account opposite "direct investment income"). As it happens, unremitted profits have accounted for a rising proportion of the recorded investment totals: in 1958 they comprised half of the total in either direction; a decade later, some two-thirds. Thus, in absolute terms, outward investment other than unremitted profits is more or less unchanged from what it was in the late 1950's (undoubtedly reflecting the stringency of British exchange restriction) and inward investment has grown only moderately.

About 55 per cent of British direct investment abroad (whether or not unremitted profits are included) is in the sterling area, about 45 per cent in nonsterling areas. By far the largest share of total investment (two-thirds to three-quarters) goes to developed rather than to developing areas — the biggest beneficiaries being rapidly growing economies such as (within the sterling area) Australia and South Africa, and (outside the sterling area) the United States, Canada, and the countries of the Common Market. Virtually all of the foreign direct investment in the United Kingdom comes from nonsterling sources, in particular from the United States. Manufacturing accounts for well over half of the total movement in either direction.[9]

Portfolio movements in recent years have resulted in net inflows of investment funds into Britain. Apart from the years immediately preceding devaluation, foreign investors have bought sterling securities on balance, including both corporate and government issues. The pound is still widely regarded as a convenient international store of value. British investors, conversely, have tended steadily to liquidate foreign security holdings on balance, except during the period immedi-

[9] For details on these and other aspects of direct investment in and out of the United Kingdom, see the successive articles on overseas investments in *Board of Trade Journal*, June 30, 1967; July 19, 1968; and May 9, 1969.

ately following devaluation. New purchases abroad are effectively dis-couraged by the obligation that they go through the so-called "invest-ment-dollar market"; the requisite foreign exchange can only be obtained from the proceeds of new sales of foreign securities by British residents. Lately the premium on investment dollars has sometimes been as high as 50 per cent over the official exchange rate. New sterling issues in the London capital market have been insignificant, averaging (after redemptions) no more than £5 million a year. Only sterling-area and (since 1963) European Free Trade Association borrowers are permitted to float new sterling issues in London, and even they must take their place on the queue and wait their turn.

However, this does not mean that British financial institutions have been shut out of the business of foreign securities issues. Quite the opposite, in fact. Nothing better illustrates Britain's evolving trans-formation from investor to investment banker than the change in the capital function of the City of London. British financial institutions have been leaders in the development of the new market for "interna-tional" bonds (Eurobonds), issues arranged by international under-writing syndicates for sale in a number of different countries. The market began only in 1963 when, with the imposition of the United States Interest Equalization Tax effectively closing the New York capital market to foreign borrowers, several London merchant banks responded by organizing a series of foreign dollar loans. Since then the market has grown by leaps and bounds, from a mere $137 million of new issues in 1963 (60 per cent denominated in dollars) to almost $1.9 billion in 1967 (90 per cent in dollars) and to well over $2 billion in 1968.[10] And while the market's growing internationalization has in-evitably diluted London's initial monopoly, the City still remains prominent in most underwriting syndicates; in fact, in the secondary market the City still remains predominant.[11] In short, British financial institutions play the classic role of middlemen, channeling foreign-owned funds to foreign borrowers, venturing none of their own capital. Indeed, that is precisely why currencies other than sterling were used

[10] Bank for International Settlements, *Annual Report, 1968,* pp. 57–58.
[11] "The Eurodollar Market: What It Means for London," *The Banker,* 119, No. 522 (August, 1969), p. 777.

in the first place: direct British resident participation in the market was to be prevented.

2

AT several points in the course of this paper I have emphasized the importance of exchange-control regulations in shaping the magnitude, direction, and composition of British capital movements. However, by no means does this emphasis imply that a constant force has been in operation. In fact, there has been a marked ebb and flow in capital restriction since it was first introduced three decades ago. Control has been eased or augmented as the general balance-of-payments situation improved or deteriorated. During the war restriction was stringent, but as soon as the war ended steps were taken gradually to loosen control, paralleling the approach to convertibility on current account in December 1958. Conversely, since 1961, and especially since the beginning of the long payments crisis lasting from 1964, the trend has been back again toward an intensification of regulation. Today (early 1970), British capital restriction is probably as tight as it has ever been.

As one might expect, most of the intensification of regulation has affected investment outside the sterling area rather than inside it. Portfolio investment is now even more thoroughly discouraged than ever by a new requirement, dating from 1965, that 25 per cent of the proceeds from sales of foreign securities be sold in the official exchange market; only 75 per cent of proceeds are thus available for sale in the investment-dollar market. And direct investment has been handicapped by a series of new administrative rulings, dating from 1961, first setting stricter criteria for the eligibility of investments abroad; then obliging investors to obtain the requisite foreign exchange in the investment-dollar market at the current premium, rather than in the regular market at the official exchange rate. However, recently even within the sterling area investment has been affected. Relative freedom of portfolio investment still prevails.[12] But since 1966 direct

---

[12] The only important exception dates from 1957 when, in order to close the notorious Kuwait and Hong Kong "gaps," the authorities prohibited British purchases of non-

investment has been regulated by a so-called "voluntary" program to limit outflows toward what is officially described as the "developed" sterling area—defined as comprising Australia, Ireland, New Zealand, and South Africa. These are the members, of course, that account for the bulk of British investment within the bloc.

All of this does not leave much room for further restriction of capital exports. Even if at some point the authorities should need temporarily to turn another screw, they may well find it difficult to locate one—unless they are willing to contemplate a virtually complete embargo on new investments abroad. But even before that point is reached a prior consideration intervenes, at least insofar as the overseas sterling area is concerned: further restrictions could endanger the very foundations of Britain's monetary region. It is well known that the outer members' privileged access to British capital is one of the few frayed threads still holding the sterling bloc together:

> The kernel of the sterling area arrangement, in so far as any arrangement formally exists, is a *quid pro quo:* that Britain should give the overseas sterling countries broadly free access to the London capital and money market, and impose no exchange control on outward payments to them—in exchange for which these countries will generally keep their external reserves at the Bank of England, rather than in dollars or in gold. . . .
>
> The fear is that, if Britain ever rescinded its part of the bargain, the sterling area countries could cause massive disturbances by liquidating their balances in London and demanding dollars and gold that Britain could not pay.[13]

The fear of a run is a real one—and remains real despite the Basle reform of the sterling area announced in 1968, which provided members with an exchange guarantee of their sterling reserve balances.[14] Sterling-area countries still regard their access to British capital as of the utmost importance. Andrew Shonfield's point has not lost its force: "The essential fact is that the sterling area has changed its

sterling securities from overseas sterling-area residents. See Peter B. Kenen, *British Monetary Policy and the Balance of Payments, 1951–1957,* Cambridge, Mass., 1960, pp. 150–152.

[13] *The Economist,* February 19, 1966, p. 721.

[14] *The Basle Facility and the Sterling Area* (Cmnd. 3787, October, 1968).

character. It has ceased to be an old-fashioned bank; its members now regard it as an investment fund." [15] In 1966, following the announcement of the voluntary program affecting the developed sterling area, the fear of a run was almost realized. Many sterling-area countries saw the program as the thin edge of a wedge. One member, New Zealand, is reported to have made a definite threat to withdraw its reserves from London.[16]

Nevertheless, suppose the United Kingdom *must* temporarily turn another screw, postponing for a time further investments overseas. What is the direct income cost of capital restriction as a means of adjusting the balance of payments in the short-term?

To attempt an answer to this question, we may concentrate on direct investment outflows, since portfolio investments have on balance been in a process of liquidation, rather than increasing, in recent years. What is striking about direct investment is its apparently low level of relative profitability. Data compiled by several different authors all point to the same conclusion, that the average return on British direct investment overseas is at best only marginally higher than the after-tax rate of return on comparable investments at home.[17] The most comprehensive study available is the *Report* by W. B. Reddaway. He found that the most important returns from foreign investment are those that accrue through the level of after-tax profits and through the net gain from "knowledge sharing" (knowledge of new techniques, new products, new methods of marketing, and so on). Together, after appropriate adjustment of depreciation rates and also after allowing for capital appreciation, these produce an operating return of just 6 per cent a year on the total of capital invested abroad, as compared with a domestic "opportunity" cost of at least 3 per cent a year. Thus the net amount of gain for Britain annually seems to be no more than approximately 3 per cent of the amount invested. Conversely, at

[15] Andrew Shonfield, *British Economic Policy Since the War,* London, 1958, p. 128.
[16] John Cooper, *A Suitable Case for Treatment: What to Do about the Balance of Payments,* London, 1968, p. 230.
[17] See, e.g., John H. Dunning, "Further Thoughts on Foreign Investment," *Moorgate and Wall Street,* Autumn, 1966, pp. 24–26; Richard N. Cooper, "The Balance of Payments," in Richard E. Caves and Associates, *Britain's Economic Prospects,* Washington, 1968, pp. 175–176; and W. B. Reddaway in collaboration with S. J. Potter and C. T. Taylor, *Effects of U.K. Direct Investment Overseas: Final Report,* Cambridge, 1968, ch. 23–26. especially pp. 333–336.

most just 3 per cent a year is lost if overseas investments are temporarily restricted.[18]

Richard Cooper calculated the medium-term "trade-offs" for the United Kingdom between capital restriction and several alternative means of achieving a given improvement in the balance of payments. Assuming a decision to maintain a fixed rate of exchange, three of the trade-offs—for capital restriction, trade restriction, and domestic demand management (expenditure reduction)—are summarized in Table 6.[19] To improve the balance of payments by £100 million when the exchange rate is fixed the authorities must reduce private capital outflows across-the-board by £112 million.[20] Alternatively, they must impose an import surcharge on manufacturers of 4 per cent, or generate a rise in unemployment of .34 percentage points. Table 6 also summarizes the direct annual cost of each of the three alternatives. (The calculations for trade restriction and domestic demand management are described in the appendix to this paper.) Capital restriction is by far the cheapest means of adjustment—3 per cent of the postponed investment, or just £3 million a year. Trade restriction is more expensive, some £45 million a year, and this is just a minimum estimate; the cost would be higher if the form of trade restriction chosen were more discriminatory than a uniform surcharge (say, differential levies or import quotas). Demand management is the costliest alternative of all—£245 million a year.

[18] The key assumption here is that if investments abroad are temporarily restricted, they will not be lost irrevocably: they will simply be postponed for a time, until the balance-of-payments situation is reversed. Such an assumption is justified by the formulation of the problem in the text, as one of *short-term* adjustment. Britain's loss would of course be greater if, in a longer-term context, it were assumed that some investments would be lost irrevocably, rather than merely postponed.

[19] Richard Cooper, *op. cit.,* p. 196.

[20] I have adjusted Cooper's calculation of this trade-off slightly. Cooper reckoned that for a payments improvement of £100 million, an across-the-board reduction of private capital outflows of £110 million would be required. This figure was based on Professor Reddaway's interim study of the effects of British overseas investment, published in 1967, which had estimated that for every £100 million of new capital outflow, British exports rise (on average) by about £9 million. (Thus, 91 : 100 = 100 : 110.) However, after Cooper wrote, Reddaway's *Final Report* (1968) increased the estimated rise of exports to £11 million. Cooper's calculation must therefore be increased to £112 million (89 : 100 = 100 : 112). Reddaway's studies also indicate that in the longer term, there will be a decline of balance-of-payments receipts equal to 4 per cent a year of the initial reduction of capital outflows. See W. B. Reddaway in collaboration with J. O. N. Perkins, S. J. Potter, and C. T. Taylor, *Effects of U.K. Direct Investment Overseas: An Interim Report,* Cambridge, 1967, p. 122; and Reddaway, *Final Report,* p. 342.

TABLE 6

Size and Cost of Alternative Methods of Improving the Balance of Payments
by £100 Million

Alternative Method	Specific Course of Action	Size of Policy Change [a]	Annual Cost
Capital restriction	Across-the-board reduction of private outflows [b]	£112 million	£3 million
Trade restriction	Import surcharges on manufacturers [b]	4 per cent	£45 million
Domestic demand management	Rise of unemployment rate	.34 percentage points	£245 million

SOURCES: Richard N. Cooper, "The Balance of Payments," in Richard E. Caves and Associates, *Britain's Economic Prospects,* Washington, 1968, p. 196; and text and Appendix.

[a] Per year, in terms of transactions levels of 1966. "Medium-term" effects, after a period of adjustment.

[b] Assumes no foreign retaliation.

The ranking of the three alternatives is about what we would expect on the basis of a priori theoretical considerations.[21] The immense width of the range, however, is surprising. The loss from restriction of capital outflows is only one-fifteenth of the least cost resulting from trade restriction; and even the latter is rather slight as compared with the loss from domestic expenditure reduction. Clearly, the optimal course for Britain at times of short-term payments crisis, given a decision to maintain a fixed rate of exchange, has been first to postpone investments abroad. For this the government has been frequently criticized: many experts have argued that if the exchange rate itself cannot be changed, then domestic expenditure reduction would be far preferable to the imposition of restrictions or controls of any kind. But perhaps, the expectations of such experts to the contrary notwithstanding, the authorities have known what they were doing after all.

[21] See, e.g., Richard N. Cooper, *The Economics of Interdependence: Economic Policy in the Atlantic Community,* New York, 1968, pp. 249–259.

APPENDIX

IN this appendix I describe my method of calculating the direct annual income-cost of trade restriction and of domestic demand management (expenditure reduction) as alternative means of adjusting the balance of payments in the short term when the exchange rate is fixed. In the text the results are summarized in Table 6.

DEMAND MANAGEMENT

Richard Cooper estimates that the trade-off between the unemployment rate and the payments balance is on the order of 0.1 additional percentage points of the former for roughly every £29 million improvement of the latter.[22] For £100 million of improvement approximately .34 additional percentage points of unemployment would be required.

As a rule, short-term fluctuations in employment tend to understate the corresponding fluctuations in gross income and output. That is, in the short-term the rate of unemployment of labor typically varies by less than the corresponding rate of employment of total capacity. There are several reasons for this.[23] The most important explanation is that the rate of utilization of labor tends to change simultaneously. Some workers, in production as well as administration, are regarded by their employers as a kind of overhead: their number is neither reduced when there is a temporary decline in output, nor raised when there is a temporary increase; instead, they simply work at a more or less leisurely pace. Additional factors include changes in the length of the work week and changes in the number of marginal workers entering or leaving the labor force.

The precise relationship between unemployment and output is not easy to identify. Frank Paish has suggested that a variation in the rate of unemployment is associated with a variation in gross output (sign changed) multiplied by a factor of five.[24] However, this seems

[22] Richard Cooper, "The Balance of Payments," pp. 156–162.
[23] See, e.g., *ibid.*, pp. 157–158; and F. W. Paish, *Studies in an Inflationary Economy*, New York, 1962, p. 318.
[24] *Ibid.*, p. 319.

an extraordinarily high figure; at any rate, Paish's evidence is sketchy and not very convincing. Much more complete and convincing is the evidence from two full-scale empirical investigations: one an international comparison by Brechling and O'Brien, the other a study of the United Kingdom by Godley and Shepherd.[25] Both sources produce a virtually identical estimate of a factor of two. That is, both agree that changes in gross output in Britain typically are about double the corresponding (opposite) changes in the rate of unemployment.

This means that an increase of .34 percentage points of unemployment will be associated with a loss of .68 per cent of real national output. In Britain in 1968 gross domestic product (which is the most comprehensive measure of the output of the economy) stood at £36,267 million. Approximately two-thirds of 1 per cent of that is some £245 million. This indicates the order of magnitude of national income that would have to be foregone (annual rate) if demand management were the alternative chosen to achieve an additional £100 million improvement of the balance of payments in the short term.

TRADE RESTRICTION

Despite a long tradition of liberal commercial policies, Britain in November 1964 unilaterally imposed a surcharge of 15 per cent on imports of most manufactured products, ostensibly for balance-of-payments purposes. Two years later (after having reduced the surcharge once, to 10 per cent, in April 1965) it was removed. There is still disagreement regarding the effectiveness of the surcharge. When first announced, it was expected to reduce imports by about £300 million a year. But according to the most systematic estimate to date, by Johnston and Henderson, imports were in fact probably reduced by only £156 million through the end of 1965, and by £72 million in 1966, both in terms of 1958 prices.[26] Converting to 1964 prices sug-

[25] Frank Brechling and Peter O'Brien, "Short-Run Fluctuations in Manufacturing Industries: An International Comparison," *Review of Economics and Statistics,* August, 1967, pp. 277–287; and W. A. H. Godley and J. R. Shepherd, "Long-Term Growth and Short-Term Policy," *National Institute Economic Review,* August, 1964, pp. 26–38. But *cf.* Richard N. Cooper, "The Balance of Payments," *op. cit.,* p. 160, n. 26.

[26] John Johnston and Margaret Henderson, "Assessing the Effects of the Import Surcharge," *Manchester School of Economic and Social Science,* May, 1967, pp. 89–110.

gests a reduction of £130 million during the year 1965 (excluding the last quarter of 1964, which is included in the £156 million) and of £80 million in 1966.[27]

However, Johnston and Henderson probably underestimated the effectiveness of the surcharge, to the extent that the full amount of the tax was not reflected in the price paid in Britain for manufactured imports. The surcharge was known to be temporary. Accordingly, many foreign exporters, wanting to maintain their position in the British market, may have absorbed some of it themselves. As Richard Cooper points out, this possibility is supported by the fact that import unit values, which had been rising steadily during the several years before 1965, stopped rising in 1965 and 1966 despite continued price increases in exporting countries. By adjusting for this possibility Cooper increases the estimated effectiveness of the surcharge.[28] His calculation of the trade-off between a control of this kind and the payments balance (on the assumption of no direct foreign retaliation) is on the order of approximately 1 additional percentage point of the former for every £25 million improvement of the latter. For £100 million of improvement a surcharge of 4 per cent would be required.

A surcharge on this order—or, indeed, any trade control at all—is bound to create an incidental loss of efficiency by protecting import-competing industries. The misallocation of resources is the cost of the improvement in the balance of payments. The magnitude of the cost will depend on the flexibility of output and demand in the economy, on the structure of prior trade restrictions, and especially on the nature of the new trade restriction. In general, the more discriminatory barriers to imports are, the greater are the distortions that are introduced into the domestic price system. Conversely, the more uniform a new barrier is, the smaller is the loss of income that will ensue.[29] Britain's surcharge in 1964 was applied uniformly to virtually all imports competing with manufacturing industries at home. We may assume, therefore, that the cost of the surcharge, or of any control like it, represents broadly the *lower* limit of the range of potential efficiency losses from trade restriction.

[27] Richard N. Cooper, "The Balance of Payments," p. 167.
[28] *Ibid.*
[29] *Ibid.*, p. 252.

There has been surprisingly little empirical research by economists into the efficiency losses of trade restrictions. However, what little work has been done suggests that in developed economies such losses tend to be very small for uniform tariffs or surcharges—certainly lower than the corresponding losses of income that are necessitated by deflations of equivalent impact on the balance of payments.[30] At the theoretical level, this suggestion has been confirmed by Harry Johnson. Using a simplified but highly plausible model, he calculates

> that both the total gains from international trade and the cost of protection are likely to be relatively small in the large advanced industrial countries, owing to their relatively flexible economic structures, probably high elasticities of substitution among the goods on which this consumption is concentrated, and relatively low natural dependence on trade.[31]

We can use Johnson's calculations to estimate the cost for Britain of a 4 per cent surcharge on manufactured imports. As it happens, the British do not have a relatively low natural dependence on trade; in fact, imports run at between 16 and 17 per cent of gross national product. But on the other hand, it happens that like other large advanced industrial countries, they do have a relatively high degree of flexibility in both output and demand. If we assume that the elasticities of substitution in production and consumption are each unity, we find that the efficiency loss created by a 4 per cent surcharge amounts to not more than 0.13 per cent of free-trade output.[32] Of course, we have no idea what free-trade output might potentially be, but as an approximation we may instead take the most comprehensive statistical measure available of actual output—namely, gross domestic product. In 1968, 0.13 per cent of gross domestic product was roughly £45 million. This is indicative of the *minimum* amount of national income that would have to be foregone (annual rate) if a uniform surcharge

[30] *Ibid.*, pp. 249–252 and 257–259. Existing empirical work on the efficiency losses from trade restriction is summarized by Harvey Liebenstein, "Allocative Efficiency vs. 'X-Efficiency,'" *American Economic Review*, June, 1966, pp. 392–394.

[31] Harry G. Johnson, "The Costs of Protection and Self-Sufficiency," *Quarterly Journal of Economics*, August, 1965, p. 371.

[32] This is composed of a consumption cost of approximately 0.06 per cent (calculated from Johnson, Table IA, p. 361) and a production cost of approximately 0.07 per cent (from Table II, p. 365).

were the alternative chosen to achieve an additional £100 million improvement of the balance of payments in the short term. If more discriminatory forms of trade restriction were chosen (e.g., differential levies or import quotas), the cost would be correspondingly greater.

INTRA-EEC CAPITAL MOVEMENTS AND DOMESTIC FINANCIAL MARKETS

ROBERT G. HAWKINS · New York University

CAPITAL markets in the continental European countries have recently been the subject of much interest and study. Part of this interest concerns the role of capital-market integration and international capital mobility in the process of integration of the EEC countries. Continued progress toward EEC integration was uncertain during 1968–69 as basic problems involving exchange-rate adjustments, the common agricultural policy, and a membership broadened to include the United Kingdom forced a reevaluation of earlier expectations. Likewise, there occurred a partial, and perhaps temporary, retrenchment on earlier liberalizations of foreign investment and a postponement of new initiatives for freeing capital movements. On the other hand, the establishment of a system of intermember credits for foreign-exchange crises and the expressed intentions to adopt a plan for currency integration among EEC members by 1980 indicate that financial integration of some form may be gaining in priority among the members.

This paper attempts to provide some evidence of the extent to which intra-EEC capital mobility has tied the financial markets of the members into a more closely integrated complex. Measures of the intensity of intra-EEC capital movements relative to other financial flows are developed and examined for trend. In addition, intercountry differences and variations in interest rates are examined for indications of an effective integration process. It is patently clear that integrating forces going beyond the confines of the EEC, particularly the Euro-currency and Eurobond markets, have played a substantial role in

NOTE: Financial support for this research from the Ford Foundation Grant to New York University for International Business and Legal Studies is gratefully acknowledged. The final version has benefited from helpful comments by Holger Engberg, Norman Mintz, Robert Platt, Ingo Walter, George Kalamoutsakis, and the discussants.

connecting more closely the EEC markets, even without an explicit connection with the Common Market integration program. This aspect is also briefly considered.

The paper is organized as follows. In Section 1 the presumed deficiencies of European financial markets and the benefits and costs of integrating them are briefly examined. In Section 2 the approach to financial integration taken by the EEC to date is outlined. Sections 3 and 4 then present some quantitative evidence as to the extent of the integration. In the former the relative intensity of intra-EEC capital movements is examined, and the latter is concerned with the harmonization of national interest-rate movements among the members.

1 ADVANTAGES AND COSTS OF FINANCIAL INTEGRATION

"UNDERDEVELOPED" CAPITAL MARKETS

Financial markets in the EEC countries are typically characterized as relatively backward in comparison with those in the United States and United Kingdom. This remains true even though continental Europe has had higher ratios of saving and fixed investment to national output than have the Anglo-Saxon countries, and despite evidence that European companies resort to external as opposed to internal finance relatively more often than is done in the United States and Great Britain.[1] The most commonly voiced complaints concerning the financial markets of the EEC countries can be summarized briefly.[2] It must be borne in mind, however, that there is considerable diversity

[1] See Ira Scott, *European Capital Markets: Present Structure and Prospects for Integration,* Washington, D.C., 1968, esp. Chapter 7.

[2] Two official studies have provided a wealth of information on European financial markets. These are the OECD *Capital Markets Study,* especially Volume III, *Functioning of Capital Markets,* Paris, 1968; and European Economic Community, *The Development of a European Capital Market* [known as the Segré Report], Brussels, 1966. See also U.S. Treasury Department, *A Description and Analysis of Certain European Capital Markets,* Washington, D.C., 1964; and Kurt Richebächer, "The Problems and Prospects of Integrating European Capital Markets," *Journal of Money, Credit, and Banking,* August, 1969, pp. 336–346.

among the markets of the Six, and easy generalizations can be only partially correct.

First, the financial markets of the EEC countries are small and relatively uncompetitive. The small size is a consequence of (1) the relatively small flow of savings and investment of the EEC members taken individually, (2) the relatively low stock of outstanding debt and resulting inadequacy of secondary markets, and (3) the failure until recently of merging to any considerable degree the separate national markets into one or more larger ones.

The submarkets within the national markets (the Netherlands being the possible exception) are generally more highly compartmentalized than is true in the United States. This results in a sluggish transmission of credit pressures from one segment to another, and a slow and constrained accommodation between the demand and supply of funds in the submarkets. The excessive domestic segmentation stems from a number of sources. Important among these are legal, administrative, and fiscal restraints on the behavior of financial institutions (and others) that limit the scope of their asset portfolios and also their ability to compete in issuing liabilities. Another factor tending to slow the transformation to a more highly developed financial system is the existence of institutional rigidities stemming from a history of currency instabilities, inflations, and government involvement in the nonbank financial sector. Also, the government often supplies services (e.g., pension plans), which has suppressed the mobilization of large amounts of funds actively seeking high returns and willing to substitute among assets on the basis of yield.

One result of this is that competition among potential sources of funds by ultimate borrowers is not very intense and particular channels of finance are heavily insulated from developments in other channels. Furthermore, the flow of funds into the long-term capital market is suppressed by the superstructure of regulations and institutional rigidities, and in some cases a distortive tax structure, which often penalizes certain types of investments. Nonbank financial institutions have not developed into the major sources of long-term funds to the financial markets that characterizes the United States and United Kingdom. As a result, secondary markets for marketable securities in most EEC countries are thin, and capital issues tend to be less liquid. This, in turn, forces borrowers to use the traditional sources of short-term finance, mainly banks, which results in a structure of private finance heavily weighted in short-term liabilities.

A reinforcing factor in most EEC countries is the proclivity of the government and government financial institutions to "preempt" funds from the long-term segment of financial markets by issuing their own securities, or securities that are subsidized or guaranteed by the government. This adds to the thinness of the markets for securities not so favored, and limits the range of choice open to the investor and the alternatives available to private borrowers.

An important reason for the perpetuation of these characteristics is that some EEC nations utilize such devices as policy tools to implement national economic programs, or at least to guide real investment into preferred channels. The use of financial incentives for such purposes occurs in each of the EEC countries to a greater or lesser degree. It poses a major problem in harmonizing monetary and fiscal policies among the members and even more of a problem in integrating capital markets.[3]

BENEFITS OF FINANCIAL-MARKET INTEGRATION

Given the characteristics of the national financial markets and the disparity among the EEC members, "integration" of financial markets (as opposed simply to free currency convertibility and removal of controls over capital outflows) involves a painful process of establishing in each member national priorities that are compatible with those of the others and of harmonizing financial regulations and structures.[4] The expected benefits must then be sizable if the EEC countries are, as it appears, willing to undertake these burdens.[5]

Integration of financial markets, taken to mean that national borrowers and lenders have meaningful alternatives for sources and uses

[3] Milton Gilbert, "Reconciliation of Domestic and International Objectives of Financial Policy: European Countries," *Journal of Finance,* May, 1963.

[4] See the Segré Report, Chapters 4 and 5.

[5] At least one eminent observer of the EEC doubts the advantage of going beyond the mere freeing of capital flows to positive steps to make national submarkets a part of a genuine EEC market. See Raymond Bertrand, "A Comment," *Journal of Money, Credit, and Banking,* August, 1969, pp. 347–349.

of funds in other countries, may give rise to at least two identifiable economic benefits as well as to other advantages in the context of economic integration in general. First, the integration of financial markets, by increasing the effective size of the market, may lead to *operational* economies of scale, i.e., to enhance the operational efficiency of the market.[6] This means that the economic resources employed in transforming a given amount of savings into investment is reduced. It may occur by means of larger underwritings of securities, narrower specialization by financial institutions, lower cost per unit of obtaining financial information, and greater competition in financial markets.

Second, financial-market integration may improve the *allocational* efficiency of the financial process. This comes about because the borrower of one nation has a broader spectrum of sources of funds open to him, and he may be able to choose a cost-repayment combination more to his liking than would be the case if he were confined to his national market. Likewise, the savers may be able to choose a more efficient risk-return combination by diversifying their asset portfolios internationally.[7] Furthermore, the risk-return spectrum faced by investors may itself be transformed as a result of the deepening and widening of financial markets. Increased secondary-market activity, which would likely accompany integration, may reduce anticipated fluctuations in yields and reduce the risk with constant return. To the extent that organized money and capital markets become more active with integration, the liquidity of marketable securities is increased and the "money risk" reduced.

Another result of improving allocational efficiency is that discontinuities in the range of available financing which existed in isolated national markets may disappear with integration. The maximum size of firm that can be financed is increased. If the rationalization of industry structure is a goal of the integration process, as it is in the EEC, an integrated financial market may be necessary to provide financing for the optimum-sized, large firms that would result.

Integration of financial markets may thus be an important complement to the integration of goods and labor markets. By equalizing bor-

[6] On these points, see A. W. Sametz, "The Capital Markets," in M. Polakoff, ed., *Financial Institutions and Markets,* Boston, 1970.

[7] See H. G. Grubel, "Internationally Diversified Portfolios," *American Economic Review,* December, 1968, pp. 1299–1314.

rowing costs among countries, competitive distortions among firms, based on nationality, are reduced. Integrated financial markets would permit the optimum location of new industry to minimize transport costs, an optimization that might not be possible with a customs union alone.

THE COSTS OF INTEGRATION

Integration carries considerable costs in independence and sovereignty over economic policy for the integrating nations.[8] Integration of financial markets involves a loss of independence in two basic areas; a loss which at least some of the EEC members have been reluctant to sustain. First, the degree to which an individual nation may influence its own monetary aggregates in the pursuit of independent economic stabilization is greatly reduced. This would be true whether a currency union were quickly established early in the integration process or a slower step-by-step removal of controls over capital flows and elimination of distortive regulations and taxation policies were used as the strategy to accomplish the integration. The ability, for example, of one member to lower interest rates while rates of other members were rising would be circumscribed if, in fact, alternative sources and uses of funds were readily available without reference to nationality. Similarly, the supply of credit within one member nation could not be independently determined if full integration existed. Despite the tendencies in the EEC to eliminate external investment controls, members retain enough independence in the formulation and execution of monetary policy to prevent an advanced state of integration of financial markets.[9]

A second facet of the loss of national policy independence involves the ability to guide the flow of saving into preferred channels of investment. Some EEC countries rely heavily on the control of the allocation

[8] These costs are succinctly described in Richard N. Cooper, "Toward an International Capital Market," Yale Economic Growth Center Discussion Paper No. 68, July, 1969.

[9] See Samuel I. Katz, *External Surpluses, Capital Flows and Credit Policy in the EEC, 1958 to 1967*, Princeton Studies in International Finance No. 22, Princeton, N.J., 1969. Also, see Scott, *op. cit.*, Part II.

of credit to influence the structure of investment spending. While, theoretically, fiscal incentives could be substituted for selective credit policies, in practice the latter are both politically and administratively more feasible.

This conflict between financial integration and independence in controlling the allocation of credit is magnified because the EEC members have rather different types of financial structures and institutions. And the structural goals that are the object of allocational credit policy also differ from member to member. Thus, a high degree of financial-market integration must inevitably reduce the efficacy of a credit policy designed to produce a desired allocation of real resources. If financial markets are to be integrated, either the selective credit controls must be given up in favor of economic efficiency or the structural priorities of the integrating members must be made compatible.[10]

2   THE EEC APPROACH TO FINANCIAL-MARKET INTEGRATION

IN THE abstract, the integration of financial markets may be accomplished via two routes, depending upon the nature of the domestic markets of the members. Take, on the one hand, a situation in which the domestic financial markets of the members are themselves highly integrated and efficient, and are without noticeably distortive regulation or monopoly elements. In such a situation, the freeing of all barriers to intraunion flows of funds in only *one* submarket (say the money market) will accomplish a high degree of integration in *all* of the financial markets of the members.

If, on the other hand, the domestic financial markets of the integrating members are compartmentalized with little communication among the submarkets, direct integration among the members of one segment of the national markets will be insufficient for full financial-market integration. Rather, two alternatives exist. One is to rationalize the domestic markets and subsequently to integrate via one submarket.

[10] The latter is precisely what is recommended by the Segré Report (Chapters 5 and 6).

The other is to attempt to integrate each of the submarkets by eliminating barriers to *international* flows while leaving largely unchanged the domestic market segmentation.

The EEC countries have more closely approximated the latter approach in the 1960's. Economists have, however, analyzed the former situation much more extensively. Their concern has been to explicate the balance-of-payments adjustment process when an abstract international investment moves frictionlessly among union members with "perfect" financial markets.[11] The EEC has avoided the alternative of establishing early in the integration process a monetary union in favor of a more piecemeal approach. This has involved the removal of explicit restrictions on capital movements and the loosening of some regulatory impediments that have tended to keep financial institutions from favoring foreign borrowers or lenders. Indeed, the Segré Report recognized the close approximation of the EEC countries to the second situation above and recommended that a broad range of members' submarkets be integrated in parallel.

The Rome Treaty is vague concerning the obligations of the members with respect to capital-market integration. It commits the members only to progressively abolish restrictions on intra-EEC capital movements to the extent necessary "to ensure the proper functioning of the Common Market."[12] Although the common market in commodities was completed in 1969, the progress toward financial-market integration has been slow, and as will be seen below, of fairly small magnitude. Furthermore, policy measures taken as a result of the currency crises and exchange-rate adjustments of 1968 and 1969 resulted in a temporary disintegration of financial markets.

The movement to eliminate explicit restrictions on *international* capital movements has been much more visible than have efforts to break down discriminatory portfolio regulations and other measures that have segmented the domestic financial markets of such members

[11] The literature here is voluminous. See particularly R. I. McKinnon and W. F. Oates, *The Implications of International Economic Integration for Monetary, Fiscal, and Exchange-Rate Policy*, Princeton Studies in International Finance No. 16, Princeton, N.J., 1966; N. M. Mintz, *Monetary Union and Economic Integration*, New York University, Institute of Finance Bulletin No. 64, New York, 1970; and Cooper, *op. cit.*

[12] Article 67 of the Rome Treaty. For a more detailed evaluation of the obligations of the members, see E. S. Kirschen *et al.*, *Financial Integration in Western Europe*, New York, 1969, pp. 42–46.

as France, Italy, and Belgium. For example, exchange controls established during World War II were gradually relaxed and free external convertibility restored in 1958. Retained, however, was a complex of controls over foreign investment by residents as well as some degree of control over investment from abroad. The vague commitment in the Rome Treaty to eliminate these controls led to the adoption of two directives of the EEC Commission (1960 and 1962). These obligated the member countries to remove restrictions on certain types of foreign investments: direct investment, dividend and interest payments and repatriations of foreign investments, loans to finance international trade, portfolio securities listed on securities exchanges, and transactions involving real estate. *Not* liberalized were new securities issues by a resident of one country on the securities markets of another, accounts (deposits) with foreign financial institutions, and certain other short-term investments. Thus, by 1969, each country (aside from Germany) still retained regulations on the sales of new foreign securities to residents and, in some instances, other types of lending to foreigners.[13] In addition, indirect discrimination against foreign borrowers in the form of double taxation on investment income still exists.

The EEC Commission attempted further to liberalize capital flows through a third directive, which would obligate each member to permit foreign new issues on its securities markets equal to a minimum percentage of all new public issues. This directive has not, however, been adopted by the member countries.

The limited success in achieving integration of financial markets plus the disruption of the process with currency crises and parity changes have contributed to recent decisions by the EEC to adopt a program of gradual monetary union. The initial steps were to create intermember credit lines and acceptance of a commitment to pool a part of international reserves and to eliminate gradually the range of fluctuation in exchange rates among the members. This avenue, if implemented, would force individual members to remove additional regulations on intra-EEC capital flows and to harmonize domestic policies with respect to credit markets. In addition, this sequence, by reducing the range (and likelihood) of changes in the exchange rate,

---

[13] See OECD, *Code of Liberalization of Capital Movement,* Paris, 1969.

would partially or wholly remove another factor tending to isolate financial markets.

It is important to note that *all* past measures to liberalize capital movements taken by EEC members have not discriminated against nonmember countries. That is, removing restrictions on certain types of foreign investment were made to apply to all such investments regardless of recipient country—EEC member or not. In addition, exchange-rate variability was the same among the member countries as it was between members and nonmembers, thus giving no relative incentive for intra-EEC capital flows. The result, which one might expect, is that the EEC has become more integrated with the financial markets of other advanced countries in general, including each other, but not simply integrated on a regional basis.

However, the question posed here is whether the EEC countries have achieved a degree of financial-market integration higher than among the developed countries generally. Some factors suggest that this might be the case, even though the policy changes made by the EEC and the major integrating devices of the Eurodollar and Eurobond markets have not been confined to the EEC countries. The very movement toward integration of product and labor markets may have been accompanied by an acceleration of intra-EEC capital flows. Improved information on investment opportunities in other member countries, some degree of tax harmonization, and attempts to harmonize antitrust laws and encourage unionwide mergers would generally tend to intensify intra-EEC financial flows. In addition, some institutions of the EEC itself—such as, the European Development Bank, the High Commission of the European Coal and Steel Community, and the Common Agricultural Fund—tend to raise the intra-EEC flow of funds. By so doing, the separate national markets are tied more closely together.

3   INTRA-EEC CAPITAL FLOWS

TWO separate bodies of evidence are examined to shed light on the degree of integration. The first is the flow of capital among the EEC members, relative to total flows of capital between the member countries and all other countries. My hypothesis is that relatively greater financial-market integration among EEC countries would be accompanied by a higher proportion of intra-EEC capital movements relative to capital movements with all countries. The second type of evidence is the similarity of interest-rate movements in EEC countries. Closer integration should, in theory, be accompanied by a narrowing of yield differentials among the members brought about by increased actual or potential intra-EEC capital flows. By extension, the narrowing of interest-rate differentials would also cause a closer coincidence (in time) of interest-rate movements among countries. The evidence on interest rates is presented in Section 4.

Consistent data on intra-EEC capital flows are notoriously deficient. Balance-of-payments figures constitute the most comparable and complete information on the matter, but even here the extent of coverage, comparability among countries, and the time span of detailed series requires that they be used with care and the usual caveats.

PRIVATE LONG-TERM CAPITAL FLOWS

Data on long-term private capital flows are available on a geographic basis for all of the EEC members for 1963 and thereafter, while comparable data for the three financially important countries — West Germany, France, and the Netherlands — extend back to 1960. The latter year is a reasonable starting point. The first steps implementing the Rome Treaty had been taken in 1959; the return to convertibility of 1958 had been absorbed; and all of the explicit measures toward liberalization of capital flows under the auspices of the EEC did not begin to occur until 1960. The unavailability of meaningful data for the period prior to 1960 precludes a comparison with the earlier period in any event.

For purposes of this paper, private long-term capital is defined to include direct investment, portfolio investment, and other loans and credits with an original maturity of one year or more.[14] Gross inflows

[14] The only exception is that long-term bank loans to foreigners are excluded, but this omission is not critical. EEC country banks make few term loans to foreigners, except for the Netherlands, and even then the flow is negligible relative to the others.

TABLE 1

Private Long-Term Capital Outflows and Inflows, EEC Countries, 1960–67

Year	Foreign Investment by EEC Countries		Foreign Investment in EEC Countries	
	Amount ($ millions)	Per Cent of Total in Other EEC Countries	Amount ($ millions)	Per Cent of Total by Other EEC Countries
Germany, France and the Netherlands				
1960	598	50	1,295	31
1961	771	37	1,254	17
1962	696	38	1,373	29
1963	522	49	1,507	23
All EEC Countries				
1963	1,023	38	2,998	15
1964	1,014	34	2,907	23
1965	1,314	43	2,450	25
1966	1,814	35	2,191	34
1967	2,349	23	2,500	31

SOURCE: Compiled from Statistical Office of the European Communities, *Balances of Payments, 1958–1967,* Brussels, 1968; EEC Commission, *The Development of a European Capital Market,* Brussels, 1966, Table 14; and *Deutsche Bundesbank, Monatsberichten, Statistische Beihefte,* September, 1969.

and outflows (net of repayments) are treated separately; the measures used, then, are flows of investment funds into and out of the individual member countries.

The summary measures are shown in Table 1. The table is divided into two parts, the lower one showing the annual inflows and outflows for all EEC countries from 1963 to 1967, and the upper one containing data only for Germany, France, and the Netherlands for 1960 to 1963. The table shows the dollar equivalent of the outflows and inflows and the percentages of each accounted for by outflows to and inflows from EEC members.

The table reflects, of course, the fact that capital inflows in the early and mid-1960's greatly exceeded capital outflows. It also reflects the absolute decline in foreign investment in the EEC countries after 1963. This decline was largely the result of the U.S. interest equalization tax and, later, the foreign-investment restrictions that reduced the volume of new American investment in the EEC. As the absolute volume of long-term capital inflows from the United States declined, the percentage accounted for by the other EEC members rose fairly consistently, so that intra-EEC investment as a percentage of total long-term capital receipts of EEC members was substantially higher in 1966–67 than earlier.

Foreign investment by EEC members was relatively stable until 1965, when a rapid expansion occurred, mainly from Germany. There is no observable trend in the proportion of outflows from EEC members going to other members. If anything, the tendency has been for the percentage to fall; i.e., EEC foreign investment in nonmember countries has tended to rise faster than such investment in member countries.

These trends are evident also in the average rate of change in the flows of private long-term investment. From 1963 to 1967, the average annual rate of growth in intra-EEC long-term capital flows was about 14 per cent. Foreign investment by EEC members in all countries grew at about 23 per cent per year, while total foreign investment in EEC countries from all sources declined by about 4 per cent per year. Thus, the evidence as to the pace of capital market integration derived from the aggregate data on private long-term capital flows is somewhat mixed. As a proportion of capital inflows, intra-EEC movements tended to increase; as a proportion of capital outflows, they tended to decline.

Some additional indication of the changes in interpenetration of financial markets can be obtained from these data by comparing them with fixed capital formation in the EEC countries, or with total domestic savings of the members. To the extent that changes in total savings and investment are accompanied by similar relative changes in financial flows, investment and saving can serve as an indication of financial flows. For the three years 1960 to 1962, the gross long-term capital inflows into EEC countries was equivalent to between 8 and

10 per cent of fixed capital formation (excluding residential construction).[15] The inflows from EEC members amounted to 2–3 per cent of fixed investment. Despite the rapid average growth in capital formation in the EEC (about 6.5 per cent per year from 1958–67) the 14 per cent annual growth in intra-EEC long-term investment was greater, thus raising the intra-EEC capital flow somewhat, but not above the relatively low figure of 5 per cent of total capital formation. This suggests that there was a very moderate increase in the interdependence of the financial markets of the EEC during the period of integration, at least until 1967–68.

The private long-term capital flows of the individual member countries are shown in Table 2. The period 1960 to 1967 (1968 for Germany) is broken into three subperiods to avoid the distortions of special factors that affect individual years.

In general, the individual country data confirm the findings based on the aggregate data that (1) there is no consistent upward movement in the relative importance of intra-EEC capital *outflows* in the total (indeed, France and the Netherlands show marked downward movements), and (2) capital *inflows* from EEC members have taken on somewhat greater importance, especially for Italy and the Netherlands.

There are two particular circumstances that distort the data in Table 2. First, the French data on capital outflows indicate a sustained net repayment on the foreign securities held by the French. Indeed, these reductions in French holdings of foreign securities were greater than gross new acquisitions in some of the earlier years, thus turning the total outflow of portfolio capital into a negative figure. At the same time, France acquired, net, some new securities of her EEC partners. This distortion explains the rapid fall in the importance of EEC outflows in the total for France from period to period. Similarly, the unusually high figure for capital inflows from the EEC to Italy in 1966–67 was again the result of a running down (repayment) of Italian debt held in non-EEC countries.

Aside from these special cases, the degree of dependence on capital flows with the EEC partners relative to the total is strikingly similar (20–30 per cent of total inflows or outflows) for each member except

[15] Calculated from data in OECD, *Statistics of National Accounts, 1952–62*, Paris, 1964.

TABLE 2

Private Long-Term Capital Flows by Country: Intra-EEC
as Per Cent of Total

	1960–63	1963–65	1966–67
Germany			
Inflows	32	24	30 [a]
Outflows	20	37	21 [a]
France			
Inflows	20	25	24
Outflows	111	57	24
Italy			
Inflows	n.a.[b]	17	83
Outflows	n.a.[b]	26	29
Netherlands			
Inflows	21	27	30
Outflows	56	42	26
BLEU			
Inflows	n.a.[b]	9 [c]	28
Outflows	n.a.[b]	56 [c]	52

SOURCE: Compiled from Statistical Office of the European
Communities, *Balance of Payments, 1958–1967*, Brussels,
1968; EEC Commission, *The Development of a European Capital Market*, Brussels, 1966, Table 14; and *Deutsche Bundesbank, Monatsberichten, Statistische Beihefte*, September, 1969.

[a] Denotes that last period covers 1966–68 rather than 1966–
67 as for other countries.

[b] Data is unavailable.

[c] Data for BLEU for 1963 and 1964 includes an unspecified
amount of short-term capital.

Belgium-Luxembourg (BLEU). The latter sends by far the highest
portion of her foreign investment to other members, but there is no
indication that this proportion has increased in the course of implementing the Rome Treaty.

To summarize, there is little evidence that a dramatic shift in the
structure of private long-term capital flows has occurred during the
period since the formation of the EEC, although it appears that the
intensity of intra-EEC flows has risen slightly relative to inflows from

outside the area. And the evidence suggests that no one country has a disproportionately large dependence on her partners as a source or a use of foreign investment funds. The possible exceptions are Italy and BLEU, on opposite sides.

It may be argued that the inclusion of direct investment together with portfolio investments and long-term credits in one category conceals potential evidence of financial integration. Direct investment flows, and their geographic structure, may depend on one set of variables, including the competition and merger policy of the EEC Commission, while indirect long-term investment is a function of other variables, including monetary policies, regulations applied to financial institutions and the like. Indirect investment may be more relevant as an indication of financial *market* integration.

Unfortunately, data that disaggregate direct and indirect investment are not available for each member for the entire period, however, consistent dissaggregation is possible for the most financially important members. This is shown in Table 3. There the average annual capital inflows and outflows for all countries are shown, and the proportion of it accounted for by direct investment. In addition, the percentages of direct and indirect investment by EEC countries are shown separately.

The data indicate that direct and indirect investment were roughly evenly split and relatively stable in their total outflows. There was a sharp rise in the proportion of direct investment by these countries going to the EEC in 1963–65, but a retrenchment in 1966–67. More relevant, however, is that portfolio outflows to the EEC as a per cent of total fell even more and were still relatively low in 1966–67.

As for capital inflows, direct investment as a per cent of total inflows rose dramatically in the middle period, and leveled off thereafter. And the proportion of direct and indirect inflows accounted for by EEC members appears to have undergone inverse cycles. The EEC indirect investment percentage rose substantially from 1960–62 to 1963–65, and then fell, but less than it had risen. This reflects partially the United States policy of stemming capital outflows, which lowered the gross flow of American portfolio investment in the EEC after 1962. Intra-EEC direct investment as a per cent of inflows, on the other hand, fell in the middle period and partially recovered in the more recent one.

TABLE 3

Foreign Direct Investment and "Other" Private Long-Term Capital Flows for West Germany, France, and the Netherlands; Total and Intra-EEC

	1960–62	1963–65	1966–67
Capital Inflows			
Total private long-term capital inflow (annual average, in millions of dollars)	1,280	1,372	1,847
Direct investment as a per cent of total inflow	36	64	60
Intra-EEC direct investment as a per cent of total from all areas	30	24	27
Intra-EEC portfolio and other long-term as a per cent of total from all areas	25	38	31
Capital Outflows			
Total private long-term capital outflows (annual average in millions of dollars)	688	858	1,409
Direct investment as a per cent of total outflow	50	52	49
Intra-EEC direct investment as a per cent of total to all areas	30	40	33
Intra-EEC portfolio and other long-term capital as a per cent of total to all areas	52	5	20

SOURCE: Compiled from Statistical Office of the European Communities, *Balances of Payments, 1958–1967,* Brussels, 1968; EEC Commission, *The Development of a European Capital Market,* Brussels, 1966, Table 14; and *Deutsche Bundesbank, Monatsberichten, Statistische Beihefte,* September, 1969.

Better evidence is available on the degree of interpenetration of capital markets from new issues data and portfolio capital flows. Integration of financial markets certainly requires that both new issues of securities and trade in secondary markets be free of national discrimination. Table 4 presents data on the total public issues of securities for the EEC countries as compared with international portfolio

TABLE 4

Portfolio Capital Inflows of EEC Countries as Related to
Net New Public Securities Issues

| Year | Public Net New Issues of Securities in EEC Countries ($ millions) | Net Inflows of Capital on Account of Portfolio Investment | | |
| | | From All Areas (as % of net securities issues) | From EEC Members | |
			($ millions)	(as % of net securities issues)
1963	8,880	14	163	1.8
1964	10,360	2	112	1.1
1965	11,670	2	152	1.3
1966	10,980	a	143	1.3
1967	12,810	3	98	0.8

SOURCES: *Net Public Issues* — European Investment Bank, *Annual Report*, various issues. *Portfolio Capital Flows* — EEC Statistical Office, *National Accounts and Balances of Payments, 1958–1967*.

ª Negligible.

investment in the EEC for the 1963–67 period. While the data are not strictly comparable, the trends shown are, no doubt, valid. The data show a steady rise of new public issues. When such issues are compared with portfolio investment in the EEC countries from outside, it is seen that there was a sharp drop after 1963, when the American market was made unattractive. From 1964 to 1967, only 2–3 per cent of new issues was accounted for by foreign portfolio issues.

The evidence is more striking when portfolio inflows from other EEC members is shown as a percentage of total securities issues. Here, the figure remained under 2 per cent for each of the five years, and was very close to only 1 per cent in four of the years. There is no indication from these data that the capital markets were highly integrated or that they became more so in this period.

The sum of the evidence remains mixed. There is *little evidence* from these admittedly inadequate data that the EEC countries forged strong new ties among capital markets and investments in the process of integration prior to 1967. But there was a perceptible tendency for a slightly larger intra-EEC flow of long-term investments to emerge, although even this may have been reversed in 1968–69.

PUBLIC AND INTERNATIONAL-AGENCY LONG-TERM CAPITAL FLOWS

While private long-term capital flows among EEC members show no marked relative increase, other types of interpenetration of markets might have occurred. Among these are capital movements resulting from public sector and international agency operations, discussed here, and short-term private movements, discussed below.

Government lending and borrowing among EEC countries has not intensified in the period since 1958. Indeed, the major changes in public long-term assets and liabilities have been with nonmembers of the EEC rather than between members.[16] Government long-term foreign assets have risen as aid to developing countries (especially Germany and France) has expanded, while claims on other EEC members have remained constant or have been repaid. Likewise, government long-term liabilities to foreigners have decreased (except for Italy) rather consistently as loans from the United States have been repaid. Liabilities to other EEC members have changed very little in absolute terms. Thus, long-term government capital flows have not been an integrating vehicle, nor have official transfer payments among EEC governments.

Besides government credits and transfers, some institutions of the EEC may themselves serve as a means of tying the financial markets of the member countries closer together.[17] These institutions may raise funds in one country and spend them in another member country. They include the European Investment Bank, the High Authority of the ECSC, the Common Agricultural Fund, and the operating budget of the EEC itself.

Although these activities may have a great future potential to

[16] Based on balance-of-payments data in EEC Statistical Office, *National Accounts and Balances of Payments, 1958–1967*, Brussels, 1968.

[17] For a general discussion of these institutions, see Kirschen, *op. cit.*, Chapter 4.

redistribute funds among EEC members, the magnitude has not been sizable as yet. By far the most important of them has been the EIB. But even it has served as much as a vehicle for capital inflows from outside the EEC as it has as a redistributor of funds. From 1961 through 1967, approximately $1 billion in loans were made by the EIB.[18] About half of these were made in Italy and another 20 per cent to nonmember countries. Of the funds raised, less than one-half was raised in the EEC countries themselves; the majority came from bond issues outside of the EEC. Thus, the scope for the redistribution of funds among the members has been relatively limited. The other EEC institutions noted above have been even less of a force.

SHORT-TERM CAPITAL MOVEMENTS

Short-term capital movements were generally decontrolled by the member countries in the early stages of the EEC. This liberalization was not, however, restricted to intra-EEC movements but was applicable to foreign assets regardless of nationality. Despite this general movement toward liberalization, there have been a number of lapses, and in 1968 and 1969 at least three countries reinstituted controls over short-term money inflows or outflows.[19]

Data are not available with which to appraise the degree of change in the interdependence of EEC money markets. It seems likely that interdependence has risen as coordination of monetary policy among the member countries became more highly developed. But there is little evidence to suggest that the member nations have given up the ability to control to a substantial degree their own short-term money market conditions. Indeed, a principal reason for the reinstitution of controls in 1968 and 1969 was to insulate the German, French, and Italian money markets from external pressures.

[18] European Investment Bank, *Annual Report, 1967,* Brussels, 1968.
[19] This is not the place to examine the measures employed by the national governments to control and manipulate short-term capital inflows and outflows. For a review of these practices, see R. H. Mills, Jr., "The Regulation of Short-term Capital Movements: Western European Techniques in the 1960's," Board of Governors of the Federal Reserve System, *Staff Study No. 46,* Washington, D.C., 1968; and Katz, *op. cit.,* esp. pp. 11–30.

THE EURODOLLAR AND EURO-ISSUES MARKETS

Without doubt, the major integrative vehicles among national money and capital markets have been, respectively, the Eurodollar and Eurobond markets. These markets have strengthened the interdependence of national interest rates and credit conditions. The Eurodollar market was the principal means by which American monetary stringency in 1966 and again in 1968–69 was transferred to Europe. Likewise the increase in borrowing by American firms in the Eurobond market in 1968 served to tighten credit supplies in the long-term credit markets.

In both instances, a closer tie between American and European financial markets was forged. But it does not necessarily follow that the Eurodollar and Eurobond markets have produced separate and additional integration of EEC financial markets beyond the generally closer common ties to American markets. A number of considerations suggest the lack of any special integrating mechanism. For example, some EEC countries have taken explicit steps to insulate their own money markets from conditions in the Eurodollar market.[20] And EEC companies have not been major issuers of Eurobonds. Exclusive of EIB issues, the peak borrowing in the Eurobond market by EEC companies was $420 million in 1967, a negligible percentage of total securities issued by such companies. On the demand side of the Eurobond market, the proportion of new issues acquired in EEC countries has been rising, but there is no precise evidence on how much of the total issues have been taken by EEC residents.[21] The lack of an active secondary market in Eurobonds limits the degree to which long-term interest rates may be tied together by this international market, although this may be changing.

Thus, while the "international" money and capital markets have been influences tending to integrate markets, they have not as yet brought about a high degree of interdependence in the EEC. They have been more effective between hemispheres than within Europe.

[20] Katz, *op. cit.,* pp. 20–29.
[21] Richebächer, *op. cit.,* pp. 342–345.

4   HARMONIZATION OF INTEREST RATES

IF SUBSTANTIAL integration of financial markets occurred during the period of establishing the EEC, one result would be that interest rates in the member countries would have moved closer together and fluctuated in more similar patterns. This could have been induced by a sizable increase in intra-EEC capital flows, or, in competitive markets, by simply the potential for such capital movements. The similarity among members in levels and movements of interest rates would have increased as integration occurred.

It is widely accepted that from the mid-1950's to the mid-1960's the differentials among national interest rates (both long and short term) of the EEC countries were somewhat reduced.[22] In 1967–69, however, the differentials widened dramatically.

Statistical measurements of a tendency for national interest rates to converge or diverge must, by nature, be somewhat arbitrary. Richard Cooper[23] has calculated the standard deviation and coefficient of variation of short- and long-term interest rates for eight countries for various years. There is an observable tendency for the national interest rates to cluster closer to the mean rate until 1968. This result, however, is partially due to the closing of the differential between European rates and rates in the United States and Canada. The latter countries were included in his sample.

I have calculated the (unweighted) average of national interest-rate differentials between each pair of EEC members for each year from 1960 to 1969. The results are shown in Table 5. From 1960 to the mid-1960's, there was a measurable tendency for interest differentials to narrow. Since 1963, however, no sustained additional narrowing has occurred. Rather, in 1966 and again in 1969, the average difference between national rates widened considerably, to levels comparable with those in the early 1960's. In sum, while there is some observed tendency for differentials between interest rates of EEC members to narrow, that tendency was not strong, irreversible, or even sustained over the period of integration.

[22] For more detail on this period, see W. D. McClam, "Interest Rates: Their International and Domestic Linkages," in OECD, *Capital Markets Study*, Volume III, pp. 655–709.

[23] Cooper, *op. cit.*

TABLE 5

Average Interest Rate Differences[a] Among EEC
Countries, 1960–69

Year	Average Differential	Year	Average Differential
1960	1.03	1965	.88
1961	1.08	1966	1.07
1962	.90	1967	.92
1963	.72	1968	.73
1964	.87	1969 [b]	1.00

SOURCE: Calculated from "Average Interest Rates for the National Economy" presented in Union Bank of Switzerland, *An International Survey of Interest Rates: Patterns and Differentials,* Zürich, 1970, Table 34. The rates presented there are averages of selected borrowing and lending rates for each country.

[a] The "average differential" is the sum of the differences between each pair of country rates for a given year divided by 10 (the total number of pairs).

[b] Through June.

While the narrowing average spreads between EEC interest rates may be a weak indication of financial integration, stronger evidence would require a greater similarity in *movements* of rates among countries. Long-term and short-term interest rate movements for each of the EEC members were, therefore, compared with each other, as well as with the United States. The interest rate series are those published by the IMF.[24] The series are for yields on short-term government securities and on long-term government bonds with roughly twenty-year maturities. Average *quarterly* yields were employed.

Three separate time periods were defined so that comparisons could be made between periods. The first period covered 1957 to 1962. This represented the period of negotiation and early implementation of the measures to establish the Common Market and is not expected

[24] International Monetary Fund, *International Financial Statistics.* Average quarterly yields on short-term and long-term government securities were the rates used.

to indicate high interconnections between EEC capital markets. The second period covers 1963 to 1967, and contains the years when financial integration was thought to be advancing rapidly. For the sake of additional comparison, a third period was defined to cover 1963 through the first quarter of 1969. The additional five quarters contained the period of the unrest in France, the ensuing franc crises, and the speculation on the revaluation of the mark. During 1968–69 there were no new initiatives toward liberalization of financial flows and some restrictions were reintroduced.

To test the degree of similarity in interest rate movements in the three periods, simple correlation coefficients were computed between each country's interest rates and those of each other EEC member (and the United States).[25] The results for the long-term government bond yields are shown in Table 6. The matrix of correlation coefficients has three entries for each combination of countries; one for each of the periods. The correlations of the United States rates with each of the EEC member's rates are also shown.

The evidence as to whether long-term interest rates moved in closer harmony in the 1963–67 period than in the earlier period is by no means definitive. For six of the pairs of coefficients, the 1963–67 is higher than earlier. In general, BLEU rates behaved much more like those of the other EEC members, and the German and Dutch rates also were more closely harmonized. On the other hand, Italian bond yields were further out of step after 1963 than earlier, as was the German with the French. Thus, in some important instances, the indication is that financial market integration was insufficient to tie bond yields much closer together.

In virtually every instance, the addition of data for 1968–69 reduced the coefficients from those for the 1963–67 period. As expected, the disruptions caused by balance-of-payments disequilibrium and foreign-exchange disturbances were disintegrative and produced divergent movements in interest rates.

The coefficients also suggest that the pairs of countries with close association between interest rates and those pairs with little correlation changed from period to period. Thus the German rate was highly correlated with those of France and Italy in 1957–62 but not in 1963–

[25] These computations were carried out by James Farrell.

TABLE 6

Similarity of Long-Term Interest Rate Movements Among Countries: Simple
Correlation Coefficients Between National Rates

	Germany	France	Italy	Netherlands	BLEU
France					
1957–62	.85				
1963–67	.56				
1963–69I	.18				
Italy					
1957–62	.87	.93			
1963–67	−.01	.10			
1963–69I	−.05	.12			
Netherlands					
1957–62	.76	.78	.76		
1963–67	.83	.79	.22		
1963–69I	.57	.83	.22		
BLEU					
1957–62	.57	.48	.41	.37	
1963–67	.66	.73	.47	.89	
1963–69I	.63	.48	.45	.85	
United States					
1957–62	−.73	−.75	−.81	−.42	−.48
1963–67	.58	.76	.10	.86	.71
1963–69I	.15	.87	.11	.84	.43

67. Similarly, there was little association between the BLEU rate and
the Dutch rate in the early period, but a high correlation later. Such
shifts also imply an absence of strong unionwide integration in financial
markets.

It is interesting to note that the coefficients between the yields
in the United States and those in all of the EEC countries were negative in the early period, as American rates generally tended upward
while the European rates generally declined. The movements in American rates from 1963 to 1967 were as much like those of the EEC
members, except Italy, as the rates in the EEC countries were similar
to each other. This would suggest that there is no additional degree of
capital-market integration among the EEC members.

TABLE 7

Similarity of Short-Term Interest Rate Movements Among Countries:
Simple Correlation Coefficients Between National Money Market Rates

	Germany	France	Netherlands	BLEU
France				
1957–62	.17			
1963–67	.39			
1963–69I	−.17			
Netherlands				
1957–62	.44	.64		
1963–67	.64	.56		
1963–69I	.40	.49		
BLEU				
1957–62	.43	−.43	−.29	
1963–67	.73	.67	.78	
1963–69I	.70	.27	.67	
United States				
1957–62	.08	−.37	.12	−.18
1963–67	.64	.53	.86	.67
1963–69I	.08	.76	.79	.36

The correlation coefficient matrix for the short-term interest rates is shown in Table 7. Italy is omitted because a comparable rate was not published for the entire period.

It appears that the money-market rates were less similar than long-term rates throughout each of the periods. Otherwise, the results in Table 7 yield the same implications as those in Table 6. There is some indication of closer connection in the 1963–67 period than earlier, but again with one notable exception—France and the Netherlands. Another important pair of countries—Germany and France—had a surprisingly low correlation between money-market rates, even in the 1963–67 period. And as one would also expect, when the data for 1968–69 is added, the coefficients are much lower, reflecting the opposite direction of movements among some of the rates, most importantly the French and German.

The coincidence of movements of short-term rates in the United States with those of the EEC countries present a pattern similar to that of the bond yields. Movements in American rates were much more similar to those in the EEC countries in 1963–67 than earlier, and, in fact, as similar to each as the EEC members' were to each other.

5 CONCLUSION

THERE is little convincing evidence that the financial markets of the EEC countries became very much more integrated during the first decade of the EEC. Although there have been positive actions taken to eliminate explicit restrictions on capital movements, to ease portfolio restrictions and other regulations that suppress capital flows, and to harmonize fiscal and financial policies among the members, most of these actions have been designed to facilitate, not intra-EEC capital flows specifically, but international flows in general. The data give no evidence whatsoever that the intensity of financial integration was greater among the members than between the members and non-members.

Capital movements statistics show some, but not a substantial, increase in the intensity of intra-EEC movements in recent years. Also, the evidence as to the degree to which EEC interest rate differentials have narrowed and the national rates move in tandem suggests only a slight increase in interconnections as the Common Market was established. Both sets of evidence, however, show a noticeable disintegration after 1967.

The slow pace of integration of financial markets within the Community is primarily the result of reluctance on the part of member governments to give up a measure of independence in aggregate credit policy or the ability to use financial markets and policies to influence the allocation of funds. The reversal of even this weak tendency toward greater integration in 1968–69 reflects the appearance of balance-of-payments disequilibria and the governments' responses to them. The costs, in policy independence, of financial integration appear low so long as there are no conflicts between policies for external and internal balance. For the EEC generally, there was no conflict until 1968, because there was an almost universal payments surplus. But once deficits became a matter of concern, measures to integrate financial markets were the first to be reversed. The costs then seemed too high.

The proposal to establish a monetary union for the EEC, if adopted and implemented, will change the picture radically. Financial integration will come about concurrently. But monetary union can be viewed as a strategy by which the sovereign independence over domestic money and credit policies is transferred to EEC institutions; i.e., given up. The reluctance to do so heretofore explains the slow pace of financial integration observed.

COMMENTS

ARTHUR I. BLOOMFIELD
UNIVERSITY OF PENNSYLVANIA

The papers by Professors Cohen and Hawkins are mainly of a factual and statistical character and are essentially noncontroversial. Cohen deals chiefly with the changing pattern of Britain's long-term capital movements, including government loans and grants, since the early 1950's. Hawkins examines the flows of long-term capital of the countries in the European Economic Community within the framework of the larger problem of EEC capital-market integration.

A major—indeed the major—theme or conclusion of Cohen's paper, recurring time and again, is that since the 1950's Britain has increasingly shifted from its traditional role as an "international long-term investor," or an "originator" or "source" of long-term capital (these are Cohen's terms), to what he variously describes as its almost exclusive role today as an "entrepôt," "middleman," or "intermediary" for long-term investment funds. Now I would at once agree that these are apt descriptions so far as concerns Britain's role in the Eurobond market. In that market Britain uses its institutional facilities to bring together foreign borrowers and investors in dollar-denominated bonds floated in London, using virtually no funds of its own. And in the Eurocurrency market it also serves as a middleman by lending to nonresidents the great bulk of the foreign-currency deposits lodged with it.

But I think it misleading to assert that Britain has become solely a middleman when considering other categories of international capital transactions. Here, it seems to me, Britain continues to perform its traditional role, despite the reduced volume of its net long-term capital exports, as a percentage of GNP and other relevant variables, compared with what it was before 1929. Cohen justifies his use of the term middleman here on what seems to me to be a number of dubious grounds.

First, he calls attention to the fact that the margin between gross long-term capital outflows and gross long-term capital inflows (by which he really means the margin between the net outflows of British capital and the net inflows of foreign capital) has been comparatively small and has been narrowing over the period. But why are the two linked or paired off? They are distinct flows and take place independently. There is nothing in an act of foreign investment in Britain that accounts directly for an act of British investment abroad. There is no middleman role here, as in the case of the Eurobond and Eurocurrency transactions. To be sure, if the inflows of foreign investment were smaller, Britain would probably have had to restrict its capital outflows more severely. But this would presumably have been equally true had other credit items in the British balance of payments been smaller than they actually were. Even less relevant is Cohen's argument that Britain's alleged middleman role is further evidenced by the geographical pattern of its long-term capital outflows — which went mainly to sterling countries — and of its long-term capital inflows — which came chiefly from nonsterling countries.

Cohen further argues in support of his use of the term middleman that Britain's net long-term capital exports are increasingly dependent upon net short-term borrowing from abroad. In general, however, Britain has not been borrowing short and lending long so far as concerns its operations in sterling. Foreign sterling balances in Britain, net of short-term sterling claims abroad and excluding holdings of the International Monetary Fund, have remained relatively constant for the past twenty years, during which Britain has been a regular net exporter of long-term capital. Of course, if foreign sterling balances had declined over the period, Britain would have undoubtedly had to cut down the scale of its net exports of long-term capital, but even this hardly seems to justify the use of the term middleman. As it happens, Cohen is able to establish his claim that net long-term capital exports have been increasingly matched by what he calls "net short-term borrowing abroad" by including in this term, not only the (relatively modest) changes in foreign sterling balances, but also the changes in Britain's gold and convertible-currency reserves, the transactions with the IMF, and even the errors and omissions item—in short, by including everything in the balance of payments except net long-term capital exports and the current-account balance.

Cohen discusses briefly Britain's "capacity" as a net exporter of long-term capital. He tells us bluntly that this capacity is limited by Britain's current-account surplus, and that the only way to increase long-term capital exports is to increase that surplus. This is one way, and a common way, of looking at the matter, but it is not one that would command universal acceptance. It could also be argued that a country's capacity to export long-term capital should be related, not to the state of its current-account balance, but to its real wealth, savings, and development; and that the current-account balance should be adjusted to the free outflow of long-term capital, thereby permitting an appropriate transfer of the real resources, rather than the other way around. However, I would admit that there are in fact many practical advantages in choosing to adjust the capital account to the current account.

At the end of his paper, Cohen attempts to measure the relative costs to Britain of restrictions on capital exports, restrictions on the trade account, and domestic-demand reduction as means of correcting balance-of-payments deficits. His calculations are in terms of national income annually foregone by use of each of these three methods. On this basis, he finds that the least costly method has been the restrictions on capital exports. Apart from the facts that this criterion may not in itself give us a complete accounting of the relative costs of capital and trade controls and that the time span he has in mind is not clear, I question his conclusion that the British authorities, by choosing the route of capital-export restrictions first at times of balance-of-payments crises, perhaps "have known what they were doing after all." If the authorities really knew what they were doing, they would, in my opinion, have devalued the pound, not in 1967, but in 1964.

The core of Professor Hawkins' paper lies in his statistical examination of EEC long-term capital movements and interest rates in an effort to determine whether appreciable progress can be said to have been made toward the integration of the capital markets of these countries since 1960. His conclusion, somewhat mixed though his statistical results are, is that no marked increase in the degree of capital-market integration has in fact occurred, despite a substantial liberalization of exchange controls and other regulations inhibiting the flow of long-term capital and despite the rapid growth of the Eurobond market, both of which have tended to make the capital markets of developed countries generally more interdependent. He attributes what he calls the slow pace of EEC capital-market integration mainly to the reluctance of individual members to relax more rapidly their direct and indirect restrictions on the flow of long-term capital, primarily from a desire to maintain a measure of autonomy in their monetary policy for purposes of domestic stabilization.

It is not entirely clear what standards Hawkins is applying, in his various tests relating to capital movements, to determine what would constitute an appreciable rate of progress towards EEC capital-market integration. Nor, in fact, does he give us a clear-cut operational definition of capital-market integration itself. It is not always evident, moreover, whether he is referring to the level or to the rate of integration, although he is presumably concerned only with the latter. And he does not make sufficiently explicit the differing degrees of significance that the different categories of long-term capital movements may have for the process of capital-market integration, a point that is stressed in the OECD report on capital markets. While these shortcomings make it somewhat difficult to evaluate his results, I believe there would be general agreement with his main conclusion.

Although aware of the limitations of the official data he uses on long-term capital movements, Hawkins does not specifically indicate that the data comprise only *net* outflows of domestic capital and *net* inflows of foreign capital. If the gross flows differ appreciably from the net flows in either direction, the data might not reflect the true degree of significance of these movements as forces integrating national capital markets.

In his various tests with the data on capital movements, Hawkins seems to be more interested in whether the EEC countries have undergone a higher rate of capital-market integration than developed countries in general, rather than in whether the rate of integration among EEC capital markets themselves has significantly increased (his originally stated intention). This is evidenced by his extensive use of percentages of intra-EEC capital flows to total EEC capital inflows and outflows, or categories thereof, as contrasted with an examination of the absolute trend of intra-EEC capital movements alone. His conclusion here that European capital markets are not becoming appreciably more integrated seems, in fact, to be based largely on the fact that the percentages show no pronounced or consistent trend. Yet the underlying data that he uses do clearly show that the *absolute* volume of intra-EEC long-term capital movements increased during the period, sharply in some categories. One must of course beware of equating the rate of growth of intra-EEC capital movements with the rate of growth of EEC capital-market integration. But, in any event, Hawkins provides us with no standard by which the two could be related.

Hawkins' preference for relative rather than absolute comparisons also shows up in his discussion of the integrative effects of the Eurobond market. He argues, though not on the basis of statistics, that the Eurobond market has been more effective in integrating the capital markets of the EEC countries with outside markets, mainly those of the United States, than with each other. This is undoubtedly true, but clearly it would not be, and has not been, inconsistent with a greater absolute (even if indirect) degree of linkage among the EEC capital markets.

Hawkins gets closer to the core of the matter when he examines the pattern of interest rates in the EEC countries. Closer integration of capital markets should show up most directly, not in any particular pattern of long-term capital movements, but in a greater similarity in levels and especially in movements of long-term interest rates in the markets concerned. While Hawkins' evidence here proved mixed among pairs of countries, so far as comparisons between the periods

1957–62 and 1963–67 were concerned, no pronounced uniform trends towards greater similarity in interest-rate patterns emerged. And in 1968–69, as he observes, there was a marked tendency for interest-rate movements to diverge. Hawkins' findings here generally confirm those of other investigators.

Making a similar set of comparisons between *short*-term interest rates in the different markets, Hawkins finds that the covariation was less than in the case of bond yields. This is a surprising result. If the comparisons were made between *covered* short-term interest rates, however, the result might have been more in keeping with expectations.

RAYMOND F. MIKESELL
UNIVERSITY OF OREGON

A common concern of these two very enlightening papers is with the benefits and costs of free or freer international capital movements, both from the standpoint of an individual country and from that of regional integration. Anticipating the entrance of Britain into the Common Market, I propose to deal with the two papers on an integrated basis.

It seems convenient to set forth in an orderly way the relevant factors in judging the case for the export of direct-investment capital. From the standpoint of the economic welfare of an individual country, direct-capital export ought to be considered on the following bases: (1) the role of foreign investment in facilitating trade; (2) a comparison of the social returns on capital investment abroad with that on domestic capital; and (3) its impact on the balance of payments. For an integrated area, such as the EEC, it is necessary to consider allocative efficiency and other benefits shared by the members of regional groups. As in the case of the benefits of free trade, the benefits from free factor movements are not going to be distributed equally among the members of the group.

With respect to the EEC, Hawkins rightly regards the freeing of capital movements as constituting an important contribution to integration, complementing the freeing of trade. The benefits from the spread of technical knowledge, improved allocative efficiency, scale economies, and the integration of markets associated with direct-investment flows are likely to be substantial even where the actual volume of capital flows among the EEC members is not large. Moreover, the generally nondiscriminatory nature of the liberalization of direct investments by the EEC makes it possible for multinational firms with headquarters in the United States to promote factor movements associated with the flow of direct investment within the EEC. I suspect that some of these direct-investment flows within the EEC are concealed in the internal accounts of multinational firms with headquarters outside the Common Market.

Hawkins suggests that financial integration within the EEC may facilitate structural adjustments required for both balance-of-payments equilibrium and stable economic growth. Thus the movement of direct-investment capital provides a vehicle for distributing technical progress and productivity growth more evenly throughout the Common Market. It may be noted, however, that there is some tendency for the more rapidly growing countries to attract more capital from abroad than they export. For example, there is considerable evidence that direct investments by the United States in manufacturing abroad have expanded more rapidly in those countries with the highest growth rates. It is also worth noting that during the period 1960–68, Germany imported more direct-investment capital from her EEC partners than she invested in them, and Germany's growth rate was somewhat higher than the average for the EEC as a whole. A tendency for those countries with the most dynamic growth to attract direct investment from the rest of the economically integrated areas could have adverse consequences for interregional balance.

The problem faced by Britain with regard to the free movement of direct-investment capital is somewhat different, at least so long as Britain remains outside the EEC. A certain amount of direct foreign investment is a concomitant of modern trade. A country cannot be a successful exporter of manufactures without investing in marketing and assembling facilities abroad; in some cases it may be forced by competition to produce certain components abroad. On the other hand, a country can be a successful exporter without massive amounts of foreign investment. The ratio of Japanese direct foreign investment to her exports of manufactures is a small fraction of that for the United States and is smaller than that for Britain as well. I strongly suspect that direct investment by American corporations through acquiring large European firms that buy relatively little from the United States does not provide social returns equal to the opportunity costs of investment in the United States. On the other hand, there are costs in trying to set up a system of direct-investment controls that would separate foreign investments that yield net social returns over opportunity costs to the investing country from those that do not.

Cohen is concerned with the net social gain or cost for the British economy of capital exports for direct investment abroad. Estimating the balance-of-payments effects of direct foreign investment, however, requires more than a simple comparison between social returns from domestic and from foreign investment. This is mainly because the investing country may be employing a higher social rate of discount to foreign exchange than to domestic income. In the face of a balance-of-payments crisis, the social rate of discount for calculating the present value of annual increments of foreign-exchange income may conceivably be 100 per cent. However, this is rarely the case, given the sources of external borrowing that are available today. But for countries with chronic balance-of-payments difficulties, the rate of discount applied to foreign-exchange income is usually substantially above that applied to domestic income.

Cohen examines the question of whether Britain should restrict direct foreign investment, in terms of the trade-off between capital restrictions on the one hand and trade restrictions or unemployment on the other. In so doing he compares the annual social costs to Britain of improving the balance of payments by £100 million under three alternatives—capital restriction, trade restriction, and domestic demand reduction. Based on a study by Richard Cooper, Cohen estimates that the annual cost to Britain of improving her balance of payments by £100 million is £3 million, if direct capital exports are restricted, and £45 million if Britain applies trade restrictions, the next best alternative. Now in making a comparison of this kind, it is important to specify whether the £100 million of direct foreign investment is only postponed for a year (and added to next year's normal foreign investment) or whether the £100 million is never restored. In the latter case, the comparison is between a once-for-all cost (£45 million) of imposing trade restrictions to improve the balance of payments by £100 million for one year, and the discounted value of £3 million per year in perpetuity, the loss from not investing abroad £100 million for one year. The choice would seen to depend upon the social rate of discount, but if we employ the 3 per cent rate assumed by Cohen (and Cooper) one would have to opt for trade restrictions and against cutting back foreign investment.[1] I might add that if a more realistic social rate of discount were used, say 10 per cent, restricting foreign investment clearly would be preferable to trade restrictions.

Now I am quite willing to admit that if a country must choose between restricting trade and restricting capital exports, the latter is preferable. But to be realistic, Britain is not faced with an absolute foreign-exchange constraint over a given time period. Given the availability of large amounts of international credit from the IMF and the Group of Ten, it is unlikely that Britain would be faced with a situation that forced her to restrict direct investment regardless of the foreign-exchange earnings from an increment of such investment. Therefore, Britain must consider whether the restriction on direct-investment outflow may not be too costly a means of securing an immediate saving of foreign exchange.

In his analysis Cohen employs the finding of the Reddaway Report that British foreign investment produces an operating return of 6 per cent a year, as compared with a domestic "opportunity" cost of capital of approximately 3 per cent per year. Both of these figures seem very low to me but I can only cite another authority in defense of my intuitive judgment. Professor J. H. Dunning, a long-time student of British foreign investment, estimates the net return on British foreign investment in manufacturing to have been 12.5 per cent per year over the 1956–63 period and the recoupment period on marginal foreign investment is estimated to be six years. Dunning believes that the Reddaway Report underestimates both the marginal return from the flow of British private direct investment and the positive balance-of-payments effects of such investment. He bases this conclusion partly on the

---

[1] In his reply to my comments Cohen stated that he meant a temporary postponement of foreign investment, *all of which would be restored,* but he admitted that his paper was not clear on this point.

grounds that the Reddaway Report takes insufficient account of the effects of not investing on the efficiency and profitability of existing investment and partly on a difference with the Reddaway Report's assumptions regarding the effects of foreign investment on imports by the host country.[2] We need more empirical evidence before judging between several possible models for determining the balance-of-payments effects of foreign investment — such as the results of the current study being undertaken at the National Bureau of Economic Research by Robert Lipsey and Merle Weiss on the relationship of American manufacturing abroad to exports from the United States. It is worth noting, however, that the British are engaged in the same type of controversy as is taking place in the United States regarding the balance-of-payments effects of direct foreign investment. Nevertheless, even if the rate of return on foreign investment estimated by the Reddaway Report can be shown to be too low, a domestic "opportunity" cost of capital of 3 per cent per year seems ridiculously low.[3] Thus, this type of comparison may well favor domestic investment over foreign investment, especially if a higher rate of discount is applied to foreign-exchange income.

Turning to flows of portfolio capital and loans, Hawkins has analyzed the benefits and costs of integrating financial markets within the EEC. Among the costs, he regards the freedom of capital movement as constraining the independent exercise of domestic monetary policies. Nevertheless, I wonder whether a larger degree of financial market integration, including the intra-EEC integration of capital submarkets, might not provide a means of easing the balance-of-payments problems associated with economic integration. Tibor Scitovsky and others have argued that the high degree of integration of asset markets, plus the ability of deficit areas to create new assets, provides a mechanism of balance-of-payments adjustment between regions within a country, which is gradual and relatively painless.[4] How much integration of financial-asset markets would be required to relieve the liquidity constraint within the EEC? Would a high degree of integration

[2] See J. H. Dunning, "Foreign Investment Controversy: II — The Effects of Foreign Investment on Resources," *The Bankers Magazine,* June, 1969, pp. 354–360.

[3] See for example, W. J. Baumol, "On the Social Rate of Discount," *American Economic Review,* September, 1968, pp. 788–802.

[4] Tibor Scitovsky, *Money and the Balance of Payments,* Chicago, 1969.

of asset markets require a common currency? I think these are important questions for the future development of the EEC.

In considering the degree to which intra-EEC financial integration has taken place during the 1960's, Hawkins finds little evidence of a strong growth of intra-EEC private long-term capital flows, either in data on the flows themselves or in any tendency toward harmonization of interest-rate movements among the domestic capital markets of the EEC countries. It seems evident that the segmented domestic capital markets of the individual countries have continued to be insulated to a substantial degree. Hawkins does point out that the major integrating vehicles are the Eurodollar and the Eurobond markets. However, he minimizes the effects of these markets by pointing to their failure to integrate the various segments of the several national capital markets. He also presents evidence that EEC companies have not been large borrowers from the Eurobond market.

I have the feeling that there has been more financial integration within the Common Market than meets Hawkins' eye. For one thing, the data on intra-EEC capital movements probably do not reflect a substantial proportion of the actual intra-EEC capital flows that take place through the intermediation of both the Eurobond and the Eurodollar markets, since many of these movements would show up in the data on EEC capital transactions with outside areas. Large international firms and large financial institutions borrow and lend in these international markets and their effects on the various segments of the domestic capital markets in the EEC countries are indirect and difficult to determine. Moreover, the domestic markets are influenced directly by national monetary policies. In addition the interest-rate differentials between the domestic markets and the international markets in assets denominated in dollars and other international currencies are affected by the swap rates, which in turn are frequently manipulated by the monetary authorities. Hawkins' findings regarding the harmonization of interest-rate movements between domestic markets are, therefore, not surprising. Nevertheless, a substantial volume of intra-EEC capital flows is taking place through the intermediation of the international markets.

Turning again to Cohen's paper and the larger issue of freeing capital movements in Britain, I am disturbed by the implication that

Britain should go on indefinitely controlling capital exports of her residents. Is this because of Britain's precarious net reserve position and the overhang of sterling balances? If so, would not a change in the role of sterling as a reserve currency along the lines suggested by Cohen in his recent Princeton essay [5] eliminate the need for controls? Or is the necessity of capital controls based on the view that Britain cannot afford to be a substantial net exporter of real capital? Britain's per capita GNP is still one of the highest in the world so that the question of whether she can *afford* to be a net capital exporter is scarcely the issue. It is a matter for national decision as to whether she is *willing* to be a net capital exporter, and by how much. Finally, is the argument that if Britain permits free capital movements, net capital exports will inevitably be larger than Britain desires or larger than her balance of payments will support? Given a general freeing of capital movements among developed countries and perhaps within a broadened EEC, might not Britain expect to enhance her role as a financial intermediary without a large net outflow of capital? Assuming such a regime, what policies would be required to keep Britain's net capital exports within the limits set by national policy without the adoption of the alternatives of domestic demand reductions or trade restriction? These appear to me to be the relevant questions.

[5] Benjamin J. Cohen, *The Reform of Sterling,* Essays in International Finance, No. 77, Princeton University, Princeton, New Jersey, December, 1969.

PORTFOLIO EQUILIBRIUM AND THE THEORY OF CAPITAL MOVEMENTS

JOHN E. FLOYD · University of Toronto

1 INTRODUCTION

THE purpose of this paper is to construct a portfolio-balance theory of international capital movements and to incorporate it in a general-equilibrium model depicting a small, fully employed economy embedded in a large trading world. Although the analysis is primarily a refinement and extension of the author's previous work on international portfolio equilibrium [1,2], the results were anticipated at a number of points by Johnson [3], McKinnon and Oates [4], and undoubtedly others.[1]

To understand fully the nature and determinants of international capital movements it is necessary to approach the problem from the point of view of portfolio equilibrium. The flow of ownership claims to capital between countries cannot be satisfactorily explained without a simultaneous explanation of the international allocation of the existing stocks. The model that is developed in this paper incorporates both stock and flow equilibria. It is shown that disturbances of equilibrium involve both once-for-all stock adjustments comprising an international transfer of ownership of part of the existing stock of capital, and changes in the allocation of the ownership of the continuous flow of additions to the stock of capital through time. The former involve

NOTE: The work for this paper was done while the author was Associate Professor of Economics at the University of Washington.

[1] Although he does not use the concept of portfolio equilibrium in deriving the capital flows in his model, R. A. Mundell's work [5, 6, 7] cannot be ignored in contemporary discussions of the monetary theory of international trade. I am indebted to him in many ways.

91

temporary short-term changes in the balance of payments, while the latter involve permanent long-term changes.[2]

After developing the theory of portfolio equilibrium and capital movements in the next section, we extend the analysis in Section 3 to a full general equilibrium model of the domestic economy. As in the author's previous work, the full model contains three equations corresponding to the three sectors of the economy: (1) the asset sector; (2) the real-goods sector; and (3) the foreign-exchange sector. In Section 4 the model is applied to the question of the ability of the government of a small country to control the level of domestic prices through the use of monetary, fiscal, and commercial policy. The results under both fixed and flexible exchange rates are examined. Particular attention is paid to the ability of such a government to insulate the country from foreign inflation. Although the general conclusions that hold in the absence of international capital mobility are also found to hold here, the introduction of interdependence of the asset sectors of the domestic and world economies results in a process of adjustment that is fundamentally different from the adjustment process as currently understood.

2   CAPITAL MOVEMENTS IN A THEORY OF PORTFOLIO EQUILIBRIUM

IN defining the assets in the portfolio, we distinguish three broad categories of wealth: money balances, skills or human capital, and machines or physical capital.

The stock of monetary wealth is denoted by the stock of real money balances, while there are at least three ways in which one could define the stock of physical capital. First, we could define it as the total value of the stock of machines (or ownership claims to machines). Second, it could be defined as an index of the quantity of machines. Third, we could define it as the number of units of real income in per-

---

[2] Since our concern is solely with international trade in ownership claims to capital, we will assume that there are no movements of capital goods across international boundaries.

petuity equivalent to the income stream yielded by the stock of machines. Our choice is the last of these definitions, largely because it is the easiest one to work with. Under the first definition, the stock of capital would vary in inverse proportion with the interest rate, a problem that does not arise when we define the stock of capital as the perpetual income-stream yielded by the stock of machines.[3] The second definition is an inappropriate measure of wealth in the sense that an improvement of the productivity of machines would make the community wealthier without increasing measured wealth.

Given our measure of physical wealth, it is appropriate to measure human wealth by the number of units of real income in perpetuity equivalent to the income stream from labor at its current level of skill. Furthermore, to allow for the possibility of uncertainty, we measure capital by the "expected" or "permanent" income stream it yields. This measure incorporates the expectations of individuals as to the future yield of the skill or machines involved.

Let us first consider the theory of asset preference with reference to a closed economy, then extend the results to a two-country situation. Also, for the moment, let us assume that the markets for both human and physical capital are perfect so that the two forms of capital can be treated as a single homogeneous asset. A representative individual in the economy thus holds wealth in only two forms: real money balances, represented by $\frac{M}{P}$, and permanent income-streams from capital, represented by permanent income and denoted by $\hat{Y}$. The reader should note that $\hat{Y}$ is both a flow of expected income and a stock of expected income-streams. The individual's situation can be depicted on Figure 1. The real money stock is on the vertical axis and the level of permanent income, or stock of permanent income streams, is on the horizontal one. The individual's wealth is denoted by the line ab.

---

[3] Even when we measure capital by the perpetual income-stream it yields, the measure is not entirely independent of the rate of interest, except where the yield of the machine in question is constant in perpetuity. Where the yield varies over time, a change in the rate of interest will alter the weights attached to the yield at various times in the future. This will change the perpetual income-stream equivalent to any variable future income-stream. This problem also arises where capital is measured by the value of the machine, since the present value will also depend on the weights attached to the income from the machine at various points in the future. Thus, the stock of capital measured in this way would not vary exactly in proportion to the rate of interest.

FIGURE 1

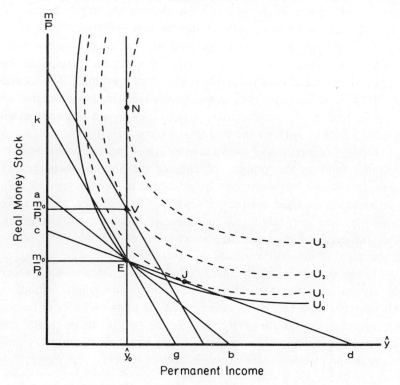

Permanent Income

Measured in units of real money balances, wealth can be expressed by

$$W = \frac{M}{P} + \frac{\hat{Y}}{\hat{i}}, \tag{1}$$

where, it will be noted, the price of a permanent income-stream in units of real money balances is the reciprocal of the rate of interest, denoted by $\hat{i}$. The individual will not be indifferent as to the mix of monetary and nonmonetary wealth in his portfolio. His tastes can be represented by a set of convex indifference curves. Given his wealth constraint ab, he will choose wealth-mix E. The interest rate facing him, given by the reciprocal of the slope of ab, is parametric.

While each individual can choose his desired wealth-mix, given his wealth restraint, all individuals taken together cannot. Suppose we regard Figure 1 as applying to society as a whole. At the wealth-mix $\frac{M_0}{P_0}$ and $\hat{Y}_0$, there will be portfolio equilibrium at the interest rate $\hat{i}_0$. At the same wealth-mix and interest rate $\hat{i}_1$, as represented by the line cd, the desired wealth-mix would be J. While an individual, by himself, could trade money balances for capital and arrive at this point, all individuals taken together cannot. The attempt to purchase assets will drive the price of income streams up and the interest rate down, rotating the line cd about the point E until it becomes coincident with the line ab, and the interest rate becomes equal to $\hat{i}_0$. Likewise, it can be shown that every wealth-mix, as represented by a point in the two-dimensional space, has associated with it an interest rate which equals the reciprocal of the slope of the indifference curve through that point. The interest rate depends on the wealth-mix and on tastes:

$$\hat{i} = A\left(\frac{M}{P}, \hat{Y}\right). \tag{2}$$

This equation can be manipulated into the more convenient form

$$\frac{M}{P} = L(\hat{i}, \hat{Y}), \tag{3}$$

which is the familiar demand-for-money equation. For our purposes, it is sufficient to express permanent income as a function of current output $Z(Y)$, so that

$$\frac{M}{P} = L[\hat{i}, Z(Y)]. \tag{4}$$

In what follows, we will assume continuous full employment with output constant at Y_0. As is well known from contemporary monetary theory, the interest rate is fixed by the real forces in the economy (in simple models), so that the price level will adjust until the desired stock of money equals the actual stock. In Figure 1, for example, a full-employment interest rate of $\hat{i}_2$, as represented by the slope of the line kg and an initial wealth-mix of $\frac{M_0}{P_0}$ and $\hat{Y}_0$, will require a fall in prices and an upward shift of the wealth restraint until equilibrium is established at the real money stock $\frac{M_0}{P_1}$ and the original full-employment level of output $\hat{Y}_0$.

Before proceeding further, it is appropriate to extend our results to include the possibility of a nonzero expected rate of inflation. The rate of interest that is relevant for the decision regarding the mix of wealth that the individual and the community will choose to hold is the money rate of interest which equals the real rate of interest plus the expected rate of increase in the price level. It is thus the money rate of interest that equals the reciprocal of the slope of the indifference curves in Figure 1.[4] If we denote the real rate of interest by i and the expected rate of increase of prices by R_p^*, we can express the money rate of interest as

$$\hat{i} = i + R_p^*, \tag{5}$$

and (4) can be rewritten

$$\frac{M}{P} = L[i + R_p^*, Z(Y)]. \tag{6}$$

These single-country results can be extended to incorporate imperfections in the market for human capital by the addition of a third axis. The three axes would then contain the real money stock, the permanent income-stream from physical capital, denoted by S, and the permanent income-stream from human capital, denoted by H. Because of imperfections in the market for human capital, human and physical capital are no longer perfect substitutes in portfolios. Given the wealth-mix in the economy as a whole, two real interest rates are generated—one on human capital, and one on physical capital. Only the latter interest rate concerns us, however, since it is assumed that no trade in human capital can occur within or between countries. The money rate of interest (which, as before, is the relevant one for portfolio decisions) is the real rate plus the expected rate of change of prices. The streams of income generated in the domestic economy by

[4] The maximum wealth position in the closed-economy case is given by the point N in Figure 1. This point, associated with a zero money rate of interest, can be attained by a negative rate of inflation equal to the real rate of interest, or by paying interest on money balances at the real rate. It is inappropriate to measure wealth in units of real money balances in this case, because the price of a unit of money balances is zero.

human and physical capital will depend upon the level of domestic output and the shares of output received by the two forms of capital. Under the assumption that the relative shares are constant (that the aggregate production function is Cobb-Douglas), the permanent income-streams from the two forms of capital will vary proportionately with permanent or expected output. Permanent output can be presumed to vary directly, though not proportionately, with current output. We can, therefore, express S and H as functions of Y:

$$S = f(Y) \tag{7}$$

and

$$H = g(Y). \tag{8}$$

The equation for portfolio equilibrium now becomes

$$i + R_p^* = A \left(\frac{M}{P}, S, H \right), \tag{9}$$

which, upon substitution of (7) and (8), yields

$$i = A \left[\frac{M}{P}, f(Y), g(Y) \right] - R_p^* \tag{10}$$

or

$$\frac{M}{P} = L[i + R_p^*, f(Y), g(Y)]. \tag{11}$$

In extending the analysis to include two countries, we assume that the domestic economy is so small in comparison with that of the rest of the world that the over-all desired wealth-mix in the world as a whole is not appreciably affected by the tastes of domestic residents, and the world stock of permanent income-streams is not appreciably affected by changes in the total stream of income generated in the domestic economy. This assumption, together with the assumption that the residents of both countries are indifferent as to whether they hold income streams from domestic or foreign-employed capital, implies that domestic residents can purchase or sell capital assets—i.e., income streams from physical capital—at what is essentially a fixed world price.[5] The world real rate of interest, which is determined by conditions in the rest of the world, is thus virtually independent of what goes on in the domestic economy. A positive anticipated rate of domestic inflation would lead to a domestic money rate of interest in excess of the world real rate, and the domestic money rate would vary directly with these inflationary anticipations. Inflationary anticipations abroad would have no effect on the domestic money rate, because they do not erode the real value of the domestic nominal money stock or assets fixed in nominal value in domestic currency.[6]

As in the case of a closed economy, the demand for money will be a function of the real interest rate (now parametric), the anticipated rate of domestic inflation, and the stocks of permanent income-streams from physical and human capital owned by domestic residents. Unlike the closed-economy case, the stock of income streams from physical capital owned by domestic residents will now differ from the stock of income streams generated from physical capital employed in the domestic economy.

The stock of income streams from physical capital owned by domestic residents will normally comprise some fraction of the stock of income streams from domestically employed physical capital plus some fraction of the stock of income streams from physical capital employed abroad. Since we are assuming that the residents of both parts of the world are indifferent as to whether they receive domestically generated income-streams, or foreign-generated income-streams, from physical capital, the inhabitants of either country would not care

[5] The basic results of the paper are unaffected by the introduction of private intermediate assets and government bonds. All that happens when private intermediate assets are introduced is that individuals have a wider range of choice as to the form in which permanent income-streams are to be held. Those who wish to avoid risk of loss of the nominal value of equities can hold their wealth in the form of bonds issued by other individuals, who, for a price, are willing to assume this risk. The size of the permanent income-stream from capital is unaffected; only the ownership of it changes. The introduction of government debt has the same effect as the introduction of private intermediate assets, as long as the future tax liabilities on this debt are fully capitalized.

[6] The interest rate at which the public will capitalize the perpetual income-stream arising from physical capital goods will be unaffected by the rate of inflation, since the rental of the machine and its price will inflate in proportion. The interest rate at which the income-stream from a debt fixed in nominal value is capitalized will adjust to include the expected rate of inflation. The former is the real, and the latter the nominal, interest rate. I would like to thank Anthony Lanyi for forcing me to clarify my argument at this point.

where the income streams they own are generated. We suppose, for the sake of convenience and determinacy, that there is some minor fixed cost to holding wealth abroad, so that the net-debtor country will never hold income streams outside its own borders.[7] We further assume that the domestic economy is a net debtor with respect to the rest of the world: domestic residents own some fraction, Q, of the total stream of income generated at home and none of the stream of income generated abroad. The remainder of the domestically generated income-stream and the entire income-stream generated abroad are owned by foreign residents.

Since there is no trade in human capital, H can be treated as a function of Y, as in the closed economy. The stream of income from physical capital owned by domestic residents will be some fraction, Q, of the total stream of income generated from physical capital employed in the domestic economy. Thus S should now be written

$$S = Qf(Y). \tag{12}$$

Substituting (8) and (12) into (9) and rearranging, we obtain

$$\frac{M}{P} = L[i_0 + R_p^*, Qf(Y), g(Y)], \tag{13}$$

where i_0 is the parametrically determined world rate of interest. This equation can be rearranged to give

$$Q = Q\left[\frac{M}{P}, Y, R_p^*\right], \tag{14}$$

where the interest rate is incorporated into the constant terms and dropped as an argument. This equation indicates the condition of equilibrium in the asset sector of the model. Given the stock of real money balances which they are forced to hold, and given the expected

---

[7] The basic reason why income-streams from domestically employed capital would not be perfect substitutes in portfolios for income-streams from foreign-employed capital is that the absence of a perfect correlation between domestic and foreign outputs leads to a gain from diversification. If the levels of output at home and abroad were perfectly correlated, there would be no basis for distinguishing between the income-streams of the two parts of the world. The assumption that there is some minor fixed cost to holding wealth abroad represents an attempt to treat the countries as separate entities, while at the same time avoiding the problem of imperfect substitutability of the two types of income-streams in portfolios.

rate of inflation and the world interest rate which they face, domestic residents will maintain portfolio equilibrium by purchasing or selling capital assets at the fixed world price. Initially, such purchases or sales of assets will involve a reduction or increase in nominal cash balances under a fixed exchange rate as the government sells or buys foreign-exchange reserves in order to preserve the external value of the currency. We assume, however, that the government always offsets the impact on the domestic money supply of these pegging operations by undertaking the appropriate open-market operations. These open-market operations are assumed to leave wealth unaffected, since the government rebates to the public the interest on any securities it owns. It is further assumed that the stock of foreign-exchange reserves is not regarded by the public as a component of wealth.

Equation (14) implies an equilibrium level of the domestic net foreign balance of indebtedness. As usually defined, the balance of indebtedness is equal to the value in current monetary units of the net ownership by foreigners of domestic capital assets or domestically generated permanent income-streams from capital. In the present context, it can be written

$$D = \frac{(1 - Q)f(Y_0)}{i_0}. \tag{15}$$

Given the parametrically determined world rate of interest and the full-employment level of domestic output, an equilibrium level of Q implies an equilibrium level of D. Shifts in the level of Q occurring at a point in time as a result of changes in the real money stock, or in the expected rate of domestic price-inflation, involve a once-for-all change in the balance of indebtedness at that point in time. This implies a one-shot capital movement induced by portfolio adjustment that must be financed either by a change in the stock of foreign-exchange reserves or by a temporary movement of the exchange rate and a temporary surplus of exports over imports.

Since equilibrium must hold through time as well as at a point in time, there will be an equilibrium time-rate of change of Q,

$$\frac{dQ}{dt} = \lambda_m \frac{M}{P} (R_m - R_p) - \lambda_y \frac{dY_0}{dt} + \lambda_r \frac{dR_p^*}{dt}, \tag{16}$$

where

$$\lambda_m = \frac{\partial Q}{\partial M/P}, \quad \lambda_y = -\frac{\partial Q}{\partial Y},$$

and

$$\lambda_r = \frac{\partial Q}{\partial R_p^*} \quad \text{from equation (14)},$$

and

$$R_m = \frac{1}{M}\frac{dM}{dt}$$

and

$$R_p = \frac{1}{P}\frac{dP}{dt}.$$

Noting that $\frac{f(Y_0)}{i_0} = P_k K^*$, where K^* is the quantity of domestically employed capital goods measured in some arbitrary units, and P_k is the real price of a unit of capital goods, we can express the differential of (15) with respect to time as

$$\frac{dD}{dt} = (1-Q)P_k \frac{dK^*}{dt} + (1-Q)K^* \frac{dP_k}{dt} - P_k K^* \frac{dQ}{dt}. \qquad (17)$$

The rate of change through time in the balance of indebtedness is related to, though not identical with, the international flow of capital per unit time, as customarily measured. The flow of capital through the balance of payments does not involve the capital gains on existing net foreign indebtedness, indicated by the term $(1-Q)K^* \frac{dP_k}{dt}$. This term must therefore be subtracted from $\frac{dD}{dt}$ to obtain the net capital inflow. Substituting (16) into (17) and letting $P_k \frac{dK}{dt} = I(i_0)$, the level of domestic investment, and $P_k K^* = \frac{f(Y_0)}{i_0}$, the expression for the domestic net capital inflow becomes

$$F = -\frac{f(Y_0)}{i_0}\left[\lambda_m \frac{M}{P}(R_m - R_p) - \lambda_y \frac{dY_0}{dt} + \lambda_r \frac{dR_p^*}{dt}\right]$$
$$+ [(1 - Q)I(i_0)]. \quad (18)$$

If the terms in the first set of brackets to the right of the equality sign vanish—that is, if $\frac{dQ}{dt} = 0$—the capital inflow will be a constant fraction of the existing flow of new domestic investment. If $\frac{dQ}{dt} \neq 0$, an additional component to the capital flow will comprise the net sale of assets to foreigners, or purchase from foreigners, consequent upon the equilibrium rate of change of Q through time.

3 CAPITAL MOVEMENTS AND PORTFOLIO EQUILIBRIUM IN A FULLY EMPLOYED ECONOMY

THE basic principles of asset equilibrium developed above can now be incorporated in a full-employment model depicting a small country embedded in a larger trading world. The full model contains three sectors, the asset sector, the income-expenditure sector, and the balance-of-payments sector, with an equation for each sector. The world real rate of interest and the price level in the rest of the world are parametric. Both domestic and foreign output are parametric by virtue of the assumption of full employment.

The conditions of equilibrium in the asset sector are given by equation (14) above. The equation determines an equilibrium level of Q for each level of the domestic nominal money-stock, prices, and expected rate of inflation. Since the equation holds at all points in time, domestic residents are also accumulating physical capital assets at an equilibrium rate relative to real money balances.

Equilibrium in the real goods market implies that planned saving minus planned investment equals the balance of trade:

$$Y - C = I + B_T, \quad (19)$$

where C is domestic consumption and B_T is the balance of trade. Although output is fixed at the full-employment level, domestic income is not. It is equal to the portions of output accruing to domestic residents. That is,

$$Y^* = Qf(Y_0) + g(Y_0), \qquad (20)$$

where Y^* is the level of income and Y_0 is the full-employment level of output.

The domestic trade balance is a function of the level of domestic income and the ratio of the price of domestic goods to the price of foreign goods, with both prices measured in domestic currency. That is,

$$B_T = B_T[P/r, \, Qf(Y_0) + g(Y_0), \, \alpha_T], \qquad (21)$$

where r is the exchange rate, α_T is a shift parameter, and the foreign price level is normalized at unity.

Similarly, the consumption function can be written as

$$C = \alpha + \beta[Qf(Y_0) + g(Y_0)], \qquad (22)$$

where β is the marginal propensity to consume.

Upon substitution of (21), (22), and the investment function $I = I(i_0)$ into (19), we obtain the condition of equilibrium in the market for real goods. A shift parameter α_d is introduced to represent a shift in expenditure on domestic goods and the shift parameter in the consumption function is dropped:

$$Y_0 = \alpha_d + \beta[Qf(Y_0) + g(Y_0)] + I(i_0)$$
$$+ B_T[P/r, \, Qf(Y_0) + g(Y_0), \, \alpha_T]. \qquad (23)$$

Finally, the balance of payments is equal to the sum of the balance of trade in goods and services and the net capital inflow minus the repatriation of the stream of income on domestically employed capital owned by foreigners. The latter equals $(1 - Q)f(Y_0)$. We can therefore write

$$B = B_T[P/r, \, Qf(Y_0) + g(Y_0), \, \alpha_T] - (1 - Q)f(Y_0)$$
$$+ (1 - Q)I(i_0) - \frac{f(Y_0)}{i_0} \left[\lambda_m \frac{M}{P} (R_m - R_p) - \lambda_y Y_0 R_{y0} \right] \qquad (24)$$

where B is the excess supply of foreign exchange and $\dfrac{dR_p^*}{dt}$ is assumed to be equal to zero.[8]

The system of three equations, (14), (23), and (24), can be solved for the three variables, P, Q, and B or r, depending upon whether the exchange rate is fixed or flexible. At this point, let us simplify it by substituting the asset equation into the other two, obtaining

$$Y_0 = \alpha_d + I(i_0) + \beta g(Y_0) + \beta Q\left(\frac{M}{P}, Y_0, R_p^*\right) f(Y_0)$$

$$+ B_T[P/r, g(Y_0) + Q\left(\frac{M}{P}, Y_0, R_p^*\right) f(Y_0), \alpha_T] \quad \text{(I)}$$

and

$$B = B_T[P/r, g(Y_0) + Q\left(\frac{M}{P}, Y_0, R_p^*\right) f(Y_0), \alpha_T]$$

$$- \left[1 - Q\left(\frac{M}{P}, Y_0, R_p^*\right)\right] f(Y_0) - \frac{f(Y_0)}{i}[\lambda_m \frac{M}{P}(R_m - R_p) - \lambda_y Y_0 R_{y0}]$$

$$+ \left[1 - Q\left(\frac{M}{P}, Y_0, R_p^*\right)\right] [I(i_0)]. \quad \text{(II)}$$

The first equation gives the combinations of r and P for which both the asset markets and the real-goods market are in equilibrium, given the values of the exogenous variables M, R_p^*, α_d and α_T. The second equation gives the combinations of r and P for which the asset markets are in equilibrium and the balance of payments is in surplus by an amount B, given the values of the exogenous variables M, R_m, R_p, R_p^*, α_d, and α_T. If we hold $B = 0$ in this equation, it represents the combinations of P and r for which the asset markets and the foreign-exchange market are in equilibrium.

We proceed to solve the system for the relative changes in the equilibrium values of the dependent variables associated with changes in the exogenous variables. Differentiating equations (I) and (II) totally, holding $B = 0$, and translating the differentials into relative changes, we obtain

---

[8] The assumption that the expected rate of inflation is constant through time will be justified in some detail later on.

$$\frac{dP}{P} = \frac{1}{\psi + \theta} \, d\alpha_d + \frac{\delta}{\psi + \theta} \, d\alpha_T + \frac{\psi}{\psi + \theta} \frac{dr}{r} + \frac{\theta}{\psi + \theta} \frac{dM}{M} + \frac{\rho}{\psi + \theta} \, dR_p^* \quad \text{(I}')$$

and

$$\frac{dr}{r} = -\frac{\delta}{\psi} \, d\alpha_T + \frac{\psi + \xi}{\psi} \frac{dP}{P} - \frac{\xi}{\psi} \frac{dM}{M} - \left(\frac{\gamma}{\psi}\right) dR_p^* + \frac{\mu}{\psi}(dR_m - dR_p), \quad \text{(II}')$$

where

$$\psi = -\left(\frac{\partial B_T}{\partial P/r}\right) P/r,$$

$$\theta = \left(\beta + \frac{\partial B_T}{\partial Y^*}\right) f(Y_0)\lambda_m \frac{M}{P},$$

$$\delta = \frac{\partial B_T}{\partial \alpha_T},$$

$$\rho = \left(\beta + \frac{\partial B_T}{\partial Y^*}\right) f(Y_0)\lambda_R,$$

$$\xi = \left(1 + \frac{\partial B_T}{\partial Y^*}\right) f(Y_0)\lambda_m \frac{M}{P} - \frac{f(Y_0)}{i}$$

$$\frac{M}{P} \lambda_m(R_m - R_p) - (I(i_0))\lambda_m \frac{M}{P},$$

$$\gamma = \left[\left(1 + \frac{\partial B_T}{\partial Y^*}\right) f(Y_0) - I(i_0)\right]\lambda_R,$$

and

$$\mu = \frac{f(Y_0)}{i_0} \lambda_m \frac{M}{P}.$$

The effects of shifts in the exogenous variables on the level of prices under a fixed exchange rate can be read directly from equation (I$'$), holding $\frac{dr}{r} = 0$. The effect on Q can be obtained by substituting this result into the total differential of (14).

The direction of the effects of shifts in the exogenous variables on the steady-state balance of payments under fixed exchange rates can be obtained by first solving equations (I$'$) and (II$'$) simultaneously for $\dfrac{dP}{P}$ and $\dfrac{dr}{r}$, and then noting that the direction of the change in the equilibrium level of r is the opposite of the effect on the balance of payments at the initial exchange rate. The solutions for $\dfrac{dP}{P}$ and $\dfrac{dr}{r}$ are

$$\frac{dP}{P} = \frac{1}{\theta - \xi}\, d\alpha_d + \frac{dM}{M} + \frac{\rho - \gamma}{\theta - \xi}\, dR_p^* + \frac{\mu}{\theta - \xi}\, (dR_m - dR_p), \quad \text{(I'')}$$

and

$$\frac{dr}{r} = \frac{\psi + \xi}{\psi(\theta - \xi)}\, d\alpha_d - \frac{\delta}{\psi}\, d\alpha_T + \frac{dM}{M}$$

$$+ \frac{\rho(\psi + \xi) - \gamma(\psi + \theta)}{\psi(\theta - \xi)}\, dR_p^* + \frac{\mu(\psi + \theta)}{\psi(\theta - \xi)}\, (dR_m - dR_p). \quad \text{(II'')}$$

The first equation gives the effect of the shifts in the exogenous variables on the price level where the exchange rate is allowed to adjust. The second gives the change in the equilibrium exchange rate. If $\dfrac{dr}{r}$ in this equation is positive, then the shift in the exogenous variable in question will produce a deficit in the balance of payments under a fixed exchange rate. If $\dfrac{dr}{r}$ is negative, a surplus in the balance of payments will be produced when the exchange rate is fixed.

Since the level of prices in the model is determined, among other things, by the level of the nominal money stock, it is wholly inappropriate to treat the percentage rate of change of prices through time as exogenous. Obviously, it will be determined partly by the percentage rate of change of the nominal money stock. Moreover, just as the relative change in the level of prices associated with given changes in the exogenous variables is different under fixed and flexible exchange rates, so the percentage rate of change of prices through time will be different under fixed and flexible rates. The equilibrium percentage rate of change of prices under a fixed exchange rate is given by equation (I'), where the derivatives are taken with respect to time, rather than with respect to some arbitrary constant at a point in time. Letting $\dfrac{d\alpha_d}{dt} = \dfrac{d\alpha_T}{dt} = \dfrac{1}{r}\dfrac{dr}{dt} = \dfrac{dR_p^*}{dt} = 0$, we have $\dfrac{1}{P}\dfrac{dP}{dt} = \dfrac{\theta}{\psi + \theta}\dfrac{1}{M}\dfrac{dM}{dt}$, the differential of which becomes

$$dR_p = \frac{\theta}{\psi + \theta} \, dR_m. \tag{IIIa}$$

When the exchange rate is flexible and $\frac{1}{r}\frac{dr}{dt}$ therefore may be non-zero, the equilibrium percentage rate of change of prices through time is given by equation (I''), where the derivatives are taken with respect to time, rather than with respect to some arbitrary parameter at a point in time. Letting $\frac{d\alpha_d}{dt} = \frac{d\alpha_T}{dt} = \frac{dR_p^*}{dt} = 0$, as before, we have

$$R_p = R_m + \frac{\mu}{\theta - \xi}\left(\frac{dR_m}{dt} - \frac{dR_p}{dt}\right).$$

This equation is satisfied by $R_m = R_p$, so that,[9] where the exchange rate is flexible,

$$dR_p = dR_m. \tag{IIIb}$$

Upon substitution of either (IIIa) or (IIIb) into (I'') and (II'') we can obtain the relative change in the price level and the equilibrium exchange rate associated with changes in the level and percentage rate of growth of the nominal money supply or exogenous changes in expenditure on domestic goods and the balance of trade. If (IIIa) is substituted, we get the results under a fixed rate or adjustable peg; if (IIIb) is substituted, we obtain the results under a flexible rate.

A DIAGRAMMATIC TREATMENT

Equations (I) and (II) can be portrayed graphically, as in Figure 2. The exchange rate is on the vertical axis and the price level is on the horizontal one. The *PP* curve gives the combinations of the price level and exchange rate for which the markets for assets and real

[9] In both equations (IIIa) and (IIIb), the rate of change in prices through time is determined solely by the rate of expansion of the nominal stock of money. If we assume that the percentage rate of expansion of nominal money balances through time is a constant determined by government policy, then the percentage rate of growth of prices is also a constant. In this event, the assumption of a constant expected rate of change of prices through time is quite appropriate.

goods are in equilibrium; it represents equation (I). The *BB* curve gives the combinations of the exchange rate and the price level for which the markets for assets and foreign exchange are in equilibrium; it represents equation (II). The intersection of the two curves gives the full equilibrium of the model.

It is clear from the facts that both ψ and θ are positive, that the *PP* curve is positively sloped. This results from the fact that a devaluation improves the trade balance and thereby increases aggregate demand. Because $\xi \gtreqless 0$, the *BB* curve may be positively or negatively sloped, as in Figures 2(*a*) and 2(*b*), respectively. The sign of its slope hinges on the effect of a rise in the price level on the balance of payments. The curve *BB* is positively sloped if a rise in prices will deteriorate the balance of payments, requiring a rise in *r* (devaluation) to preserve equilibrium; it is negatively sloped if a rise in *P* will improve the balance of payments, requiring a fall in *r* (upward valuation) to maintain equilibrium. The usual view of economists is that a rise in the price level will hurt the balance of payments because it worsens the balance of trade. This view does not consider the effect of the price rise on the capital flow. The increase in the price level reduces the real money stock, leading to a portfolio adjustment which takes the form of sales of assets to foreigners against additions to foreign-exchange reserves. This leads to a reduction in the fraction of domestically employed physical capital owned by domestic residents and an increase in the fraction owned by foreign residents. This increase in the fraction owned by foreigners will imply, ceteris paribus, that a larger fraction of the flow of new domestic investment will be sold to foreigners. This will improve the balance of payments and may offset the effect of the rise in the level of prices on the balance of trade. The over-all effect of a rise in the price level on the balance of payments will therefore be ambiguous.[10]

Stability of the system implies that a rise in *r* improves the balance

---

[10] At this point, it is important to notice that the area above the *BB* curve represents the combinations of *r* and *P* for which there is a surplus in the balance of payments (since at any *P*, *r* is too high), and the area below the curve represents the combinations for which there is a deficit. Similarly, the area to the left of the *PP* curve represents conditions of excess demand in the real goods market (since at any *r*, *P* is too low), while the area to the right gives the combinations of *r* and *P* for which there is excess supply.

FIGURE 2

(a)

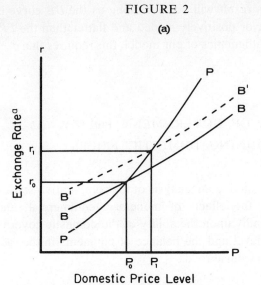

Domestic Price Level

(b)

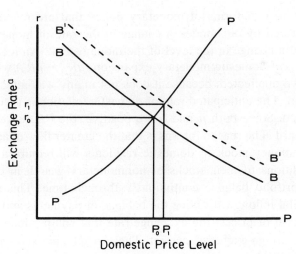

Domestic Price Level

ᵃ Price of foreign currencies in units of domestic currency.

of payments. This result will occur as long as the *BB* curve is either negatively sloped, or positively sloped and flatter than the *PP* curve. In terms of the mathematics of our model, this requires that $\theta - \xi > 0$.

4 THE ROLE OF GOVERNMENT POLICY IN DETERMINING DOMESTIC PRICES

THIS section is devoted to an analysis of the comparative-static results, focusing first on the effects of monetary, commercial, and fiscal policies, and secondly upon the ability of the domestic government to control the price level and the balance of payments in the face of inflationary pressure from abroad.

MONETARY POLICY

There are two forms of monetary policy that are relevant in a world described by our model: a change in the rate of monetary expansion and a change in the level of the money stock. An increase in the rate of *real* domestic monetary expansion $(dR_m - dR_p)$ will leave the *PP* curve unaffected, because it does not in any way affect aggregate demand. The anticipated rate of domestic inflation is assumed to be unaffected. Since both μ and ψ are positive, the *BB* curve will be shifted upward. The reason for this is that the greater flow of additions to the real money stock of domestic residents will require a greater flow of additions to their stocks of nonmonetary wealth in order to maintain portfolio balance continuously through time. This reduces the net capital inflow, worsening the balance of payments and raising, for every level of prices, the exchange rate that will produce equilibrium in the foreign-exchange market. These results are shown in Figures 2(*a*) and 2(*b*).

Two possibilities arise with respect to the effect of an increase in the rate of expansion of nominal money balances on the rate of expansion of real money balances. If the exchange rate is fixed, equation

(IIIa) implies that $dR_m - dR_p = \dfrac{\psi}{\theta + \psi} \, dR_m$ and, since θ and ψ are both positive, an increase in the rate of nominal money expansion will result in a less than proportional increase in the rate of real money expansion. If the exchange rate is flexible, equation (IIIb) implies that $dR_p = dR_m$, so that the rate of real monetary expansion is unaffected by the rate of nominal money expansion. In this case, there are no effects on the BB curve in Figures 2(a) and 2(b), and an increase in the rate of nominal expansion will raise the rate of price inflation and of reduction in the exchange value of the currency but will have no effect on the level of prices or on the level of the exchange rate, as long as the increased rate of inflation is unanticipated.

In the case of a fixed exchange rate, it can be seen from Figures 2(a) and 2(b) that the level of prices will be unaffected by the monetary policy. A long-run deficit in the balance of payments will result, as evidenced by the fact that the domestic currency is overvalued at r_0. There will be a continuous *rate of loss* of foreign-exchange reserves. Since the real money stock is unaffected at the point in time under consideration (only its rate of change through time is increased) there will be no portfolio adjustment.

If the exchange value of the domestic currency is reduced to remove the long-run disequilibrium, the trade balance will improve, aggregate demand will increase, and the price level will rise. This reduces the real money stock, leading to a once-for-all sale of assets to foreigners and, hence, a one-shot capital inflow, as portfolio equilibrium is reestablished. Thus, while an exchange rate of r_1 will produce long-run balance-of-payments equilibrium, it will be too high in the short-run while the resulting portfolio adjustment is occurring, and there will be a one-shot accumulation of foreign-exchange reserves.

As long as the exchange rate is held at r_0, however, no portfolio adjustment and no price changes will result from an increase in the rate of nominal money expansion. Changes in the rate of increase in the money supply are thus effective and costless ways of maintaining external balance in the short-run. They are not a costless way of maintaining external balance in the long run, however, for two reasons.

First, any increased rate of expansion of the nominal money stock, and the associated increased rate of expansion of prices, will eventually become anticipated and the *expected* rate of inflation will increase. This will make money balances less attractive than other assets and lead to a net purchase of assets abroad by domestic residents. Since the community's capital assets are increased in exchange for foreign-exchange reserves (which are not a part of wealth), permanent income and aggregate demand will increase. The *PP* curve will thus shift to the right. This is indicated by the fact that ρ, ψ, and θ are positive in equation (I'). The effect of the increase in the expected rate of inflation on the balance of payments at the initial level of prices is ambiguous. The increase in Q resulting from the purchase of capital abroad will reduce the flow of repatriated income to foreigners and improve the balance of payments. This effect may be more than offset, however, by the reduction in the flow of sales of new capital to foreigners, resulting from the fact that foreigners now own a smaller equilibrium share of the stock of domestically employed capital. The *BB* curve can there-fore shift either up or down. The increase in the rate of monetary ex-pansion would thus raise the domestic level of prices if the resulting increase in the *rate* of inflation were anticipated, and the stability of domestic prices would thereby be sacrificed in controlling the balance of payments by manipulating the rate of nominal money expansion. Furthermore, since the *BB* curve may shift in either direction, it is uncertain whether an increase in the rate of monetary expansion would, under these circumstances, improve the balance of payments at the initial exchange rate. The second reason why manipulation of the rate of monetary expansion would lead to longer-term changes in prices is that a higher rate of change of prices for some period implies a higher level of prices at the end of that period.

An increase in the level of the nominal money stock at a point in time will increase the level of aggregate demand and shift the *PP* curve to the right, as evidenced by the fact that ψ and θ are positive in equations (I') and (II'). This result follows from the fact that the rise in M stimulates a purchase of securities abroad in return for foreign-exchange reserves. Permanent income rises and, with it, aggregate demand and the price level. It should be noted that the rise in prices will, under conditions of constancy of the exchange rate, be less than proportional to the increase in the nominal money stock, so that the real money stock will increase. This result follows from the fact that the rise in the price level not only reduces aggregate demand for the same reason that the rise in M increases it, but reduces it, in addition, by worsening the balance of trade.

Because $\xi \gtrless 0$, an increase in the nominal money stock may have either effect on the BB curve. The increase in permanent income resulting from the rise in Q will lead to a reduction in the income from domestically employed capital repatriated abroad. This will tend to improve the balance of payments. However, the fall in $(1 - Q)$ will also reduce the fraction of the current flow of new investment being sold to foreigners, tending to deteriorate the balance of payments.

As can be seen from an examination of Figures 3(a), 3(b), and 3(c), the price level will rise from P_0 to P_1 if the exchange rate is fixed. On the basis of the directions of the shifts of the PP and BB curves, it is not possible to say whether the balance of payments would improve or deteriorate, whether the equilibrium exchange rate would be higher or lower, or whether the price level would rise, on balance, if the exchange rate were flexible. However, from equations (I'') and (II''), the changes in the equilibrium levels of P and r associated with a relative change in M can be shown to equal

$$\frac{dP}{P} = \frac{dr}{r} = \frac{dM}{M}.$$

This implies that the shifts in the PP and BB curves will be such that the equilibrium combinations of P and r will always fall on a ray through the origin.

An increase in the level of the money stock will thus produce a long-run deficit in the balance of payments. The change in the price level at the initial exchange rate is associated with a once-for-all purchase by domestic residents of capital assets from foreigners, financed by a one-shot decline in the stock of foreign-exchange reserves. The domestic foreign-exchange authority will also suffer thereafter a continuous rate of decline in the stock of foreign-exchange reserves through time. If the foreign-exchange peg is adjusted upward to r_1 to eliminate the deficit, the price level will rise further to P_2, lowering the real money stock to its initial level and wiping out both the portfolio adjustment and the long-term flow deficit in the balance of payments.

FIGURE 3

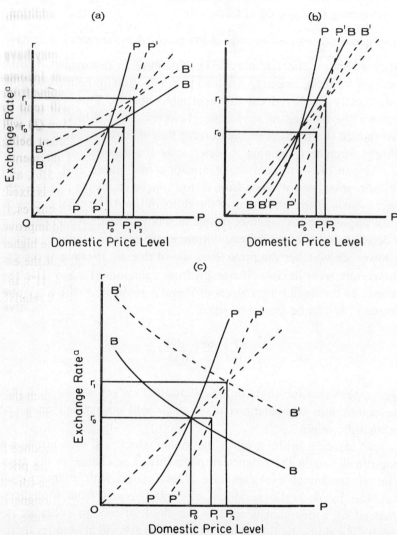

(a)

(b)

(c)

[a] Price of foreign currencies in units of domestic currency.

It is clear that, if the exchange rate is flexible, the increase in the nominal money stock merely results in a proportional rise in the level of domestic prices and a proportional fall in the external value of the domestic currency.

We can conclude that the government, through manipulation of the level of the money stock, has full control over the price level under a flexible exchange rate and at least some control under a fixed rate. This control is limited, in the case of a fixed exchange rate, by the government's willingness and ability to have its foreign-exchange reserves fluctuate.

The only reason why the domestic government has any control at all over the price level under a fixed exchange rate is that a rise in the nominal money stock results in a purchase of productive assets abroad in return for "unproductive" foreign-exchange reserves, leading to a change in income, consumption, and aggregate demand. Surely this overstates the change in wealth, since foreign-exchange reserves should, to some extent, be considered as wealth. The fact that the reserves are held involuntarily, however, implies that the members of the community, as individuals, would not choose to hold them if confronted with the alternative of trading them for capital. Thus, while a reduction of these reserves in return for income streams from physical capital would increase wealth, it would do so by less than the value of physical capital assets obtained. The changes in the price level under fixed exchange rates would therefore presumably be much smaller than indicated in the above analysis.[11]

COMMERCIAL POLICY

The term commercial policy refers to policies which directly affect exports and/or imports. A government-induced reduction in expenditure on imports results in an improvement of the trade balance and can be interpreted in our model as a positive change in α_T. Since

[11] If one was to assume that the level of wealth is unaffected by a change in the stock of foreign-exchange reserves, the PP curve would become a ray through the origin and would not shift with changes in the level of the money stock. Aside from the fact that the level of domestic prices would be independent of the domestic money stock under a fixed exchange rate, the results obtained earlier would still hold.

δ, ψ, and θ are positive, the effect will be to shift the PP curve to the right and the BB curve down. The improvement of the trade balance increases aggregate demand, raises prices, and improves the balance of payments at the initial exchange rate. The rise in prices reduces the real money stock and leads to a sale of capital assets to foreigners by domestic residents as portfolio equilibrium is reestablished. There will thus be a one-shot increase in the stock of foreign-exchange reserves in the short-run, as well as a continuous rate of accumulation through time, thereafter. To determine which way the price level will move if the exchange rate is allowed to adjust, we must refer to equations (I″) and (II″). It can be seen that for any given change in α_T

$$\frac{dP}{P} = 0 \text{ and } \frac{dr}{r} = -\frac{\delta}{\psi} < 0.$$

As shown in Figures 4(a) and 4(b), the commercial policy can be viewed as shifting both curves downward by the same amount. If the exchange rate is flexible (or is adjusted downward to eliminate the surplus), the balance of trade, flow of capital, stock of capital domestically owned, and domestic price level all remain at (or return to) their initial positions.

FISCAL POLICY

Finally, we will define fiscal policy as a government-induced shift in the domestic demand for domestically produced goods.[12] An expansionary shift is represented by a positive change in α_d in our model. Aggregate demand increases and the PP curve shifts to the right. The BB curve remains unchanged because the balance of trade is, by assumption, unaffected. A rise in the price level occurs at the initial exchange rate, reducing the real money stock and leading to a one-shot sale of capital assets to foreigners. This short-run accumulation of foreign-exchange reserves will be followed in the long run by either accumulation or decumulation, depending upon whether the BB curve is positively or negatively sloped. If the exchange rate is flexible, its

---

[12] If the demand for foreign goods is also directly affected, we would interpret the policy as a combination of fiscal and commercial policy.

FIGURE 4
(a)

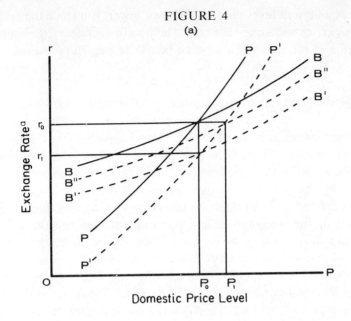

Domestic Price Level

(b)

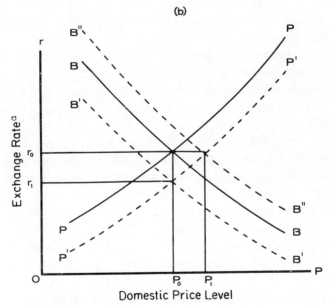

Domestic Price Level

^a Price of foreign currencies in units of domestic currency.

long-run equilibrium level may be higher or lower. But since the price level always rises and a one-shot capital inflow always occurs, the short-run position of the rate will always be below its long-run position.

FOREIGN INFLATION AND THE DOMESTIC ECONOMY

We can now analyze the effects of inflation abroad on the domestic price level and the ability of the government to offset it. A once-for-all increase in the nominal money stock in the rest of the world, occurring either at a point in time or over an interval of time, will lead to a temporary fall in the world interest rate and an increase in investment. This drives up the foreign price level, returning the interest rate to its initial level and eliminating the increase in investment. Since the world interest rate does not ultimately change, the level of domestic investment will remain at (or return to) its former level. The rise in the foreign price level will lead to an increase in domestic exports and a reduction in imports. This shifts the BB curve down and the PP curve to the right, as in Figures 4(a) and 4(b). The results are identical with those of a positive shift of α_T, so as we have already shown, an appreciation of the domestic currency from r_0 to r_1 will reestablish equilibrium without a change in the domestic price level. The domestic government will thus have no problem of inflation in the face of inflation abroad as long as the exchange rate is flexible. Since none of the real variables, at home or abroad, are affected, there will be no portfolio adjustment.

As shown in Figures 4(a) and 4(b), under a fixed exchange rate the improvement of the trade balance will create excess aggregate demand in the domestic economy and increase the price level from P_0 to P_1. The rise in the domestic price level increases imports relative to exports, moderating the improvement in the balance of trade induced by the rise in prices abroad. In addition, it reduces the real money stock, leading to a one-shot sale of assets abroad. In the long run, the fall in the fraction of domestically employed capital assets owned domestically leads to a rise in the proportion of new domestic investment being purchased by foreigners, and results in an increase in the continuous inflow of capital.

The domestic government is now confronted with two problems: a problem of inflation, and the problem of a payments surplus. The latter problem is significant because the surplus implies that wealth is being transferred to other countries every time a dollar of foreign-exchange reserves is accumulated.

The continuous payments surplus can be relieved for a short period by an increase in the rate of monetary expansion, which would—in order for portfolio equilibrium to be maintained continuously through time—reduce the flow of sales of capital assets abroad. This would shift the BB curve to BB'' in Figures 4(a) and 4(b), equilibrating the long-term balance of payments. However, nothing would be done to reverse the one-shot gain of foreign-exchange reserves associated with the portfolio adjustment. Nor would there be any immediate effect on the domestic price level.

The balance-of-payments problem can better be handled by an increase in the level of the money stock at a point in time or over an interval of time. This would reduce the steady-state-equilibrium surplus in the balance of payments and create a portfolio adjustment that would bring about a net purchase of assets and a one-shot reduction in the stock of foreign-exchange reserves. The payments surplus, both short run and long run, will be offset when Q, the fraction of domestically employed assets owned by domestic residents, has returned to its initial (pre-foreign-inflation) level. For this to occur, all real variables must return to their initial preinflation levels. The fact that the balance of trade must return to its initial level implies that the domestic price level must rise proportionately with the initial rise in the foreign price level. For the real money stock to be returned to its preinflation level, therefore, the domestic nominal money stock must be increased proportionately with the initial rise in the foreign money stock. The domestic government has validated the inflationary pressure on the domestic economy from abroad by increasing the domestic money stock in proportion. The problem with this policy is that it sacrifices the objective of eliminating the inflation in favor of eliminating the surplus in the balance of payments.

To eliminate the rise in the price level would require a contraction of the nominal money stock at a point in time or over an interval of time. The fall in prices is accomplished, however, at the cost of further capital inflows in both the short run and long run and a further rise in the stock of foreign-exchange reserves.[13] The reason for this is that the reduction in the money stock leads to a sale of capital assets abroad in order to maintain portfolio equilibrium, resulting in a further short-term capital inflow and accumulation of foreign-exchange reserves. The resulting fall in Q and equivalent increase in $(1 - Q)$ increases the fraction of the flow of current domestic investment being sold to foreigners, further accentuating the long-term capital inflow and the rate at which foreign-exchange reserves will accumulate in the long run.

An alternative policy would be to attempt to control the domestic price level by reducing government expenditure on domestic goods. This would reduce aggregate demand, shifting the PP curve to the left in Figures 4(a) and 4(b). If there was no leakage to imports, the BB curve would be unaffected. The price level would fall, eliminating for the time being the problem of inflation. The real money stock would rise, leading to a portfolio disequilibrium that would be eliminated by a purchase of assets abroad by domestic residents. This would cause a one-shot loss of foreign-exchange reserves that would tend to offset the initial accumulation consequent upon the foreign inflation. The government could, therefore, accomplish its objective of reducing the price level and, at the same time, reduce its excess stock of foreign-exchange reserves. In the long run, however, the surplus in the balance of payments and the *rate* of accumulation of reserves may either increase or decrease, depending upon whether the BB curve is positively or negatively sloped. Thus, while the short-run balance-of-payments problem is eliminated, this policy could accentuate the long-run balance-of-payments problem. It should be noted, in addition, that if the foreign inflation continues over a long period, this method of control over the domestic price level will, in the long run, imply regular additional cuts in government expenditure. Such a contraction of the government sector may be unacceptable.[14]

Finally, the government could prevent the foreign inflation from

[13] If the public regards a dollar's worth of foreign-exchange reserves as equivalent in portfolios to a dollar's worth of capital, it would not be possible to reduce the price level by reducing the nominal money stock.

[14] The alternative fiscal course of increasing taxes operates through effects on wealth, which are ruled out in the model used here.

raising the domestic price level and causing an inflow of capital by applying direct controls to the trade balance. This would have the same effect on prices and the balance of payments as a devaluation. Indeed, it is a devaluation which is not applied to all goods in proportion to their prices, but rather to individual commodities on a selective basis.

5   CONCLUSIONS

THE central concern here has been the construction of a portfolio-balance model of international capital movements and its application to a small, fully employed economy embedded in a large trading world. The paper's main contribution lies in its ability to explain both the international allocation of the existing stock of ownership claims to physical capital and the international allocation of the flow of additions to that stock in a single model.

A major conclusion that arises out of this formulation is that there are two distinct types of international movements of ownership claims to capital: first, once-for-all portfolio shifts arising from changes in the level of the nominal money stock or the level of prices at a point in time; and second, continuous capital flows through time arising out of the requirement that portfolio equilibrium be maintained through time in the face of positive (or negative) rates of expansion of the nominal money stocks, prices, and the level of real output. The treatment of international capital movements as a function of interest-rate differentials, a formulation that is common in much of the current literature, is inconsistent with the theory of portfolio equilibrium developed in this paper.

The effects of monetary and fiscal policy differ in fundamental ways from the standard zero-capital-flow analysis. The usual theorem that an increase in the nominal money stock results in a proportional rise in the domestic price level and, if the exchange rate is flexible, in a proportional depreciation of the domestic currency, still holds, as does the theorem that an increase in the money stock or an expansionary fiscal policy will result in a rise in prices and a deficit in the balance of payments. But the details of the process by which these results arise are fundamentally different. In the analysis assuming zero capital flow, an increase in the nominal money stock results in a temporary fall in the interest rate, which is removed by a proportional rise in prices. The balance of payments deteriorates via a worsening of the balance of trade. If the exchange rate is flexible, the domestic currency falls in inverse proportion to the increases in the money stock and price level, eliminating the deterioration of the trade balance and the balance of payments deficit. Once the assumption of zero flow of capital is dropped and interdependence between domestic and foreign portfolio equilibria is introduced, a rise in the money stock does not result in a proportional rise in the price level at the initial exchange rate. It results in a portfolio disequilibrium that is resolved by a purchase of assets abroad. The interest rate does not change. The only reason that the price level rises at all is that the sale of foreign-exchange reserves for capital assets raises wealth, and this raises spending. To the extent that the domestic price level rises, the trade balance deteriorates; and to the extent that foreigners now own a smaller equilibrium fraction of the stock of domestically employed capital, they will be purchasing a smaller fraction of the flow of new additions to that capital stock. On both these counts, the balance of payments will deteriorate in long-run equilibrium. This deterioration is accentuated in the short-run by the one-shot purchase of capital required to maintain portfolio equilibrium. Where the exchange rate is flexible, the depreciation required to eliminate the payments deficit puts upward pressure on prices, which reverses the portfolio adjustment resulting from the rise in the nominal money stock. Prices rise until the real money stock has returned to its initial level, at which point the short-term portfolio adjustment and the increase in the long-term capital flow are completely reversed. The deterioration of the trade balance resulting from the rise in prices is prevented by the depreciation of the currency. All real variables are thus unaffected by the monetary expansion: only the nominal magnitudes, the price level and the exchange rate, are affected.

In the typical models where no trade in ownership claims to capital is allowed, a change in the rate of monetary expansion changes only the rate of price change through time and the rate at which the balance of payments is deteriorating. The introduction of trade in ownership claims to capital and the specification of conditions of portfolio equilibrium through time result in a direct relation between the rate of monetary expansion and the level of the balance of payments. More specifically, if the rate of expansion of the nominal stock of money is increased, and domestic residents are therefore being forced to add to their stock of money balances at a more rapid rate, the maintenance of portfolio equilibrium through time will require that they add to their ownership of capital at a higher rate. This will result in a greater flow of purchases of ownership claims to new capital from foreigners and a deficit in the balance of payments under a fixed exchange rate. Since aggregate demand and the level of prices are unaffected, changes in the rate of monetary expansion are a simple way of maintaining balance in foreign payments in the short run. Such changes will not be effective in the long run, both because changes in the *rate* of price increase will become capitalized into expectations, and because a change in the *rate* of price increase will result in a different, and possibly undesirable, level of prices at some time in the future.

Finally, the results of this paper suggest that the conflict between domestic and foreign stability inherent in systems of fixed exchange rates and adjustable pegs may pose even greater problems than is currently thought. Since changes in the exogenous variables in the system result in short-term portfolio shifts, as well as long-term "fundamental" disequilibria, one might expect a rather variable path of balance-of-payments adjustment to exogenous changes. Substantial short-term movements of capital among countries may be caused by nonspeculative forces alone. Since we know nothing about the timing of these short-term portfolio adjustments, nor about speculative capital movements that might accompany them, the problem of predicting the equilibrium level of the exchange rate and any required readjustment of the peg may be even more difficult than we now think.

REFERENCES

1. Floyd, John E., "International Capital Movements and Monetary Equilibrium." *American Economic Review*, Vol. LIX, No. 4, Part I (September, 1969), pp. 472–492.

2. ———— "Monetary and Fiscal Policy in a World of Capital Mobility." *Review of Economic Studies,* Vol. XXXVI (4) (October, 1969), pp. 503–517.
3. Johnson, Harry G., "Toward a General Theory of the Balance of Payments," in *International Trade and Economic Growth: Studies in Pure Theory.* Cambridge, Harvard University Press, 1958.
4. McKinnon, Ronald I., and Oates, Wallace E., "The Implications of International Economic Integration for Monetary, Fiscal, and Exchange Rate Policy." *Princeton Studies in International Finance,* No. 16 (1966).
5. Mundell, Robert A., "The Monetary Dynamics of International Adjustment under Fixed and Flexible Exchange Rates." *Quarterly Journal of Economics,* Vol. 74 (May, 1960), pp. 227–257.
6. ———— "Flexible Exchange Rates and Employment Policy." *Canadian Journal of Economics and Political Science,* Vol. 27 (November, 1961), pp. 509–517.
7. ———— "Capital Mobility and Stabilization Policy under Fixed and Flexible Exchange Rates." *Canadian Journal of Economics and Political Science,* Vol. 29 (August, 1963), pp. 475–485.

CAPITAL MOBILITY AND PAYMENTS EQUILIBRIUM

EDWARD S. HOWLE · University of North Carolina

IN HER recent survey article, Anne Krueger notes that "the first problem of balance-of-payments theory is to formulate the nature of the external constraint. Since theory allows for, and countries are, running deficits (however defined) it is not sufficient to say that the external constraint means there can be no deficits."[1] Also, "any balance-of-payments model which precisely formulated the external constraint would, of necessity, be intertemporal. Since most models to date are static, the issue of the nature of the constraint is avoided by focusing upon current-account transactions and assuming that deficits must eventually be corrected."[2] Krueger states that growth models, with increasing asset demand and changing flows, hardly exist.[3] This paper represents an effort to develop such a model for the fixed exchange-rate case; a model in which the external constraint is endogenously determined from demand and debt-servicing requirements. (Table 1 provides a listing of symbols employed therein.)

In the real world the liquidity constraint, or the constraint upon the amount deficit countries can borrow, is imposed for at least three reasons: (1) countries do not wish to lend their savings in more than limited amounts; (2) countries are fearful of imported inflation; and (3) we all recognize intuitively that even if unlimited lending were available to offset imbalances, a system of fixed exchange rates would

NOTE: Research support was provided by National Science Foundation Grant GS940 and by the Business Foundation of North Carolina, Incorporated. I am greatly indebted to James C. Ingram for his original suggestion that I do research on capital mobility and for his comments on earlier versions of this analysis. George Schieren gathered empirical data, did much of the computer work, and made useful suggestions. Comments by Marina v. N. Whitman and Dennis Appleyard were helpful in making the final revision. Blame for the remaining deficiencies is mine.

[1] Anne O. Krueger, "Balance-of-Payments Theory." *Journal of Economic Literature,* March, 1969, p. 2.

[2] *Ibid.*

[3] *Ibid.,* p. 23.

TABLE 1

List of Symbols

Stocks and flows in real units of domestic goods:

B The current-account balance. $B \equiv X - M - (r - p)D$.

D Net external indebtedness of the region. A negative D value indicates that the region is a creditor. $D_n \equiv \sum_{j=1}^{n-1} B_j$.

I Physical investment in the region.

K The capital stock physically located in the region. $K_n \equiv \sum_{j=1}^{n-1} I_j$.

M Imports expressed in terms of equivalent units of domestic goods at the current price ratio.

T The current account minus net external investment earnings. In the model this is identical to the trade balance. $T \equiv X - M$.

W Income. Output minus the interest burden. $W \equiv Y - (r - p)D$.

X Exports.

Y Output.

Y^* Full capacity output.

Ratios, coefficients, and rates:

d D/K.

d^* The equilibrium d ratio.

e Elasticity of demand for exports.

e' Elasticity of demand for imports.

f The rate of growth of export demand in the absence of different rates of inflation between regions.

g The rate of growth of K and of capacity.

k The output-to-capital ratio.

n The natural growth rate of the region's capacity; n can be interpreted as the growth rate of labor with no innovation, or the rate of growth of labor plus the rate of increase in capacity output per laborer if labor-saving innovation is assumed to exist.

p The rate of increase in the price of goods produced in the region.

p' The rate of increase in the price of imports.

r The nominal rate of interest. The region's real rate of interest is $(r - p)$.

s The average propensity to save. The saving function is assumed to be linearly homogeneous, but s need not be constant with respect to short-run changes in income or the growth rate.

still restrict a country's ability to use expansionary fiscal policy. With regard to the third point, the ultimate constraint of fixed exchange rates is not the liquidity constraint; it is the constraint imposed by the growing debt and deteriorating trade balance of any nation, or region, that expands faster than is warranted by world demand for her goods. But because of the theoretical gap that Krueger notes, we have not been able to specify what sort of limitations the latter constraint imposes on a region, and this makes it difficult to determine what the liquidity constraint should be—and whether, indeed, it is necessary.

An initial step in bridging this gap was taken by Robert A. Mundell in his analysis of the short-run characteristics of a payments system involving fixed exchange rates, perfect interregional mobility of capital (funds), and separate regional fiscal programs.[4] The liquidity constraint is effectively relieved by capital mobility in this case—except that the region must maintain the same interest rate as that existing elsewhere. Although this prevents monetary policy from being used for internal balance, fiscal policy can be used for this purpose, while capital flows are induced that offset any resultant current-account imbalance. This gets rid of the liquidity constraint, and that is a necessary step if a model is to be developed in which the balance-of-payments constraint is to be an endogenously determined part of the analysis, rather than being an arbitrary limit upon the current account that is imposed exogenously at the outset. It remains to find out what happens in the long run in this Mundellian world—to determine what happens to the debt and the trade balance once the region is freed of the liquidity constraint.[5]

Interregional differences in interest rates or credit constraints do not play a major role in maintaining balance-of-payments equilibrium between regions of, say, the United States. Nevertheless, demand forces, acting through the multiplier and accelerator, evidently limit inflation or expansion in a region to a rate warranted by demand for the region's goods, but this demand relationship does not insure a balance-of-payments equilibrium in the conventional static sense. A re-

[4] Robert A. Mundell, "Capital Mobility and Stabilization Policy under Fixed and Flexible Exchange Rates." *Canadian Journal of Economics and Political Science,* November, 1963, pp. 475–485.

[5] Krueger, *Journal of Economic Literature,* March, 1969, pp. 20–21.

gion may run a current-account deficit indefinitely, but not a deficit of unlimited size.[6] The indebtedness of the region may also grow for an indefinite time, but both the deficit and the debt remain in some sort of reasonable proportion to the output capabilities of the region.

The preceding arguments suggest the direction that might be taken by an analysis in which the external constraint is endogenously determined. A dynamic model will be presented in which perfect capital mobility relieves the liquidity constraint à la Mundell, and the only remaining payments-equilibrating force is the demand effect of changes in the interregional interest burden and the trade balance. It is well known that the demand effects of balance-of-payments changes do not insure an equilibrium within the static Keynesian framework. But considered within an intertemporal framework, they do lead to something that can be called a dynamic equilibrium — an equilibrium in which the level of external debt and the current-account imbalance *grow* at a rate that is compatible with the growth rate of the region. After the characteristics of this equilibrium are described, the model will be used to determine the nature of the external constraint imposed by this ultimate requirement that the debt level or trade imbalance remain in proportion to the economic size of the region.

The analysis presented here is based upon several versions of a rather complex difference-equation model, a variant of which is shown in the Appendix. The text of the paper uses a more intuitive presentation. This analysis will be presented in two steps. First, the concept of an equilibrium ratio of regional external debt to capital, labeled d^*, will be discussed. A determinate d^* value will be shown to exist for any set of values of the following coefficients:

1. The rate of capital formation: g.
2. The real interest rate: $(r - p)$.[7] The nominal rate is r, and p is the rate of price increase of domestically produced goods.

---

[6] Richard G. Davis and Lois Banks, "Interregional Interest Rate Differentials." *Federal Reserve Bank of New York Monthly Review,* August, 1965, pp. 165–174.

[7] Actually, $(r - p)$ is only an approximation of the real rate of interest, which is more accurately stated as $(r - p)/(1 + p)$. An inaccuracy also results from the fact that p is the rate of increase in the price of domestically produced goods, and what is actually needed is an expression for the rate of increase in the price of domestically consumed goods.

3. The output to capital ratio: k.
4. The saving to income ratio: s.

It will be shown that if these values remain constant, the debt-level to capital ratio, d, will approach the equilibrium level d^*. This is not to imply that the values of all of these coefficients will, in fact, remain constant during the adjustment process.

In the second part of the analysis it is affirmed that a change in the trade-balance to capital ratio, T/K (or, in one version, the export to capital ratio, X/K), must be accompanied by changes in g, k, s, and/or p. This is definitional. Consequently, a change in T/K will alter d^*. But it is argued that any change in T/K will be self-limiting. A worsening of T/K (increase of the deficit relative to the capital stock) will depress demand relative to capacity to produce, and this deflationary effect will increase until the deterioration of T/K is halted. By a similar process, any increase in T/K is eventually self-limiting. Therefore, an approach to a dynamic balance-of-payments equilibrium involves an approach of T/K to its limiting, or equilibrium, value at the same time as d approaches an equilibrium value. Then both the external-debt level and the current-account imbalance of the region will tend to grow at the same rate as the region's capital stock or capacity to produce.

The deflationary or inflationary process through which changes in T/K are self-limiting can involve long-run price, and/or income, changes.[8] If labor, as well as capital, is highly mobile between regions, the adjustment will come primarily through income changes; but if labor is not mobile, price changes will play the primary role. In considering the effect of changes in T/K, therefore, two limiting cases will be considered: the case of perfect interregional mobility of labor, and that of perfectly immobile labor. In both cases, of course, capital is assumed to be perfectly mobile, so that the liquidity constraint in the usual sense does not exist.[9]

---

[8] This analysis is related to export-based growth models and a number of other long-run theories. A complete bibliography cannot be provided here; see Marina von Neumann Whitman, "International and Interregional Payments Adjustment: A Synthetic View," *Princeton Studies in International Finance*, No. 19, 1967.

[9] Space will not permit a detailed response to discussants. However, extreme or limiting-case assumptions are used by the theorist not because they are encountered in reality, but because they are a useful starting point in attempting to understand reality. Perfect competition and perfect monopoly are examples; the assumptions are never fulfilled, but

While this paper is too brief to describe completely the dynamic adjustment process following a variety of disturbances, I will use the model to analyze the options that might have been open to France in 1968 and 1969 had not that country been faced by a limit on reserves and borrowing. Symbols will be defined as they are introduced, but they are also listed for quick reference in Table 1 above.

1 THE EQUILIBRIUM RATIO OF EXTERNAL DEBT TO CAPITAL

THE following assumptions will apply throughout the remainder of this discourse:

1. The world consists of small region A and large region F. Region A is sufficiently small so that foreign repercussions of changes within A can be ignored.

2. The balance-of-payments adjustment process in region A will be considered, while the rest of the world (region F) grows at a constant rate.

3. Region F maintains a constant money rate of interest (r).

4. No change of exchange rates is possible and capital is perfectly mobile between regions in the Mundellian sense. An infinitesimal deviation of region A's interest rate from the rate in F will induce a flow of funds of whatever size is needed to make up the difference between internal investment and saving and so offset an existing current-account imbalance. As Mundell has pointed out, this means that region A's nominal interest rate cannot deviate from the rate r existing in F. All investment takes the form of riskless bonds with the nominal yield

the models have provided a norm with which to compare reality and a background for the construction of models of oligopoly and monopolistic competition. In balance-of-payments analysis, the limiting case of zero factor mobility with fixed exchange rates has been well developed in the specie-flow and open-economy multiplier models. The assumptions (i.e., zero capital mobility) are not realistic, but the models have provided a background for the consideration of more realistic cases. In contrast to studies in micro-economics, the opposite extreme of perfect capital mobility has not been adequately developed. An automatic adjustment process is at work in that case, as in the specie-flow case, and examining it provides a different perspective. In addition, many of the conclusions reached are surprisingly unaffected by changes in assumptions.

r. The debt (D) of region A will always mean the net debtor position of region A vis-á-vis region F. A negative D value means that A is a creditor.

5. No assumption is necessary concerning the exact institutional arrangement that facilitates the perfect mobility of capital. With a unified currency, a well-developed banking system can facilitate the transfer of savings. With separate currencies and a highly developed capital market, open-market operations by region A's monetary authorities can produce the transfer, as has been explained by Mundell. An agreement involving a uniform interregional interest rate and a commitment by each region's central bank to establish interbank lending to offset any current-account imbalance will also do it. Any of these three arrangements will make the excess saving of the surplus region available, at the world rate of interest, in an amount sufficient to cover the excess investment of the deficit region.

Region A will run a deficit on current account whenever the investment needs of firms within that region exceed the saving done by residents. With the assumptions just specified, the needed additional saving will be provided by residents of F, and A will accumulate a net indebtedness (positive D value). Considered within a static model, the accumulating debt appears to be a cause for concern; the debt and the interest burden grow over time. But with a given rate of saving, the debt only results from the expansion of the region's capital stock and capacity at a rate which cannot be accommodated by domestic saving. Given certain parameters, a particular relationship between the growth of the debt and the growth of the capital stock will exist, and the debt-to-capital ratio (d) of the region will tend to approach an equilibrium value (d^*).

One way to express this equilibrium ratio is [10]

$$d^* = 1 - \frac{S}{I}. \tag{1}$$

Thus, if saving is 90 per cent of net investment, there will be one unit addition to the debt for each 10 units addition to capital, for that por-

[10] Mathematical derivations are omitted throughout the paper to conserve space. They are available from the author.

tion of investment funds must come from another region. The d ratio will tend to approach 10 per cent.

It will be more useful to express d^* in terms of the growth rate of the region's capital stock (g), the average propensity to save (s), the output-to-capital ratio (k), and the real rate of interest ($r - p$). Since these parameters imply a particular relationship between S and I, the d^* value can be expressed in these terms by a simple translation of equation (1):

$$d^* = \frac{g - sk}{g - s(r - p)}. \tag{2}$$

If the d ratio is at this value, it will remain unchanged as long as the values on the right do not change. It is easy to show that equation (2) represents a stable equilibrium in the sense that should the values on the right be constant and within the relevant range, any existing d value will approach d^*. But the adjustment process is not likely to involve an approach of d to d^* while the values on the right side of equation (2) remain constant. In fact, any change in the trade balance of a region must affect investment and/or saving; hence it must affect s, g, and/or k. It may also affect p. Now it must be shown how the trade balance of the region will tend to approach some limiting magnitude relative to the size of the region, and how it will influence s, g, k, and/or p in the process. When this is done, we will have an equilibrium model of the balance of payments that does not depend upon liquidity constraints.

2 THE ADJUSTMENT PROCESS — PERFECTLY MOBILE LABOR

WITH liquidity constraints removed, trade imbalances are limited only through price and income effects. The open-economy multiplier and price relationships do not insure an equilibrium in the conventional static sense, but they obviously do limit the relative size to which a trade imbalance can grow. A long-run change in the trade balance of region A may affect the region through income, and/or price, changes.

Given perfect mobility of capital, the degree of mobility of labor is crucial in determining which will be the primary effect. In this section the limiting case of perfect mobility of labor will be considered. In order to do this, the assumptions stated at the beginning of the preceding section will be expanded as follows:

1. Labor (as well as capital) is perfectly mobile between regions. Thus the wage rate in region A must conform to the constant rate assumed to exist in F. Labor and capital are the only two factors of production.

2. There is no technological change. Because of this and the constant factor prices, the ratio of full-capacity output to capital will remain constant. There is no assumption, however, that capital will always be used to capacity.

3. The rate of price inflation in region A cannot deviate from the zero rate existing in F for the reasons just mentioned: constant factor prices and no technological change. Because of perfect factor mobility, region A can expand capacity sufficiently to produce, at a constant price, any quantity of goods demanded.

4. Interregional commerce consists of goods traded, interest payments on outstanding bonds, and the sale of bonds. The "trade balance" includes the first category of transaction only, while the "current-account balance" includes the first and second.

5. The consumption and import functions of the region are linearly homogeneous with respect to its long-run growth. The homogeneous consumption function means that there is no secular tendency for s to increase. This does not imply that s is unaffected by short-run demand changes or even by changes in the *rate* of growth.

6. The investment function, likewise, is linearly homogeneous with respect to long-run growth. The rate of investment (g value) is assumed to be determined by, and to vary directly with, the ratio of demand to capital.[11]

Since labor is instantaneously mobile, the only short-run restriction upon the size of the region is K, its capital stock. K is therefore used as a proxy for the size of the region. In conventional static multi-

[11] James S. Duesenberry, *Business Cycles and Economic Growth*. New York, 1958, pp. 179–276.

plier-analysis, given the consumption, investment, and import functions, there is an equilibrium income level and an equilibrium rate of investment corresponding to each level of exports. This reasoning is familiar. To convert it to a dynamic framework, we can say that given the same three functions, there is an equilibrium ratio of demand to capital and an equilibrium rate of investment, or g value, corresponding to any given ratio of exports to capital. This result is obtained by dividing all values by K. With the homogeneity assumption, a doubling of exports and of capital should leave the demand-to-capital ratio, and the g rate, unaffected. Demand is twice as great, but so is capacity, and the same rate of investment is induced as before. Thus g is directly related to X/K:

$$g = g(X/K). \tag{3}$$

An expansion of exports relative to capital results in an expansion of total demand relative to capital (capacity) through the usual multiplier relationship. This induces a higher rate of investment; that is, a higher g value. Because of the homogeneity assumption, the relationship between X/K and g remains constant over time.

Changes in the debt level of the region also affect demand. An increase in debt increases the interest burden of the region and reduces income relative to output. This reduces the level of domestic consumption. An increase in D, therefore, affects g in the same direction as a decrease in X. Following the same reasoning as before, an increase in D/K, or d, decreases g, while a decrease in d increases g. Thus, both d and X/K affect g, and function (3) must be rewritten as

$$g = g(X/K, -d). \tag{4}$$

Equation (4) is expressed graphically in Figure 1 by the growth contours g_1 through g_4. The slowest growth rate represented is g_1, and the fastest is g_4. Each growth contour depicts the various X/K and d combinations that generate sufficient demand, relative to the capital stock, to produce that particular rate of growth. An increase in X/K, or a decrease in d, will increase the growth rate. Thus, the contours slope upward to the right.

Region F grows at the exogenously determined rate f, and the demand for A's exports is also assumed to grow at that rate. Since region

FIGURE 1

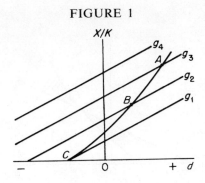

A can, in the long run, supply any quantity of exports demanded, supply considerations do not limit the growth rate of exports. With f, the growth rate of X, exogenously determined; the X/K ratio, which appears in the demand equation (4), can remain constant only when the growth rate of the region's capital stock (g) has adjusted to equal the growth rate of exports (f). This adjustment of g will, in fact, be induced by the demand effects of the changes in X/K, as expressed in equation (4). If g exceeds f, K grows faster than X, and X/K will decline. This is deflationary, reducing total demand relative to capital or capacity. A reduction in investment is induced and g declines. The adjustment mechanism will continue to operate, and the export-induced reduction in the ratio of demand to capacity will become progressively greater, as long as K continues to grow faster than X; that is, as long as g exceeds f. Once X/K has decreased sufficiently to cause g to equal f, that particular X/K ratio will tend to be sustained. The vertical arrows in Figure 2 represent the demand pressure exerted by changes in X/K when f is equal to g_2. Thus, with the factor mobility and homogeneity assumptions, the growth rate of the region must adjust to that of exports. Even if the homogeneity assumption is discarded, a given f value, along with specific consumption, investment, and import functions, will imply a particular equilibrium g value, although the identity of the two values will be lost. This occurs simply because a region cannot forever outrun the level of world demand for its goods, nor can its capacity forever lag behind demand. And with factors mobile, it is g, not f, that will adjust.

It has been shown that region A will adjust vertically in Figure 1

FIGURE 2

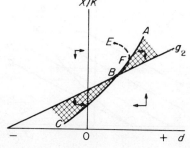

or 2 to approach the g contour at which g equals f. In Figure 2 this g value was arbitrarily assumed to be g_2. What will happen to the debt-to-capital ratio d, and how the region moves horizontally in the diagram, have not yet been indicated. The equilibrium d value, d^*, was expressed in equation (2). If the growth rate of export demand (f) is altered, it must affect the coefficients in this equation. It has already been shown that g will be altered; s and k may be also. Export-induced *short-run* changes in demand may affect s considerably, but in most developed countries the average propensity to consume has shown considerable stability over the long run. In a long-run analysis of developed regions it seems realistic to assume that export-induced changes in g do not affect s or k greatly, and that the change in g, itself, will be the predominant effect in equation (2).

The assumption that changes in g will predominate in equation (2) is not crucial to the argument. The dynamic equilibrium will occur anyway. However, this is not an innocent assumption as far as the nature of the adjustment path is concerned. If s and k do not respond greatly to export-induced g changes, then an increase in the growth rate of exports, in expanding total demand, will increase investment more than saving. A larger investment inflow will be needed. The expansion will cause imports to rise more than the original rise in exports, facilitating a real transfer of resources. With mobile capital, the capital account will adjust to the current account, and an investment inflow will be induced. A relatively greater proportion of investment must be financed by outside saving, and d will rise. Thus, with s and k relatively unresponsive to demand-induced g changes, an increase in the growth rate of export demand and the resulting increase in g will lead to a deterioration of the current account and a rise in d^*.

That effect of a change in exports upon the current account is just the opposite of what we would expect from the conventional static model; an increase in exports is generally assumed to increase saving more than investment, thereby improving the current account. This is the familiar "stability in isolation" requirement that demand changes affect saving more than investment. But the condition for stability in isolation is not likely to obtain where factors are highly mobile; investment will be too responsive. All regions of a mobile-factor area can be "unstable in isolation," that is, dependent upon export demand for stability; while the area as a whole, because factor supply is limited, may be perfectly stable. Consequently, it will be assumed that an increase in f affects I more than S, although this assumption is not crucial to the establishment of the dynamic equilibrium.

We shall now examine how the value of d^* is related to the demand-determined value of g, as illustrated in Figure 3. Note that in equation (2), since k is the output-to-capital ratio, it can be expected to be numerically larger than $(r - p)$, the interest rate. This means that sk in the numerator of (2) is larger than $s(r - p)$ in the denominator. In the extreme case of an unrealistically rapid growth-rate of capital, $(g - sk)$ will be almost as large as $[g - s(r - p)]$, and d^* will have a value of almost unity. If the growth rate of a region creates such a demand for investment funds that only a small portion of such funds can be obtained internally, then the external debt will be nearly as large as the capital stock. Because the rapid growth rate of exports has induced a high internal growth rate, investment is high relative to saving, the

FIGURE 3

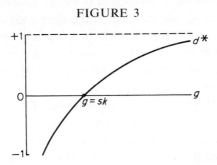

trade balance is passive, capital flows in, and a high positive $d*$ value results. Of course, more realistic g values will produce $d*$ values considerably less than unity, and $d*$ will equal zero when g is as small as sk, since the numerator on the right side of equation (2) will be zero at this point; but with sk greater than $s(r - p)$ the denominator will still be positive. When g is smaller than sk but larger than $s(r - p)$, the expression assumes a negative value; the region will be a net lender.

We also see that $d*$ is nearly minus infinity if g is only slightly above $s(r - p)$. It turns out, however, that the growth rate of the region will always be driven up to well above $s(r - p)$. If the growth rate approaches a level as low as $s(r - p)$, this will cause the $d*$ ratio to grow to a large negative value. Thus, interest income will grow in relation to the capital stock, causing domestic demand to increase relative to K. This relative expansion in demand will continue as long as $(-d*)$ increases. It will induce an increase in investment and push the growth rate up long before $d*$ approaches minus infinity. (Due to this the growth rate of capital may remain permanently above the growth rate of exports — an exceptional case to be considered below.) Thus, it appears that reasonable values for the parameters s, k, p, r, and g will produce an equilibrium ratio of debt to capital that is between a positive value of considerably less than unity and a relatively small negative value; $d*$ will vary with g, as shown in Figure 3.

Since a unique $d*$ value corresponds to each g value, there is some $d*$ value corresponding to each growth contour in Figure 1. Whenever the region is on that particular growth contour, the d ratio will tend to approach this equilibrium value. Point A in Figure 1 is assumed to be the equilibrium d point on contour g_3. Only at point A on that contour will d remain constant. If the region is on the g_3 contour above and to the right of point A, the increase in the debt which results from the current-account deficit will cause D to grow at a slower rate than g_3 (the rate of growth of K), and therefore d will decline toward $d*$. Conversely, if the region is on the g_3 contour to the left and below point A, the d ratio will rise.

Of course, there is an equilibrium d ratio for every other growth rate. At slower growth rates the lower g value will bring about a smaller value of $d*$, for less investment is required, and a larger proportion of it can be obtained from internal saving. Thus, B and C in Figure 1 can be assumed to represent points at which the d ratio is in equilibrium when the growth rates of the region are g_2 and g_1, respectively. The ABC line is a nexus of all points at which the growth rate of capital, as determined by the demand factors d and X/K, coincides with the growth rate of the debt, as determined by the current-account imbalance. If the region's position falls below and to the right of this line, the d ratio will decline; if it lies above and to the left, the d ratio will rise. Point C should be noted. Here the d ratio is in equilibrium with no commodity exports whatever, the value of $(-d)$ being sufficiently high for interest income to replace export income completely. But more on that later.

The ABC line also appears in Figure 2. The horizontal arrows pointing toward the ABC line indicate the movement of the d ratio toward its equilibrium value. If this is combined with the changes in the X/K ratio that are represented by the vertical arrows, the adjustment path of the region toward equilibrium can be traced. To illustrate, assume that the growth rate of exports is equal to g_2, but that the initial X/K and d ratios put the region at point E in Figure 2. Demand conditions (equation (4)) generated by the existing X/K and d ratios cause the region's capital stock to grow faster than g_2, as is indicated by the fact that the region is above the g_2 line. This means that the growth rate of capital will be greater than the growth rate of exports, and that the X/K ratio will decline. As it does so, the total demand for the region's goods relative to capital will decrease. This is the familiar foreign-trade multiplier relationship. The relative decrease in demand causes a decrease in g, which is represented by the movement of the region to lower growth contours as it moves down the X/K axis. The X/K ratio will continue to decline and to depress the growth rate until the g_2 contour is reached, for f is assumed to be equal to g_2. Given the homogeneity of the demand functions, this must occur. As noted earlier, the vertical arrows in Figure 2 indicate the change in the X/K ratio that pushes the region toward the contour at which g will equal f.

Of course, the region will not move directly downward to the g_2 contour, for changes in d will occur. Note that an essential difference between the present analysis and the static multiplier model is already evident. In the latter analysis, a decrease in the demand for exports also induces downward pressure on aggregate demand; but once this pressure is spent, it is assumed that no further automatic corrective forces are available. Thus, there is no assurance of a current-account equilibrium. On the other hand, if the multiplier analysis is considered within a growth framework, it is assured that there will be an increasing downward pressure on demand as long as the growth rate of the economy is greater than that of exports. Thus, unless exports become negligible first, the corrective forces continue to lower the growth rate of capital until it is the same as that of exports. This is not necessarily a current-account equilibrium, but it is a dynamic equilibrium in the sense that the tendency for the region to outgrow the demand for its exports has been eliminated.

Now consider the d ratio. At point E in Figure 2 the region is above the ABC line. This means that the d ratio is below the equilibrium ratio (equation (2)) for the existing growth rate of capital. The increments to the debt (which are relatively large owing to the high g value and the resultant large current-account deficit) cause it to increase more rapidly than the capital stock does, and d rises toward d^*. The path of adjustment for the region is, therefore, in the direction of the broken line moving away from E. Its direction is a combination of the vertical vectors, propelling the region toward the g_2 line where X/K will be in equilibrium; and the horizontal vectors, propelling the region toward the ABC line where d will be in equilibrium. Only where both lines intersect at B will the growth rate of the region remain constant, for only there will both ratios remain unchanged. The path of adjustment is not directly to point B, for the force vectors initially cause d to rise. As soon as the growth rate has slowed sufficiently, however, the d ratio will reach a temporary equilibrium at point F on the ABC line. The growth rate of capital at that point is still above the growth rate of exports, and X/K will continue to decline, pushing the growth rate below the ABC line. As soon as this happens, the debt level is above the equilibrium position, and both X/K and d decline toward the equilibrium point B, at which X, K, and D are all growing at the rate f.

For an additional example, consider the adjustment from point B to a new equilibrium following a change in f, as illustrated in Figure 4. Point B is initially the equilibrium position, for f is equal to g_2. K and D are growing at the same rate as X. Now the growth rate of export demand (f) increases to a value equal to that of g_3. An adjustment must

FIGURE 4

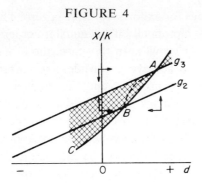

occur to a new equilibrium at point A. For a time, K continues to grow at the rate g_2, but X is growing at the rate g_3, and X/K rises. This is expansionary. The region shifts upward in the diagram to a higher g value. The resulting increase in demand for investment funds causes imports to increase more than exports, the trade balance deteriorates, and d starts rising, shifting the region to the right in the diagram and back to the ABC line. The new equilibrium is reached at point A, with a faster growth rate, a larger current-account deficit and d value, and K and D once again growing at the same rate as X.

In general, the adjustment process from any point in the diagram is as described here. As long as the region is outside the shaded area, the force vectors will take it to that area. Once within the area, the vectors take it directly toward the equilibrium point, which is the intersection of the ABC line and whichever g contour happens to equal the value of f. A high value of f leads to a correspondingly high g value, a current-account deficit, and a positive d^* value, while a low f value will lead to a surplus and a negative d^*. In either case, however, an equilibrium will normally result in which the debt level, current-account imbalance, and capital stock will grow at the same rate as export demand. While the relaxation of the homogeneity assumption would destroy the exact equality of these growth rates, the nature of the adjustment process and the self-limiting nature of excessive changes in the relative size of the current-account imbalance and the relative size of the debt level would not be affected.

There is an exception to the above conclusions. As noted earlier, point C in Figure 1 involves the complete substitution of external investment earnings for exports, for X/K is zero. This equilibrium may be approached asymptotically if f is equal to, or less than, g_1, which is a very slow rate of growth. In this case, the low rate of investment causes the region to achieve a considerable current-account surplus during the adjustment process, and the gradually rising $(-d)$ value causes investment earnings to replace export income eventually. The region's growth rate will then continue to outrun the growth rate of exports, and X will eventually become insignificant relative to K. Then the region is close to point C, which is the equilibrium point. K and $(-D)$ will grow at the same rate, but X (now insignificant) may grow at a slower rate; that is, a rate less than g_1. This type of equilibrium will always come about if f is as low as the value of $s(r - p)$. (I believe that the zero X/K equilibrium is unlikely to occur in reality because of the sustained low level of f that is required to bring it about.)

Further description of the adjustment process and the dynamic equilibrium will be postponed until after the presentation of the immobile-labor case, for that case is surprisingly similar to the case of mobile labor.

3   THE ADJUSTMENT PROCESS — CAPITAL COMPLETELY MOBILE AND LABOR COMPLETELY IMMOBILE

IN THE preceding analysis, the growth rate of the region's output could respond to changes in the long-run growth rate of demand without affecting factor costs. Both factors were available from the other region. Thus, an unlimited-supply and constant-price analysis seemed appropriate. In such a case, the rate of growth of the region's capacity eventually adjusted to the growth rate of export demand. The equilibrium growth path involved growth of both the region's capital stock and its debt at the same rate as the growth of export demand. The fact that region A was small, and the lack of induced differences in the rates of inflation between regions, made it reasonable to assume that the growth of export demand was exogenously determined. If labor is immobile, on the other hand, g cannot adjust to f, at least not at constant prices.

Considering the opposite extreme, it is apparent that if labor is immobile and factor proportions cannot be varied, then the region's capacity can be expanded only as fast as the growth rate of the labor force, or the natural growth rate of the region. But if the homogeneity assumption is retained, there must still be an adjustment to equalize g and the rate of growth of externally generated demand. (Even with specific nonhomogeneous functions, some given relationship between the two rates is indicated.) This adjustment is likely to occur through the establishment of a rate of inflation in region A that will cause the rate of growth of demand (and the rate of growth of the trade imbalance) to adjust to the unresponsive g value. This is just the opposite of the previous case, in which g did all the adjusting, but many of the characteristics of the two examples are similar. To consider this limiting case, we may discard the assumptions specified at the beginning of Part 2 and assume the following:

1. Labor is immobile between regions, and region A's labor force grows at an exogenously determined and constant rate. Capital, as before, is completely mobile. With the supply of one factor limited, the assumption of unlimited capacity must be discarded. If demand tends to exceed that which can be supplied with the existing labor force, wages and prices will be driven up. Conversely, if a low level of demand causes a sufficiently high level of unemployment, and some downward wage and price flexibility exists, wages and prices will decline. With the present assumptions of immobile labor, therefore, the previous assumption of constant prices will be replaced by the assumption of a Phillips Curve kind of relationship between the rate of unemployment and the rate of demand-induced inflation. Since there is some evidence that the long-run Phillips Curve might be vertical, it may seem more appropriate to assume that the rate of change in the rate of inflation is a function of the rate of unemployment. This, however, would insure that fiscal policy was ineffective in altering the long-run rate of unemployment, and since the same conclusion can be reached on other grounds, the latter assumption will not be used here.

2. All terms in the following analysis will be expressed in real units of domestic goods. Imports will be expressed in terms of the equivalent number of units of domestic goods at the then-existing price ratio. The import term, therefore, is actually the total real amount

spent on imports. To avoid an index-number problem, it is assumed that all investment goods are domestically produced. Thus, a change in the price level in region A will not alter K. The symbol p is defined as the rate of increase in region A's wages and prices per time period. Region F's prices, and the price of region A's imports, increase at the constant and exogenously determined rate p'. Since capital is mobile, the money rate of interest is exogenously determined. The real rate of interest $(r - p)$, however, varies inversely with the rate of price inflation. Although the real interest rate to a resident of A is likely to be different from the real rate to a resident of F, the real rate to a resident of a given region will not be affected by where he invests; it is the rate of price inflation in his own region that determines his real return.

3. No technological change occurs and factor proportions cannot be varied, so that the region's natural growth rate (n) is equal to the growth rate of the labor force. This places an absolute limit on the rate of expansion of capacity and makes the present case precisely the opposite of the mobile labor case. Incidentally, an alternative assumption that would not alter the analysis is to postulate that exogenously determined technical progress increases the efficiency of labor at a specific rate, increasing the ratio of output to labor while not affecting the ratio of output to capital. Then n would become the sum of the rate of growth of labor and the rate of technical progress, but the rate of growth of capacity would still be absolutely limited by the value of n. (However, since the assumption of no technological change will tax my explanatory ability less, that is the one which I shall use.[12])

4. The difference-equation models that have been used to develop this analysis have made the rate of investment a function of the ratio of demand to capital, with allowances for the effects of changes in the real interest rate.[13] With such an investment function and with stability conditions met, the growth rate of capital, g, will not vary long from the growth rate of labor, n. For g to remain above n, demand must grow faster than labor. But if capital and demand grow faster than labor, unemployment will fall, $(p - p')$ will rise (an increase in the rate of

[12] Professor Lanyi suggests in his discussion that n can also be interpreted as the target growth rate of the region. This is correct.
[13] Duesenberry, pp. 179–276.

domestic inflation relative to foreign inflation), foreign goods will be substituted for domestic goods, and in this way the inflation will lower the rate of growth of demand in region A. The rate of inflation can only cease to increase when g and n are equal, for only then will the rate of unemployment cease to decline. For a similar reason, g will not long lie below n. The rate of unemployment will rise until $(p - p')$ is decreased sufficiently to cause the rate of growth of demand, and of capital, to rise to equal the rate of growth of labor capacity. Given the fact that g automatically adjusts to equal n in the model, it will be assumed in the presentation that follows that g always equals n as a long-run approximation, and that the capital-to-labor ratio is always at a level such that the full employment of capital and of labor occur simultaneously. Although this assumption is not explicit in the mathematical model, it is used here because it reduces the number of variables and allows the use of K as a proxy for the size of the entire region, including the labor force. In spite of the short-run inaccuracy of the "g equals n" assumption, from a long-run perspective it is in keeping with the assumptions of immobile labor and mobile capital; the ultimate restriction on the growth rate of the region is not capital, which has unlimited availability, but labor, which does not.

5. A change in p is assumed to have no effect upon s. With g constant, the effect of g upon s that was possible in the analysis of mobile labor does not occur here. Therefore, s can be assumed constant. As before, however, an increase in demand relative to capital will result in more complete utilization of capital at the same time as it raises p. An increase in p, therefore, is correlated with an increase in the effective value of k, as well as with a decrease in the rate of unemployment. Of course, such a change in k is due to a change in the utilization of capacity, not to a change in the ratio of *full-capacity* output to capital.

6. All other assumptions, including the linear homogeneity of all internal relationships with respect to long-run changes in the economic capacity of the region, are the same as in the mobile-labor analysis. As before, the growth rate of foreign demand for exports, in the absence of different rates of inflation, is f. That is, X increases at the rate f per time period if $(p - p')$ is zero. Price changes, of course, will now

enter the picture, and both the exogenously induced tendency for export demand to grow and the endogenously determined rate of inflation affect the actual growth rate of export demand.

In the case of mobile labor, the growth rate of exports was constant throughout and g adjusted to it. Such an adjustment of the growth rate can no longer take place. That equilibrating force no longer exists. But with labor immobile, and different regional rates of inflation possible, adjustment will be brought about by the rate of price inflation. The adjustment will, in a sense, be the opposite of the earlier one; the rate of growth of the trade imbalance will now adjust to the natural growth rate that is imposed upon the region by the immobility of labor, again without liquidity constraints.

The adjustment process can be described with the aid of modified versions of demand equation (4) and the diagrams used earlier. Of course, g no longer responds to demand, but p does, for this is implied by the Phillips Curve. With consumption, import, and investment functions given and linearly homogeneous, as before, the two factors determining the ratio of demand to capital are the ratio of the interest burden to capital and the ratio of the trade balance to capital (T/K). An increase in d increases the interest burden, decreases income and demand relative to capacity, and therefore decreases p. This effect is intensified because the lower p value itself increases the real interest burden for residents of A, for it increases the real interest rate ($r - p$). In a similar way, a decrease in T/K reduces total demand relative to capacity, hence reducing p. Thus, a function for p can be expressed in the form

$$p = p(T/K, -d). \tag{5}$$

This is similar to the demand function (4) except that now p, not g, is affected. Also, in the constant-price version the average propensity to import could be assumed constant, and X/K, rather than T/K, could be used. With price changes, however, imports and exports will both be affected during the adjustment process, and T/K must be adopted.

Now consider Figure 5, which is similar to Figure 1 except that T/K replaces X/K, and the two demand factors T/K and d influence p rather than g. Each p contour represents the various T/K and d combinations that will generate a particular rate of inflation. The lowest

FIGURE 5

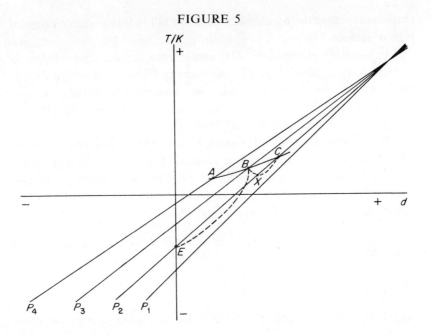

rate is p_1, and the highest p_4. An increase in T/K, or a decrease in d, is inflationary, involving a movement to a higher p contour. With g predetermined and s unresponsive to demand changes, a relatively small change in T/K or d is likely to produce a large change in p, resulting in p contours that are relatively close together. As a result, all of the contours of reasonable p values *may* fall on one side or the other of the zero T/K axis. If this is the case, it simply means that the internal investment and savings relationship (g and s) is such that a zero T/K value will involve an unrealistically severe inflationary or deflationary condition; the dynamic equilibrium must involve a current-account imbalance in that case.

Higher p contours are more horizontal than lower ones, because a higher p value results in a lower real interest rate, so that changes in the debt level have less effect on demand. The p contours may even intersect on the right side of the diagram. If investment is very high relative to internal saving, the equilibrium may fall in the area to the right of the intersection of the p contours, and price instability may result. This possibility will be discussed below. For the time being, we shall assume that the equilibrium does not fall in this unstable range of high d^* values.

It has been shown how T/K and d influence demand relative to capacity, hence altering p. The contours in Figure 5 illustrate this. It will now be shown how changes in p react upon the trade balance, alter T/K, and hence alter demand relative to capacity. In this way, changes in T/K and p will tend to be self-limiting.

It is assumed, as before, that exports tend to grow at an exogenous rate (f) if prices in region A are constant. But prices affect both imports and exports, in accord with the usual elasticity relationship. Assuming that the influences of price and income are additive, it can be shown that T/K will be in equilibrium (constant) when

$$p = \frac{\left(\frac{M}{T} + 1\right)(f - g)}{e - \frac{M}{T}(1 - e - e')} + p'. \tag{6}$$

M/T is the ratio of imports to trade balance, f is the rate that exports would tend to grow in the absence of price effects, e' is the elasticity of demand for imports, and e for exports. The right side of this equation reduces to $(f - g + ep')/e$ if e' is unity, or to approximately $(f - g + ep' + e'p' - p')/(e + e' - 1)$ if trade is nearly balanced.

Equation (6) is not difficult to interpret. If f exceeds g, the region's exports, in the absence of price effects, tend to grow faster than the region's capacity. With the import function linearly homogeneous, the trade balance therefore tends to improve relative to capacity. And if T/K tends to improve when $(p - p')$ is zero, there is some value of p higher than p' that will exactly offset this tendency and will hold T/K constant. Equation (6) states that p value. With the sum of the two elasticities greater than unity, p will exceed p' if f exceeds g, and p will be less than p' if f is less than g. The equilibrium p value may change slowly over time, for a nonzero $(p - p')$ value together with a nonunitary elasticity of demand for imports may cause M/T in equation (6) to change gradually. This effect did not occur in the difference-equation model because of the nature of the import function, but other equally plausible functions would have caused it. The change in the equilibrium value of p will, however, be so slow that it can be ignored in the description of the adjustment process.

Let us assume that p_3 in Figure 5 happens to be the p value that will cause T/K to remain constant, as expressed in equation (6). When the region is above the p_3 contour, the existing T/K and d ratios will generate a level of demand relative to capacity that will cause a greater inflation than p_3 (demand equation (5)). Then the high level of p relative to p' will cause the trade balance to deteriorate relative to capacity, although not necessarily in absolute value. This will cause the usual multiple reduction in demand relative to capacity, and the region will shift downward toward p_3. T/K declines, demand decreases, the rate of inflation also decreases; the decrease in the rate of inflation, in turn, reduces the decline in T/K. Eventually p_3 is reached, and the value of $(p_3 - p')$ is just enough to offset whatever tendency would have otherwise existed for T to grow at a rate different from that of K. On that contour, T will grow at the same rate as K, and T/K will remain constant. The tendency for demand to grow at the same rate as capacity will then sustain the existing rate of inflation.

Now turn once again to equation (2) and consider the adjustment of d to its equilibrium. Since labor is immobile, the values of g, s, and r are now given, and it is p that responds to demand changes. Because capital tends to be better utilized when demand is great, the effective value of k will be related to p. As long as the nature of this relationship is known, an equilibrium d value, d^*, can be calculated for each p contour in Figure 5, and as before, the ABC line can represent the nexus of such points. As in the earlier analysis, this line represents all points at which the existing current-account imbalance will cause the debt to grow at the same rate as capital, thus holding d constant. In the case of mobile labor it seemed likely that the ABC line would slope upward to the right; a higher f value would increase g and this would result in a shift in the ratio of the current account to capital toward a deficit, and thus an increase in d^*. In the present case the ABC line may have almost any slope; it may fall in any of the four quadrants of Figure 5, or it may pass through several of them. In the next section it will be shown that the equilibrium will fall in the upper right quadrant if $sk < g < r - p$, in the lower right quadrant if $sk < g$ and $r - p < g$, in the lower left quadrant if $g < sk$ and $g < r - p$, or in the upper left quadrant if $r - p < g < sk$.

To summarize, each p contour in Figure 5 represents the various combinations of T/K and d that will generate the amount of demand necessary to create that particular rate of price change (equation (5)). The p value that will cause T to grow at the same rate as K (equation (6)) is assumed to be p_3 in the diagram. The d^* value corresponding to each p contour is determined from equation (2), and these d^* values result in the ABC line. The intersection of p_3 and ABC is the equilibrium point where both T/K and d will tend to remain constant. This point (B) happens to fall in the upper right-hand quadrant, but different parameter values could cause it to fall in any of the other quadrants.

Let the region initially be at point E. At that point, region A has a trade deficit that results in the rate of inflation p_2, which falls short of the equilibrium rate p_3. In other words, the existing rate of inflation is less than the rate that would cause the trade deficit to grow at the same rate as the capital stock. Thus, $(-T/K)$ becomes smaller, causing the region to shift upward in the diagram. The improvement in the ratio of the trade balance to capital is inflationary; a movement directly up from E leads to higher p contours, but offsetting changes in d will occur in this particular case. The d value cannot remain at zero, for a trade deficit exists. Thus d rises. This increases the interest burden, lowers domestic income relative to capacity, and is therefore deflationary. In the illustration, the deflationary effect of the rightward shift in d is initially greater than the inflationary effect of the upward shift in T/K, so that the region drops below p_2. The decrease in p further contributes to the improvement in T/K. Eventually T/K becomes positive. In spite of this, d continues to increase in value, for the interest burden creates a current-account deficit in spite of the favorable trade balance. The trade balance continues to improve until a rate of inflation is reached that will cause T to grow no faster than K. This is p_3. Similarly, D will grow faster than K until d reaches a stable value on the ABC line (equation (2)). Both conditions are met only when point B is reached.

Although the direction of change in d and T/K will be different, depending upon the location of the equilibrium point and upon the initial T/K and d values, the preceding case does illustrate the nature of the adjustment forces that push the region toward the intersection of the line ABC and the equilibrium p contour; the intersection of those two lines is the only point at which T/K and d will both remain constant. However, as in the case of mobile labor, there is an instance in which the equilibrium just described will not result. This may occur if the natural growth rate of the region is slow enough to cause the numerator in equation (2) to approach zero or to assume a negative value. In other words, it may occur if $s(r - p)$ is almost as large as g or larger. In this case, the internal demand for investment funds is so small that $(-d)$ will grow very large. The increasing investment earnings may compensate for the deteriorating trade balance, and the dynamic equilibrium as described here may never be reached, or it may be reached with such a large $(-d)$ value as to make the result unrealistic.

Another kind of problem may occur if internal saving is very small relative to investment; the resulting high d^* value may fall to the right of the intersection of the p contours in Figure 5, which might cause price instability. To consider this possibility, suppose that the region is in equilibrium with a very high d^* value, perhaps .50 or so. If p for any reason rises above the equilibrium point, the real rate of interest, $(r - p)$, will be reduced. Because of the large external debt, this reduces the real interest burden, which result means an increase in real income. Thus, an increase in p produces an inflationary influence that may cause an even further increase in p should this inflationary effect be strong enough to offset the deflationary influence of the increase in p upon the trade balance.

There are a number of reasons why this possible instability does not seem likely to be a problem in reality. First, a relatively high level of d^* is required in the model to produce that result. In addition, it is assumed that a change in the real rate of interest is immediately recognized by debtors as a change in their real income, and the introduction of a lag in this relationship would appear to add stability.

Before leaving the analysis of the adjustment process in the case of immobile labor, the reader may wish to consider the adjustment from point B in Figure 5 to a new equilibrium, following a change in f. With the region initially in equilibrium at B, let f decrease. With the lower f value, T can be made to grow as fast as K only with a p value of less than p_3. Let us say that the new equilibrium p value is p_2. The existing rate of price inflation, p_3, causes T to deteriorate relative to

K, and T/K declines. This deterioration of the trade balance involves an increase in the increments to the debt each time period, and d rises. Thus the region moves along the dotted line. The deterioration of T/K ends as soon as the contour p_2 is reached at point x, for p_2 is now the rate of inflation that will cause T to grow exactly as fast as K. But the T/K value at point x is too low for the debt to grow at the same rate as capital, and d continues to rise. The region moves to the right, and since an increase in d is deflationary, this involves a drop in p below p_2. Then T/K rises. As p_2 is approached a second time, the increase in T/K slows to a stop, and this time the region also approaches ABC, for now the value of T/K is high enough for D to grow as slowly as K. The new equilibrium is reached at C.

4   THE EXTERNAL CONSTRAINT AND THE CHARACTERISTICS OF THE EQUILIBRIUM

THE preceding material has been an attempt to describe the forces that bring about a dynamic equilibrium in several variants of an open-economy model, a version of which is in the Appendix. In both cases, with mobile labor and with immobile labor, a dynamic equilibrium generally comes about in which the region's debt level, current-account balance, and capital stock grow at the same rate. Capital mobility removes the short-run liquidity constraint of limited reserves, but the analysis describes other external constraints operative in the long run. With both factors mobile, the constraint is upon the growth rate of the region, which with linearly homogeneous functions must equal the growth rate of exports. (Of course, with both factors mobile the rate of price inflation and the rate of unemployment are controlled by factor mobility.) At the other extreme, with immobile labor and fixed factor proportions, the growth rate of the region is constrained internally and the external constraint is upon the rate of inflation; $(p - p')$ must assume a value that will keep the trade balance growing at the same rate as the region.

Now consider the characteristics of the dynamic equilibrium.

These characteristics are not dependent upon the more restrictive assumptions of the model, but merely follow from the fact that changes in T/K and D/K will influence the ratio of demand to capacity in such a way that the T/K and D/K changes will be self-limiting. Given values of certain parameters, only one balance-of-payments configuration can result, for there will be only one configuration that is compatible with the stability of the T/K and D/K ratios. It is not even necessary to assume a fixed exchange rate to reach the conclusions that follow in this section, and they apply to both the mobile, and immobile, labor cases.

Since it is the current-account balance (B) that keeps D growing at the same rate as K in equilibrium, the equilibrium relationship of B/K to D/K, or d, must be

$$\frac{B}{K} = -gd^*. \tag{7}$$

Thus, the current-account balance and the debt level must have opposite signs in equilibrium. But T may have a different sign from B. The relationship of the equilibrium T/K value to the d^* value can be determined by considering that the current-account balance $[B = X - (r - p)D - M]$ must be equal to the increase in the stock of external investments $(-\Delta D)$ in the stipulated time period. Since the debt grows at the rate g in equilibrium, $[X - (r - p)D - M]$ must equal $(-gD)$ in equilibrium. Rearranging this equality, dividing by K, and substituting d^* for D/K and T for $(X - M)$ produces

$$\frac{T}{K} = (r - p - g)d^*. \tag{8}$$

The relationships expressed in equations (7) and (8) result from the fact that B, T, D, and K all must grow at the same rate in equilibrium.

Thus we relate the equilibrium B/K and T/K values to d^*; d^* was previously related to g in equation (2). It can now be shown how the values of B/K, T/K, and d^* relate to each other in equilibrium at different growth rates. First, whether the growth rate that equals the real rate of interest is greater or less than the growth rate that equals sk must be known. Figure 6 shows the former case. In area (1) of that diagram, the slow growth rate g, measured along the horizontal axis, produces the conditions $(g < sk, g < r - p)$. The $(g < sk)$ condition

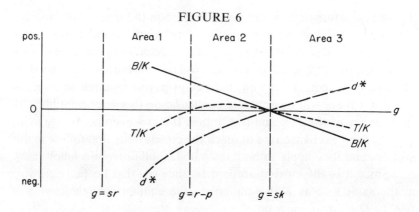

FIGURE 6

is another way of saying that domestic investment is less than domestic saving; the slow growth rate implies a low level of investment demand and excess savings. A current-account (B) surplus must exist. It was explained earlier that if export demand tends to be incompatible with this required B value, either g will change through induced investment (if labor is mobile), or export demand will change through induced price changes (if labor is immobile). In either case, a current-account surplus must come about or the region must shift to a g value greater than sk, which means a shift out of area (1) in the diagram.

With the region's growth rate in area (1), therefore, a current-account surplus must exist. Since capital is perfectly mobile, this is offset by a capital outflow, and a negative D/K value accompanies the positive B/K value, as is expressed in equation (7). Equation (8) states that this equilibrium, with g less than $(r - p)$, must involve a negative T balance along with the positive B balance. Interest payments, of course, make up the difference. To see why T must be negative, assume for a moment that T equals zero. $(-D)$ will grow at the interest rate $(r - p)$. But the diagram shows g (the growth rate of K) to be less than $(r - p)$, and if D grows at the rate $(r - p)$ the value of $(-D/K)$ will rise. This increase in demand relative to capacity, acting through the usual relationships, will cause the trade balance to deteriorate. D/K will continue to increase until T/K has established a sufficiently negative value to drain away some of the external interest income and reduce the growth rate of $(-D)$ from $(r - p)$ to g. Then $(-D/K)$ can remain constant and a dynamic equilibrium can exist. The negative T/K ratio must accompany the positive B/K ratio, because with g less than $(r-p)$, the value of $(-D/K)$ would otherwise grow without limit.

In area (2) of Figure 6 the growth rate exceeds sk, so that insufficient internal saving is available, d^* (equation (2)) is positive, and B/K (equation (7)) is negative. Since g is less than $(r-p)$, the value of T/K expressed in equation (8) is positive; its sign has changed because the sign of d^* has changed. T/K must be positive for D to grow at the rate g, for a zero T/K value would cause D to grow at the faster rate $(r-p)$. If g is faster than both $(r-p)$ and sk, the debt grows faster than the interest rate, and T/K must assume a negative value to cause D to grow that fast, as is stated in equation (8).

Figure 7 is like Figure 6, except that in Figure 7 it is assumed that the growth rate that will exceed $(r-p)$ is less than the growth rate that will exceed sk. The curves are determined from equations (2), (7), and (8) as before.

Borts and Kopecky, in a paper appearing in this volume, present empirical results that support the conclusions stated here. They examine data from OECD countries in an attempt to explain the value of the ratio of external interest income to GNP for each country. (With constant k and $(r-p)$ values, this is, of course, the same as attempting to explain the value of D/K.) Their findings imply that the D/K ratio is strongly influenced, as expected, by the growth rate, the savings ratio, the capital coefficient, and the government-spending rate.

FIGURE 7

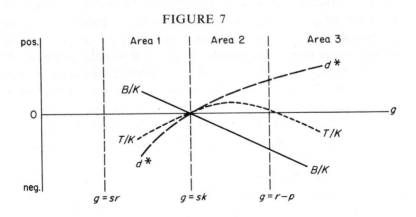

5   THE EXTERNAL CONSTRAINT AND FISCAL POLICY

EVERYONE is familiar with the way in which liquidity requirements restrict a nation's ability to use fiscal policy within today's international monetary structure. As noted earlier, the liquidity constraint exists for at least three reasons: (1) countries wish to limit the amount of their saving that they lend to others, (2) countries fear inflation, and (3), as we all recognize intuitively, even if unlimited lending were available to offset imbalances, a system of fixed exchange rates would still restrict a country's ability to use expansionary policy.

But we have only the vaguest notion of what the external constraint should be, for balance-of-payments theory has taken for granted that the constraint exists. In this paper, instead of following that course, an attempt has been made to describe the type of equilibrium that tends to develop when liquidity is not constrained and the only external constraint is demand for the region's goods. It now remains to determine how much this constraint of external *demand* limits the usefulness of regional fiscal policy. In doing so, we may get a clearer view of what is, and what is not, possible with fixed exchange rates.

A region's capacity or price level cannot indefinitely outrun the level warranted by world demand for the region's goods. Hence the ultimate determinant of the rate of growth or rate of price inflation in the region must be the value of f. If one accepts the assumption that f is exogenously determined, then it follows that fiscal policy cannot indefinitely keep a region's rate of growth or rate of inflation above the equilibrium level. If fiscal expansion temporarily raises g or p above the equilibrium rate, a deterioration in T/K will be induced which will offset the expansion, and g or p will drop back to equilibrium. If labor is mobile, this fall in g or p will occur because the rate of growth of K exceeds that of exports; if labor is immobile, the excessive p value will reduce T relative to K. Thus, g or p can be maintained above the equilibrium level only so long as the fiscal deficit can be continually increased relative to the size of the region, for this is what is required to offset the deterioration in T/K. Since an increasing fiscal deficit means that less internal saving is available for investment, this expansionary effort will be accompanied by a rising d level.

The above is not the only limitation on the effectiveness of fiscal policy. Serious balance-of-payments problems may result even from using fiscal policy to prevent fluctuations in g or p around the equilibrium value. It will be shown that the debt level, current-account balance, and the required fiscal imbalance are all likely to explode if the fiscal goal is to maintain a given p or g value, even if that value is the equilibrium one. Specifically, such instability will occur if the growth rate of the region is less than the real rate of return on interregional investment. This conclusion (as far as I can determine) is a very general one and is not dependent upon the more specialized assumptions of the model.

Assume that region A, a small part of an area in which capital is mobile, has the fiscal goal of preventing economic fluctuations around the dynamic equilibrium. If labor is mobile, the region will attempt to keep g exactly at its long-run equilibrium value; in other words, at the value warranted by the rate of increase in export demand. If labor is immobile, the goal will be to keep unemployment continuously at a level that will cause p to remain at its equilibrium value, which is the p value that will cause T to increase at a rate compatible with the natural growth rate of the region. In either case, the effect of fiscal policy will be to keep T/K at its equilibrium value. However, part of the process through which the d level is stabilized involves the adjustment of T/K through the demand effects of changes in the interest burden, and the d value may be unstable if its influence upon T/K is eliminated by using stabilizing fiscal policy. This can be easily shown.

Consider first the case in which g is less than $(r - p)$. For illustrative purposes, assume a positive debt and a current-account deficit. If T/K is zero, the debt will grow at the real rate of interest. The equilibrium must involve a positive T/K value of the size needed to reduce the rate of growth of D from $(r - p)$ to g. Now assume that for some unexplained reason an increment is added to D to cause it to exceed its equilibrium value, and consider the growth of that increment separately from the growth of the rest of D. The T/K ratio will still be of the correct amount to cause the rest of the debt to grow at the same rate as K, but the increment will grow at the rate $(r - p)$ because of compounding interest. It will become larger and larger relative to K, which is only growing at the rate g. Normally, the deflationary effects of this would increase T/K, reduce the rate at which the debt accumulates, and bring

D/K back to equilibrium. But the commitment of the region to offset income or price fluctuations prevents the adjustment. D/K explodes.

On the other hand, if g exceeds $(r - p)$, the use of fiscal policy to prevent income or price fluctuations around the equilibrium path poses no problem. Any increment to D above or below its equilibrium value grows at the rate $(r - p)$; but since K is growing at the faster rate g, the increment becomes less and less significant, and D/K reapproaches its equilibrium value, even though fiscal policy offsets the tendency for the change in D/K to influence price or income.

The above argument was framed in terms of a positive debt, but the case of a negative debt is analogous. The debt may explode either positively or negatively when g is less than $(r - p)$ and stabilizing fiscal policy is employed.

To summarize, it has been found that fiscal policy within a system of fixed exchange rates has two major limitations. First, while it can effectively prevent large deviations of p or g from the equilibrium value, it cannot permanently alter the value of p or g unless it affects f or causes a continuous substitution of domestic for imported goods. In addition, if g is less than $(r - p)$, those small fluctuations in p or g around the equilibrium value which are necessary to stabilize d must be permitted.

The above analysis of fiscal policy has been applied to a particular policy problem. In 1968, France was faced with an exceptional increase in wages and prices following a round of strikes in May through June. This led to a balance-of-payments problem and an eventual devaluation. The model was used to examine the policy alternatives that might have been open to France if that country (1) had been forced to maintain a permanently fixed exchange rate (as with a monetary union), and (2) had not been faced with a liquidity limit.

It was found that even with unlimited lending, a readjustment of prices was inevitable following the disturbance. The rate of employment and the rate of inflation had to fall temporarily below their long-run equilibrium values.[14] Moreover, any given increase in the ratio of fiscal deficit to income would offset this adjustment only temporarily. Efforts to use fiscal policy to postpone the required adjustment of

[14] With fixed exchange rates there is nothing peculiar about a large autonomous increase in prices leading to a subsequent lowering of the rate of inflation; even the specie-flow model produced this result.

prices indefinitely would require an ever increasing ratio of fiscal deficit to income; both that ratio and the ratio of debt to capital would explode.

As noted above, this situation resulted from the fact that the rate of growth in France was less than the rate of return on international investment; g was less than $(r - p)$. It should be observed, however, that fiscal policy could be effectively used to spread the adjustment process over a greater number of years, thus reducing the amount of price adjustment and unemployment occurring in any one year.

The application of the model to this particular policy problem produced some other interesting findings. For example, it became evident that the imposition of a liquidity constraint considerably complicated the adjustment process by necessitating policy actions that moved the region further away from its equilibrium path, thus creating a need for offsetting actions in the future. To generalize, it appears that the requirements for a balance-of-payments equilibrium in the liquidity sense may often conflict with the requirements for a long-run, or dynamic, equilibrium. When this happens, policies that necessitate offsetting policy actions at some future date must be pursued for liquidity reasons.[15]

6   CONCLUSION

THE simple specie-flow analysis endogenously generates a type of balance-of-payments equilibrium—the zero current-account balance. The liquidity constraint is the modus operandi which produces that equilibrium. More recent analysis has begun with the assumption of some particular equilibrium concept; the nature of the constraint is assumed at the outset rather than being generated by the analysis. This trend has evolved because the ultimate external constraint, which involves demand rather than liquidity, cannot be endogenously determined within a static model.

The external-demand constraint, like the liquidity constraint, can bring about a condition that can be called a balance-of-payments equilibrium—but an equilibrium in a dynamic sense, not in a static one. The

[15] Duesenberry, pp. 179–276.

static open-economy multiplier model analyzes demand forces, but a static model cannot describe the intertemporal equilibrium that those demand forces tend to produce. Inevitably, the equilibrium concepts that have been assumed have not been greatly different from the equilibrium generated by the specie-flow analysis. Efforts to modify the equilibrium concept have generally involved distinguishing between different kinds of capital flows, but the liquidity constraint remains the central focus. Thus, static balance-of-payments analysis has not been able to determine what sort of liquidity limits should be imposed upon a nation.

The present effort to develop a model in which the external constraint is endogenously determined initially employed the same static assumptions as did Mundell in his analysis of perfect mobility of capital with fixed exchange rates. This procedure eliminated the liquidity constraint and permitted the examination of the long-run adjustment process of the balance of payments where demand remained as the only constraint upon the expansion of the region. The resulting adjustment process and dynamic equilibrium were then analyzed. Certain inadequacies of the current analysis are evident. Only a few types of disturbances have been considered. Many details of the adjustment process and the equilibrium remain to be explored. Alternative assumptions need to be evaluated. Nonetheless, a number of conclusions have been reached:

1. The demand constraint limits the size, relative to capacity and output, of a region's current-account imbalance and of its net debtor or creditor position. The result can be described as a dynamic balance-of-payments equilibrium.

2. If both capital and labor are mobile between regions, the demand equilibrium tends to be established by the adjustment of the growth rate of the region's capacity and output to a rate that is compatible with the growth of the demand for its exports.

3. Capital formation within a region is likely to be highly responsive to demand changes when capital and labor are both mobile between regions. In this case it seems unlikely that the individual region will meet the familiar "stability in isolation" postulate that an increase in demand increases saving more than investment. An increase in the growth rate of the demand for exports is therefore likely to cause a

deterioration of the current-account and an increase in the relative size of the debt.

4. If labor is immobile between regions and the marginal factor-proportions ratio is unresponsive to demand influences, the region's growth rate cannot adjust to suit export demand. The equilibrium then comes about through the establishment of an induced rate of price change that will cause the trade imbalance to expand at a rate that is compatible with the growth rate of the region.

5. With reasonable long-run stability of the ratio of output to capital, the propensity to save, and the growth rate, the dynamic equilibrium will approximate the characteristics shown in Figure 6 and Figure 7. One of the most interesting features is that the T balance (current account minus net investment earnings) will tend to adjust to a positive value with an intermediate growth rate, but to a negative value if the growth rate is either fast or slow.

6. Regional fiscal policy cannot have a sustained influence upon demand unless it can influence export demand or cause domestic goods to be substituted for imports. A current-account deterioration will otherwise offset any given expansionary effort. The new dynamic equilibrium resulting from a fiscal expansion will involve an increased equilibrium ratio of debt to capacity and a more negative equilibrium ratio of current-account balance to capacity.

7. A rapid growth rate appears to have a definite stabilizing influence upon the region's balance of payments, for it makes d more stable. In fact, if the growth rate of the region is less than the real rate of return on interregional investment, the stability of d depends upon induced changes in T/K. In this case, efforts to use fiscal policy to prevent fluctuations around the long-run trend line of prices or growth will produce an unstable d ratio.

8. A region can prevent the adjustment to the dynamic equilibrium only by an ever increasing ratio of fiscal deficit to capital (and capacity). A secular rise in this ratio is a signal that the region cannot sustain the existing rate of expansion (g or p); it is a warning that the equilibrating forces are being thwarted.

9. A tendency to approach an equilibrium with zero exports may occur if a low equilibrium g value severely limits internal demand for investment funds. (Due to limited space, this equilibrium was not discussed in detail.)

APPENDIX

THE analysis is based upon several versions of a difference equation model. One of the more useful variants is presented here. The reader should refer to Table 1 for the definition of terms. The subscript t indicates the time period.

First, the immobile labor case. The Phillips Curve assumption is

$$p_t = a_7 \frac{Y_t}{Y_t^*} - a_8. \tag{A-1}$$

Full-capacity output is limited by the labor supply and grows at the natural rate

$$Y_{t+1}^* = Y_t^*(1 + n). \tag{A-2}$$

Consumption is a function of income

$$C_{t+1} = a_1 W_{t+1} = a_1[Y_{t+1} - (r - p_{t+1})D_{t+1}]. \tag{A-3a}$$

An alternative version of (A-3a) can be used to make C less responsive to short-run income changes. This involves reducing the value of a and adding $a_{14}K_{t+1}$, where K_{t+1} is a proxy for the long-run income level of the region

$$C_{t+1} = a_1[Y_{t+1} - (r - p_{t+1})D_{t+1}] + a_{14}K_{t+1}. \tag{A-3b}$$

Investment is a function of the ratio of income to capital and of the real rate of interest [16]

$$I_{t+1} = a_3 Y_{t+1} - a_4 K_{t+1} - a_5(r - p_{t+1})K_{t+1}. \tag{A-4}$$

For the export and import functions, the income and price effects are added together to obtain

$$X_{t+1} = X_t(1 + f - ep_t + ep'), \tag{A-5}$$

and

$$M_{t+1} = a_2(C_{t+1} - C_t) + M_t[1 + (e' - 1)(p_t - p')]. \tag{A-6}$$

The price effect on M takes the form $[1 + (e' - 1)(p_t - p')]$ because M

[16] *Ibid.*

is actually the value of imports expressed in real units of domestic goods.

The system is completed with the following definitions:

$$D_{t+1} = M_t + D_t(1 + r - p_t) - X_t, \qquad (A\text{-}7)$$

$$K_{t+1} = K_t + I_t, \qquad (A\text{-}8)$$

and

$$Y_t = C_t - M_t + I_t + X_t. \qquad (A\text{-}9)$$

The mobile-labor model is identical except that equation (A-1) is replaced by $(p - p' = 0)$ and equation (A-2) is deleted.

A general solution could be obtained only in a simplified version of the model. Instead, a variety of parameter values were selected and computer simulations were run.[17]

COMMENTS

ROBERT Z. ALIBER

UNIVERSITY OF CHICAGO

The capital-market problems analyzed by Professors Howle and Floyd in terms of portfolio-balance models can be examined in the context of a new and imaginary state, the Kingdom of Brookings. This kingdom is initially part of a unified-currency area, Howledom. Later it joins a multiple-currency area known as Floyddom. Both Howledom and Floyddom are parts of a Mundellian world. One aspect of this world is the extremely high sensitivity of financial capital to small differences in interest rates offered in different parts of the world.

My comments on the two papers under discussion are organized into three sections. First, the papers will be reviewed briefly. Then, the models of national economies in the world will be compared with the problems of a firm in an exclusively national economy. Finally, concluding comments will be directed to the relevance of these papers to the policy problems of the international economy.

[17] Details are available from the author.

The major problem for the Kingdom of Brookings in Howledom is how much to borrow from foreign sources, knowing that increasing current expenditure relative to current income means that future expenditure must fall relative to future income. The tradeoff is between the present balance-of-payments constraint and the future balance-of-payments constraint. The kingdom has an equilibrium debt-to-capital ratio. Deviations from this path induce variations in the growth rate, movements in factors, or changes in relative prices. The interest rate paid on a loan is independent of the amount borrowed.

Certain theorems, both formal and informal, are derived from this model. Some of these theorems have Fisherian properties — increases in the yield on capital and reductions in the interest rate lead to more borrowing. Several other theorems relate to the impact on the amount borrowed abroad of changes in the growth of foreign demand for domestic goods. Thus, a decline in the growth of export demand leads to a reduction in the growth of debt; apparently the impact of the reduction in export demand on the growth rate dominates its impact on the supply of foreign exchange. The model shows the limitations on the use of fiscal policy, for the trade effects of induced changes in income cause a payments imbalance that will necessitate an offsetting change in the fiscal balance. This model is useful in its demonstration of which variables adjust under a variety of assumptions about factor mobility and fiscal policy.

The Floyd world differs from the Howle world in having more policy variables and fewer real variables. The Kingdom of Brookings issues and operates an exchange-stabilization fund, a monetary policy, a fiscal policy, and a commercial policy. Floyd is concerned with changes in the distribution of the ownership claims of additions to this stock in response to imbalance in the trade accounts. Redistributions of these claims between the residents of the small country and the rest of the world reflect the necessity of getting the trade deficits financed. These ownership claims appear to be denominated in the same currency — if they are denominated in any currency. Yields on this claim are necessarily identical, regardless of whether the issuers are in the country with the trade deficit or in the one with the trade surplus.

This model leads to the usual proportionality theorems under floating exchange rates. Thus, an increase in the money supply leads to an increase in the price of local goods and in the price of foreign exchange; the distribution of ownership claims among residents of the several countries does not change.

In a world of pegged exchange rates, however, disturbances have different consequences. An increase in money supply in the small country leads to an increase in the demand for imports and in the demand for ownership claims. The price of ownership claims increases. This price increase has a real-balance effect, which leads to a shift in the demand-function for goods. This conclusion depends on several assumptions, one of which is explicit. The explicit assumption is that no wealth effects are attached to the ownership of officially held international reserves, so that when the demand for foreign exchange rises, the resulting loss of reserves does not raise the unit value of the reduced holdings. If it did, owners of these reserves might realize a capital gain as the demand for foreign exchange increased. An implicit assumption is that the increase in the money supply has no wealth effect vis-à-vis goods, while it has a wealth effect vis-à-vis ownership claims. One inference from Floyd's model is that the difference in the conclusion about adjustment paths with pegged and floating rates reflects the assumptions about the differential wealth effects of the ownership of different financial assets, including the exchange-stabilization fund.

A comparison between the Kingdom of Brookings and the Brookings Clothespin Company (BCC) illustrates the international dimensions of the worlds of Howle and Floyd, and the relevance of their use of portfolio-balance models. Within the international economy, adjustment occurs through trade in goods, bonds, and money. A country adjusts to changes in the external demand for its goods by changes in the selling prices for its goods, bonds, or money. Within a domestic economy, a company adjusts to changes in the demand for its goods by changes in its issue of bonds and by changes in its money-holdings. Adjustments in the bond and money markets reflect changes in the goods market. BCC issues liabilities in the domestic capital market— a unified-currency area—to finance excesses of expenditures over incomes. Within the domestic economy the theory of portfolio balance suggests that the more debt BCC issues, the higher the interest rates on its marginal debt issues. Buyers of Monday's bonds require that

Tuesday's bonds be given inferior claims on the BCC. The theory of portfolio balance focuses on the relations between the prices of different financial assets in the bond market and the money market.

Countries in the worlds of Floyd and Howle face simpler problems than does BCC in a domestic economy, when the introduction of an international component might be expected to complicate the portfolio problem. The worlds of Howle and Floyd are domestic worlds in the sense that all financial assets are denominated in the same currency; their worlds have only one money and only one nonmoney financial asset. The lenders in these worlds passively adjust their demands for supplies generated by borrowers without any allowance for risk. Changing the name of the borrower from a company to a country does not automatically make the problem international.

The uniqueness of the world of international finance is the division of the world into currency areas. Each country has its own currency. The market applies different prices to securities denominated in these several currencies. The differences in these prices reflect expected exchange rates and the prices demanded by investors for bearing exchange risk. Howle intentionally sidesteps this problem. Floyd operates in a pseudo-multiple-currency world—*pseudo* in the sense that the ownership claims issued by borrowers in different countries do not differ in terms of currency denomination.

Papers on the international mobility of capital which fail to acknowledge the division of the world into currency areas and the consequences of that division for asset pricing may be excellent papers, but they are in the wrong ball park. Portfolio analysis appears well designed to deal with the pricing of assets denominated in different currencies. Instead, these papers caricature international finance and portfolio balance. They caricature international finance because they operate within a unified-currency area, and they caricature portfolio balance because the yield on financial assets appears independent of their value relative to other assets, and to the chain of prior claims on the borrower.

ANTHONY LANYI
PRINCETON UNIVERSITY

An important piece of unfinished business in international economics is the development of an economically meaningful and operational concept of external balance or external constraint. For an age of special drawing rights and greater flexibility of exchange rates, it will be of limited usefulness to define imbalances in terms of institutionally imposed constraints on international liquidity and on the frequency of changes in exchange rates. External balance should no longer be thought of as an end in itself but as a means toward the achievement of national and international economic goals. The latter must then be incorporated into our definition of external balance, with necessary account being taken of international economic interdependence and the likely incompatibility of different nations' economic objectives. As yet, we have not come very far along these lines.[1]

In view of this hiatus in the literature, and in our thinking, Howle's contribution is suggestive. His definition of external constraint is endogenously determined in a long-run model whose crucial variables are the long-run equilibrium ratio of foreign debt to capital stock, an endogenously determined rate of interest, the saving rate, the capital-output ratio, and the rate of growth of foreign demand for the country's exports. In the case of internationally immobile labor, an additional determining factor is the "natural rate of growth," given by exogenously determined rates of growth of the labor force and technical change. It is argued that fiscal policy cannot evade this constraint for more than a temporary period of time, and this argument is supported by a numerical illustration purporting to describe French economic problems following the *événements* of May, 1968. In the limited space available, I should like to mention what I believe are the major difficulties with this approach.

First, I doubt that it is appropriate to define external constraint in terms of a small region unable to affect the rest of the world. In fact, the world is made up of many such regions. The interest rate is exoge-

---

[1] However, several writers—including Richard Cooper, John Letiche, and Tibor Scitovsky—have argued that our criteria of external balance should incorporate the notion of stabilization policy on an international scale.

nously determined in Howle's model but is not so in the real world; the same is true of the rate of growth of foreign demand. To ignore international economic interdependence in such a model is to beg some major questions inherent in the present international monetary dilemma. The real situation presents a multiplicity of possible solutions and, therefore, a far greater range of policy choice than Howle's model would suggest. The real problem is not to find a theoretical equilibrium but to define tradeoffs and to use welfare criteria to find the best feasible position.

Long-run equilibrium analysis tends to be irrelevant to the mainstream of policy concerns, not only because there is in reality no unique solution to the system, but also because such analysis is nonoperational. Howle never defines the appropriate time horizon for defining an external constraint—unless, by implication, the time horizon is infinity. However, for periods shorter than the long run in which we are all dead, once-for-all changes of an unpredictable nature are likely to dominate putative equilibrium magnitudes.[2] Even if this were not so, there would still be the problem of translating long-run equilibrium values into guidelines based on short-run statistics. How can policymakers identify Howle's external constraint when they see it?

Finally, I am uneasy about some of the variables around which Howle has chosen to construct his analysis. I wonder why the ratio of foreign debt to physical capital is more appropriate than the ratio of foreign debt to total financial assets: Raymond Goldsmith's recent work shows that these two ratios do not change in tandem. Moreover, the "natural rate of growth" is a fictional magnitude; Edward Denison's empirical studies have certainly shown this. I suggest that n might be interpreted as a *desired* rate of growth, in which case Howle's model depicts the tradeoff between the rate of growth and the rate of price inflation. An interesting extension of this model would be to assume floating exchange rates, in which case a fall in the exchange rate could be substituted for some, or all, of the price inflation, depending on one's assumptions about the relationship between the two.

---

[2] This fact does not disturb Howle, who, in discussing the French case, is able to ignore an initial price *rise* of six per cent and analyze ensuing developments on the assumption of an initial rate of price *deflation* of one per cent. Such, however, is the ineluctable logic of long-run equilibrium analysis.

While Howle's problem springs from the application of a model of long-run equilibrium to the issues of short-run policy, Floyd's lies in extending a comparative-static model to explain long-run changes. The strength of Floyd's model is its inclusion of portfolio adjustment, a consideration omitted from Howle's analysis. This difference in assumptions produces at least one interesting difference in results, namely that in Floyddom the ratio of foreign debt to real national wealth depends on monetary as well as real variables; while in Howledom, it depends on real variables alone. On the other hand, Floyd's model as it now stands is inadequate for the exploration of long-run relationships. One reason for this is the assumption of constant output, which is not only inconsistent with an annual nonzero flow of new domestic investment, but also entails the omission of a most important variable from the analysis of portfolio adjustment over time. Another reason is the curious assumption that the expected rate of price inflation is independent of the actual rate. Although the author has mentioned verbally that the expected rate might adjust to the actual rate, this point of view is not incorporated into the mathematical model, which consequently enjoys a somewhat deceptive aura of dynamic stability.

A further oversight in the specification of Floyd's model is the assumption that the domestic *real* rate of interest is determined by the *real* rate of interest prevailing abroad. In fact, foreign investors compare the *nominal* rate of interest in their countries (i_n^f) with the *nominal* rate of interest in the home country (i_n) *minus* the expected rate of depreciation of the home-country currency (R_r^*). In a world of perfect capital mobility, then, we would expect that

$$i_n^f = i_n - R_r^*.$$

Only when exchange rates are flexible *and* the expected rate of depreciation of the home-country currency is exactly equal to the difference between the expected rates of price inflation at home and abroad will the *real* interest rates be equated. Incorporating this correction into Floyd's model produces significant changes. For instance, Floyd predicts that under fixed exchange rates, a foreign inflation will raise aggregate demand in the domestic economy, thereby inducing domestic price inflation and a sale of domestic assets to foreigners. In fact, if foreign inflation drives up nominal interest rates abroad, one would expect foreigners to wish to sell *their* holdings of domestic assets as well. The adjustment process then becomes considerably more complicated – and more realistic – than the one Floyd describes.

In Figure 2 of his paper, Floyd neatly exhibits the process by which simultaneous equilibrium is achieved in the markets for assets, goods, and foreign exchange through changes in the exchange rate and the price level. Once long-run rates of change of variables are incorporated into the analysis, however, the result is somewhat confusing. In one place we are told that the price level is unaffected by monetary policy under fixed exchange rates, since an increase in the *rates* of monetary expansion and price inflation will have no effect on the *levels* of the money supply and prices during the present period. Elsewhere, it is asserted that higher rates *do* have an effect on the levels by the end of the period during which they are changed. This confusion apparently stems from the author's interpretation of the short run as a period whose length asymptotically approaches zero – a concept corresponding to the time derivatives in Floyd's model. But in such a short run, the rates of change *also* approach zero asymptotically. The author should have taken greater care to distinguish between a verbal description of his mathematical model and the way terms like short run are commonly understood in policy analysis.

Thus, while Howle's analysis of the short run suffers from paying excessive attention to the near-infinite *long* run, Floyd concentrates inordinately on the near-infinite *short* run. Needless to say, neither of these periods is of much interest to the makers of economic policy. That neither of these papers has much to say about the short or medium runs, as commonly understood, implies criticism either of the models employed or of the way in which interpretations have been drawn (or have *not* been drawn) from them. There is a lesson in this. Just as mathematics is a way of checking the logical validity of our economic analysis, so must economic analysis be used to check the economic validity and relevance of our mathematical models. We must be careful to avoid the bad (and increasingly widespread) habit of letting mathematical models do our economic thinking for us.

PROBLEMS IN THE THEORY AND EMPIRICAL ESTIMATION OF INTERNATIONAL CAPITAL MOVEMENTS

EDWARD E. LEAMER · Harvard University
ROBERT M. STERN · University of Michigan

THE goal of our paper is to elucidate some of the important problems currently at issue in the theoretical conceptions and empirical estimations of international capital movements. Following our introductory remarks, we discuss the theoretical orientation of models of capital movements, contrasting what we call activity models and transactor models. We then indicate some of the important considerations that affect the choice of explanatory variables for particular capital items. After that there is a discussion of problems arising in the empirical estimation of capital movements plus whatever implications may be drawn for formulating economic policy.

We should like to emphasize at the outset that our paper does not by any means offer the last word on many of the problems touched upon and that we offer no new empirical evidence. While many of our remarks may appear critical, they should not be interpreted as denigrating the work that has been done to date. Rather, we hope that our discussion will stimulate a search for continued improvement in the theoretical design and empirical implementation of models of capital movements.

NOTE: We are indebted to Robert Holbrook, J. David Richardson, Warren L. Smith, Harold T. Shapiro, and members of the Research Seminar in International Economics at the University of Michigan for helpful comments on an earlier draft of this paper.

171

INTRODUCTION

THE study of capital-account relationships involves many more difficulties than does a study of the current account.[1] Most of these difficulties arise from the fact that capital movement is a monetary, not a real, phenomenon. For example, the relative stability of tastes will assure the relative stability of the import and export demand for goods and services as a function of price. Certain capital movements, in contrast, will be influenced significantly by changes in expectations regarding rates of return, thereby suspending the usual dependence on observed returns. It is also true that nonprice allocative variables such as credit rationing and capital controls will have a much more important impact on capital movements than is the case for the current account.

Analysis of capital movements is further complicated by certain special characteristics of the foreign-exchange and credit markets that must be taken into account in constructing theoretical models. To illustrate, the forward-exchange market may vary considerably at times in terms of its depth and availability, depending upon commercial-bank practices, government regulations, and the nature of speculative activity. Banks and other creditors may attempt to discriminate among borrowers on the basis of credit worthiness, in which case the loanable-funds market will be fragmented and thus not amenable to aggregative analysis. Credit rationing by banks may also occur, with the result that some customers may be denied servicing altogether. In this event, the suspension of the normal supply-and-demand mechanism will pose great analytical difficulties.

The foregoing remarks presage the numerous difficulties that beset the analysis of capital movements. Let us now turn to some of the theoretical problems at issue in this analysis.

[1] See Edward E. Leamer and Robert M. Stern, *Quantitative International Economics,* Boston, 1970, Chaps. 2–4, for an extended discussion of the theory and empirical measurement of current and capital-account relationships.

THEORETICAL PROBLEMS OF INTERNATIONAL CAPITAL MOVEMENTS

THEORETICAL models of economic systems are ordinarily constructed by categorizing the set of relevant economic exchanges into more-or-less homogeneous subsets. Each subset is analyzed individually, and the resulting independent parts are put together to form a model. Two general principles of categorization may be used to establish these subsets. The first requires us to categorize events according to the activity that is occurring—say, consumption or investment. The second principle requires a categorization according to the transactor involved—say, households or business firms.

Historically, most economic models have started out with an activity orientation, which has given way to a transactor orientation as minor and major flaws were discovered in these activity models. Current theoretical and empirical analysis of international capital transactions is, for the most part, oriented towards activities. We will discuss below several reasons why the shift to a transactor orientation might be better.

ACTIVITY MODELS

Most existing models of international capital transactions are based upon a set of independent activities, which are categorized typically into short-term (consisting of trade, interest arbitrage, and forward-market speculation) and long-term (consisting of portfolio and direct investment). In the case of capital movements, concern over the balance of payments leads to concern over capital *flows*. This leads, naturally enough, to the consideration of various capital-flow activities within the activity framework. Thus, at least until the mid-1960's, models of the foreign-exchange market included capital-flow items that were thought to respond primarily to interest-rate differentials. This was true not only of the early empirical studies of short-term capital movements, typified especially by Kenen's work,[2] but of the theoretical literature as well, particularly in Mundell's development of the assignment problem.[3]

The activities framework constructed for capital flow was increasingly subjected to attack as it became questionable whether one could identify any transactors who might conceivably behave as implied by the flow equations. Accordingly, more sophisticated activity models were developed, in which speculation and interest arbitrage, especially, were combined into a single activity – portfolio adjustment.[4] Moreover, commercial traders were allowed to acquire bank-financing for their operations in the context of a portfolio model. The logical conclusion of this approach was, therefore, to view all capital movements, including long-term transactions, as arising from the adjustment of portfolios. Thus, capital-flow activities were replaced by portfolio adjustment or capital-stock activities.

The portfolio view, which is now widely accepted,[5] suggests that the concrete specifications required for empirical analysis may be constructed in two comparatively easy steps. First, a decision must be made regarding the assets which substitute for the particular asset under examination. The corresponding rates of return are then to be included in the asset-demand equation. Secondly, one must define precisely the wealth variable that is relevant to the particular asset.

[2] See Peter B. Kenen, "Short-Term Capital Movements and the U.S. Balance of Payments," in *The United States Balance of Payments,* Hearings before the Joint Economic Committee, Washington, 1963.

[3] See Robert A. Mundell, *International Economics,* New York, 1968, especially pp. 217–71.

[4] An excellent example of such a model is to be found in the work of Jay H. Levin, *Forward Exchange and Internal-External Equilibrium,* Ann Arbor, 1970. This formed the basis of our own earlier treatment of capital movements (see Edward E. Leamer and Robert M. Stern, *op. cit.,* Chap. 4).

[5] At least judging from the works of William H. Branson, *Financial Capital Flows in the United States Balance of Payments,* Amsterdam, 1968; Ralph C. Bryant and Patric H. Hendershott, "Capital Flows in the U.S. Balance of Payments: The Japanese Experience, 1959–1967" (in process); John E. Floyd, "International Capital Movements and Monetary Equilibrium," *American Economic Review,* September, 1969; Herbert G. Grubel, "Internationally Diversified Portfolios," *American Economic Review,* December, 1968; C. H. Lee, "A Stock-Adjustment Analysis of Capital Movements: The United States–Canadian Case," *Journal of Political Economy,* July/August, 1969; Jay H. Levin, *op. cit.;* Norman C. Miller and Marina v. N. Whitman, "A Mean-Variance Analysis of U.S. Portfolio Investment," *Quarterly Journal of Economics,* May, 1970; and Thomas D. Willett and Francesco Forte, "Interest Rate Policy and External Balance," *Quarterly Journal of Economics,* May, 1969.

This presumably is straightforward, depending only upon the level of aggregation being employed.

Since the pendulum seems to have swung now so much in favor of the portfolio-adjustment view of activities, it is appropriate to consider whether this view has any important drawbacks. In our judgment, there are at least two worth mentioning. The first stems from the static conception of portfolio adjustment, in which net worth is taken as given. This may enable portfolio models to explain, say, the ratio of foreign to domestic assets, but such models will reveal very little about the scale of portfolio-holdings. The point is that capital flows may be more the result of decisions that influence net worth than of the allocation of net worth among potential assets.[6] The second drawback is that it appears doubtful that the complex activities occurring in any economy operate to bring about a portfolio balance in the aggregate. This is not merely an aggregation problem, since if all units were operating under portfolio-balance rules, there would exist a weighting scheme for the wealth items that would produce an accurate portfolio-adjustment equation for the aggregate. Rather, what we are asserting is that there are some important economic transactors that do not behave, at least in the short run, according to portfolio-adjustment prescripts.

One difficulty with activity models, therefore, is that they lead us into thinking that corresponding to each activity there exists an identifiable transactor behaving in the specified way. This simply may not be so, for transactors cannot be identified strictly on the basis of such activities as commercial trade, arbitrage, speculation, and long-term investment.

A second difficulty with activity models is the lack of independence of the various activities being undertaken. This suggests that activities may not form useful separate units for analytical purposes. It seems logically superior to begin by making the various transactors, themselves, the focus of the analysis, and then proceeding to analyze their activities. In actuality, this is what the stock models have done,

---

[6] Two further comments on this point are appropriate. Portfolio models tend to ignore the impact of policy on the growth rates of the net-worth variables and therefore tend to give misleading policy implications. In addition, the seemingly important question of repatriation of earnings is not handled very well within the portfolio framework, since it is more a question of whether to consume, or to save, earnings than a question of allocation of net worth.

since their superiority over flow models can be established only by an implicit appeal to the behavior of the relevant transactors. Consequently, we consider that stock models mark an important step in the right direction in their focus on transactors, although these models may not be applicable to transactors of all kinds.

TRANSACTOR MODELS

It is interesting to note that transactor-oriented models are comparatively rare in international financial analysis, whereas such models are commonplace in domestic analysis. In constructing a transactor model of capital movements, we should separate the relevant economic decision-making units according to how homogeneous or diverse the decision procedures are within and between groups. A categorization of transactors which may be relevant to the international transactions of any given country is as follows:

1. Nonfinancial corporations
2. Commercial banks
3. Other institutional investors
4. Government and official institutions
5. Households

Let us examine briefly some of the salient behavioral characteristics of the various transactors to see in what ways they may differ with regard to decision procedures.

Nonfinancial corporations are primarily concerned with production and sales, both at home and abroad. In order to carry out this primary function, firms will have to accumulate capital stock. The portion of this stock located abroad is, of course, what we designate as direct investment. The financing of the accumulation may be effected by way of bank loans, new security issues, or retained earnings. Each of these methods will have a direct, or indirect, impact on international capital transfers. Firms will also hold liquid assets at home and abroad for transactions and speculative purposes. Funds held in liquid form will compete against other demands, such as dividends and capital accumulation. Moreover, some firms will extend commercial credit to other firms as a sales inducement.

Given the complexity of the firm's decisions and the fact that there will surely be important constraints upon firm behavior in the short run, it is difficult to see how the attainment of a long-run portfolio balance can be anything but a rather distant objective. By eschewing the portfolio view of firm behavior, we may be able to focus more directly on the factors that determine the size — rather than simply the allocation — of a firm's net worth.

Commercial banks, whose principal activities consist of accepting demand and time deposits and allocating the incoming funds to a set of potential assets, may — in contrast to business firms — appropriately be viewed in a portfolio-adjustment context. In this regard, however, Hester and Pierce have suggested that the ease of acquisition and disposal varies considerably among assets.[7] Unusual deposits (withdrawals) are likely to have an initial impact on the most easily acquired (disposed of) assets. With the passage of time, this impact will be spread more evenly among the financial assets to achieve portfolio balance. It should be noted that the formulation of the adjustment process amounts to much more than simply adding lagged variables, since it must allow for the important short-run constraints affecting bank behavior.

International capital movements associated with banks are the result of deposits by foreign banks, business firms, and governments, and of deposits in foreign banks, loans to foreign firms, and claims on foreign governments (e.g., treasury bills). The various loans and government-security holdings can be accommodated easily in the portfolio-balance framework. The interbank deposits present some theoretical problems, however. These deposits are designed to facilitate the clearing process. Thus, for example, a foreign firm wishing to discharge a dollar obligation will have its bank perform the transaction by drawing down the firm's account and drawing a check on the bank in the United States. In the absence of a dollar demand deposit, funds would have to be transferred through the foreign-exchange market or by way of a dollar loan. The dollar demand deposit thus serves a convenience function and may be thought of as representing a transactions demand

[7] See Donald D. Hester and James C. Pierce, "Cross Section Analysis and Bank Dynamics," *Journal of Political Economy,* July/August, 1968.

which responds primarily to the level of transactions in dollars. It is noteworthy in this connection that banks in the United States do not hold deposits of similar magnitude in foreign banks, since the level of American transactions in foreign currencies is comparatively small.

The third group of transactors is composed of *other institutional investors,* including life-insurance companies, savings and loan associations, pension funds, nonprofit foundations, universities, and so on. These institutions behave in a fashion analogous to the commercial banks, accepting inflows and allocating the incoming funds to potential portfolio investments. They must be distinguished from banks, however, since they do not ordinarily accept demand deposits or grant commercial credit. Moreover, their portfolio profiles are considerably different from commercial-bank profiles. Thus, for example, increases in demand deposits will not engender additional foreign long-term portfolio claims, while similar flows into life insurance companies will.

Governments and official institutions form a fourth class of transactors. A portfolio-adjustment view of such transactors is not clearly plausible, inasmuch as there appears to be no obvious way to specify the wealth variable. Total claims on foreigners suggests itself. But such claims are certainly influenced by changes in government policy and may therefore be exogenous. Furthermore, allocation of claims among gold and other assets may be more a function of a country's world trading position, especially vis-à-vis the United States and changes in the political climate affecting the dollar, than of expected returns.[8]

Households form a residual category, including all units that are not identified above. These units are unimportant here, since, ordinarily, they do not hold significant amounts of foreign claims.

The foregoing sketches of some of the behavioral characteristics of different transactors are meant to illustrate three important points. In the first place, there is significant variation in asset preferences among transactors. It is important to take this variation into account, especially when there is any sizeable wealth redistribution among them. This is essentially a problem of aggregating different decision-making units. Secondly, short-run constraints upon behavior vary considerably

---

[8] See Helmut A. Hagemann, "Reserve Policies of Central Banks and Their Implications for U.S. Balance of Payments Policy," *American Economic Review,* March, 1969, for a recent study of central bank behavior that corroborates this view.

from transactor to transactor, and appropriate decision models vary as well. This means that it will be extremely difficult to construct a single comprehensive model of the capital account capable of capturing all of the structural characteristics of the different transactors. Thirdly, when individual transactors engage in multiple activities, the implicit interdependent decision-making will require a joint analysis of all of the interdependent activities for the transactors in question. Viewed in this light, disaggregation based on activities may be misleading insofar as activities that are presumed to be independent may not, in fact, be so.

The bulk of the research to date on international capital movements has sought to explain these movements by analysis of a set of hypothetical activities. This approach is deficient, since transactors cannot readily be identified to correspond to the different activities hypothesized, and since activities do not form naturally independent units of analysis. Consequently, generation of appropriate models must be based upon the behavioral considerations that are most pertinent to the actual transactors, themselves.

CHOICE OF EXPLANATORY VARIABLES

It should be evident from the preceding discussion that a variety of explanatory variable sets may be chosen for different models of capital movements. We shall now discuss some of the theoretical issues involved in this choice. We have just argued that the appropriate starting point for model construction is to consider the set of relevant transactors. However, since such transactor models have yet to be constructed, we shall divide our discussion according to the traditional activities of short-term capital, portfolio investment, and direct investment. Nevertheless, our intention is still to draw upon those insights offered by a transactor orientation. We trust that in time it will be possible to integrate many of the points adduced here into explicit transactor models.

1. Short-Term Capital. Three main categories of explanatory variables are relevant in explaining short-term capital movements. These are: (*a*) return variables; (*b*) trade variables; and (*c*) wealth variables. We shall discuss each of them in turn.

Risk factors aside, the competition between two assets will generally center upon the return associated with each one. A more-or-less acceptable restriction on the nature of this competition is to constrain asset-demand relations to be functions of return differentials rather than of the returns appraised individually. Taking this for granted, a more difficult question arises concerning whether to use the covered or uncovered return differentials in explaining short-term capital movements. If covered differentials are used, it is with the assumption that forward cover is available at the quoted market rate. If uncovered differentials are used, additional costs such as margin requirements intervene when arbitrageurs seek to cover their holdings, and these costs effectively prevent them from obtaining forward contracts.

In fact, the appropriate differential probably depends on the characteristics of the period under study. In very stable periods marked by the absence of pressure on the exchange-rate limits, forward cover will be relatively cheap but unneeded. The discrepancy between covered and uncovered differentials would be relatively small at such times. In less stable periods marked by expectations of exchange-rate adjustments and significant speculation in forward markets, the desire for forward cover will be greater. In the least stable periods, forward cover may become either relatively expensive because of increased margin requirements, or banks may ration it in some form. This suggests that the presence or absence of exchange-market pressures will be the determining factor affecting the need for, and cost of, forward covering. Since an uncovered asset may be thought of as a covered asset together with an offsetting speculative position in the forward market, we may regard all assets as covered in the forward market. Thus, asset demand will depend on the return on covered assets and on the expected return to speculation, an alternative portfolio choice. This implies that the best procedure might be to use the covered differential together with some variable that will reflect any additional cost of forward-covering, and a similar variable reflecting returns to forward-market speculation. If these latter variables are impossible to construct, we may, instead, divide the data periods into normal and abnormal groups—a procedure to be discussed more thoroughly below.

A large amount of short-term capital movement is connected with the financing of international trade. In view of this close link between the trade and capital accounts, a question arises concerning the propriety of using the level or changes in exports and imports, their sum, or their difference, in explaining the relevant capital movements. Banks and corporations are, of course, the two main sources of credit for the financing of private commercial trade. As far as banks are concerned, the link between trade flows and the volume of credit supplied seems tenuous. Banks will be accumulating claims on foreigners on the basis of returns to such claims. It is by no means clear how aggregative trade flows are linked with returns from the standpoint of banks, although such flows may have some bearing upon how banks evaluate risk factors such as capital controls. In addition, banks may grant credit related to trade flows as a service to foster good customer relations.

A much clearer link exists between trade flows and corporate willingness to lend. Extensions of credit will be made by corporations to foreign customers primarily as an enticement for sales. Increases in exports will therefore tend to be associated with increases in the credit outstanding. However, assuming that the corporation has profit objectives, credit extensions are properly linked with the profits from the sale, not the sale itself. Higher-profit sales are likely to be associated with much greater credit extensions than lower-profit sales of the same volume. Furthermore, there may be a strong causal relationship going the other way, with credit extension influencing sales.[9]

Just as there is no clear-cut link from exports to credit supply *to* foreigners, credit demand *by* foreigners is not straightforwardly related to exports. A foreign firm engaged in importing will have certain inventory needs. Credit to finance those inventories may be obtained from domestic sources, foreign sources, or through internal cash flows. It is probably true that smaller, less-well-established importing firms are likely to rely more on external sources of funds than do larger, well-established firms. We might expect, therefore, to observe relatively large credit extensions when new markets are being opened up, as, say, in the case of Japanese trade in the late 1950's and early 1960's. In contrast, increases in exports to more mature markets may engender

[9] In such a case, an ordinary least-squares regression of credit extensions on sales will be subject to simultaneity bias. More will be said about this below.

somewhat less credit demand, since importing firms in such circumstances may have greater access to internal financing. Pinches on internal funds will, of course, reestablish the link between imports and credit demands. However, just as in the case of credit supply, credit demand is properly linked to profits, not sales. One further point of interest is that the link between credit demand and sales may be broken if the credit extension is used to finance additional real investment or portfolio accumulation. The desire to obtain credit for these purposes naturally depends on the return involved.

While we have discussed the well-known but questionable link between short-term claims on foreigners and exports, it should be noted that there is a possible link between such claims and imports. That is, importers – and/or the banks with whom they deal – may hold balances in the foreign currency for transactions purposes. Import increases will therefore stimulate larger transactions balances and, thus, larger claims on foreigners. In the case of the United States, importers will not need such balances since imports are commonly financed in terms of dollars. Firms and banks in other countries which undertake trade denominated in dollars will maintain transactions balances in banks in the United States, both for trade with the United States and for trade with other countries.

Our discussion suggests that merchandise-trade variables are not well suited to explain credit extensions, because they may reflect only indirectly the profitability motivations of the transactors on both the supply and demand sides, and because the direction of causation is unclear. However, lacking information relating to profitability, it may be necessary to rely on some measure of sales for explanatory purposes. Whether exports and/or imports should be used will depend upon the circumstances under study. What should be emphasized is that the primary variable for explaining trade-financing should be expressed in terms of *changes* in sales rather than level of sales.[10] The reason for this is that rapid growth in sales, which reflects favorable profit opportunities, will engender increases in trade credit. When sales

[10] It should be pointed out that the position taken here departs from the traditional one, in which the stock of trade credit was related to the flow of goods. The traditional view, which was essentially ad hoc, was developed within an activity framework, which, as we have argued, obscures the relevant behavioral characteristics of banks and corporations in the case of trade credit.

and profit opportunities level off, there will be a tendency for firms to rely more on internal financing and domestic credit sources. The result will be an evening off, and perhaps even a decline, in the use of foreign credits.

Wealth variables comprise the third variety of important variables for explaining short-term capital movements, especially in the context of a model of portfolio adjustment. On the most highly aggregative level, wealth may be defined to include capital stock, plus government debt, plus net claims on foreigners. Such a definition may not be particularly revealing, however, insofar as it fails to represent accurately the behavioral constraints on the relevant economic transactors. As we have argued previously, models of capital movements should focus on the behavior of unique transactors and seek to identify the wealth and other constraints that influence such behavior. Thus, for example, we noted that while banks may regard their deposit flows as given when making asset choices, they may allocate demand and time deposits to generally different assets. Furthermore, unexpected deposit variation is most likely to have an initial impact on the more liquid assets. We also observed that corporations may have important cash-flow and other constraints in the short run; and that given the complexity of corporate decisions, a portfolio-equilibrium view of corporate behavior seems inadequate.

2. Portfolio Investment. To the extent that purchases of foreign bonds and equities represent short-term investments, the points made earlier with respect to employing uncovered, or covered, return differentials would be applicable. Exchange-rate expectations may be less important, however, for strictly long-term investment, although the timing of this investment might be sensitive to such expectations. Since it seems quite appropriate to use a portfolio model for this kind of investment, the choice of the wealth variable should closely reflect those constraints which are most binding on the behavior of the transactors involved.

3. Direct Investment. In pursuing profits or sales goals, corporations are required to make a great number of intertwined decisions, one of which is the quantity of direct investment. A superficial view has direct investment depending upon expected returns to the investment, expected returns to alternative uses of funds, and the availability of funds. Unfortunately, each of these three items depends in a very complicated fashion on the other decisions which the firm has made or is making. Returns to the investment depend upon current and projected export sales. Alternative uses of funds include dividends, domestic investment, postponed investments, and so on. Sources of funds include internal cash flows and external borrowing. The problem is further complicated by the impact of current investment decisions on future flexibility.

The construction of a theoretical model that deals with all of these problems is clearly outside the range of this paper. However, we wish to reiterate our position that a portfolio-adjustment view of the corporation, and of direct investment, is not particularly revealing. In the first place, it tends to ignore all of the short-run financial constraints upon the behavior of the firm. Secondly, it can easily lead to a definition of returns that ignores the complex interrelationships in the decisions of the firm. Thirdly, it ignores the fact that the investment decision is fundamentally a question of whether to increase net worth, not a question of how to allocate a given net worth.

EMPIRICAL PROBLEMS IN ESTIMATING INTERNATIONAL CAPITAL MOVEMENTS

HAVING set forth various theoretical considerations important to the construction of models of international capital movements, we turn now to several significant problems in the empirical implementation of the models. These problems are concerned generally with how best to represent the behavioral characteristics subsumed in the different models, and how to handle some purely statistical matters. We shall deal in particular with the following: (1) measuring expected returns and risk; (2) handling of speculative activity; (3) capital controls and credit rationing; (4) disaggregation schemes; (5) data inadequacy; (6) lag structure; (7) functional form; and (8) simultaneity.

MEASURING EXPECTED RETURNS AND RISK

Since the expected returns and risk variables used in most theoretical descriptions of asset accumulation are ordinarily unobservable, it is necessary to adopt some procedure that will make these concepts operational. We can either seek proxy variables to represent expected returns and risk, or else construct models of expectations-formation concerning these phenomena. It may be possible, in addition, to identify time periods separately on the basis of important changes in expectations that affect behavior.

Uncertainty over returns stemming from the holding of foreign debt instruments is associated primarily with the possibility of devaluation and/or capital controls. The proxy variables sought should, therefore, reflect pressure on the authorities induced by balance-of-payments difficulties. Expected returns and risks of equities and direct investments may also be affected by such balance-of-payments considerations, but will, furthermore, depend upon business-climate variables.[11]

An alternative to using proxy variables is to construct a model of expectations-formation. Ordinarily, this involves the assumption that expected future returns/risk are a constant function of current and historical values of the rates in question. This assumption is clearly inapplicable to the spot rate in a pegged-exchange-rate system, although it may be acceptable in this system when applied to the forward rate and to returns to equities and direct investment.[12]

A further alternative is to identify turbulent periods in which changes in expectations had an important effect upon behavior. This may be done by exploring the regression residuals in an interest-parity model, as Stein did,[13] assuming that large residuals from interest

[11] See Norman C. Miller and Marina v. N. Whitman, *op. cit.*, for a more extensive discussion of proxy variables for returns/risk which relate to portfolio investment. Their model included the lagged value of the U.S. balance-of-payments liquidity deficit and deviations of U.S. GNP from trend. They also experimented, unsuccessfully, with changes in aggregate exchange reserves of selected foreign countries, the ratio of forward and spot rates, and a ratio of the spot rate in period $t + 1$ to the spot rate in period t.

[12] Branson, *op. cit.*, is especially noteworthy in his effort to incorporate expectations into his model.

[13] See Jerome L. Stein, "International Short-Term Capital Movements," *American Economic Review*, March, 1965.

parity reflected a suspension of the normal behavior pattern in favor of speculation. Rather than concentrating on the residuals, however, it might be preferable, as will be discussed more fully below, to separate the data on an a priori basis into "normal" and "speculative" periods and perform regression analysis separately on each set of data.

SPECULATIVE ACTIVITY

It is well known that in a system of pegged exchange rates, speculative activity may fundamentally alter the nature of the foreign-exchange markets. During periods of substantial speculative activity, the forward market may dry up, existing credit lines may be curtailed and new ones denied, credit rationing may become more prevalent, inventory speculation may become pronounced, and so forth. In such circumstances, expectations may increase so much in importance that they dominate behavior. This means that the behavior relations applicable during a "normal" period may be effectively suspended, since responses will be swamped by expectational forces that are not fully incorporated in the usual empirical models of capital movements. What is suggested, then, is that we separate "normal" from "speculative" periods according to the absence or presence of expectations concerning exchange-rate changes outside the official limits.

If normal periods dominate the sample, the speculative eras could be treated as outliers and discarded. Unfortunately, there is no sound statistical way of doing this without a great deal of effort. Still, the inconvenience does not justify a resort to ad hoc procedures which are potentially dangerous from the standpoint of data interpretation. In this regard, we have already taken note of Stein's construction of a speculative-pressure variable based on the residuals of a regression of the forward premium on the uncovered interest-rate differential.[14] This procedure was criticized in separate comments on Stein's work by Heckerman and Laffer,[15] who contended that the residuals may reflect other things besides speculative pressure.[16]

[14] *Ibid.*

[15] See Donald G. Heckerman, Arthur B. Laffer, et al., "International Short-Term Capital Movements: Comments," *American Economic Review,* June, 1967.

[16] Stein's procedure may be all the more questionable since, as Jay H. Levin has pointed

An alternative to Stein's approach would be to identify periods of exchange-market turbulence on some a priori basis. One such possibility would be to seek out expert opinion concerning periods during which currencies were felt to be especially affected by substantial speculative transactions. Rather than relying on informed judgment, it might be preferable to use data on forward exchange rates. Theoretical considerations suggest that speculative confidence in the limits of spot exchange rates in the pegged-rate system will be reflected by infinitely elastic speculative activity in the forward market at these limits. The forward rate may move outside the limits only if speculators lack confidence in the government's willingness and ability to maintain the spot rate and if there is no official counter-speculation to peg the forward rate.[17] A reasonably objective method for separating speculative from normal periods might be a division based on whether or not the forward rate for a given period lay inside or outside the official support limits designated for the spot rate.[18]

In order to evaluate how this criterion performed, in Chart 1 we plotted the ninety-day forward rates for the pound, mark, and French franc as a per cent of the official spot peg on an end-of-month basis for the period 1960–69 (September). The official spot support points are shown as 99 per cent and 101 per cent. The chart suggests that the pound was under speculative pressure to devalue periodically throughout the period. The speculative attack on the pound in 1961 was accompanied by opposite pressure on the mark. The years 1968 and 1969 were very turbulent, with pressure on all three currencies. We conclude, therefore, that empirical studies which include assets in the United Kingdom will necessarily have to deal with the speculation problems more or less throughout the 1960's. Analysis of the mark and

out in private discussion, Stein's model of the foreign-exchange market makes inadequate provision for hedging by traders in the forward market and does not clearly distinguish the stock of investor short-term capital which represents covered-interest arbitrage.

[17] Note that Stein's analysis implicitly assumes the forward rate to be determined by interest-arbitrage considerations. We, however, regard the forward rate as being determined primarily by speculative activity, at least outside the support points.

[18] It might be thought that dummy variables could be introduced to handle these speculative occurrences in a single analysis, rather than separating the time periods. Dummy variables would not do the job, however, because the assumption would still be made that the usual explanatory variables were applicable, when, in fact, they may not be during speculative periods.

CHART 1

Ninety-Day Forward Rates (End of Month) of Pound Sterling, Mark, and
French Franc 1960–69

(*per cent of spot peg*)

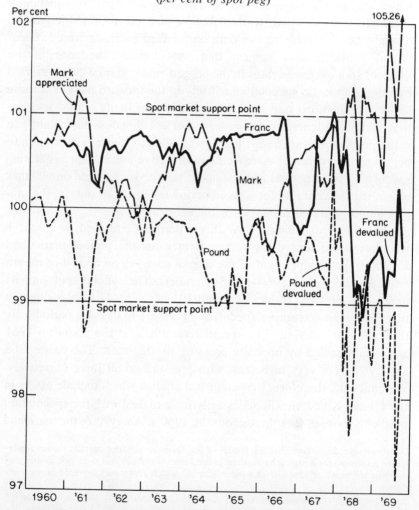

SOURCE: International Monetary Fund, *International Financial Statistics,* various issues.

the franc will have to deal with speculation particularly in 1968 and 1969. As is suggested above, these points in the series of data might best be analyzed separately. (See Tables 1, 2, and 3.)

CAPITAL CONTROLS AND CREDIT RATIONING

We have already mentioned that controls and credit rationing will have an impact on capital movements. When controls result in the reduction of effective returns, a suitable variable may be introduced to take this into account. However, when controls take the form of quotas, the model may have to be abandoned altogether, since the observed points in the series of data may bear no relationship to the true underlying demand or supply schedule being estimated. This is also the case when credit rationing occurs.

The presence of capital controls and credit rationing thus poses very serious difficulties, since the relationships that we usually formulate are predicated on the assumption that they will correspond with the observed data. It is possible to assume, as Bryant and Hendershott have done,[19] that the effect of capital controls is to reduce the observed quantity by a proportion depending on the existing controls. Their rationale for doing so was that the capital controls in question were voluntary, and that the observed responses to other stimuli were reduced but not eliminated. To proceed in this way requires, of course, much detailed knowledge of the controls and their effects, and there may not be any straightforward way to allow quantitatively for the reductions in responses. This is an unfortunate situation since — particularly in the case of capital movements — interferences of various kinds may well be the rule and not the exception.

DISAGGREGATION SCHEMES

Capital assets of varying maturities are issued and acquired in many different countries by many different transactors. The potential

[19] See Ralph C. Bryant and Patric H. Hendershott, *op. cit.*

TABLE 1

Ninety-Day Forward Rate: Pound Sterling (1960–69)

(per cent of spot peg)

	1969	1968	1967	1966	1965	1964	1963	1962	1961	1960
January	98.96	99.82	99.58	99.93	99.06	99.84	99.96	99.80	99.96	100.07
February	99.06	99.45	99.58	99.75	99.09	99.75	99.89	99.86	99.60	100.09
March	99.06	98.28	99.71	99.51	98.93	99.75	99.66	99.98	99.38	100.09
April	98.20	98.76	99.71	99.58	99.38	99.80	99.82	100.07	99.39	100.09
May	98.08	97.60	99.66	99.55	99.09	99.73	99.84	100.16	99.24	99.91
June	98.85	98.02	99.53	99.49	99.26	99.58	99.89	100.11	98.66	99.78
July	98.93	99.27	99.35	99.26	99.22	99.40	99.93	100.02	98.79	99.80
August	97.13	98.67	99.29	99.31	99.04	99.29	99.91	99.91	99.22	99.87
September	98.36	99.14	99.24	99.46	99.71	99.22	99.88	99.89	99.55	99.89
October		99.43	99.15	99.55	99.80	99.26	99.86	99.96	99.84	100.11
November		98.54	100.50 [a]	99.44	99.86	98.97	99.86	99.79	99.78	100.11
December		98.36	99.58	99.46	99.82	98.97	99.84	99.64	99.64	99.89

SOURCE: Calculated from International Monetary Fund, *International Financial Statistics*, various issues.

[a] Devaluation.

TABLE 2

Ninety-Day Forward Rate: German Mark (1960–69)

(per cent of spot peg)

	1960	1961	1962	1963	1964	1965	1966	1967	1968	1969
January	100.70	100.89	100.30	100.00	100.86	100.76	99.63	100.55	100.50	100.81
February	100.75	100.89	100.25	99.98	100.91	100.76	99.68	100.65	100.45	100.50
March	100.69	101.24 a	100.28	100.15	100.85	100.78	99.63	100.65	101.21	100.40
April	100.69	101.19	100.10	100.23	100.76	100.65	99.55	100.68	101.11	102.01
May	100.67	101.14	100.27	100.40	100.76	100.30	99.65	100.70	101.32	101.65
June	100.73	101.16	100.30	100.45	100.91	100.05	99.85	100.60	101.01	101.34
July	100.68	100.88	100.30	100.40	100.81	99.80	100.20	100.25	100.30	100.96
August	100.74	100.45	100.15	100.55	100.73	99.70	100.30	100.35	101.32	101.96
September	100.89	100.30	100.10	100.40	100.63	99.67	100.27	100.25	101.14	105.26
October	100.82	100.25	99.90	100.55	100.60	99.80	100.45	100.30	101.16	
November	100.75	100.15	99.95	100.55	100.67	99.90	100.55	100.93	101.01	
December	100.84	100.35	100.15	100.70	100.58	99.92	100.55	100.91	101.06	

SOURCE: Calculated from International Monetary Fund, *International Financial Statistics*, various issues.

a Appreciation.

TABLE 3

Ninety-Day Forward Rate: French Franc (1960–69)

(per cent of spot peg)

	1969	1968	1967	1966	1965	1964	1963	1962	1961	1960
January	99.53	100.49	99.74	100.80	100.78	100.63	100.76	100.61	100.65	
February	99.63	100.41	99.85	100.80	100.73	100.59	100.71	100.65	100.69	
March	99.49	100.67	99.82	100.82	100.80	100.51	100.69	100.67	100.65	
April	99.07	100.32	100.02	100.84	100.80	100.50	100.73	100.59	100.55	
May	99.37	a	100.05	100.80	100.82	100.22	100.65	100.59	100.53	
June	99.35	99.08	100.80	100.80	100.76	100.45	100.51	100.65	100.65	
July	99.31	99.23	100.73	101.00	100.80	100.48	100.59	100.73	100.59	
August	100.25 b	99.19	100.75	100.96	100.80	100.51	100.67	100.76	100.28	
September	99.60	98.86	100.84	100.55	100.80	100.52	100.59	100.76	100.26	
October		99.17	100.87	100.10	100.78	100.69	100.71	100.77	100.22	100.71
November		99.44	101.04	99.86	100.78	100.76	100.57	100.82	100.55	100.71
December		99.50	100.96	99.83	100.80	100.73	100.57	100.76	100.73	100.65

SOURCE: Calculated from International Monetary Fund, International Financial Statistics, various issues.

a Not quoted.

b Franc devalued.

for disaggregation is, therefore, substantial. The simplest rule that can be stated in this regard is that if a certain category of capital movements is theoretically important, disaggregation should be carried at least as far as that category. Whether disaggregation should be carried even further involves the questions of whether a better understanding or a clearer explanation would be obtained, and how one deals with the vectors of variables describing microunits, which are implicit in the aggregate relation.

One ordinarily argues that the returns from disaggregation will be greatest when distinctly different responses can be isolated for the transactors in question. This assumes, however, that we employ the usual index-number solution to the problem of how to handle the long vectors of microvariables in the relationships specified, in which case we would be assuming, in effect, that all responses were identical within the category chosen. If this were not in fact true, a specification error would have been made and further disaggregation might be in order. While the procedure just described is a common one, it is by no means satisfactory. That is, it is possible to construct index numbers that do not assume identical responses.[20] Moreover, treating the issue as a specification error overlooks important statistical questions concerning the proliferation of data points as disaggregation is pursued further.

Unfortunately, there is no way to resolve all of the statistical issues involved in choosing disaggregation schemes. For this reason, ad hoc procedures must be employed. It might be reasonable to continue disaggregating as long as improved (or perhaps only different) estimates of the aggregative relationship are obtained, given the budget constraint upon research resources.

INADEQUACY OF DATA

We have already noted that micromodels of asset accumulation will ordinarily contain several different exogenous variables on rates of return, many of which will enter implicitly into the relevant aggre-

[20] This involves determining the proper weights to be used. See Edward E. Leamer and Robert M. Stern, op. cit., Chap. 2, Appendix, for a discussion of this matter in the context of estimating import-demand functions.

gate relationships. Consequently, the total number of explanatory variables may be rather large. At the same time, however, substitutions between assets are likely to be sufficiently important so that no return variable may move independently of the others. We will thus be faced with an extreme case of data inadequacy in the form of a large collinear set of explanatory variables. This is an unfortunate occurrence because it makes for great difficulties in interpreting the data.

Multicollinearity plagues much econometric work, capital movements being no exception. This may, nevertheless, be an appropriate place to register our strong disapproval of the common practice for dealing with multicollinearity: fitting the equation, discarding the variables that are "not significant statistically," and then refitting the equation. This procedure is undesirable on two counts. In the first place, *statistical* significance must be carefully distinguished from *economic* significance. What is often forgotten is that an "insignificant" coefficient results from a combination of a small true coefficient and a large standard error, whereas multicollinearity is ordinarily associated with large standard errors. This means that a coefficient may be judged insignificant even when it is of substantial size. What must be emphasized is that terms such as *small* or *large* and *significant* or *insignificant* take on precise meaning only when put in a particular decision-making context. It is thus quite conceivable that an investigator who rejects "large" coefficients because they have "large" standard errors may be imposing an interpretation on the data that is, in fact, economically unwarranted.[21]

An additional objection to the refitting of equations in the manner cited is that such "specification searches" have no theoretical basis.[22]

---

[21] This can be illustrated by a simple example. Suppose that we were interested in reducing domestic interest rates by one per cent to stimulate the domestic economy. If this change induced, say, up to $5 million in capital outflow, we might be unconcerned. From $5 to $50 million, our concern might grow increasingly. And, maybe, after a $50 million outflow, we would discard the proposed interest-rate change altogether. In this example, an "insignificant" coefficient is one that leads to less than a $5 million outflow. This may be quite different from the conclusion to be drawn from a test based on statistical significance.

[22] That is, least-squares axioms allow only a single fit, and where specification searches based on the discarding of variables have been analyzed (as in Edward E. Leamer, "Inference with Non-Experimental Data: A Bayesian View," University of Michigan, Doctoral Dissertation (unpublished), 1970), they have been found detrimental to the validity

The only approach with established statistical validity is interpretation of the data directly from the full, unconstrained equation. While it is true that the presence of extreme multicollinearity implies fairly useless information about individual coefficients, there may, nonetheless, be useful information about sets of coefficients. In order to obtain that information, estimates could be calculated of sums, or averages, of coefficients and their standard errors.[23]

LAG STRUCTURE

Lagged variables will be required to reflect both the adjustment mechanism and the formation of expectations. A common procedure is to attempt to capture these effects simply by adding lagged explanatory or dependent variables to the basic model. This implicitly involves the assumption of a fixed but unknown response pattern. In the case of capital movements, this technique may be found lacking in at least two respects. One is that it makes little or no distinction between the two types of lags. Such a distinction could be important from a policy standpoint since, for example, expectations could be altered significantly by virtue of the announcement effects stemming from policy changes. It might be desirable, therefore, to employ explicit models of adjustment and expectations in order to be able to distinguish these influences from one another.[24]

of the data interpretation so afforded. It is not difficult to see why this is so. By constraining some of the coefficients to be zero, we force other correlated variables to take over the role played by the discarded variables. There would be a tendency, therefore, to overestimate the impact of the included variables and, of course, to underestimate the impact of the excluded ones.

A different search procedure than the one usually followed might be to constrain the coefficients in a way which is more or less justified on a priori grounds. In this case, we could construct an index number for the return variables, thereby implicitly assuming a relationship between the regression coefficients. Leamer is presently investigating this procedure in the context of empirically weighted price indexes constructed for use in estimating import-demand functions.

[23] One further possibility is to interpret the data by exploring multidimensional confidence intervals. See Edward E. Leamer and Robert M. Stern, *op cit.*, Chap. 2, for an illustrative example using income and price coefficients from an import-demand regression.

[24] Roger N. Waud in "Misspecification in the 'Partial Adjustment' and 'Adaptive Expectations' Models," *International Economic Review*, June, 1968, has pointed out that in simple models of partial adjustment and adaptive expectations, it may be impossible

Mechanical use of lagged variables also ignores potentially useful information concerning the determinants of the response pattern. One of our basic objections to portfolio-adjustment models is that they tend to ignore short-run constraints upon behavior which determine methods and speeds of adjustment. In some cases, these constraints may become so important that the long-run portfolio-balance considerations are barely reflected in the findings.

In constructing a model of expectations-formation, it is possible to allow for adaptations in the expectations. Such a model leads to a set of fixed weights on past observations.[25] This is not a completely acceptable procedure, since the extent to which future projections are adjusted in the light of the discrepancy between current projection and current observation is not a fixed fraction but depends instead upon current and past information. Also, risk factors, as well as expectations, will be adjusted in response to current evidence. To the extent that his projections come to fruition, an investor may justifiably gain confidence in his ability to project, and shift his portfolio to more risky assets. Clearly the problem of expectations-formation is in need of further study.[26]

---

to identify the two elements separately. Edgar L. Feige in "Expectations and Adjustments in the Monetary Sector," *American Economic Review,* May, 1967, has shown, however, that more complex models permit such identification.

[25] See *ibid.* for a discussion of adaptive expectations models.

[26] A Bayesian view of expectations-formation could prove useful. Suppose, for example, that an investor establishes a subjective multivariate normal distribution on a vector of future returns, r. At time t, he will have observed the first t elements in r, say r_1. He then updates his subjective measure on the remaining elements, say r_2, according to Bayes Rule, $p(r_2 | r_1) = p(r_1, r_2)/p(r_1)$. In the case of the multivariate normal distribution (see Howard Raiffa and Robert Schlaifer, *Applied Statistical Decision Theory,* Boston, 1961, p. 250) with mean $m = [m_1, m_2]$ and variance

$$V = \begin{bmatrix} V_{11} & V_{12} \\ V_{21} & V_{22} \end{bmatrix},$$

the updated measure on r_2 is also multivariate normal with mean $m_2 + V_{21}V_{11}^{-1}(r_1 - m_1)$ and variance $V_{22} - V_{21}V_{11}^{-1}V_{12}$, indicating that the discrepancy between the projection m_1 and outcome r_1 is used to update the mean on r_2 according to a set of fixed weights $V_{21}V_{11}^{-1}$. The discrepancy does not affect the variance. This is precisely what the usual adaptive expectations-model assumes.

Other models of expectations within the Bayesian framework will not reduce to the usual adaptive expectations-model, however. For example, the investor may regard the set of returns to be a sample from a normal process with mean m, variance σ^2, and autocorrelation coefficient ρ. The observations r_1 will provide information about all parameters. Although the updated projection is rather complicated, it is clearly not the simple adaptive expectations-projection.

CHOICE OF FUNCTIONAL FORM

The use of simple linear-regression techniques requires that the hypothetical relationship be linear in its parameters. Within that linear class, there is an infinite variety of functional forms from which to choose. Economic theory often provides little, if any, basis for choice, and researchers commonly select linear or log-linear forms, perhaps considering the problem unimportant for the inferences and decisions to follow. However, in the case of asset accumulation, economic theory does suggest a more restrictive class of functional forms.

A general asset-demand function relates the stock of assets A to a set of scale variables W (which determine the portfolio size) and to a set of preference variables r (which determine the allocation of the portfolio among competing assets), $A = f(r, W)$. The associated capital flow at a fixed interest rate is $F = dA/dt = (\partial f/\partial W)dW/dt$. Policy analysis will, of course, be concerned with the flow induced by a change in interest rates, $dF/dr = (\partial^2 f/\partial W \partial r)dW/dt$. Functional forms such as $A = g(r) + h(W)$, which constrain $\partial^2 f/\partial W \partial r$ to zero, also constrain the flow induced by interest-rate policy to zero, thus presupposing the answer to an important policy question. Since portfolio increases are almost certainly allocated among assets according to the constellation of interest rates, such forms should be avoided. The very popular form $A = f(r)W$, on the other hand, remains acceptable.

SIMULTANEITY

The spot and forward exchange rates and the interest rate will not necessarily be fixed independently of variations — especially those in the size of the large capital items. There may also be other demand-and-supply interactions (particularly in the extension of trade credit) that make for ambiguities in the direction of causation. Quite clearly, theoretical models will have, and should have, simultaneous elements. It is well known that the presence of such simultaneity implies biases in the estimated coefficients, the extent of the biases depending upon both the seriousness of the simultaneity and the stability of the relationship being analyzed. In order to plot a course relative to this issue, we must ask not only if simultaneity is present, but also if there might be more pressing problems than the necessity of perfecting estimating techniques to handle the simultaneity. In our judgment, in the case of capital movements, it is premature to worry too much about sophisticated statistical techniques to handle simultaneity. There are, indeed, other more important problems to be resolved, not the least of which is the specification of a model which is itself appropriate.

THE EMPIRICAL EVIDENCE

THE study of international capital movements should be a prelude to coping with certain important questions of economic policy. Thus, for example, we might want to know how the balance of payments is affected by changes in monetary and fiscal policies, whether selective capital controls are effective, what the impact will be of official counter-speculation in the forward market, how changes in domestic policies will affect other countries, how their policies will affect us, and so on. While there is an abundance of theoretical literature dealing directly with questions such as the foregoing, this recognition is, unfortunately, much less prevalent in the empirical literature. Many empirical studies of capital movements have aimed primarily at justification of a particular model, rather than at drawing policy implications regarding the model parameters from the available empirical evidence. Moreover, the evidence in many studies is summarized in a confusing manner which makes it very difficult to reach meaningful conclusions.

We thought that it would be useful to survey the empirical literature on movements of short-term and portfolio capital for the United States and Canada in any event, with two fairly simple but important questions in mind: what effect would a one per cent change in interest rates have on the capital accounts, and what is the impact of the merchandise-trade variables on these accounts? We were not able to make a comparable survey for direct investment, the existing studies being rather limited in number and scope.

INTEREST-RATE IMPACTS

Tables 4 and 5 contain summaries of the evidence regarding the impact of a one per cent change in interest rates on capital movements of various kinds for the United States and Canada. We have taken the regression estimates of the interest-rate coefficient noted in the individual studies as the best guess at the impact of interest-rate adjustments. Where an interest rate was reported to be not significant statistically, we assumed that the investigator had concluded that it had a zero effect.[27] No reference is given in Tables 4 and 5 to studies in which the regression results did not lend themselves easily to the question being posed, or in which the investigator excluded the particular relationship from his analysis.[28] One important caveat must be noted with regard to these tables: they ignore the other repercussions of the interest-rate change which considerably dampen the effect of the assumed policy. That is, other explanatory variables such as foreign interest rates and forward-exchange rates are assumed to be unaffected by the interest-induced capital flows.

It will be observed that stock and flow effects are distinguished in Table 4. The reason for this is that in a stock model there will be a stock adjustment to an interest-rate change and a continuing flow effect. The flow effect results from an altered allocation of the assumed increments to any scale variables. Not all of the stock models shown embody a flow effect. As noted earlier, there are certain functional forms that constrain the flow effect to zero. Branson's use of a linear form is a case in point.[29] Some of the results cited are based only on flow models which assume that the induced capital flows will continue indefinitely. This arrangement is not very plausible; the results in question have to be interpreted as some combination of stock and flow effects.

Some interesting points emerge from Table 4. There are evidently substantial differences in the estimates based upon Branson's quarterly and monthly models. He had no ready explanation for these differ-

[27] Note, however, as discussed earlier, that we regard this use of significance tests to be inappropriate.
[28] Note also that the coverage of the capital items may differ between studies.
[29] William H. Branson, op. cit.

TABLE 4

Summary of Estimated Effects of a One Per Cent Per Annum Increase
in Interest Rates upon the Capital Account of the United States
(*millions of dollars*)

Capital Item [a]	Source of Estimate [b]	Stock Effect [c]	Flow Effect [c]
U.S. claims			
Short-term:			
Total	Branson	−468	0
	Branson [d]	−253	0
	Kenen [e]		−270
	Prachowny		−170
	Laffer	0	0
	Laffer		0
Banking claims	Stein	−27	0
	Stein		−69
Claims on Japan	Bryant and Hendershott	−600	−25
Long-term:			
Total	Branson	−315	0
	Branson [d]	−800	0
	Miller-Whitman	−1,073	−21
	Prachowny		−124
Claims on Canada	Lee	−1,619	−20
Bank loans	Branson	0	0
U.S. liabilities			
Short-term:			
Total	Branson	260	0
	Branson [d]	540	0
	Kenen [e]		260
	Laffer	0	0
	Laffer		0
Banking liabilities	Stein	0	0
	Stein		46
Long-term:			
Total	Branson	693	0
	Branson [d]	2,000	0
	Prachowny		100

Notes to Table 4.

NOTE: Flow effects are given per quarter.

[a] Coverage of the items noted may not be exactly comparable in different studies.

[b] Based upon results contained in: William H. Branson, *Financial Capital Flows in the United States Balance of Payments,* Amsterdam, 1968; Peter B. Kenen, "Short-Term Capital Movements and the U.S. Balance of Payments," *The United States Balance of Payments,* Hearings before the Joint Economic Committee, Washington, 1963; Martin F. J. Prachowny, *A Structural Model of the U.S. Balance of Payments,* Amsterdam, 1969; Arthur B. Laffer, "Short-Term Capital Movements and the Voluntary Foreign Credit Restraint Program" (in process); Jerome L. Stein, "International Short-Term Capital Movements," *American Economic Review,* March, 1965; Ralph C. Bryant and Patric H. Hendershott, "Capital Flows in the U.S. Balance of Payments: The Japanese Experience, 1959–1967" (in process); Norman C. Miller and Marina v. N. Whitman, "A Mean-Variance Analysis of U.S. Foreign Portfolio Investment," *Quarterly Journal of Economics* (forthcoming); C. H. Lee, "A Stock-Adjustment Analysis of Capital Movements: The United States–Canadian Case," *Journal of Political Economy,* July/August, 1969.

[c] Calculated at point of sample means, excluding feedbacks.

[d] Estimated with monthly data.

[e] Calculated on the assumption that regressions not reported showed zero interest-rate effects.

ences, but believed the results of the quarterly model to be the more reasonable. It can also be seen that the results of the flow models tend to lie within the range of the comparable stock and flow effects based on stock models. We may note, finally, that the relatively large estimates of interest rates for the two items, disaggregated by country in the works of Bryant and Hendershott, and Lee, suggest that a component of a capital item is more sensitive to interest rates than is the entire item, itself. At first glance, this appears to bear upon the problem of disaggregation, suggesting that effort could be expended profitably in disaggregating the capital items by country. However, there may also be an important element of data misinterpretation, caused by the highly collinear data set required at that level of disaggregation.[30]

[30] To illustrate, assume that country 1's (U.S.) asset demand (A_1) for the claims of country 2 (Canada) will depend upon returns (r) in countries 1, 2, and 3 (U.K.), subject to country 1's wealth constraint (W_1):

$$A_1 = A_1(r_1, r_2, r_3, W_1).$$

If the capital instruments of countries 2 and 3 are good substitutes from the point of

TABLE 5

Summary of Estimated Effects of a One Per Cent Per
Annum Increase in Canadian Interest Rates upon the
Capital Account of Canada
(*millions of Canadian dollars*)

Capital Item	Source of Estimate [a]	Flow Effect
Canadian liabilities		
Short-term:		
Total	Rhomberg	183
Net Canadian capital movements (claims − liabilities)		
Short-term:		
Total	Helliwell et al.	−102
	Arndt	−125
Long-term:		
Total	Helliwell et al.	−177
Canada–U.S.	Rhomberg	−149

NOTE: Flow effects are given per quarter.

[a] Based upon results contained in: Rudolf R. Rhomberg, "A Model of the Canadian Economy Under Fixed and Fluctuating Exchange Rates," *Journal of Political Economy,* February, 1964; John F. Helliwell et al., "The Structure of RDX1," Bank of Canada, Staff Research Studies No. 3, Ottawa, July, 1969; Sven W. Arndt, "International Short Term Capital Movements: A Distributed Lag Model of Speculation in Foreign Exchange," *Econometrica,* January, 1968.

view of country 1 investors, then the marginal responses to r_2 and r_3 will be very large. At the same time, the three rates may be highly collinear and the usual search procedure of discarding insignificant variables could well lead to a form such as:

$$A_1/W_1 = a + b(r_2 - r_1).$$

The misspecification involved in such a form necessarily provides biased estimates. In the case of the impact of country 1's (U.S.) rate, there is a presumption of overestimation. This is, in fact, precisely what C. H. Lee, *op. cit.,* did. In an equation in which the U.S., Canadian, and U.K. interest rates were used separately, the impact of the U.S. rate was but a fraction of the implied value in his misspecified relation. This argument does not apply to Ralph C. Bryant and Patric H. Hendershott, *op. cit.,* who did not fit such a constrained form.

In view of the apparent dearth of reliable results for the component capital items listed in Table 4, it must be concluded that we are still much in the dark with regard to the over-all balance-of-payments effects of an interest-rate increase by the United States.[31] Clearly, much remains to be done. The situation for Canada is no better. It can be seen in Table 5 that all of the three studies cited have employed a flow model,[32] and that the two sets of flow results for the net movement of Canadian short-term and long-term capital are reasonably close to one another. These results may not be reliable for policy purposes, however, in view of the theoretical objections pertaining to a flow model.

IMPACTS OF MERCHANDISE TRADE

The evidence concerning the impact of merchandise-trade flows on capital movements is summarized for the United States in Table 6. The sparseness of entries, compared with Table 4, is indicative of the exclusion of trade credit influences in many empirical studies. Branson's results showed that an assumed $100 million increase in the quarterly flow of exports from the United States will induce a $90 million increase in the stock of short-term claims held by the United States in the form of trade credit. His comparable figure, using monthly data, was only a third as large. Prachowny's results indicated that the assumed increase in exports from the United States would generate a continuing flow of claims against foreigners equal to $21 million per

---

[31] It may, nevertheless, be of interest to note William H. Branson's conclusion, *op. cit.*, p. 160, that a one per cent change in the U.S. interest rate, inclusive of feedback effects, would result in a net capital inflow of $2.5 billion based on his quarterly model, and a $3.0 billion inflow based on his monthly model. These are presumably total stock effects, since he has constrained the flow effect to be zero. The flow equations in Martin F. J. Prachowny, *A Structural Model of the U.S. Balance of Payments*, Amsterdam, 1969, pp. 119–20, suggest that a one per cent interest-rate change will improve the U.S. balance of payments by $161.2 million in the first quarter, but that this improvement will not be perpetuated when the lag structure of the model is taken into account. Such evidence as the foregoing is, in our judgment, too meager for use in formulating policy decisions for the balance of payments.

[32] This is the case, also, with the work by Stanley W. Black, "Theory and Policy Analyses of Short-term Movements in the Balance of Payments," *Yale Economic Essays*, Spring, 1968. Since his model involved a number of complex interactions, it was not possible to derive a simple interest-rate effect for inclusion in Table 5.

TABLE 6

Summary of Estimated Effects of a $100 Million Increase Per Quarter in
Merchandise-Trade Flows upon the Capital Account of the United States
(*millions of dollars*)

Capital Item	Source of Estimate [a]	Exports	Imports	Trade Balance
U.S. claims				
Short-term:				
Total	Branson	94		
	Branson [b]	30		
	Prachowny	11 [c]		
	Laffer			32 [c]
Claims on Japan	Bryant and Hendershott [d]			
U.S. liabilities				
Short-term:				
Total	Branson		72	
	Branson [b]		112	
	Laffer		50 [e]	

[a] See references cited in Table 4.
[b] Fit with monthly data.
[c] Per quarter.
[d] Constrained to unitary elasticity.
[e] With respect to world exports.

quarter. Laffer's results, also based on a flow model, implied that an increase in the trade balance of the United States of the given amount would increase short-term claims of the United States by about one-third on a continuing basis. Bryant and Hendershott did not measure the influence of exports on trade credit, since they constrained the relationship to be of unitary elasticity. The results for short-term liabilities of the United States can be interpreted in a similar manner.

The results in Table 6 are thus very sketchy, indicating that much remains to be done here as well.[33] This is especially the case since we

[33] In this instance, the only result that we can report for Canada comes from Sven W. Arndt (see reference in Table 5), who estimated from a flow equation that a $100 million increase in Canada's trade balance would induce a $41 million reduction in the quarterly flow of Canadian net short-term capital.

consider the relationships underlying Table 6 to have been misspecified. That is, the stock of trade credit implied by a fixed flow of goods is not likely to be very large. Rather, credit extension is related to increases in the flow of goods associated with the profit possibilities of new and rapidly expanding markets, and with the limitations experienced by new firms—especially with regard to their ability to generate internal cash flows and to borrow domestically.

DIRECT INVESTMENT

We have already indicated that the theoretical analysis of direct investment is still very much in its infancy. It is not surprising, therefore, that most of the quantitative work that has been done to date, except perhaps for Stevens',[34] is rather impressionistic and ad hoc.[35]

IMPLICATIONS FOR FURTHER RESEARCH

IN GENERAL, we conclude that both the theoretical and empirical analysis of international capital movements require considerable improvement before an adequate understanding of these phenomena can be claimed. We have suggested that theoretical views of capital flows of all varieties can be improved by an explicit analysis of the transactors involved. Perhaps the greatest shortcoming of the usual activity framework is the failure to recognize the importance and complexity of national and international corporations.

The absence of an appropriate theory has led empirical workers to ad hoc and questionable specifications of their models in several instances. We must, therefore, view these empirical results with con-

[34] Guy V. G. Stevens, "Fixed Investment Expenditures of Foreign Manufacturing Affiliates of U.S. Firms: Theoretical Models and Empirical Evidence," *Yale Economic Essays,* Spring, 1969.

[35] See, for example, the equations fitted in the studies for the U.S. by Martin F. J. Prachowny, *op. cit.,* and Anthony E. Scaperlanda and Laurence J. Mauer, "The Determinants of U.S. Direct Investment in the EEC," *American Economic Review,* September, 1969. For Canada, see John F. Helliwell, et al. and Rudolf R. Rhomberg (references cited in Table 5).

siderable skepticism. In addition, there are numerous empirical problems which could profit by further work. We have tried to catalogue these problems and, wherever possible, to indicate possible solutions.

We began by noting that our paper does not purport to offer the last word on the problems discussed, and that we have made no empirical estimates of our own. Rather, our primary objective has been to elucidate the most important problems in a way that may stimulate efforts toward their solution. Too often, researchers, rushing to the data, have either failed to identify, or chosen to ignore, many theoretical and empirical problems. Such premature use of the strictly limited data forces empirical work to assume an hypothesis-generating role rather than the much more important role of selecting among alternative hypotheses.[36]

[36] See Edward E. Leamer, *op. cit.,* for an extended discussion of this point.

EMPIRICAL ANALYSIS OF CAPITAL FLOWS: SOME CONSEQUENCES OF ALTERNATIVE SPECIFICATIONS

RALPH C. BRYANT · Federal Reserve Board
PATRIC H. HENDERSHOTT · Purdue University

WE HAVE three specific objectives in this paper. First, we wish to incorporate lagged time responses into the theoretical framework set out in an earlier work [6]. Second, we report the results of subjecting our earlier empirical analysis to further tests. These include some testing of our earlier assumptions that (a) the lags in the portfolio adjustment of borrowing by Japanese foreign-exchange banks are short; (b) the desired borrowing relationship is homogeneous of degree one in bank net worth and Japanese imports; and (c) equations estimated for the entire 1959–67 period hold approximately for the 1964–68 period. Finally, we give some examples of how the estimation of equations attempting to explain capital movements are affected by alternative specifications, including some cases of theoretical misspecification. As in our earlier paper, we are concerned here primarily with the theoretical framework and the empirical methodology that are appropriate for the analysis of international capital movements. All of the empirical results reported in both of our papers refer to short-term borrowing from American banks by Japan, but we believe that the inferences we draw from our intensive study of this particular capital flow have wide applicability for the empirical analysis of all international capital flows. To begin with, we summarize our basic framework and preliminary results, as described in [6].

1 SUMMARY OF BASIC FRAMEWORK AND PRELIMINARY RESULTS

THE basic empirical relationship employed in our study of short-term borrowing from banks in the United States by Japanese banks expresses the Japanese banks' long-run desired level of borrowing, Bus^*,[1] as a function of the Japanese banks' net worth, NW, Japanese imports, M, and numerous borrowing and lending rates:

$$Bus^* = f(\overset{+}{NW}, \overset{+}{M}, \overset{-}{RBus}, \overset{+}{RLld}, \overset{+?}{RBj}, \overset{+?}{RBe\$}). \qquad (1)$$

The specific interest rates employed in (1) are: the "own" rate on borrowing from the United States, $RBus$ (calculated as a weighted average of the rate charged on U.S. bankers' acceptances and the rate charged by U.S. banks on short-term business loans); the return earned by Japanese banks on their lending, $RLld$ (calculated as a weighted average of the rates charged on all loans and discounts); the cost to Japanese banks of borrowing funds in Japan, RBj (calculated as a weighted average of the discount rate of the Bank of Japan and the rate in the call-money market in Tokyo); and the cost to Japanese banks of borrowing in the Eurodollar market, $RBe\$$ (approximated in our study by the rate paid by London banks on ninety-day Eurodollar deposits). The theory of the demand and supply of financial instruments and the empirical approximations used to derive equation (1) are spelled out in some detail in our earlier work.[2] The intellectual lineage of functions of this sort goes back to the theory of portfolio choice as worked out by Markowitz [16] and Tobin [24], [25].

---

[1] Much the greatest portion of Japanese short-term borrowing from banks in the United States is carried out by Japanese banks. The exact proportion is not known but is probably well in excess of 90 per cent. For this reason we treat the time series as though it were entirely borrowing by Japanese banks, even though small amounts of borrowing by Japanese nonbanks may be included. In our earlier paper [6, pp. 27, 44, 53] we tested to see whether an episode of large official borrowing in 1961–63 (there referred to as LOJ) substituted for private borrowing that might otherwise have taken place. Since our test seemed to indicate that this official borrowing had no significant impact on the remainder of Japanese borrowing, the variable Bus in the present paper is defined as total short-term borrowing from American banks less these special official loans in 1961–63.

[2] Ideally, (1) should contain some additional variables—most notably some proxy variables for the risks which Japanese banks associate with the holding of the different liabilities and assets on their balance sheets. See [6, pp. 5–15, 34–46].

The signs of the partial derivatives of *Bus** with respect to its determinants are noted above the symbols in (1). Increases in the net worth of the Japanese banks should, by reducing the risk associated with portfolios of given size and composition, lead to an expansion of all forms of borrowing and lending. The positive relationship between Japanese imports and borrowing from American banks reflects the institutional fact that—perhaps because there is a lower risk associated with lending against trade documents as collateral—American banks prefer to lend to Japan in the form of bank acceptances based on import-trade bills. Thus, increases in Japanese imports lead, other things being equal, to greater borrowing from the United States. The economic rationale for this institutional relationship may have been particularly strong in the early 1960's, when Japanese banks were still establishing their overseas financial contacts and their credit-worthiness in international financial markets. Later in the decade, one might have expected the importance of this relationship between borrowing from American banks and Japanese trade bills to have declined. Some of our further experiments, reported in Part 3 below, do suggest such a diminution in importance.

Increases in the own interest rate, *RBus*, obviously make the Japanese banks less eager to borrow from the United States. Increases in the returns earned by Japanese banks on their loans and discounts should unambiguously induce increases in desired borrowings. The directional impact on *Bus** of increases in other borrowing rates is ambiguous. Increases in the costs of borrowing funds at home in Japan or in the Eurodollar market will induce familiar substitution effects (more borrowing from American banks relative to other sources), but they will also produce what might be termed an "income" effect (a reduction in total borrowing, some portion of which falls on borrowing from the United States). One cannot conclude a priori that the substitution effects will outweigh the income effect, but this seems to us the more likely outcome.

In most of our empirical work so far, we have modified equation (1) by assuming that the long-run desired function is homogeneous of degree one in net worth and imports:

$$Bus^* = g\left(RBus, RLld, RBj, RBe\$, \frac{M}{NW}\right) NW. \qquad (2)$$

We find this multiplicative form appealing because it makes the impact of increments in the scale variable on the desired quantity dependent on the levels of the interest rates, and the impact of changes in the interest rates dependent on the level of the scale variable.[3] Although we cannot directly justify the assumption of linear homogeneity in terms of the Markowitz-Tobin theory,[4] we regard the assumption as a practical modification of (1) that given the present state of our theoretical and empirical knowledge, is as plausible as any other specific modification we might choose to make. The functional form of (2) allows for easy estimation of an equation where $g(\quad)$ is approximated by a linear relationship. Such an approximation is:

$$Bus^* = \left(\theta_0 + \theta_1 RBus + \theta_2 RLld + \theta_3 RBj + \theta_4 RBe\$ + \theta_5 \frac{M}{NW}\right) NW, \quad (3)$$

where θ_1 is expected to be negative; θ_2 and θ_5 are expected to be positive; and θ_3, θ_4, and θ_0 could be either negative or positive. In Part 3 below, we report some results that seem to confirm the suitability of the assumption of linear homogeneity.

If actual Japanese borrowing, Bus, always coincided with long-run equilibrium borrowing, Bus^*, it would be appropriate to estimate (3) directly. For at least two reasons, however, a substitution of Bus for Bus^* in equation (3) may not be valid. First, desired borrowing in the short run, designated here as Bus^s, may differ from long-run equilibrium borrowing because of the presence of lagged responses (see Part 2 below). Second, and more important in the case of Japanese borrowing from American banks, Japanese and American capital restrictions have significantly influenced the actual level of borrowing attained. For much of the 1959–68 period, only a fraction of desired short-run borrowing was effectively demanded or supplied. Algebraically,

---

[3] These responses can be most easily seen by taking the first difference of equation (2):

$$\Delta Bus^* = g(\quad)\Delta NW + NW_{-1}\Delta g(\quad), \quad (2')$$

since $\Delta(AB) = A\Delta B + B_{-1}\Delta A$. In a growing (or declining) economic world—$\Delta NW \neq 0$—changes in interest rates bring about both "existing-stock" (through the second term), and "continuing-flow" (through the first term) impacts on capital flows. Given a "once-for-all" change in one or more interest rates, the existing-stock effect produces capital flows that are also once-for-all in nature (a reallocation of existing portfolios), while the continuing-flow impact persists indefinitely as long as $\Delta NW \neq 0$. See [6, pp. 11–13].

[4] See [6, pp. 10–11].

$$Bus = \alpha Bus^s; \ 0 < \alpha \leqslant 1, \tag{4}$$

where α equals unity when capital restrictions are absent or not binding.

The fraction α is itself related to three different phenomena. The first is the basic relaxation during 1959 and 1960 of restrictions which the Japanese government had imposed on external transactions throughout the 1950's, denoted by the variable BR. The second is a "learning process" (on the part of both Japanese banks and foreign lenders) and the growth of Japanese credit-worthiness in international financial markets during 1961–64, triggered by the earlier relaxation; this group of phenomena is designated by the variable CW. The third phenomenon is the introduction and varying effectiveness of the American Voluntary Foreign Credit Restraint program during 1965–68, summarized in the variable V.[5] Expressing the fraction α as a linear function of these three variables, we have

$$\alpha = 1.0 + \beta_1 BR + \beta_2 CW + \beta_3 V; \ \beta_i < 0 \text{ for all } i. \tag{5}$$

Assuming that $Bus^s = Bus^*$ (an assumption used in our earlier paper but relaxed in this one), we substitute the equations for α and for Bus^* into (4) to give an equation which relates actual borrowing to both the economic variables and the variables representing the effects of capital restrictions:

$$\frac{Bus}{NW} = (1.0 + \beta_1 BR + \beta_2 CW + \beta_3 V)$$

$$\times \left(\theta_0 + \theta_1 RBus + \theta_2 RLld + \theta_3 RBj + \theta_4 RBe\$ + \theta_5 \frac{M}{NW} \right). \tag{6}$$

Numerous variants of this equation have been estimated on quarterly data from the 1959–67 period. Four of them are given in Table 1. In the table we report nonlinear regression estimates together with their standard errors (below and in parentheses). Because estimates with unconstrained interest-rate coefficients seemed implausible [6, p. 52], the sum of the interest-rate coefficients was constrained to equal

[5] For a more detailed discussion of these three phenomena, see [6, pp. 13–15, 36–44, D1–D4]. The variable V is defined as zero (prior to 1965) or as the ratio of foreign claims of American banks at, or over, their individual ceilings to the aggregate ceiling for all American banks reporting in the Voluntary Foreign Credit Restraint program.

TABLE 1

Estimates of the

Equa-tion	BR	CW	V	Con-stant	RLld minus RBus
(1.1)	−.349	−.437	−.199	.060	.426
	(.049)	(.036)	(.119)	(.399)	(.099)
(1.2)	−.410	−.402	−.231	.350	.183
	(.161)	(.146)	(.082)	(.844)	(.107)
(1.3)	−.370	−.415	−.158	.316	.336
	(.044)	(.032)	(.114)	(.333)	(.040)
(1.4)	−.397	−.393	−.202	.345	.184
	(.142)	(.142)	(.073)	(.719)	(.075)

NOTE: The dependent variable is Bus/NW. See text and [6] for exact specification of equation and definitions of variables. Bus and M are measured in

zero by the use of interest-rate differentials. We show for each equation the standard error of estimate (SEE), the Durbin-Watson test statistic for serial correlation in the residuals (DW), and the parameter ρ used in an autoregressive transformation that we employ when a low DW figure suggests high positive serial correlation in the residuals. In general, ρ is estimated by assuming that the serial correlation follows a first-order autoregressive scheme [6, p. 54], but occasionally it is specified a priori.

Equations (1.1) and (1.2) are estimates of equation (6) with and without the autoregressive transformation. The capital control variables, the principal interest-rate differential, and the imports-net-worth variable all seem to work reasonably well. Also as expected, given the offsetting nature of the income and substitution effects, the other two interest-rate coefficients are very small; these variables contribute nothing to the explanatory power of the equation. If these two variables are omitted from the equation, we obtain equations (1.3) and (1.4).[6]

[6] Omission of the rate spreads is the result of applying the theory of second best; it is not the preferred procedure. All variables implied by the theory ought to be retained in the equation unless they have coefficients that are clearly less plausible than zero. However, when we add variables to the equations in Section 3-A (below) to test for lagged responses, these insignificant rate spreads would likely generate substantial multicollinearity problems.

Basic Equation

RBj minus RBus	RBe\$ minus RBus	M/NW	ρ	SEE	DW
−.043	.182	.503	–	.134	.83
(.055)	(.174)	(.162)			
−.011	−.022	.650	.99	.105	2.05
(.053)	(.093)	(.146)			
		.485	–	.134	.76
		(.160)			
		.668	.98	.105	2.11
		(.140)			

billions of dollars, NW is in trillions of yen, and interest rates are expressed in per cent per annum. The period of estimation is 1959–67.

2   ESTIMATION OF LAGGED RESPONSES

THE importance of capital restrictions as a factor causing observed quantities of financial instruments to diverge from their long-run desired levels was discussed at some length in our earlier paper. A second source of discrepancy between observed and long-run desired quantities is the fact that economic units may fully adjust their holdings of financial instruments to changes in the determinants of long-run desired holdings only after some significant period of time has elapsed. We give here reasons for expecting lagged responses and describe methods of estimating them. (Some of these methods are employed in the estimation reported in Part 3.)

A. REASONS FOR LAGGED RESPONSES

It seems unlikely that an assumption of instantaneous adjustment would be appropriate in studies of most international capital flows. Recent empirical studies of domestic financial behavior, when they have been designed so as to allow for the presence of lagged responses, have generally reported the apparent existence of significantly long lags.

The reasons for lagged adjustment in financial behavior are at least two, one of which is dependent on the other. First, portfolio adjustment necessarily entails transactions costs; both time and money must be expended in obtaining the necessary information and in implementing the adjustment. Particularly large transactions costs are incurred when financial instruments with inferior secondary markets and/ or penalty rates for prepayments or redemption before maturity are involved. Since a significant proportion of both pecuniary and nonpecuniary transactions costs tends not to vary with the size of transactions, there are economies in making less frequent adjustment.

Second, it is expected future yields and risks that are relevant to investors, but only observed yields are generally available for use as regressors. Given the existence of transactions costs, a change in the yield (or the risk associated with the yield) on short-term or fixed-valued financial assets must be of some permanence if adjustment of one's portfolio is to be at all profitable. While the permanency of changes in the yields on long-term or variable-valued assets is not of importance,[7] future expected values of these yields still are. For example, if the yield on a variable-valued asset rises, an investor will not move into that asset if he expects the yield to continue rising. To do so would invite future capital losses. Since investors may extrapolate recent interest-rate changes into the future and/or expect future rates to regress toward long-run "normal" rates, a weighted average of current and lagged values of yields may be a good proxy for the expected yield. This implies that current changes in yields and risks will lead to portfolio adjustments in future periods.

Transactions costs may be relatively less important for financial institutions whose costs for obtaining information and making adjustments are probably less than those of other economic units. Also, transactions costs stemming from inferior secondary markets and/or penalty rates for prepayments or earlier redemption can be avoided by short delays only, when short-term instruments are involved. Thus, we would

[7] Even if the yield movement is reversed, a capital gain is made (if the yield has risen) or a loss is avoided (if the yield has fallen).

expect responses to be most rapid for financial institutions rearranging their short-term portfolios, and least rapid for nonfinancial units rearranging their long-term portfolios.

B. METHODS OF ESTIMATION

A complete theory of the demand and supply of particular financial instruments would require an explicit utility-maximization treatment of the manner in which economic units attempt to adjust short-run desired quantities to long-run equilibrium levels.[8] We do not have such a theory and know of no study of financial behavior containing one. What we do here is merely outline some of the empirical procedures that can be used in estimating lagged responses.

It is useful to begin by considering how an equation would have to be specified (how the variables would have to be measured) if one wished to assume no lags, i.e., instantaneous adjustment. Clearly, the dependent variable at any point in time should be related to the independent variables at the same point in time. It is customary to use average values of the dependent variable during an interval in order to eliminate fluctuations that are extremely short-run. Thus, in our case, the assumption of instantaneous adjustment would be enforced (temporarily ignoring the existence of capital controls) by estimating

$$\overline{Bus} = f(\overline{NW}, \overline{M}, \overline{R}), \tag{7}$$

where average (mean) values are denoted by a bar over the variables and, for notational purposes, the interest rates are combined into a single-rate vector. If the observation period is a quarter, $\overline{Bus}$, $\overline{NW}$ and $\overline{R}$ are average values during the quarter and $\overline{M}$ is the cumulative flow of imports during that quarter. If some of the data are measured only as of the last day of the quarter, a simple average of beginning and end of quarter values could be employed.[9]

Consider now the case where lagged responses are expected to be

[8] If there were no relevant capital restrictions and no other discrepancies between actual and short-run desired quantities, the part of the theory concerned with lagged responses would explain the adjustment of actual quantities to long-run equilibrium levels.

[9] For a careful discussion of how continuous-time models should be approximated in discrete time for the purposes of empirical research, see H. Houthakker and L. Taylor [12, pp. 11-21].

not much, if at all, longer than the observation period itself. Here the best procedure to follow is probably to assume a uniform *intraperiod* lag distribution. This is achieved by measuring the dependent variable (a stock) at the end of the observation period and measuring all independent variables as averages during the period. (This, in fact, was the procedure we employed for the equations reported in [6]). Equation (8) reflects this measurement.[10]

$$Bus = g(\overline{NW}, \overline{M}, \overline{R}). \tag{8}$$

This case is not as rare as one might imagine. In fact, where the main research objectives do not include the rigorous investigation of lagged responses, it may be good strategy to select the observation period so as to correspond as closely as possible with the expected length of lag. One might employ monthly data, for example, if it were expected that adjustment would be completed in a month, or a month and a half. Quarterly data could be used if it were thought that one to one-and-a-half quarters were required for full adjustment, while annual data could be used if one to one-and-a-half years were required. Conversely, if one is particularly interested in studying lagged responses, obviously a short enough observation period must be chosen.

The general case (still ignoring capital controls) expresses *Bus* as a function of current and lagged values of all of its determinants:

$$Bus = h(\overline{NW}, \overline{NW}_{-1}, \ldots, \overline{NW}_{-r},$$

$$\overline{M}, \overline{M}_{-1}, \ldots, \overline{M}_{-s}, \overline{R}, \overline{R}_{-1}, \ldots, \overline{R}_{-t}). \tag{9}$$

If lagged responses are significantly long in relation to the observation period, direct estimation of (9) could prove to be impossible, owing to the limited degrees of freedom or the high collinearity among the regressors, or both. However, in the case where lags are thought to be short relative to the length of the observation period, a direct approach may be feasible. For those explanatory variables being tested for lags, one-period, and possibly two-period, lagged values can be explicitly entered in the regression equation. In Part 3, we report some illustrative equations where this procedure has been followed.

[10] If the dependent variable were a flow, each independent variable would be correctly measured as the average of its values in the current period and the previous period.

Perhaps the most popular method of estimating lagged responses is use of the Koyck-Nerlove "stock-adjustment" model.[11] In this model, a constant proportion of the gap between actual and long-run desired quantities is assumed to be closed each period:

$$\Delta Bus = \lambda(\overline{Bus^*} - \overline{Bus}), \tag{10}$$

where λ is the proportion closed and must lie between zero and unity. Since any gap between actual and desired quantities is being closed continuously through time, the relevant gap to use in a discrete-time model is the *average* gap prevailing during the period. If $\overline{Bus}$ is approximated as $\frac{1}{2}(Bus + Bus_{-1})$, then equation (10) can be algebraically rewritten as:[12]

$$\Delta Bus = \gamma(\overline{Bus^*} - Bus_{-1}) \tag{10'}$$

or

$$Bus = \gamma\overline{Bus^*} + (1 - \gamma)Bus_{-1}, \tag{10''}$$

where $\gamma = 2\lambda/(2 + \lambda)$.

If one wishes to use this method in a context such as ours, the existence of capital controls complicates matters, but it can be handled as follows. First, we express equation (10″) in terms of the value of Bus that would have existed in the absence of capital controls, Bus^s:

$$Bus^s = \gamma\overline{Bus^*} + (1 - \gamma)Bus^s_{-1}. \tag{11}$$

Then, we substitute for Bus^s and Bus^s_{-1} from equation (4) and multiply through by α. This yields

$$Bus = \alpha\left[\gamma\overline{Bus^*} + (1 - \gamma)\left(\frac{Bus}{\alpha}\right)_{-1}\right]. \tag{11'}$$

Equation (11′) differs from the usual form of the stock-adjustment

---

[11] For a discussion of the implied lag structures in several of the early empirical studies in terms of the stock-adjustment model, as well as of shortcomings of that model, see Hendershott's comment [10] on Stein [21].

[12] In many empirical studies, γ has been interpreted incorrectly as the "speed of adjustment." As the text illustrates, the estimate of $\lambda = 2\gamma/(2 - \gamma)$ should be interpreted as the speed of adjustment. For slow speeds of adjustment, the differences between γ and λ are small, but the difference becomes more important, the larger the estimate for γ. (Note that an estimate of γ greater than .67 is theoretically inadmissible.)

model because instantaneous adjustment to changes in α, the capital controls construct, is assumed.[13]

A disadvantage of the Koyck-Nerlove type of model is that it places relatively severe constraints on the lag distributions. Lag weights for each explanatory variable are assumed to decline geometrically, and the rate of decline is adjudged the same for all variables.[14] Another problem with the stock-adjustment model is that the coefficient on the lagged stock will be biased upward toward one (γ and therefore λ, will be biased downward) to the extent that autocorrelation of the residuals exists.[15] What is worse, even though the "desired" stock (or α) may be seriously misspecified, the stock-adjustment model can generate superficially plausible estimates. In the extreme case, the lagged values of a dependent variable – if it is a rather smooth series – will alone "explain" the dependent variable quite well, suggesting a "significant" slow speed of adjustment, even though there are no theoretically correct variables in the equation to which the dependent variable is adjusting.[16] Some examples of the use (and misuse) of the stock-adjustment model are given in the next two sections.

The technique of polynomial approximation first used by Almon [1] is a general method of estimating longer lag distributions that also conserves degrees of freedom.[17] In this method, the distributed lag weights are assumed to lie along a polynomial of given degree; both the

[13] In most cases (though conceivably not with all types of capital controls), it would seem preferable to assume that changes in capital controls bring about very rapid adjustments. Any a priori knowledge about lagged responses to capital controls, if these lags were thought to be important, might most appropriately be taken into account when the proxy variables for capital controls are themselves being constructed. (This is the procedure we followed in [6].)

[14] These constraints can be relaxed somewhat if the function for the "desired" stock is defined to include recent lagged values, as well as current values, of its theoretical determinants.

[15] The bias in the estimate of λ will be present if the "true" relationship is of the form

$$y_t = \gamma\beta x_t + (1 - \gamma)y_{t-1} + u_t,$$

and the u_t are serially correlated.

[16] See Griliches' note [7] on serial-correlation bias in estimates of distributed lags, and also his recent survey article [8], for a discussion of these points. Procedures have been suggested for obtaining a consistent estimate of the coefficient on the lagged dependent variable when autocorrelation is present and major misspecification errors have been avoided. See, for example, the references cited in Griliches [8, pp. 40–42] and Wallis [26]. Still, no technique of estimation, however sophisticated, can give valid results if the specification of the desired stock is itself seriously incorrect.

[17] See also Tinsley [22], [23].

degree of the polynomial and the length of the lag are preselected by the researcher. Here we do not report any equations which make use of the technique of polynomial approximation, and therefore do not discuss it. Nonetheless, we believe that it is a method which ought to be given at least equal prominence with the Koyck-Nerlove Model.

3 FURTHER RESULTS

THE results of three types of test are presented below. First, we test for the existence of significant lagged responses in the borrowing behavior of Japanese foreign-exchange banks. Second, we report on a sample test of the linear homogeneity assumption. Third, we present three equations estimated on data from the 1964–68 period only.

A. LAGGED RESPONSES

The equations reported in our earlier work [6] and summarized in Table 1 assumed that the response to a disturbance was completed in the quarter following the disturbance. Table 2 contains eight equations testing for longer responses. In equations (2.1) and (2.2), current and lagged-one-period values of the imports–net-worth ratio, and the spread between the Japanese lending rate and the American borrowing rate, are employed as regressors. Equation (2.2) differs from (2.1) in that the autoregressive parameter is estimated. Both of these equations suggest that there is a lagged response to changes in interest rates, but not apparently to changes in the import–net-worth ratio. Another finding of interest is the small estimated impact of the VFCR variable; the current estimates are only about a third of those in equations (1.1)–(1.4).

Equations (2.3) and (2.4) are partial-adjustment equations using the form of equation (11′). Equation (2.4) differs from (2.3) in that the lagged, as well as current, value of the interest-rate spread is employed as a regressor. These equations are very similar. The only meaningful difference seems to be that the current interest-rate coefficient in (2.3) is divided between the current and lagged coefficients in (2.4). While

TABLE 2

Lagged Adjustment

Equation	BR	CW	V	Constant	RLld minus RBus	(RLld minus RBus)$_{-1}$	M/NW	(M/NW)$_{-1}$	γ	ρ	SEE	DW
(2.1)[a]	−.365 (.039)	−.420 (.029)	−.064 (.118)	.004 (.376)	.091 (.100)	.267 (.096)	.680 (.183)	−.099 (.191)	—	—	.121[a] (.099)	.66
(2.2)[a]	−.333 (.187)	−.348 (.177)	−.083 (.105)	.043 (1.185)	.150 (.082)	.116 (.091)	.735 (.159)	−.059 (.135)	—	.99	.101[a] (.083)	2.08
(2.3)	−.298 (.110)	−.462 (.075)	0 (.064)	−1.010 (.727)	.423 (.058)		1.026 (.369)		.322 (.071)	—	.073	1.79
(2.4)	−.300 (.105)	−.464 (.067)	0 (.066)	−1.011 (.654)	.277 (.162)	.140 (.148)	1.021 (.330)		.365 (.087)	—	.073	
(2.5)	−.246 (.139)	−.442 (.069)	−.032 (.063)	−.205 (.631)	.303 (.163)	.169 (.139)	1.376 (.425)	−.810 (.379)	.379 (.100)	.20	.067	1.94
(2.6)	−.302 (.093)	−.456 (.060)	−.031 (.061)	−.341 (.586)	.359 (.160)	.121 (.137)	1.531 (.421)	−.902 (.379)	.351 (.078)	—	.064	1.68
(2.7)	−.213 (.177)	−.425 (.088)	−.033 (.061)	.004 (.642)	.234 (.128)	.215 (.112)	1.152 (.341)	−.675 (.328)	.467 (.110)	.5	.067	2.25
(2.8)	−.187 (.218)	−.380 (.121)	−.035 (.062)	.166 (.640)	.185 (.110)	.220 (.100)	.990 (.293)	−.555 (.299)	.549 (.130)	.7	.070	2.33

NOTE: See Table 1 for measurement of variables. Period of estimation: 1959–67.

[a] Since the dependent variable in these equations is Bus/NW, while that in the remainder of the equations is Bus, the SEE's of these equations are not comparable to those of the others. The product of the SEE's of these equations and the mean value of NW is somewhat comparable to the SEE's of the other equations. Thus it is reported in parenthesis below the SEE.

the standard errors of the equations are roughly 10 per cent below that of equation (2.2), the equations exhibit a theoretically undesirable property: the response of borrowing to a change in imports is estimated to be more than one for one. The short-run response is almost exactly one for one, while the long-run response (the short-run response divided by the estimated speed of adjustment) is three times the change in imports. Since the rationale behind the variable is that import trade bills can be used as collateral, a greater than one-for-one relationship between borrowing and imports seems highly implausible.

Other somewhat surprising results are the zero coefficient on the VFCR variable (it was constrained a priori to be nonpositive) and the relatively low estimate of the speed of adjustment.[18] The latter implies that it takes eight quarters for 95 per cent of the adjustment to occur. As we noted above, the estimate is biased downward to the extent that, say, the exclusion of relevant explanatory variables from the equation tends to introduce autocorrelated residuals into that equation.

In an attempt to remove possible downward bias in the estimate of the speed of adjustment, we have estimated a partial-adjustment equation including the first-order autoregressive parameter. More specifically, the equation is of the form

$$Bus = \alpha \left[\hat{\gamma} Bus^* + (1 - \hat{\gamma}) \left(\frac{Bus}{\alpha} \right)_{-1} \right]$$

$$+ \hat{\rho} \left\{ Bus_{-1} - \alpha_{-1} \left[\hat{\gamma} Bus^*_{-1} + (1 - \hat{\gamma}) \left(\frac{Bus}{\alpha} \right)_{-2} \right] \right\} + \epsilon, \quad (12)$$

where $\hat{\gamma}$, $\hat{\rho}$, and the parameters in α and Bus^* are all estimated, and where ϵ is a disturbance term assumed to have the customary desired properties.[19] To the extent that the estimate of the speed of adjustment increases, this inclusion is likely to reduce the estimate of the long-run

---

[18] The "true" speed of adjustment, λ (see page 217, note 12), is only .38 in equation (2.3).

[19] Equation (12) is derived by assuming that the error term in direct estimation of (11') is first-order positively autocorrelated. In other words, with u_t as the error term in (11'), we assume

$$u_t = \rho u_{t-1} + \epsilon_t$$

where $0 < \rho \leq 1$ and ϵ_t is a disturbance term that is not serially correlated. Lagging equation (11') one period, multiplying through by ρ, and subtracting the resulting equation from (11') yields equation (12), in which the disturbance term is ϵ_t.

response of borrowing to a change in imports. Another possible means of reducing the long-run value of this estimate is to employ the lagged imports–net-worth ratio as an explanatory variable. Since the lagged ratio assumed a negative coefficient in equations (2.1) and (2.2), it would appear that the response to changes in imports is faster (possibly even instantaneous) than the response to changes in interest rates.

Equation (2.5) suggests that these modifications, while having the desired influence, are not enough. The autoregressive parameter assumes a low value of 0.2, and its inclusion does not seem to have significantly raised the estimate of the speed at which banks respond to changes in interest rates (compare (2.5) with (2.4)). However, the combination of this parameter and the lagged-imports variable provides estimates that banks adjust very rapidly to changes in imports; the long-run partial of borrowing with respect to imports, 1.49, only slightly exceeds the short-run partial, 1.38.

The impact on these partials of including the autoregressive parameter is shown most clearly by comparing equation (2.5) with (2.6). The short-run partial implied by the latter exceeds that implied by the former by 10 per cent, and the difference in long-run partials exceeds 20 per cent. Even though including the autoregressive parameter worsens the equation in the sense that it raises the standard error of estimate (from .064 to .067), the more plausible (lower) estimates of the partials with respect to imports are enough to lead us to prefer equation (2.5) to (2.6). In fact, we are willing to trade off additional explanatory power in order to obtain more reasonable estimates of the import partials. Thus, a priori, we have estimated the basic equation constraining the autoregressive parameter to assume successively higher values.

Equations (2.7) and (2.8) are sample results. As was expected, increasing the value of ρ lowers the estimates of both the short- and long-run partials with respect to imports. In fact, equation (2.8) implies that American banks initially finance all of Japanese imports, but that perhaps a fifth of imports are eventually financed in some other manner; that is, imports act, at least partially, as an "impact" variable [11, pp. 48–49]. Also, as expected, the estimate of the time taken for adjustment diminishes. This estimate, in conjunction with the interest-rate coefficients, implies that 66 per cent of the eventual response to changes in interest rates occurs within two quarters, 85 per cent occurring within three. A much slower response in the adjustment of short-term portfolios by financial institutions would seem unlikely. At the same time, very rapid adjustment would be surprising, given the lack of a secondary market in bank loans.

To summarize, at the cost of a 10 per cent fall in the standard error of our equation (compare (2.6) and (2.8)) we have obtained theoretically acceptable estimates of the response of borrowing to changes in imports, and we have estimated what we consider to be a plausible time-response of borrowing to changes in interest rates.

Since equation (2.8) is our preferred equation, it might be useful to discuss some of its implications. The principal difference between it and the "best" equation reported in [6] (equation (1.2) in the present paper) is the largeness of the long-run interest-rate elasticities. By ignoring lags in our earlier paper, we forced the long-run elasticities to equal the short-run (one quarter) elasticities. In fact, the former (-1.9 for the United States rate, and 2.5 for the Japanese lending rate) seem to be about four times the latter.[20] The estimates from equation (2.8) imply that a 50 basis-point rise in the American rate would tend to reduce borrowing, at the end of 1967 values of Bus and α, by $140 million, $220 million, and $100 million for the current and two future quarters, respectively. Lastly, the VFCR program seems to have mattered little. The estimates in equation (2.8) imply that the end of 1967 Japanese short-term borrowing was only $25 million less than it would have been in the absence of the VFCR program. This estimate is substantially less than the $160 million implied by equation (1.2).

B. THE LINEAR HOMOGENEITY ASSUMPTION

Linear homogeneity in the scale variable (or in all dollar magnitudes) has been assumed in recent work on international capital flows by Lee [15], Miller and Whitman [17], and ourselves [6].[21] In none of these studies has the assumption been explicitly tested, although it

[20] For a discussion of the mechanics of this and the other calculations in this paragraph, see [6, pp. 56–57].
[21] This has been a common assumption in empirical work on domestic financial behavior for some time.

was implicitly tested by Miller and Whitman.[22] We report here a test of our assumption that Japanese short-term borrowing from American banks is homogeneous of degree-one in Japanese imports and the net worth of Japanese foreign-exchange banks.

Given the use of a nonlinear regression program, testing the linear homogeneity assumption would appear to be a simple matter. Equation (2.1) was of the basic form

$$\frac{Bus}{NW} = \alpha \frac{Bus^*}{NW} NW^\phi, \tag{13}$$

where $\phi = 0$. To test the homogeneity assumption, we simply estimate ϕ. A value of ϕ insignificantly different from zero would support the homogeneity assumption. Equation (2.2) is of the same general form, but with the autoregressive parameter; thus, the homogeneity assumption could be tested in the same manner. Equation (2.8) was of the form

$$Bus = \alpha \left[\gamma \frac{Bus^*}{NW} NW^\phi + (1 - \gamma) \left(\frac{Bus}{\alpha}\right)_{-1} \right]$$
$$+ .7 \left\{ Bus_{-1} - \alpha_{-1} \left[\gamma \left(\frac{Bus^*}{NW}\right) NW^\phi_{-1} + (1 - \gamma) \left(\frac{Bus}{\alpha}\right)_{-2} \right] \right\}, \tag{14}$$

where $\phi = 1$. This time an estimate of ϕ insignificantly different from unity would support the homogeneity assumption.

As simple as these tests appear, the large number of intricately

---

[22] Miller and Whitman's equation (18) is of the form

$$\log K = .8447 \log A_1 + .7245 \log W_{t-1} + \cdots,$$

where K is the stock of foreign portfolio assets held by American residents, A_1 is the scale variable (K plus various domestic long-term portfolio assets), and W is the ratio K/A_1. The short-run elasticity of K with respect to A_1 is .8447, not far below unity. To obtain the long-run elasticity, we express W_{t-1} in terms of K and A_1. Slight manipulation yields

$$\log K = .7245 \Delta \log A_1 + .1202 \log A_1 + .7245 \log K_{-1} + \cdots.$$

The estimated long-run elasticity is $.1202/(1.0 - .7245) = .44$. Thus, it appears from this equation that A_1 acts partially as an impact variable; increases in A_1 temporarily raise K substantially above its new equilibrium level. (At first glance, this seems somewhat implausible.) Further, the estimated long-run elasticity appears to be substantially less than unity.

related parameters to be estimated seemed to raise insurmountable difficulties for our nonlinear regression program.[23] However, equation (13) has been approximated by iterating on the parameter ϕ.[24] When values of ϕ in the ± 1.0 range were selected, the equation with $\phi = 0.01$ yielded the lowest SEE. This equation is

$$\frac{Bus}{NW} = \underset{(.039)}{(1.0 - .366BR} \underset{(.029)}{- .418CW} \underset{(.118)}{- .069V)}$$

$$\left[\underset{(.377)}{-.018} + \underset{(.100)}{.092(RLld} - RBus) + \underset{(.096)}{.270(RLld} - RBus)_{-1} \right.$$

$$\left. + \underset{(.183)}{.688} \frac{M}{NW} - \underset{(.191)}{.101} \left(\frac{M}{NW}\right)_{-1} \right] NW^{.01}. \qquad (13')$$

$$SEE = .121274. \ DW = 0.67.$$

The closeness of this estimate of ϕ to 0.00 and the minor reduction of the SEE (compared with .121280 in equation (2.1)) lends some support to our use of the linear homogeneity assumption in [6] and in this text.

C. 1964–68 ESTIMATES

We test the stability of the regression estimates over time by estimating equations on data from the 1964–68 period. These equations could conceivably provide a more accurate estimate of the basic behavioral relationship, and of the impact of the American Voluntary Foreign Credit Restraint program, since the data for this period were not affected by either the relaxation of Japanese restrictions or the responses which ensued.

Equations (3.1)–(3.3) in Table 3 (which are analogous to equations (2.1), (2.2), and (2.8)) are based on data from the 1964–68 period. They imply a 25–50 per cent smaller total borrowing response to changes in imports than do the equations based on the total 1959–67 period. This

---

[23] For reasons that are not yet clear to us, the program failed to iterate away from the initial guesses of the parameters.

[24] Even with ϕ specified a priori in equations of the form of (2.2) and (2.8), the program failed to iterate away from the initial guesses of the other parameters.

TABLE 3

Tests on

Equation	Constant	V	$RLld$ minus $RBus$	$(RLld$ minus $RBus)_{-1}$
(3.1)	.143	−.146	.155	.299
	(.464)	(.102)	(.107)	(.100)
(3.2)	.307	−.025	.148	.117
	(.556)	(.089)	(.077)	(.078)
(3.3)	.572	0	.329	.111
	(.947)		(.140)	(.116)

NOTE: Bus/NW is the dependent variable in equations (3.1) and (3.2); Bus is the dependent variable in (3.3). See Table 1 for measurement of var-

is consistent with our expectation that the bias of American lenders in favor of acceptances based on import trade bills would decline during the period as the Japanese established their credit-worthiness. Regarding interest-rate responses, the total responses implied by equations (3.1) and (3.3), respectively, are about 25 per cent greater than those implied by their 1959–67 counterparts. The coefficients in (3.2), however, are virtually identical to those in (2.2). The stock-adjustment parameter in (3.3) is noticeably (although probably not significantly) lower than in equation (2.8) (.44 compared with .55), and the time pattern of interest-rate responses is also different. These two changes offset each other to some extent, so that equation (3.3) implies an adjustment to interest-rate changes that is almost as rapid as that implied by (2.8).

These estimates reinforce our earlier finding that the impact of the VFCR program on American short-term bank lending to Japan has apparently been negligible. The estimate of the V coefficient in (3.1) is substantial, but that in (3.2) is negligible, and that in (3.3) has to be constrained from assuming a positive value. Since equation (3.1) is probably the least reliable of the three, we conclude that the impact of the program has been slight.

1964–68 Data

M/NW	$(M/NW)_{-1}$	γ	SEE	ρ	DW
.758	−.343	−	.111	−	1.04
(.221)	(.233)				
.509	−.039	−	.086	.87	1.60
(.180)	(.161)				
.804	−.617	.439	.075	.70	2.60
(.380)	(.411)	(.141)			

iables. The variables BR and CW are equal to zero throughout the period.

4 ALTERNATIVE SPECIFICATIONS

IN THE course of our research, extending over several years, we have more than once revised our notion of the proper theoretical and empirical specification of international capital demand and supply equations. To put it more bluntly, we have estimated a number of equations that, in retrospect, were poorly specified. Many of these equations were, of course, patterned after existing work in the literature. The fact that these earlier equations often yield at least superficially plausible results while improperly specified in important respects has aroused our curiosity.

We will now put forward some examples of alternative specifications for equations purporting to explain Japanese short-term borrowing from the United States. In every case we consider these alternative specifications inferior to those already discussed—inferior in the sense either that they are less acceptable on theoretical grounds, or that they seem less likely to provide valid empirical approximations to the underlying behavioral relationship. In several instances we deliberately employ obvious misspecifications. Our purpose in presenting these additional equations is to shed some light on a general question of interest to all researchers in this and other fields: How sensitive are one's conclusions to the equation specification employed?

A. TREATMENT OF CAPITAL CONTROLS

We have argued in [6] that there are probably few countries in which changes in governmental restrictions on capital flows have been negligible enough to be ignored. The importance of these controls in the case of the particular capital flow examined here is incontrovertible. It is not surprising, therefore, that a specification of the relationship determining Japanese borrowing from American banks which completely ignores these controls is incapable of providing meaningful estimates of the effects of the economic determinants. Equation (4.1) in Table 4 is an estimate of such an equation; it is identical to equation (1.3) except for the fact that α has been set equal to unity throughout the entire 1959–67 period. The coefficient on the import ratio is unexpectedly negative; the coefficient on the interest-rate spread, while positive, is less than its standard error; and the explanatory power of the equation is exceptionally low.

It is somewhat surprising, however, that simply adding a time trend [25] and a dummy variable to reflect the American VFCR program [26] yields results which are superficially plausible. Equation (4.2) includes a time trend [27] T_{68} and (4.3) includes a VFCR dummy variable as well. The latter variable is zero until the second quarter of 1965; in that and subsequent quarters, it is unity. The time trend greatly improves the equation. The standard error of estimate is nearly halved; the coefficient on the import ratio changes to the correct sign and is

[25] For examples of the use of a time trend in capital-flow equations, see [5], [18].

[26] For examples of the use of dummy variables to capture the impact of the United States Interest Equalization Tax and the VFCR program, see [5], [17], [19]. This method will not yield accurate estimates except in the unlikely event that the impact of the programs are constant over time.

[27] The trend variable T_{68} is equal to unity in the first quarter of 1959 and rises by 1 each quarter throughout the entire 1959–67 period.

TABLE 4

Estimates Ignoring Capital Controls

Equation	Constant	RLld minus RBus	M/NW	T_{68}	T_{64}	D_V	SEE	DW
(4.1)	2.448	.123	−.419				.616	.11
	(1.013)	(.139)	(.560)					
(4.2)	−3.236	.669	.576	.087			.323	.47
	(.812)	(.094)	(.313)	(.009)				
(4.3)	−2.397	.518	.440	.095		−.596	.297	.49
	(.814)	(.104)	(.292)	(.009)		(.230)		
(4.4)	−2.451	.365	.620		.116	−.057	.151	.83
	(.405)	(.051)	(.150)		(.005)	(.111)		

NOTE: *Bus/NW* is the dependent variable. See the text for the definition of variables and Table 1 for their measurement. Period of estimation: 1959–67.

nearly twice its standard error; and the coefficient on the interest-rate spread is seven times its standard error. While the inclusion of a time trend can presumably be rationalized as an attempt to mitigate the influence of excluded variables, such as Japanese capital controls, on the estimates, it is still surprising to us—and also disconcerting—that the trend variable seems to perform so well in a case where the excluded variables are clearly so important. Inclusion of the VFCR dummy also appears, superficially, to be a success. Its coefficient in equation (4.3) is negative, as expected, and it is twice its standard error. Moreover, this inclusion lowers the standard error of estimate of the equation by nearly 10 per cent.

In comparison with the equations in Tables 1 and 2, however, equation (4.3) does not stand up well. Its SEE is more than twice that of its closest analogue, equation (1.3). Further, the large coefficient on the VFCR dummy variable in equation (4.3) suggests that the program has had an implausibly large impact on bank lending to Japan. This equation implies that lending was approximately $1 billion less at the end of 1967 than it would otherwise have been. In contrast, equa-

TABLE 5

Equations with Misspecified

Equation	$RLld$	$RBus$	$RBe\$$	Constant
(5.1)	−.151	−.108		1.641
	(.067)	(.036)		
(5.2)		−.205	.136	.291
		(.071)	(.065)	(.163)
(5.3)	−.003	−.098		.371
	(.057)	(.026)		(.501)
(5.4)	−.048	−.102		.621
	(.095)	(.035)		(.894)
(5.5)	−.057	−.107		.919
	(.058)	(.029)		(.495)

NOTE: The change in *Bus* is the dependent variable. See Table 1 for measurement of variables. Period of estimation: 1959–67.

tion (1.3) implies that the impact was only $160 million; and in numerous equations, the impact has been estimated to be negligible.

Equation (4.4) illustrates that a more plausible estimate of the impact of the VFCR program can be obtained even within the current simplistic framework. The equation differs from (4.3) only in that a truncated time-trend, rather than the "complete" trend, appears as a regressor. The truncated-trend variable rises by 1 each quarter through the first quarter of 1964 and thereafter remains at that level. The use of this variable might be rationalized along somewhat the same lines as we rationalized the *BR* and *CW* variables in our earlier research.[28] This switch alone slashes the SEE by half and yields an estimate of the impact of the VFCR program of only $90 million. The important point is that without the earlier equations reflecting the explicit consideration of Japanese capital controls, one might have been convinced that the VFCR program had a substantial impact on bank lending to Japan.

[28] See [6, pp. 39–44].

Desired Stock

ΔT_{64}	ΔNW	ΔM	M	SEE	DW
.027				.094	1.96
(.049)					
.047				.095	1.48
(.053)					
.043	2.209	.542		.069	2.05
(.041)	(.854)	(.104)			
.091			.102	.093	1.85
(.065)			(.069)		
−.004		.468		.076	1.56
(.040)		(.109)			

B. MISSPECIFICATION OF THE DESIRED STOCK

The most flagrant possible misspecification of the desired stock consists of relating capital *flows* to the *levels* of interest rates and nothing else. This framework combines the infamous "flow theory" of capital movements with an absence of theory on the scale of economic units. At a lower order of magnitude, errors of specification can be committed in the choice of interest rates and the scale variable.

Table 5 contains five misspecified equations, each having the change in American short-term bank lending to Japan as the dependent variable. In an attempt to isolate misspecifications of the desired stock from the problems of measuring the impact of capital controls, all equations contain the change in the truncated-trend variable.[29] The effect of including the truncated trend is to allow the constant term in the flow equations to be larger in the 1959-I–1964-I period than in the later period.

[29] It was established in the previous section that the truncated-trend approximately accounts for the impact during the 1959–64 period of Japanese controls on the level of bank lending. The closeness of the coefficient of the VFCR dummy variable to zero in equation (4.4), and the equations in Tables 2 and 3, suggest that omission of variables representing American controls will not seriously alter the results.

All of the equations in the table include the levels of interest rates, rather than the increments, as regressors. Given this basic misspecification,[30] we have not attempted to document in any systematic manner the effect of using the wrong set of rates as regressors; in all equations except one we have employed the two theoretically most important rates — the cost of borrowing in the United States, and the return from lending in Japan. In general, earlier researchers have only considered the yields on the "own" and substitute instruments. In our case this would mean including only borrowing rates (i.e., the cost to Japanese banks of borrowing in the American, Japanese, and Eurodollar capital markets). A more fundamental error is to include rates prevailing in international financial centers only.[31] This would require the exclusion of all Japanese interest rates from the set of regressors.

Turning to Table 5, equations (5.1) and (5.2) exclude all scale variables.[32] They differ only in that the former includes the Japanese lending rate, while the latter includes the Eurodollar borrowing rate. Quite deceptively, even though interest rates are incorrectly measured as levels rather than increments, the United States and Eurodollar rates are statistically significant, with the expected sign. The Japanese lending rate, however, is significant with the unexpected sign.

Equation (5.3) includes the net-worth scale variable and the import-distribution variable. Both variables enter significantly, substantially reducing the standard error of estimate. In addition, they eliminate the misspecified Japanese lending rate that was entering with the unexpected sign.

Another misspecification suggested by some of the earlier literature is the use of the level (rather than increment) of imports in an equation where the dependent variable is *changes* in borrowing.[33] If the level of Japanese borrowing is actually related to the level and increment in imports, as equation (2.8) suggested, the change in borrowing should be related to the first- *and* second-difference in imports, hardly the level. Equation (5.4) is the misspecified equation; (5.5) is

---

[30] Studies containing this misspecification include [2], [4], [9], [13], [14], [18], [19], [20], [21]. See also the Dobell-Wilson chapter in this volume.
[31] See [21] for an example of this error.
[32] Investigations ignoring scale variables altogether include [2], [4], [18], [20], [21].
[33] See [14] for an example. More generally, this misspecification would relate capital flows to the level of export or import "distribution" variables.

reported for purposes of comparison. As expected, the change in imports performs much better than the level of imports.

. The equations listed in Table 5 are disturbing in an important respect. The standard errors of estimate of these equations compare favorably with those reported earlier. The relevant comparison is probably with the SEE of equation (1.4), appropriately adjusted. (Since the dependent variable in (1.4) is the ratio of borrowing to net worth, the SEE of that equation should be multiplied by .82, the mean value of net worth, to make it roughly comparable to those of the equations in Table 5. Such a multiplication yields a value of .086.) As can be seen, the SEE's of equations (5.3) and (5.5) are, in fact, below that of (1.4). Disconcertingly, the SEE of (5.3) is below even that of our preferred equation, (2.8). A corollary to the low SEE's is, of course, the fact that the misspecified interest-rate variables are often quite significant. A partial explanation for the relatively low SEE's in Table 5 is that all of the equations reported earlier employed interest-rate differentials. The use of differentials will raise the SEE when the individual rates would otherwise tend to assume coefficients that are much different in absolute magnitude; such is clearly the case with our data [6, Table 5].

While the equations in Table 5 explain the data quite well in a purely statistical sense, they all imply that the long-run elasticity of bank lending to Japan with respect to interest rates is infinite (plus or minus). Such an inference is, of course, inconsistent with observed diversified asset-and-liability portfolios.

C. SOME PARTIAL ADJUSTMENT EQUATIONS

In Part 2 we emphasized some problems associated with the partial-adjustment model. More specifically, we noted that "even though the determinants of the 'desired' stock (or α) may be seriously misspecified, the stock-adjustment model can generate superficially plausible estimates." In addition, the estimate of the speed of adjustment in such an equation is almost certain to be biased downward. In Table 6, we report four "typical" partial-adjustment equations. The principal misspecification of the equations is the complete absence of

TABLE 6

Misspecified Partial-

Equation	Constant	RLld	RBus	M
(6.1)	.766	−.069	−.090	.223
	(.755)	(.089)	(.036)	(.126)
(6.2)	.194		−.089	.255
	(.123)		(.031)	(.057)
(6.3)	1.102	−.113	−.089	.169
	(.792)	(.095)	(.035)	(.132)
(6.4)	.160		−.083	.268
	(.129)		(.032)	(.059)

NOTE: *Bus* is the dependent variable. See Table 1 for measurement of variables. Period of estimation: 1959–67.

any variables reflecting the impact of Japanese capital controls ($\alpha = 1$ throughout).

Equation (6.1) contains all the determinants of the desired stock — the principal borrowing and lending rates, net worth, and imports — and a dummy variable purporting to capture the impact of the American VFCR program. According to some standards, the equation looks "reasonably" satisfactory. All coefficients have the expected signs except the coefficient on the Japanese lending rate and the practically zero coefficient on net worth; the coefficients on both the borrowing rate and the dummy variable are significantly less than zero at the .05 level, while that on imports is significantly greater than zero. In addition, the standard error of estimate of the equation is respectable; for example, it is lower than that of the "best" equation published in our earlier paper (.086 on a comparable basis). Equation (6.2), which does not include the variables that were statistically insignificant in (6.1), looks even better. The regression coefficients are more significant, and the SEE is marginally lower.

On closer inspection, however, these equations exhibit a number of disturbing characteristics. First, with respect to imports, the equations imply that the long-run partial derivative substantially exceeds 2.0. This result seems economically implausible. Second, the equations

Adjustment Equations

NW	Dv	Dv_{-1}	Bus_{-1}	SEE	DW
−.012	−.138		.904	.082	2.11
(.303)	(.074)		(.045)		
	−.125		.892	.080	1.97
	(.058)		(.034)		
.152	−.068	−.133	.885	.081	2.15
(.326)	(.088)	(.104)	(.047)		
	−.065	−.080	.885	.080	1.90
	(.062)	(.090)	(.035)		

suggest that the VFCR program succeeded in reducing lending to Japan by more than $1¼ billion by the end of 1967. We noted earlier that an estimate as large as this is implausible. Third, the estimated speed of adjustment of these equations is less than three-tenths of the already slow speed of adjustment estimated in equation (2.3), a typical partial-adjustment equation including variables reflecting Japanese capital controls. This is, of course, exactly what was anticipated.

Equations (6.3) and (6.4) reflect an attempt, within the limiting constraints imposed by the employment of an on/off dummy variable, to obtain a more plausible estimate of the impact of the VFCR program. Not only is the estimate of the total impact of the program in equations (6.1) and (6.2) implausible, so also is the timing of the impact. The equations imply that 10 per cent of the impact was felt during the quarter the program was imposed, 9 per cent the next quarter, 8 per cent the following quarter, and so on. This obviously unacceptable result simply reflects the low estimate of the speed of adjustment, and the fact that the typical partial-adjustment equation forces the speed of adjustment in response to all variables to be identical. In general, one would probably expect the imposition or removal of any government restrictions to have a relatively rapid impact. To test for a more rapid impact of the VFCR program, we include the lagged value of the dummy variable in the equation. If the lagged value were to assume a coefficient with sign opposite to that of the current value, the effect would be to reduce the lag. However, since the lagged coefficient is also negative, equations (6.3) and (6.4) suggest an even slower response to the imposition of the controls than to changes in the underlying economic determinants.[34]

The fact that equations ignoring Japanese capital controls – probably the most important determinant of bank-lending to Japan during the period – look reasonably appealing, even at first glance, is disturbing. It is also worrisome that such equations might lead policymakers to overestimate greatly the impact of the VFCR program, and to underestimate the impact of interest-rate changes in the short run (due to the low estimate of the speed of response). If these results offer any general guide to problems encountered with other capital flows, and we suspect that they do, estimators and users of partial-adjustment equations would be well advised to proceed cautiously.

5 CONCLUDING NOTE

OUR objectives in this paper and in [6] have been primarily methodological. Working intensively with a single set of data, we have tried to pose, and to resolve as adequately as possible, many of the theoretical and econometric problems arising in the empirical analysis of all international capital flows.

As we noted in our earlier paper, our research has not led us to an optimistic assessment of the ease with which valid substantive conclusions can be reached in this field. The difficulties to which we have drawn attention are serious and cannot be easily overcome. Although we doubt that useful empirical knowledge of the behavior relationships determining capital flows can be acquired rapidly and at small cost, we

---

[34] An example of the successful measurement of a more rapid response to changes in government regulations than to changes in the economic determinants is given in [11]. Sixty per cent of the response of the commercial bank time-deposit rate to changes in the ceiling rate on time deposits is estimated as occurring in the first quarter, while only about 13 per cent of the adjustment to changes in economic determinants seems to occur within this time limit.

are not, on the other hand, so pessimistic as to want to discourage econometric research in this area. In our view, substantial research efforts are warranted, simply because many important problems of domestic and international financial policy cannot be dealt with wisely without a much better quantitative grasp of the determinants of capital flows.

It seems appropriate to conclude with a comment of a general nature about the priorities that we feel ought to be observed in future research. There is no doubt in our minds that the major investment of resources in future research should go, first, into the judicious selection of the particular capital flows to be studied; second, into the development of well thought out theoretical specifications appropriate in the particular circumstances; and, third, into the careful collection of high-quality data. The actual estimation of many additional equations for many types of capital flows should have a lower priority. Theory and techniques are both still in a relatively primitive state and reliable data are scarce. In this situation, the need is for intensive research, not for extensive application of existing (but meager) knowledge. In any empirical work, of course, one should always formulate a convincing theoretical framework, developing strong opinions on the type of results that would be theoretically acceptable before estimating any equations. This principle, honored more in the breach than in the observance in the existing literature (we cannot claim purity on this score ourselves), should be adhered to more strictly if it is to serve as a practical guideline for future empirical work on capital flows.

The pitfalls that lie in wait for the researcher unarmed with strong a priori theoretical views have been amply illustrated here. Many different specifications for a relationship—with widely varying implications—may, superficially, seem to work. Our experience with the data that we have been discussing certainly suggests that frequently one may be unable to discriminate clearly, in purely statistical terms, between alternative imperfect specifications. Fishing expeditions are virtually bound to be "successful" if a researcher is satisfied with merely finding some specification that will give a good statistical fit. If it does nothing else, this paper ought to underline the need for a much more robust definition of "success" than the customary tests of statistical significance. One well researched relationship based on prior development of a sound theoretical framework, and on careful matching of empirical counterparts to theoretical constructs, will usually prove more useful and interesting than scores of equations with good fits but weak theoretical underpinnings.

REFERENCES

1. Almon, Shirley, "The Distributed Lag Between Capital Appropriations and Expenditures." *Econometrica,* Vol. 33 (January, 1965).
2. Arndt, Sven W., "International Short-Term Capital Movements: A Distributed Lag Model of Speculation in Foreign Exchange." *Econometrica,* Vol. 36 (January, 1968).
3. Bell, Philip W., "Private Capital Movements in the U.S. Balance of Payments Position," in *Factors Affecting the U.S. Balance of Payments,* Joint Economic Committee Compendium of Papers. U.S. Government Printing Office, 1962.
4. Black, Stanley, "Theory and Policy Analysis of Short-term Movements in the Balance of Payments." Unpublished doctoral dissertation, Yale University, 1965. Abridged version published in *Yale Economic Essays,* Vol. 8 (Spring, 1968).
5. Branson, William H., *Financial Capital Flows in the U.S. Balance of Payments.* Amsterdam, North-Holland Publishing Co., 1968.
6. Bryant, Ralph C., and Hendershott, Patric H., *Financial Capital Flows in the Balance of Payments of the United States: An Exploratory Empirical Study.* Princeton Studies in International Finance No. 25. Princeton, 1970.
7. Griliches, Zvi, "Notes on Serial Correlation Bias in Estimates of Distributed Lags." *Econometrica,* Vol. 29 (January, 1961).
8. ——— "Distributed Lags: A Survey." *Econometrica,* Vol. 35 (January, 1967).
9. Hawkins, Robert G., "The Stability of Flexible Exchange Rates — The Canadian Experience." *The Bulletin,* New York University Institute of Finance, Part II of No. 50–51 (July, 1968).
10. Hendershott, Patric H., "Comment IV." *American Economic Review,* Vol. LVII (June, 1967).

11. ——— "Recent Development of the Financial Sector of Econometric Models." *Journal of Finance* (March, 1968).
12. Houthakker, H., and Taylor, L., *Consumer Demand in the United States, 1929–70.* Cambridge, Massachusetts, Harvard University Press, 1966.
13. Kenen, Peter B., "Short-term Capital Movements and the U.S. Balance of Payments." Included in *United States Balance of Payments,* Hearings before the Joint Economic Committee, 88th Congress, First Session. U.S. Government Printing Office, 1963.
14. Laffer, Arthur B., "Comment III." *American Economic Review,* Vol. LVII (June, 1967).
15. Lee, C. H., "A Stock-Adjustment Analysis of Capital Movements: the United States-Canadian Case." *Journal of Political Economy,* Vol. 77 (July/August 1969).
16. Markowitz, Harry H., *Portfolio Selection.* New York, Wiley and Sons, 1959.
17. Miller, Norman, and v. N. Whitman, Marina, "A Mean-Variance Analysis of United States Long-term Portfolio Foreign Investment." *Quarterly Journal of Economics,* Vol. LXXXIV (May, 1970).
18. Powrie, T. L., "Short-term Capital Movements and the Flexible Canadian Exchange Rate, 1953–61." *The Canadian Journal of Economics and Political Science,* Vol. XXX (February, 1964).
19. Prachowny, Martin F. J., *A Structural Model of the U.S. Balance of Payments.* Amsterdam, North-Holland Publishing Co., 1969.
20. Rhomberg, Rudolf R., "A Model of the Canadian Economy under Fixed and Fluctuating Exchange Rates." *Journal of Political Economy,* Vol. 72 (February, 1964).
21. Stein, Jerome L., "International Short-term Capital Movements." *American Economic Review,* Vol. LV (March, 1965).
22. Tinsley, Peter, "An Application of Variable Weight Distributed Lags." *Journal of the American Statistical Association* (December, 1967).
23. ——— "On Polynomial Approximation of Distributed Lags." Unpublished, 1968.
24. Tobin, James, "Liquidity Preference as Behavior Towards Risk." *Review of Economic Studies,* Vol. XXV (February, 1958).

25. ——— "The Theory of Portfolio Selection," in F. Hahn and F. P. R. Brechling, eds., *The Theory of Interest Rates*. New York, Macmillan, 1965.
26. Wallis, Kenneth F., "Lagged Dependent Variables and Serially Correlated Errors: A Reappraisal of Three-Pass Least Squares." *Review of Economics and Statistics*, Vol. XLIX (November, 1967).

COMMENTS

STANLEY W. BLACK

PRINCETON UNIVERSITY

Professors Leamer and Stern regard the portfolio-adjustment model of capital flows as a logical development of the older *activities* framework, which used the concepts of speculation, arbitrage, and trade flows of short-term capital. While they apparently regard the portfolio model as an improvement, they sound a useful warning of the limitations of the model. Not only does the portfolio model neglect changes in net worth, it also ignores liquidity considerations. However, changes in net foreign worth of a country are easily allowed for, since they are identical with net exports. Leamer and Stern's strictures against the portfolio model for nonfinancial corporations seem well taken.

The authors suggest that the *stock* of short-term capital be related to covered interest differentials, speculative variables, and *changes* in exports or imports as measures of changes in sales. This last suggestion disagrees with the practice advocated by Bryant and Hendershott, as well as by Branson: use of the *change* in exports or imports in capital-*flow* equations, or the *level* of exports or imports in *stock* equations. Furthermore, the use of changes in sales to explain the stock of a financial asset goes against the logic and history of the treatment of stocks and flows. Equilibrium stocks can logically be related to both

NOTE: The author has accepted a position at Vanderbilt University.

the level *and* change of an appropriate flow variable, but not to the change in flows alone.

I am particularly pleased that Leamer and Stern raise the simultaneous-equations problem in regard to exports and imports, a topic which I will discuss later. One point of contention is that the portfolio-adjustment equations *can* be modified to take account of short-run cash-flow constraints, as de Leeuw did for the monetary sector of the Brookings Model.

Concerning the treatment of speculative periods, I have two suggestions. Dropping out speculative periods throws away valuable information on demand functions. An alternative to the Stein approach to residuals is to estimate a function in a nonspeculative period and then calculate the residuals from that function *for the speculative period only*. The implied expectation can then be used to estimate other functions for the speculative period. I have done this with some success for the Canadian devaluation. Dummy variables can also be used with more imagination, especially if the data are for short time periods, such as weekly data. An exponential distribution of speculative impact suggests itself on several grounds, including Muth's "rational expectations." Thus, an unanticipated disturbance would have impact 1, λ, $\lambda^2, \ldots$, while an anticipated disturbance would have impact $\ldots \lambda^2$, $\lambda, 1, \lambda, \lambda^2, \ldots$.[1]

I found inappropriate Leamer and Stern's conclusion that disaggregation should be pursued only if it offers improved estimates of the *aggregate* relationship. It seems to me that economists should be willing to disaggregate as long as different *micro*behavior patterns turn up. Bryant and Hendershott give us a particularly good illustration of the value of disaggregation.

On multicollinearity, Leamer and Stern confuse me. This is not a case of dropping variables with *t*-ratios less than two. Rather, if A is dropped, B is significant; and conversely. Thus, as they say, neither coefficient is estimated accurately, but some linear function of the coefficients is. If A is left out, for example, the coefficient of B measures the effect of *both* A and B together. In that sense, A has not really been discarded.

[1] See my paper, "The Use of Rational Expectations in Models of Speculation, *Review of Economics and Statistics,* Vol. LIV, No. 2 (May, 1972).

Concerning the simultaneous-equations problem, Leamer and Stern remind us that exports and imports may be simultaneously determined with capital flows. However, as the paper progresses, they appear to be saying that specification of the model is a more important problem than simultaneity. I believe that *understanding* the simultaneity is one of our most pressing problems of specification. It is clear that the treatment of interest rates as exogenous is not correct in some cases. In recent works on Eurodollar liabilities of the United States, I have found it essential to regard the interest rate as jointly determined, and have estimated reduced-form equations for both the rate and the liabilities. In a paper presented at this conference, Miller and Whitman take a similar approach.

Once interest rates become endogenous, it can be seen that the issue is really the interaction of the real and monetary sectors of the international economy. Current practice regards the monetary sector as being affected by changes in the real sector, but as having no converse influence. For example, monetary tightening should reduce incomes and, therefore, imports. Financing costs may be crucial at the margin of some trade decisions, interest-rate "pessimism" to the contrary. We are not ready for three-stage least squares, but our models should begin to reflect a larger view of what is jointly determined.

Leamer and Stern's compilation of empirical estimates is interesting partly for its entertainment value. We clearly have our work cut out for us in reducing the uncertainty about interest-rate and trade impacts. Unfortunately, in some places they have inserted the wrong figures for Branson's work. The monthly estimates of interest-rate effects on short-term claims and liabilities given in the original version of Table 1 allow for an increase in the Eurodollar and Canadian interest differentials, respectively, vis-à-vis the United States. However, as Branson points out, interest differentials vis-à-vis the United States are unlikely to change because foreign rates follow the American ones. Branson's Table 1, equation (10), and Table 3, equation (11), in Chapter 4, indicate impacts of $253 million and zero for a one point change in the American rate on short-term claims and liabilities, respectively. Branson's over-all figures for interest-rate impacts given in their footnote 30 are cited incorrectly by Leamer and Stern. The correct figures are $3.1 billion for the monthly model and $2.5 billion for the quarterly model, including errors and omissions in the latter. The discrepancies are disturbing.

	Monthly	Quarterly
Short-term claims	$ 253 [a]	$ 468
Long-term claims	800	315
Short-term liabilities	0	260
Long-term liabilities	2,000	693
Errors and omissions	n.a.[b]	794
	$3,053	$2,530

SOURCE: Branson, Reference [5], Bryant and Hendershott.
[a] All figures in millions.
[b] Not available.

Furthermore, can one believe that impacts of this magnitude would have no influence on the real-sector exports and imports? It is also disturbing that disaggregation increases impacts markedly. Can this be related to the increased substitution possibilities allowed by disaggregation? Professors Leamer and Stern are to be congratulated for raising and discussing cogently so many issues important for econometric work on capital flows.

Ralph Bryant and Patric Hendershott discuss some of the same problems as Leamer and Stern, but with the advantage of a well-tested model and a well-understood set of data with which to demonstrate many of their propositions. The result is an especially valuable "how to do" (or "how not to do") guide for empirical workers. I will not discuss their basic model except to say that it represents a remarkable blend of theory and knowledge of institutional detail.

The model, as given in Table 1, contains no lags. After a brief discussion of the Koyck-Nerlove lag structure, the authors present some estimates allowing this type of lag structure in Table 2. Several questions should be raised about the estimates in this table. The original model was of the ratio form

$$B/NW = \alpha f(R, M/NW).$$

In equations (2.3) to (2.7), Bryant and Hendershott drop, without explanation, the ratio form for the dependent variable. They have informed me that the original equation was multiplied through by net worth and estimated so as to retain homogeneity.

The authors note the existence of bias in the Koyck-Nerlove Model with autocorrelated residuals, and in fact reject the unconstrained results from this model (equation (2.5)). Thus, their preferred equation (2.7) has a coefficient for the lagged stock that is *higher* than the unconstrained version, which was biased downward. It would have been preferable had Bryant and Hendershott written out their statistical assumptions more explicitly. Their estimating equation (10) seems to imply rather special assumptions. Using β to represent their *Bus*, they seem to assume

$$\beta_t = \alpha_t \beta_t^s + u_t, \tag{1}$$

$$\beta_t^s = \gamma \beta_t^* + (1 - \gamma)\beta_{t-1}^s, \tag{2}$$

or

$$\beta_t = \alpha_t[\gamma \beta_t^* + (1 - \gamma)\beta_{t-1}^s] + u_t. \tag{3}$$

Since

$$\beta_{t-1}^s = (\beta_{t-1} - u_{t-1})/\alpha_{t-1}, \tag{4}$$

we have

$$\beta_t = \alpha_t \left[\gamma \beta_t^* + (1 - \gamma)\frac{\beta_{t-1}}{\alpha_{t-1}}\right] - (1 - \gamma)\frac{\alpha_t}{\alpha_{t-1}} u_{t-1} + u_t. \tag{5}$$

It is this last combination-disturbance term that is assumed to be first-order autocorrelated, which must imply that u_t satifies approximately

$$u_t - (\rho + \Delta)u_{t-1} + \rho\Delta u_{t-2} = \epsilon_t, \tag{6}$$

where $\Delta = (1 - \gamma)\dfrac{\alpha_t}{\alpha_{t-1}}$ and ϵ_t is a random term. Thus, u_t is approximately second-order autocorrelated, instead of first-order.

Bryant and Hendershott give an informal test of the stability of their equation in Table 3. One wonders why they did not use the Chow test for stability, which, although formulated for a linear model, should hold approximately for a nonlinear one.

I find it difficult to do more than commend the rest of Bryant and Hendershott's paper as an illuminating catalogue and demonstration of pitfalls due to improper model formulation. Everyone should examine their results on capital controls, the flow theory, the scale variable, and the insensitivity of the Koyck-Nerlove Model to specification error. It is particularly instructive that they find it impossible to distinguish statistically between the stock and flow theories of effects of interest differentials. It should be noted that Miller and Whitman, in their contribution to this volume, find theoretical basis and empirical evidence for both stock *and* flow effects. Although I am included in the list of miscreants in footnote 30 (Bryant and Hendershott), I will point out that my work contains both stock and flow components.[2] The authors are to be thanked for pursuing the implications of their data set far beyond the call of duty, to our benefit and instruction.

ELINOR B. YUDIN
INTERNATIONAL BANK FOR RECONSTRUCTION AND DEVELOPMENT

To anticipate the most probable single conclusion of this conference: capital-account transactions are amorphous phenomena that do not easily lend themselves to formal economic analysis or measurement. Only through painstaking care and precision, both of thought and of observation, can understanding of these phenomena advance. Even then, the results obtained are often replete with ambiguity. Both papers on which I shall comment provide evidence supporting these contentions. Both focus on evaluating and reconsidering current analytical approaches to capital movements. That of Professors Leamer and Stern does so in rather general terms. They correctly question—but for reasons I find incorrect—the "activity" orientation of prevalent analytical models, advocating its replacement by a "transactor" orientation. They list quite completely, and defend rather generally, their selection of explanatory variables relevant to capital-flow analysis. Finally, they consider certain of the manifold problems that

NOTE: The views expressed are those of the author. They in no way reflect those of the International Bank for Reconstruction and Development.
    [2] See equation (4.11), Reference [4], Bryant and Hendershott.

arise in the process of empirical estimation. Bryant and Hendershott, because they place their study in the concrete context of United States banks' short-term lending to Japan, necessarily confront problems of estimation more directly. But, like Leamer and Stern, their primary concern lies with the fundamental theoretical analysis of capital movements and the problems encountered in econometric application of a priori theory.

There is much in both papers that is well done and stimulating. Nonetheless, I have chosen to concentrate on two points and to comment briefly on a third. First, I focus on the activity-transactor choice in orientation that Leamer and Stern raise. My second point touches on issues that are more pervasive: I draw particularly on the Bryant-Hendershott paper to question just how much—if any—progress has been made in the econometric analysis of short-term capital movements. Finally, I attempt to verbalize my uneasy reaction to the concluding note of the Bryant-Hendershott presentation.

ACTIVITY VERSUS TRANSACTOR

Leamer and Stern argue that capital-account analysis will be improved by switching to an orientation based on "transactors" (that is, households, businesses, government, and so on) from the one based on "activities" (consumption, investment, and others) that they find dominant in current work. Such shifts in perspective may jog thinking out of old ruts, thereby providing new insights. Two instances in other areas of economic analysis where changes in perspective seem particularly fruitful come to mind. Barbara Bergmann, at the December meetings of the American Economic Association, advocated an analogous, but opposite shift—*to* an activity orientation—for analysis of social, environmental, and government problems.[1] Gilbert and Kravis, in 1954, recommended the merits (albeit with reservations) of the same shift for international comparisons of national accounts.[2]

[1] B. R. Bergmann, "The Urban Economy and the 'Urban Crisis.' " *American Economic Review,* Vol. LIX (September, 1969).

[2] M. Gilbert and I. B. Kravis, *An International Comparison of National Products and the Purchasing Power of Currencies.* Paris, Organization for European Economic Cooperation, 1954.

In the context of the Leamer-Stern paper, the shift in perspective does isolate certain subtleties of capital-account analysis, thereby providing new insight. However, I question whether this particular adjustment in perspective is needed.

First, if, as the authors suggest, the activity approach gives rise to analytical flaws because there is no one-to-one correspondence between activity and transactor, how does the shift they propose avoid the same problem? Transactors frequently embark on several activities simultaneously. Stern and Leamer do recognize this difficulty: "This means, therefore, that it will be extremely difficult to construct a single model of the capital account that will capture all the structural characteristics of the different transactors." More important, simultaneous activities of a single transactor are interdependent events. This interdependence provides the authors with their strongest argument in defense of their preference for the transactor approach.

Second, if one aim of disaggregation by transactor, not activity, is to impose greater homogeneity of behavior in the categories analyzed, would this be attained? Asset preferences (and attitudes toward risk) tend to vary markedly, even among nominally identical transactors. Viewed in this light, the transactor approach may prove too aggregated for predictive purposes. In addition, homogeneity is even more difficult to obtain in an international study. One must assume that each type of transactor behaves similarly with respect to the same activity, regardless of nationality. For example, one would have to assume that an American businessman and a Japanese businessman will make identical decisions when faced with a given option. But suppose that official restrictions (or traditional behavior) differed between the United States and Japan; then the decisions of the two men would be likely to differ. Since restrictions do differ, I see no a priori reason to expect like behavior patterns for like transactors in different countries.

Bryant and Hendershott contend that, ideally, one needs different approaches for different transactors *and* different instruments (activities). In examining capital flows between two countries, their first step in disaggregation is by country. By disaggregating in this manner, they treat each nationality as a homogeneously responding group. Strictly speaking, this treatment raises questions analogous to those raised by Leamer and Stern's criterion for disaggregation. Neither assures homogeneity of behavior within each group.

Third, and basic, has the switch to a transactor orientation already occurred? It seems to me that it has. The questions raised with respect to the behavior implications of the early capital-flow models by Kenen, Stein, et al., effectively set the pendulum in motion, swinging it completely to portfolio or stock-adjustment models. But a portfolio is a diversified collection of securities held by a single institution or investor. In consequence, *portfolio analysis already embodies a transactor orientation.*

These stock-adjustment models transpose the Tobin-Markowitz utility-maximization models, conceived originally in a national context, into an international one. In the later studies, however, several analyses do take account of Stern and Leamer's valid criticism that portfolio models do not allow for continuous-flow adjustments. Recent studies modify the Tobin-Markowitz framework, allowing both stock *and* continuous-flow adjustments. Among others, Willett and Forte,[3] Miller and Whitman,[4] and Bryant and Hendershott (in the paper now under scrutiny) have all attempted to deal with that criticism. Bryant and Hendershott comment:

> In a growing (or declining) economic world, changes in interest rates bring about both "existing stock" . . . and "continuing flow" . . . impacts on capital flows. Given a "once-for-all" change in one or more interest rates, the existing-stock effect produces capital flows that are also once-for-all in nature (a reallocation of existing portfolios), while the continuing-flow impact persists indefinitely as long as [the change in net worth is not zero].[5]

These attempts do suffer from some of the shortcomings that Leamer and Stern note. For example, to obtain this relationship in econometric form, Bryant and Hendershott invoke homogeneity assumptions that they are unable to defend rigorously within the Tobin-

[3] T. D. Willett and F. Forte, "Interest Rate Policy and External Balance." *Quarterly Journal of Economics,* Vol. LXXXIII (May, 1969).

[4] Norman C. Miller and Marina v. N. Whitman, "A Mean-Variance Analysis of U.S. Portfolio Investment." *Quarterly Journal of Economics,* Vol. LXXXIV (May, 1970). See, too, their article in this volume.

[5] See their footnote 3.

Markowitz framework. Nevertheless, there appears to be a centering of the pendulum in models that combine both stock-adjustment and continuous-flow relationships, an approach that seems curiously conformable with the very nature of the capital account.

Leamer and Stern do offer a most damaging criticism of the portfolio approach. But they do so in a brief assertion: "Some important economic transactors do not behave . . . according to portfolio-adjustment prescripts." This pronouncement clearly deserves elaboration or demonstration if their position is to prevail.

PROGRESS IN ECONOMETRIC ANALYSIS

Both of these papers demonstrate that analysis of capital accounts is advancing, however haltingly, as a result of recent theoretical developments. Bryant and Hendershott's work makes it abundantly clear that the empirical aspects of this subject confront large and (as yet) apparently immovable stumbling blocks. Their choice of explanatory variables is one of the first examples of this point. The discussion of the structural equations, particularly in their earlier paper,[6] acknowledges (as do Leamer and Stern) the influence of risk and expectation variables — the cost of forward cover, the risk of change in asset and liability prices — on exchange rates. Their estimating equations, by contrast, include no proxies for these variables. This exclusion represents a serious shortcoming of the study, limiting the possibilities of generalizing it to analyses of other capital flows.

The exclusion also stresses a general "state of the arts" problem: Given limited information, how can these variables be quantified? Nonetheless, experimentation with some proxies for them would seem a worthwhile endeavor.

Turning briefly to a few results which Bryant and Hendershott do present, several questions come to mind. They begin their paper with what they regard as a rather successful equation (1.4), modified from the earlier work in which they focused on estimating the impact of

[6] Published subsequently as: R. C. Bryant and P. H. Hendershott, *Financial Capital Flows in the Balance of Payments of the United States: An Exploratory Empirical Study*. Princeton Studies in International Finance No. 25. Princeton, 1970.

capital controls. In that equation, the key anomaly is the strength, measured by the t-ratio, shown by the United States Voluntary Credit Restraint program (V). The two additional variables which indicate the effectiveness of capital controls are the objective "basic relaxation" of Japanese restrictions between 1959 and 1960 (BR) and the more subjective "learning process" and growth of credit-worthiness of the Japanese in the American market (CW). As expected, both BR and CW effectively distort capital flows. In the equations experimenting with lags, however, the t-ratios for all variables change: that for V now suggests that the program had little impact; those for CW and, particularly, for BR decline. One suspects that if the autoregressive coefficient were set even nearer its level of the first experiments, these variables would evince no power at all. Since many people regard the Japanese case as exemplary in the use and effectiveness of capital controls, this result would be particularly disconcerting. Although the authors comment only on the change in V, it would seem that the "gain" in lags has been offset by the "loss" in capital controls. Which is better?

The "misspecified desired-stock equations" in Section 4.B and the partial-adjustment equations in Section 4.C emphasize this confusion. In Section 4.B, equations (5.1)–(5.5) employ levels, instead of increments, of interest rates, and imports as regressors, excluding all scale variables. Both these papers comment on the theoretical inadequacy of this specification. In Section 4.C, equations (6.1)–(6.4), the Japanese capital-control variables are absent. There, the strong import response and impact of the Voluntary Credit Restraint program, as well as the slow speed of adjustment, are implausible. Unfortunately, these findings are surrounded by low standard errors of estimate and regressors with appropriate signs and significant t-values. If Japanese controls are as important as the authors contend, one does wish even more that they had reconsidered their own earlier equations, particularly equation (2.8).

Other aspects of their comparison of their own work with alternative specifications based on the work of others are also intriguing. Equation (4.4), for example, yields results quite similar to those yielded by their own equation (1.3). Evidently this is because the equation (4.4) takes account of the authors' study of time patterns of specific controls. Yet the similarity between the two results, it would seem, argues better for careful thought and observation than for a particular form of equation.

It is indeed disconcerting that in the absence of Bryant-Hendershott's work, one might find these alternative specifications econometrically, if not theoretically, gratifying. Their experiments, like the discussion in the Leamer-Stern paper, should set off signals warning of the need for great caution in future work.

UNEASY REACTIONS

Bryant and Hendershott's concluding note is a forthright statement of their fundamental position. But, basically, it evokes an uneasy reaction, one that merits much more thought and discussion than is possible here.

They argue that a researcher must arm himself with "strong, a priori theoretical views." This is a valid and quite well-accepted point. But they have, at another time, come close to arguing that data are to be "forced" into the predetermined — and "correct" — theoretical mold.[7] If this is what they intend to suggest, I am uneasy.

First, there is an obvious danger: strong, a priori views can, all too easily, become armor complete with blinders instead of the first weapon of attack that the authors envisage. Second, and more fundamentally, data are malleable; they can be fitted into many molds. Economic theory is a logical construct; there is one mold for each set of initial assumptions. But there may be more than one set of assumptions — particularly where those assumptions relate to behavior. In consequence, more than one "correct" theoretical mold can be formulated. Third, and not unrelated to the first two, forcing data into *any* mold contradicts the very purpose of empirical analysis. Meaningful empirical testing requires the opposition, possibly implicit, of alternative hypotheses. The probability of accepting one hypothesis when an alternative is true — the *beta* error — plays a vital role in empirical analysis. To the extent that data are forced into a strong, a priori

[7] This position is not explicitly stated in their paper. In discussion during the conference Mr. Hendershott expressed this view. Admittedly, his views may have undergone modification since then, and Mr. Bryant may disagree — with either or both of us.

theoretical mold, the purpose of empirical testing is vitiated. The researcher who forces data into a mold says, in effect: "I'll be judge; I'll be jury."

I am far more comfortable with the authors' plea for a "more robust definition of 'success' than the customary tests of statistical significance." This is, perhaps, their key contribution. It focuses on a need well and clearly demonstrated in their own empirical work.

THE OUTFLOW OF SHORT-TERM FUNDS FROM THE UNITED STATES: ADJUSTMENTS OF STOCKS AND FLOWS

NORMAN C. MILLER · Carnegie-Mellon University
MARINA v. N. WHITMAN · University of Pittsburgh

1 INTRODUCTION

IN THIS paper, we develop a two-equation model of short-term capital outflows from the United States, in which Americans' demand for short-term foreign assets and foreigners' supply to us of their liabilities are both determined by considerations of relative yield (in the case of foreign liabilities, relative cost) and relative risk. The reduced-form solution of this model is tested empirically (using quarterly data for 1959–1967), following Willett and Forte [24] and Miller and Whitman [19], by breaking the total capital flow into its "stock-adjustment" and "flow-adjustment" components.

A number of empirical studies of the short-term capital account have been conducted, most of them utilizing a single-equation approach which rests on the assumption, explicit or implicit, that American lenders' demand for foreign assets of this type is infinitely elastic; i.e., that Americans are willing to lend foreigners all they want to borrow at the going price. In this group are the studies of Bell [2], Kenen [14, 15], and Bryant and Hendershott [5]. Arndt [1] and Hawkins [11] use another variant of a single-equation approach by estimating *net* flows of short-term capital in the Canadian balance of payments, rather than developing separate equations for transactions conducted by Canadians and those conducted by foreigners.

In a pioneering study, Stein [21] has developed a theory of capital

NOTE: The authors are grateful to A. Maeshiro of the University of Pittsburgh for his assistance. The research was financed by National Science Foundation Grant No. S-80238.

253

flows in which American short-term claims on foreigners are assumed to equal American holdings of foreign exchange, and vice versa for foreign short-term claims on us.[1] Using this "foreign-exchange market" approach to capital flows, he arrives at a reduced-form equation for American claims on foreigners by first solving a set of equations for the exchange rates consistent with simultaneous equilibrium in the spot and forward markets. He then substitutes the equilibrium spot rate into an expression that defines the current supply of foreign exchange to Americans as equal to their previous holdings, plus or minus the basic balance of payments of the United States (this latter depending on the equilibrium spot rate). The very low R^2's generated when Stein tested the model for flows of short-term capital might be due, in part, to the fact that the model does not contain an explicit behavior equation for the amount that foreigners wish to borrow from us. The problem is that although Stein's model is in simultaneous-equation form, he implicitly includes the foreign supply of assets to us in the aggregate basic-balance variable.

In a recent book which represents the most exhaustive investigation of the financial capital account of the United States to date, Branson [3] assumes implicitly that American short-term claims on foreigners are strictly of the "trade-credit" variety. His model utilizes a risk-and-return approach to derive a function for the supply of foreign assets to the United States. The American demand for such assets does not appear explicitly in the model. Branson, like Stein before him, solves a model of the foreign-exchange market to show that the equilibrium spot and forward exchange rates will depend on (among other things) the expected future spot rate. Again following the lead of Stein, Branson develops an empirical estimate of such expectations and uses this as one of many explanatory variables in his estimating equation. In empirical tests of this model for American short-term claims on foreigners, Branson obtained $\bar{R}^2$'s that range between .42 and .55.[2]

---

[1] Stein actually developed and tested two separate models, one of which was based on the assumption that interest-rate differentials determine capital *flows,* and the other on the more reasonable assumption that interest-rate differentials determine the *stock* of claims on foreigners.

[2] We are reporting here only on that portion of Branson's extensive work on the capital account of the United States that relates to this paper.

Our study differs from previous efforts in two important ways. First, we assume that the stock of short-term claims on foreigners is determined by the simultaneous interaction of the American demand for such assets and the foreign supply of same to us. These demand and supply functions are derived from utility-maximization assumptions for American creditors and foreign debtors, along Tobin-Markowitz lines [23], [17].[3] The foreign supply of assets to us will depend in part on the need to finance trade and in part on any of the other sundry reasons why a debtor may need money. Of particular interest is the fact that the American demand for foreign short-term assets (and, hence, the flow of short-term capital abroad) depends in part on the business cycle in the United States, a relationship which has found its way into recent macroeconomic models by H. G. Johnson [13] and Floyd [8], but which has been verified empirically only for flows of long-term portfolio capital by Miller and Whitman [19] and by Branson [3]. Second, the empirical tests here do not estimate the flow of capital with a single equation (as have all other studies) but follow the suggestion of Willett and Forte [24] and the study of long-term capital flow by Miller and Whitman [19] in dividing the total flow into two components. The first is the stock-adjustment component, which arises when changes in exogenous variables cause alterations in either the American creditors' desired ratio of short-term foreign assets to total assets in their portfolios, or in the foreign debtors' desired ratio of borrowings from America to total borrowings. The second is the flow-adjustment component, which arises when American creditors increase the total size of their portfolios and, hence, buy more foreign assets. When this technique of separating stock adjustment and flow adjustment is combined with the simultaneous-equation approach, geared to take account of risks and returns, the result is a theory of short-term

[3] Grubel [10] has pointed out that the "risk-return" approach is required in order to explain the simultaneous two-way flows of international capital observed in the world. Bryant and Hendershott [5] apply a Tobin-Markowitz model to the statistical investigation of Japanese short-term borrowing from the United States. A statistical investigation of long-term portfolio capital outflows from the United States to Canada, using the mean-variance framework, has recently been published by Lee [18]. A paper by the authors [19] applies this approach to the investigation of aggregate long-term portfolio investment by the United States. Levin [16] and Feldstein [7] also use the mean-variance approach in theoretical work on capital flows.

flows of capital that holds up much better under empirical testing than have previous efforts along these lines.

2 THE MODEL

A. DEMAND FOR SHORT-TERM FOREIGN ASSETS

In terms of a risk-and-return theory of portfolio selection, the ratio of foreign to total risky assets held in the portfolios of American investors depends on both relative rates of return and the relative riskiness associated with each group of risky assets—foreign and domestic. The expected rate of return, R_A^e, on a portfolio "A," containing both risky short-term foreign assets (K) and risky domestic assets (D), and the standard deviation of this rate of return can be expressed as

$$R_A^e = WR_K^e + (1 - W)R_D^e, \tag{1}$$

$$\sigma_{R_A} = [W^2\sigma_K^2 + (1 - W)^2\sigma_D^2 + 2W(1 - W)\Gamma\sigma_K\sigma_D]^{1/2}, \tag{2}$$

where W is the ratio of short-term foreign to total risky assets in the portfolio, i.e., $W = K/(K + D) = K/A$, and where R_K^e and R_D^e are the expected returns on short-term foreign assets and domestic risky assets, σ_K^2 and σ_D^2, are the variances of R_K^e and R_D^e, and Γ is the simple correlation coefficient between R_K^e and R_D^e.[4] (Definitions of all symbols are summarized in the Appendix.)

The determination of the desired combination of domestic and foreign assets, characterized by the parameters for risk and return given above, is presented very briefly here, since we have discussed it in detail elsewhere [19]. The locus of all efficient portfolio combinations, such that σ_{R_A} is a minimum for any given R_A^e, is indicated graphically by the opportunity locus LL in Figure 1. The optimum among this infinity of efficient combinations is determined by the point

---

[4] The mean-variance approach to the theory of portfolio choice requires one of two alternative assumptions: that investors' utility functions are quadratic, or that they view the range of probable outcomes from a financial investment in terms of a normal distribution. See Tobin [22].

FIGURE 1

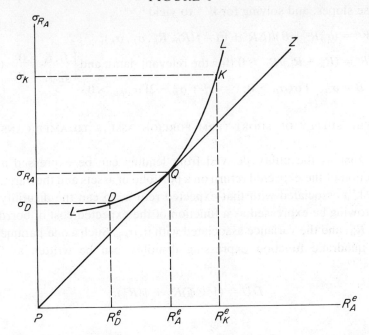

of tangency between the LL locus and the capital-market line, PZ, which represents the locus of attainable combinations of risk and return from various portfolio combinations of risky and riskless assets.[5] At the equilibrium point Q, the marginal tradeoff between risk and return in the optimal bundle of risky assets is equated with the risk-return tradeoff between homogenous bundles from this optimal set of risky assets and the riskless asset.[6] Algebraically, the optimum W^* represented at Q is found by substituting (1) and (2) into the expression for the slope of the capital-market line, σ_{R_A}/R_A^e, and into the expression

[5] For a concise summary and critique of the Sharpe model [20], in which the concept of the capital market line is developed by applying Tobin's separation theorem, see Fama [6]. Note that the fact that the capital market line goes through the origin assumes that the riskless asset has zero yield, e.g., cash.

[6] Note that each investor may choose a different optimum position along PZ, but following Tobin's separation theorem [23], the optimum combination of risky assets, W^*, does not depend upon this final resting place. That is, W^* is independent of the ratio of risky to riskless assets in the investor's total portfolio.

for the slope of the opportunity locus, $(d\sigma_{R_A}/dW)/(dR_A^e/dW)$, equating these slopes, and solving for W^* to yield [7,8,9]

$$W^* = (\sigma_D^2 R^e + B)/(BR^e + c) = f(R_D^e, R_K^e, \sigma_D, \sigma_K); \tag{3}$$

$$R^e = (R_K^e - R_D^e)/R_D^e > 0 \text{ (for the relevant data); and} \begin{cases} f_2, f_3 > 0 \\ f_1, f_4 < 0 \end{cases} \tag{3a}$$

$$B = \sigma_D^2 - \Gamma\sigma_K\sigma_D > 0; \quad c = \sigma_K^2 + \sigma_D^2 - 2\Gamma\sigma_K\sigma_D > 0. \tag{3b}$$

B. THE SUPPLY OF SHORT-TERM FOREIGN ASSETS TO AMERICANS

Just as the utility derived from lending can be expressed as a function of the expected return on a portfolio of assets and the variance ("risk") associated with that expected return, so can the disutility of borrowing be expressed as a function of the expected cost of borrowing, R_B^e, and the variance associated with it, σ_{R_B}. Such a one-parameter (ψ) quadratic function expressing disutility can be written as follows: [10]

$$DU = (1 + \psi)R_B + \psi(R_B^2), \tag{4}$$

and

$$E(DU) = (1 + \psi)R_B^e + \psi[\sigma_B^2 + (R_B^e)^2]. \tag{4'}$$

On the assumption that ψ is a positive constant, this function yields a family of indifference curves of the type depicted in Figure 2. These curves are negatively sloped, implying that higher borrowing costs must be associated with a lower variance in these costs in order to keep the level of disutility constant. They are concave to the origin, implying an increasing marginal rate of substitution between risk and ex-

---

[7] This formulation is based in the simplifying assumption that $r = $ constant.

[8] The $f_4 < 0$ holds when $R^e < 1/W^*$, a condition that is always fulfilled in this study.

[9] The B term could be either positive or negative, since an $R_K^e > R_D^e$ implies $\sigma_D < \sigma K$. If $B < 0$ (as when $r = 1$), then W^* could conceivably be negative, reflecting the fact that it might pay to go long in one asset and short in another when their yields are perfectly correlated. However, since we observe only positive W's in the data, we assume that $B > 0$, which insures that $W > 0$.

[10] Levin [16, Ch. 3], Branson [3, Ch. 2], and Bryant and Hendershott [5] have independently utilized an approach to the theory of foreign supply of assets similar to ours. Note that none of our conclusions would be changed if we used a two-parameter quadratic function.

FIGURE 2

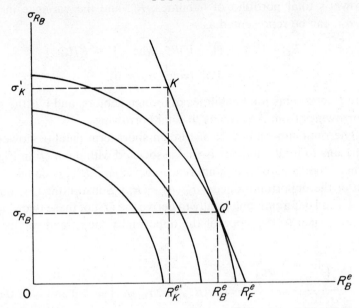

pected borrowing costs. Finally, the indifference curves represent higher levels of disutility as one moves out from the origin.

The opportunity locus faced by each potential foreign borrower is depicted by the straight line connecting points R_F^e and K, representing the various combinations of borrowing from other foreigners (associated with an expected borrowing rate of R_F^e and zero variance) and borrowing from Americans (associated with an expected borrowing rate of $R_K^{e'}$ and a variance of $(\sigma_K')^2$ in that rate). This variance is associated with the expected borrowing rate on loans from Americans for two reasons. First, there is the chance of an exchange gain or loss if the loan is denominated in dollars and the foreign borrowers do not cover in the forward market. Second, there is the possibility that borrowing from Americans could alienate or dry up home sources of credit for the foreign debtor. Thus, in order to keep his home lines of credit open, it is conceivable that the foreign debtor may never want to do all his borrowing from the United States.[11]

[11] Bryant and Hendershott argue [5, p. 7], that the variance associated with borrowing costs may lead to the diversification of liabilities even domestically.

Under these assumptions, the expected cost of borrowing on the borrower's total portfolio of liabilities, R_B^e, and the variance in that rate, σ_B, can be represented as

$$R_B^e = VR_K^{e'} + (1 - V)R_F^e, \text{ where } V \equiv K/L; \qquad (5)$$

$$\sigma_B = V\sigma_K' \text{ (since } \sigma_F \equiv 0), \qquad (6)$$

where L represents total liabilities of foreign debtors, and V is the ratio of borrowings from Americans to total borrowings.

The optimum ratio, V^*, of foreign short-term liabilities owed to Americans to total liabilities is that associated with point Q' in Figure 2, where the slope of the indifference curve, $d\sigma_B/dR_B^e$, is equal to the slope of the opportunity locus, $\sigma_K'/(R_K^{e'} - R_F^e)$. Substituting (5) and (6) into (4′) and differentiating totally to derive the first of these two slopes, setting it equal to the slope of the opportunity locus, and solving for V^*, gives

$$V^* = \frac{\left(\dfrac{1+\psi}{-2\psi} - R_F^e\right)}{\dfrac{(\sigma_K')^2}{R_K^{e'} - R_F^e} + (R_K^{e'} - R_F^e)} = g(R_K^{e'}, R_F^e, \sigma_K', \psi). \begin{cases} g_3, g_4 < 0; \\ g_1 < 0 \text{ and } g_2 > 0 \quad (7) \\ \text{if } \sigma_K' > (R_F^e - R_K^{e'}) \end{cases}$$

The stated algebraic condition required for the partial derivatives to have their expected signs ($g_1 < 0$ and $g_2 > 0$) can be represented in terms of Figure 2 by the requirement that point Q' be such that the equilibrium slope of the price line will have an absolute value greater than one. This condition is necessary to ensure that the well-known "perverse wealth effect" associated with quadratic preference functions (implying that risk-aversion increases as the net wealth level rises or net debt decreases) does not swamp the substitution effect stemming from the change in the relative costs of borrowing at home and abroad.[12] The satisfaction of this condition is assumed throughout the analysis in this paper and is supported by the empirical results.

Finally, we must explain the role of the shift-parameter, ψ. From (4′), above, the derivative of the slope of the indifference curve with respect to this parameter, $\delta \left(\dfrac{d_B^\sigma}{dR_B^e}\right)\bigg/ \delta\psi$, is positive, implying a "flatten-

[12] For a discussion of this and other problems associated with the quadratic utility function, see Levin [16, Appendix B].

ing," or counterclockwise rotation, of each indifference curve as ψ increases. An increase in ψ, in other words, implies a greater weight given to the expected cost of borrowing, R_B^e, as compared to the weight given the variance in that cost, σ_B, in the borrower's disutility function. Since the expected cost of borrowing abroad is smaller, and the variance associated with this cost greater than for domestic borrowing, an increase in ψ implies a reduction in V^*, the desired ratio of foreign to total borrowing.

3 IMPLEMENTATION OF THE MODEL: THE ESTIMATING EQUATIONS

A. THE GENERAL FORM

The portfolio-balance approach to foreign investment implies that, at any point in time, the stock of short-term foreign assets held by American lenders K, is equal to $K = (W)(A)$, so that the observed capital flow, ΔK, over any time interval is equal to

$$\Delta K \equiv (\Delta W)(A) + (W)(\Delta A) \equiv FS + FF, \tag{8}$$

where the first term, FS, is defined as the *stock-adjustment* component and is the change in American holdings of foreign short-term assets caused by changes in the determinants of the portfolio ratio; and the second term, FF, is defined as the *flow-adjustment* component, or the steady-state flow which results from the need to maintain the desired portfolio ratio as the size of the portfolios of Americans increases. More precisely, with time subscripts added, we have

$$\Delta K_t \equiv FS_t + FF_t, \qquad \left\{ \begin{array}{ll} \Delta K_t \equiv K_t - K_{t-1} & (9) \end{array} \right.$$

$$FS_t \equiv (\Delta W_t)(A_{t-1}), \text{ and} \qquad \left\{ \begin{array}{ll} \Delta W_t \equiv W_t - W_{t-1} & (10) \end{array} \right.$$

$$FF_t \equiv (W_{t-1})(\Delta A_t). \qquad \left. \begin{array}{ll} \Delta A_t \equiv A_t - A_{t-1} & (11) \end{array} \right.$$

In estimating the stock- and flow-adjustment components of the total flow of short-term capital, we require some relationship between the desired ratio, W^*, and the observed ratio, W. We postulate such a relationship in the form of a partial-adjustment model, assuming that asset-holders adjust their portfolio ratio in any given time-period by some fraction of the difference between the desired proportion of foreign assets, W_t^*, and the proportion held at the beginning of the period, W_{t-1}.[13] That is,

$$\Delta W_t = \phi(W_t^* - W_{t-1}) + \mu_t, \qquad (12a)$$

where ϕ is the speed of adjustment, and

$$W_t = \phi W_t^* + (1 - \phi)W_{t-1} + \mu_t. \qquad (12b)$$

The model described in Section 2 above generates not a desired stock of foreign assets in absolute terms but a desired portfolio *ratio* of foreign to total risky assets. When a linearized version of the resulting equation (12b) is utilized for estimating purposes, it carries an implicit assumption that the wealth elasticity of demand for such foreign assets is unity, when the total portfolio of risky assets, A, is taken as the appropriate measure of wealth.[14] We are assuming, in other words, that any increase in the scale-variable A will, ceteris paribus, increase the desired stock of foreign short-term assets in the same proportion. Furthermore, the formulation of the adjustment mechanism between actual and desired stocks given in (12a) and (12b), above, implies that this scale-adjustment, unlike adjustments to changes in the determinants of the desired portfolio-ratio, takes place without any lag, entirely within one quarter.[15]

To derive a reduced-form solution for our system, we first redefine W^* as $W_d^* = K_d^*/A$, the Americans' desired demand for foreign short-term assets as a fraction of all risky assets held by them. Then we transform the foreign debt ratio, $V^* = K_s^*/L$ (where K_s^* is foreign desired short-term borrowings from Americans) into $W_s^* = (L/A)$ $(K_s^*/L) = K_s^*/A$, the foreign desired supply of short-term assets to us

[13] Experiments utilizing a distributed lag, rather than a one-period lag, version of the partial-adjustment model suggested that the latter assumption correctly reflects investors' behavior.

[14] See Bryant and Hendershott [5, pp. 10–12], for a discussion of this linear-homogeneity assumption in the mean-variance framework.

[15] In order to check for the possibility of a lag in the adjustment of W to changes in its denominator, A, the variable $\Delta A/A_{t-1}$ was included as an explanatory variable in a number of equations. It was never significantly different from zero; indeed, the t-ratio associated with it was always less than one. We are grateful to Patric Hendershott for this suggestion.

as a fraction of the total *American* portfolio. We then assume that L/A can be considered a constant over the time-period under consideration. This assumption is an arbitrary one, of course, but it is necessitated by the lack of direct information on the universe of foreign liabilities, L. Some indirect and very general evidence on the extent to which this assumption conforms with, or deviates from, reality may be inferred from the success or failure of the estimating equations based on it.

Next, assume that foreign debtors use a partial-adjustment process in adjusting to changes in the explanatory variables in (7) but adjust instantaneously to changes in L, so that we can write

$$V_t = \delta V_t^* + (1 - \delta)V_{t-1}, \tag{13a}$$

or

$$W_{s_t} = \delta W_{s_t}^* + (1 - \delta)W_{s_{t-1}}, \tag{13b}$$

since $W_{s_{t-k}} = (L/A)_{t-k}(V_{t-k})$ for all k, and $(L/A)_t$ is assumed to be constant for all t.

B. THE EXPLANATORY VARIABLES: DEMAND

In order to utilize equation (3) in developing an estimating equation for the portfolio-ratio, W, we require measurable proxies for the arguments of that function, R_D^e, R_K^e, σ_D, and σ_K. We have chosen the current yield on ninety-day U.S. Treasury bills as the proxy for R_D^e, the expected yield on domestic assets.

In acquiring a short-term foreign asset, the American potential lender has three choices: he can purchase foreign assets denominated in dollars, in which case the expected rate of return is the stated rate of interest on such loans, defined here as i_K; he can purchase an asset denominated in foreign currency and hedge by purchasing a forward contract, in which case his expected return depends on the relationship between the spot and forward rates of exchange, r_f/r_s (both in dollars per unit of foreign exchange), as well as on i_K; or he can purchase an asset denominated in foreign currency without hedging, in which case his expected rate of return depends not only on i_K but on the relationship between the present spot rate of exchange and the rate he expects to prevail at the time the asset matures, r_s^e/r_s. Thus, the expected rate of return on a portfolio of foreign assets can be expressed as

$$R_K^e = \alpha_1 i_K + \alpha_2[(r_f/r_s)(1 + i_K) - 1] + \alpha_3[(r_s^e/r_s)(1 + i_K) - 1], \quad (14)$$

where the α's represent the proportions of dollar-denominated, hedged-foreign-currency-denominated, and unhedged-foreign-currency-denominated assets, respectively, in the total portfolio of short-term foreign assets. In general functional form we have

$$R_K^e = \rho(i_K, r_s^e/r_s, r_f/r_s). \qquad \rho_1, \rho_2, \rho_3 > 0 \qquad (15)$$

Note that i_K is not observable, but since i_K is determined endogenously in the model, it can be eliminated in the process of deriving a reduced-form equation for W. This, however, prevents us from estimating an equation for i_K and, consequently, we lack sufficient information to obtain empirical estimates of the coefficients in the behavior equations. Discussion of the proxies for r_s^e/r_s and r_f/r_s is postponed until later in this paper.

One of the basic assumptions of our model is that the riskiness of domestic assets, σ_D, is inversely correlated with deviations in the Gross National Product of the United States from its long-term trend. We have discussed the a priori reasons for postulating such a relationship, as well as the statistical evidence in support of it, elsewhere [19]. Here we simply hypothesize that one of the major determinants of the riskiness of American assets, taken as a whole, is the deviation of GNP from its long-run trend value in a given quarter.

Finally, since risk is a manifestation of imperfect information, the risk-estimate associated with an asset should diminish as information concerning the probable return on the asset increases. For this reason, we hypothesize that there has been a secular downward trend in σ_K, stemming from the increase in knowledge and communications, which symbolizes the gradual movement toward integration of international short-term capital markets since World War II. Finally, the Voluntary Credit Restraint program (VRP) imposed by the United States government in the second quarter of 1965 and expanded several times since then, can be assumed to have increased the riskiness of foreign lending because of considerable uncertainty about its application and enforcement. Furthermore, the VRP should also raise σ_K, because these restrictions prevent lenders from allocating their foreign portfolios in what they regard as an optimal manner; it is frequently asserted that these regulations have lowered the quality of foreign assets in American portfolios by discriminating against low-risk borrowers in the advanced countries. For VRP we use a dummy variable, which is zero until the first quarter of 1965 and unity from the second quarter of 1965 on.[16]

Substituting the various proxies just described for R_D^e, R_K^e, σ_D, and σ_K into (3), we have

$$W_d^* = F(i_K, r_s^e/r_s, r_f/r_s, R_D^e, Y, VRP, T). \qquad \begin{cases} F_1, F_2, F_3, F_7 > 0 \\ F_4, F_5, F_6 < 0 \end{cases} \quad (16)$$

If we now linearize, and transform the expression for W_d^* into one for W_d by means of the partial-adjustment mechanism of (12a) and (12b), the demand equations for W, the ratio of short-term foreign to total risky assets in the portfolios of American lenders, and for the change in that ratio, ΔW, are [17]

$$W_d = a_0 + \overset{+}{a_1 i_K} + \overset{+}{a_2(r_s^e/r_s)} + \overset{+}{a_3(r_f/r_s)} + \overset{-}{a_4 R_D^e}$$

$$+ \overset{-}{a_5 Y} + \overset{-}{a_6 VRP} + \overset{+}{a_7 T} + (1 - \phi)W_{d_{t-1}}, \quad (17)$$

[16] The use of a dummy variable for VRP, along with the partial-adjustment assumption given in (12a), implies that the VRP did not exert its full effect immediately. This is consistent with the statements of A. Brimmer [4], who, as Assistant Secretary of Commerce for Economic Affairs, was the first administrator and "salesman" of the VFCR program.

[17] In order to obtain the expressions for each of the a_i coefficients, it is necessary to obtain linear approximations to each of our equations, notably (3) and (15), by using a Taylor's expansion for each, and dropping all higher-order terms. Define such expansions for (3) and (15) as (3') and (15'). The discussion in the text implies (omitting the constant terms in Taylor's expansions)

$$\sigma_D = \sigma_D(Y) = \sigma_{D_1}Y,$$

and

$$\sigma_K = \sigma_K[VRP, T] = \sigma_{K_1}VRP + \sigma_{K_2}T. \qquad \begin{cases} \sigma_{D_1} < 0 \\ \sigma_{K_1} > 0 \\ \sigma_{K_2} < 0 \end{cases}$$

Substituting these two equations and (15') into (3'), and then placing (3') into (12b) and (12a), gives the following coefficients for equations (17) and (18)

$$a_1 = \phi f_2 \rho_1 > 0; \quad a_2 = \phi f_2 \rho_2 > 0; \quad a_3 = \phi f_2 \rho_3 > 0;$$

$$a_4 = \phi f_1 < 0; \quad a_5 = \phi f_3 \sigma_{D_1} < 0; \quad a_6 = \phi f_4 \sigma_{K_1} < 0;$$

$$a_7 = \phi f_4 \sigma_{K_2} > 0.$$

and

$$\Delta W_d = a_0 + a_1 i_K \overset{+}{+} a_2 (r_s^e/r_s) \overset{+}{+} a_3 (r_f/r_s) \overset{-}{+} a_4 R_D^e$$

$$\overset{-}{+} a_5 Y + \overset{-}{a_6} VRP + \overset{+}{a_7} T - \phi W_{d_{t-1}}, \quad (18)$$

where the expected sign of the effect of each explanatory variable's impact on W_d is given above that variable's coefficient.

C. THE EXPLANATORY VARIABLES: SUPPLY

From (7), and the additional assumption that L/A can be regarded as a constant, we have W_s^* as a function of $R_K^{e'}$, R_F^e, σ_K' and the shift-variable, ψ. σ_F, the variance associated with the costs of borrowing by foreigners in their own countries, is excluded because it is zero by assumption.

In determining the appropriate proxies for $R_K^{e'}$, the debtors' expected cost of borrowing in the American market, we must remember that the potential foreign borrower, like the potential American lender, has three alternatives. He can contract a loan from an American lender denominated in his own currency, in which case the expected cost is the going rate of interest on such loans, i_K.[18] He can make a contract denominated in dollars and hedge in the forward market, making the ratio between forward and spot exchange rates part of his expected borrowing costs. He can make a dollar-denominated contract without hedging, in which case his expected costs are a function of the relationship between the expected future spot rate and the present spot rate, r_s^e/r_s, as well as of i_K. Thus, the expected borrowing costs (in percentage terms) associated with his total liabilities to Americans can be expressed as

$$R_K^{e'} = \gamma_1 i_K + \gamma_2 \left[\frac{1}{r_s^e/r_s} (1 + i_K) - 1 \right] + \gamma_3 \left[\frac{1}{r_f/r_s} (1 + i_K) - 1 \right], \quad (19a)$$

---

[18] This formulation assumes that the nominal rate of interest, i_K, on loans from the United States is the same for dollar-denominated and foreign-currency-denominated liabilities of the same type, with any differences in expected costs among the three alternative ways of borrowing from the United States being reflected in the forward premium or discount and/or the expected change in the spot rate.

where, analogous with (14), the γ's represent the proportions of foreign-currency-denominated loans, unhedged dollar-denominated loans, and hedged dollar-denominated loans, respectively.[19] In general functional form, we have

$$R_K^{e'} = \Omega(i_K, r_s^e/r_s, r_f/r_s). \qquad \begin{cases} \Omega_1 > 0 \\ \Omega_2, \Omega_3 < 0 \end{cases} \qquad (19b)$$

As a proxy for R_F^e, the expected cost of short-term money in the home markets of the short-term borrowers, we use a simple arithmetic average of representative short-term rates of interest in four major recipient countries. For Canada and the United Kingdom this rate is the Treasury bill rate; for Japan and West Germany it is the call money rate.[20]

Our implementation of the model is incomplete because we have no observable proxy for $(\sigma_K')^2$, the variance that foreign debtors associate with borrowing from Americans. There are reasons to believe that this variance, like that on the lenders' side, may bear some relationship to aggregate economic variables in the borrowers' home country,[21] but we have not been able, as yet, to specify the nature of these relationships in a testable form.

Finally, we must offer some economic interpretation of the shift-variable ψ, representing the relative importance assigned to expected cost as opposed to considerations of risk in the foreign borrowers' preference functions. Any increase in the need for dollars (as opposed to a need for funds in general) should increase the debtors' preference for borrowing from Americans; that is, decrease ψ. To test this hypothesis, we utilize here three alternative proxies of "the demand for dollar-import financing": exports from the United States; "net" exports from

[19] Note (a) that the relationship between these weights and those of equation (14), namely, the proportion of U.S. short-term foreign assets denominated in dollars, α_1, must equal the proportion of foreign liabilities denominated in dollars, $\gamma_2 + \gamma_3$, and vice versa; (b) that this formulation rests on the simplifying assumption that borrowers in the rest of the world do not contract foreign liabilities in any market other than that of the United States; and (c) that R_K^e in (14) would necessarily equal $R_K^{e'}$ in (14a) only if expectations were the same for creditors and debtors, and if all the γ's in (19a) and α's in (14) were equal to $\frac{1}{3}$.

[20] We are grateful to Patric H. Hendershott of Purdue University for making the Japanese interest-rate series available to us.

[21] Bryant and Hendershott [5, pp. 32–33] suggest, for example, that the aggregate ratio of deposits to net worth for all Japanese banks is one of the determinants of their short-term foreign borrowing.

268 · INTERNATIONAL MOBILITY AND MOVEMENT OF CAPITAL

the United States, defined as exports minus American direct investment abroad (reflecting the assumption that exports associated with such investment are automatically financed and, therefore, generate no additional demand for short-term trade credit); and imports of the rest of the world (world imports as reported by the International Monetary Fund minus imports into the United States), on the assumption that much of the world's trade is financed by dollar loans from the United States. The hypothesis is, of course, that an increase in any of these proxies will decrease ψ and increase W_s^*. We shall refer to the trade variable as X.

Linearizing and making substitutions into (7) and (13b) analogous to those for (16) and (17), we derive the equations for W_s and ΔW_s:[22]

$$W_s = b_0 + \overset{-}{b_1 i_K} + \overset{+}{b_2 r_s^e/r_s} + \overset{+}{b_3 r_f/r_s} + \overset{+}{b_4 R_F^e} + \overset{+}{b_5 X} + (1 - \delta)W_{s_{t-1}}, \quad (20)$$

$$\Delta W_s = b_0 + \overset{-}{b_1 i_K} + \overset{+}{b_2 r_s^e/r_s} + \overset{+}{b_3 r_f/r_s} + \overset{+}{b_4 R_F^e} + \overset{+}{b_5 X} - \delta W_{s_{t-1}}, \quad (21)$$

where δ is the speed-of-adjustment coefficient.

D. THE REDUCED-FORM ESTIMATING EQUATION

Although $W_s^* = W_d^*$ only under conditions of full equilibrium, W_s and W_d must, under the assumptions made here concerning the relationship between V and W_s, be equal during all observation periods. This fact enables us to derive an estimating equation for $W = W_s = W_d$ by solving equations (17) and (20) for i_K, setting the two expressions equal to each other, and then solving the resulting expression for W

---

[22] Again, use a truncated Taylor's expansion for (7) and (19b)—call them (7′) and (19b′)—then note that our discussion implies

$$\psi = \psi(X) = \psi_1 X, \qquad \begin{cases} \psi_1 < 0 \\ k = \text{constant} \end{cases}$$
$$L/A = k.$$

Substitute these and (19b′) into (7′) and the resulting equation into (13b) (noting the transition from V^* to W_s^* given on page 262) to get the following coefficients for the b_i in (20) and (21):

$$b_1 = \delta k g_1 \Omega_1 < 0; \quad b_2 = \delta k g_1 \Omega_2 > 0; \quad b_3 = \delta k g_1 \Omega_3 > 0;$$
$$b_4 = \delta k g_2 R_F^e > 0; \quad b_5 = \delta k g_4 \psi_1 > 0.$$

$(\doteq W_s = W_d)$. The resulting reduced-form equation for W, and the corresponding one for ΔW, are [23]

$$W = A_0 + \overset{+}{A_1 r_s^e / r_s} + \overset{+}{A_2 r_f / r_s} + \overset{-}{A_3 R_D^e} + \overset{+}{A_4 R_F^e} + \overset{-}{A_5 Y}$$

$$+ \overset{-}{A_6 VRP} + \overset{+}{A_7 X} + \overset{+}{A_8 T} + \overset{+}{A_9 W_{t-1}}, \quad (22)$$

and

$$\Delta W = A_0 + \overset{+}{A_1 r_s^e / r_s} + \overset{+}{A_2 r_f / r_s} + \overset{-}{A_3 R_D^e} + \overset{+}{A_4 R_F^e}$$

$$+ \overset{-}{A_5 Y} + \overset{-}{A_6 VRP} + \overset{+}{A_7 X} + \overset{+}{A_8 T} + \overset{-}{A_9' W_{t-1}}, \quad (23)$$

where the signs over each of the coefficients have the meaning already described and are derived from the signs associated a priori with the coefficients of the underlying demand and supply equations.

The proxies used to represent the independent variables of equations (22) and (23) have been described in the two preceding sections. We must still, however, describe the measures used to calculate observed values of the dependent variable, W, the ratio of short-term foreign assets to total risky assets in the portfolios of American lenders. The numerator of W is K, the outstanding stock of short-term foreign assets held by American banks and nonfinancial institutions at the end of each quarter. Unfortunately, this series, as published, involves serious problems of comparability. The reporting coverage changed several times during the period under investigation, with a particularly sharp increase in the number of banks reporting taking place in 1964-

---

[23] The A_i coefficients in (22) and (23) are

$$A_0 = \frac{b_1 a_0 - b_0 a_1}{b_1 - a_1} \gtreqless 0, \quad A_1 = \frac{a_2 b_1 - b_2 a_1}{b_1 - a_1} > 0, \quad A_2 = \frac{a_3 b_1 - b_3 a_1}{b_1 - a_1} > 0.$$

$$A_3 = \frac{a_4 b_1}{b_1 - a_1} < 0, \quad A_4 = \frac{-a_1 b_4}{b_1 - a_1} > 0, \quad A_5 = \frac{a_5 b_1}{b_1 - a_1} < 0,$$

$$A_6 = \frac{a_6 b_1}{b_1 - a_1} < 0, \quad A_7 = \frac{-b_5 a_1}{b_1 - a_1} > 0, \quad A_8 = \frac{a_7 b_1}{b_1 - a_1} > 0,$$

$$A_9 = \frac{b_1 (1 - \phi) - a_1 (1 - \delta)}{b_1 - a_1} > 0, \quad A_9' = (A_9 - 1).$$

270 • INTERNATIONAL MOBILITY AND MOVEMENT OF CAPITAL

IV.[24] We have taken this problem into account by utilizing two alternative measures of K, and therefore of W, which represent the two extreme assumptions regarding the nature of the discontinuity involved. The first measure of W simply uses the published data without adjustment, making the implicit assumption that firms reporting for the first time are also holding short-term foreign assets for the first time. The second, or revised, measure of W uses a K series adjusted by a technique based on the assumption that the newly reporting firms would have increased the total stock of foreign short-term assets in all periods (prior to the one in which they first report) by the same proportion as they raise the total in the first period in which they do report.[25] It is highly probable that the truth lies somewhere between these extreme assumptions, but as we shall see, the qualitative nature of our regression results is not affected when we substitute the adjusted for the unadjusted K in the dependent variables W and ΔW.

The denominator, A, of W is the outstanding end-of-quarter stock, not of *all* risky assets held by American investors, but of a subset of such assets which, in our judgment, is representative of the universe of assets considered as alternatives by actual or potential holders of short-term foreign assets.[26] Actually, we have tested here two alternative subsets of the relevant universe of assets. The first, which places a relatively greater weight on short-term assets, includes short-term U.S. government securities and the "bank loans, n.e.c." and "other loans" categories of the flow-of-funds tables compiled by the Board of Governors of the Federal Reserve System. The second, more inclusive grouping, containing more long-term assets, consists of the foregoing plus long-term securities of the U.S. government, state and local

[24] Bryant and Hendershott [5, Appendix B] explain the reason for this jump: "When banks learned in February, 1965, that their allowable voluntary 'ceilings' for foreign assets would be expressed as a percentage of a base taken as their total foreign assets at end-December, 1964, the banks showed somewhat more interest in reporting their foreign assets carefully than they had shown in the past. . . . Total claims on all foreigners were increased by over 8 per cent in the December 1964 revisions."

[25] The difference between the unrevised and the revised figures for any period is that the totals for the former exclude, and those for the latter include, the value of assets held by institutions reporting for the first time. The adjustment technique used here is a special case of the one used by Bryant and Hendershott [5] and described in detail in their Appendix B.

[26] The reasons for using such a "representative subset," and the difficulties associated with its selection, are discussed in Miller and Whitman [19].

government securities, mortgages, and corporate and foreign bonds.

Obviously, the choice of *any* particular combination of assets as the denominator of W is somewhat arbitrary, since we do not know for certain what the actual or potential holders of short-term foreign assets regard as relevant alternatives; our choice of assets has been guided, however, by the fact that American banks hold most (70 per cent–80 per cent) of the American short-term claims on foreigners. Fortunately, the relationships suggested by our regression analysis are apparently not very sensitive to the precise specification of the relevant universe of risky assets.[27]

In summary, we have four measures of the portfolio ratio: W, WR, W', and WR'. The WR and WR' measures use the adjustment process for K described above. W uses the more inclusive denominator, while the denominator of W' is heavily weighted toward short-term assets.

4   EMPIRICAL RESULTS

A. REGRESSIONS FOR ΔW

We report in Table 1 a number of ordinary least-squares regression estimates of the reduced-form equation for ΔW, using several variants of the foreign-asset ratio, W, and several different proxies for a number of the explanatory variables described above. The coefficients and associated t-ratios in the corresponding equations for W are identical to those shown, except for that associated with W_{t-1}. We have chosen to report the equations for ΔW rather than those for W because we feel that R^2's associated with the latter are more meaningful; those associated with W are all over .98, as is often the case with time-series regression.

The adjusted coefficients of determination tend to be slightly higher

---

[27] Obviously, the *magnitude* of the coefficient associated with each explanatory variable will differ with different specifications of W, if for no other reason than that the magnitude of the dependent variable, W, itself varies.

TABLE 1
Regression Equations

Dependent Variable	Constant ×10³	Time ×10³	Y ×10³	Y* ×10³	VRP ×10³	R_F^e ×10³	R_D^e ×10³	WIMP ×10³	NEXP ×10³	EXP ×10³	W_{t-1}	$\bar{R}^2$	DW
1 ΔW	4.71 (1.76)	.118 (1.74)	-.046 (2.69)		-.669 (3.10)	.228 (1.67)	-.337 (3.72)	.032 (1.94)			-.32 (4.74)	.76	2.46
2 ΔW	-.972 (.70)	.043 (.09)		-.043 (1.71)	-.718 (2.98)	.249 (1.67)	-.339 (3.28)	.032 (1.82)			-.29 (3.97)	.72	2.35
3 ΔW	4.99 (2.27)	.154 (3.26)	-.045 (2.85)		-.592 (3.35)	.356 (3.57)	-.264 (3.15)		.351 (3.11)		-.30 (4.84)	.80	2.44
4 ΔW	-.523 (.65)	.043 (2.07)		-.048 (2.18)	-.616 (3.24)	.377 (3.57)	-.247 (2.63)		.381 (3.24)		-.25 (4.32)	.78	2.27
5 ΔW	4.46 (1.95)	.130 (2.53)	-.040 (2.52)		-.727 (3.76)	.242 (2.18)	-.268 (3.18)			.485 (3.03)	-.30 (4.84)	.80	2.51
6 ΔW	-.578 (.71)	.027 (1.12)		-.042 (1.85)	-.770 (3.75)	.250 (2.13)	-.255 (2.72)			.532 (3.21)	-.26 (3.21)	.78	2.40
7 ΔWR	7.70 (2.59)	.160 (2.20)	-.064 (3.39)		-.698 (2.98)	.411 (1.45)	-.218 (4.15)	.035 (1.94)			-.41 (5.58)	.74	2.04
8 ΔWR	-.215 (.13)	.004 (.08)		-.059 (2.11)	-.742 (2.74)	.241 (1.42)	-.400 (3.43)	.035 (1.76)			-.33 (4.48)	.68	1.94
9 ΔWR	8.92 (3.48)	.220 (4.24)	-.066 (3.64)		-.588 (2.86)	.364 (3.13)	-.346 (3.50)		.302 (2.39)		-.41 (5.99)	.76	2.10
10 ΔWR	.717 (.73)	.059 (2.58)		-.068 (2.59)	-.612 (2.65)	.392 (3.05)	-.316 (2.75)		.336 (2.42)		-.34 (5.07)	.71	1.94
11 ΔWR	8.45 (3.15)	.200 (3.51)	-.062 (3.33)		-.697 (3.10)	.271 (2.08)	-.351 (3.52)			.404 (2.22)	-.41 (5.88)	.75	2.09
12 ΔWR	.671 (.67)	.045 (1.64)		-.062 (2.33)	-.744 (3.00)	.280 (1.97)	-.323 (2.82)			.463 (2.36)	-.34 (5.06)	.70	2.00

13 $\Delta W'$	20.8 (2.17)	.500 (2.06)	−.185 (3.00)		−2.61 (3.38)	.546 (1.11)	−1.14 (3.48)	.103 (3.38)			−.36 (5.11)	.69	2.39
14 $\Delta W'$	−1.40 (.27)	.065 (.35)		−.185 (2.01)	−2.68 (3.08)	.671 (1.25)	−1.14 (3.02)	.101 (1.55)			−.31 (4.28)	.64	2.29
15 $\Delta W'$	21.0 (2.84)	.597 (3.84)	−.181 (3.41)		−2.41 (3.94)	.943 (2.75)	−.880 (3.06)		1.34 (3.51)		−.33 (5.58)	.77	2.37
16 $\Delta W'$	−1.06 (.38)	.161 (2.31)		−.204 (2.64)	−2.42 (3.63)	1.06 (2.88)	−.818 (2.50)		1.43 (3.52)		−.29 (4.91)	.74	2.23
17 $\Delta W'$	19.8 (2.46)	.531 (3.00)	−.167 (2.96)		−2.84 (4.13)	.558 (1.41)	−.912 (3.02)			1.69 (2.98)	−.34 (5.42)	.74	2.51
18 $\Delta W'$	−.774 (.25)	.119 (1.39)		−.182 (2.24)	−2.76 (3.25)	.622 (1.48)	−.864 (2.54)			1.84 (3.09)	−.30 (4.86)	.71	2.43
19 $\Delta WR'$	40.5 (2.91)	.851 (2.51)	−.309 (3.50)		−2.45 (2.20)	.991 (1.39)	−1.77 (3.77)	.106 (1.25)			−.53 (5.40)	.64	2.15
20 $\Delta WR'$	3.03 (.40)	.125 (.49)		−.319 (2.43)	−2.44 (1.92)	1.18 (1.49)	−1.70 (3.09)	.102 (1.09)			−.45 (4.46)	.56	1.99
21 $\Delta WR'$	44.2 (3.60)	1.03 (4.20)	−.314 (3.45)		−2.11 (2.08)	1.44 (2.55)	−1.58 (3.30)			.901 (1.46)	−.54 (5.63)	.64	2.15
22 $\Delta WR'$	5.53 (1.13)	.274 (2.56)		−.344 (2.73)	−2.08 (1.85)	1.60 (2.61)	−1.43 (2.61)			1.05 (1.57)	−.45 (4.83)	.58	1.98
23 $\Delta WR'$	41.9 (3.35)	.949 (3.62)	−.301 (3.46)		−2.53 (2.36)	1.10 (1.79)	−1.57 (3.32)			1.40 (1.62)	−.53 (5.64)	.65	2.21
24 $\Delta WR'$	4.55 (.96)	.210 (1.66)		−.324 (2.59)	−2.59 (2.19)	1.19 (1.79)	−1.43 (2.66)			1.64 (1.78)	−.45 (4.88)	.59	2.09

NOTE: The first number in each block gives the magnitude of the A_i coefficient in equation (23) in the text. The number given in parentheses is the t-value, which is significant here at the 5 per cent level for values greater than 1.71 and at the 1 per cent level for t greater than 2.49. WIMP, NEXP, and EXP are rest of world imports, net U.S. exports, and U.S. exports respectively. (See the Appendix for the definitions and sources for all variables.) W_{t-1} refers to the lagged value of an appropriate measure of W, i.e., W_{t-1}, W'_{t-1}, WR_{t-1}, or WR'_{t-1}.

for the ratio with the more inclusive group of "alternative" domestic assets in the denominator, ΔW and ΔWR, than for $\Delta W'$ and $\Delta WR'$; and they are somewhat higher for the unrevised than for the revised series in each case, but in no case is the $\overline{R}^2$ difference substantial. The Durbin-Watson statistics, on the other hand, are more frequently closer to 2.0 in the case of the equations based on revised W's, suggesting that the procedure of adjusting for discontinuities has somehow served to destroy some of the correlation in the residuals. But, given the bias inherent in the Durbin-Watson statistic in equations of this type, we cannot make much of these differences.[28] In general, our results suggest that neither the particular arbitrary group of assets chosen to represent the alternatives considered by short-term foreign lenders, nor the unavoidable discontinuities in the data on stocks of short-term foreign claims, affect the basic nature of the reduced-form relationships suggested by our analysis.

Before discussing each of the explanatory variables in turn, we should note that all data used were without seasonal adjustment, and that quarterly dummy variables for the first three-quarters of each year were included in every equation. These coefficients have been omitted from Table 1 to save space, but they were always highly significant with negative coefficients. This is consistent with Branson's findings [3, p. 89] that the so-called "window-dressing" withdrawal of foreign short-term funds from America at the end of each year applies also to foreign borrowers. Evidently, foreign banks intending to borrow in the United States will, if possible, time their borrowings to occur at year-end.

The hypothesis that there is an inverse relationship between the proportion of short-term foreign assets which American investors want to hold in their portfolios and the state of the American economy, as measured by the deviation of GNP from its long-run trend (one of the central hypotheses of our model), is apparently corroborated by our regression results. Two variants of this measure were used: GNP itself, designated as Y, and a detrended measure of GNP, Y^*.[29] About

---

[28] The value of the Durbin-Watson statistic is biased toward 2 in equations which include the lagged value of an endogenous variable among the explanatory variables.

[29] The Y^* series represents deviations from a trend value of Y, calculated as Y minus the antilog of the estimated value of the dependent variable in the following regression equation: $\ln Y = at$, for the period 1959–1967.

the only difference the substitution of Y^* for Y makes is to reduce the significance of the constant term always and sometimes the significance of the coefficient associated with time, T. This effect on the coefficient of T is what we might expect, since when Y is used, T plays two roles in the equation: to detrend all the other explanatory variables, and to pick up any secular decrease in σ_K associated with increasing information and familiarity with short-term foreign investment. Since none of the other explanatory variables has as strong a positive time trend as Y, the substitution of Y^* eliminates much of the first role of T. The fact that its coefficient then becomes insignificant in some of the equations raises some question about the existence of a secular learning effect associated with short-term foreign investment.

All of the equations reveal the expected positive relationship between changes in W and foreign interest rates, as measured by an average of the short-term rates prevailing in each of four major recipient countries.[30] The t-ratio associated with the average rates of interest abroad does, however, fall below the 5 per cent significance level in several equations. We also find the expected negative relationship with the domestic short-term interest rate;[31] this coefficient is consistently significant at the 1 per cent level in a one-tailed test.[32]

Of the three variants of the proxy for the shift variable.ψ: world imports, exports from the United States, and these exports net of American direct investment abroad, the latter two have the expected sign, and are significant at the 5 per cent level in most equations. World imports has the expected sign, but its t-value tends to be lower. The significance of net exports suggests that direct-investment outflows from the United States do indeed finance some part of its exports, whereas the inferiority of "world imports" raises some question about the importance of "third-party" trade-financing in American short-

[30] The Eurodollar rate, tested as an alternative proxy for borrowing costs in "the rest of the world," proved far less successful than the one used in the equations reported here. Kenen [14], who also found the Eurodollar rate surprisingly poor as an explanatory variable, suggests that this result may stem from the inaccuracy of published figures on the Eurodollar rate, particularly for the early years of its existence.

[31] An alternative proxy for American interest rates, the yield on corporate bonds, almost always turned out to be insignificant, whatever the variant of W used as the dependent variable.

[32] In cases where the expected sign of the relationship is known a priori, a one-tailed, rather than a two-tailed, test of significance is appropriate.

term lending abroad. But these subsidiary conclusions are highly tentative. The general pattern of relationships leaves little doubt, however, of the positive relationship between trade variables and the desired foreign-asset ratio.[33]

Conspicuous by their absence from Table 1 are any variables relating to the foreign-exchange market, namely r_f/r_s and r_s^e/r_s. The absence of r_f/r_s is due to the fact that the equilibrium value for r_f/r_s depends in part on domestic and foreign rates of interest, as well as on the expected future spot rate, r_s^e. (See, e.g., Branson [3, p. 10], Stein [21, p. 51], and Grubel [9, Chap. 6].) Thus, r_f/r_s does not belong as an explanatory variable in any regression equation that also contains American and foreign interest rates and r_s^e/r_s as explanatory variables.

The r_s^e/r_s variable is omitted from Table 1 because we could not find a proxy for r_s^e/r_s that had a statistically significant coefficient. We tried two approaches. First, we followed the lead of Branson [3, Chap. 3] by obtaining estimates, $\hat{r}_s^e/r_s$, of r_s^e/r_s. In doing this, we regressed r_s^e/r_s against American and foreign interest rates, exports and imports of the United States, and lagged values of r_s^e/r_s. The estimates $\hat{r}_s^e/r_s$ were then used as an explanatory variable in the regression equations for ΔW, but the coefficient of $\hat{r}_s^e/r_s$ was never significant. Similar results were obtained when we used the observed $r_{s_{t+1}}/r_{s_t}$ as a proxy for r_s^e/r_s, on the assumption that all spot rates are correctly anticipated.

One shortcoming of this technique for obtaining a proxy for r_s^e/r_s is that a regression equation of this nature can never generate an estimated $\hat{r}_s^e/r_s$ that anticipates a major change in the exchange rate if (ex post) such a change did not occur. Consequently, we tried an alternative approach, wherein variables that might reasonably be expected to influence expectations about exchange rates were substituted for r_s^e/r_s. Those other proxies were the balance of payments of the United States, measured on a liquidity basis and lagged one quarter, and changes in the combined international-reserve position of the four major recipient countries. Neither of these was successful. In conclusion, either we have not found the correct proxy for r_s^e/r_s or else exchange-rate expectations do not significantly affect the behavior of

---

[33] Regressions were also run which tested the hypotheses: (a) that trade credit may lead or lag behind the trade flows; and (b) that trade credit lasts longer than ninety days, i.e., that a moving sum of trade determines the stock of trade credit outstanding. Neither of these hypotheses was supported by the data.

American citizens and foreign debtors in the market for short-term loans from the United States.

The dummy variable for the Voluntary Credit Restraint program (VRP), which affects the riskiness of foreign assets, gave better results. It was always significant at the 5 per cent level, and usually at the 1 per cent level, with the expected *negative* sign. Finally, the coefficient of the lagged value of the dependent variable, W_{t-1}, is always highly significant, with the negative sign implied by our partial-adjustment hypothesis. In a structural equation, the absolute value of this coefficient is the "speed of adjustment," the proportion of the discrepancy between the desired and the actual W that is eliminated in any given quarter. In our reduced-form equation, the coefficient of W_{t-1} is a type of weighted average of the speeds of adjustment of the borrower and the lender, so that its absolute value lies between that of the speed-of-adjustment coefficient in the Americans' demand equation, ϕ, and that of the corresponding coefficient in the foreigners' supply equation, δ. The absolute value of this coefficient ranged from .25 to .54.[34]

If, as our theory implies, the equilibrium W^* depends on the levels of the explanatory variables in the American and foreign behavior equations, then the total change in W (from one equilibrium position to another) will depend on changes in these explanatory variables. Thus, in a growing world, if speeds of adjustment were very high, i.e., if $\phi = 1$ in (17) and $\delta = 1$ in (20), then the observed ΔW would depend on changes in the explanatory variables but not on W_{t-1}. If, however, the speeds of adjustment are low (as our regression coefficients for W_{t-1} suggest), then ΔW is determined by W_{t-1} and by the levels of the explanatory variables, rather than by changes in them. This does not, however, contradict the view that the portfolio decision (for both debtor and creditor) is essentially a stock phenomenon. If a once-for-all change in an explanatory variable took place in a situation of steady-

---

[34] The speeds of adjustment implied by these coefficients seem rather low for short-term capital transactions; such a puzzling long adjustment-lag has been noted by a number of investigators using estimating equations containing an autoregressive term. That these lags must be taken with more than a grain of salt is suggested by the fact that they are extremely sensitive to the period of observation. Typically, regressions based on quarterly data will imply slower speeds of adjustment than those based on monthly data, and those based on annual data yield even larger estimates of the adjustment lag.

state growth, the value of the resulting ΔW would (if we abstract from any time trend in W) gradually approach zero, since the negative influence of W_{t-1} in our regression equation (23) eventually would just cancel the positive influence of all the other explanatory variables.

B. ESTIMATING THE SHORT-TERM CAPITAL FLOW

Our model requires that we do not directly estimate the aggregate outflow of short-term capital from the United States, ΔK, but, rather, the stock-adjustment (FS) and flow-adjustment (FF) components taken separately. To do this, we calculate the *observed* values of FS and FF, using the observed values of W, ΔW, A, and ΔA, following (10) and (11) above. These values are given in Table 2 below. The mean of FF is \$132.8 million, while the algebraic mean of FS is \$109 million, which implies that on the average, the flow-adjustment component accounted for 55 per cent of the quarterly capital outflow. Note, however, that the mean of FS is low because FS has many negative values. The mean of the absolute values of FS is \$255.2 million, so that fluctuations in the total flow are determined primarily by FS.

Next, we calculated a series of *estimated* values, $\hat{FS}$ and $\hat{FF}$, using the observed values of A and ΔA — since these are determined exogenously — but the estimated values of $\Delta \hat{W}$ for each time-period yielded by the regression equation (4) in Table 1, and estimates of $\hat{W}$ from the corresponding equation for W. The resulting regression equations are

$$FF = 1.0006\hat{FF}, \qquad \begin{cases} \bar{R}^2 = .999 \\ DW = 2.314 \end{cases} \tag{24}$$
$$(379.46)$$

and

$$FS = .9758\hat{FS}. \qquad \begin{cases} \bar{R}^2 = .832 \\ DW = 2.223 \end{cases} \tag{25}$$
$$(13.8305)$$

The coefficient of the independent variable is, in each case, positive, highly significant, and not significantly different from one, as is implied by our specification of the underlying model.

The final step is to see how well our theory and the regression equations that are derived from it explain the total quarterly flow of

TABLE 2

A Breakdown of Short-Term Capital Outflows
from the United States, 1959–1967
(*billions of dollars*)

Period	$FS = A(\Delta W)$	$FF = W(\Delta A)$
1959–II	−.0145	.0749
III	−.1180	.0778
IV	.1944	.0629
1960– I	.0639	.0222
II	.1314	.0402
III	.4216	.0465
IV	.9315	.0728
1961– I	.1492	.0080
II	.3142	.0842
III	.0472	.1259
IV	.3726	.1411
1962– I	.2382	.0740
II	.0293	.1419
III	−.0080	.1337
IV	.1128	.1520
1963– I	−.0516	.0663
II	.3740	.1563
III	−.1875	.1178
IV	.2181	.1976
1964– I	.5611	.0777
II	.3678	.1993
III	.0529	.1672
IV	.9586	.2458
1965– I	−.4317	.1451
II	−.5071	.2201
III	−.3913	.1362
IV	−.0591	.2789
1966– I	−.2118	.1448
II	−.1074	.1680
III	−.2756	.1166
IV	.3879	.1953
1967– I	−.0118	.0948
II	.1199	.0937
III	−.1823	.2368
IV	.3277	.3314

short-term capital owned by residents of the United States. This is done in two ways: first, by adding our estimates of $\hat{FF}$ and $\hat{FS}$ together to form an estimate of the capital flow and regressing this sum against the observed flow; and second, by including $\hat{FF}$ and $\hat{FS}$ as separate variables in a regression equation with the actual flow. The results are

$$\Delta K = .986(\hat{FS} + \hat{FF}), \qquad \begin{cases} \bar{R}^2 = .838 \\ DW = 2.19 \end{cases} \qquad (26)$$
$$\quad (17.0)$$

and

$$\Delta K = .971\hat{FS} + 1.03\hat{FF}. \qquad \begin{cases} \bar{R}^2 = .834 \\ DW = 2.19 \end{cases} \qquad (27)$$
$$\quad (13.1) \qquad (6.5)$$

The results are virtually the same, with none of the regression coefficients differing significantly from unity.

C. SOME IMPLICATIONS OF CHANGES IN EXPLANATORY VARIABLES

This section attempts to suggest the relative effects of changes in the GNP of the United States, the U.S. Treasury bill rate, and foreign short-term interest rates on the quarterly flow of American short-term capital. This will be done, using the empirical results from equation (4) in Table 1, by first calculating the long-run effects of these three explanatory variables on W (by dividing each of the relevant regression coefficients by the coefficient of W_{t-1}) and then tracing the influence of this change in W on FF and FS. The resulting magnitudes give only the roughest type of estimates, since they fail to take into account the effects on FF and FS of changes in other explanatory variables that might be induced by changes in GNP and foreign or domestic rates of interest.

To find the effects of changes in R_F^e and R_D^e on capital flows, ΔK, we must compute

$$\delta(\Delta K)/\delta R_F^e = \delta FS/\delta R_F + \delta FF/\delta R_F$$
$$= (\delta \Delta W/\delta R_F)(\bar{A}) + (\delta W/\delta R_F)(\bar{\Delta A}) = 1.162 + .020,$$

and

$$\delta(\Delta K/\delta R_D^e) = \delta FS/\delta R_D + \delta FF/\delta R_D$$
$$= (\delta \Delta W/\delta R_D)(\bar{A}) + (\delta W/\delta R_D)(\overline{\Delta A}) = -.542 - .009.$$

The bars over A and ΔA indicate that we have taken their average values. Notice that an increase in the foreign rate of 1 per cent will ultimately increase the stock-adjustment component of the capital flow, FS, by $1,162 million, and will increase the flow-adjustment component, FF, by $20 million per quarter for each succeeding period. In contrast, an increase in the domestic rate of 1 per cent will eventually decrease FS by $542 million and FF by $9 million, the latter for each succeeding quarter. Finally, we have estimated the importance of a change in Y_t^* on capital flows and have found that

$$\delta(\Delta K)/\delta Y^* = \delta FS/\delta Y^* + \delta FF/\delta Y_t^* = -.148 + 0.$$

Thus, an increase of $1 billion in the GNP of the United States will lower FS by a total of $148 million and will have no significant effect on FF.[35] The domination of the stock-adjustment terms, noted in each of the three estimates just given, is consistent with the simulated findings of Willett and Forte [24] for short-term flows and with the estimated results of Miller and Whitman [19] for long-term portfolio flows.

APPENDIX: DEFINITIONS OF VARIABLES
AND SOURCES OF DATA

R_A^e Expected return on the portfolio of risky assets held by American investors who are actual or potential holders of short-term foreign assets

$\sigma_{R_A}^2$ Variance of R_A^e

R_D^e Expected return on risky U.S. assets; approximated by

---

[35] The term $\delta FF/\delta Y^* = (\delta(W)/\delta Y^*)\Delta A + (\delta(\Delta A)/\delta Y^*)W = 0$ because the first term is negative and various regression estimates of $\delta(\Delta A)/\delta Y^*$ give a positive second term that, on the average, just cancels the first.

	the U.S. Treasury bill rate. Source: *International Financial Statistics*
σ_D^2	Variance of R_D^e
R_K^e	Expected return on foreign short-term assets, from the point of view of U.S. lenders
σ_K^2	Variance of R_K^e
$R_K^{e'}$	Expected cost of borrowing from the United States, from the point of view of foreign borrowers
$\sigma_K'^2$	Variance of $R_K^{e'}$
R_F^e	Expected cost of borrowing from foreign lenders, from the point of view of foreign borrowers; approximated by a simple arithmetic average of the following rates: Canada and United Kingdom, Treasury bill rate; Germany and Japan, call money rate. Sources: Canada, Germany, United Kingdom, *International Financial Statistics;* Japan, unpublished data provided by P. Hendershott
σ_F^2	Variance of $R_F^e = 0$
R_B^e	Total expected cost of borrowing for those foreign debtors who are actual or potential short-term borrowers from the U.S.
σ_B^2	Variance of R_B^e
K	End-of-quarter stock of short-term claims on foreigners held by American banks and nonfinancial insitutions. Source: *U.S. Treasury Bulletin*
D	Domestic risky assets held by U.S. investors
ΔK	Change in K; the quarterly net-outflow of short-term U.S. capital
A'	End-of-quarter stock of: short-term U.S. government securities; bank loans, n.e.c.; and other loans. Source: unpublished data of the Board of Governors of the Federal Reserve System, provided by S. Taylor and J. Berry of the Flow of Funds Section
A	A' plus end-of-quarter stock of: long-term U.S. government securities; state and local government securities; mortgages; and corporate and foreign bonds. Source: same as for A'

W	$= K/A$; $W' = K/A'$
WR & WR'	W and W', using the K adjusted for discontinuities by the procedure described in the text
L	Total liabilities of those foreign debtors who are actual or potential borrowers from the U.S. on a short-term basis
V	$= K/L$
W_d & W_s	The portfolio ratio demanded by American creditors and supplied by foreign debtors
W^* & V^*	Desired values of W and V
ϕ & δ	Speeds of adjustment for American investors and foreign debtors in reaching their optimum portfolios
i_K	Nominal rate of interest on short-term loans of U.S. capital to foreigners
ψ	Parameter in foreign debtors' disutility functions that shifts with the need for dollar loans for financing international trade
X	Theoretical measure of the trade that foreigners wish to finance via short-term loans from the United States; empirical proxies are $WIMP$, EXP, and $NEXP$
r_f/r_s	Ratio of the forward rate to the spot rate of exchange, in dollars per unit of foreign exchange
r_s^e/r_s	Ratio of the expected future spot rate to the current spot rate
FF	$= (W)(\Delta A) = $ the flow-adjustment component of the total capital flow
FS	$= (\Delta W)(A) = $ the stock-adjustment component of the total capital flow
$\hat{FF}$ & $\hat{FS}$	Estimated values of FF and FS
T	Time
Y	Quarterly U.S. GNP, not seasonally adjusted. Source: *Survey of Current Business*
Y^*	Deviations of Y from its time trend over the period 1959-I–1967-IV, calculated by method described in footnote 29
VRP	Dummy variable for U.S. Voluntary Credit Restraint program

WIMP   Rest of world imports = world imports minus U.S. imports; not seasonally adjusted. Source: *International Financial Statistics*

EXP   Merchandise exports from the United States; not seasonally adjusted. Source: *Survey of Current Business*

NEXP   *EXP* minus direct foreign investment by residents of the United States. Source: *Survey of Current Business*

REFERENCES

1. Arndt, Sven W., "International Short Term Capital Movements: A Distributed Lag Model of Speculation in Foreign Exchange." *Econometrica,* Vol. 36, No. 1 (January, 1968), pp. 59–70.
2. Bell, Philip W., "Private Capital Movements and the U.S. Balance of Payments," *Factors Affecting the U.S. Balance of Payments.* Washington, D.C., U.S. Government Printing Office, 1962, pp. 395–481.
3. Branson, William H., *Financial Capital Flows in the U.S. Balance of Payments.* Amsterdam, North-Holland Publishing Co., 1968.
4. Brimmer, Andrew F., "Direct Investment and Corporate Adjustment Techniques Under the Voluntary U.S. Balance of Payments Program." *Journal of Finance,* Vol. 21 (May, 1966), pp. 266–283.
5. Bryant, Ralph, and Hendershott, Patric H., "Financial Capital Flows in the U.S. Balance of Payments: An Explanatory Empirical Study." Mimeographed, August, 1969.
6. Fama, Eugene, "Risk, Return and Equilibrium: Some Clarifying Comments." *Journal of Finance,* Vol. 23, No. 1 (March, 1968), pp. 29–40.
7. Feldstein, Martin S., "Uncertainty and Forward Exchange Speculation." *Review of Economics and Statistics,* Vol. L, No. 2 (May, 1968), pp. 182–192.
8. Floyd, John E., "International Capital Movements and Monetary Equilibrium." *American Economic Review,* Vol. LIX, No. 4, Part 1 (September, 1969), pp. 472–491.
9. Grubel, Herbert G., *Forward Exchange, Speculation and the*

International Flow of Capital. Stanford, Stanford University Press, 1966.

10. ―――― "Internationally Diversified Portfolios." *American Economic Review,* Vol. LVIII, No. 5 (December, 1968), pp. 1299–1314.

11. Hawkins, Robert G. "International Capital Movements Under Canada's Flexible Exchange Rate." Unpublished paper, 1967.

12. Hendershott, Patric H., "Recent Development of the Financial Sector of Econometric Models." *Journal of Finance,* Vol. 23, No. 1 (March, 1968), pp. 41–66.

13. Johnson, Harry G., "Some Aspects of the Theory of Economic Policy in a World of Capital Mobility," in Tullio Bagiotti, ed., *Essays in Honor of Marco Fanno.* Padua, 1966.

14. Kenen, Peter B., *Portfolio Capital and the United States Balance of Payments* (forthcoming).

15. ―――― "Short-Term Capital Movements and the U.S. Balance of Payments," *U.S. Balance of Payments, Hearings,* Joint Economic Committee, 88th Congress, 1st Session. Washington, D.C., U.S. Government Printing Office, 1963, Part 1, pp. 153–191.

16. Levin, Jay H., "Forward Exchange and Internal-External Equilibrium." Seminar Discussion Paper No. 1, Research Seminar in International Economics, Department of Economics, University of Michigan, 1968.

17. Markowitz, Harry, *Portfolio Selection.* New York, John Wiley & Sons, 1959.

18. Lee, Chung Hoon, "A Stock-Adjustment Analysis of Capital Movements: The United States–Canadian Case." *Journal of Political Economy,* Vol. 77, No. 4, Part 1 (July/August, 1969), pp. 512–523.

19. Miller, Norman C., and Whitman, Marina v. N., "A Mean-Variance Analysis of United States Long-Term Portfolio Foreign Investment." *Quarterly Journal of Economics,* Vol. LXXXIV, No. 2 (May, 1970), pp. 175–196.

20. Sharpe, William F., "Capital Asset Prices: A Theory of Market Equilibrium." *Journal of Finance,* Vol. 19 (September, 1964), pp. 425–442.

21. Stein, Jerome, "International Short Term Capital Movements."

American Economic Review, Vol. 55, No. 1 (March, 1965), pp. 40–66.

22. Tobin, James, "Comment on Borch and Feldstein." *Review of Economic Studies,* Vol. 36 (January, 1969), pp. 13–15.

23. ——— "Liquidity Preference as Behavior Toward Risk." *Review of Economic Studies,* Vol. 25 (February, 1968), pp. 65–86.

24. Willett, Thomas D., and Forte, Francesco, "Interest Rate Policy and External Balance." *Quarterly Journal of Economics,* Vol. 83 (May, 1969), pp. 242–262.

POLICY TOWARD SHORT-TERM CAPITAL MOVEMENTS: SOME IMPLICATIONS OF THE PORTFOLIO APPROACH

WILLIAM H. BRANSON · Princeton University
THOMAS D. WILLETT · Cornell University

1 INTRODUCTION: CAPITAL FLOWS AND POLICY

THE SOURCES of policymakers' interest in international financial capital movements can be divided into three major categories: the actual or potential effects of such capital movements on (a) the balance of payments; (b) domestic monetary management; and (c) the efficiency of resource allocation. While the same capital movement, or policy toward capital movements, may have effects under all three categories, it is useful to keep the three conceptually distinct.

Concern over the *balance-of-payments effects* of capital movements ranges from the desire to prevent or offset potential capital flows themselves to the active manipulation of capital movements to offset a net surplus or deficit in the rest of a country's balance of payments. Discussions of the *effects on domestic monetary management of financial capital movements* are usually concerned with the reduced ability to follow an independent monetary policy implied by high capital mobility, although it should be noted that some countries manipulate the foreign asset and liability positions of their commercial banks in lieu of open-market operations to influence the domestic money market.[1]

NOTE: This paper was written while the authors were senior staff economists at the Council of Economic Advisers, on leave from Princeton and Harvard Universities, respectively. They wish to acknowledge the financial assistance of the National Science Foundation (Research Grant No. GS 1972) and the Ford Foundation. They especially wish to thank Raymond D. Hill for his assistance on the empirical aspects of the paper.

[1] See, for instance, Katz [13].

Concern over the *resource-allocation effects* of financial capital movements results from the fact that for numerous reasons, including the existence of disequilibrium exchange rates, the private and social costs and returns from international financial capital movements will often not be the same. International differences in interest rates often do not adequately reflect international differences in the productivity of capital; thus, false signals may be given to private investors and borrowers. Furthermore, deficiencies in the adjustment mechanism can cause a transfer problem — "desirable" net movements of financial capital may not generate commensurate movements of real resources.[2]

In many cases, these distortions are the result of poor functioning of the international monetary system. For instance, greater flexibility of exchange rates should substantially reduce the type of large, volatile movements of capital observed recently when parities came under suspicion, and, likewise, should reduce the distortions (pointed out by Lutz [17]) caused by differential inflation premiums in the interest rates of countries connected by temporarily fixed exchange rates. Similarly, the transfer of real resources in response to net capital movements would be facilitated.

In such a situation, the best solution would be reform of the exchange-rate system. But if this is not possible, there is a case for the use of selective measures as a second-best policy. In addition, selective

---

[2] We use *desirable* deliberately, as a weasel word without full definition. An attempt to give a precise definition would raise enough controversial questions to last a full paper if not a volume. (What, for instance, was the social productivity of the speculative capital flows which preceded the British devaluation in 1967, and how does this compare with the productivity of the movements in earlier crises? Obviously, it would be difficult to secure general agreement on the answers to these questions.)

The productivity gains from international capital movements have often been assumed to occur only when net movements result in the transfer of real resources. There are additional sources of potential economic gain, however. Cross flows of capital which result in no net direct resource transfers may still increase economic efficiency. Specialized knowledge and complementarity between specific economic activities (such as possible benefits from internal financing) explain much of the cross flows between countries. Another possible source of gain from gross flows (unconnected with real resource transfers via the trade balance) is differences in liquidity preference such that a country may, for instance, lend short and borrow long. Such international financial intermediation has been pointed to by Despres, Kindleberger, and Salant [3], and has been the subject of refinement and empirical investigation by other authors, such as Laffer and Salant in this volume. See also the critical commentary by Halm [10] and Triffin [22]. A third type of gain comes from the possibility of reducing aggregate risk through portfolio diversification. See, for instance, Grubel [8].

measures may correct market imperfections not connected directly with the exchange-rate system. For example, while the Interest Equalization Tax was enacted primarily for balance-of-payments reasons (as a second-best policy to exchange-rate adjustments), it has given infant-industry protection to the development of European capital markets. Thus, it probably has had a beneficial long-run effect on the efficiency of resource allocation.

Within any given exchange-rate system, policy measures toward movements of financial capital can be grouped into four major categories:

1. General monetary (interest-rate) policy can be adjusted to induce or prevent capital movements.

2. Selective measures can be used for this purpose. These can range from attempting to twist the structure of interest rates or the use of official forward intervention or swaps, through moral suasion (voluntary controls), to formal requirements or controls and fiscal (tax and/or subsidy) measures designed to influence the relative profitability of investing, or borrowing, at home and abroad. These may be applied in a general or discriminating manner and may be used either to affect particular capital movements directly or to offset them by inducing private capital movements in the opposite direction.

3. Capital movements may be financed by reserve movements or official borrowing and lending.

4. Other components of the balance of payments may be allowed, or forced, to adjust to capital movements.

In addition, as we have briefly indicated above, changes in the exchange-rate system may have important influences on capital movements. For example, moving toward a system in which exchange rates are changed frequently – or even continuously – in small amounts should reduce the frequency of sudden, large capital shifts as the viability of existing rates comes into question under the present system of adjustable pegs. In turn, assurance that exchange rates will remain fairly close to equilibrium should make official financing of transitory flows of capital more acceptable than under the current system.

The feasibility of using official financing to offset undesired capital movements in place of preventing them by the adjustment of interest rates, or by the use of selective measures, will be crucially affected by the size and duration of such movements. Where capital movements are primarily of the nature of stock adjustments, or their size is fairly small relative to activity in domestic money markets, ample reserves or official borrowing facilities would allow countries to maintain a reasonable degree of monetary independence without the need to resort to selective measures. A change in interest rates or other incentives for capital movements would lead primarily to a one-shot adjustment of portfolios. This adjustment would exert a temporary effect on the balance of payments and could probably be handled by the use of reserves. On the other hand, if large quantities of capital would continue to move internationally as long as differential incentives remained, official financing could not provide substantive monetary independence. The magnitudes and stock-flow relationships of internationally mobile funds are thus of critical importance in determining a desirable policy strategy. These factors also influence the relative desirability of using interest-rate policy or selective measures to suppress capital movements. The greater is the interest sensitivity of international capital movements and the greater are continuing flows, the less are the costs of using interest-rate policy.[3]

Thus, in formulating policies toward financial capital movements it is important to have a proper theoretical view of the nature of these movements and some idea of their likely magnitudes. Obtaining reasonable quantitative estimates of these magnitudes depends in turn on the proper specification of the estimating equation, i.e., upon the use of a proper theoretical framework.

In Section 2 we briefly outline the portfolio-balance model of capital movements and discuss some implications of this model for balance-of-payments policy and for research on capital movements. In Section 3 we describe the empirical implementation of the portfolio model to estimate an equation for changes in short-term American claims on foreigners, using quarterly data for 1960–64; in Section 4, the data sample is extended to 1968 and the effects on short-term claims of the capital-controls program of the United States are examined. Finally, in Section 5, as another illustration of the importance of the portfolio approach for the formulation of policy concerning cap-

---

[3] For further discussion of this point, see, for instance, Willett [26], and Willett and Forte [28].

ital movements, we consider its implications for the existence of the constraint on domestic interest rates which many writers have suggested would occur under an exchange-rate system of sliding parities.

2 THE PORTFOLIO-BALANCE MODEL OF CAPITAL MOVEMENTS

THE portfolio approach to capital flows relates equilibrium holdings of stocks of assets to levels of interest rates. This is a simple application of the portfolio-distribution model developed by Tobin [21] and Markowitz [18]. This approach to international capital movements has been applied by a number of authors in recent years, including ourselves in earlier work, and by still others in several of the papers published in this volume.[4] Hence our present treatment of this concept can be brief.

For any given constellation (or vector) of rates of return, each individual has an equilibrium distribution of various types of assets in his portfolio. If this distribution is not itself dependent on the size of the portfolio, then the fraction of the portfolio held in each type of available asset can be written as a function of the vector of rates of return:

$$\frac{V_t^j}{V_t} = g(I_t). \tag{1}$$

V^j/V is the fraction of net worth, V, held in asset j, and I is a vector of interest rates $i^1, \ldots, i^n$. As i^j rises, V^j/V will generally rise.[5] We would expect that after some point this relationship would become nonlinear, with successive increments calling forth progressively smaller adjustments in V^j/V.

---

[4] References to many of these papers may be found in Officer and Willett [19]. In addition to the papers in this volume, see also Levin [16] and Lee [15].

[5] It is, of course, theoretically possible for wealth effects to offset substitution effects so that V^j/V would fall, but we consider such dominance to be unlikely empirically. However, wealth effects may make the absolute level of interest, as well as interest differentials, an important factor in portfolio allocation. See Willett [25]. For a recent, more general treatment of wealth effects, see Stiglitz [20].

Interpreting this equation in the case of American holdings of foreign securities, V^f, we have

$$\frac{V_t^f}{V_t} = g(i_t^f, i_t^d; Z_t), \qquad (2)$$

where i^f is "the" foreign interest rate, i^d is "the" domestic rate, and Z includes variables such as evaluation of risk and exchange-rate expectations, which are held constant while we look more closely at the relationship between asset holdings and interest rates.

Multiplying (2) by the "scale variable" V gives a relation determining the equilibrium holdings of foreign assets [6]

$$V^f = Vg(i^f, i^d; Z). \qquad (3)$$

(Time subscripts will be included from here on only where they are needed to avoid confusion.)

We should note that for empirical estimation this function will have to be modified to account for any special information we have about the determinants of holdings of the particular series we choose for V^f. For example, in estimating equations for short-term claims on foreigners, we would want to add exports to the explanatory variables in (3) to account for the role of short-term lending in financing foreign trade. Since this is not particularly related to the size of the portfolio, we would add terms in exports to the right-hand side of (3), rather than including exports in Z, which pertains only to the distribution of the portfolio. For the present we shall stick to the formulation in (3) to focus on relationships between the interest rates and capital flows. Complications will be added and discussed when we come to an example of empirical estimation.

What, now, is the effect of a change in interest rates on holdings of foreign assets, V^f? At a *given level* of portfolio size, V_0, the effect of a rise in "the" foreign rate is given by

$$\frac{dV^f}{di^f} = V_0 \frac{\partial g}{\partial i^f}. \qquad (4)$$

---

[6] Equations (1)–(3) give the usual specification of an asset demand-equation in the literature on financial models. See, for instance, equations (1)–(4) of the prototype model of Brainard and Tobin [1, p. 101].

The increase in the foreign rate causes a stock shift in the equilibrium distribution of the portfolio toward foreign assets. With a given portfolio size, and ignoring transactions costs for the moment, this *stock-shift* effect is a once-for-all change in portfolio distribution.

But portfolios grow over time, and the higher foreign rate should raise the fraction of portfolio growth that goes to accumulation of foreign assets.[7] With a given vector of interest rates, the growth in foreign assets is given by

$$\frac{dV^f}{dt} \equiv \dot{V}^f = \dot{V}g(i^f, i^d; Z).$$ (5)

An increase in the foreign interest rate will increase $\dot{V}^f$ — the equilibrium flow into foreign assets from portfolio growth — by

$$\frac{d\dot{V}^f}{di^f} = \dot{V}\frac{\partial g}{\partial i^f}.$$ (6)

The most interesting point here is not that there is a *continuing flow* effect, but that the fairly general model of portfolio distribution given by (1) implies a very rigid relationship between the continuing flow and the stock-shift effects. Dividing (6) by (4) we obtain

$$\frac{\text{Flow effect}}{\text{Stock effect}} = \frac{d\dot{V}^f_t/di}{dV^f_t/di} = \frac{\dot{V}_t}{V_t}.$$ (7)

The ratio of the flow effect to the stock effect is equal to the rate of growth of the "scale variable."[8] Assume that portfolios are growing at, say, 10 per cent per year; then if an increase in the foreign rate of 1 per cent gives a stock shift of, say, $500 million, the initial effect on the continuing annual outflow would be $50 million per year. This effect itself would, of course, also grow at 10 per cent annually.

However, the presence of this continuing flow effect does not imply that an increase in foreign interest rates will necessarily lead to worsening in the balance of payments. This is because the continuing outflow

---

[7] The model developed by Grubel [8] is essentially the same as ours, but in his conclusions he failed to recognize this continuing flow effect. See Willett and Forte [28, p. 249]. An earlier application of portfolio theory to aspects of international short-term capital movements is given in Grubel [7].

[8] Equation (7) is simply a mathematical equivalent of the assumptions behind equation (3). This equation contains no new information beyond that in (3).

due to the increase in i^f may be offset by the increase in interest earnings both on the existing stock of claims on foreigners, V_0^f, and on the increase on that stock, dV^f. Earnings on the existing stock would rise by $V^f di^f$. In addition, the stock that is shifted abroad, $dV^f = V_0^f \dfrac{\partial g}{\partial i^f} \, di^f$, will earn interest at the rate i^f, so that the total annual interest earnings would be approximately

$$V_0^f di^f \left(1 + i^f \frac{\partial g}{\partial i^f} \right).$$

This amount would act as an offset to the continuing flow effect, $d\dot{V}^f = \dot{V}^f \dfrac{\partial g}{\partial i^f} \, di^f$. Thus the continuing-flow effect would outweigh the increment to interest earnings if

$$\left(\frac{\dot{V}^f}{V^f} - i^f \right) \frac{\partial g}{\partial i^f} > 1. \tag{8}$$

Thus the growth rate of V must be sufficiently greater than the foreign interest rate, i^f, that condition (8) is met if the continuing flow effect is to outweigh the effect on interest earnings. If this is not the case, an increase in foreign rates may, on balance, improve the sum of the capital account plus investment income once the stock-shift is completed.

While presented in terms of the effects of interest rates on the portfolio allocation of assets, the same point has general applicability to other types of expected return, such as expected movements in exchange rates; and to decisions concerning borrowing, spot, and forward speculation, and the movement of funds by leading and lagging commercial payments.[9, 10]

[9] Spot speculation and uncovered interest arbitrage are, of course, the same thing. On the application of portfolio theory to forward exchange speculation, see Feldstein [5]. A stock-adjustment approach to trade financing, which can be used to consider the effects of speculative changes in leads and lags, is presented in Willett [24]. On capital movements via changes in leads and lags, see Einzig [4], Hansen [11], Katz [12], and White [23].

[10] For discussions of the balance-of-payments costs of such policies in terms of increased interest payments, speculative profits of foreigners, and a worsened trade balance see, for instance, Grubel [7, chap. 16], Hansen [11, chap. 9], and Willett and Forte [28]. In the last-named paper it is estimated that for the United States, the long-run balance-of-payments effects of an increase in domestic short-term interest rates will probably be negative, with increased interest payments exceeding induced capital in-

The stock/flow relationship implicit in the theory of portfolio distribution has a number of interesting implications for balance-of-payments policy and research. First, since the flow effect is small relative to the stock-shift, interest-rate policy for external purposes is more a policy influencing levels of reserves than balance-of-payments flows. It is *changing* interest rates that produce large continuing flows in the balance of payments; *high* rates primarily affect reserve positions. As was previously indicated, this relationship also means that the balance-of-payments costs of high interest rates, or forward intervention, may exceed the continuing balance-of-payments gains, once the stock adjustment has been substantially completed.

The second point is that continuing flow effects in the data on capital movements will probably be very hard to see if the portfolio theory is correct. With interest rates continually changing, the stock-shift effects would tend to swamp the continuing flow effects. Thus, the existence of continuing flow effects will be hard to confirm empirically, and will probably have to be built into econometric models by assumption.

Finally, if the portfolio model is correct, the concept of an elasticity of capital flows with respect to interest-rate changes is a bit fuzzy. There is an elasticity of equilibrium stock with respect to interest rates, and an elasticity of continuing flow with respect to interest-rate changes. The two are related by the rate of growth in portfolios.

As suggested above, application of the portfolio model to the data requires numerous modifications. First, the existence of complications like transactions costs and tax laws implies that adjustment to changes in interest rates will be lagged and incomplete. Since additions to portfolios impose costs, whether acquisitions are made at home or

flows. H. Peter Gray [6] has recently pointed out that there may be an upward bias in the Willett and Forte calculations of interest costs because of an implicit assumption in their calculations that net interest costs on official dollar holdings were not reduced as a result of the induced stock adjustment of private funds. However, the Willett and Forte calculations also erred in the opposite direction by treating as non-interest-bearing demand deposits a large quantity of liabilities of American commercial banks to foreign branches which are, in fact, predominantly financed at Eurodollar rates. Since Eurodollar rates tend to follow American short-term interest rates upward very quickly (see, for instance, Branson [2, p. 102]), the original calculations understated interest costs on this score. As it happens, these two biases are roughly equal in magnitude, so that the original estimates can stand.

abroad, redistribution of a portfolio by reallocating additions—leaving the existing stock unchanged—can spread the stock-shift effect over several months. If empirical work does not take this lag into account, it may appear that one is observing a relation between interest-rate *levels* and capital *flows*.[11]

Next, if we use balance-of-payments data on capital flows in empirical work, we must recognize that observable variables other than interest rates also affect the measured flows. In the example to be given below, exports clearly affect short-term claims on foreigners through trade finance, and moreover, we must allow for the effect of the balance-of-payments programs of the United States. In addition, there are variables that are more difficult to observe (which we have included in the Z variable of equation (3)), such as the effects of speculative expectations and of the availability of credit. The best we can get, at least in the current state of the economist's art, are estimates of the differential effects of changes in interest rates and foreign trade on short-term claims, for instance—not a complete explanation of what moves short-term claims.

There are also problems concerning the relevant measure of portfolio size, V, and possible effects from changes in the composition of V (such as might be brought about by an open-market operation, for instance), and problems involving the interaction between capital flows and interest rates at home and abroad. The equations for capital flows are part of a world characterized by simultaneity, in which capital flows affect interest rates, as well as vice versa. Furthermore, an increase in domestic rates of interest will, at least in theory, be associated with a fall in portfolio size as bond prices fall. If a rise in domestic rates is due to the domestic authorities' tightening action, the reduction in portfolio size will add to the effect of higher rates in reducing capital outflows. But if the rise in domestic rates is due to a capital outflow caused by a rise in rates abroad, the drop in portfolio size will reduce the increase in outflow.

[11] This may have led several authors to reject the stock-adjustment theory on the basis of empirical results which were, actually, not inconsistent with a better specification of the portfolio model. For discussions of the specification problems involved in the early published studies of financial capital flows from the United States, see Willett [27, chap. 5] and the papers in this volume by Stern and Leamer and by Bryant and Hendershott.

Even with all of these empirical difficulties, we can find fairly regular relationships between interest rates and capital flows in the data for the United States.[12] Here we will give an example of the application of the portfolio theory to the determination of changes in American short-term claims on nongovernmental foreign contacts. This will give us an idea of the expected magnitude of the stock and flow effects of changes in interest rates.

3 ESTIMATION OF AN EQUATION FOR SHORT-TERM CLAIMS, UNITED STATES, 1960–64

AS WE suggested above, several modifications and assumptions concerning the form of equation (3) must be made before we can get on to estimating its coefficients. First, we will modify the equation by adding current and lagged terms in exports to the set of explanatory variables. Next, we assume that the function $g(i^f, i^d; Z)$ is linear, and that all variables include both current and lagged values. Finally, we will estimate the equation in first-difference form so that it is an equation for *changes* in short-term claims on foreigners—a capital *flow* equation.

With these modifications, the basic form of the estimating equation is

$$\Delta V_t^f = \alpha_0 + \alpha_1 \Delta V_t + \sum_{j=0}^{J} \beta_j \Delta (V i^d)_{t-j}$$

$$+ \sum_{k=0}^{K} \delta_k \Delta (V i^f)_{t-k} + \sum_{n=0}^{N} \tau_n \Delta X_{t-n} + \epsilon_t. \quad (9)$$

This form of (3) assumes that $g(\cdot)$ includes a constant term, accounting for the presence of ΔV_t alone in (9). Definitions and units of variables are given in Table 1.[13] Various rates of interest were experimented

---

[12] This is not at all to say that further research attempting to take into account the types of difficulties mentioned above is not needed. For an in-depth study of one bilateral flow that examines such problems, see Bryant and Hendershott in this volume.

[13] A listing of the data used in Sections 3 and 4 can be obtained from William Branson, Department of Economics, Princeton University.

TABLE 1

Definitions and Units of Variables in Equation (9)

Variable	Definition	Units
ΔV^f	Changes in American short-term claims on private foreigners	$ million, quarterly rates
ΔX	Changes in merchandise exports from the United States	$ million, quarterly rates
V	Net worth of American households	$ trillion
i	3-month Treasury bill rates	Percentage points

with; the only ones with significant explanatory power that we discovered were the American 3-month bill rate, i^{US}, the British 3-month bill rate, i^{UK}, and the Canadian 3-month bill rate, i^{C}.[14]

We also experimented with forms of (9) that use changes in exports, ΔX, as the scale variable, and that insert the export term into the equation in a way interrelated with ΔV. But as a single scale-variable ΔV performed much better than ΔX, while scarcity of observations prevented the use of more complex forms of the equation that interrelate ΔX and ΔV but also add variables to the right-hand side. As more data become available, this defect can be remedied, and presumably more interest rates will be identified as significant in estimation.

Equation (9) was first estimated on quarterly data from 1960 through 1964. This was done for two reasons. First, these data fall in time between the formal reestablishment of European convertibility in 1958 and the emergence of the Eurodollar market in 1959, on the one side; and the beginning of the American program of controls over capital flows in 1965, on the other. Second, the estimated equation can be compared with earlier work by Branson [2] that did not recognize the role of the scale variable and the "continuing flow" effect of changes in interest rates. The comparison will tell us if the explanation of capital flows is improved by this refinement.

---

[14] We should note that the contemporaneous value of the rate in the United States was not significant in any of our estimates. This has been a persistent result of our study of capital flows. See [2, p. 150].

TABLE 2

Coefficients of Equation (9) Estimated on Quarterly Data, 1960–64

Variable	Coefficient (Standard Error)	Variable	Coefficient (Standard Error)
Constant	116.30 (73.30)	$\Delta(Vi^{US})_{t-2}$	−149.8 (44.1)
ΔV_t	4131.7 (2212.9)	$\Delta(Vi^C)_t$	54.2 (44.1)
ΔX_t	0.584 (.139)	$\Delta(Vi^C)_{t-1}$	69.4 (43.8)
ΔX_{t-1}	0.403 (.158)	$\Delta(Vi^{UK})_t$	81.4 (41.5)
$\Delta(Vi^{US})_{t-1}$	−181.2 (95.0)		

$R^2 = .73$.
Durbin-Watson statistic = 1.93.
Standard error of estimate = 180.4.

Table 2 gives the coefficients and statistics of equation (9), estimated on quarterly data, 1960–64. Several features of the estimated equation are of interest:

1. The equation fits much better than it did before the scale-variable V was introduced. The earlier equation [2, p. 150] had $R^2 = 0.58$.

2. The American and British rates on short-term bills are quite significant in explaining short-term flows from, or into, the United States, while the Canadian rate is only marginally significant.

3. The sum of the coefficients in the American bill rate, −331.0, is larger than that of the foreign rates, 205.0. This suggests that an increase of the same magnitude in all rates will *reduce* capital outflows from the United States.

4. The total coefficient on ΔX, 0.98, corresponds fairly closely to the earlier estimate [2, p. 150], of 0.94.

With a total coefficient of −331.0 for the American interest rate, and V_t at $2.20 trillion in the fourth quarter of 1964, a 1 percentage point increase in i^{US} (with foreign rates unchanged) in 1964-IV would give a stock-shift toward the United States of

$$\Delta V^f = (331.0)(2.20)(1.0) = \$730 \text{ million.}$$

This shift would be completed three quarters after the change in the interest rate.

The continuing flow effect of an increase in i^{US} of 1.0 in 1964-IV, with V growing at 7 per cent per year, would be

$$\Delta \dot{V}^f = (331.0)(2.20)(.07)(1.0) = \$51 \text{ million.}$$

Thus, the annual flow effect would be 7 per cent of the stock shift, as shown by the earlier arithmetic.

If foreign rates adjusted fully to changes in American rates, the net coefficient of -126.0 would substitute for -331.0 in the example, giving a stock-shift toward the United States of

$$\Delta V^f = (126.0)(2.20)(1.0) = \$277 \text{ million,}$$

and a continuing flow effect of $19 million per year.

These estimates may be closer to actuality than the "no-reaction" estimates, so that we might conclude that a 1 percentage point increase in the U.S. Treasury bill rate near the end of the 1960–64 period would yield a reduction in the outstanding stock of short-term claims on foreigners of about $300–$400 million in three quarters, and reduce the subsequent outflow by about $20–$30 million per year.

4   THE IMPACT OF THE CAPITAL CONTROLS PROGRAM: AN EXTENSION OF THE EQUATION TO THE 1965–68 PERIOD

IN FEBRUARY of 1965, the Administration imposed voluntary restraints on short-term lending to foreigners; these restraints were made mandatory in January, 1968. In general, the program initially required banks to limit their *increase* in short-term claims to 5 per cent in 1965, and 4 per cent in 1966, leaving the ceiling at the end of 1966 at 109 per cent of claims outstanding at the end of 1964. During this period, short-term outflows were reduced substantially (with negative outflows in some quarters), so that outstanding claims were well below the ceiling at the end of 1966.

With this leeway in mind, the Administration held the ceiling on outstanding claims constant at 109 per cent of the 1964 level in 1967, and reduced it to 103 per cent in 1968, with controls becoming mandatory. We can get a rough picture of the effects of the program by using our estimate of equation (9) on the 1960–64 data to predict what outflows there would have been from 1965 through 1968, and then comparing these predicted values with the actual flows. This comparison is shown in Chart 1, where the dotted line shows predicted values, and the solid line shows actual values.

CHART 1

Actual and Predicted Changes in Short-Term Claims on Nongovernmental Foreigners from the 1960–64 Equation

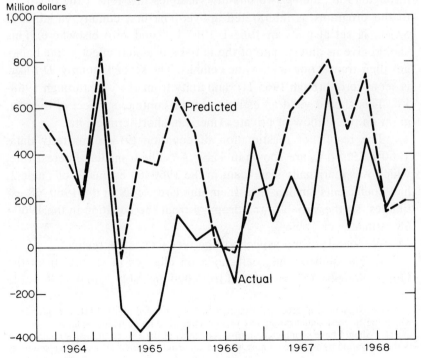

Chart 1 shows that a large gap opened between actual and predicted outflows in 1965, with actual figures below predicted ones. The gap narrowed somewhat in late 1965, and from then on, movements in capital flows (quarterly changes in flows) were fairly similar in the two series, with actual figures below predicted ones until late in 1968.

Our interpretation of these results is that during 1965 the banks reduced outflows enough to get their transactions well below the ceiling, producing the leeway that so bothered the Administration in 1967 and 1968. Once the stock of claims was sufficiently below the ceiling, the banks could then react "normally" to *changes* in capital *flow* determinants, rather than having to worry continually about bumping up against the ceiling. Capital flows were then kept at an average level below normal, but continued to react to changes in interest rates, trade flows, and total assets in the usual way.

With this view of movements in the data from 1965 to 1968 in mind, we can now extend the period of estimation of equation (9) through 1968, adding two dummy variables that reflect the reactions to the programs as interpreted above. The first dummy variable, *D Stock,* is set at unity in 1965-I–1965-III, and zero elsewhere. This should give us an estimate of the initial stock-shift effect as the banks got their transactions below the ceilings. The second dummy, *D Flow,* is set at zero through 1965-III, and unity from 1965-IV through 1968-IV. This should yield an estimate of the continuing effect of the program on the outflow of private American short-term capital.

The results of reestimation of equation (9) on quarterly data, 1960-I–1968-IV, are shown in Table 3.[15] The Canadian interest rate, which was marginally significant in the 1960–64 estimates of Table 2, had coefficients smaller than their standard errors in the 1960–68 estimates, so the variable was dropped from the equation in the 1960–68 estimates of Table 3.

We found several aspects of the reestimates interesting:

1. The sum of the coefficients on changes in exports from the United States $-\Delta X-$ is reduced from 0.99 in Table 2, to 0.63 in Table

---

[15] In reestimation, a large negative residual was noticed in 1964-III, the quarter in which the Interest Equalization Tax was introduced. With no ready explanation of why the IET should have so affected short-term claims of the United States, we eliminated that observation by adding a dummy with the value unity in 1964-III and zero elsewhere.

TABLE 3

Coefficients of Equation (9) Estimated on Quarterly Data, 1960–68

Variable	Coefficient (Standard Error)	Variable	Coefficient (Standard Error)
Constant	195.85 (53.39)	$\Delta(Vi^{US})_{t-2}$	−140.0 (41.5)
ΔV_t	2890.4 (1087.3)	$\Delta(Vi^{UK})_t$	53.2 (23.8)
ΔX_t	0.371 (.095)	D Stock	−584.3 (111.9)
ΔX_{t-1}	0.260 (.096)	D Flow	−163.2 (69.6)

$R^2 = .72$.
Durbin-Watson statistic = 2.12.
Standard error of estimate = 172.9.

3. This may reflect the impact of the capital restraint program on trade financing by American banks.

2. The interest-rate coefficients are smaller in the 1960–68 estimate than in the 1960–64 estimate. The United States bill rate lagged one quarter was thoroughly insignificant and was dropped from the estimate.

3. The coefficient of the American rate of interest, −140.0, is still greater (in absolute value) than that of the foreign rate, 53.6, so that an equal increase in all rates still gives a reduced outflow of short-term capital.

4. The stock-shift effect of introducing the program on short-term claims was apparently about $600 million per quarter for three quarters. The effect on continuing quarterly outflows was to reduce them by about $160 million. These are *not,* however, net gains from the program, because there were probably offsets in decreased inflows of foreign capital.[16]

[16] See, for instance, the discussion in Haberler and Willett [9, pp. 14–18] and the econometric work by Laffer [14].

The 1960–68 estimates suggest that the program reduced the sensitivity of short-term capital to changes in interest rates. With the estimates of Table 3, a 1 percentage point increase in i^{US} (with foreign rates unchanged) in 1968-IV, with V_t at \$2.91 trillion, would give a *stock shift* toward the United States of

$$\Delta V^f = (140.0)(2.91)(1.0) = \$407 \text{ million},$$

and a continuing flow effect of \$28 million per year with net worth growing at 7 per cent per year.

An equal one-point increase in both the American and British rates would give a stock shift toward the United States of

$$\Delta V^f = (86.8)(2.91)(1.0) = \$252 \text{ million}.$$

Thus, the program may well have damped the interest sensitivity of American funds, but the interest-rate variables were still significant.

As we said earlier, these estimates of equation (9) clearly do not provide a complete explanation of flows of private American short-term capital. For that, a much more painstaking and detailed empirical study, such as that reported by Bryant and Hendershott in this volume, will probably be necessary. But these estimates do give a rough idea of the *differential* effect of changes in interest rates on short-term capital, and also give us an idea of the quantitative effect of the restraint program of the United States.

The results also show that a proper specification of an equation such as (3), incorporating both the stock and flow effects, gives reasonable econometric results. This adds one more shred to the mounting evidence that capital flows are a tractable subject for econometric research.

5 THE CONSTRAINT ON INTEREST RATES UNDER A SLIDING-PARITY SYSTEM OF EXCHANGE RATES

ONE familiar argument against a sliding-parity system of exchange rates is that relative interest rates would have to adjust to the rate of change of parity to prevent large outflows of capital from the devaluing country. This argument thus says that there is no (or little) gain from a sliding-parity system in terms of freeing monetary policy to meet domestic targets; monetary policy must still compensate for movements in parity.

In this section we extend the model developed in Section 2 to consider exchange-rate expectations, and show that on a portfolio-adjustment view of capital movements, this "interest-rate constraint" is much weaker than would be implied by a flow theory. Essentially, the capital outflow that results from a change in the expected rate of change of parity from zero to, say, the maximum negative rate of change allowed in the system, is a one-shot affair. Furthermore, it will be reversed if and when the expected rate of change returns to zero as the exchange rate reaches a new equilibrium.

Expected changes in the exchange rate should enter decisions on portfolio allocation analogously to interest rates. The expected return from uncovered capital movements depends on (a) differences between interest rates at home and abroad, and (b) expectations concerning the spot exchange rate at the time of maturity of the financial instrument in question. The relative importance of these two components depends on the length of time to maturity (or the anticipated time to repatriation). The shorter the time period in question, the more important are expected movements in the spot rate. On a one-month loan, the movement of the spot rate from the bottom to the top of a ¾ per cent band in each direction around parity would be the equivalent of an 18 percentage point difference in interest rates expressed in annual rates. On a three-month loan such a movement would be the equivalent of a 6 percentage point difference in interest rates. And on a ten-year loan, such an exchange-rate movement would be the equivalent of a difference in interest rates of only 15 basis points (0.15 percentage points).

This relationship between the time to maturity and the relative importance of interest-rate differentials and exchange-rate movements illustrates the importance of the smoothness of a parity movement in situations in which the spot rate is confidently expected to move in line with changes in parity. Suppose that adjustments in parities are made only quarterly. Then for one-month loans, each ½ per cent jump, *when it occurred,* would be the equivalent of a 6 percentage point difference in interest rates. A discrete 2 per cent jump under a

New Look Bretton Woods system would be the equivalent of an 8 percentage point difference in interest rates on three-month loans during the quarter in which it occurred.[17]

In the case of fairly smooth, continuous movements in exchange rates, as should occur under a system of sliding parities, we can extend the model of Section 2 to include exchange-rate expectations specifically by adding the expected rate of change of the price of domestic currency, $\dot{r}_e$, to the explanatory variables in the portfolio-distribution function (2). We can then rewrite (2) as

$$\frac{V^f}{V} = g(i^d, i^f, \dot{r}_e; Z'). \tag{10}$$

With any given i^d and i^f values, and exchange rates expected to remain constant so that $\dot{r}_e = 0$, a given proportion of portfolios will be held abroad. As portfolio size, V, grows, claims on foreigners, V^f, will grow, giving "normal" capital flows with given interest rates.

If, in this situation, the domestic currency begins to fall and the rate of decrease is expected to continue, $\dot{r}_e$ becomes negative and the desired proportion of portfolios held abroad, V^f/V, will rise, generating a stock-shift outflow of capital. To prevent this outflow, the domestic interest rate would have to rise relative to the foreign rate. This is the interest-rate constraint, in the framework of the stock-adjustment model.

But once this initial stock-shift is completed — over perhaps three quarters, on the evidence of Sections 3 and 4 — the continuing capital outflow due to the continuing crawl of the parity will be only a fraction of the initial shift. Furthermore, if the crawl slows, a reflow of capital will begin, and when the exchange rate reaches a new equilibrium, so that $\dot{r}_e$ returns to zero, this return flow should, ceteris paribus, be equal to the initial stock-shift plus the accumulated continuing flow effect of the temporary downward crawl of the parity.

This result simply says: if I hold a given proportion of my assets abroad with a given set of interest rates and a constant exchange rate, when the price of the domestic currency begins to fall I will transfer

---

[17] For further discussion of the comparative speculative incentives for short-term capital movements under alternative exchange-rate systems, see our contribution to Willett, Katz, and Branson [29].

more of my assets abroad to increase my return, and I will also transfer abroad a larger fraction of any additions to my portfolio. When the exchange rate stabilizes again, if interest rates have not changed and my portfolio was in equilibrium to begin with, I will transfer back both the initial asset-shift and the assets accumulated abroad due to the drop in the exchange rate.[18]

The estimates of Section 3 suggest, for example, that the initiation of an upward crawl in the dollar price of foreign currencies of 1 per cent a year would lead to a stock-shift outflow of American short-term capital of about $0.7 billion, since this would be comparable to a one-point drop in the American interest rate relative to foreign rates. This would be followed by a continuing outflow of perhaps $50 million a year as long as the crawl continues. If the rate reached a new equilibrium after two years, the return flow would include both the original flow and the accumulation of the continuing flow *that was due to the crawl.*[19]

The constraint on interest rates should be compelling, therefore, only if the country's reserves were dangerously threatened by the temporary stock-shift outflow due to initiation of the crawl. When the rate reaches a new equilibrium, capital that left the country *due to expected exchange-rate movements* would return.

One way to ensure that countries retain freedom of monetary policy—freedom from the "interest-rate constraint"—would be to arrange for official recycling of funds that flow in response to changes in r_e under a sliding parity. Our estimates in Section 3 indicate that such movements would not be so large that they could not usually be handled in this manner. The prospect that the loans under a recycling agreement would be repaid when the rate reaches a new equilibrium should reduce opposition to recycling, and a recycling agreement should reduce opposition to a sliding-parity system, thus improving both the short-run and long-run stability of the system.[20]

---

[18] A numerical example of this process is given in Willett, Katz, and Branson [29, p. 9].

[19] We should note that the appropriate measure of the interest-rate constraint is how much interest rates would have to be raised above the level desired for domestic purposes in order to keep capital from flowing in response to a change in $\dot{r}_e$. Often the factor leading to a change in $\dot{r}_e$ would also move the desired level of domestic interest rates in the direction dictated by the change in $\dot{r}_e$. See Willett, Katz, and Branson [29, pp. 5–6].

[20] This is discussed at greater length in Willett, Katz, and Branson [29, pp. 31–34].

REFERENCES

1. Brainard, William C., and Tobin, James, "Pitfalls in Financial Model Building." *American Economic Review,* Vol. LVIII, No. 2 (May, 1968).
2. Branson, William H., *Financial Flows in the U.S. Balance of Payments.* Amsterdam, North-Holland Publishing Co., 1968.
3. Despres, Emile, Kindleberger, Charles R., and Salant, Walter S., "The Dollar and World Liquidity: A Minority View." *The Economist* (London), February 5, 1966, reprinted with additional material by The Brookings Institution as Reprint 115, April, 1966.
4. Einzig, Paul, *Leads and Lags.* New York, St. Martin's Press, 1968.
5. Feldstein, Martin S., "Uncertainty and Forward Exchange Speculation." *Review of Economics and Statistics,* Vol. L, No. 2 (May, 1968).
6. Gray, H. Peter, "Fiscal-Monetary Mix and Full Employment External Balance: Two Addenda." Unpublished manuscript.
7. Grubel, Herbert Gunter, *Forward Exchange, Speculation and the International Flow of Capital.* Stanford, Stanford University Press, 1966.
8. ——— "Internationally Diversified Portfolios: Welfare Gains and Capital Flows." *American Economic Review,* Vol. LVIII, No. 5 (December, 1968).
9. Haberler, Gottfried, and Willett, Thomas D., *U.S. Balance-of-Payments Policies and International Monetary Reform.* Washington, D.C., American Enterprise Institute for Public Policy Research, 1968.
10. Halm, George N., "International Financial Intermediation: Deficits Benign and Malignant." *Princeton Essays in International Finance,* No. 68 (June, 1968). Princeton, Princeton University Press, 1968.
11. Hansen, Bent, *Foreign Trade Credits and Exchange Reserves.* Amsterdam, North-Holland Publishing Co., 1961.
12. Katz, Samuel I., "Leads and Lags in Sterling Payments." *Review of Economics and Statistics,* Vol. XXXV, No. 1 (February, 1953).

13. —— *External Surpluses, Capital Flows, and Credit Policy in the European Economic Community, 1958 to 1967.* Princeton Study in International Finance, No. 22, 1969.
14. Laffer, Arthur B., "Short-term Capital Movements and the Voluntary Foreign Credit Restraint Program." Unpublished manuscript.
15. Lee, Chan H. "A Stock-Adjustment Analysis of Capital Movements: The United States–Canadian Case." *Journal of Political Economy,* Vol. 77, No. 4 (July-August 1969).
16. Levin, Jay H., *Forward Exchange and Internal-External Studies Equilibrium.* Ann Arbor, Michigan International Business Studies, No. 12, 1970.
17. Lutz, Friedrich, "Monetary Rates of Interest, Real Rates of Interest and Capital Movements," in Fellner *et al., Maintaining and Restoring Balance in International Payments.* Princeton, Princeton University Press, 1966.
18. Markowitz, Harry M., *Portfolio Selection: Efficient Diversification of Investments.* New York, John Wiley, 1959.
19. Officer, Lawrence H., and Willett, Thomas D., "The Covered Arbitrage Schedule: A Critical Survey of Recent Developments." *The Journal of Money, Credit, and Banking* (May, 1970).
20. Stiglitz, Joseph E., "The Effects of Income, Wealth, and Capital Gains Taxation on Risk-Taking." *Quarterly Journal of Economics,* Vol. LXXXIII, No. 2 (May, 1969).
21. Tobin, James, "Liquidity Preference as Behavior Towards Risk." *Review of Economic Studies* (February, 1958).
22. Triffin, Robert, "The Balance of Payments and the Foreign Investment Position of the United States," *Princeton Essays in International Finance,* No. 55 (September, 1966). Princeton, Princeton University Press, 1966.
23. White, William H., "Interest Rate Differences, Forward Exchange Mechanism, and Scope for Short-Term Capital Movements." *International Monetary Fund Staff Papers,* Vol. X, No. 3 (November, 1963).
24. Willett, Thomas D., "The Influence of the Trade Balance and Export Financing on International Short-Term Capital Movements: A Theoretical Analysis," *Kyklos,* Vol. XXII, fasc. 2, 1969.
25. —— "Interest Arbitrage and the Absolute Level of Interest

Rates." *Revista Internazionale de Scienze e Commerciali,* No. 2, 1968.

26. ——— "Official Versus Market Financing of International Deficits." *Kyklos,* Vol. XXI, fasc. 2, 1968.

27. ——— *A Portfolio Theory of International Short-Term Capital Movements, With a Critique of Recent U.S. Empirical Studies.* Unpublished Ph.D. dissertation, University of Virginia, 1967.

28. ——— and Forte, F., "Interest-Rate Policy and External Balance." *Quarterly Journal of Economics,* Vol. LXXXIII, No. 2 (May, 1969).

29. ——— Katz, Samuel I., and Branson, William H., "Exchange-Rate Systems, Interest Rates, and Capital Flows." *Princeton Essays in International Finance,* No. 78, January, 1970.

COMMENTS

M. JUNE FLANDERS

PURDUE UNIVERSITY

Studies such as these are welcome additions to the literature on optimum policies for an open economy. In the conventional neo-Keynesian theory, the monetary authorities in a closed economy can control either the money supply or the rate of interest. In the models of an open economy built by Mundell and others — and represented at this conference by Floyd's paper, for example — the monetary authorities can influence either the exchange rate or the balance of payments. They have, however, no power to affect (let alone determine) domestic monetary magnitudes. The reason for this, of course, is the assumption that international capital movements are infinitely elastic with respect to interest-rate differentials.

In the real world of the 1970's there are probably few countries which are either completely "closed" or "small" in the Mundellian sense. Thus, for example, the Federal Reserve Board has been understandably chagrined but not-so-understandably surprised that a tight-

COMMENT BY FLANDERS • 311

ening at home has induced an inflow of short-term capital from abroad. While the Federal Reserve Board decries the weakening of its control over domestic monetary conditions, neither the Board nor anyone else has denied that its influence remains substantial. We have, therefore, neither of the two extremes of the models described above: the elasticity of demand for foreign assets is clearly neither zero nor infinity. Qualitative solutions to the model are therefore nonexistent and we must seek quantitative solutions. Now the precise size of the elasticities is important. Note, however, that in both papers only part of the international capital flow is being measured, namely the response of movements of American capital to differentials in interest rates here and abroad. Foreign claims on the United States are excluded. There is no reason to assume that the elasticities are the same in both directions, so that predictions as to the balance-of-payments impact of changes in interest rates could be misleading.

Both studies incorporate the notions of portfolio theory into an analysis of international capital movements and attempt to settle finally the stock versus flow argument which has persisted in this area. It turns out, after all, that everybody has been partly right. To the question, "Is the response of short-term capital to international differences in interest rates a stock adjustment or a flow?" the answer is, "Both." There is a stock adjustment as asset-holders find themselves out of equilibrium when the structure of world interest rates changes. There is a flow as the total portfolio of the asset-owners grows and a constant share of the increase is allocated to foreign assets. When interest rates change at home or abroad, this share of the increase changes. The flow thus generated is, however, small relative to the size of the initial stock adjustment. Changes in the flow are smaller yet in importance. In order to increase the international "flow" of capital (in the conventional sense), it is necessary to change interest rates repeatedly and thus to elicit continual stock adjustments. A more general model would, of course, have to allow for the impact of these changes in interest rates on the "scale variable" through a change in bond prices (which Branson and Willett recognize but do not treat) and perhaps, also, on its rate of increase if borrowing and investing decisions are influenced by the rate of interest.

Finally, in this general vein, we note that although the discussions here (and elsewhere) are in terms of responses to interest-rate *differentials*, neither of these studies specifies this formally. In both, desired holdings of foreign assets are functions of both foreign and domestic interest rates, but not necessarily of the difference between them. According to Branson and Willett, the coefficient of changes in foreign interest rates is smaller than that of domestic interest rates (in absolute value). The policy implication of this is that a rise in domestic interest rates would lead to a backflow of American capital even if foreign interest rates rose by the same number of percentage points; that is, even if the United States were a "large" (indicating the opposite of "small") country. It does not follow from this, of course, that the United States should continually boost its own, and therefore the world's, interest rates in order to eliminate or ameliorate its balance-of-payments problem. First, such a policy has numerous implications for growth rates, income distribution, and economic welfare in general. Second, these results of Branson and Willett are not entirely con-sonant with those of Miller and Whitman. In the latter paper, the co-efficient of foreign interest rates (the average of rates in four recipient countries), when significant, is somewhat greater than the absolute value of the coefficient of domestic interest rates. Whether the differences are significantly nonzero is not clear. In any case, the Branson and Willett result is not repeated here.

The similarities and differences between the empirical results of the two studies raise interesting questions. I shall state some of them (it being clearly understood that they are indeed questions). As far as I can tell, the major dependent variable is the same in both estimations: the stock of short-term claims on nongovernmental foreigners held by Americans at the ends of quarters. The denominator (Miller and Whitman) or scale variables (Branson and Willett) differ, however. Miller and Whitman have two alternatives. The first, A', is short-term U.S. government securities plus "bank loans, n.e.c." and "other loans," as reported in the Federal Reserve flow-of-funds tables. The second, A, is A' plus long-term U.S. government securities, state and local securities, mortgages, and corporate and foreign bonds. The former seems to perform somewhat better, but the difference is not dramatic. Branson and Willett, on the other hand, get good results using a much broader category, namely "net worth of households." One explanation of the similarity of results, despite the apparent differences in variables, is that the two variables used as normalizers are highly correlated with one another.

A second difference, more puzzling, is that Branson and Willett estimate a demand equation (at any rate, they call it a demand equation), and Miller and Whitman say that they are estimating a reduced form of two equations, demand and supply. Yet the results are similar, and the estimating equations are similar, at any rate in the major independent variables. That is, the coefficient of the domestic interest rate is expected to be negative; the coefficient of the foreign interest rate is expected to be positive. To be sure, there are differences between the estimating equations, but not, it seems, in any important respect that distinguishes between a demand equation and a reduced-form equation. One possible explanation of this is that the supply of foreign assets to Americans is infinite. The analytical model of Miller and Whitman emphasizes "borrowing" on the part of foreigners. The supply of assets matters, because foreigners choose where to borrow, and they worry about the variance of the expected rate they must pay for loans from the United States (including both expected changes in the exchange rate and the cost of being cut off from domestic sources of funds at some point in the future if they become too dependent on American lenders). The reduced-form equation, like Branson and Willett's demand equation (and like my own view of the world), pictures Americans taking the initiative and anonymously purchasing transferable financial assets in the money and capital markets of foreign countries, or simply making deposits in foreign banks. The Miller and Whitman view of the world may be more accurate, but they have been unable to test it, since they substitute rates on treasury bills and call money for the "loan rate" which they were unable to observe, and are, moreover, unable to find a suitable proxy for expected changes in the exchange rate. At the same time, neither Miller and Whitman nor Branson and Willett are able, in their estimations, to assure us that there is, in fact, no simultaneity; that American lending does not affect foreign interest rates (which according to the foreign press, it does)—in short, that the United States is not a "large" country.

Finally, as a general reaction to both studies, it is disturbing that things should apparently work out so well in the absence of any consideration in the estimations of actual or expected exchange rates. First, the interest rates used in the estimations are uncovered rates, and yet differences in recipient countries' forward-rate policies (both between countries and over time) do not appear to have mattered. Perhaps, however, they did. This may be the reason why, in general, foreign interest rates are poorer explanatory variables than domestic rates, and why the studies get different results with respect to the relationship between the coefficients of domestic and foreign rates of interest. Secondly, expectations of changes in exchange rates appear not to have mattered. This may be fortuitous, however. The worst of the flights from sterling, for example, do not coincide with the divergences between actual and predicted values for capital outflow in the 1964–68 period, as computed by Branson and Willett. This may be due to the fact that the United Kingdom is evidently not a major recipient of United States short-term capital. But this, in turn, raises the question of why the United Kingdom Treasury bill rate is the only foreign interest rate to yield satisfactory results in the Branson and Willett study. Possibly this bill rate is a proxy for something else, perhaps the Eurodollar rate. In short, at the risk of appearing ungracious, I would argue that it is incumbent upon the authors to explain why their results are so good.

RUDOLF R. RHOMBERG
INTERNATIONAL MONETARY FUND

The two papers presented in this session are concerned with the sensitivity of the outflow of short-term capital from the United States to factors influencing it, such as changes in interest rates and merchandise exports, or the Government's capital restraint program. Estimation of these influences is the main purpose of the paper by Miller and Whitman. Branson and Willett also estimate equations explaining these short-term capital flows and use them to illustrate certain general conclusions for policy toward capital movements. This comment will be divided into: (1) some remarks on general methodological questions raised by these papers; (2) a review of the econometric techniques and results; and (3) observations on the policy conclusions drawn by Branson and Willett.

GENERAL METHODOLOGICAL PROBLEMS

The first question concerns a fundamental point: Should the determinants of short-term capital flows be assessed in isolation from the movements of other capital-account items and (most) current-account magnitudes? A number of reflections render this approach dubious.

First, movements of short-term capital are directly dependent not only on merchandise exports (trade financing), but also on other items of the balance of payments. For instance, changes in long-term capital flows may induce, or be accompanied by, short-term capital flows in the opposite direction when the proceeds of long-term loans are not immediately transferred.

Second, short-term capital movements and the rest of the balance of payments are indirectly interdependent through the adjustment mechanism. Under freely fluctuating exchange rates, without official intervention in the exchange market, short-term movements, which (especially in the very short run) tend to show a higher responsiveness to the exchange rate than other components of the balance of payments, are determined by the sum of the other components, with the exchange rate moving so as to achieve this balance. The par-value system is characterized by a combination of official intervention (reserve changes) and exchange-rate movements within permitted margins. Compared with a system of floating rates, under this system the balance-of-payments adjustment function of short-term capital movements (through response to changes in exchange rates) is somewhat lessened, but it is not entirely absent. If components of the balance of payments were to be ordered in sequence from the most nearly autonomous (say, private remittances or contractual interest payments) to the most nearly "accommodating," the category of short-term capital movements as a whole would doubtless hold a place near the "accommodating" end of the list. This accommodation is achieved partly through the exchange-rate mechanism and partly in other ways. Even if the equation for the flow of short-term capital adequately reflected these relations, there would still be the problem of consistent estimation of its coefficients within this system of simultaneous equations; a single-equation approach would be found wanting.

Third, the same question could be raised within the framework of the portfolio approach, which is employed in both papers under discussion: Is the over-all portfolio of domestic and foreign assets decomposable in this particular way, and can the portfolio approach be separately applied to long-term and short-term assets without explicit allowance for any interaction between these portfolios? To be sure, the size of each of the two portfolios, short-term and long-term — or for that matter, the size of any other subportfolio — may be known ex post. It may also be possible to explain the distribution of such a subportfolio among component assets by reference to variables expressing rates of return and riskiness. But it will not be possible to explain or forecast changes in one of the components — say, short-term capital movements — because the size of each of these subportfolios cannot be explained or forecast unless the problem of the distribution of the total portfolio among the various subportfolios has been solved.

These reflections suggest that econometric work on short-term capital movements should ultimately be based on a general-equilibrium model covering the entire balance of payments and all domestic and foreign assets, real and financial. This observation is not, however, meant as a criticism of the pioneering work under discussion, even though it may fall short of ideal, as yet unattainable, standards.

I now turn more briefly to three other general questions. What has been said so far acquires additional weight in view of the fact that exchange rates, though in principle part of the models used in the two papers, do not in practice enter the functions expressing short-term capital flows. In the theoretical formulation, both papers include exchange-rate influences (Miller and Whitman explicitly, Branson and Willett in the catchall variable) but are forced to leave them out of the estimating equations for lack of a satisfactory proxy for expected exchange rates. The resulting equations would thus properly reflect short-term capital movements in a single-currency area. If exchange-rate expectations play an important role in the explanation of short-term capital movements (and they could hardly fail to do so), and if they are correlated with changes in interest rates (as is also likely), the estimated sensitivity of short-term capital movements to changes in interest rates is likely to be biased. For instance, a downward bias would result if foreign interest rates were raised when foreign currencies were expected to depreciate vis-à-vis the U.S. dollar. The conceptual and statistical difficulties of finding appropriate exchange-rate variables for inclusion in equations for short-term capital movements are clearly formidable.

In econometric work on capital movements, the question of geographic aggregation, or disaggregation, is particularly troublesome. On the one hand, there is no easy way to express divergent financial conditions in various partner countries through a few summary variables, like the interest rate, or the expected exchange rate, in the rest of the world. On the other hand, a bilateral model estimating capital flows to a particular partner country (as in Bryant and Hendershott's paper in this volume) must be essentially incomplete, since it is implausible to suppose that financial conditions—say, interest rates—in third countries would not influence the bilateral capital movements in question. Branson and Willett use interest rates in two foreign countries, dropping one of them in the course of the investigation. Miller and Whitman use an unweighted average of four foreign interest rates. To make further progress in this regard, it may be necessary to develop an explicit multinational model without, at the same time, running afoul of the constraint imposed on statistical estimation by the available degrees of freedom. Conceivably such a development could follow the lines of the market-shares approach used in trade models, with the shares assumed to be influenced by relative interest rates, expected exchange rates, and similar factors.

A final methodological comment relates to the practice of "estimation by proxy." Models are often being constructed to a large extent in terms of unobservables, actual estimation being carried out with the help of a set of proxy variables. Sometimes the relation between the theoretical variable and its proxy is quite tenuous (e.g., Miller and Whitman use deviations from trend of GNP for the riskiness of domestic assets and a time trend for the riskiness of foreign assets). Statistical tests cannot confirm or refute the postulated relation between the unobservable theoretical variables and their proxies. The estimated structure is consistent with any theory that could have been tested with the help of the same set of proxies, and conclusions with respect to the confirmation of the theory presumably being tested must be drawn with caution. It has been found that econometric work must often be preceded by a reconstruction of received theory so as to make it testable in terms of observable phenomena. In the area of capital movements, this reconstruction of theory has not yet been brought to a very satisfactory level of development.

ECONOMETRIC TECHNIQUES AND RESULTS

Branson and Willett follow a portfolio approach, which is simplified by omission of any explicit representation of the riskiness of assets. This formulation of the model, by itself, allows them to draw some interesting conclusions with respect to the distinction between stock-shift and flow effects of changes in interest rates. In the application, however, they deviate from a strict portfolio approach by introducing, in addition to portfolio considerations, separate effects of changes in exports, reflecting trade financing apparently unrelated to rates of return and portfolio size. Although this separation of trade financing from the remainder of the portfolio may be indicated for practical reasons, logically it is not fully satisfactory. For one thing, it is difficult to think of the volume of export financing as being unaffected by the total volume of funds available for placement. Moreover, once exclusions from the portfolio model are allowed, there is no reason to stop at export financing: variables explaining many other types of borrowing that may at first glance appear to be independent of the size of the lender's total portfolio could be introduced as separate additive factors determining capital movements. In order to preserve a consistent portfolio approach, the possibility of allowing the volume of export financing to be determined within the portfolio model may be worth considering. The yield of this type of investment would then have to be represented by a shadow rate of return, reflecting the profit on the exports that are being financed.

The choice of interest-rate variables and their lag structure seems to have been determined largely by statistical criteria. In the equation estimated by Branson and Willett for the period 1960–64 (Table 2), the American interest rate lagged by one and two periods, the Canadian interest rate not lagged and lagged by one period, and the British interest rate not lagged are taken to affect outflows of U.S. short-term capital (although only the American interest rate lagged by two periods seems to be statistically significant at the 95 per cent confidence level). In the corresponding equation estimated for the period 1960–68 (Table 3), only the American interest rate, lagged by two periods, and the British interest rate, not lagged—both significant—are retained as interest-rate variables. Moreover, the effect of the American interest rate, though long delayed, is quite strong, while the effect of the British interest rate, though immediate, is relatively weak. It would be difficult to find a theoretical justification for such a time pattern of interest-rate effects. It may be that an explicit formulation in terms of distributed lags might be preferable. In both equations the effect of the domestic interest rate on movements of American short-term capital is stronger than the effect of foreign interest rates; but in view of the uncertainties with respect to the time pattern of these effects, of the selective use of only one or two foreign interest rates, and of the low level of significance of the estimates, undue importance should not be attached to this finding.

In the equation fitted to data extending to 1968, it would be desirable to take cognizance of the gold and exchange-rate crises that occurred during the last part of the period, which must be presumed to have had effects on flows of American short-term capital. It is true, however, that the equation explains a large proportion of the variation in capital outflows, even without any allowance for the effects of changes in exchange-rate expectations. In this equation the effect of the Government's capital-control program is indicated by two additive dummy variables. Here, again, the question arises as to whether it might not be preferable to test for these effects within the framework of the portfolio approach (which would require a modification of the portfolio ratio, rather than a reduction of the capital outflow by an absolute amount, as a result of the restraint program).

Miller and Whitman develop a very imaginative double-portfolio approach, in which the demand side is represented by the asset-portfolio ratio, which depends on yields of domestic and foreign short-term assets and their respective riskiness, and the supply side by a liabilities-portfolio ratio, which depends on the cost of borrowing in the United States and elsewhere, and on the respective riskiness associated with these borrowing costs. Under the assumption that the ratio of the total American portfolio of short-term assets to the total foreign portfolio of liabilities is constant, a reduced-form equation for the equilibrium ratio in the American short-term portfolio is derived and a pattern of adjustment of actual to optimal portfolio ratios specified.

Be it for reasons of the inherent merit of this sophisticated model or because of a wise choice of proxy variables, the empirical results appear quite promising. It is remarkable that an explanation of up to three-fourths of the total variation in changes in the portfolio ratio is achieved (although the explanatory power of the equation may be aided by the use of seasonally unadjusted data and the inclusion of seasonal dummy variables). The preferred equation for the portfolio ratio implies an explanation of quarterly flows of American short-term capital amounting to over 83 per cent of the total variations in this flow over the observation period.

A comparison of some of the results of the two papers shows that considerable uncertainty still exists regarding the magnitude of some of the estimated effects. For instance, Branson and Willett estimate that the effect of a change of 1 percentage point in the domestic interest rate has a much larger effect on the flow of American capital than does a change of 1 per cent in the foreign interest rate; Miller and Whitman estimate that the opposite is the case. While the results obtained by Miller and Whitman, working with the period 1959–67, for the effect of changes in domestic interest rates are roughly comparable with the equation estimated by Branson and Willett for the period 1960–64, their stock-shift effect is about three times that found by Branson and Willett in the equation applying to the longer period, 1960–68. An even larger discrepancy is found in the estimates of the effect of a change in foreign interest rates. Here the difficulties in connection with geographic disaggregation and the choice of foreign interest rates discussed above may play a major role.

POLICY IMPLICATIONS

Branson and Willett draw some interesting conclusions that follow directly from the portfolio approach to the explanation of movements of short-term capital (rather than from the particular parameter estimates contained in their paper). This approach implies that the continuing (flow) effects of changes in interest rates would tend to be small relative to the once-for-all stock-adjustment effects of such changes. What is true for the effects of interest-rate changes would also apply to the impact of changes in the rate of change of the exchange rate. With this thought in mind, the authors make an interesting contribution to the current discussion on interest-rate policy under the crawling-peg system. In order to offset through interest-rate policy the effect of an expected change in the exchange rate on movements of short-term capital, the difference between domestic and foreign interest rates would have to be adjusted by the expected annual percentage change in the exchange rate. But only a temporary adjustment is required. Once the exchange rate has found its new equilibrium level, the interest differential can, other things being equal, be returned to its former value. Moreover, if the effect of exchange-rate expectations under the crawling-peg system were not to be offset by interest policy, expected changes in exchange rates would only temporarily affect monetary reserves through movements of short-term capital, this effect being reversed as soon as the exchange rate is no longer expected to continue its rise or decline. As a result, monetary authorities would tend to be more favorably disposed, Branson and Willett feel, toward "recycling" the funds that may at times move temporarily in one direction or another in response to expectations regarding the direction and rate of change of crawling movements of par values.

This point is well taken, as far as it goes, and its acceptance would appear to weaken one objection to the crawling-peg system; namely, that it would severely constrain national interest-rate policy. There are, however, two sides to this consideration. Since the mere cessation of a previous trend in the exchange rate will tend to reverse the short-term capital flow that was induced when that trend came to be expected, it is unlikely that the exchange rate will remain close to its new equilibrium level following a period during which it had been rising or falling; instead, it will tend to reverse its course. In view of the uncertainty that exists with respect to the magnitude and timing of the sensitivity of short-term capital movements, one cannot exclude the possibility that a crawling-peg system, under which the par value responds by formula to past exchange rates or reserve movements, may be unstable — at any rate, within the limits imposed by the speed with which the par value would be adjusted and the permitted margins on either side of par. Proponents of the crawling-peg system are attracted by the notion that exchange rates would gradually drift in a direction indicated by longer-run tendencies of the balance of payments. If this consideration were to cause par values to fluctuate around a constant level, or around their longer-run trend, in response to movements of short-term capital induced by the very expectation of these fluctuations, the performance of this system would be impaired, even though the effects of these fluctuations on reserves could be mitigated through the technique of recycling operations among monetary authorities.

CAPITAL MOBILITY AND THE INTERNATIONAL FIRM

GUY V. G. STEVENS · Federal Reserve Board

1 INTRODUCTION

THE explanation and prediction of the capital flows associated with the international firm is a timely and long-neglected undertaking. Direct foreign investment by corporations from the United States has long been a part of our program to encourage foreign economic development and, more recently, the object of progressively more stringent regulation in the name of protecting the balance of payments, yet the theoretical and empirical study of the relations between capital flows and the activities of the international firm has barely begun. Symptomatic of this state of affairs is the fact that, after five years of government controls on direct investment, we have yet to have any econometrically defensible estimates of the impact of these controls.

This paper has three goals:

1. to develop a theoretical model, consistent with the maximization of the market value of the firm, in order to explain some important capital flows associated with the international firm—those flows financing asset accumulations abroad;

2. to test the above model and an alternative suggested by the Department of Commerce against aggregate data for direct investment in manufacturing, the one sector for which minimally adequate data are available; and

3. to estimate the impact of the voluntary and mandatory balance-of-payments programs on asset accumulations and their financing by foreign manufacturing affiliates of firms in the United States.[1]

[1] The author gratefully acknowledges the comments and constructive criticism of Michael Adler, Phillip Berlin, Edward Ettin, George Kopits, Peter Tinsley, Walter Salant, and the discussants Sidney Robbins and Robert Stobaugh. His thanks go to the Federal Reserve Board and the Brookings Institution for supporting this research. Needless to say, none of the above individuals or institutions are responsible for the author's opinions or the paper's remaining errors.

CAPITAL FLOWS TO BE CONSIDERED

The capital flows this paper will seek to explain are the flows popularly called "direct investment," its components, and the borrowing by foreign affiliates from foreign sources.

The flow of direct investment, as that term is used in this paper (and as defined by the U.S. Department of Commerce), is a measure of the change in the ownership position of the United States—or the change in net worth of the United States—in the foreign affiliates of American firms; the stock corresponding to this flow will be called the stock of direct investments or, as named by the Commerce Department, the value of direct investments abroad (V).[2] The flow of direct investment (ΔV) is broken up by the Department of Commerce into the U.S. share of retained earnings of foreign affiliates (RE) and the net capital outflow from the United States (NKO).[3] The first of these, of course, is the difference between the American share of the subsidiaries' earnings (E) and repatriated dividends (DIV).

Capital flows, and particularly the flow of direct investment, have been, and should be, of major policy interest. In measuring the net flow of financial resources from the United States to the host country, the flow of direct investment is an important indicator of the contribution of foreign affiliates to the development of the host country, the oldest goal of direct-investment policy. Currently, the regulation of the flow of direct investment is a major part of our balance-of-payments policy. The immediate alternative cost for the balance of payments of a given flow of direct investment is precisely equal to the value of that flow—although only a part of it directly enters the balance of payments as officially reported. This observed balance-of-payments effect is equal to the net capital outflow minus repatriated dividends.

[2] Unfortunately there seems to be no unambiguous reference to the official definition of "the flow of direct investment" or the "value of direct investments." See, however, U.S. Department of Commerce, *U.S. Business Investments in Foreign Countries*. Washington, D.C., 1960, pp. 77–78.
[3] The net capital outflow consists of changes in American claims on all liability accounts of foreign affiliates (with the exception of bank loans from the United States and certain commercial claims reported elsewhere in the balance of payments) *plus* all changes in the share of net worth and surplus accounts of the United States which are unaccounted for by the American share of retentions.

2 THEORETICAL CONSIDERATIONS

THE SCOPE OF PREVIOUS ADVANCES

Starting in the very recent past, there has been a slow accumulation of theoretical and empirical findings about the foreign operations of American firms.[4] These studies have demonstrated that theoretical ideas successful in explaining domestic business operations – especially investment activity – can be applied to the activities of foreign affiliates. However, none of these studies, including one by this author, has fully incorporated the implications of recent advances in the theory of corporate finance for the explanation of capital flows associated with the international firm.

Further, probably because of the paucity of time-series data, most of the empirical work so far completed has been limited to the analysis of cross sections, thus circumscribing its applicability to forecasting and policy problems. Of previous empirical studies, only one has been used for the purpose of explaining and predicting the aggregate capital flows associated with international firms. That study was developed, appropriately enough, by the Department of Commerce, the government agency in charge of the various balance-of-payments programs as they affect direct investment.[5] Although little publicized, the model

[4] Here is a partial list of recent contributions: Gary C. Hufbauer and F. M. Adler, *Overseas Manufacturing Investment and the Balance of Payments,* Washington, D.C., 1968; Stephen Hymer, *The International Operation of National Firms: A Study in Direct Foreign Investment,* unpublished Ph.D. dissertation, MIT, 1960; Samuel Morley, *American Corporate Investment Abroad Since 1919,* unpublished Ph.D. dissertation, University of California, Berkeley, 1966; Joel Popkin, *Inter-Firm Differences in Direct Investment Behavior of U.S. Manufacturers,* unpublished Ph.D. dissertation, University of Pennsylvania, 1965; Alan K. Severn, "Investment and Financial Behavior of American Direct Investors in Manufacturing," this conference, 1970; James Moose, *U.S. Direct Investment Abroad in Manufacturing and Petroleum – A Recursive Model,* unpublished Ph.D. dissertation, Harvard, 1968; Guy V. G. Stevens, "Fixed Investment Expenditures of Foreign Manufacturing Affiliates of U.S. Firms: Theoretical Models and Empirical Evidence," *Yale Economic Essays,* Spring, 1969.

[5] This model is partially described in Andrew F. Brimmer, "Direct Investment and Corporate Adjustment Techniques Under the Voluntary U.S. Balance of Payments Program," *Journal of Finance* (May, 1966), pp. 266–282. Details have been supplied to the author in conversations with members of the Balance of Payments Division, Office of Business Economics, Department of Commerce.

has special importance, having been put to forecasting use, and thereby becoming instrumental in the formulation of the balance-of-payments programs of 1965–67. The model, however, has serious deficiencies. As is argued below, it is not complete enough to allow any estimation of the impact of economic policies like the balance-of-payments programs on the capital flows considered in this paper. Moreover, in my opinion, it is completely without theoretical justification.

AN AGGREGATIVE TIME-SERIES MODEL

The flow of direct investment and its components, which we have singled out for explanation, constitute a subset of the numerous alternative methods for financing the asset changes of foreign affiliates. We shall argue here for some causal relationships between the changes in assets and the accompanying financial flows. In addition, we propose an accounting identity linking the changes in the value of asset accumulations (ΔA) to changes (flows) in the various liability (ΔL) and net-worth (ΔNW) accounts of foreign affiliates:

$$\sum_i \Delta A_i = \sum_i \Delta L_i + \sum_i \Delta NW_i. \qquad (1)$$

We shall construct a model, simple enough to be estimated, using aggregate time-series data, which breaks down the asset and liability sides of the above identity into five variables:

(a) the change in current assets (ΔCA);

(b) the change in net fixed assets (ΔNK), which, in turn, equals plant and equipment expenditure (PE) minus depreciation (DEP);

(c) the flow of direct investment, that is, the change in liabilities and net worth owed to the parent company (ΔV);

(d) the change in liabilities and net worth owed to foreigners (ΔF), i.e., non-U.S. residents; and

(e) a residual flow of liabilities (u_0), small in magnitude and here hypothesized to be essentially random, made up of changes in certain commercial claims and bank loans to foreign subsidiaries.[6]

[6] See Appendix B for the estimated size of this residual, 1957–65.

As indicated above, the flow of direct investment can be broken down into its component parts if such a breakdown is desired.

At the minimum, then, we have four endogenous variables and a random residual, linked by an accounting identity:

$$\Delta CA + \Delta NK = \Delta V + \Delta F + u_0. \tag{2}$$

To close the system we need three additional independent equations.

Financial Equations and the Modigliani-Miller Theorem

Any attempt to construct equations that explain financial flows must deal immediately with the now famous propositions of Modigliani and Miller, the first of which states that, given certain assumptions, the financing mix of the firm as between equity and liabilities is indeterminate.[7] In a Modigliani-Miller world, any financial plan chosen by the firm is as good as any other in maximizing the market value of the firm. In particular, it does not matter how the firm divides the financing of its foreign assets (ΔA) between capital flows from the United States (ΔV) and foreign sources (ΔF).

The implication is that, given the goal of maximizing the market value of the firm, we can derive equations for the optimal level of each asset, but we can derive none for the liabilities and equity in our model, the primary variables of interest.

If one wishes to derive equations for foreign funds and/or the flow of direct investment, he must choose one of the following courses:

1. reject the Modigliani-Miller theorem, either (a) by rejecting the maximization of the market value of the firm or (b) by rejecting one or more of the assumptions on which its rests (identical supply curves of finance for investors and firms; no transactions costs or bankruptcy costs; no interest deductions for the purpose of company taxation, and so on); or

2. accept the Modigliani-Miller theorem and the maximization of the present value of the firm, but use the extra degrees of freedom presented by financial indeterminacy to impose additional constraints or goals on the firm—constraints that will lead to financial determinacy

[7] Franco Modigliani and M. H. Miller, "The Cost of Capital, Corporation Finance and the Theory of Investment." *American Economic Review*, Vol. XLVIII, No. 3 (June, 1958), pp. 261–297.

but that are not inconsistent with the maximization of the present value of the firm.

Here I am going to take the second course. The financial indeterminacy implied by the acceptance of the Modigliani-Miller theorem will be overcome by postulating a secondary goal of the firm, the minimization of the risk of losses due to exchange-rate fluctuations. The empirical results presented later in this paper indicate that this hypothesis is broadly consistent with the available data. It should be emphasized, however, that this consistency does not imply that the data necessarily are inconsistent with models based on a rejection of the Modigliani-Miller theorem or their assumptions. That question is still open—one of many in this field on which much more research should be done.

Minimization of Exchange-Rate Losses and the Determination of Financial Flows

In the normative literature on financing international operations, there has been considerable emphasis on self-protection against capital losses caused by devaluations.[8] Major emphasis is frequently put on borrowing in the same currency in which assets are denominated.

According to the Modigliani-Miller propositions, such hedging activity should not lead to any increase in the market value of the firm, because the corporation has no advantage in this sort of financial operation over ordinary investors—or some investors. However, given the degrees of freedom the firm has in its financial policy, a goal of minimizing exchange-rate losses is quite compatible with maximizing the market value of the firm.

In Appendix A, I shall formalize this model and derive specific equations for the optimal value of borrowings in a given foreign currency. I postulate that the measure of risk the company uses is the variance of its worldwide profits—operating profits plus capital gains. The hypothesis is that the company tries to minimize this variance subject to its balance-sheet constraint.

In this simplest of risk models, the firm borrows in each currency

---

[8] See, e.g., William D. Falcon, ed., *Financing International Operations*. New York, American Management Association, 1965.

up to the point where foreign borrowings are equal to the sum of net profits (after interest payments) earned in the foreign currency and the value of capital *denominated in that currency*. Thus, we have the following equation for borrowings (D_i) in a given foreign currency:[9]

$$D_i = \frac{GP_i}{1 + r_i} + \frac{qK_i}{1 + r_i},$$ (3)

where GP_i is profit exclusive of interest costs in a given currency i; qK_i is the value of assets denominated in currency i; r_i is the interest rate in market i.

Given rapid adjustment of actual borrowings to the equilibrium levels, we would expect the flow of foreign-currency borrowings to be a function of *changes* in the level of foreign-denominated assets and profits.

In the empirical section of this paper, I shall identify the changes in borrowings in foreign currencies with the observed magnitude (ΔF), the change in liabilities and net worth owed to foreign residents. The latter is an imperfect measure, since it contains some borrowings in dollars—e.g., Eurodollar borrowings for subsidiaries.[10] However, there is no way to correct for this deficiency. I shall assume further that the change in the value of assets denominated in foreign currencies is proportional to the change in the value of total assets (ΔA).

Asset Equations

What *does* matter for the maximization of value of the firm is the proper policy for the investment in real assets. As set out in Appendix A (and in more detail by others, for example, Jorgenson and Siebert),[11] the firm should invest in any asset, foreign or domestic, fixed or current, up to the point where the marginal-revenue product of each type of capital is equal to its shadow price—the latter a function of the

[9] The value of assets, qK_i, and the level of profits exclusive of interest costs, GP_i, are both determined by the process of maximizing the market value of the firm; therefore, they are predetermined with respect to borrowings.

[10] But it does not include the recent great quantities of Eurodollar borrowings by the U.S. *parent firm*.

[11] Dale W. Jorgenson and Calvin Siebert, "Optimal Capital Accumulation and Corporate Investment Behavior." *Journal of Political Economy*, Vol. 76, No. 6 (November/December, 1968), pp. 1123–1151.

firm's discount rate, the depreciation rate on the asset, and the prices of the capital goods and output. Assuming a Cobb-Douglas production function and some of the other simplifying assumptions proposed by Jorgenson, we get the following equations for the desired (equilibrium) levels of fixed (NK^*) and current assets (CA^*):

$$NK^* = \frac{a_1 pQ}{s + d_1},$$

and

$$CA^* = \frac{a_2 pQ}{s + d_2}, \tag{4}$$

where Q, p, and s are the firm's output and its price and discount rate; a_1 and a_2 are the elasticities of output with respect to fixed and current assets; d_1 and d_2 are the respective rates of depreciation.

Capital need not adjust instantaneously to its new equilibrium level. If it does not, observed investment may be a distributed lag of past changes of the independent variables.

COMPARISON WITH THE COMMERCE DEPARTMENT MODEL

The one direct-investment model so far put to practical use, the above-mentioned model by the Department of Commerce, has been described in print only once — and then only partially — in a 1966 article by Andrew Brimmer, then Assistant Secretary of Commerce.[12] This article makes it clear that the Commerce model, particularly its equation for net capital outflow, played a role in determining the form of the voluntary restraint programs for direct investment in 1965 and 1966.[13]

When described in its entirety, the Commerce model is sufficient to explain the flow of direct investment and of all its components — i.e., virtually all the capital flows from the United States associated with the international firm.[14]

The construction of the model is markedly different, however, from the one presented above. There are three equations, one each for

[12] Andrew F. Brimmer, *op. cit.*, pp. 262–282.
[13] *Ibid.*, Section VI, pp. 278–79.
[14] See footnote 5, above.

the three components of the flow of direct investment: net capital outflow, dividends repatriated to the United States, and the American share of the foreign subsidiaries' earnings. The explanation or prediction of direct investment is built up constructively as the sum of the three component variables.

The key causal equation in the Commerce model is one explaining net capital outflow (NKO) as an approximately constant proportion of the level of plant and equipment expenditures by foreign affiliates. A second equation explains repatriated dividends as a linear function of the American share of foreign subsidiaries' earnings. Finally, in an admittedly rough approximation, for forecasting purposes the American share of the subsidiaries' earnings was assumed to be a constant function of the stock of direct investments (or, perhaps, net fixed capital abroad).

To my knowledge, no theoretical justification has ever been offered for the model; nor can any be provided here. The preceding section discussed the hurdles that must be surmounted in order to derive capital-flow equations within the general framework of the maximization of the present value of the firm. These problems were not faced in the Commerce model. Moreover, it seems to me impossible to relate the key equations in the model—the equations for net capital outflow and repatriated dividends—to *any* reasonable goals that might be pursued by an international firm. Rather, the equations seem to be an arbitrary matching of financial and real flows. The equation for net capital outflow, for example, fails to indicate why, in financing plant and equipment expenditure, the firm discriminates among the seemingly perfect financial substitutes: net capital outflow, depreciation, and the retained earnings of subsidiaries. With respect to the dividend equation, again it is not clear why such a relationship should hold between two parts of the same business organization—even if it is operative between the firm and its stockholders.

Besides having these theoretical defects, the model is not complete enough to allow us to estimate the impact of recent balance-of-payments programs. No equation for plant and equipment expenditure appears in the Commerce model; the Department obtained its plant and equipment forecast directly from the major foreign investors. Hence there can be no estimate within the model of the impact of ac-

332 · INTERNATIONAL MOBILITY AND MOVEMENT OF CAPITAL

tual or proposed policies on plant and equipment expenditure. Without
such an estimate, there can be no estimate of the total effect of a policy
on net capital outflow or the flow of direct investment, even if the proposed equations are valid.

3 EMPIRICAL RESULTS

ANNUAL DATA AND SAMPLE [15]

The models developed in the previous section are tested below
against data for the aggregate international operations of the manufacturing sector. Where possible, the official data collected by the Office
of Business Economics have been used. Since some of the important
independent variables are unavailable for the period after 1965, these
official data were augmented by those collected by the McGraw-Hill
Company.[16] The period of fit varies, depending on data availability,
from 1957–65 to 1957–68.

RESULTS FOR THE PROPOSED MODEL

Plant and Equipment Expenditures

The maximization of the present value of the firm, as formulated
in Appendix A, leads to an equation for desired fixed capital in current
dollars (NK^*) in terms of expected output (Q), the elasticity of output
with respect to capital (a), the firm's discount rate (s), the rate of depreciation (d), and the price of output (p):

$$NK^* = \frac{apQ}{s+d}. \tag{5}$$

Alternatively, we might assume that there is a fixed (desired) ratio of

[15] For a list of the data used, see Appendix B.
[16] McGraw-Hill Department of Economics, *Survey of Foreign Operations,* annual
surveys, 1959 to present.

output to capital, due to fixed coefficients in production or lack of variation in the ratio of factor costs.[17]

The firm may not adjust completely to its level of desired capital within our period of observation, one year. Hence, in testing alternative investment functions, I have allowed for simple forms of lagged adjustment—due to building lags, costs dependent on the rate of investment, or differences between expected output and observed output.

Models with fixed or variable desired capital/output ratios performed about equally well. The time series is too short, the price data are too deficient, and the performance of the models is too similar, to permit a choice of one as clearly superior to the others.

The Jorgenson model, coupled with a distributed lag which is geometrical after the second year, led to the following estimated results: [18]

$$(PE_t - dNK_{t-1}) = -161.2 + 0.015(NK_t^* - NK_{t-1}^*)$$
$$(2.54)$$

$$+ \; 0.031(NK_{t-1}^* - NK_{t-2}^*) + 0.58(PE_{t-1} - dNK_{t-2}). \quad (6)$$
$$(4.59) \qquad\qquad\qquad (8.26)$$

$$R^2 = .98 \qquad SEE = 158.3 \qquad \text{No. Obs.} = 10$$

This function implies that a unit change in desired capital leads to $.015/a$ units of investment in the first year, $.031/a + .58(.015/a)$ in the second and, thereafter, 58 per cent of the previous year's change. Using realistic values for a, the elasticity of output with respect to capital, this rate of adjustment seems very low.

---

[17] Since the data on foreign capital-goods prices, actual rates of depreciation, and so forth are questionable or nonexistent, it will be important to test this kind of alternative model—for comparison purposes, at least.

[18] This functional form was first suggested to me by Sung Y. Kwack in some research he has done for the Brookings Econometric Model on the determinants of direct investment (preliminary manuscript, June, 1969).

In this and all subsequent equations, the t-ratios are presented in parentheses under each estimated coefficient. R^2 is the coefficient of determination; SEE is the standard error of the estimate; No. Obs. is the number of observations. Durbin-Watson statistics were calculated, but because of insufficient degrees of freedom, no tests could be performed. All asset regressions were done using undeflated value figures for the dependent variable. Bias in the estimated coefficients can therefore be introduced, especially in the NK terms, because additions to the existing capital stock were valued at prices of capital different from $q(t)$.

A simpler flexible accelerator with a constant output/capital ratio does just as well, or better.[19]

$$PE = -1111.0 + 0.42S_{t-1} + 0.081(S_t - S_{t-1}) - 0.92NK_{t-1}. \quad (7)$$
$$(10.82) \qquad (2.62) \qquad\qquad (8.44)$$

$$R^2 = .99 \qquad SEE = 120.5 \qquad No.\ Obs. = 11$$

The coefficient of the net-capital variable is the estimate of the depreciation rate minus the speed of adjustment. The estimated coefficient of $-.92$ indicates that the speed of adjustment of expected sales to actual sales is quite fast; expected sales during period t equal approximately $.19S(t) + .81S(t-1)$.[20]

Although this equation fits the data very well for the whole period 1958–68 — and, in fact, for all subperiods — it has its share of drawbacks. The intercept is unexplainably large in absolute value. The estimated coefficients, particularly the speed of adjustment, vary widely, though not in sign, when the regression is fitted on subperiods.

A final comment is in order concerning estimates of the impact of the various balance-of-payments programs that have constrained direct-investment activities in the past four years. To preview the evidence presented in the final section, virtually no impact of the various balance-of-payments programs on plant and equipment expenditures in manufacturing is shown. This conclusion was also reached for all of the other dependent variables in this model — but not, of course, for some important flows not covered here, especially parent company borrowing in foreign money markets.

Investment in Current Assets

Explanation of changes in the current assets of foreign manufacturing affiliates is hampered by the unusual shortness of the time se-

---

[19] This distributed lag was conceived as the result, not of building lags, but of lags created by expectations. Here we assume that the firm's expected sales at time t is a function of sales at times t and preceding periods. After the first term, the weights decline geometrically. See Zvi Griliches, "Distributed Lags: A Survey." *Econometrica,* Vol. 35, No. 1 (January, 1967), p. 24.

[20] $S^*(t) = aS_t + wS_{t-1} + wzS_{t-2} + wz^2S_{t-3} + \cdots + wz^nS_{t-n-1} + \cdots$. Here are the coefficients of the various terms: the coefficient of ΔS is ba, where b is the desired capital/output ratio; the coefficient of S_{t-1} is $bw + ba(1 - z)$; the coefficient of NK_{t-1} is $-(1 - z - d)$, where d is the rate of replacement of the capital stock. We assumed that $d = .08$ for the calculation in the text; then $z = 0$, $a = .19$. We assume that $a + w = 1$, so $w = .81$.

ries and the impossibility of breaking down the series into its component parts. The data on the level and changes in current assets are available from 1957 to 1965 only.

It is standard practice to assume that the desired level of each component of current assets — and, thus, the sum — is some function of expected output or sales. In Appendix A, I shall derive one such function in rather unsophisticated fashion. As far as the adjustment process is concerned, I would expect no building lags but admit the possibility of a degree of lagged adjustment due to expectational considerations.[21]

In fact, we can explain current-asset changes fairly well as a linear function of the change in sales — assuming no lags in adjustment and a constant capital/output ratio:

$$\Delta CA = 280.7 + 0.46 \Delta S.$$
$$(6.32)$$

$$R^2 = .87 \qquad SEE = 317.7 \qquad \text{No. Obs.} = 8$$

The fit can be improved somewhat by allowing for lagged adjustment:

$$\Delta CA = -478.9 + 0.29 S_t - 0.47 CA_{t-1}. \tag{8}$$
$$(2.79) \qquad (1.88)$$

$$R^2 = .95 \qquad SEE = 208.4 \qquad \text{No. Obs.} = 8$$

The Financial Flow Equations

One more behavior equation permits us to close our four-variable model. As detailed above and in Appendix A, we can obtain this equation by assuming that, in addition to attempting to maximize the firm's present value, the managers of the firm also seek to minimize the risk of losses due to devaluation. If all hedging against devaluation is done by borrowing in foreign currencies, we obtain the following equation for finance raised from foreign sources: [22]

---

[21] There is no term for unintended accumulations in the current-asset equation, even though such is normal when fitting equations for the individual current assets, taken alone. The reason is that the positive and negative unintended accumulations of the component current assets can be shown to cancel out.

[22] Funds borrowed from foreign sources is an imperfect measure of funds raised by subsidiaries in foreign currencies; some of the former can include dollar borrowings from foreigners or other foreign affiliates of American companies. This is, however, our only measure of foreign currency borrowings.

$$\Delta F = a\Delta A + \Delta E,$$

where a is the percentage of total asset changes denominated in foreign currencies, and ΔE is the change in foreign earnings or profits.

The results strongly support the role of asset changes in explaining borrowing from foreign sources, but reject that of earnings changes:

$$\Delta F = -292.1 + 0.58\Delta A - 0.47\Delta E.$$
$$(7.52) \qquad (0.54)$$

$$R^2 = .94 \qquad SEE = 209.6 \qquad No.\ Obs. = 9$$

Dropping the earnings-change variable, we obtain:

$$\Delta F = -281.3 + 0.55\Delta A. \tag{9}$$
$$(10.04)$$

$$R^2 = .94 \qquad SEE = 198.7 \qquad No.\ Obs. = 9$$

The empirical results only partly confirm the hypothesized risk-reduction theory of finance. Two reasons can be offered to explain the total insignificance of the change in earnings. It may be that other techniques, such as operations in the forward market, are used to protect the dollar value of profits denominated in foreign currencies. A further consideration, suggested by Robert Stobaugh, one of the discussants of this paper, is that the change in total assets may already measure the effect we are trying to capture by the use of the change in earnings. If, for example, earnings are accumulated and held in liquid balances abroad until the beginning of the new year before being transferred to the United States, the value of the change in total assets, measured as it is at year-end, would already incorporate the change in earnings. It can be shown, also, that this implication holds when profits are transferred to the United States more than once a year. In any case, whatever the significance of the poor result for the earnings-change variable, we have discovered a very strong regularity between funds raised from foreign sources and asset changes.[23]

Given the behavior equations for fixed and current assets and for

[23] While the discussants do not seem to attack the theoretical hypothesis that some debt denominated in foreign currency is raised to hedge losses on assets held abroad, they do object to the *empirical measure* for the change in assets denominated in foreign currencies: a constant proportion of the change in the value of total assets. In particular,

funds from foreign sources, if we make use of the approximate identity (2), $\Delta A = \Delta F + \Delta V + u_0$, the flow of direct investment (ΔV) is determined as a function of the other three variables and u_0. In view of our primary interest in ΔV and the unknown nature of u_0, we can go further and fit the implied equation for ΔV. Using the approximate identity and the final equation for ΔF, the following equation is implied:

$$\Delta V = a + (1 - b)\Delta A - u_0 - u_1, \tag{10}$$

where $\Delta F = -a + b\Delta A + u_1$. If the residual sources of finance, u_0, are indeed random with zero mean and, further, if u_0 is independent of the change in total assets, then the estimated coefficients of the two financial equations should be related to each other, as indicated in equations (10) above.

The fitted equation for the flow of direct investment shows a very close dependence on changes in total assets abroad:

$$\Delta V = 244.9 + 0.45\Delta A. \tag{11}$$
$$(22.3)$$

$$R^2 = .98 \qquad SEE = 72.0 \qquad No.\ Obs. = 9$$

The size of the estimated coefficients in relation to those from the equation for funds raised from foreign sources is strong evidence for

the discussants hypothesize that no fixed assets, and only a part of current assets, are affected by changes in exchange rates.

Theoretically, their argument is plausible. The model developed in Appendix A of this paper is a one-period model, which implicitly assumes that all capital gains and losses are realized at the end of each period. If a fixed asset is to be held with certainty until it falls apart, then, contrary to the implications of the above model, no capital losses will be realized. However, where there is the *possibility* of the sale of the fixed asset for foreign currency, then exchange-rate hedging makes sense.

In fact, despite the results presented by the discussants, the data that we all used indicate that a part of fixed-asset changes *is* hedged. Breaking down the change in total assets into the change in fixed assets (ΔNK) and current assets (ΔCA), we find upon rerunning equation (9) above that funds from non-U.S. sources (ΔF) are significantly related to changes in *both* current and fixed assets:

$$\Delta F = -339.9 + 0.76\Delta NK + 0.47\Delta CA$$
$$(6.49) \qquad (6.85)$$

$$R^2 = .99 \qquad SEE = 76.0 \qquad No.\ Obs. = 9$$

One surprise in the above material is that the coefficient on the fixed-asset term is larger than that for the current-asset term. All I can venture on this point is the statement that it is a surprise and a suitable question for further research.

our hypotheses about the nature of the residual sources of finance, u_0.[24]

Up to this point there has been no attempt to explain individually the three components of the flow of direct investment: net capital outflow, repatriated dividends, and foreign profits. In terms of the devaluation-risk-avoidance theory of finance, there is no warrant to do so and no implication that it can be done. However, it does seem justifiable to break out foreign profits and derive an equation for net capital outflow minus repatriated dividends ($NKO - DIV$), the part of the flow of direct investment that directly affects the balance of payments.[25] Subtracting E, the U.S. share of foreign earnings, from both sides of equation (11) above, we derive an equation for $NKO - DIV$. Estimating its coefficients, we get:

$$NKO - DIV = 290.3 + 0.47\Delta A - 1.08E. \qquad (12)$$
$$(5.05) \qquad (3.61)$$

$$R^2 = .91 \qquad SEE = 77.3 \qquad No.\ Obs. = 9$$

PERFORMANCE OF THE DEPARTMENT OF COMMERCE MODEL

Despite our strong theoretical objections to the model used by the Department of Commerce, and its incompleteness, it will be of interest to see how this model performs relative to the model suggested above.

The two main equations of the Commerce model are those for net capital outflow (as a function of plant and equipment expenditure) and repatriated dividends (as a function of the American share of subsidiaries' earnings). The results show that for the period for which the requisite data are available, 1958–67, the ability of the Commerce equations to explain the variations in the dependent variables is at least fair to good:

$$DIV_t = 113.7 + 0.41E_t + 0.083(E \times DV65\text{--}67);$$
$$(4.07) \qquad (1.84)$$

$$R^2 = .94 \qquad SEE = 76.2 \qquad No.\ Obs. = 10$$

[24] Additional evidence is provided in the table for u_0 in Appendix B.
[25] Once the change in assets is determined, the level of affiliate earnings would seem dependent on market conditions abroad and quite insensitive to any random variables that might affect the flow of direct investment. Hence the error term in (11) must affect mainly NKO and DIV.

$$NKO_t = 108.8 + 0.30PE_t + 0.022(PE_t \times DV65\text{--}67).$$
$$(2.30) \qquad (0.30)$$

$$R^2 = .84 \qquad SEE = 212.7 \qquad \text{No. Obs.} = 10$$

The last term in each equation is a dummy variable multiplied by the independent variable in each equation; as such, the coefficient of the term tests for a change in relationship during the years of the voluntary balance-of-payments program. The estimated coefficients indicate that there was no effect on net capital outflow, but that there seemed to be an increase in the dividend/payout ratio; this latter change just misses significance at the 5 per cent level.

The above equations do not permit a direct comparison of the explanatory ability of the two alternative models. However, since there seems to be no reason why one cannot assume that the two independent variables above are independent of the error term in *both* of the equations under discussion, we can construct the Commerce equations for the flow of direct investment (ΔV) and the part of that flow that passes through the balance of payments ($NKO - DIV$). Subtracting the first equation above from the second leads to the Commerce equation for $NKO - DIV$. The equation is fitted for the period 1957–65, so the results will be comparable to those for the alternative model. Comparison of the coefficient of determination and the statistical significance of the estimated coefficients of equation (13), below, with those of equation (12), shows that the alternative model is clearly superior for this equation and period:

$$NKO - DIV_t = -396.8 + 0.45E_t - 0.095PE_t + 285.3DV65. \quad (13)$$
$$(0.82) \quad (0.38) \qquad (1.04)$$

$$R^2 = .59 \qquad SEE = 175.9 \qquad \text{No. Obs.} = 9$$

Adding the value of foreign earnings to both sides of equation (13) gives the Commerce equation for direct investment. The Commerce results are again inferior to the alternative model's—equation (11) above:

$$\Delta V = -396.8 + 1.45E_t - 0.095PE_t + 285.3DV65. \qquad (14)$$
$$(2.64) \quad (0.38) \qquad (1.04)$$

$$R^2 = .94 \qquad SEE = 175.9 \qquad \text{No. Obs.} = 9$$

4 THE IMPACT OF THE VOLUNTARY AND MANDATORY BALANCE-OF-PAYMENTS PROGRAMS OF 1965–68

FOR the most part, the balance-of-payments programs for direct investment have sought to regulate only the financing of the asset accumulations of foreign affiliates. Except for some secondary exhortations about postponing marginal fixed-investment projects and reducing working capital abroad, no direct controls were put on affiliates' investment in real assets.[26] The voluntary programs attempted to work primarily through the attainment of targets (limits) for the flow of direct investment – or, rather, the flow of direct investment as defined above *minus* the value of securities placed on international markets by the parent companies.[27] More stringent versions of the voluntary targets were made mandatory in 1968 and form the foundation of the program since that year.

Theoretically, one should not expect this type of restraint program to have any effect on asset changes. As long as the program leaves unaffected such variables as the firm's discount rate, and sales and price expectations in foreign markets, one can appeal again to the Modigliani-Miller propositions and from them conclude that a program which hits financing directly – and only financing – will not affect the market value of the firm or its investment strategy. Theoretically, the effect of such a program should be exactly the amount by which it shifts the financing of a given level of asset changes from the (net) flow of direct investment to funds from foreign sources (including the value of the parent company's securities placed abroad). Although limited to the manufacturing sector, almost all of the empirical results of the present study support this conclusion.

[26] See A. F. Brimmer, *op. cit.;* also, annual releases from the Office of the Secretary, U.S. Department of Commerce, on the Balance of Payments Program for the foll)wing year, December, 1965; December, 1966.

[27] The published figures for net capital outflow do not net out the value of foreign funds raised by the foreign borrowing of the parent firm. These are treated as foreign purchases of American liabilities and appear elsewhere in the balance of payments.

EXPENDITURES FOR PLANT AND EQUIPMENT

A preliminary indication of the programs' lack of effect on the plant and equipment spending of foreign manufacturing affiliates is given by the residuals from the best-fitting equation (7) discussed above:

$$PE = -1111.0 + 0.42S_{t-1} + 0.081(S_t - S_{t-1}) - 0.92NK_{t-1}.$$

$$R^2 = .99 \qquad SEE = 120.5 \qquad \text{No. Obs.} = 11$$

The unexplained fixed investment residuals for 1965–68, in millions of dollars, are as follows:

| 1965 | −140.7 | 1967 | +31.4 |
| 1966 | +196.5 | 1968 | −84.0 |

All of the residuals are easily less in absolute value than two times the standard error of the estimate (120.5), and thus could have arisen purely by chance. Further, the negative and positive residuals for the four years of balance-of-payments programs just about cancel each other out. With one exception, more formal tests confirm this negative result.

If it is hypothesized that each of the respective programs had a constant impact on plant and equipment spending for each year of its existence, then the effect should be estimated by a dummy variable. The following is the best-fitting equation for plant and equipment, with dummy variables added for the voluntary restraint program (DV_V) and for the first year of the mandatory program (DV_M). As suggested by the above table of residuals, neither coefficient is significantly different from zero, but the coefficient for the effect of the mandatory program is close:

$$PE = -963.47 + 0.25S_{t-1} + 0.12\Delta S - 0.44NK_{t-1}$$
$$(3.32) \qquad (4.35) \qquad (2.15)$$

$$+ 244.7DV_V - 413.5DV_M. \quad (15)$$
$$(1.26) \qquad (1.85)$$

$$R^2 = .99 \qquad SEE = 95.3 \qquad \text{No. Obs.} = 11$$

However, when the insignificant dummy variable for the voluntary program years is suppressed, the effect of the mandatory program becomes, statistically, significantly different from zero. The estimate of the effect is $511 million, equal to an 11 per cent decrease in plant and equipment expenditures. Although this result is plausible, it must be accepted with caution. The plant and equipment expenditure equations have a tendency to overpredict in the later years of the sample period and beyond; hence, we see negative residuals for the last year in the sample period in almost every case. Thus, the dummy variable for the mandatory program may just be picking up this tendency to overpredict. On the other hand, such an effect is plausible, especially in light of the suddenness with which this stringent mandatory program was instituted at the beginning of 1968; it could well be that parent firms were unable to arrange alternative foreign financing for all previously planned foreign investment expenditures. One would then expect some postponement of 1968 plant and equipment expenditures, and higher levels of such spending in 1969. A pattern of residuals consistent with this explanation was observed for the first two years of the voluntary program: a negative effect in 1965, more than offset by a positive effect in 1966.

Concerning the effect of the voluntary program, it could be argued that the effect should not be measured as a constant for each year of the program, but as some function of the level of desired plant and equipment expenditures. In particular, the program could affect either the desired capital/output ratio or the adjustment process, or both. A number of different tests were run along these lines, the results of each supporting a rejection of any significant differences between program and nonprogram years. As an example, there being independent evidence that the desired capital/output ratio did not change,[28] the desired capital/output ratio was constrained at its pre-1965 level (.455) and a simple, flexible accelerator investment equation was estimated, allowing for different speeds of adjustment in program and nonprogram years. The coefficient of the term $[DV(.455S_{t-1} - NK_{t-1})]$ in equation (16) is the estimate of the *difference* between speeds of adjustment in program and nonprogram years. The coefficient is insignificantly different

[28] See Appendix B, Part 3.

from zero, indicating no effect of the voluntary restraint program on the speed at which actual fixed capital is adjusted to the desired level.

$$PE = -1380.1 + 0.95(.455S_{t-1} - NK_{t-1})$$
$$(3.64)$$
$$- 0.032[DV(.455S_{t-1} - NK_{t-1})] + 0.053NK_{t-1}. \quad (16)$$
$$(0.50) \qquad\qquad (0.67)$$

$$R^2 = .98 \qquad SEE = 188.1 \qquad No.\ Obs. = 10$$

CURRENT ASSETS AND FINANCIAL FLOWS

The series for current-asset changes, total-asset changes, and funds raised from foreign sources go up to 1965 only. So, at best, we can get a direct measure of the effect of the balance-of-payments program for only the first year of the voluntary program, 1965. As the following equations show, when a dummy variable for 1965 ($DV65$) was added to the best-fitting equation for current-asset changes, for funds from foreign sources, and for the flow of direct investment, no significant effect for 1965 was detected.

$$\Delta CA = -270.3 + 0.29S_t - 0.47CA_{t-1} + 278.5DV65. \quad (17)$$
$$(2.67) \quad (1.86) \qquad\qquad (0.89)$$

$$R^2 = .96 \qquad SEE = 213.0 \qquad No.\ Obs. = 8$$

$$\Delta F = -200.0 + 0.51\Delta A + 215.0DV65. \quad (18)$$
$$(6.07) \qquad (0.67)$$

$$R^2 = .94 \qquad SEE = 207.0 \qquad No.\ Obs. = 9$$

$$\Delta V = 217.2 + 0.46\Delta A - 73.3DV65. \quad (19)$$
$$(14.84) \qquad (0.63)$$

$$R^2 = .99 \qquad SEE = 75.3 \qquad No.\ Obs. = 9$$

The above results are of limited usefulness. We can, however, take another tack and get a picture of the effect of the balance-of-payments programs after 1965 by predicting from the model for 1966–68 and comparing the predictions to realized values for those variables for which post-1965 data are available. In particular, the data for the flow of direct investment [29] are available for 1965–68. The predictions for the flow of direct investment come from equation (11): $\Delta V = 244.9 + 0.4453\Delta A$. Using the reported values for plant and equipment expenditures, and predicted values for changes in current assets and for depreciation, the change in total assets ($\hat{\Delta A}$) is predicted. This is all we need to apply equation (11) and derive a forecast for the flow of direct investment. The various forecasts and the comparision of actual and predicted flows of direct investment for manufacturing are presented in the following table:

Predicted ($\hat{\Delta V}$) and Actual (ΔV) Direct Investment
in Manufacturing
(*millions of dollars*)

	$\hat{\Delta A}$	$\hat{\Delta V}$	ΔV	$\Delta V - \hat{\Delta V}$
1966	5672	2770	2720	−50
1967	4443	2223	2069	−154
1968	4256	2140	2144	+4

SOURCES: *Survey of Current Business;* equations (11), (8).

The above forecasts are remarkably close to the observed values for the flow of direct investment, even for three years beyond the sample period. Given that estimated values are used for the independent variable in equation (11), the largest deviation (for 1967) is well within the range of chance variation.

The implication of the above exercise is that the flow of direct investment has not been affected by the restraint programs of 1965–68. The pre-1965 relationship between direct investment and asset changes holds up very well for the years of the various balance-of-payments programs. If the above relationship is unchanged, then so is that between the subsidiaries' borrowing from foreign sources and changes in total assets.

The final and most important implication is that, for foreign affil-

[29] Frederick Cutler *et al.,* "The International Investment Position of the United States in ——." *Survey of Current Business* (October usually), Vol. 47–49 (1967–69).

iates in manufacturing, the major—if not the only—impact of the recent balance-of-payments programs has been in the stimulation of borrowings abroad by the parent companies and their domestic finance subsidiaries (incorporated in the United States). Since the restraint programs strongly encouraged such borrowing, and since pre-1965 levels were virtually zero, it is probably correct to attribute all such borrowing since 1965 to the balance-of-payments programs. The total impact of the programs in this field would then be the manufacturing share of the total of such borrowings—i.e., the manufacturing share of: $191 million in 1965; $594 million in 1966; $446 million in 1967; and $2129 million in 1968.[30] If the above conclusions can be shown to hold for foreign investors in *all* industries, then the direct effect of the balance-of-payments programs would be equal to the totals shown.

As has been noted, there is the possibility of an additional effect of the 1968 mandatory program on plant and equipment expenditure ($−511 million). The net reduction of the flow of direct investment attributable to such an effect would be $230 million—.45(511), the estimated plant and equipment reduction times the proportion of that financed by the flow of direct investment. However, a number of reasons were noted why such an effect may be spurious or, if not spurious, subject to reversal in the near future.

5   CONCLUSIONS

A THEORETICAL model has been constructed to explain four real and financial capital flows associated with the international firm: spending for plant and equipment abroad; the change in current assets held abroad; the flow of direct investment; and the flow of funds raised abroad by foreign affiliates. Equations for the first two variables were derived from considerations related to the maximization of the market value of the firm. Equations for the financial flows were derived from a theory of minimization of devaluation risk, subsidiary to, and consistent with, the maximization of the market value of the firm.

[30] David T. Devlin and Frederick Cutler, "The International Investment Position of the United States: Developments in 1968." *Survey of Current Business,* Vol. 49, No. 10 (October, 1969), Table 4, p. 27.

The equations were estimated for aggregate data for foreign affiliates in manufacturing. They explain past data well and do so significantly better than the major existing alternative model developed by the Department of Commerce.

An application of the model developed here is the estimation of the impact of recent balance-of-payments programs on the capital flows associated with the international firm. No significant effects of recent programs were detected for any of the four dependent variables, with the possible exception of plant and equipment spending in 1968. The implication of this finding is that, for the manufacturing sector, the major impact of recent programs has been the stimulation of large foreign borrowings by the parent firms. Further, the impact of this development on the balance of payments does not seem to have been weakened by a lessening of foreign borrowing by the foreign subsidiaries themselves.

APPENDIX A: THEORETICAL MODELS

1. TABLE OF FREQUENTLY USED SYMBOLS

Variables

Q = quantity produced

L, K = inputs of labor and capital services, respectively

D = level of debt

M = Lagrangian multiplier

I = investment in capital services or goods

Parameters

p, w, q = prices of output, labor services, investment goods, respectively

s = firm's discount rate

x = exchange rate ($ per unit of foreign currency)

r = interest rate on debt

d = depreciation rate of capital goods

a = the elasticity of output with respect to capital

---

2. DETERMINATION OF THE DESIRED LEVEL OF CURRENT AND FIXED ASSETS

We assume that the firm chooses the level of capital services and labor services in each location with the goal of maximizing the market value or wealth of the firm. The treatment below follows that of D. W. Jorgenson in "Anticipations and Investment Behavior," *The Brookings Quarterly Econometric Model of the United States.*[31] The reader should refer to the Jorgenson article for a detailed discussion of the various mathematical derivations. Below we discuss only those points where our treatment differs from Jorgenson's.

We assume that the firm operates in n locations throughout the world. Net revenue at any time in a given location is (assuming no taxes):

$$x[pQ(K_1, K_2, L) - wL - q_1 I_1 - q_2 I_2],$$

where K_1 is the level of services from fixed capital and K_2 is the level of services from current assets. Current assets are assumed to provide services that enter the production function in a way similar to fixed assets; this, of course, is a simplistic view of the role of current assets. In all locations but the United States, profits are realized originally in foreign currencies; multiplication by the exchange rate, x, transforms these into U.S. dollars.

The firm attempts to maximize its market value, i.e., the present value of all future net revenues:

$$\int e^{-st} \left\{ \sum_i x_i [p_i Q_i(K_{1i}, K_{2i}, L_i) - w_i L_i - q_{1i} I_{1i} - q_{2i} I_{2i}] \right\} dt.$$

Each of the above variables has an implied time subscript. The above maximization is constrained by a Cobb-Douglas production function for each location, and by the relationship between the rate of change of capital and investment. Following Jorgenson, this expression for the optimal level of real capital service j (1 or 2) in location i can be deduced:

$$K_{ji}^* = a_{ji} p_i Q_i / q_{ji}(s + d_{ji} - \dot{x}_i/x_i - \dot{q}_{ji}/q_{ji}),$$

[31] Chicago, Rand McNally, 1965, pp. 43–47.

where a_{ji} is the elasticity of output with respect to capital service j. The only difference between the above expression for desired capital and Jorgenson's is the presence of the percentage rate of change of the exchange rate, $\dot{x}/x$, which, in addition to changes in the price of capital goods, leads to speculative gains or losses from the holding of assets. To obtain the level of desired capital *in current dollars* one multiplies both sides of the equation by q_{ji}.

3. MINIMIZATION OF THE RISK OF DEVALUATION LOSSES AND THE DETERMINATION OF THE LEVEL OF BORROWING IN FOREIGN CURRENCIES

We assume that the firm has already chosen its optimal level of current and fixed assets, labor, and output so as to maximize its market value. Subject to these predetermined variables, we assume that the firm determines its financing arrangements so as to minimize the risk of losses due to devaluation.

To simplify matters we make the following further assumptions:

1. The only random variable the firm faces is the exchange rate in each market, x_i. The U.S. market is numbered 0, and $x_0 = 1$.

2. The firm need look only one period ahead and minimizes its risk by taking actions at the beginning of each period.

The firm reaps two kinds of return in each market: operating profits (OP) and capital gains (CG). Since the only random variable is the exchange rate, capital gains cannot be reaped in the U.S. market. We will define operating profits inclusive of interest costs on debt:

$$OP = \sum_i x(pQ - wL - dqK - rD),$$

where each variable has a location subscript. Without loss of generality, we now neglect to differentiate current and fixed assets. We also implicitly assume that all assets held in a foreign location are valued in foreign-currency units; this, too, can be easily relaxed.

Capital gains result when the value of capital goods and/or debt changes because of price changes; since we assume that only the exchange-rate changes, capital gains in any foreign location, $i = 1, \ldots, n$, equals:

$$CG = [x(t) - x(t - 1)](qK - D),$$

where $x(t - 1)$ is the value of the exchange rate at the beginning of the period, and $x(t)$ is the rate at the end.

Total profits in any period is the sum of operating profits and capital gains in each location. Total profits contains n random variables, $x_1, \ldots, x_n$; $x_0 = 1$.

The firm wishes to minimize the risk of the dollar value of total profits. We assume that the variance is the measure the firm chooses as the indicator of risk. Assuming, for simplicity, that the firm expects no correlations among exchange-rate changes in different locations, the over-all variance, or risk, of total profits is

$$VAR = \sum_{i=0}^{i=n} var(x_i)(p_iQ_i - w_iL_i - dq_iK_i - r_iD_i + q_iK_i - D_i)^2.$$

This expression is to be minimized subject to the firm's balance sheet:

$$\sum_i q_iK_i = \sum_i D_i + \text{net worth},$$

where net worth is constant.

The marginal equations for D_i, $i \neq 0$ are:

$$-2var(x_i)(p_iQ_i - w_iL_i - dq_iK_i - r_iD_i$$
$$+ q_iK_i - D_i)(1 + r_i) - Mx_i(t - 1) = 0,$$

where all variables have t subscripts unless otherwise noted. The Lagrangian multiplier, M, equals 0, since $dV/dD_0 = 0 - M(1) = 0$, for debt in the United States. We thus arrive at the following for D_i:

$$D_i = (1/1 + r_i)(p_iQ_i - w_iL_i - dq_iK_i) + (1/1 + r_i)q_iK_i.$$

This is equation (3), appearing in Section 2.

APPENDIX B: DATA SOURCES AND ESTIMATES: FOREIGN MANUFACTURING AFFILIATES

1. CURRENT ASSETS (CA), FINANCIAL FLOWS $(\Delta F, \Delta V, u_0)$, AND TOTAL ASSET CHANGES (ΔA)

Year	NKO $-DIV$ [a]	CA [b]	ΔA [c]	ΔA [c] (unad-justed)	ΔF [d]	ΔV [e]	u_0 [f]
1957	−10	9180	1526	1526	567	865	94
1958	−190	9822	1168	1302	472	730	100
1959	−79	11073	1828	1703	575	1050	78
1960	251	12410	2332	1955	717	1427	−189
1961	−260	13553	1638	2036	977	943	116
1962	−34	14771	2327	2200	933	1273	−6
1963	118	16690	2998	2942	1273	1659	10
1964	141	19227	4039	3957	1973	1993	−9
1965	431	22336	5027	5137	2437	2453	247

NOTE: Figures in millions of dollars.

SOURCES: Data for 1957 and earlier: U.S. Department of Commerce, *U.S. Business Investments in Foreign Countries,* Washington, D.C., 1960; data for 1958–68 from annual articles in the *Survey of Current Business* entitled (1) "The International Investment Position of the United States in . . . ," (2) "Plant and Equipment Expenditures of Foreign Affiliates . . . ," and (3) "Financing and Sales of Foreign Affiliates . . . ." Where possible the latest published revised data were used.

[a] Source: article (1), above, in the *Survey of Current Business.* For *DIV*, I took the figure "Income" from direct investments. Although this item includes some interest income, it was used in preference to the alternative item "Income Paid Out" in (3) because of its availability for recent years, and because of the more complete sample of firms from which it is constructed.

[b] Source: for recent years, article (3) in the *Survey.* The *change* in current assets can be constructed from the data reported in annual articles (3). It was constructed as the sum of the following items reported annually: the change in inventories, receivables and other assets. The latter was included because it was assumed to reflect largely changes in the holdings of cash and securities. The *level* of current assets is available for 1957 in *U.S. Business Investments in Foreign Countries,* Table 16, p. 104. The level figure for 1957 of 9180

(million dollars) is the sum of 8207 for current assets plus 322 for "Investments in Affiliates" and 651 for "Other Assets." These last two items were included (1) for completeness, so that the sum of current and net fixed assets would equal total assets, and (2) for consistency, because changes in these categories are probably reflected in the annual figures for changes in other assets. If the second reason should be invalid, the regression results reported above would not be affected by this procedure for 1957; the addition of this constant amount to reported current assets for 1957 (and all later years) does not change the correlations between current assets and the other variables. The levels for years later than 1957 were constructed by adding current-asset changes to the previous year's level figure, starting in 1957.

    c Source: article (3) in the *Survey*. The unadjusted figure (ΔA unadjusted) is the sum of changes in current assets and net fixed assets. Using this figure for total asset changes omits the value of purchases of existing enterprises or take-overs. For only part of the period 1957–65, the Commerce Department has constructed a measure of this latter item (see, e.g., the table on "Reconciliation of Data on Capital Flows and Earnings," *Survey*, October, 1964, p. 11). By inspecting this "Reconciliation" table, one finds that the value of take-overs is approximately equal to Net Capital Outflows (NKO) *minus* Total Funds from the United States (from the Sources and "Uses of Funds" table in (3)) *plus* U.S. financing from sources other than the parent firm (e.g., U.S. bank loans, also from (3), where available). Only the first two of these items are available throughout our period. The difference of the two available items has been used above, of necessity, as an estimate of the value of take-overs. This estimate, therefore, is probably an underestimate. The adjusted figure (ΔA) was used as the measure of asset changes in the equations presented in the paper; however, the fitted equations for ΔF and ΔV and the predictions for ΔV change little if the unadjusted figure for asset changes is used. One set of results is considerably inferior if the unadjusted figure is used: that for $NKO - DIV$, equation (12).

    d Source: article (3), above. The figure for our estimate for funds raised from non-U.S. sources is the sum of the Commerce items "Funds Obtained Abroad" and "Miscellaneous Sources." The latter item was included for consistency; in some years this item was lumped with funds obtained abroad, and in some it was not.

    e Source: article (1), above. These figures are equal to $NKO + E - INC$ as reported in the *Survey*, rather than the first-difference of reported level figures. The latter procedure is unsatisfactory because of periodic adjustments in the levels to reflect previous exchange losses, expropriations, and so on. Thus, the difference between the above measures for ΔV and $NKO - DIV$ is E (the U.S. share of foreign-affiliate earnings).

    f By its construction, our estimate of u_0 also includes errors and omissions.

2. SALES AND INVESTMENT DATA, 1957–68

Year	PE	DEP	NK_{t-1}	S_{COMM} [a]	S_{McG-H} [b]	CU_{McG-H} [c]
1957	1347	539	5009	18331		
1958	1300	640	5817	19384 [e]	19693	
1959	1147	695	6477	20634	21071	
1960	1397	779	6929	23315	22927	88
1961	1782	889	7547	25111	25493	84
1962	2042	1060	8440	27923	27745	
1963	2251	1228	9422	31769	32296	88
1964	3007	1587	10445	37270	34721	90
1965	3893	1864	11865	42377	41502	87
1966	4583	2209 [d]	13893	48408 [e]		85
1967	4513	2681	16267 [f]	51325		81
1968	4178	3046	18099	57227	58533	85

NOTE: Figures in columns 2–6 in millions of dollars; column 7, data in per cent.

SOURCES: For Commerce Department data, see the first footnote to the previous table; for McGraw-Hill data: McGraw-Hill annual *Survey of Foreign Operations* (see footnote 16).

[a] Sales: Commerce Department; official figures except for 1958 and 1966–68; these figures are used as S_t in regressions.

[b] Sales: McGraw-Hill.

[c] CU: capacity utilization from McGraw-Hill.

[d] Depreciation estimated, 1966–68.

[e] Sales estimated 1958, 1966–68.

[f] Net capital estimated, 1967–68.

(For estimation methods, see below.)

3. ESTIMATING SALES AND DEPRECIATION FOR FOREIGN AFFILIATES IN MANUFACTURING

For depreciation, it was found that there is a very high correlation between depreciation expense in period t and the value of the net capital stock (NK) in period $t - 1$:

$$DEP_t = -556.0 + 0.199NK_{t-1}.$$

$$\bar{R}^2 = .98$$

Thus it was possible to estimate DEP for 1966 and, along with the reported value for PE in 1966, to construct $NK_{66} = NK_{65} + PE_{66} - DEP_{66}$, and so on for successive years.

The McGraw-Hill sales and capacity-utilization figures were used to construct estimates of total foreign sales for manufacturing affiliates in those years for which no official figures are available: 1958, 1966–68.

First, it was observed that there was a very high correspondence between the two sales series where both figures were available:

$$S_{COMM} = -1774.19 + 1.075 S_{McG\text{-}Hill}.$$
$$(19.4)$$

$$R^2 = .99$$

Given this close relationship, I felt it permissible to interpolate the same change in the Commerce data as in the McGraw-Hill data for the one year, 1958, where the latter was available, but not the former.

For the estimates of Commerce sales for 1966–68, the McGraw-Hill capacity-utilization data were used. Capacity utilization is defined as actual sales or output divided by optimal sales for the present plant: i.e., $CU = S/Smax$. $Smax$ is also related to the firm's desired capital/output ratio for a particular period: $Smax = c^*(t) \times NK(t)$. (Our only measure of actual capacity is the Commerce Department net-capital figure.) We assumed that $c^* = a + bt$. Then we can get the following equation:

$$CU = S/Smax = S/(a + bt)NK.$$

These equations, in turn, imply: $S = CU(a + bt)NK$, which is a linear equation in the variables, $CU \cdot NK$ and $tCU \cdot NK$.

In fitting this equation for years when each variable was available, the coefficient of the second independent variable proved insignificant. The best fitting equation:

$$S = 3.508 CU \cdot NK.$$
$$(125.8)$$

$$R^2 = .99$$

Thus, given CU and NK, one can estimate S, as was done for 1966–68.

COMMENTS

SIDNEY ROBBINS
COLUMBIA UNIVERSITY

ROBERT B. STOBAUGH
HARVARD UNIVERSITY

Stevens has combined an elaborate network of theory into a series of models that he has tested empirically. Through this methodology he has concluded that neither the voluntary nor mandatory restraint program of the United States has exerted much effect on the flow of foreign direct investment or on plant and equipment expenditures by foreign subsidiaries, but that these programs did stimulate substantial borrowings abroad by the American parents and their domestic financial subsidiaries.

Our own investigations corroborate these conclusions.[1] The consensus of the financial managers of multinational enterprises in the United States whom we interviewed clearly indicated that they were able to consummate their overseas investment plans. Although there was some doubt on this score in the early days of the voluntary program, it is now well known that their ability to do so stemmed from the very substantial borrowings undertaken abroad, especially in the Eurodollar markets.

Moreover, Stevens is correct in asserting that prior studies have not focused adequately on the multinational firm in assessing international capital movements. Analysts have been discouraged from such undertakings by the admitted absence of suitable data. Stevens does not share this timidity, probably because of his talent at making imaginative use of the statistics that are available. We admire this quality and endorse his efforts to combine theory and empiricism, as applied to the firm, in explaining capital movements. With this judgment rendered, we should like to concentrate on what appear to be gaps in the

[1] The results of our research will be published in 1972 under the title *Money in the Multinational Enterprise: A Study of Financial Management,* as part of a joint Ford Foundation–Harvard University study of multinational enterprises coordinated by Professor Raymond Vernon.

presentation, feeling that while in some instances the queries may represent oversights or misunderstandings on our part, in others, they may have significance. In either case, it is only by concentrating on such apparent, or real, shortcomings that ideas can be sharpened and further avenues of exploration opened. With this thought in mind, we have allowed differences rather than agreements to predominate in our review.

IMPLICATIONS FOR THE INTERNATIONAL AREA OF THE FIRST MODIGLIANI-MILLER THEOREM

At the outset, let us examine Stevens' theoretical concatenation. His initial point of reference is the first of the Modigliani-Miller propositions, according to which the market value of any firm is independent of its capital structure, or put another way, the average cost of capital to any firm is completely independent of its capital structure. Underlying the Modigliani-Miller thesis is the assumption of perfect markets where rational investors offset, through self-created leverage, the effects of corporate leverage on the market price of equities. Stevens relies on this thesis to justify his statement that it does not matter how the firm divides the financing of its foreign operations between capital flows from the United States and foreign sources.

At best, there is no unanimity with respect to the validity of the Modigliani-Miller proposition,[2] while in the international area its application is even less relevant. For example, it is not uncommon for multinational enterprises to have subsidiaries which borrow heavily without parent-company guarantees, but which are not included in the consolidated statement; this added leverage, therefore, ordinarily does not come to the attention of the investment community despite the fact that it influences both the company's capital structure and earnings. Indeed, the art of international reporting is still so primitive that the parent firm, itself, may not be fully aware of the total amount of over-all system borrowing. Moreover, the assumption of perfect markets, when applied to the confines of a single country, is a bold one;

[2] Joseph E. Stiglitz, "A Reexamination of the Modigliani-Miller Theorem." *The American Economic Review,* Vol. LIX, No. 5 (December, 1969), pp. 784–93.

when stretched to cover the whole world, the assumption becomes daring to the point where its credibility is taxed. For example, the differential interest rate fully covered for exchange risk has sometimes exceeded 1 per cent between New York and London—and these represent two major money markets with excellent communication links.[3]

The Modigliani-Miller logic used by Stevens presupposes a tax-free world, a limitation, of course, that these authors later acknowledged.[4] In the international arena, where a multinational firm operates in many different countries with a variety of tax structures, some above and others below the average level in the United States, taxation very clearly enters the picture. As a matter of fact, we know that the more adroit financial managers of firms active in this field have been able to save their firms considerable sums through effective tax-minimization programs. Accordingly, our feeling is that in the very real world of the multinational firm, the distribution of the subsidiaries' capital structures has a very real influence on the level of after-tax earnings. Along these lines, we have calculated that in certain cases the parent company will have substantially higher after-tax earnings if it invests both debt and equity in a subsidiary, instead of just equity, despite the fact that the consolidated balance sheet at the time of the investment will be the same.[5] In the light of these conditions, it becomes important for the international firm to select the appropriate policy for the liability side as well as the asset side of its subsidiaries' balance sheets.

MINIMIZATION OF EXCHANGE-RATE LOSSES

In accordance with Stevens' interpretation of the Modigliani-Miller theorem, the parent company in the multinational system may select any debt/equity ratio for its foreign subsidiaries without affect-

[3] For a discussion of the reasons for this lack of a perfect equilibrium, see Raymond Vernon, *Manager in the International Economy.* Englewood Cliffs, New Jersey, Prentice-Hall, Inc., 1968, pp. 47–48.

[4] Franco Modigliani and Merton H. Miller, "Corporate Income Taxes and the Cost of Capital: A Correction." *American Economic Review*, Vol. LIII, No. 3 (June, 1963), pp. 433–43.

[5] Robert Stobaugh, "Financing Foreign Subsidiaries of U.S.-Controlled Multinational Enterprises." *Journal of International Business Studies*, Vol. I (Summer, 1970), pp. 43–64.

ing the system's cost of capital or market value. Accordingly, he hypothesizes that the firm will establish as its goal the minimizing of exchange losses. To meet this goal, the firm, in turn, borrows in each foreign currency a sum approximately *equal* to the subsidiary's net profits and total assets denominated in the foreign currency. While in his theory Stevens does not specify the length of time over which profits should be protected, in his empirical tests he uses one year. Since these empirical results show that profits have little significance in explaining the level of borrowing, he discards the profit variable, devoting his final equation to relating foreign borrowings to total assets. We question the theoretical implications of this relationship on several grounds. For one thing, the equivalent dollar value of fixed assets often remains constant in spite of a devaluation of the local currency; and therefore, it is not usually necessary for the firm to protect itself against exchange losses due to changes in the dollar value of these assets. This fact is recognized by the accounting profession, which, for the parent company's statement, values fixed assets at historical exchange rates, i.e., those existing at the time the fixed assets were obtained. Then again, the value of certain current assets, such as imported inventory, also often remains constant in terms of dollars, a fact that has led many companies to value such inventories at historical exchange rates. For these reasons, one might theorize that foreign borrowing will be some function of current assets, rather than equal to total assets. To some extent, this conclusion is corroborated by Stevens' regression equation, which indicates that annual changes in foreign borrowings were about 55 per cent of annual changes in total assets.

In accordance with his hypothesis, however, a much higher percentage than 55 per cent should prevail, because the firm wants to borrow 100 per cent; and, of course, it is possible for the foreign subsidiaries of multinational firms to borrow a substantially higher portion of their total assets than 55 per cent should the parent company so desire. While his regression coefficient is statistically significant, we suspect that this may have been true because of the significant correlation which prevailed during this period between total and current assets ($R^2 = .97$).[6] Such a relationship cannot be assumed to continue

[6] The equation, using data in Stevens' paper, with the *t*-ratios presented in parentheses under the estimated constant and coefficient, is:

invariably, and therefore, a more accurate predictor could probably be obtained by employing the more appropriate causal variable. In this connection, using data in Stevens' paper, we performed a regression which shows that annual changes in foreign borrowing equal approximately 80 per cent of annual changes in current assets; this relationship is not only significant but is also consistent with our hypothesis.[7] We recognize that the factors determining subsidiary borrowing are much more complicated, because many firms hedge externally, as well as borrow, and also take into account the perceived weakness of an individual currency in deciding whether protection against exchange risk is desirable.

Another variable that might be important is time. It is plausible to believe that firms in the United States might have financed abroad a greater percentage of their foreign subsidiaries' assets in the mid-1960's than in the late 1950's because of improvements in local money and capital markets abroad and an increasing awareness of foreign sources of finance on the part of the firm. That this was so is indicated by the data used by Stevens, which show an increase in foreign borrowing from the 34–37 per cent range in the late 1950's up to the 43–50 per cent range in the mid-1960's; as our regression model indicates that this trend is statistically significant at an annual increase of about 1.8 per cent,[8] a model incorporating the trend would be more realistic than a model based on the hypothesis that subsidiary foreign borrowing is a constant percentage (55 per cent) of total assets for all years.

$$\Delta CA = -78 + .64\Delta A; \ R^2 = .97 \qquad SEE = 160 \qquad \text{No. Obs.} = 9$$
$$(.62) \quad (14)$$

where ΔCA = annual change in current assets; ΔA = annual change in total assets.

[7] The equation is:

$$\Delta F = -129 + .80\Delta CA: R^2 = .94 \qquad SEE = 183 \qquad \text{No. Obs.} = 9$$
$$(.96) \quad (10)$$

where ΔF = annual change in liabilities and net worth owed to foreigners; ΔCA = annual change in current assets.

[8] The equation is:

$$\frac{\Delta F}{\Delta A} = '+ 33 + 1.8 TIME; \ R^2 = .67 \qquad SEE = 3.6 \qquad \text{No. Obs.} = 9$$
$$\phantom{\frac{\Delta F}{\Delta A} = '+ 3}(13) \quad (3.8)$$

where $\dfrac{\Delta F}{\Delta A}$ = percentage of annual change in total assets financed by annual change in liabilities and net worth owed to foreigners.

$TIME$ = years, with 1957 = 1.

Despite the significant correlation between annual changes in current assets and annual changes in total assets ($R^2 = .97$), there is some doubt about the existence of an upward trend in changes in foreign subsidiaries' borrowing as a percentage of changes in current assets; the fact that the t value of the regression coefficient is less than one creates this doubt.[9]

FOREIGN DIRECT INVESTMENT

Stevens employs the relationship between changes in total assets and changes in foreign borrowing to derive an equation for predicting flows of direct investment. Because the actual flows of direct investment during the years of the restraint program are close to his estimated flows (which were calculated from an estimate of changes in total assets during this period), he concludes that the restraint program has had little influence on direct-investment flows.

In assessing the effect of the restraint program by predicting from his model for the years 1966–68 and comparing the predictions with actual values for the same period, Stevens encounters a common problem in the international area—absence of data. While he has actual statistics for direct investment, his predictive equation requires total-asset figures, which are not available for the 1966–68 period. Accordingly, he estimates sales, depreciation, and current assets and uses these data, along with reported values for plant and equipment, to derive estimates for total assets. He then inserts these estimates of total assets into his predictive equation to derive the forecasts of direct investment that he compares with reported data. His forecasts of direct investment, therefore, depend not only upon the reliability of the predictive equation but also upon the reliability of his estimate of sales, current assets, and depreciation. It seems to us that this series of es-

---

[9] The equation is:

$$\frac{\Delta F}{\Delta CA} = +65 + 1.3 TIME; \quad R^2 = .066 \qquad SEE = 14 \qquad No. \ Obs. = 9$$
$$\phantom{\frac{\Delta F}{\Delta CA} = } (6.4) \ (0.70)$$

where $\dfrac{\Delta F}{\Delta CA}$ = percentage of annual change in current assets financed by annual change in liabilities and net worth owed to foreigners.

$TIME$ = years, with 1957 = 1

timates strung together to provide a predictive figure is carrying empiricism beyond the call of duty—particularly when one realizes that even reported data in the international area must be employed with extreme caution. As a result, our net reaction is that his models related to flow of foreign direct investment are interesting more because of the adroit handling of the underlying statistics than for their usefulness as predictive devices.

EXPENDITURES FOR PLANT AND EQUIPMENT

It is well recognized that the determinants of the investment decision represent a controversial area of economic theory. Although Stevens initially uses the neoclassical model which Jorgenson and Siebert found superior to a number of alternatives, including the accelerator,[10] he eventually abandons it in favor of a simpler accelerator with a constant capital/output ratio.

In this model he relates total net fixed assets in time t to sales in time t and $t - 1$. The premise underlying this relationship is that the firm's expected sales may, in turn, be gauged by the sales in the current and preceding periods. While we realize that this approach has been used for tests of data derived essentially for domestic operations, we are skeptical about its usefulness in the international area. There are various reasons for this opinion.

Changes in the sales of companies in the international area are characterized by abrupt and discontinuous increases as know-how available in the United States is used abroad to add new product lines or to extend the degree of integration in the production process. International investment decisions are often the outcome of governmental political determinations that are in no way related to prior subsidiary sales. As a matter of fact, we have found that in the budgeting process such factors as these, plus marketing strategies and expected environmental changes, are characteristically given mcre weight than changes

[10] Dale W. Jorgenson and Calvin D. Siebert, "Optimal Capital Accumulation and Corporate Investment Behavior." *Journal of Political Economy* (November/December 1968), pp. 1123–1151.

Also, *idem*, "A Comparison of Alternate Theories of Corporate Investment Behavior." *The American Economic Review* (September, 1968), pp. 681–712.

in prior sales. Therefore, in developing a model based upon historical data to be applied for testing purposes to a period when sales are also known, it might have been more logical to employ a relationship between capital expenditures in one period and sales in future periods. Still, we must keep in mind that because of the difficulty companies have in adjusting for risk in the international environment,[11] the international investment decision is even more likely than a domestic investment decision to be dependent on strategy considerations, rather than on a single number such as calculated return on investment or estimated future sales.[12]

Besides these theoretical shortcomings, Stevens' equations for plant and equipment do not consistently confirm his own conclusions. For example, he mentions the problem of explaining a very large intercept and the tendency for the model to overestimate in the terminal years of the sample. As a result, he cannot affirm that the model is necessarily correct in its indication of a significant effect of the mandatory restraint program on foreign investment in 1968.

QUESTION OF ACCOUNTING

Another problem area in Stevens' paper is accounting. Since his analysis must be based upon reported data, which, in turn, are used to deduce the estimates necessary for his equation, it is important to recognize the precariousness of these reported figures.

As an illustration, Stevens obtains various estimates based on the assumption that change in net fixed assets during a period equals plant and equipment expenditures of the current period minus depreciation of the current period. While this relationship is often true, it could be significantly affected by the accounting policies of the companies involved. To test for this contingency, we applied Stevens' reasoning to a single company, IBM, a major participant in the international area.

The midyear of Stevens' study was chosen arbitrarily for this cal-

---

[11] Robert Stobaugh, "How to Analyze Foreign Investment Climates." *Harvard Business Review,* Vol. 45, No. 5 (September/October 1969), pp. 100–108.

[12] This process is described in Yair Aharoni, *The Foreign Investment Decision Process.* Boston, Division of Research, Graduate School of Business Administration, Harvard University, 1966.

culation, but similar results would be obtained for other years. According to Stevens' method of calculation, the net fixed assets of IBM should have increased between the end of 1960 and the end of 1961 by $137,345,655, or the difference between IBM's reported capital expenditures of $386,526,082 and reported annual depreciation of $249,180,427. However, according to the IBM Annual Report, net fixed assets rose by only $87,214,072 during this period. The reason for this discrepancy between the estimate made using Stevens' method and the IBM reported figures is that IBM follows a policy of charging partly to cost of sales and partly to its accumulated depreciation allowance the substantial amounts of dismantled and obsolete equipment which it retires annually. Accordingly, to obtain the change in net fixed assets reported by IBM, there would have to be deducted from the $137,345,655 figure indicated above (representing the difference between capital expenditures and depreciation) an additional $50,131,583 representing the amount of dismantled or obsolete assets that was written off during the year and charged to cost of sales rather than accumulated depreciation. This calculation is shown with data from Appendix B of Stevens' paper.

Since this $50,131,583 difference is more than half of the actual change in IBM's net fixed assets for that year, it is significant and cannot be readily dismissed from any analysis of the company's reported data. The company, in turn, has considerable control over this figure, which can have an important effect on reported earnings and the market value of its shares. Moreover, this policy is followed by other computer companies. Consequently, mixing their reported results with those of companies in other areas that do not follow this policy could produce a nonhomogeneous set of statistics as the analytic base.

THE HOMOGENEITY OF THE SAMPLE

This comment leads to what may be our major concern, and that is the danger of employing aggregate statistics that are not homogeneous. Our own studies have revealed that all firms do not respond in the same way to similar events, but that there are certain major characteristics which may be employed as variables to obtain more homo-

Calculations for Net Fixed Assets

Accounting Procedure	All Foreign Manufacturing Affiliates of U.S. Firms (Appendix B of Stevens' paper) (1)	Expected Results for IBM Calculated by Stevens' Method (2)	Actual Results Shown in IBM Annual Report (3)
Net fixed assets, end of 1960	7,547 [a]	849,690,933 [b]	849,690,933 [b]
Add plant and equipment expenditures in 1961	1,782	386,526,082	386,526,082
Subtotal	9,329	1,236,217,015	—
Subtract depreciation in 1961	889	249,180,427	—
Net fixed assets, end of 1961	8,440	987,036,588	936,905,005
Difference between totals of columns (2) and (3) equals retirements charged to cost of sales rather than depreciation			50,131,583

[a] In millions of dollars.
[b] In dollars.

geneous groupings. Therefore, in any major effort to identify the effect of national policies on corporate practices in the international area, it is important to recognize the need to disaggregate the statistics into more meaningful combinations.

Along these lines, Stevens, in developing his model, takes the firm's objective to be maximization of its market value, which, in turn, he identifies with the present value of future earnings. We recognize that this is an accepted approach. At the same time, we think it desirable to point out that in the international area, particularly, objectives may not be so clear-cut and may vary. For example, when devaluation occurs, managers often are much more concerned about unrealized exchange losses than about changes in the earning power of their subsidiaries. This concern with reported book-values suggests that many managers may be more interested in the appearance of their current financial statement than in their long-run cash flows.

Even if we assume that all firms have the same maximizing objective, the policies adopted to reach this objective differ substantially. We now know that managers of very large firms tend to adopt rule-of-thumb procedures, such as the remission of a specified portion of earnings to the parent company, because they find their corporate system so complex that they doubt their ability to reach an over-all optimum. The relatively small firms, on the other hand, follow to a much greater extent the policy of "every tub on its own bottom." As a result, they give considerable freedom to managers overseas because the headquarters personnel do not have the experience to develop decision rules or a central staff at their disposal to control overseas activities. We believe that financial flows developed from the group of large companies would differ substantially from those of small companies; to mix them into a single aggregate produces an odd statistical brew.

CONCLUSION

Empirical evidence that a program aimed directly at financing does not affect investment strategy appears eminently reasonable, as the firms have been able to raise funds through alternative methods. That the program did cause a substantial stimulation of borrowings in the Eurocapital markets is evident from these reported amounts, and it is equally clear that such borrowings would lead to capital expenditures, since the companies would hardly have kept the funds idle for any substantial length of time; although, as Stevens points out, there may be an adjustment lag. We are much less sure that the program had no effect on market value of the firms, as Stevens states; we have seen no empirical evidence to demonstrate that conclusion. Indeed, to the extent that the program produced changes in the cost of capital and in tax payments, or resulted in even temporary postponement of an expansion, there might very well have been an effect on the market price. In short, we are much more respectful of the liability side of the balance sheet than is Stevens. Accordingly, despite the reasonableness of his conclusions, we are not sanguine about the reliability of his models in providing consistently useful results.

ROBERT E. LIPSEY

QUEENS COLLEGE AND NATIONAL BUREAU OF ECONOMIC RESEARCH

Stevens suggests that a firm can be expected to borrow in each currency up to the point where foreign borrowings are equal to the sum of net profits earned in that foreign currency and the value of capital denominated in that currency, in order to protect itself against the risk of devaluation. Such a policy might be both definable and sensible with respect to monetary assets, but really has no meaning as applied to direct investments. Direct investments are not denominated in any currency and the earnings from the affiliate are not necessarily in the currency of the host country.

In the case of a foreign monetary asset, the face value would not increase as a result of an inflation, and the value in the home country's currency would fall as a result of a devaluation. It is these characteristics that make protection against devaluation losses desirable. An equity asset, however, would tend to rise in price in inflation, and a corresponding devaluation would only offset the rise in price. It is not even clear that the value of a direct investment is reduced by devaluation, especially if the affiliate is producing for export. A devaluation might increase the value of the investment by making complementary local resources cheaper. Would we expect an American oil company in Saudi Arabia to borrow in Saudi currency to protect itself against a devaluation?

Another curious feature of the Stevens model is the explanation of plant and equipment expenditure of an affiliate by the affiliate's sales growth, lagged sales, and desired capital stock. The implication of the equation is that no firm not already established abroad would ever begin foreign investment. If this reasoning were applied to investments in individual countries, as would seem logical, it would imply that no American firm not already established in that country would ever begin to invest there. We can say that the equation performs well if we judge by the R^2 and the significance of the coefficients, but it presumably does so because of the aggregation of all foreign countries. This aggregation means that we often explain investment in one country by the growth of sales in another country, a relationship that is not very appealing in theoretical terms.

INVESTMENT AND FINANCIAL BEHAVIOR OF AMERICAN DIRECT INVESTORS IN MANUFACTURING

ALAN K. SEVERN · Federal Reserve Board

THIS paper integrates foreign direct investment and other activities of the American-owned, international firm. It deals with period-to-period variations in direct investment activity, rather than with the firms' average level of activity abroad. Thus, it examines the short-run impact of direct investment on selected items in the balance of payments of the United States.[1]

Since the use of parent-controlled funds is closely related to expenditures for plant and equipment abroad, an equation is estimated for such spending. Equations for two other uses of funds are also estimated; one for domestic spending for plant and equipment, and one for the parent company's dividend payments to stockholders. The immediate impact on the balance of payments of the United States is represented by capital outflows minus repatriated foreign profits (referred to here as net outflow).

The unit of observation is the firm. Within it the decision variables relate to the foreign sector, the domestic sector, or the firm as a whole. The firm has several groups of managers, whose desires are made consistent by top management. Thus, decisions of each group affect the other groups. For this reason, the equations are estimated simultaneously.

Data on the level of the individual firm show a wide range of ex-

NOTE: The author is Economist, Division of International Finance, Board of Governors of the Federal Reserve System. Opinions expressed are not necessarily those of the Board.
[1] The greatest impact of government direct-investment policy is in the short-run, since capital outflows in any given year are offset by income receipts and other balance-of-payments items in subsequent years. For a full discussion of these effects, see G. C. Hufbauer and F. M. Adler, *Overseas Manufacturing Investment and the Balance of Payments,* U.S. Treasury Department, Tax Policy Research Study Number One. Washington, U.S. Government Printing Office, 1968.

367

perience during a short period, allowing the researcher to ignore any institutional changes that affect all firms over a longer span.[2] At the same time, the results of this study should reflect direct investment in manufacturing in the aggregate, since the sixty-three firms in the sample account for about half of such activity by American firms.

Since the data cannot be broken down for specific foreign areas, a two-country model is required.[3] Furthermore, foreign sales include goods exported from the United States. Hence, the model is based on the theory of investment and financial behavior of the firm, rather than on the considerations of comparative advantage, tariffs, and so on, usually encountered in international economics.[4]

THE MODEL

FORMULATION of the investment equations follows the typical approach of balancing marginal efficiency against marginal cost of funds.[5] Shifts in the schedule of the marginal efficiency of investment (MEI) are determined by actual and expected increases in sales. Thus, an accelerator is used, modified by various factors affecting the cost of funds.[6] These include internal funds, competing uses of funds, debt position, and the interest rate.

[2] The difficulties of using aggregate time series are illustrated in R. E. Krainer, "Resource Endowment and the Structure of Foreign Investment." *Journal of Finance,* March, 1967, pp. 49–57. For further discussion see Alan K. Severn, "The Structure of Foreign Investment: Comment." *Journal of Finance,* December, 1967, pp. 653–654.

[3] This level of aggregation appears behaviorally appropriate in light of Stevens' findings. Basing his argument on plant and equipment equations at the subsidiary level, he rejects several variants of the subsidiary-independence hypothesis. See Guy V. G. Stevens, "Fixed Investment Expenditures of Foreign Manufacturing Affiliates of U.S. Firms: Theoretical Models and Empirical Evidence." *Yale Economic Essays,* Spring, 1969, pp. 137–198. Interview studies also suggest that authority for large capital expenditures is not delegated to the individual foreign affiliate. See A. W. Johnstone, *United States Direct Investment in France: An Investigation of the French Charges.* Cambridge, M.I.T. Press, 1965.

[4] The data used were assembled from corporate annual reports and from confidential reports to the U.S. Department of Commerce. The latter were made available to the author as an employee of the Department.

[5] See J. S. Duesenberry, *Business Cycles and Economic Growth.* New York, McGraw-Hill, Inc., 1958, Chapters 4 and 5.

[6] This form can be derived by assuming profit maximization, given demand conditions, input prices, and a production-function constraint.

The "pure" rate of interest affects the alternative cost of internal or external funds. It is the same for all firms in any given year and is controlled by time dummies; therefore, it does not enter the model explicitly.

Internal funds are income and depreciation in the domestic and foreign sectors of the firm. Although internal funds can generally be used anywhere in a firm, the decision process may be such that funds generated in a given part of the firm tend to be used in that part. In the large firm, there is usually at least one level of management between subsidiaries and top management. Authority for large capital expenditures is generally delegated to this level rather than to subsidiaries, especially if such investment can be made without borrowing or without additional funds from the parent organization. Consequently, foreign and domestic income are entered separately, current as well as lagged values being employed.[7] In the foreign-investment equation, net outflow is a cost-of-funds variable, representing the availability of parent-controlled funds for foreign investment.

Foreign and domestic income may affect investment diversely if changes in expected profits affect the marginal efficiency of investment. For example, an increase in the expected profitability of foreign investment will raise the foreign MEI schedule relative to the domestic one.

Depreciation allowances are an internal-funds variable but also represent the need for replacement investment. However, firms typically use methods of accelerated depreciation, which concentrate depreciation allowances in the early years of a capital good's service life, when replacement expenditures are least. For this reason, and because interfirm differences in durability are controlled by firm dummies, depreciation represents cost of funds, not marginal efficiency of (replacement) investment.

Investment in the rest of the firm and dividends are cost-of-funds variables, since both compete for funds with foreign investment. In the domestic-investment equation, net outflows are a substitute vari-

---

[7] In an annual model, income in a year may affect the realization of investment plans later in the same year. While investment can increase income and thereby bias its coefficient, this effect is offset by start-up costs, higher interest costs, and depreciation allowances (especially where accelerated depreciation is used).

able for foreign investment, since domestic investment competes with net outflow, which is, in turn, associated with foreign investment.

Leverage (outstanding debt in relation to assets) affects the cost of further debt. The effect of a given amount of leverage is peculiar to each firm, owing to differences in basic business risk, accounting definitions, and other institutional considerations.[8] These long-run factors are controlled by firm intercepts.

Marginal efficiency of investment is represented in part by changes in sales for the preceding two periods. The other marginal-efficiency variable is the firm's stock price as a proxy for expected growth of sales.[9,10] In this context, stock prices are proxies for management expectations of sales, as well as profits. Nerlove has found that ex post rates of return on investment in common stocks are associated with investment opportunities generated by growth of sales and financed by retention of earnings.[11] Since stock prices are determined directly by investors, not by management, it must be assumed that investors learn of management expectations via securities analysts and the financial press.

Stock prices are affected by extraneous factors. Still, any relation between stock prices and investment should reflect expectations of long-run increase in profits via increased sales, since income in the two succeeding years is explicitly included.[12] The usefulness of stock price as a proxy for expected sales is an empirical question: Does the

[8] Leverage is assumed to affect the firm's cost of capital, owing to institutional considerations such as margin requirements, unlimited liability, and higher cost of borrowing by individuals. These factors limit the compensating leverage by individuals, which is central to the familiar Modigliani-Miller propositions.

[9] Measured as the ratio of the price at the beginning of year $t - 1$ to average price over the sample period, adjusted for splits and stock dividends. Then a similar ratio of market averages is subtracted to control for general changes in market valuation.

[10] Share prices have frequently been used in similar contexts, for forecasting and because they may allow more reliable estimation of the effect of other variables. See, for example, R. W. Resek, "Investment by Manufacturing Firms: A Quarterly Time Series of Industry Data." *Review of Economics and Statistics,* August, 1966, pp. 322–333; Z. Griliches and N. Wallace, "The Determinants of Investment Revisited." *International Economic Review,* September, 1965, p. 325.

[11] M. Nerlove, "Factors Affecting Differences Among Rates of Return on Investments in Individual Common Stocks." *Review of Economics and Statistics,* August, 1968, pp. 312–331.

[12] Stock price should not affect investment via cost of funds, since equity financing was a small proportion of manufacturers' new financing in the sample period.

expectational component overcome the "noise" caused by extraneous elements?

The dividend equation has the standard form of partial adjustment, in which desired dividends are a function of income and, perhaps, depreciation allowances. Current dividends depend on lagged dividends and desired dividends. In addition, debt position, domestic investment, and foreign investment, or net outflow, represent implicit cost to the firm of dividend payments. One modification completes the specification: dividends are assumed to adjust fully to expected changes in income and partially to the remaining "transitory" change.

The net-outflow variable reflects the impact of direct investment on the balance of payments of the United States. Its two components are combined, because both are determined by top management and the management of the international division. It is irrelevant to the over-all balance of payments whether capital outflows rise or repatriated profits fall. In addition, there are offsetting data errors in the two components.[13]

The net-outflow equation starts from the premise that net outflow is related primarily to fixed-asset expenditures of foreign affiliates. It is in the net-outflow equation that a direct substitution between domestic investment and an element of foreign investment is most likely. While investment in the United States is in the foreign-investment equation, these two variables are direct substitutes only insofar as (1) foreign investment is financed by a change in net outflow; (2) a given stage of production can be carried on at equal cost at home or abroad; or (3) the imputed cost of borrowing in one place is affected by the amount of borrowing elsewhere. Net outflow should have a stronger negative reaction to domestic investment than does foreign investment. This argument is based on the assumption that the firm borrows simultaneously in both domestic and foreign markets, owing to upward-sloping cost-of-borrowing schedules in both foreign and domestic capital markets. The situation is depicted in Figure 1, where the cost-of-borrowing schedules for foreign and domestic operations

---

[13] It must be noted that the net-outflow variable does not include all of the immediate balance-of-payments impact of direct-investment activity, let alone the cumulative effect during the years following such activity. For example, capital outflows may be matched by exports of machinery.

FIGURE 1

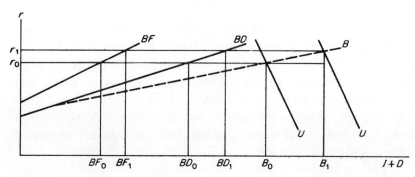

are shown separately as BF and BD, and their horizontal sum, B, is the cost-of-borrowing schedule for the entire firm.[14] The firm-wide cost-of-borrowing schedule is intersected at r_0 by the uses-of-funds curve U; the latter is equal to the sum of the MEI and desired-dividend schedules, less internally generated funds and decrease in cash assets. The firm then equates its marginal interest cost by borrowing amount BF_0 in the foreign market and BD_0 in the domestic market. These borrowings enter into the determination of net outflow as follows.

Assume a shift in either the domestic or foreign MEI schedule. The uses-of-funds curve shifts to U' and the firm borrows BF_1 and BD_1 in the appropriate markets, equating the imputed interest cost to r_1. Defining the difference between BF_1 and BF_0 as ΔBF, and so on, the additional amount borrowed in all markets is equal to the total change in investment:

$$\Delta B = \Delta BF + \Delta BD = \Delta I^f + \Delta I^d. \tag{1}$$

The change in net outflow can be defined either as outflow from the parent or inflow to the foreign sector:

$$\Delta F = -(\Delta I^d - \Delta BD) = +(\Delta I^f - \Delta BF). \tag{2}$$

Thus, net outflow consists of additional domestic borrowings not used

[14] For simplicity, these are represented as linear. At each level of the interest rate r, the imputed cost of foreign borrowing is determined by assuming domestic borrowing in the amount appropriate to the given level of the interest rate, and vice versa. Thus the two schedules are interdependent.

for domestic investment, or of additional foreign investment not financed by foreign borrowing.

If, for example, the domestic MEI schedule shifts rightward, domestic investment would increase and foreign investment might decrease. But net outflow would decrease by a larger amount than would foreign investment, because ΔBD is positive as the firm borrows more in both markets. Thus, the reaction of net outflow to domestic investment is the sum of the reaction of foreign investment and of borrowing. Therefore, net outflow should react more strongly to domestic investment than does foreign investment.[15]

In the net-outflow equation, only current foreign and domestic income are used, because financial decisions are assumed to be made with no appreciable lag. Finally, dividends are included as a use of parent-company funds which competes with net outflow.

The model consisting of the four equations discussed above is as follows (symbols are defined in Table 1).[16]

Foreign fixed asset expenditure:

$$I_t^f = a_0 + a_i + a_1 k \Delta S_{t-1}^f + a_2 k \Delta S_{t-2}^f + a_3 P_{t-1} + a_4 R_{t-1}^f + a_5 Y_t^f$$
$$+ a_6 Y_{t-1}^f + a_7 Y_{t-1}^d + a_8 I_t^d + a_9 D_t + a_{10} L_{t-1} + a_{11} F_t + b_t + u_t. \quad (3)$$

Domestic fixed asset expenditure:

$$I_t^d = a_0 + a_i + a_1 k \Delta S_{t-1}^d + a_2 k \Delta S_{t-2}^d + a_3 P_{t-1} + a_4 R_{t-1}^d + a_5 Y_t^d$$
$$+ a_6 Y_{t-1}^d + a_7 Y_{t-1}^f + a_8 F_t + a_9 D_t + a_{10} L_{t-1} + b_t + u_t. \quad (4)$$

Dividend policy:

$$D_t = a_0 + a_i + a_1 D_{t-1} + a_2 Y_t^d + a_3 Y_{t-1}^d + a_4 Y_t^f + a_5 Y_{t-1}^d$$
$$+ a_6 R_t^d + a_7 R_t^f + a_8 L_t + a_9 I_t^d + a_{10} F + b_t + u_t. \quad (5)$$

---

[15] The same conclusion is reached if the international division of the firm is sufficiently independent so that foreign and domestic borrowing rates are not equalized. In this case, foreign investment would be independent of domestic investment, except to the extent that it is financed by changes in net outflow. But this is an institutional argument which requires the discarding of the assumption of a profit-maximizing firm.

[16] All variables refer to firm i, but the firm subscript has been dropped to simplify the expression, except on the firm intercept (a_i) where it has been retained for emphasis.

Net outflow:

$$F_t = a_0 + a_i + a_1 I_t^f + a_2 I_t^d + a_4 Y_t^f + a_5 Y_t^d + b_t + u_t. \tag{6}$$

These equations involve different portions of the firm. Consequently, to use cross-sectional data in estimating this model, one must control two elements of scale: size of the over-all firm, and relative foreign involvement.

The size of the firm must be controlled in order to eliminate heteroscedasticity introduced by wide variations in size. Therefore, each

TABLE 1

List of Variables

Jointly Determined

$I_t^f =$ expenditures (gross) on fixed assets abroad
$I_t^d =$ domestic expenditures (gross) on fixed assets
$D_t =$ dividends paid to stockholders
$F_t =$ net outflow (capital outflow less repatriated profits)

Exogenous

$\Delta S_{t-1}^f =$ change in foreign sales in the preceding year $(S_{t-1}^f - S_{t-2}^f)$
$\Delta S_{t-2}^f =$ change in foreign sales lagged two periods $(S_{t-2}^f - S_{t-3}^f)$
$\Delta S_{t-1}^d =$ change in domestic sales in the preceding year $(S_{t-1}^d - S_{t-2}^d)$
$\Delta S_{t-2}^d =$ change in domestic sales lagged two periods $(S_{t-2}^d - S_{t-3}^d)$
$R_{t-1}^f =$ foreign depreciation allowances in the preceding year
$R_{t-1}^d =$ domestic depreciation allowances in the preceding year
$P_{t-1} =$ price of the firm's stock at the beginning of year $t-1$, as a ratio of average price during the sample period
$Y_t^f =$ foreign income during the current period
$Y_{t-1}^f =$ foreign income during the preceding period
$Y_t^d =$ domestic income during the current period
$Y_{t-1}^d =$ domestic income during the preceding period
$Y_t^t =$ income of the entire firm during the current period
$Y_{t-1}^t =$ income of the entire firm during the preceding period
$K^f =$ gross fixed assets abroad at the beginning of year t
$K^d =$ domestic gross fixed assets at the beginning of year t
$K^t =$ total gross fixed assets at the beginning of year t
$L_t =$ debt-equity ratio
$k =$ ratio of gross fixed assets to sales

equation will be normalized by the appropriate capital stock, K_{t-1}; i.e., all dollar magnitudes in an equation will be divided by the capital stock of the sector to which the dependent variable refers.[17] Capital stock is used as a normalizing variable, because it is the best available measure of activity in each firm and sector. A sales variable has been used for this purpose in a similar model,[18] but sales include intermediate goods purchased from other firms or from other sectors within a given firm. Value added would be a suitable criterion, but such data are not available. The capital-output ratio, k, appears in the sales terms of the model specified above, but not in the normalized model below, because its numerator and the normalizing variable cancel out. The capital-output ratio of the foreign or domestic sector of any firm is assumed constant and equal to K_{t-1}/S_{t-1}, where capital stock and sales refer to the sector of the firm in question.[19] Therefore, the normalized sales terms are simply $\Delta S_{t-i}/S_{t-1}$, $i = 1, 2$.

The other scale problem is making the jointly determined variables mutually compatible within each firm.[20] This must be done because the proportions of domestic and foreign involvement differ among the firms in the sample. It imparts random "noise" to variables relating to other sectors of the firm, and would therefore bias their coefficients toward zero if an adjustment were not made.[21] Therefore, each jointly determined explanatory variable will be scaled by the size of the sector to which the dependent variable refers as a ratio of the size of the sector of the explanatory variable.

This scaling is justified as follows. A rightward shift in any of the desired-expenditure curves (e.g., the MEI in the investment equations)

[17] Capital stock is defined as estimated gross fixed assets at the end of the preceding year. Gross, rather than net, assets are used, owing to the vagaries of depreciation-accounting, and the dichotomy between physical decay and economic obsolescence.

[18] Dennis C. Mueller, "The Firm Decision Process: An Econometric Investigation." *Quarterly Journal of Economics*, February, 1967, pp. 58–87.

[19] Capital-output ratios of manufacturing establishments have been observed to be remarkably stable over periods considerably longer than the six-year period used here. The inventory-sales ratio for any firm is assumed to be constant or to change in an orderly way over time.

[20] These remarks also apply to the use of income generated in the other portion of the firm as explanatory variables in the investment equations.

[21] Firm intercepts help to adjust for this "random" element, but the larger the sector to which an endogenous variable refers, the larger should be the deviations around the mean level represented by the firm dummy.

FIGURE 2

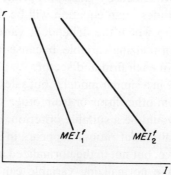

will cause all categories of expenditure to be reduced as the imputed cost of funds rises. The larger the sector in which the shift occurs, the greater will be the proportion of adjustment occurring in that sector, with a correspondingly smaller proportion falling in the others. The absolute amount of the reduction in each category depends upon the slope of the desired-expenditure curve. But the slope of such curves should be less, the larger the sector concerned.[22] In Figure 2, MEI_1^f refers to the foreign sector of Firm 1, which has foreign operations which are twice as large as those of Firm 2 (represented by MEI_2^f). If the domestic operations of the two firms are of equal size, the foreign investment of Firm 1 would be expected, on the average, to respond more strongly than that of Firm 2 to a change in the imputed cost of funds caused by a given shift in their respective domestic MEI curves. Failure to adjust for this difference would bias the coefficient of domestic investment in the first equation above (a_8) toward zero. Therefore, all firms must be adjusted to a comparable basis, regardless of the existing division of their operations between foreign and domestic activities.

The adjustment can be rationalized by assuming that the elasticity with respect to the imputed cost of funds of any desired-expenditure curve (MEI^f, MEI^d, desired dividends, or desired net outflow) is identical for all firms.[23] The coefficient of I^d in the foreign-investment equa-

---

[22] This is so because the MEI curve for any sector of the firm is equal to a rightward summation of the MEI curves for any of the individual establishments within the sector (after adjustment for any interdependence).

[23] Note that it is not assumed that each of the four curves has the same elasticity within

tion is equal to $\partial I^f/\partial I^d$. However, this reaction varies with the size of the foreign sector relative to the domestic, while the elasticity of foreign investment with respect to any factor causing a change in the imputed cost of funds does not. Therefore, the coefficient of I^d is converted into an elasticity by multiplying it by the relative size of the foreign and domestic sectors (K^f/K^d):

$$a_s(K^f/K^d)I^d = (\partial I^f/\partial I^d)(K^f/K^d)I^d. \tag{7}$$

Other jointly determined variables will be handled in an analogous way.

Since each equation is to be normalized (i.e., divided through) by the capital-stock variable relevant to the dependent variable, a variable relevant to another sector is simply divided by the capital stock of the sector to which it refers. That is, the capital stock relevant to the dependent variable appears in both numerator and denominator on the right-hand side of the equation, and is, accordingly, canceled out. For example, the domestic-income variable in the normalized foreign-investment equation is Y^d_{t-1}/K^d.

Several variables, namely leverage, stock price, and the intercept terms, were not expressed in dollar terms in the original single-firm equations above. If the model were estimated without normalization in cross section, these variables would be weighted by the size of the firm and sector concerned. For example, a given rise in a firm's stock price should affect domestic investment in proportion to the size of that firm's domestic sector. Here, the normalizing variable in the denominator cancels out the identical weighting variable in the numerator.

The normalized and scaled model to be estimated is as follows.

Foreign fixed asset expenditure:

$$\frac{I^f_t}{K^f} = a_0 + a_i + \frac{a_1\Delta S^f_{t-1}}{S_{t-1}} + \frac{a_2\Delta S^f_{t-2}}{S_{t-1}} + a_3P_{t-1} + \frac{a_4R^f_{t-1}}{K^f} + \frac{a_5Y^f_t}{K^f}$$

$$+ \frac{a_6Y^f_{t-1}}{K^f} + \frac{a_7Y^d_{t-1}}{K^d} + \frac{a_8I^d_t}{K^d} + \frac{a_9D_t}{K^t} + a_{10}L_{t-1} + \frac{a_{11}F_t}{K^f} + b_t + u_t. \tag{8}$$

a firm. Furthermore, the variables used to represent any of the four curves primarily determine the position of the given curve, rather than its shape. Only as cost-of-funds variables change independently of the other variables can one deduce anything about the shape of the desired-expenditure curves from empirical data.

Domestic fixed asset expenditure:

$$\frac{I_t^d}{K^d} = a_0 + a_i + \frac{a_1 \Delta S_{t-1}^d}{S_{t-1}^d} + \frac{a_2 \Delta S_{t-2}^d}{S_{t-1}^d} + a_3 P_{t-1} + \frac{a_4 R_{t-1}^d}{K^d} + \frac{a_5 Y_t^d}{K^d}$$

$$+ \frac{a_6 Y_{t-1}^d}{K^d} + \frac{a_7 Y_{t-1}^f}{K^f} + \frac{a_8 F_t}{K^f} + \frac{a_9 D_t}{K^t} + a_{10} L_{t-1} + b_t + u_t. \quad (9)$$

Dividend policy:

$$\frac{D_t}{K^t} = a_0 + a_i + \frac{a_1 D_{t-1}}{K^t} + \frac{a_2 Y_t^d}{K^d} + \frac{a_3 Y_{t-1}^d}{K^d} + \frac{a_4 Y_t^f}{K^f} + \frac{a_5 Y_{t-1}^f}{K^f}$$

$$+ \frac{a_6 R_t^d}{K^f} + a_8 L_t^- + \frac{a_9 I_t^d}{K^d} + \frac{a_{10} F_t}{K^f} + b_t + u. \quad (10)$$

Net outflow:

$$\frac{F_t}{K^t} = a_0 + a_i + \frac{a_1 I_t^f}{K^f} + \frac{a_2 I^d}{K^d} + \frac{a_3 D_t}{K^t} + \frac{a_4 Y_t^f}{K^f} + \frac{a_5 Y_t^d}{K^d} + b_t + u. \quad (11)$$

An intercept dummy for each firm (with a_0 constrained to zero) could have been employed as an alternative to the use of deviations around firm means. The two methods are equivalent, and both give results which represent short-run behavior.[24] Observation effects are common in various types of behavior, and the data used here show similar effects in the exogenous variables.[25] The legitimacy of pooling data from several cross sections depends upon whether the response of jointly dependent variables to the predetermined variables is sufficiently similar between the various years so that they can reasonably be regarded as being from the same universe.[26] An approximate co-variance-test showed that such pooling was acceptable and that separate year intercepts were unnecessary. Similarly, pooling data from firms having a wide range in size was acceptable, when firm intercepts were used. Therefore, the sample was pooled across firms and years,

[24] See Lewis Schipper, *Consumer Discretionary Behavior*. Amsterdam, 1964, pp. xiii–xix.

[25] While outside the scope of this paper, the full effect of sales growth, income, and similar factors, on investment behavior could be studied by relating average investment to average levels of the exogenous variables.

[26] See A. M. Mood and F. A. Graybill, *Introduction to the Theory of Statistics* (2nd ed.). New York, McGraw-Hill, Inc., 1963, pp. 352–356.

without year intercepts.[27] Estimates were made for the period 1961–66, with a combination of publicly reported annual data and confidential OBE annual data.

Preliminary simultaneous estimation provided evidence about the effect of changes in sales on investment. Positive changes lagged one period had the expected effect on investment, while negative changes had virtually no effect; in addition, changes in sales lagged two periods had no noticeable effect. Thus, it appears that negative changes in sales were regarded as transitory. It would, therefore, be wrong to assume that investment responds positively to an increase in sales which merely offsets all or part of a preceding decline. In other words, a firm which experiences a one-period drop in sales, offset in the following period, should have the same induced investment in the subsequent period as it would have had if sales had remained constant during the two preceding periods. The absence of a reaction to negative changes in sales during one period does not imply, however, that the firm's investment will not decline if the lower level of sales persists over two or more periods.[28]

For these reasons, a revised sales-change variable was constructed. If the change in sales in the preceding period is negative, its effect on investment is constrained to zero. If positive, any decrease in the second preceding period is offset against the increase, up to the full amount of the increase in the immediately preceding period.

After normalization, the size of residuals did not appear to be associated with the size of the firm or with any of the explanatory variables.[29]

In preliminary estimates, current depreciation was not significant in the dividend and net-outflow equations, and was dropped from the model. It was already excluded from the investment equations, be-

---

[27] These tests were based on two-stage least-squares results. The dummy for 1966 was retained in the net-outflow equation, however, because the voluntary balance-of-payments program for that year had specific targets for the corporations covered.

[28] Given a protracted loss in sales, the firm makes an appropriate long-run adjustment in its investment behavior. This long-run adjustment is accounted for by the firm intercept.

[29] S. M. Goldfeld and R. E. Quandt, "Some Tests for Homoscedasticity." *Journal of the American Statistical Association,* June, 1965, pp. 539–541.

cause investment leads to higher depreciation allowances in the same year.

The firm's debt-asset position indicates the availability, cost, and imputed risk associated with external funds. Various forms of this leverage variable were tested, the most useful being the ratio of the book value of debt to the book value of equity (assets less debt). Owing to decision lags, the leverage variable used in the investment equations is the debt-equity ratio at the beginning of the preceding year. It is the balance-sheet position of the firm at the time when investment decisions are assumed to be made. In contrast, leverage at the beginning of the given year was used in the dividend equation, since dividend decisions can be carried out with little lag. To test this specification, the alternative variable was used in each equation, both in addition to the existing leverage variable and as a substitute for it. In all cases, the alternative was statistically less significant. Preliminary estimates also showed similar reactions of dividends to foreign and domestic income, so these variables were combined to reduce multicollinearity.

With the changes noted, the model was reestimated in two-stage least-squares, as presented in Tables 2–5.

EMPIRICAL RESULTS

FIRM dummies control the stable element of firm behavior. Their effect can be seen by comparing $\bar{R}^2$'s before and after their adoption. Only in the dividend equation do variables other than firm dummies account for more than half of the total "explained" variation in the dependent variable. Eisner describes this type of regression as "firm time-series." He argues that firms react less strongly to the transitory component of sales change, income, and so forth.[30] For example, sales-change coefficients of .25, and .18 (in the equations for foreign and domestic investment, respectively) are compatible with full adjustment to a rate of growth of sales regarded as permanent. But a time-

[30] R. Eisner, "A Permanent Income Theory for Investment: Some Empirical Explorations." *American Economic Review,* June, 1967, pp. 363–390.

series model is more appropriate to short-run balance-of-payments policy, so firm dummies are retained here. Because of the transitory nature of deviations from six-year means, the respective effects of the independent variables are more difficult to discern than they would be in pure cross-section. Therefore, any variable is retained in the model if its t-value exceeds unity and if its sign is appropriate.

Tables 2–5 each present a basic equation for one jointly determined variable, followed by alternative versions. A discussion of these four tables follows.

The basic foreign-investment equation (Version 1) includes four variables which together determine appropriations, and one variable (F) relevant to their modification. All five coefficients take the expected sign. This version is preferable to Version 4, which uses current foreign income as a modifications variable. While the availability of funds for net outflow, as represented by the endogenous variable F, is not statistically significant, it does make a small contribution to the over-all explanation of foreign investment.

The stock-price variable also makes a small contribution to this equation. This is all that can be expected. Even if the stock price is a good index of expectations, it represents those of the firm as a whole, rather than its foreign operations alone. Attempts to weight this variable by the foreign proportion of the firm's total capital stock were unsuccessful.

The debt-equity ratio lagged one period is superior to its value at the beginning of the current year, as indicated by Versions 2 and 3. This is to be expected, since the cost of funds should be more germane to capital appropriations than to realizations. The foreign-depreciation variable proved useless (Version 5), perhaps because of poor data.

Jointly determined explanatory variables other than net outflow, i.e., domestic investment and dividends, took the wrong sign (Versions 6 and 7). Thus, there is no evidence in this model that foreign and domestic investment were substitutes during the 1961–66 sample period. However, domestic investment and the use of American-controlled funds to finance foreign investment may be.

The basic domestic-investment equation (Table 3, Version 1) also has five explanatory variables. As in the foreign-investment equation, there are three cost-of-funds variables. The marginal cost of funds

TABLE 2

Coefficients for Foreign-Investment Equation [a]

Version	ΔSf_{t-1}	Yf_{t-1}	L_{t-1}	P	F	Additional Variable	R^2 with Dummies	$\bar{R}^2$ After Dummies
1	.254 (4.699)	.146 (1.613)	-.136 (-2.961)	.179 (1.572)	.122 (1.113)		.461	.103
2	.273 (5.056)	.154 (1.693)		.189 (1.653)	.202 (1.968)	L_t : -.097 (-2.454)	.457	.096
3	.259 (4.775)	.139 (1.526)	-.108 (-2.148)	.191 (1.678)	.113 (1.028)	L_t : -.060 (-1.380)	.462	.105
4	.249 (4.589)	.099 (1.176)	-.158 (-3.835)	.168 (1.481)		Yf_t : -.014 (-.203)	.459	.100
5	.253 (4.650)	.147 (1.616)	-.133 (-2.869)	.180 (1.582)	.127 (1.145)	Rf_{t-1} : .073 (.300)	.460	.101
6	.246 (4.541)	.093 (.969)	-.138 (-3.018)	.031 (.218)	.093 (.841)	I_t^a : .288 (1.760)	.464	.108
7	.252 (4.661)	.104 (1.073)	-.137 (-2.982)	.103 (.801)	.085 (.751)	D_t : .267 (1.224)	.462	.104

NOTE: The column labeled "$\bar{R}^2$ After Dummies" in Tables 2 through 5 indicates the proportion explained of variation remaining after adjustment for interfirm differences. The "R^2 with Dummies" column is the proportion explained of the original variation, adjusted for number of firms and explanatory variables other than dummies.
[a] With implicit firm dummies; t-values in parentheses.

TABLE 3

Coefficients for Domestic-Investment Equation [a]

Version	ΔS_{t-1}^d	P	Y_{t-1}^d	Y_{t-1}^f	Y_t^d	Additional Variable	$\bar{R}^2$ with Dummies	$\bar{R}^2$ After Dummies
1	.177 (3.990)	.188 (2.365)	.129 (1.621)	.115 (2.498)	.204 (3.496)		.603	.304
2	.178 (3.997)	.190 (2.382)	.127 (1.588)	.117 (2.513)	.204 (3.499)	L_{t-1} : −.008 (−.312)	.602	.302
3	.178 (3.875)	.189 (2.350)	.127 (1.562)	.115 (2.497)	.204 (3.489)	L_t : −.002 (−.100)	.602	.302
4	.173 (3.912)	.167 (2.086)	.124 (1.558)	.111 (2.404)	.215 (3.671)	R_{t-1}^d : −.416 (−1.682)	.605	.307
5	.171 (3.678)	.184 (2.301)	.132 (1.653)	.112 (2.393)	.199 (3.358)	I^f : .034 (.396)	.602	.302
6	.169 (3.689)	.174 (2.145)	.122 (1.527)	.138 (2.760)	.225 (3.472)	F_t : −.053 (−.745)	.602	.303
7	.153 (3.147)	.201 (2.508)	.196 (2.005)	.086 (1.438)	.256 (3.496)	D_t : −.325 (−1.179)	.603	.304

NOTE: See note to Table 2 for definitions.
[a] With implicit firm dummies; t-values in parentheses.

(to the firm as a whole) should be a more important determinant of investment when the marginal efficiency of investment is relatively elastic. In the domestic-investment equation, the three cost-of-funds variables all represent income, i.e., internally generated funds, while leverage has no discernible effect. This suggests that domestic marginal efficiency was more elastic at the lower imputed cost of funds represented by internally generated funds than at the higher marginal cost represented by reliance on external funds. Neither of the internal-funds variables (F_t and Y_{t-1}^f) in the basic foreign-investment equation was statistically significant, while leverage was highly significant. Thus, the opposite pattern of elasticity appears to hold for foreign investment. The fact that domestic income did not affect foreign investment, although foreign income affected domestic investment, can be explained by a foreign MEI curve which was less elastic than its domestic counterpart in the lower range of expected return on investment.

The positive effect of foreign income on domestic investment [31] also tends to refute the "gambler's winnings" hypothesis of Barlow and Wender.[32] Funds available throughout the corporation are balanced against requirements of the firm as a whole.

In general, the foreign MEI appears to be less elastic than the domestic MEI. For the sample, the mean change in annual sales was 9.7 per cent for foreign operations and 5.4 per cent for domestic. This difference is reflected in a larger sales-change coefficient in the foreign-investment equation. A larger proportion of domestic investment than of foreign investment appears to have been motivated by factors other than increasing demand. If one assumes that there was a lower imputed rate of return on such investment, the result is a short-run function for domestic MEI of the hypothesized shape: more elastic at low levels of expected return.[33]

[31] Foreign income could be a proxy for foreign sales; and foreign sales affect the demand for parts, components, and finished goods supplied by the parent. Therefore foreign income could be a proxy for a domestic demand variable. Such was not the case, however, since lagged foreign-sales change was clearly insignificant when added to the basic U.S. investment equation, while lagged foreign income retained its significance.

[32] E. R. Barlow and I. T. Wender, *Foreign Investment and Taxation*. Cambridge, Harvard Law School International Program in Taxation, 1955, p. 161.

[33] This assumption results from the firm's flexibility in the timing of such investment. Ultimately, all investment is made to reduce costs, but the added cost of postponing the replacement of obsolete or worn-out capital goods should be less than the cost of foregoing additional sales.

In contrast, most of the foreign MEI curve appears to reflect investment induced by changes in sales, with the greater elasticity at high rates of return reflecting expansion to take advantage of increased demand.[34] If the foreign affiliates of American firms tend to specialize in technologically advanced products and to operate in oligopolistic markets, as Vernon and Hymer, respectively, have claimed,[35] then cost-reducing investment should be relatively less important for foreign investment.

Thus it appears that as a low firm-wide marginal cost of funds rose, owing to an upward shift in the cost-of-funds schedule, the largest proportional reduction of investment expenditures occurred in the domestic sector. As it continued to shift upward, the cuts were more nearly equal; during the sample period, domestic reductions may still have been proportionately larger, owing to the greater elasticity of the domestic MEI schedule, in general. Finally, as the cost of funds rose to the highest observed levels, the foreign sector incurred the larger proportional reductions in investment.

The stock-price variable, representing expected sales, was significant in all versions of the domestic-investment equation. Omitting this variable (not shown) raised the coefficient of the lagged (but not current) income terms, owing to collinearity between stock price at the beginning of year $t - 1$ and income during that year. Stock price appears partially to reflect expectations of short-run changes in income. But its significance in the presence of lagged income variables suggests that it also reflects longer-term sales expectations.

The depreciation variable takes an unexpectedly negative sign (Version 4). This result probably stems from depreciation accounting practices and from firm dummies which control interfirm differences in such practices. Since the depreciation variable represents deviations around firm means, the effect of consistently high depreciation allowances (i.e., of high replacement requirements) is reflected in the firm

[34] Take-overs of existing firms are excluded from the data; hence they are not reflected in the implied MEI curves.

[35] R. Vernon, "International Investment and International Trade and the Product Cycle." *Quarterly Journal of Economics,* May, 1966, pp. 190–207; S. Hymer and R. Rowthorn, "Multinational Corporations and International Oligopoly: The Non-American Challenge," in C. P. Kindleberger, ed., *The International Corporation.* Cambridge, M.I.T. Press, 1970, pp. 57–91.

TABLE 4

Regression Coefficients for Dividend Equation [a]

Version	L_t	D_{t-1}	Y_t^t	Y_{t-1}^t	I_t^d	F_t	Additional Variable	$\bar{R}^2$ with Dummies	$\bar{R}^2$ After Dummies
1	-.013 (-2.477)	.674 (18.499)	.189 (10.961)	.100 (4.082)	-.034 (-1.191)	-.016 (-1.503)		.987	.845
2	-.014 (-2.500)	.674 (18.487)	.188 (10.877)	.099 (4.029)	-.032 (-1.105)	-.013 (-1.105)	L_{t-1}: .004 (.595)	.987	.845
3	-.016 (-2.952)	.679 (18.678)	.187 (11.138)	.096 (3.934)	-.005 (-.177)		I_t : -.045 (-2.415)	.988	.846

NOTE: See note to Table 2 for definitions.
[a] Including implicit firm dummies; t-values in parentheses.

TABLE 5

Regression Coefficients for Net-Outflow Equation [a]

Version	Y_t^t	Y_t^d	I_t	I_t^d	D_t	1966 Dummy	$\bar{R}^2$ with Dummies	$\bar{R}^2$ After Dummies
1	-.494 (-3.788)	.948 (3.714)	.453 (1.704)	-1.608 (-3.259)	-.559 (-.823)	.230 (1.168)	.403	.080
2	-.513 (-3.963)	.918 (3.612)	.441 (1.660)	-1.281 (-3.150)	-.766 (-1.168)		.403	.079

NOTE: See note to Table 2 for definitions.
[a] Including implicit firm dummies; t-values in parentheses.

intercepts. Reestimation without firm intercepts showed that this was true in both investment equations. The depreciation coefficients were close to unity and highly significant statistically. At the same time, many of the sample firms used accelerated depreciation accounting, whereby a large portion of the price of a capital good is allocated to cost during the early years of its expected service life.[36] Thus higher-than-average depreciation allowances reflect higher-than-average investment in prior years. Therefore, the depreciation variable used may reflect investment in previous periods, taking the negative sign which one would expect.

The coefficient of foreign investment is insignificantly positive (Version 5), with little effect on the coefficients of other variables. This result supports the conclusion that there is no evidence that foreign and domestic investment were substitutes during the sample period. The apparent lack of substitution may result from high cash flow and relatively low interest rates during this period, combined with the relatively slow growth of domestic demand noted above. A different set of domestic circumstances during this time might well have resulted in a noticeably negative relationship between foreign and domestic investment.

While the coefficient of foreign investment is nonsignificant and positive, the outflow variable at least takes the right sign, although it is not significant (Version 6). Nor is the dividends variable significant, though, again, the sign is as expected (Version 7).

The dividend equation is generally consistent with the results obtained by other authors.[37] The point estimates of Version 1 (Table 4) imply a reaction speed of .326, a desired payout ratio of .580, and a coefficient of expected change of income of .256. These estimates appear reasonable, except for the implied coefficient of the expected change of income. The firms in the sample experienced an average

---

[36] This bunching of depreciation allowances in the United States was furthered by the shorter service-lives allowed from 1962 on.

[37] For example, Fama and Babiak used unpooled annual firm time-series, 1946–64, to estimate Version 1, less leverage and the endogenous variables. Their median coefficients were .598 for lagged dividends, .150 for current income, and .043 for lagged income. They also found small and erratic coefficients for a depreciation variable. See E. F. Fama and H. Babiak, "Dividend Policy: An Empirical Analysis." *Journal of the American Statistical Association,* December, 1968, pp. 1139–1140.

increase in income of 12.7 per cent per year, about half as large as the expected increase implied by the estimates of Table 4. Since the expected-income-increase coefficient is derived from the coefficients of Y_t, Y_{t-1}, and D_{t-1}, its sampling error is large enough to include the rate experienced.[38] As a test for the effect of data and sampling error, it would be desirable to estimate 1967 dividends for comparison with realized dividends, or to estimate the model with an entirely new set of firms. Both of these approaches are ruled out by lack of suitable data.

Leverage at the beginning of the current year also helped to explain dividends, while lagged leverage did not (Version 2). Domestic investment and outflow take the expected negative sign but are not statistically significant.

This equation thus supports the finding by Fama and Babiak that dividend policy is based more on permanent, than on transitory, changes in income;[39] in addition, balance-sheet position is a useful, but secondary, determinant of dividends.[40] The dividend equation also suggests (inconclusively) that expansion of foreign operations may inhibit dividend payments.

In the net-outflow equation (Table 5), all coefficients but one have the expected sign, although the explanatory power of the equation is low. As in the foreign-investment equation, most of the total variation accounted for is attributable to the firm intercepts. Thus, a large proportion of corporate behavior with respect to foreign operations reflects the influence of long-run factors peculiar to each firm; such behavior is only marginally influenced by macroeconomic policy as it impinges on the firm in the short run.

The two income coefficients together suggest that at the margin, in the absence of capital controls, corporations allocate funds without regard to origin. The coefficient of domestic income implies that in-

[38] This result might also be due to a more complicated lag structure, which would require additional lagged values of income and/or dividends to estimate. Such data are not available, so no such model was formulated here.

[39] Fama and Babiak, op. cit., pp. 1139–1140.

[40] Brittain found that liquidity (cash plus government securities) and realized investment were useful in explaining target payout over time. Since liquidity is an offset to debt, leverage and liquidity both represent ability to make dividend payments without incurring further debt. See J. Brittain, Corporate Dividend Policy. Washington, The Brookings Institution, 1966, p. 186 and passim.

creases in domestic income are allocated in approximately equal proportion to foreign operations, with the remainder being divided between domestic operations and dividends. Thus, changes in current income were allocated to foreign operations in an amount more than proportionate to their size. This allocation of funds reflects the fast growth of the foreign sector relative to the domestic sector; it represents a shift in the relative share of financing from foreign external funds (or retained earnings) to domestic internal funds (since foreign income is included separately in the equation). The reaction of net outflow to current domestic income represents primarily a shift in financing, not a modification of foreign investment plans. This follows from the finding that when current domestic income is added to the basic foreign-investment equation, its coefficient is a nonsignificant .096.

On the other hand, the elasticity of net outflow with respect to current foreign income is $-.494$. Thus, foreign affiliates were allowed to retain just over half of every additional dollar of income earned abroad. Since the short-run reaction of dividends to income is only .189, this implies that .317 of changes in foreign income were used for general corporate purposes other than dividends.

The dummy variable for 1966, representing the "voluntary balance-of-payments program for direct investment," takes an unexpectedly positive sign. Most of the firms in the sample were in the program. Apart from sampling or data error (the coefficient is not significant), this result must be attributed either to accelerated outflows in anticipation of tighter controls and/or to outflows not reported. A newspaper article suggested that part of the errors and omissions item in the balance of payments represented capital outflow: "Monetary specialists suspect that some companies not only don't report all their investments abroad but actually go to some length to conceal them—so as not to advertise their unwillingness to comply with the Administration's guidelines for restraint."[41] Since most of the net-outflow data used here are derived from annual reports, rather than from data submitted to program authorities, such "hidden" outflows are likely to be included.

[41] "Missing Dollars," *Wall Street Journal,* May 4, 1967, pp. 1, 22.

Domestic investment has a more-than-proportionate negative effect on net outflow. In contrast, domestic investment took a positive sign in the foreign-investment equation. Thus the relationship of substitution of net outflow with domestic investment expenditures is stronger than that between investment expenditures abroad and at home. The fact that the coefficient for domestic investment exceeds unity in the outflow equation, while there is no negative reaction between foreign and domestic investment, suggests that foreign borrowing rises more than in proportion as domestic investment rises.

The reaction of net outflow to foreign investment is a near-significant .453, indicating that, at the margin, about 55 per cent of foreign expenditures for plant and equipment are financed from sources other than capital outflows and/or reduction in repatriated earnings. Since such expenditures were far too large in the sample period to be financed by liquid assets abroad, and since virtually no equity financing was used there, this result suggests that foreign debt financing was quite important. For all foreign direct investment in manufacturing (of which the sample accounts for about half), the mean ratio of capital outflow to foreign expenditures for plant and equipment during the 1962–65 period was .357. Since profit repatriation undoubtedly responds at the margin to foreign investment, the average and marginal reactions of net outflow to foreign investment appear to be of the same order of magnitude. When the same equation is estimated with no allowance for individual-firm intercepts, the reaction of net outflow to foreign investment is .575; thus firms which are expanding abroad rapidly tend to finance a larger proportion of this expansion with funds from domestic sources.

The reaction of net outflow to dividends was negative but not statistically significant. However, the relationship is slightly stronger when the 1966 dummy is omitted (Version 2, Table 5). Apart from its statistical significance, this fact hints that, in 1966, in the context of tighter money and capital markets, firms increased capital outflows at the expense of dividends.

SIMULATIONS

GIVEN the model as discussed above,[42] its implications for balance-of-payments policy of the United States are now explored by simulations based on two sets of assumptions about domestic macroeconomic policy.

Several qualifications must be made about any simulation. First, the model is one of short-run reaction to developments at the level of the individual firm. The policies simulated must be those which are likely to be perceived as transitory by management, and macroeconomic policy leads to interactions among firms that may strengthen or weaken its effect on the jointly determined variables. For example, Eisner demonstrates that changes in demand which affect an entire industry have a stronger effect on investment than do changes which affect only one firm.[43] On the other hand, changes in the desired investment of an entire industry or economy lead to supply constraints in the capital-goods industry, thereby offsetting all, or part, of additional investment planned. For lack of further information, such interactions are assumed to have a zero net effect on the jointly determined variables. Second, policy changes which affect the manufacturing sector in the United States also affect the rest of the domestic economy, as well as the world economy. For example, changes in foreign investment affect the level of economic activity abroad through foreign demand for capital goods; in addition, changes in domestic demand affect imports, thereby affecting indirectly foreign demand for the products of American affiliates abroad, as well as for exports from the United States. Third, any defects in the model used clearly affect the simulation results. Arbitrary choices had to be made about data, specification, and estimation. In particular, capital movements were relatively free during the 1961–66 period, and foreign investments of American firms grew rapidly, partly because of the establishment of the European Common Market. For these reasons, the results pre-

[42] The order condition for identification did not indicate that the structure of the model was inappropriate to the jointly determined variables under consideration. See J. Johnston, *Econometric Methods*. New York, McGraw-Hill, Inc., 1963, pp. 240–264.

[43] R. Eisner, *op. cit.*

sented below must be regarded merely as indicative of orders of magnitude.

As a control solution for comparison, the model consisting of Version 1 of each equation (Tables 2–5) was simulated on the basis of mean values of all predetermined variables. Since these variables are ratios, it was not necessary to adjust for growth within the sample period.

The first policy assumption is that the economy of the United States was allowed to go into a brief recession comparable to that of 1960–61, except that full recovery is assumed to have taken place by the end of the year. Simulations were made for the recession year and the following year, since some of the predetermined variables are lagged. Sample means for 1961 were used in place of over-all means for current or lagged values, as appropriate. For example, ΔS_{t-1}^d went from its mean of .054 to a recession value of .022, and Y_t^d went from .160 to .140.[44]

The resulting effect on net outflow is small (Table 6). Based on capital stock at the beginning of 1961, the net effect is about $2.4 million for all foreign direct investment in manufacturing. In comparison, the balance-of-payments deficit of the United States (liquidity basis) for 1961 was $2.4 *billion*. The effect of the simulated recession on net outflow is a combination of a large decrease in net outflows during the recession year, followed by a larger increase in the following year. Outflows decrease with income during the recession year; this offset outweighs the positive effect of current declines in dividends and domestic investment. But outflows rise in the following year as a result of the lagged decrease in investment and dividends. Thus, this model does not suggest that the level of economic activity in the United States has a strong effect on the balance of payments by means of direct investment outflows and repatriated profits.

The second set of policy assumptions involves a one-year surcharge on the corporate income tax. It is assumed that a 10 per cent surtax was imposed early in the given year, retroactive to the beginning of the year, in order to allow added government expenditures without raising prices or interest rates. Additional government pur-

[44] These numbers are small because they are expressed as normalized ratios (of sales level or capital stock, as appropriate).

TABLE 6

Policy Simulations
(*ratios of dollar values to the appropriate capital stock*)

Variable	Control Solution	Current Reaction	Lagged Reaction	Average Reaction	Average Reaction Less Control Solution
		1. Brief Recession			
I^d	.1074	.1033	.0998	.1016	−.0058
I^f	.1268	.1257	.1283	.1270	.0002
D	.0875	.0797	.0834	.0816	−.0059
F	−.0367	−.0452	−.0215	−.0384	−.0017
		2. One-Year Corporation Income Tax Surcharge [a]			
I^d	.1074	.1038	.1056	.1047	−.0027
I^f	.1268	.1254	.1276	.1265	−.0003
D	.0875	.0819	.0814	.0816	−.0059
F	−.0367	−.0430	−.0300	−.0365	.0002

[a] Partially offset.

chases are assumed to offset the decline in sales of investment goods. These policies should increase outflows in other capital accounts in the balance of payments, in comparison with a reliance on tighter monetary policy. But there is no effect on the capital outflows and repatriated profits of manufacturing firms. The decline in internally generated funds is offset, in both years, by lower dividends and domestic investment than would otherwise have occurred. Since these compete with net outflow for available funds, a larger proportion of such funds is available for foreign affiliates.

Thus, within the qualifications discussed above, there is little apparent impact of domestic economic policy on the United States balance of payments via direct investment in manufacturing.

This negative result occurs despite the positive coefficient of domestic income in the net-outflow equation. This contrast occurs because domestic policy affects net outflow both directly, through the domestic income variable; and indirectly, through other jointly determined variables (domestic investment and dividends).

One must recall, however, that the model was estimated for a period in which foreign economic activity was growing rapidly. The accelerator influence was stronger in the foreign-investment equation than in its domestic counterpart, suggesting that American firms gave high priority to foreign capital requirements while cutting back, if necessary, on domestic uses of funds. Clearly, the short-run reaction to economic policy might have been different if foreign demand had been rising less strongly relative to domestic demand.

Also relevant is the fact that the model deals with short-run reactions. For example, a fiscal stimulus expected to be permanent, such as a tax cut carried out in two or more annual instalments, should have a negative impact (via dividends and domestic investment) on net outflow which outweighs the positive effect via domestic income.

For these reasons, and also because of interactions among firms and the indirect effects of investment activity, the finding of negligible impact of domestic economic policy on direct investment outflows must be regarded as a highly tentative conclusion, limited to the institutional and economic circumstances prevailing in the early 1960's.

CONCLUSIONS

THE following conclusions can be drawn about the corporate decision process as it bears on foreign investment and other corporate actions:

1. Only a small portion of the variation in investment and financial behavior of firms can be attributed to year-to-year variation in financial variables at the firm level. About twice as much of the variation in foreign investment and net outflow can be explained by the levels of such financial variables, as opposed to their year-to-year changes. For dividends and domestic investment, however, year-to-year variations explained nearly as much as did levels. Thus, the distinction between "permanent" and "transitory" elements of income,

sales increase, and other factors, was even more important for foreign operations than for over-all investment or dividends. But separate tests, not shown above, indicate that firm dummies account for more than differences in the average levels of the variables.

2. Little substitution is evident between foreign and domestic investment. Both variables take a positive sign but are not statistically significant in the corresponding equations. It is interesting to note, however, that firm intercepts control various factors common to both foreign and domestic investment (e.g., rate of technological progress). Without them, the investment coefficients become positive and significant in the investment equations.

3. There is considerable flexibility in financial behavior, with respect both to shifting of funds across national boundaries and to utilization of external sources of funds when justified by prospective return of investment.

Several strands of evidence support this conclusion. First, the sum of the reaction of net outflow to foreign investment and that of foreign investment to lagged foreign income is only .6, leaving the remainder to be accounted for by current, retained foreign earnings, foreign external funds, and reduction of liquidity abroad. Second, foreign and domestic investment do not appear to be substitutes, yet net outflow has a strong negative reaction to domestic investment. This combination of results suggests that when total investment exceeds internally generated funds less dividends, firms reduce net outflows and compensate by increased use of foreign external funds or by reducing cash balances abroad. Finally, foreign income affects domestic investment, and domestic income affects net outflow; these results confirm the expectation that, in the absence of controls, firms allocate funds without regard to national origin.

4. At the same time, however, changes in the domestic economic circumstances of individual firms appear to have little direct impact on the balance of payments of the United States, since domestic liquidity offsets the substitution between net outflow and domestic investment plus dividends.

5. The performance of the chosen proxy for sales expectations (stock prices) is striking. Its coefficients are quite similar in the two

investment equations, and its statistical significance in the domestic investment equation undoubtedly results from the fact that domestic operations are usually larger than foreign.

6. The relative performance of internal funds, external funds, and marginal efficiency as variables in the two investment equations confirms previous theoretical and empirical work on the subject.[45] Given the rising demand experienced by direct-investment enterprises, only lagged foreign income and net outflow (a proxy for current availability of funds) contributed to the foreign-investment equation, and neither was statistically significant. On the other hand, all income variables, except current foreign income, were useful in explaining domestic investment.

In contrast, the imputed cost of external funds was useful only in the foreign-investment equation, where the reaction to increases in sales was also stronger than in the domestic-investment equation.

7. Domestic investment appears to affect dividend payments, but the converse appears to be true only to a smaller extent. The reason apparently lies in the greater lag in decision-making about investment than in dividend policy. As each quarterly dividend decision is made, the firm considers competing claims on available resources, including previously planned investment projects. As these projects are in the process of completion, there is little flexibility, since the firm has contractual commitments to make specified payments. But as investment appropriations are made, there is no immediate impact on dividend payments, except to the extent that the firms set aside financial resources pending completion of such projects.

In summary, this study shows that methods of investigation typically applied to domestic investment also apply to foreign investment, although the latter varies even more widely among firms. Foreign and domestic investment are interrelated primarily through the financing mechanisms used, whereby top management allocates internally generated funds in such a way as to maximize profit; thus, in the absence of controls, the multinational firm freely allocates funds across national borders.

[45] For example, J. S. Duesenberry, *Business Cycles and National Income.* New York, McGraw-Hill, Inc., 1958, Chapters 4 and 5. J. R. Meyer and E. Kuh, *The Investment Decision.* Cambridge, Harvard University Press, 1957. J. P. Bennett, "Cyclical Determinants of Capital Expenditures." *Southern Economic Journal,* January, 1966, p. 340.

THE POLICIES OF ENGLAND, FRANCE, AND GERMANY AS RECIPIENTS OF FOREIGN DIRECT INVESTMENT

ROBERT W. GILLESPIE · University of Illinois at Urbana

INTRODUCTION

THE growth of long-term international capital movements is widely recognized as one of the important economic phenomena in the postwar world economy. Long-term capital movements have, of course, played an important historic role in earlier periods of the world economy. One aspect of the postwar period that distinguishes it from the earlier experience is the quantitative importance of foreign direct investment and the emergence of the multinational firm as an important agent in the capital-transfer process.[1] Another aspect unique to the

NOTE: The author gratefully acknowledges research support provided by the University of Illinois' Center for International Comparative Studies and the valuable assistance of Mr. Willard Radell, who carried out much of the library research.

[1] It has been suggested that the multinational firm exists and grows quite independently of any capital movement in the traditional sense. There is much to be said for this view, particularly since the United States government imposed restrictions on American direct investment financed in the domestic capital market. To the extent that foreign-ownership control, per se, of domestic firms affects economic policy or behavior, the emphasis is correctly placed on this aspect rather than on the capital movement aspect. This view has been developed and expounded by S. Hymer. See C. P. Kindleberger, *American Business Abroad,* New Haven, 1969, pp. 11 ff. Also see Christopher Layton, *Trans-Atlantic Investment,* Paris, 1968, for a good review and critique of this discussion.

397

postwar period is the rapid growth of capital movements in the form of foreign direct investment between developed nations. In earlier periods, the flow was primarily from developed to underdeveloped countries or from mother countries to colonies. Flows of direct investment between developed nations not only raise new issues, but the old issues assume a different significance in the new setting.[2]

The purpose of this paper is to review some of these issues by examining the policies of England, France, and Germany toward direct investment by foreign firms during the postwar period. We shall seek to determine the degree to which these policies have been restrictive in nature, and the rationale behind these restrictive aspects. This rationale is of interest because the governments of all three countries — through their participation in postwar international agreements — have explicitly endorsed freedom of capital movements as a desirable policy.

We shall examine the policy actions and the rationalizations for these actions on their own terms, and within their own frame of analysis, rather than attempting an independent specification of the relevant economic effects. The latter approach, though extremely valuable, would be difficult, and it is not attempted here. Rather, we restrict ourselves to an examination of the effects suggested by policymakers as the important ones. Their views may not be accurate, or not even relevant, within certain frames of reference; nevertheless, they are strongly held and, consequently, become a reality in the formulation of policy. For this reason, evaluating and understanding them is important.

The three countries that we are dealing with have been selected to permit a comparative analysis. They obviously have much in common as the three major industrialized nations in Western Europe. But, as we shall show, there are also significant differences, which have affected their policies toward foreign direct investment.

---

[2] The discussion of the "technology gap" is intimately related to the emergence of the modern multinational firm. The literature is quite extensive on this but for a general summary see Organization for Economic Cooperation and Development, *Gaps in Technology: General Report,* Paris, 1968. For one view of the sovereignty aspect, see Raymond Vernon, "Economic Sovereignty at Bay," *Foreign Affairs,* October, 1968.

REVIEW OF POLICIES

THE ENGLISH CASE

A. Legislative Basis for the Control of Inward Investment [3]

Of the three countries being studied, only the United Kingdom still exercises formal control of inward investment by means of exchange-control regulations — regulations which derive from the Exchange Control Act passed in 1947. The Act itself gives the Treasury very broad and substantial powers for controlling payments between United Kingdom residents and nonresidents of the sterling area. As is not unusual in the United Kingdom, the legislation leaves great powers of interpretation to the discretion of the Treasury, which, in turn, delegates operational control to the Bank of England. This procedure permits substantial flexibility in policy, since the Treasury is able to alter policy by issuance of directives, without recourse to Parliament.

As this is being written, exchange-control regulations technically permit free inward investment by nonresidents if the investment is being effected through the purchase of securities quoted on the Stock Exchange. A formal exception is the stipulation that Treasury permission is required if the purchase will result in transfer of control (more than 50 per cent of the voting shares) from the domestic company to a nonresident. As a practical matter, however, the "complete" freedom of inward investment is only nominal, since, without specific approval, any subsequent repatriation would have to be made through an exchange rate of the pound sterling at a discount from the official rate. Thus, even if a purchase involves less than 50 per cent of the shares, permission must still be obtained to insure repatriation rights.

The effects of these regulations are twofold. First, they insure that foreign investments are financed by a capital inflow rather than by borrowing in the London capital market; hence, they produce an immediate increase in foreign-exchange reserves. The second effect, and

---

[3] This discussion benefited greatly from Leslie F. Murphy, "Investing in the United Kingdom," Conference on Financial and Economic Decisions for United Kingdom Operations, American Management Association, New York, September, 1966.

one more relevant for the discussion which follows, is that they prevent loss of control to foreigners of firms in industries considered vital
to the interests of the United Kingdom. We shall now turn to an examination of what the interests of the United Kingdom are felt to be, and
what methods other than outright prohibition of foreign investments
are used to protect these interests.

B. The Conservative Government's Policy, 1952–65

Given the very general legislative basis for controlling foreign investment, one must look to specific cases to determine how the
granted authority has been applied in practice. This method is admittedly selective, for it leaves out any potential investments which
have been either submitted for approval, failing to receive it — or else
so coolly received that the applications were subsequently withdrawn
without the publicity that a formal disapproval might evoke. There is
no way to document the precise number of such cases, since the applications need never become a matter of public record. Judging from off-
the-record answers to inquiries about the number of such cases given
by government officials, one would conclude that the number is small —
and may even be zero.

During this period, several cases of foreign investment were important enough to precipitate a Parliamentary debate, thus requiring
the Government to take an explicit policy position: the Texas Oil
Company's purchase of Trinidad Oil Company (1956); the American
Ford Company's purchase of the minority equity in British Ford held
by residents of the United Kingdom (1960); and the purchases by the
Chrysler Corporation that finally gave it controlling interest in British
Rootes Motors (1964, 1967). These cases are well known; only the
policy position that emerged need be summarized here.[4]

The Conservative Government studied each of these requests
with some care but ultimately approved all three of them uncondi-
tionally. The major factors cited by the Government in support of its
policy were the strengthening of the balance of payments that would
result; the benefits that American technology would bring to the

[4] *Hansard,* Vol. 554, June 14 and June 20, 1956; Vol. 731, July 12, 1966. *The Trinidad
Oil Company: Proposed Purchase by the Texas Company* (1956), Cmd. 9790, p. 5.

economy; and the need to protect British investment abroad from retaliatory restrictive policies.

C. The Labour Government's Policy, 1965–69

Although the Labour Party's opposition to Government approval of the transfers cited above was spirited,[5] it was not based upon a closely reasoned argument, rather it was inherently a dislike of foreign control of British firms. Nevertheless, the Labour Party's own policy after 1965 was not significantly different.[6] Doctrinaire standards were not applied; the policy was to judge each case on its individual merits.

The first major application of Labour policy came in 1967 when the Government approved Chrysler's proposal to increase its minority holdings in Rootes Motors to a controlling interest. What differentiated this approval from similar actions by the Conservative Party Government was the attachment of several conditions regarding export efforts and the stipulation that the majority of the Directors would remain British. Even more significant was the further stipulation that the Government would participate in the firm as a minority stockholder, with representation on the Board of Directors. This move was designed to insure that the "national interest" would be formally represented in the Board room. Financial participation by the Government represents a major departure from Conservative practice, which in similar circumstances was limited to attempts to induce private British capital sources to aid domestic firms in financial difficulty.

Apart from this, the policy of the Labour Government differed little from that of its predecessor when faced with similar foreign take-overs. Both Governments were equally constrained by immediate balance-of-payments needs, by fears that the investment might be transferred to a European competitor, and by a desire not to precipitate restrictive treatment of British investment abroad. Faced with these constraints, the Labour Government expressed its somewhat greater concern over possible deleterious effects of foreign investment by adopting policies designed to strengthen the structure of domestic industry.

[5] *Ibid.*
[6] *Hansard,* Vol. 731, July 12, 1966, p. 1196. Compare with the statement of the Conservative Government in the Trinidad Oil White Paper, p. 9.

One form which this policy took was the establishment of legislation giving the Government significant power both to prevent mergers and to stimulate reorganization. Two major parts of this legislation are the Monopolies and Mergers Act of 1965 and the Industrial Reorganization Corporation Act of 1966. Interestingly, one of the first cases referred to the Monopolies Commission under the 1965 act—the take-over of Pressed Steel Company by British Motors Corporation—resulted in a favorable report, at least in part because the proposed merger was between two domestic firms. One reason that the Commission saw this merger as desirable was that it would prevent a take-over of Pressed Steel by a foreign firm.[7]

Another effort by the Labour Government to strengthen the structure of domestic industry was the creation in 1966 of the Industrial Reorganization Corporation. The IRC was charged to promote or assist the reorganization or development of any industry on its own initiative, or upon request by the Secretary of State,[8] through the market purchase of equity shares, or by loans (either direct or arranged with private lenders). The IRC began operation with its participation in the Chrysler-Rootes take-over. Since then it has sought to promote rationalization of various sectors of British industry. The general goals are to create larger and more efficient British-owned industrial firms that will (not incidentally) be less vulnerable to foreign take-overs. The recent IRC involvement in promoting a merger of the three largest British bearing manufacturers was at least partly motivated by a prospective foreign take-over of one of these firms.[9]

In summary, when one looks at the policy of the United Kingdom toward foreign direct investment during the postwar period (where this policy is strictly defined to encompass only legal or administrative restrictions and major official statements), the policy would have to be characterized as basically and consistently liberal or unrestrictive. Concern over investments by foreign firms—especially when these would involve take-overs of British-owned firms—has, instead, been

[7] The Monopolies Commission, *The British Motor Corporation Ltd. and the Pressed Steel Company Ltd.: A Report on the Merger,* London, 1966, p. 16.
[8] *Industrial Reorganization Corporation Act, 1966,* London, 1966, p. 2.
[9] "IRC Statement on the U.K. Ball and Roller Bearing Industry," printed in full in *The Economist,* May 24, 1969, p. 76.

manifested in attempts to restructure industries that are vulnerable to take-overs and in which domestic ownership is felt to be in the "national interest." In such industries, policy has been aimed at maintaining intact a significant vertically integrated share under domestic ownership.

Certain broad criteria for defining the national interest emerge from these recent actions. Industries which are large and produce traded goods (i.e., exports and import substitutes) are felt to involve the national interest both through their implications for the balance of payments and through their quantitative importance in the over-all level of economic activity (e.g., the automotive and petroleum industries). The national interest has also become associated with domestic control of industries which are experiencing rapid technological change — in particular, all science-based industries. This association has thus become more extensive than the accepted concern for protecting the traditional "national-defense industries" — a fact to which we shall return later.

THE FRENCH CASE

During the period under consideration, French policy toward foreign investment has been characterized by major shifts. Furthermore, these policy changes were more often hinted at than explicitly announced by new legislation or directives. For both of these reasons, it will be necessary to review French policy in somewhat greater detail.

The volatility of French policy is the more surprising when one considers that France has entered into several international agreements designed to liberalize capital movements, and which, technically, should have significantly restrained the policies of that nation. Among these are the bilateral treaty between France and the United States guaranteeing the right of establishment to each other's nationals (1959); the Code of Liberalization of Capital Movements of the Organization for Economic Cooperation and Development (1960); and Articles 52, 58, and 67 of the Treaty of Rome (1958). Although the legal implications of these agreements are undeniably important, they lie beyond the scope of this paper.[10]

A. Policy Under Finance Minister G.-d'Estaing, 1962–65

In the postwar period up to 1962, French officials were clearly hospitable to new foreign investments, both for the immediate balance-of-payments effects and for the creation of real capital that was generally directly associated with the financial flow. The balance-of-payments effect was insured because new foreign investments had to be financed with funds brought in from abroad. This, however, was a common feature of the exchange-control systems of Western European countries during this period. The policy during this era could be characterized as favorable but restrained,[11] and a steady increase in foreign direct investment in France took place.

Beginning in late 1962, and continuing through 1965, French policy entered a new and decidedly more hostile phase. To recognize this change, it is necessary to refer to particular cases, each of which has received sufficient publicity to make it somewhat of a *cause célèbre*. Although the events are well known, and some have been subjected to extensive analysis,[12] they will be briefly summarized here for purposes of interpretation.

Two American-owned plants, a GM-Frigidaire plant near Paris and a Remington Rand plant at Lyons manufacturing portable typewriters and office furniture, announced substantial layoffs. Official French reaction to these layoffs was prompt and highly critical.[13] The official criticism emphasized a common theme—the irresponsibility of foreign control. The action of these firms did not conform to the ac-

[10] *Conventions of Establishment Between the United States of America and France,* signed at Paris, November 25, 1959. For a legal view of recent French policy in the light of the obligations of this treaty, see Charles Torem and William L. Craig, "Control of Foreign Investment in France," *Michigan Law Review,* February, 1968, pp. 669–720.

[11] See Rosine Dusart, "The Impact of the French Government on American Investment in France," *Harvard International Law Journal,* Winter, 1965, pp. 75–112, for the development of these regulations.

[12] Allan W. Johnstone, *United States Direct Investment in France: An Investigation of French Charges,* Cambridge, Massachusetts, 1965 and Dusart, *op. cit.,* p. 78.

[13] Both the Minister of Industry, M. Maurice Bokanowski, and the Minister of Finance, M. Valéry Giscard-d'Estaing, commented critically on these layoffs. *Christian Science Monitor,* October 6, 1962, p. 5.

cepted French practice of prior consultation by management with the State when significant layoffs were planned.

The dispassionate analysis of these events by Allan W. Johnstone confirms the charge that no prior consultation was made; however, the actions of the firms were not nearly so callous as press reports and official indignation suggested. The labor market was quite tight, so that layoffs would result in only temporary unemployment for most workers, and the firms themselves had undertaken to find employment for many workers in anticipation of the layoffs.

In retrospect, the facts strongly suggest that the official reaction was motivated by considerably more than the events themselves. Not only were the firms not publicly credited with the concern they did show, but the economic forces that initiated the firms' actions were generated within the EEC. The Remington Rand decision was a move to rationalize their production facilities within the EEC, and the GM-Frigidaire redundancy was caused by refrigerator imports from Italy.

Within a few months of these two events, it was announced that the Chrysler Corporation had acquired a controlling interest in the Simca automobile firm. Chrysler had purchased a 25 per cent share in 1958, and now had purchased another 38 per cent from other foreign owners. Had the owners been French, the approval of the French government would have been required, but since the owners who were selling to Chrysler were not French, no such approval was necessary under existing French law. The official French reaction to the transaction in question was publicly critical.[14] Moreover, as noted below, French regulations were subsequently changed to bring such transactions within the reach of French law.

The official concern expressed during late 1962 and early 1963 was in sharp contrast to the lack of specific criticism during the earlier postwar period.[15] Numerous unattributed reports and public statements by French officials now extended the criticism from these specifically

---

[14] *The Economist,* February 9, 1963, pp. 495–496.

[15] This is not to say that U.S. economic influences had evoked no earlier public concern. See, for example, the *New York Times,* October 19, 1961, p. 8, for a rejection of a "gadget civilization" and the "creation of artificial needs," both of which characterize the "American Way of Life."

French experiences to the broader issue of foreign economic domination of the entire EEC.[16]

This sudden fear of foreign—that is, American—domination can be better understood if viewed simultaneously with other events of the period, especially the application of Great Britain for entry into the Common Market. Preliminary negotiations had been under way for several months when President de Gaulle abruptly announced the French veto on January 14, 1963. The threat of American domination was posed in two ways: first, through the "special relationship" existing between the United States and England; and second, through American firms operating within the EEC. The French veto unilaterally countered the first threat. However, a similar "French solution" to the second problem was much more difficult to achieve.

During 1963, the French attempted to raise direct investment by American firms to the level of a Community problem by bringing the issue before the meetings of the EEC finance ministers.[17] The ministers, however, gave little support to the French position that a Community policy was needed to prevent excessive American investment. The consensus of the other members was that any Community response to the question of foreign investment could only be based upon Community Competition Policy—Article 86 of the Treaty of Rome, which provides for Community action in the case of the abuse of a dominant position by a firm or group of firms. Community control on any other basis would be contrary to Article 52, which establishes as Community policy the expansion and encouragement of capital movements.[18]

The French effort to raise their concern over increasing foreign direct investment to the level of a Community problem requiring Community action was thus a failure. The lack of response to this issue by the other members can be attributed to the advantages each saw in con-

[16] Speech by Prime Minister M. Pompidou, reported in the London *Times,* April 25, 1963, p. 18. See also statements by Minister of Finance Valéry Giscard-d'Estaing expressing similar sentiments, reported in the *Christian Science Monitor,* February 7, 1963, p. 4.

[17] *New York Times,* January 25, 1963, p. 13; March 25, 1963, p. 2; *Christian Science Monitor,* February 7, 1963, p. 14.

[18] *European Community,* April–May, 1963, p. 9. See also D. Swann and D. L. McLachlan, *Concentration or Competition: A European Dilemma?* London, 1967, pp. 46ff., for an analysis of Article 86.

tinuing American investment in its own economy; and, perhaps, in some degree, to resentment at the way France had dealt unilaterally with the question of British entry.[19]

Although French officials had indicated that their policy was to protect vulnerable sectors, they did not specify what sectors these were. The French response to the bid by General Electric to take over Machines Bull revealed that the French electronic-computer industry was among those considered vulnerable.[20] An elaboration of French policy was given by Finance Minister G.-d'Estaing at the end of 1964. He stressed two points: that French industry required protection during the transition period 1965 to 1970; and that in affording this protection, the government would make a distinction between foreign take-overs of French firms, and investments which created new productive facilities in France. The former were to be strictly controlled during the transition period, while the latter would be permitted on condition that they conformed to the objectives of French policy, particularly the National Plan.[21]

During 1965, the French policy of discouraging American investment reached its apex. The philosophical basis was expounded by President de Gaulle in his New Year's speech as he warned the French people that great economic efforts would be required if they were to avoid "being engulfed in painful mediocrity and . . . being colonized by foreign interests, inventions and capability."[22] A few months later, he made the same point even more clearly: "We must see that our activities of the essential part remain under French management and French control."[23] Although never officially acknowledged, it was

---

[19] It should be noted, however, that concern at the Community level had previously been hinted at. The Memorandum of the Commission on the Action Programme of the Community for the Second Stage, published in October, 1962, makes a brief reference to foreign investment in the discussion of sector investment policy: "In certain special cases foreign investments in the Community may raise special problems" (p. 59).

[20] *New York Times*, February 5, 1964, p. 44. The negotiations involved a major reorganization and division of the corporate structure. The defense-oriented work of the firm was absorbed by a newly created and wholly French-owned corporation. For an extensive treatment of the details of this affair, see Robert D. W. Landon II, "Franco-American Joint Ventures in France: Some Problems and Solutions," *Harvard International Law Journal*, Spring, 1966, pp. 238–285.

[21] Speech by Minister of Finance Giscard-d'Estaing, December 16, 1964.

[22] "Nationalism and Cooperation," address given December 31, 1964.

[23] "The Independence of France," address given April 27, 1965.

widely reported that all applications for approval of new investments were blocked—simply by not being acted upon.[24]

The effort to sponsor an EEC policy along French lines having failed, during 1965 the French government carried out an extensive review of its national policy toward foreign direct investment. Part of this effort included the first official compilation and analysis of statistics measuring, by sector, the magnitude of foreign direct investment in the French economy. Until this time, the most detailed published statistics were those collected by the U.S. Department of Commerce, but these were limited to American capital only and the figures were not broken down into sectors. The report,[25] prepared by the Ministry of Industry, introduced into the policy discussion facts as well as some analysis—both of which had heretofore been largely absent.

The report noted both the macrodimensions of foreign investment and its distribution by sectors. By the macromeasures, the scale of American investment was acknowledged to be small—2.8 per cent of American productive investments abroad and only 1.7 per cent of the French GNP. The main stress, however, was on the sector breakdown, where percentage of sales in 1963 was the measure of participation. The report's definition of sectors seemed at best capricious: the list ranged from standard sectors, such as automobiles and agricultural machinery, to hybrids such as razor blades and elevators. There is no sense in which these latter two could reasonably be considered to be of equal economic importance to the former pair. The classification scheme appears to have been selected largely to achieve dramatic effect by singling out classes of industry narrowly defined in such a manner that the degree of American participation seems particularly high.

The data and analysis notwithstanding, the conclusions of the report were moderate and balanced, in contrast to many earlier official evaluations of direct investment and its implications for France. The report advised against a strict ban on foreign investment. It argued

[24] It is ironic that the International Monetary Fund's *Annual Report on Exchange Restrictions for 1964* had for the first time stated that foreigners were now freely permitted to make direct investments in France (p. 176).

[25] Ministére de l'Industrie, *Rapport sur Les Investments Etrangers Dans L'Industries Francaises* (Bokanowski Report), 1965.

that since the foreign firms could invest elsewhere within the EEC and freely supply the French market, such a policy, although possible, would leave French industry ultimately facing the same competition. Furthermore, the French economy would lose the advantages of investment in France, such as balance-of-payments effects and the introduction of new technology. This cost of French policy was pointed out by other observers each time an applicant for French approval withdrew and invested elsewhere in the EEC.

By the fall of 1965, the French had relaxed their ban on investment applications, although no take-overs were being approved.[26] During this year there also developed more publicly expressed concern within the Community institutions. Early in the year, President Hallstein addressed himself to the question of American direct investment in an address given before a conference on "Europe, America, and World Trade"; his concern, too, was "excessive sectorial concentration of American investment." [27] The Monetary Committee also expressed concern in its report issued in 1965.[28] The committee, however, stressed the need to control inflation within the EEC. Capital inflows, the report stated, made this control more difficult to achieve, particularly when the inflows were direct investment and affected demand directly.

Over-all, during the period 1963–65, we observe a shift in policy from unrestricted approval of foreign investment to a careful screening of applications and a much more frequent rejection of requests. The method of rejecting the applications was generally that of prolonged delay in acting upon the applications. Both the method used for screening — administrative secrecy — and public interpretations of the policy reflect a lack of any consistent criteria except a strong, if not overriding, preference for investments creating new productive facilities rather than take-overs of existing French-owned firms, and a special concern for certain "key sectors."

Although a distinction between new capital investments and take-overs is made so frequently that its significance seems always to be

---

[26] *New York Times* (International edition), September 17, 1965, p. 7; *The Economist,* November 6, 1965, p. 633.

[27] Address delivered in Amsterdam, February 4, 1965.

[28] *Seventh Report of the Monetary Committee* (English edition), March, 1965, pp. 7ff.

taken as self-evident, in fact it is not possible to differentiate clearly between the economic effects of these two forms of investment. Both a take-over bid and the direct creation of new capital have identical initial balance-of-payments effects, and theory alone offers no guidance regarding long-run balance-of-payments effects. The widely held view that the one has "real" effects on the economy, while the other is purely a financial transaction, is fallacious. The previous French owners of the firm that has been purchased will use the funds for consumption, other domestic investment, or foreign investment. The mass consumption of capital under the prevailing economic conditions seems unreasonable as a general assumption; foreign investment does not seem to have been a major concern during this period, as foreign-exchange controls were being relaxed; the form of new domestic investment might, however, be a cause for official concern.

The French planning mechanism relies heavily upon the control of credit to insure that domestic investment conforms to the plan. Thus, it is possible that foreign take-overs could indirectly finance domestic investment that credit institutions would discourage, e.g., land speculation. Of the three possible explanations, this one is the most plausible, although official emphasis has not been placed upon it to rationalize the ban on take-overs.

The rationale that does seem implicit in the French attitude toward foreign take-overs is that the remaining French firms in the industry will be less able, or willing, to compete with the firms that have been taken over than they would be had the foreign investment created a new firm. Although it is true that French firms would have more time to adjust before feeling the competitive impact, this—when it does occur—may well be stronger, due to the incorporation of the most modern technology into a new plant.[29] Alternatively, if the barriers to entry of new firms are very high in an industry, preventing take-overs may effectively prohibit all foreign investment in that industry. Hence, a ban on take-overs is a convenient device for banning all foreign investment.

[29] The ban on take-overs may also be interpreted as one method of encouraging the merger of French firms, in an effort to put them in a stronger competitive position vis-à-vis the much larger American corporations. With the option of selling out to foreign interests closed, merging with other firms may become the only alternative for the financial survival of small firms.

Let us turn now to the other major factor that appears to have dominated French policy toward foreign direct investment during the period under consideration: the desire to protect certain "key" sectors from foreign investment. All references to key – or advanced – sectors indicated that they were those in which the most rapid technological change was taking place. The electronics industry generally, and the computer branch specifically, is the example that comes most readily to mind as the archetypal key sector in French policy.

This key-sector criterion for screening applications for foreign investments proved to be at least as inconsistent and unworkable as the new versus take-over criterion. A recurring dilemma was created as the policy of excluding investment in key sectors met head-on with a policy of encouraging investments which introduced new technology, simply because key sectors were most often those in which French technology was lagging. Furthermore, foreign investors with a technological advantage were obviously unwilling to invest unless they could retain management control.[30] *L'affaire Bull* presents an excellent example of this latter conundrum: in this instance, French authorities opted to have the technology even at the expense of increased foreign participation in a key sector.

B. *Policy Under Finance Minister M. Debré, 1966–68*

By 1966, it was clear that France lacked any viable long-run policy, both because its membership in the EEC left the French economy vulnerable to imports from American subsidiaries in other member countries, and because the cost of developing French technology in all fields was too high.

The replacement of Valéry Giscard-d'Estaing as Minister of Finance by Michael Debré in January of 1966 initiated a reformulation of French policy. The strident official commentary on the threats to French independence posed by foreign investment ceased. Whereas formerly one received the impression that foreign investment was

---

[30] Evidence also indicates that introduction of new technology through licensing agreements would be no more acceptable to the French government than to the American firms involved. This official concern over the purchase of foreign technology is reflected in the fact that such agreements also required government approval.

presumed to be harmful unless the merits of a particular case were especially strong, official statements now indicated that foreign investment was desirable unless the demerits of a particular case were strong.[31]

Although explicit new criteria were not issued,[32] the legal structure by which foreign investments were controlled was substantially altered by a new law introduced in December of 1966.[33] The new law replaced the complex structure of foreign-exchange controls dating from as far back as 1939. Although this new law was popularly proclaimed as a major step toward freedom of capital movements, in fact it intensified the controls over direct foreign investment in the French economy. New foreign investments still required approval by the Finance Ministry although the Ministry could no longer block an application by indefinite inaction. Two months after filing, applications were to be considered automatically approved, unless the Ministry explicitly disapproved the application or requested a postponement.

The scope of the investments subject to a declaration procedure has, however, been substantially increased. For example, the transfer of ownership of firms located in France from one foreign owner to another requires approval. Similarly, the merger of two foreign firms would require official approval if one of the merging firms owned a French subsidiary, on the ground that the merger would change the ownership of this subsidiary; existing foreign subsidiaries must now obtain approval of the Finance Ministry to expand using new capital from abroad—either equity or loans.

The law fails to provide a general definition of what constitutes a controlling foreign interest in a French firm, except to exempt purchases on the Bourse of less than 20 per cent of existing shares. Further, other factors than percentage of ownership may be considered in the definition. The Ministry of Finance lists these other factors as follows: loans or debt instruments held by the investor, real-property rights, leases and mining rights, technical-assistance agreements, and licensing of industrial-property rights.[34]

[31] London *Times*, January 31, 1966, p. 15.
[32] *International Financial News Survey*, April 15, 1966, p. 120.
[33] The following summary of the legal aspects of the problem relies heavily upon the excellent article by Torem and Craig, "Control of Foreign Investment in France," previously cited.
[34] *Ibid.*, p. 685.

A decree issued at the same time as the new regulations for foreign investments provides for government control of purchases by French firms of foreign industrial-property rights and know-how. All French firms must now obtain the approval of the Ministry of Industry before acquiring foreign industrial-property rights, know-how, or technical assistance. Further, if such acquisition is approved, annual reports of expenses are required.

In summary, these new regulations provide a legal basis for exceedingly close control of all economic activity of foreigners in the French economy — control which is actually more stringent than under the previous structure of foreign-exchange controls. None of the foreign investments mentioned earlier in this account of French policy could have been made without explicit approval. For example, the purchase of controlling interest in Simca by Chrysler was beyond reach of the exchange controls because both parties were foreign. The new law clearly brings such transactions under government control.

This law has, however, recently been seriously challenged by the Commission of the European Economic Community. As was noted above, French membership in the EEC legally subordinates French policy to the provisions of the EEC treaty governing capital movements; the Treaty of Rome and subsequent directives clearly establish freedom of capital movements within the EEC — including direct investment. The Commission has notified the French government that it considers the French authorization procedure for major foreign investments in France to be in violation of EEC regulations. The French have replied that although authorization is required, it is automatic for EEC companies, but this has not satisfied the Commission. Although not explicitly raised, an important issue here is whether the European subsidiaries of American firms are "European companies." To the French, they are clearly not. This dispute will be resolved by the Court of Justice of the European Communities, as the Commission has formally charged that the French law governing capital movements is a violation of the treaty.[35]

French policy continues to permit foreign investment on a selective basis, with a strong bias against foreign take-overs.[36] There is also,

[35] *Wall Street Journal,* February 10, 1969, p. 12, and October 20, 1969, p. 12.
[36] For a recent example see *The Economist,* December 13, 1969, p. 75.

however, some tangible evidence that other types of foreign investment are actively welcomed—at least in development regions. The French government has again opened an office in New York to stimulate the interest of foreign investors.[37] Such an office existed previously but was closed in the early 1960's.

The viability of current French policy depends very much on the outcome of the legal case brought by the European Commission, and on the form and speed of the evolution of the EEC itself. We shall return to the implications of the latter in the section on comparative analysis.

THE GERMAN CASE

The German policy toward direct foreign investment has been exceptionally liberal, especially when contrasted with the policies of France and Great Britain. This liberality has been evidenced both by the complete lack of restrictions on such investment in Germany itself, and by the opposition of Germany, within the EEC, to French efforts to create a Community-wide policy to control foreign investment. Further evidence is to be found in the absence of any German law giving the government legal power to prohibit direct foreign investment or to require prior notification.[38] The law does, however, require registration of the investment.[39] The openness of the government policy extends to the regular publication of data on the magnitude and distribution of foreign participation in the German economy.[40] It is the only one of the three countries to do so. Because the policy has been so unrestrictive, our discussion can be much more brief than it was in the previous two cases.

Although German officials have not indulged in the strong implicit and explicit criticism of foreign investment that has been evident in

[37] *Wall Street Journal,* September 11, 1965, p. 1.

[38] Admittedly, governments of nations as large and modern as Germany do not, in fact, need a legal base for preventing foreign investments. The mere expression of government dissatisfaction with a proposed investment would normally be sufficient to dissuade any foreign investor.

[39] *Verordnung zur Durchführung des Aussenwirtschaftsgesetzes,* paragraphs 57 and 58.

[40] *Monthly Report of the Bundesbank,* May, 1965; November, 1966; and May, 1969.

France, there have been occasional expressions of concern.[41] These, however, have been moderate in tone, and have tended to stress the economic rather than the political implications of excessive foreign investment. In particular, such comments have drawn attention to the possible reduction in competition that might be caused by highly concentrated industries, whether this concentration is foreign or domestic or both.[42]

The official policy toward foreign investments was extensively outlined, in December, 1966, in a statement by the Minister of Economics, Professor Schiller, responding to a question raised by a member of the Bundestag. Professor Schiller stated that participation of foreign capital in the German economy does not have prejudicial effects; rather, it strengthens the economy by stimulating competition and introducing new ideas and techniques. The only problem that might arise, he stated, would be due to concentrations that reached monopolistic levels. Although he felt that no such concentrations then existed, the government was closely observing key industries such as oil.[43]

The only publicly reported instances of government intervention to prevent a foreign take-over involved the oil industry. Early in 1966, a bid was made by the Texas Oil Company for a controlling interest in the ailing firm Deutsche-Erdöl. Negotiations were broken off, owing to government opposition. However, for reasons not known, the government soon withdrew its objections, and the transfer of ownership was ultimately accomplished.[44]

A similar situation arose again in the oil industry when the Dresdner bank sought to find a buyer for its 30 per cent share in one of the only three remaining German-owned oil firms, Gelsenkirchner Bergewerk (GBAG). Both American and French firms were said to be in-

[41] It should, perhaps, be added that Germans not holding official government positions have been rather more apt to criticize the Government's liberal policy toward direct foreign investment. See, for example, "The New American Invasion of Germany," *Der Spiegel,* October, 1965; and the remarks of a key member of the German Parliament, reported in the *Wall Street Journal,* April 6, 1966, p. 5.

[42] See "Foreign Investments in Germany," a statement by Government Director Waldemar Muellar-Enders, Federal Ministry of Economics, in the *Bulletin of the Federal Press Office,* August 26, 1966.

[43] Drucksache, v/1249 of December 19, 1966.

[44] *Wall Street Journal,* May 2, 1966, p. 5; and May 13, 1966, p. 32; *The Economist,* May 14, 1966, p. 743.

terested. However, the German government actively sought a German buyer and succeeded in finding one. GBAG was finally taken over by Germany's largest electrical producer.[45]

The German government's sensitivity to foreign investment in the domestic oil industry reflects considerably more than a fear of economic concentration per se. First, it is not clear that concentration in the German market would have been increased by any of the proposed foreign purchases. Secondly, any definition of the relevant market should start at the level of the EEC and then be limited as other economic factors suggest. To start with, the German market — particularly to the exclusion of French purchasers — indicates that nationalist sentiments, although less of a factor in German policy, are nevertheless not completely absent. We shall return to some implications of German policy for the European Economic Community in our final section, "Summary and Conclusions."

COMPARATIVE ANALYSIS

STATISTICAL ANALYSIS

It is of some interest to review the quantitative changes in foreign investment in the three countries during the postwar period. To the extent that policies have differed significantly among them, these differences should be reflected in the data for this era. We shall restrict our attention to the period 1958 to 1968; 1958 provides a natural starting point because the European Economic Community formally came into existence in that year, and because there was a significant move toward greater convertibility of European currencies at this time. Both factors represent important structural changes affecting foreign investment, and differentiate these years from the earlier postwar period.

Our attention will be restricted to flows from the United States to Europe, to the six countries of the European Economic Community,

[45] *The Economist,* August 12, 1967, p. 595; June 17, 1967, p. 1264; October 5, 1968, p. 99; February 8, 1969, p. 77.

and to each of the three countries selected for this study. The reasons for this restriction are the availability of comparable data, the over-riding importance of American investment, and the obvious economic homogeneity of Europe, as contrasted with other areas of the world. Further, we are only concerned with relative shifts in the flow of American investment to these parts of Europe.

Adopting these restrictions, the available data have been assembled into two tables. Table 1 gives the annual net capital outflow from the United States and Table 2 records the book value of American investment abroad at the end of each year.

The general statistical picture that emerges from these two tables is well known: the flow of American investment to Europe increased quite rapidly early in this period but declined at the end of it as U.S. controls over direct investment in Europe came into effect. There was, nevertheless, more than a fourfold increase in the book value of American investments in Europe in this ten-year period.

The data on book values are of interest primarily because they provide historical perspective. These data reflect both the relative attractiveness of countries for American investors over long periods and the residual effects of major upheavals in the international economy, such as wars.

Within Europe, the United Kingdom and the countries of the European Economic Community combined accounted for 89 per cent of all American investments in 1958, and 81 per cent in 1968. The decline notwithstanding, the two areas have clearly dominated the European picture both historically and over this recent period. Among individual nations, the United Kingdom similarly dominates with 47 per cent of all American investments in Europe in 1958, and 35 per cent in 1968. This dominance reflects the historical preferences of American investors for Britain, although, since 1958, the creation of the EEC has tended to alter this pattern. In 1957, the British share was 48 per cent, as compared with the 40 per cent share of the EEC countries; by 1968 these shares had changed to 35 per cent and 46 per cent.

Although the book values are arrived at over this period as a cumulation of net flows, the flows are also of interest because they quickly highlight important shifts in investment—shifts which produce notice-

TABLE 1

American Direct Investment Abroad, Including Net Capital Outflow and Undistributed Earnings of Subsidiaries

	1958	1959	1960	1961	1962	1963	1964	1965	1966	1967	1968
					(millions of dollars)						
Europe	428	750	1,325	1,057	1,161	1,443	1,776	1,867	2,244	1,749	1,437
EEC	219	283	436	406	566	733	907	854	1,243	893	526
France	76	77	101	104	157	204	191	184	143	142	−1
Germany	81	130	209	168	290	279	294	317	631	420	285
U.K.	172	330	749	318	261	343	373	559	576	434	583
					(percentages)						
France as a % of EEC	35	27	23	26	28	28	21	22	12	16	0
Germany as a % of EEC	37	46	48	41	51	38	32	37	51	47	54
U.K. as a % of EEC	79	117	172	78	46	47	41	65	46	49	111
U.K. as a % of Europe	40	44	57	30	22	24	21	30	26	25	41
EEC as a % of Europe	51	38	33	38	49	51	51	46	55	51	37

SOURCE: *Survey of Current Business*, September, 1967; October, 1968; and October, 1969.

TABLE 2

Book Value of American Direct Investments Abroad

	1957	1958	1959	1960	1961	1962	1963	1964	1965	1966	1967	1968 [a]
	(millions of dollars)											
Europe	4,151	4,573	5,323	6,681	7,713	8,930	10,340	12,109	13,985	16,209	17,882	19,386
EEC	1,680	1,908	2,208	2,644	3,087	3,722	4,480	5,426	6,304	7,584	8,405	8,992
France	464	546	640	741	857	1,030	1,240	1,446	1,609	1,758	1,904	1,910
Germany	581	666	796	1,006	1,177	1,476	1,780	2,082	2,431	3,077	3,487	3,774
U.K.	1,974	2,147	2,477	3,231	3,542	3,824	4,172	4,547	5,123	5,657	6,101	6,703
	(percentages)											
France as a % of EEC	28	29	29	28	28	28	28	27	26	23	23	21
Germany as a % of EEC	35	35	36	38	38	40	40	38	39	41	42	42
U.K. as a % of EEC	118	113	112	122	115	103	93	84	81	75	73	75
U.K. as a % of Europe	48	47	47	48	45	43	40	38	37	35	34	35
EEC as a % of Europe	40	42	41	40	40	42	43	45	45	47	47	46

SOURCE: *Survey of Current Business*, September, 1966; September, 1965, p. 24; August, 1964, p. 10; August, 1963, p. 18; September, 1958; August, 1957, 1961, 1962, and 1959; September, 1960.
[a] Preliminary data.

able effects in the stock figures only over longer periods of time. Because of the sharp changes in French policy during this period, the flows relating to France are of particular interest.

In 1958, the flows of American investment to Germany and France were approximately equal, each representing about 36 per cent of American investment in the countries of the Community. In combination, they represented only slightly less than American investment going to England. For the remainder of the period, Germany's share of foreign investment in the Community was significantly larger than the French share. In 1968, Germany received half of all American investment in the Community, while the French share was zero. The impact of the more restrictive policy is clearly seen in the steady decline of France's share of American investment in the countries of the Community after 1963. The precipitous drop from 1967 to 1968 was, however, no doubt attributable to the civil disorders in 1968.

The data for the United Kingdom are complicated by several large individual investments, especially Ford's purchase of the minority interest in British Ford in 1960, and Chrysler's final purchase of Rootes Motors in 1965. Making an allowance for these, from 1958 to 1961 the flow into the United Kingdom was approximately 80 per cent of the flow to the Community, although this flow exceeded the combined flow to Germany and France. In 1962, the flow into the United Kingdom relative to that into the Community declined abruptly and then, through 1967, remained constantly in the range of 40 per cent to 50 per cent of American investment in the Community. During this same period, American investment in France and Germany combined was in the range of 60 per cent to 70 per cent of the investment in the Community, with the share going to Germany steadily increasing over that going to France. By 1966–67, Germany and the United Kingdom were receiving equal amounts.

The data for 1968 are substantially at variance with the trends established during the previous five years. The jump in investment in Britain relative to that in the Community reflects the impact of three major events: the complete cessation of further investment in France (resulting in part from French domestic political instability); the devaluation of the pound in the fall of 1967 (making assets in the United Kingdom cheaper); and, finally, political uncertainties aroused by the invasion of Czechoslovakia. One can only conjecture as to the relative weights that should be assigned to each of these happenings.

In spite of the difficulties in accurately assessing causes of the 1968 data, the impact of French policy is still clear: no other explanation adequately explains the intra-Community shifts of American investment away from France. During this same time, American investment in the Community as a whole did not show any decline relative to American investment in Europe. From 1962 to 1967, the Community's share of all American investment in Europe has remained very stable at around 50 per cent.

This brief analysis of the data indicates that French policy has been both too effective (with respect to discouraging American investments in France) and quite ineffective (not achieving any significant reduction in American investment in the Community). French policy has only redirected American investment from France to the other countries of the Community — especially Germany.

ECONOMIC DETERMINANTS

In this section we consider in turn those economic variables which have appeared most frequently in the discussions of foreign investment policy, our objective being to evaluate their actual importance in the decision-making of each of the three countries. In the subsequent section we shall consider those variables that could be classified as economic but which, we feel, have in actuality been shaped more by political considerations.

A. Balance of Payments

During the whole postwar period, the balance of payments has been a major factor in the economic policy of the United Kingdom, and certainly, as we have noted, any official discussion of foreign investment always mentions the favorable balance-of-payments effects. Nevertheless, it seems extremely unlikely that the weak balance of payments was a crucial determinant of the generally unrestrictive United Kingdom policy; rather, it served primarily to rationalize it.

Should the balance-of-payments problem of the United Kingdom be "solved," this would be more likely to lead to a removal of government restrictions on foreign investment by British firms than to the adoption of a more restrictive policy toward foreign investment in the United Kingdom. The United Kingdom is too important a foreign investor itself to risk an overtly restrictive policy.

In Germany, the balance of payments was typically in surplus over this period, frequently combined with problems of inflation. Restriction of foreign direct investment would have assisted in ameliorating both of these problems. Nevertheless, no restrictions were imposed or mooted in public.

Early in the period, France was experiencing balance-of-payments deficits, and the liberal foreign-investment policy of this time encouraged capital inflows, which assisted in the financing of these deficits. In the mid-1960's, when foreign-investment policy became highly restrictive, French reserves were rising, thus permitting the balance-of-payments impact of this reversal of policy to be ignored. Subsequently, the balance of payments returned to a deficit. Nevertheless, there has been no return to the earlier liberal policy. Foreign investments that would involve the take-over of French firms are still discouraged.

On the basis of these three different situations, we conclude that the balance of payments has generally played a peripheral role, rather than an overriding one, in determining policy toward foreign direct investment.

B. Economic Planning

The literature makes frequent reference to the complications created for national economic planning by direct foreign investment in Europe. Usually such references take the complications as self-evident; hence, no supporting evidence is offered. Here, we shall critically review the potential importance of these complications for the countries in our study. Of these three, only two are of interest in this respect, Germany having no significant, detailed national economic planning. The United Kingdom and France do have forms of economic planning, although implementation of the British plan has not been vigorously pursued. We shall discuss each in turn.

A review of the planning mechanism in the United Kingdom is

beyond the scope of this paper.[46] We are primarily interested in potential and actual conflicts between planning goals, the means for achieving them, and foreign participation in the British economy. With this in mind, it is interesting to observe the role and the problems that the planners themselves anticipated. The basic document for the British effort at detailed planning was issued in 1965, a time of manifest concern over foreign investment.[47] Although this document runs to over four hundred pages, there is only one significant reference to foreign investment:

> New productive investment by foreign companies, especially in underemployed areas of the United Kingdom, will continue to play an important part in the creation of new industrial capacity. A special effort will be made to attract those companies whose exports to Britain have already secured them a firm base in the British market to start local production. There will continue, of course, to be regulation of the acquisition of control of existing British companies.[48]

Taken at face value, this statement indicates that conflicts between economic planning and foreign direct investment are not at issue. Further, in the regional planning of the United Kingdom, the significant role played by American investment is well recognized. If planning encompasses the alteration of the structure of industries, both to create larger production units and to preserve a substantial degree of domestic ownership, then the potential for conflict is significant. As we noted earlier, British policy regarding the structure of industry places considerable emphasis on protecting domestic ownership.

In France, the planning issue is more complex than in Britain, because it has been an important guiding force in the French economy during the whole postwar period; [49] it is an integral part of the economic

---

[46] For a thorough discussion of the development of United Kingdom planning, see Everett E. Hagen and Stephanie F. T. White, *Great Britain: Quiet Revolution in Planning*, Syracuse, N.Y., 1966. For a comparative analysis of planning among the countries of interest here, see M. MacLennon, M. Forsyth, and G. Denton, *Economic Planning and Policies in Britain, France, and Germany*, New York, 1968.

[47] *The National Plan*, Cmd. 2764, London, 1965.

[48] *Ibid.*, p. 10.

[49] See MacLennon *et al.* for a brief review and analysis of French planning.

fabric of the nation. Further, the plan is much more detailed in that output targets are set for individual industries rather than just for macrovariables. For implementation, the plan relies upon both government intervention and an *économie concertée* achieved through cooperation between industry and government. Government intervention takes place through both fiscal and monetary incentives — particularly the latter. Extensive government control of the capital market and major credit institutions is a basic factor in insuring compliance with the plan.

With this institutional structure of planning in the French economy, one can readily see that a large disruptive influence might be wielded by foreign-controlled firms.[50] Such firms can be expected neither to identify with the plan as a national goal nor to depend as much upon French credit sources as do French-owned firms. This point has been frequently reflected in the public criticism of foreign investment. The closures of the plants of Remington Rand and Frigidaire cited earlier gave credence to the alleged indifference of American firms to accepted modes of French socioeconomic behavior.

Because of this widely accepted presumption that direct investment has been incompatible with the French planning mechanism, the statement of Oliver Giscard-d'Estaing before a Congressional committee is of particular interest. In listing the significance of American investment for the French economy, he stated that subsidiaries of American firms have been responsive to French economic-planning policies.[51] The major concern expressed by Oliver Giscard-d'Estaing related to the technology gap and American investments. We shall return to this issue below.

Another factor that reduces the disruptive potential of foreign investments for French planning is the wide power for regulating this investment embodied in the law passed in 1967. This piece of legislation effectively prevents foreign firms from escaping French credit these gaps. Nevertheless, the report suggests that member countries

[50] MacLennon *et al.*, p. 362.

[51] *International Aspects of Anti-trust*, Part I. Hearings before the Subcommittee on Antitrust and Monopoly of the Committee on the Judiciary, U.S. Senate, 89th Congress, 2nd Session, April 28, 1966, p. 205. M. Oliver Giscard-d'Estaing should not be confused with his brother Valéry, who was Minister of Finance just prior to this time. At the time of his testimony, Oliver Giscard-d'Estaing was Director General of the European Institute for Business Administration, Fontainebleu, France. He has also achieved the rank of Inspector of Finance within the French Civil Service.

controls through borrowing abroad. The law, however, does not restrict self-financing of these firms through retained earnings. This stand is consistent with a move toward more flexible planning; the Fifth Plan, in fact, encourages more self-financing by firms, in spite of the loss of government influence which results.[52]

To summarize, the complications created for French planning by foreign direct investment seem, upon examination, to have been more potential than actual. Further, as French membership in the European Economy Community increases French interdependence with the other member economies, the implications for French national planning raised by this new situation will greatly overshadow any complications caused by American investments.

POLITICAL DETERMINANTS AND THE TECHNOLOGY GAP

Our review of the economic determinants has failed to suggest any general framework which builds upon them to explain the policy actions described earlier. In fact, our analysis has suggested that, collectively, these strictly economic factors have played at most a minor role. In this section, we seek a better understanding of these policies by taking a broader view—one that encompasses the political context.

Since the mid-1960's, one of the major topics dominating the discussion of American-European relationships has been the "technology gap."[53] Concern over this problem has been widespread in Europe, and it has placed American direct investment and technology in a different perspective. The policymaker's view of the interrelationship between transfer of technology and foreign direct investment has undergone a radical change during the postwar period. The earlier view (frequently reflected in the policy statements reviewed above)

[52] MacLennon et al., p. 167.

[53] Most of this discussion has been distressingly vague—a term searching for a phenomenon, and frequently not even finding a definition. The important parts of this discussion have now been masterfully pulled together and given a clear framework by Robert Gilpin in his book *France in the Age of the Scientific State*, Princeton, N.J., 1968. Much of the discussion which follows here draws directly on his basic conceptualization. Anyone interested in the literature should refer to his book; the subsequently published OECD reports in *The Gaps in Technology Between Member Countries* series; and Christopher Layton, *European Advanced Technology: A Programme for Integration*, London, 1969.

was an extremely positive one: the benefits to the domestic economy of new technology were unquestioned, and foreign investment was a uniquely important device for transmitting this technology.

By the mid-1960's, a significant counterview began to emerge in the context of a broader reassessment of science and technology, and their implications for the evolution of the nation-state. This view has been articulated most extensively by the French; it is, however, by no means an exclusively French concern.[54]

Robert Gilpin has recently synthesized the French views and generalized them into a most useful and interesting conceptual framework. In Gilpin's view, this new and overriding concern over technology on the part of European political leaders marks the beginning of the age of the "Scientific State" and the end of the "Industrial State." From the 19th century to the mid-20th century, industrialization was the step through which a nation-state could achieve the status of a Great Power.[55] Even the rhetoric of the 1950's reflects this: size and growth of GNP, amount of steel capacity, and so on, were the indices of Great Power status. But in the age of the Scientific State, the institutionalization of science and technology provides nations with the essential ingredient for Great Power status, as it is now conceived.[56]

Similar ideas appear in the study by the Organization for Economic Cooperation and Development on *Gaps in Technology,* but without Gilpin's conceptual framework. After reviewing the evidence, the OECD report concludes that technological gaps *have had no undesirable effects on the trade or on the economic growth* (paramount goals in the age of the Industrial State) of the countries experiencing these gaps. Nevertheless, the report suggests that member countries

---

[54] See, for example, the famous "industrial helotry" speech by Harold Wilson, delivered to the Council of Europe on January 23, 1967. See also earlier remarks on a European Technological Community, London *Times,* November 15, 1966, p. 1, and December 1, 1966, p. 12.

[55] Gilpin, *op. cit.,* p. 5.

[56] *Ibid.,* p. 25. J.-J. Servan-Schreiber is also concerned with achieving Great Power status for Europe through technology. This idea is clearly stated in his influential book *The American Challenge,* although it is buried in a footnote on page 111 of the English edition. In explaining why selective specialization in science-based industries, on the Swedish model, will not do, he states, "The Swedish model is rich in social potential, but Sweden has no ambitions to be a world power."

desire to control their own technology.[57] Great Power aspirations require far greater national control over science and technology than is possible if foreign firms dominate the domestic science-based industries.

If this thesis is correct, the differences in the policies toward American investment demonstrated by the three countries reflect differences in the gaps dividing the Great Power aspirations and the resources of each. This gap has been greatest for France and relatively smaller in the cases of Germany and the United Kingdom, although not altogether insignificant in either.

The United Kingdom has both a broader base in the technologically advanced industries and an easier entree to American technology in certain fields, most notably that of atomic development.[58] Germany has also had a special political relationship with the United States because of its defense problems; this relationship has negated any technological independence.[59]

In spite of these differences, an independent European technology and science has emerged as a common concern, with implications that may ultimately lead to a common policy toward foreign direct investment. As was noted earlier, France failed in 1963 to obtain support from other members of the European Economic Community in establishing a Community-level policy to control American investment. By 1965, however, the other European countries were moving much closer to the French view of the importance of science and technology — and the attendant need for action. We shall return to the implications for Community policy in the next section.

FOREIGN INVESTMENT POLICY OF THE EUROPEAN
ECONOMIC COMMUNITY

No discussion of the policies of France and Germany would be complete without reference to their membership in the European

[57] Organization for Economic Cooperation and Development, *Gaps in Technology: General Report*, Paris, 1968, p. 31.
[58] Gilpin, *op. cit.*, p. 54.
[59] *Ibid.*, p. 437.

Economic Community, both because economic interdependence imposes constraints on the national policies of any member, and because the Community has the long-range goal of harmonizing all national economic policies. However, insofar as a firm policy of the Community is still being formulated, we can do little more than suggest which lines of development appear to be the most significant for the future.

On the Community level, it seems unlikely that any policy explicitly restricting American investment will be adopted. This approach, though urged by France, has never received public support from other members. However, the French have stimulated common concerns which are now receiving Community attention in two distinct ways.

First, concern for European technology has led to numerous national cooperative efforts (e.g., the Concorde) and to some efforts on the Community level (e.g., Euratom), but no comprehensive framework has yet emerged, nor is it yet clear what types of cooperation are most successful. The obstacles have been extensively analyzed and numerous proposals advanced, but nationalistic sentiments and rivalries have continued to prevent a comprehensive approach.[60]

The second policy of the Community that is evolving deals with nationalizing the industrial structure—a response similar to that taken by the United Kingdom in creating the Industrial Reorganization Corporation.[61] The Medium-Term Economic Policy Committee of the Community is formulating a policy concerning the industrial structure which aims to improve the competitiveness of firms in the countries of the Community vis-à-vis American firms, especially those with large investments in Community countries.[62]

One of the goals of the industrial-structure policy is to create larger European firms on a scale comparable to the major international firms.[63] To carry out such a policy at the Community level is an undertaking vastly more difficult than doing so within a single nation. Many other Community policies must be formulated and implemented si-

[60] Both Gilpin and Layton (1969) provide comprehensive analyses of these problems. Layton also provides an extensive review of the specific efforts at technological cooperation that have been undertaken.

[61] European Communities, *Second General Report on the Activities of the Communities* (1968), Brussels, February, 1969, p. 199.

[62] European Economic Community Commission, *Tenth General Report on the Activities of the Community*, Brussels, June, 1967, p. 179.

[63] *Second General Report*, pp. 181–182.

multaneously to permit modification of the industrial structure; these include a European company law, a detailed Community antitrust policy, a more efficient Continental capital market, and a decision on the admission of new members to the Community.[64]

These are, of course, major obstacles to the evolution of the Community itself, and complete discussion of them is beyond our limits here. If these obstacles are surmounted, a policy of the Community regarding its industrial structure could have a most significant impact on foreign direct investment. If this policy is implemented by discrimination against existing foreign firms — through discriminatory government purchasing, for example — the postwar trend away from economic nationalism could well be reversed.[65]

SUMMARY AND CONCLUSIONS

OUR "Review of Policies" has shown none of the three countries willing to permit complete freedom of foreign direct investment in its economy, international agreements to this effect notwithstanding. The methods of restricting foreign investment have been quite different among the three. The English have abided by the letter of the agreements but have also undertaken domestic policies clearly designed as defensive measures aimed at preventing foreign investment in certain industries. The French were initially less subtle in their methods for restricting investment. Apparently, the restrictions were carried to excess, necessitating the subsequent revision of policy. With the single exception of oil, German policy has been highly unrestrictive. This policy will be tested in the future by the support and direction that Germany gives to the developing policy of the European Economic Community.

[64] European Communities, *First General Report on the Activities of the Communities* (1967), Brussels, February, 1968, pp. 193–194. Many of these points are also developed by E. M. J. A. Sassen, a member of the Commission, in his article, "Competition Policy: More than 'Anti' Trust," *European Community,* October, 1969, pp. 3–5.

[65] See the view of Commission member M. Guido Colonna di Paliano in "Industrial Policy: Problems and Outlook," *Bulletin of the European Communities,* February, 1969, pp. 5–8.

One important question raised by our study concerns the real motivation behind restrictive policies. The "Comparative Analysis" section above failed to uncover any official economic rationale solidly based on factual and theoretical economic analysis. On the contrary, the official rationale was typically devoid of factual evidence and of any solid base of sound economic theory. The general policy bias against foreign take-overs as opposed to "real" investment is a major example of bad theorizing.[66]

For an explanation, one is tempted to attribute restrictive policies to simple economic nationalism. Such an explanation now has a secure place in the corpus of economic theory, as a result of the work of Breton and Johnson.[67] Their approach suggests that domestic ownership of economic assets within a country is a collective, or public, good from which psychic income is derived by the populace or significant segments of it. Restriction of foreign direct investment can thus be interpreted as rational economic behavior. While this approach has general appeal, it seems inadequate for the cases at hand, because it does not adequately emphasize the increasing focus of these restrictive policies on the science-based industries.

The concept of the Scientific State may provide a more insightful and richer explanation. It is more insightful through its particular relevance to the three countries under discussion, given their state of economic development and their historical experience. It is also a richer explanation because it simultaneously encompasses other important contemporary phenomena peculiar to these countries—for example, their national concern with science and educational policy, and the interrelationships of these with foreign direct investment.[68]

Because of the growing common elements in these three national

[66] One might argue that new foreign firms are preferable to take-overs because a larger number of firms will reduce industrial concentration and increase competition. This, however, would be empirically inappropriate here, inasmuch as all three governments have generally been concerned to *increase* concentration of the domestically owned firms.

[67] Albert Breton, "The Economics of Nationalism," *Journal of Political Economy,* 72 (1964), pp. 376–386. H. G. Johnson, "A Theoretical Model of Economic Nationalism in New and Developing States," *Political Science Quarterly,* 80 (June, 1965), pp. 169–185.

[68] H. G. Johnson, *Comparative Cost and Commercial Policy Theory for a Developing World Economy,* Wicksell Lectures, 1968; Stockholm, 1968. See especially the second lecture.

policies, and because of the overwhelming likelihood that Britain will join the European Economic Community, attention naturally turns to the Community for the future implications of these policies.

A major implication for the future is the Community's policy regarding its industrial structure. If this policy moves to create European firms in science-based industries through overtly discriminatory and protectionist devices, it will have undesirable consequences for free trade in the Atlantic Community and for the economic benefits derived from this trade — not to mention the political friction that it would generate.

It nevertheless seems likely that, by some means, larger European firms are going to be created. Two major economic issues for the future then follow. The first of these will be a need to arrive at an international agreement defining and limiting the scope for discriminatory governmental "Buy American" or "Buy European" policies. Policies of this nature already represent substantial barriers to efficient resource allocation on the international level, and if unchecked, promise to raise even greater obstacles in the future. Further, as two-way direct investment grows, it will become more and more difficult to make ethnoeconomic distinctions.

A second consideration for the future lies in the fact that a greater number of large European firms will mean a greater number of large multinational firms. The world is a big market, but economic concentration can threaten competition in this market just as it can in national markets. To avoid this, there will be a growing need for internationally agreed upon and enforced "competition policy."

Both of these issues will require the attention of economists. The threat of economic nationalism is still with us, but it now appears with a new impetus and a new rationale in the age of the Scientific State. The Scientific State, like the Industrial State before it, has a tremendous potential for benefiting mankind through the systematic application of new scientific knowledge according to comparative advantage. But this potential may well be lost if the Scientific State reverts to the narrowly nationalistic pattern that characterized the early development of the Industrial State.

COMMENTS

MERLE YAHR WEISS
NATIONAL BUREAU OF ECONOMIC RESEARCH

Although the title of Severn's paper, "Investment and Financial Behavior of American Direct Investors in Manufacturing," is a fairly accurate description of the content of his paper, his intention in analyzing the behavior of foreign investors is to appraise the impact of American direct investment on certain items in the balance of payments of the United States. By his methods, he finds that domestic economic circumstances and policies have negligible effects on direct-investment outflows. This conclusion is warranted on the basis of his analysis, but his work cannot be used to estimate the over-all effect of direct investment on the balance of payments.

Other than capital outflows and remitted earnings, Severn's paper ignores all effects of direct investment on the balance of payments. There is no reason to believe that the secondary effects of direct investment—for example, multiplier effects on income in the host country, changes in the demand by subsidiaries for capital goods produced in the United States, the substitution of goods produced by subsidiaries for exports from the United States, changes in the demand for parts and components imported from the United States, and even changes in exports to the United States of goods produced by subsidiaries—are negligible, or that their net effect on the balance of payments is very small. In addition, subsidiaries might provide information about other American products not produced by subsidiaries, and by this means increase exports from the United States. Although, at present, we do not know the magnitudes of these effects, I feel that Severn's approach to the appraisal of the impact of direct foreign investment on the balance of payments is incomplete and, moreover, addresses itself to analyzing an aspect of foreign direct investment that could have but little effect on the balance of payments.

Certainly the view of the U.S. government in changing the voluntary controls on direct investment to mandatory controls was that potential future inflows could be sacrificed to reduce present outflows.

We do not know whether the government view has been warranted, but Severn's analysis cannot yield the information we need to appraise the costs of the government's action.

Severn's paper is divided into two parts: in the first, he estimates a model of investment and financial behavior of multinational firms. His intention here is to assess the importance of various factors within an individual firm as determinants of the firm's division of expenditures between foreign and domestic investment. Because he views payments of dividends to stockholders as competing with other possible uses of the firm's funds, he also estimates the determinants of variations in dividends. In yet another equation, he estimates the determinants of the relative allocation of firm funds between domestic and foreign uses.

Severn's main interest is in determining whether firms will use their internally generated funds for domestic, or for foreign, investment expenditures. Correctly, he views the firm's managers as dividing their investment funds between foreign and domestic uses, depending on where the marginal efficiency of investment is higher. However, his proxy variable for the marginal efficiency of investment is the change in the firm's sales in each location. Changes in sales represent, at most, only the changes in the demand factors that the firm faces in each location, totally ignoring the cost conditions which, together with the demand conditions faced by the firm, determine the marginal efficiency of investment. These cost conditions are unlikely to remain constant during the annual periods which Severn takes as his short run. Possibly, one could argue that cost conditions are relatively homogeneous within the United States and that change in sales is a good proxy for the marginal efficiency of investment in different locations. Among countries, though, a large body of statistics indicates that costs of production, including wages and the prices of raw materials, differ greatly. Furthermore, because of the unavailability of certain specialized factors of production in some countries, production of certain products may be impossible. Is it reasonable to assume, then, that the marginal efficiency of investment can be measured by sales changes alone, or by adding lagged sales changes to the model to take account of more long-run effects? I think not. Furthermore, Severn's model assumes that the firm's output is sold in *either* the foreign or the domestic market exclusively, and that output produced in a given area is sold in that area. Exports are not a part of his model, and their omission appears to be inconsistent with the view that firms maximize worldwide profits.

In the second part of his paper, within the context of his model of behavior of the firm, Severn uses the results of his estimating techniques to measure the impact of macroeconomic policy on the balance of payments of the United States. He finds that domestic economic policy has a negligible net effect on direct-investment outflows. A recession in the United States causes a large decrease in net outflows during the recession year and an increase in the next year. His results are not surprising: multinational firms undertake investment in order to maximize long-run worldwide profits. If a recession limits the ability of these firms to finance foreign investments, they will either increase their capital outflows in the following year or will attempt to finance their foreign expansion by borrowing abroad. This latter action is entirely ignored in Severn's model, and almost entirely ignored in his paper. Does not the maximization of worldwide profits of the firm imply that firms will utilize foreign borrowing as a source of funds if they are cheaper or, as in the case of the present restrictions on capital outflows, if they are sometimes the only means by which multinational firms can expand abroad.

Severn's data cover the period 1961–66. The voluntary restraint program was begun in 1965 and was extended in 1966. Thus, during two years of this six-year period, the U.S. government was urging firms to finance any expansion of their productive capacity abroad by foreign borrowing. Firms not only had a rational basis for borrowing abroad when it was cheaper for them to do so, but, in 1965 and 1966, they had fewer choices and were often forced to expand their foreign capacity by this means.

In one version of his model, Severn does include a dummy variable for 1966. This variable takes a positive sign, but it is not significant. The positive sign implies that foreign-investment expenditures increased in response to the restraint program. Although the positive coefficient could be attributed to errors in the data, Severn believes that it is indicative of the actual behavior of firms, reported in their annual reports (the source of his data), these errant firms successfully concealing their behavior from the U.S. government. An article in the *Wall Street Journal* suggested that part of the errors-and-omissions item in the balance of payments represented capital exports by American firms. This appears to be possible. However, I doubt that these same firms would then reveal large capital exports in their annual reports to their stockholders.

At present, we have very little empirical information about the determinants of foreign investment. Severn has attempted to fill this gap in our knowledge by developing and estimating a model of the international firm's investment behavior. His paper provides a useful beginning. After reading it, other authors will be better able to understand the international firm. However, I submit that much additional work needs to be done before we shall be able to estimate the balance-of-payments effects of foreign investment.

Gillespie examines the policies of three important host countries of American foreign investment, namely, England, France and Germany, to obtain an understanding of the economic determinants of these countries' policies toward foreign investment. His objective is a valuable one: if we knew the economic conditions that determined policy, we would be better equipped to predict policy changes and to appraise the appropriateness of specific policies.

The main body of his paper is a review of the policies of England, France and Germany toward direct foreign investment during the post-World War II period. He cites the laws regulating foreign investment in each of these countries and briefly recounts how they were interpreted for specific American foreign investments that provoked public debate and controversy. Gillespie is aware that this approach leads him to ignore many potential investments that were immediately rejected and others that were not undertaken because the American investor withdrew his request in anticipation of its being rejected. However, Gillespie is not aware that his approach also fails to analyze the total investment climate in any of these countries resulting from the existence of rules and regulations which restrict the activities of foreign investors. We do not know how many American firms did not request the privilege of investing in England, France, or Germany because they anticipated that they would not be able to operate freely in these countries.

Gillespie compares the quantitative changes in foreign investment in the three countries during the 1958–68 period. He believes that the policies of each of these countries should have determined, to some degree, the capital flows received by each country during this period. Undoubtedly this is true; however, American firms should also have responded to other conditions prevailing in these countries before undertaking foreign investments—considering primarily their incentive to maximize worldwide profits. We cannot tell from these data what factors motivate American firms to invest in each of these countries, and the relative strength of these factors.

However, Gillespie's principal concern is not with why investment takes place but with the economic determinants of host-country policies toward foreign investment. He concludes that economic conditions, specifically balance-of-payments problems and internal economic planning, have had only a minor role in determining the policies toward foreign investment of these three countries. Although this is a possible conclusion based upon the experience in the countries under discussion, it does not convince me. He reasons that since Britain is a significant foreign investor herself, she will never use balance-of-payments conditions as a basis for restricting foreign investment. This conclusion implies that Britain will not restrict foreign-investment activities, as she will always be conscious of her own role as a foreign investor.

Although national economic planning could provide a basis for restricting foreign investment, Gillespie concludes that this factor did not motivate France, the principal planning nation of the three, to limit foreign investment. Britain, which has a somewhat less planned economy than France, did not find that foreign investors had goals that were inconsistent with the British planning goals. In short, neither balance-of-payments problems nor economic-planning goals motivated Britain, France, or Germany to regulate foreign investment.

What, then, provided the incentive for regulations? Gillespie cites nationalism as the principal factor. In his view, these three countries and the European Economic Community are very much concerned with developing their own large firms, which will successfully compete with the already significant and large American firms. If this is correct and the Europeans are successful, American firms can expect more competition from European producers and greater restrictions on their expansion in Europe. American firms would do well to study Gillespie's conclusions and appraise their impact on company activities.

ARNOLD W. SAMETZ

NEW YORK UNIVERSITY

Severn's study is essentially an extension to foreign direct investment of a theory of corporate investment decision-making that has been applied to domestic investment. By treating the international firm's decision in a noncompartmentalized way, he has been able to develop a testable model of the financial behavior of direct investors abroad that is analytically appealing and that promises to predict well. I think we are going to see much more work following the lines set out in this paper; and a reevaluation of other approaches is in order.

On the one hand, the variety of residual-fund theories that relate foreign investment too closely to the earnings of foreign subsidiaries, or even treat those earnings as wholly reserved for foreign investment, are refuted. Indeed, earnings of the foreign subsidiary seem to have more effect on *domestic* investment of the firm, and on investment of the firm as a whole. There seems to be even less reluctance to go outside for funds to finance investment opportunities abroad than for those at home.

On the other hand, the usual approach of comparing the marginal efficiency of investment (MEI) with the cost of funds, as applied to cyclical expansion, would seem to be supported by Severn's findings. For example, considering that, over the period covered, the investment boom was abroad rather than at home, and given a Lintner dividend function, the share of external finance of subsidiaries both from the parent and from local sources abroad increases. (Sources-of-funds data for direct investment in European manufacturing show a rising role of external finance during this period, even before the imposition of direct-investment controls.)

If I interpret Severn's model correctly, considering the period *since* 1966, we would say that the shift rightward of the domestic MEI schedule (relative to foreign-investment opportunities) would lead to a shift in the mix of foreign subsidiaries' borrowing toward borrowing abroad (as well as some reduction in investment abroad) even in the absence of controls over direct investment. It will be interesting to see how well the model works with 1967–69 data. Is it not likely that foreign and domestic investment behave more like substitutes under these conditions, even though they did not do so during Severn's period — that is, 1961–66?

Next, I want to draw attention to two aspects of the foreign-investment decision that are slighted in this model but which, I think, could easily and fruitfully be explicitly incorporated. Severn regards increases in sales as more permanent (or less transitory) when sales have been growing steadily for some time in the past. I wonder whether some of the greater so-called permanence of the demand for foreign investment, as compared with domestic investment, may not be explained by the greater oligopoly power of the subsidiaries in their overseas markets vis-à-vis the parent in the domestic market. The relative substitutability of domestic investment and the danger of spoiling the domestic market are, of course, the central concern here.

In a longer-run model, domestic and foreign investment may well be more directly substitutable, in that domestic investment plus exports is the alternative to new foreign direct investment. (From the point of view of national welfare — that is the next area for a seminal paper — the domestic-investment alternative is probably preferable.)

Second (and last), a word on leverage. In this model, leverage turns out to be more helpful in explaining foreign investment than domestic investment. Why? I am not satisfied with the typical cost-of-capital approach (see, e.g., p. 393). Nor can it be attributed merely to the surge of foreign investment in the last decade: the debt-equity ratio of (European manufacturing) subsidiaries vis-à-vis parents was greater even before that. (The 1957 Census showed a 1:1 debt-equity ratio for manufacturing subsidiaries versus a 1:2 ratio for the parent corporation.) Here again, we return to the risks of devaluation (and confiscation) and to the use of local debt as an offset. Or are there nontransitory institutional factors, differing tax structures, and personal preferences that make it cheaper, or more attractive, for foreign direct investors to borrow abroad than at home?

Gillespie's paper is essentially a review of the official policies of the United Kingdom, France, and Germany toward direct foreign investment, and an attempt to measure the effects of those policies on the actual stocks and flows of direct investment from the United States to those countries over the last decade.

My principal over-all reaction to the paper is that he has given far too much consideration to the *stated* national policies (to the neglect of other likely determinants) and too little consideration to the data and to quantitative analyses. In general, I believe it is more fruitful to pay greater attention to what economic (and political) units *do* than to what they *say*. And this is especially true in the present case, since, unlike the author, I do not see much influence of stated policy goals on actual flows of direct foreign investment to these three countries. It is not demonstrated, for example, that Gaullist rhetoric and indicative planning in France have significantly inhibited the flow of direct foreign investment to France. Nor are other hypotheses formulated, much less tested.

1. Gillespie concludes that "the impact of the more restrictive policy is clearly seen in the steady decline of France's share of American direct investment in the EEC countries after 1963 . . ." and presumably through 1967 (since 1968 was France's year of "relevance"). But this is not so clear or impressive to me.

Between 1959 and 1965 (the apex year for French stated restrictions) France's share of direct-investment flows was in the (trendless) range of 21 per cent to 28 per cent of the total of such flows to the European Economic Community. The drop from that range to 12 per cent and 16 per cent in 1966 and 1967, respectively, can be attributed to a variety of factors other than stated policy toward direct foreign investment. Among those factors worth considering are the following: (*a*) short-run balance-of-payments problems in the United States (as well as in France) during a sharp cyclical expansion, with resultant cost-of-capital effects. For example, direct foreign investment by the United States (hereafter referred to as DI) may have shifted from France to Germany because pressures to finance DI abroad increased, and finance was cheaper and more available in Germany than in France; (*b*) shifts in investment opportunities toward Germany from France due to disparate rates of growth of the economies or to differences in current and expected returns.

Moreover, it should be noted that the absolute amount of direct-investment flows from the United States to France was twice as high in 1966/67 as it was in 1958/59. (True, they were three times as high in 1963–65.) In reading this paper, one is led to forget that a boom in foreign direct investment was occurring throughout Europe. The data on stocks (Table 2) reveal little change in France's position vis-à-vis the European Economic Community; it is the relative decline in the share of the United Kingdom that impresses. But here one is likely to attribute that shift to the evolution of the Common Market rather than to controls over DI flows.

In short, the role of national policy on direct investment can only be reasonably isolated in a model that at least accounts for the principal causal factors.

2. A study of policy alone, it seems to me, could be more helpful to the extent that it treated specific cases and did so quantitatively. In the case of France, Gillespie stresses that the specific targets of the investment controls were take-overs and the protection of particular sectors, e.g., electronics. But the role of these types of direct investment in total direct investment in France is not (perhaps cannot be) explored. Nor is it at all clear to me that (as Gillespie assures us) it is "not possible to differentiate the economic effects" of take-overs from new corporate investment overseas.

The two types of investment have different effects on the use of real resources in the host country, even if only in the short run; and there are surely differences in the effects on the structure of industry, unless the opening up of a new unit overseas is ruled out as an alternative form of direct investment. The volume (as well as the composition) of investment in the host country will be different if take-over is substituted for new foreign direct investment. There will also be differences in the number of firms, as when entry into the banking system is permitted via merger rather than requiring the establishment of a new branch.

There are also differences in the economic effects on the investing country when it expands overseas investment by the take-over route instead of the new-investment path. Take-overs slur the distinction between foreign portfolio and direct investment; while having the "control" element associated with direct investment, they share the "financial" (rather than "real") asset attribute of portfolio investment. Of course, in the long run, the origins of the subsidiary become irrelevant. But that is not to say that the short-run distinction is unimportant.

3. One final matter: I fear that Gillespie attributes too much aggregate effectiveness to direct-investment controls of the United States. On the basis of sources-of-funds data (rather than preliminary balance-of-payments data), one cannot conclude that American direct investment in Europe has declined at all through 1968. What one sees is a shift toward external financing of such investment—from sources at home to sources abroad. Again it is the *structural,* like the sectoral, aspects that tend to be slighted in the paper, though they are probably just the areas where the effects of the controls are most significant.

Note that I do not claim that the controls have had no effects. I do claim, however, that the effects were seldom the advertised or intended ones, and, in any case, can hardly be determined outside of a reasonably complete model of the investment process.

DIRECT INVESTMENT AND THE BALANCE OF PAYMENTS OF THE UNITED STATES: A PORTFOLIO APPROACH

MARTIN F. J. PRACHOWNY · Queen's University

1 INTRODUCTION

THE active control and operation of firms in other countries implied by direct foreign investment has dominated the international investment position of the United States vis-à-vis the rest of the world. At the end of 1967, 73 per cent of the long-term foreign assets owned by residents of the United States were held in the form of direct investment. On the other side of the coin, 35 per cent of foreign-owned long-term assets in the United States were in this category.

The purpose of this paper is to explain the demand for these direct-investment assets, both those arising from investments abroad by U.S. residents and those from investments in the United States by foreign residents. It should be emphasized that the demand analysis involves specifying and estimating structural relationships for a given level of these assets, rather than for changes in those levels as measured by flows in the balance of payments. In this regard there has been a major shift of emphasis from models designed to estimate the flow per period of time to those models that view an international capital flow as an attempt to close the gap between the actual and desired stock of

NOTE: The author wishes to acknowledge with gratitude the financial assistance of the Institute for Economic Research and the Interim Research Committee, both of Queen's University. Brian Gallivan performed admirably as my research assistant and Mrs. Ellen McKay typed many drafts without complaint. Helpful comments and suggestions were made by John P. Harkness, Peter H. Lindert, Gordon R. Sparks, Hiroki Tsurumi, Robert M. Stern, and members of the Research Seminar in International Economics at the University of Michigan. In addition, Robert E. Lipsey and Ronald I. McKinnon, the discussants of the paper at the conference, provided the stimulus to tighten the analysis and correct a number of errors.

assets, the latter based on optimum-portfolio models. It is unfortunate that there was a lag of approximately a decade between the appearance of general portfolio models, as drawn up by Markowitz [9] and Tobin [16], and their application to international capital assets. Nevertheless, in the recent past this lapse has been partially remedied. Theoretical investigations include the pioneering work of McKinnon and Oates [8], and other studies by McKinnon [7], Harkness [3], and Leamer and Stern [5]. Also, some empirical work on certain aspects of the problem has been undertaken by Branson [1], Grubel [2], Lee [6], and Miller and Whitman [10]. But these studies have been concerned with portfolio, or financial, investment and not with direct investment. Only when reliable estimates of all major private foreign assets have been obtained can a complete and consistent model of the balance of payments be constructed.

2 A MODEL OF FOREIGN DIRECT INVESTMENT

A. THE DETERMINANTS OF THE OPTIMUM STOCK

The derivation of the optimum-stock equation is based on a Tobin-Markowitz portfolio model. Assume that a corporation has a utility function, $U = U(R)$, so that $U' > 0$ and $U'' < 0$, where R is the rate of return on its wealth. It can hold two types of assets: A_1, the value of direct foreign-investment assets; or A_2, the value of domestic assets.[1] Then we can write the demand for A_1 as

$$A_1 = A_1(R_1, R_2, \sigma_{R_1}, \sigma_{R_2}, \sigma_{R_{12}}, \sigma_e, W), \qquad (1)$$

where A_1 is the desired or optimum holdings of direct-investment assets abroad, R_1 and R_2 represent the expected rates of return on the two types of assets, σ_{R_1} and σ_{R_2} represent some measure of the risk attached to the two expected rates of return, $\sigma_{R_{12}}$ is the covariance of

[1] The exposition will be in terms of an American firm holding assets at home and abroad. An analogous treatment of foreign direct investment in the United States would involve a foreign firm holding assets in the United States, A_1^*, and assets in the domestic economy, as well as in other countries except the United States, A_2^*.

the rates of return,[2] σ_e represents external risk factors which arise because the investment takes place in a foreign country, and W ($= A_1 + A_2$) is the total portfolio of wealth owned by the corporation, or in other words, its net worth. (Put yet another way, W represents the shareholders' equity in the corporation, which equals assets minus liabilities. Since we can derive an optimum portfolio of assets as well as of liabilities, shareholders' equity is also optimized. In the remainder of the paper, the term "assets" refers to net assets or shareholders' equity.)

This demand equation does not rely on any specific theory of direct investment. Instead, its underpinning is the eclectic assumption that corporations maximize profits under conditions of risk and subject to constraints. Kindleberger [4, pp. 389–407] summarizes a number of views on direct investment, and—although they stress different aspects of the behavior underlying international firms—it would be difficult to conceive of a theory that denies categorically the assumption made here. Nevertheless, no claim is made that equation (1) can completely capture the behavior of every corporation with foreign assets. There are times and places when other arguments (some economic, some noneconomic) enter the decision-making process and require modifications of the approach taken in equation (1). But in view of the aggregation involved in the empirical estimates in this paper, one can justifiably relegate these factors to secondary status without at the same time denying their existence. Indeed, it is not necessary to assume that every direct-investment decision is made within a portfolio framework; all that is necessary is that the decision be consistent with the predictions of a portfolio model. For instance, the specific decision for a direct-investment venture may reflect the desire to get inside a newly erected tariff wall. But this stimulus can be viewed as an increase in the expected rate of return on production abroad or a reduction in the rate of return on domestic assets. In essence, the appeal of a portfolio model of direct investment is its generality, that is, its ability to subsume a number of specific reasons for direct investment.

---

[2] The effect of $\sigma_{R_{12}}$ on A_1 is ambiguous. If rates of return become more harmonious, diversification in asset-holding becomes less important. In the extreme, the investor will buy only the asset with the higher expected rate of return.

There remains the argument that direct-investment assets are not sufficiently liquid to allow for alterations in a corporate portfolio to maintain its efficiency when underlying conditions change. While it is true that it is easier to create real assets than to destroy them, thus creating problems of liquidity, the same does not hold true for titles to these assets, which can be bought and sold with not much more difficulty than other long-term portfolio assets.

B. CAPITAL FLOWS AND CHANGES IN THE STOCK OF ASSETS

Once we accept equation (1) as the correct behavioral hypothesis, we encounter difficulties in translating changes in the stock of an asset into balance-of-payments entries. For illustrative purposes, assume that direct investment abroad by U.S. residents is the only capital asset. Then we can write the balance-of-payments identity as

$$B \equiv X - M + Y - S - Q, \tag{2}$$

where B is the defined balance of payments, X and M are the values of exports and imports, $Y - S$ represents repatriated profits ($Y =$ earnings on foreign direct investment and $S =$ reinvested earnings) and Q is the flow of new direct-investment capital. But a change in the stock of direct-investment assets is not necessarily equal to a flow. Thus the reconciliation between changes in stocks and flows can be written as

$$\Delta A_1 \equiv Q + S + C, \tag{3}$$

where C represents all other changes in the stock of A_1 during the given time period. These changes may be caused by physical depreciation, expropriation of foreign assets, changes in the market value of the assets, changes in the value of the foreign currency, and other exogenous changes.

Although these "other adjustments" were quite small in most years, they have been as large as −$953 million in 1960 and −$916 million in 1957, and thus cannot be ignored. Hence there is no simple transformation from a portfolio model to a balance-of-payments model. Since a portfolio can be adjusted by any one, or combination, of these components, it is necessary to specify the determinants of any two components (the third being determined residually) so that Q and S, which enter the balance of payments directly or indirectly, can be separated from C, which does not. While it is possible to make this specification on a theoretical level, it would not be empirically testable. This unfortunate result emanates from the treatment of profits of branches and subsidiaries in the data compiled by the Department of Commerce. Whereas retained profits of subsidiaries are not entered in the balance of payments, retained profits of branches enter twice, once as repatriated earnings (line 11 of Table 1 in *Survey of Current Business*, June, 1968) and again as new capital outflows (line 33).[3]

3 EMPIRICAL ESTIMATION OF THE MODEL

A. THE GENERAL ESTIMATION EQUATIONS

Based on equation (1), the following equations will be used to estimate the optimum stock of direct-investment assets abroad owned by U.S. residents and direct-investment assets in the United States owned by foreigners:

$$D_t/W_t = \alpha_0 + \alpha_1(R_t^*/R_t) + \alpha_2(\sigma_{R*}/\sigma_R) + \alpha_3\sigma_{R*,R} + \alpha_4 B_{t-1} + u, \quad \text{(I)}$$

and

$$D_t^*/W_t^* = \beta_0 + \beta_1(P_t/P_t^*) + \beta_2(\sigma_P/\sigma_{P*}) + \beta_3\sigma_{P,P*} + \beta_4 B_{t-1} + v, \quad \text{(II)}$$

where:

D_t = stock of direct-investment assets abroad owned by United States residents, billions of dollars, end of period

W_t = value of American corporate stock, billions of dollars, end of period [4]

---

[3] This latter procedure has been recommended by the Bernstein Committee [14], but the asymmetrical treatment of branch and subsidiary profits, although not affecting the balance of payments, leads to difficulties in estimating stock adjustments in direct-investment assets.

[4] Since this variable, as reported in the flow-of-funds accounts, is dominated by stock prices at the end of the year, it does not adequately reflect the net worth that American corporations have at their disposal during the year. Hence $W_t = VCS \times SP_y/SP_D$ where VCS is the value of corporate stock as reported in the flow of funds, SP_y and SP_D are the Standard and Poor industrial stock price-indexes for the year and December, respectively.

$R_t^* = Y_t/D_{t-1}$ (where Y_t is earnings on direct investment abroad by United States residents after foreign taxes but before United States taxes), in per cent

R_t = after-tax rate of return on net worth in American manufacturing, in per cent

$$\sigma_{R*} = \left(\frac{1}{3}\sum_{i=0}^{3}(\bar{R}^* - R_{t-i}^*)^2\right)^{1/2} \text{ where } \bar{R}^* = \frac{1}{4}\sum_{i=0}^{3}R_{t-i}^*$$

σ_R = same calculation as for σ_{R*}

$\sigma_{R*,R} = r \times \sigma_{R*} \times \sigma_R$ where r is the correlation coefficient for the four observations of R^* and R

B_{t-1} = United States balance of payments on liquidity basis in the previous year, billions of dollars

D_t^* = stock of foreign direct investment in the United States, billions of dollars, end of period

W_t^* = value of corporate stock in Canada and the United Kingdom, billions of dollars, end of period [5]

$P_t = Y_t^*/D_{t-1}^*$ (where Y_t^* is the earnings on foreign direct investment in the United States), in per cent

P_t^* = simple average of after-tax rates of return on net worth in Canadian and United Kingdom manufacturing, in per cent

σ_P = same calculation as for σ_{R*}

σ_{P*} = same calculation as for σ_{R*}

$\sigma_{P,P*} = r \times \sigma_P \times \sigma_{P*}$

u, v = disturbance terms

Before we proceed with the estimates of these equations, the form of the equation and the variables should be discussed. In the first place, the dependent variable is the ratio of foreign assets to total assets. This is consistent with the mathematical derivation of optimum

[5] Since neither country publishes flow-of-funds accounts, this variable had to be "manufactured." In both cases, the book value of corporate stock is obtained from taxation data. These series are then multiplied by the relevant stock price-index (yearly average, 1956 = 100) and then converted to U.S. dollars and aggregated. Since an index number is involved in the calculations, only in the loosest sense can the final figure be said to be denominated in dollars. Various other forms of W^* were investigated without better results. Canada and the United Kingdom are the largest holders of direct-investment assets in the United States. In 1967, Canada's proportion of the total was 26 per cent, and the United Kingdom owned 32 per cent. For other countries, the breakdown is as follows: Netherlands, 15 per cent; Switzerland, 11 per cent; other European countries, 13 per cent; and all other areas, 3 per cent.

FIGURE 1

Determination of Expected Rate of Return and Risk

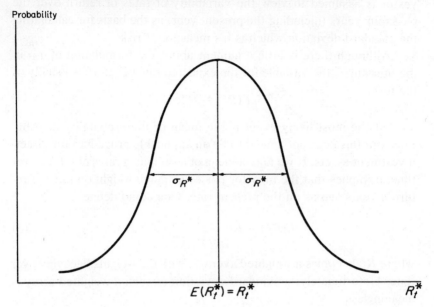

portfolios, but it makes the implicit assumption that the elasticity of D with respect to W is one.

Next, the variables for expected rate of return and risk considerations must be examined.[6] Although there are a number of plausible methods by which investors are assumed to formulate these variables, the following procedure will be used in this study. An investor deciding how much of corporate net worth to hold in foreign direct investment will consider the present rate of return on that investment as the most likely event. This is shown in Figure 1 as $E(R_t^*) = R_t^*$.

In determining the expected rate of return, the investor must make some projection. R_t^* cannot be known definitely until the end of the year, and yet he will be making investments on the basis of this information during the course of the year. Because of this uncertainty, and because the investor is aware of other outcomes (but all less likely to

---

[6] Only the formulation of R_t^* and σ_{R^*} will be dealt with in detail, since the other rates of return and risk variables are determined in a like manner.

come to mind), he forms a probability distribution around R_t^*. One parameter of that distribution is its dispersion. In this instance, the investor is assumed to view the variability of rates of return over the past four years (including the present year) as the basis for calculating the standard deviation which is his measure of risk.

Although there is little argument about the formulation of σ_{R*} in the literature,[7] the variable for the expected rate of return is usually of the form

$$E(R_t^*) = \bar{R}^*, \tag{4}$$

so that the most likely event is the mean of the probability distribution. But this does not appear to be an applicable procedure for direct-investment assets. If we take a mean of a sample of rates of return over time, it implies that the investor places as much weight on rates of return n years ago as on the present rate. One could define

$$E(R_t^*) = \bar{\bar{R}}^* = \frac{1}{\Sigma \lambda_i} \sum_{i=0}^{n} \lambda_i R_{t-i}^*, \tag{5}$$

where $\bar{\bar{R}}^*$ becomes a weighted average, with the weights decaying over time. Unfortunately, a standard deviation of such a weighted array is meaningless.[8]

As a result of this process of elimination, the variables chosen to represent the expected rate of return and risk, although not elegant from a theoretical point of view, appear to be the best a priori approximations of the decision-making process of investors involved in foreign direct investment.[9, 10]

[7] One could argue whether σ_{R*}, which is an objective measure of dispersion, can adequately convey the subjective evaluation of uncertainty that investors must make.

[8] Assume, for instance, $R_{t-i}^* = 10$ ($i = 0, \ldots, 3$). Then $\bar{R}^* = 10$ and $\sigma_{R*} = 0$. But if we assign weights of, say, .10, .15, .25, and .50, then $\bar{\bar{R}}^* = 10$ but $\sigma_{R*} = 1.78$. However, it is possible to define the standard deviation as follows: $\sigma'_{R*} = \left(\sum_i \lambda_i (\bar{\bar{R}}^* - R_t^*)^2 \right)^{1/2}$ where $\sum_i \lambda_i = 1$, so that with the given observations, $\sigma'_{R*} = 0$.

[9] The discussion up to this point has been in terms of a probability distribution based on historical data. But cross-section data are also a possibility. In a sense R_t^* is a weighted average of rates of return across all industries or countries. But the dispersion of cross-section rates of return may not be an applicable measure of risk, since the deviation of the rate of return in industry y from the mean may be of no importance to a firm in industry x.

[10] Ratios of the rates of return and risk variables were used rather than differences.

Finally, B_{t-1} enters the equation as a proxy variable for "external risk." [11] Aside from the variability of the rates of return, foreign investment is subject to a number of risks with no comparable counterpart in domestic investment. These risks include the probability of expropriation, changes in the exchange rate of the foreign country, and controls on the repatriation of earnings. Although these risks are likely to appear at discrete time intervals, it is necessary to have a continuous variable or a complex set of dummy variables. It is assumed that the balance-of-payments position of the United States will capture some of these effects. An improvement in the balance of payments implies a strengthened reserve position for the United States and a weakened reserve position for other countries. Under these conditions, the United States is less likely to devalue or impose capital controls, and other countries are more likely to take these actions. Hence an investor (domestic or foreign) will shift his portfolio to larger holdings of assets in the United States and smaller holdings of assets abroad. A deterioration in the balance of payments of the United States will, of course, have the opposite effect. In order to avoid the problem of simultaneous determination, the balance has been lagged one year.[12]

Although not specifically dealt with in the equations, the establishment of convertibility of the European currencies in the late 1950's may have influenced both American and foreign owners of direct-investment assets. But this influence is neither easy to define nor easy to measure.[13] In any case, it was decided to use a dummy variable, $CONV$ (1959 onwards equals 1) in both equations.

The assumption underlying this procedure is that the elasticity of the dependent variable with respect to the numerator of any independent variable is equal to the elasticity with respect to the denominator, except for sign.

[11] The question arises whether the external-risk variable influences the dependent variable directly, or through the variables for rates of return or risk, or both. The answer depends on the type of anticipated risk. Restrictions on the repatriation of earnings, devaluation, and so forth, are likely to influence the optimum stock directly, whereas changes in taxes, profit-sharing agreements, and similar measures will influence the rate of return. Since most of the relevant risks are in the first category, a separate external-risk variable is used.

[12] For a similar discussion of the use of B_{t-1}, see Miller and Whitman [10, p. 181]. However, McKinnon has pointed out that the simultaneity problem is not resolved if there is autocorrelation in the B variable.

[13] For a fuller discussion of this point, see Prachowny [13, p. 73].

B. DATA, LAGS, AND ESTIMATING TECHNIQUES

The equations for direct-investment assets will be tested with annual data for 1953 to 1964. Although flow data are available on a quarterly basis, the stock data have been compiled only on an annual basis, and because of the volatility of "other adjustments," the interpolation of nonflow data would be a dangerous procedure. [All original data and their sources are available from the author upon request.]

Portfolio theory requires that stocks of assets, and thus the total portfolio, be defined as market values. For W_t and W_t^*, market values are used, but for stocks of direct-investment assets it is likely that the series more closely approaches book value than market value, mainly because these assets rarely enter the market, and their market price is difficult to establish. This lack of symmetry in the valuation of the numerator and denominator of the dependent variable is probably the most serious problem in estimating direct investment in a portfolio framework.[14]

The lag structure in the system seems quite complicated. For new investment in fixed assets, the sequence of events would appear to be: first, the appropriation; then, the expenditure; and finally, at the end of the accounting period in which the expenditure is completed, the adjustment of the stock of assets. The length of time covered by this sequence could be two to three years. For take-overs of existing foreign firms, the time lapse may be shorter. The precise nature of the difficulty can be seen as we attempt to relate the last step in the sequence, the change in assets, to the decision-making variables (rates of return, risk, and so on), when, in fact, the causal relationship should be between appropriations and the decision-making variables. One way to sidestep this difficulty is to assume that the lags in the sequence described above are constant through time, and then to incorporate a lag structure in equations (I) and (II). But, given the shortage of degrees of freedom, the experimentation with lag structures is severely limited, and hence only a Koyck-type lag will be introduced.

---

[14] Various ad hoc procedures involving stock price-indexes for converting the book value of direct investment to market value were attempted without success. The fact that the Department of Commerce has not yet reported any market-value series indicates the difficulty of such conversions.

Since the optimum stock of direct-investment assets fits into the much larger framework of the foreign sector of American economic activity, which in turn is only one part of the whole economy, this study can be viewed as partial-equilibrium analysis, with the independent variables treated as exogenously given.[15] Hence, simultaneous estimating techniques are not appropriate, and both equations will be fitted with ordinary least squares.

C. FINDINGS ON AMERICAN DIRECT INVESTMENT ABROAD

Table 1 summarizes the regression results for estimating the optimum stock of direct foreign investment by residents of the United States. First of all, it should be noted that the last observation was for 1964. Later years were excluded from the regression on the assumption that a structural change took place at this time, mainly in response to the voluntary restraint program (VRP). Theoretically, the effect of VRP is that the actual stock of foreign direct-investment assets remains lower than the optimum stock. One could approximate this structural change by the use of a dummy variable, but since the requirements of VRP changed every year, a separate dummy variable for each observation after 1964 would have to be used. However, this procedure is undesirable on statistical grounds, and thus the decision was made to measure the effect of VRP by extrapolating the results of the equation for 1953–64 and comparing the estimated optimum stock of assets with the actual one.

The coefficient of the lag variable is not reported in Table 1, since in no case was it significant at the 10 per cent level. This seems to imply that in making decisions on foreign investment, the expected rates of return and other variables are projected into the future for the period in which the investment is expected to be completed. But,

---

[15] The interactions within the balance of payments and between the foreign and domestic sectors of the economy of the United States are more fully dealt with in Prachowny [13]. However, even within this single-equation model, it may not be quite appropriate to treat the independent variable as exogenous. For instance, an increase in direct-investment assets may reduce the rate of return. Also R^* and R are not independent, since increased foreign profits which are remitted to the parent firm also increase domestic profits.

TABLE 1

Regression Results for American Direct Investment Abroad, 1953–64

	Coefficients and t-Ratios							
Equation	Constant (1)	R_t^*/R_t (2)	σ_{R*}/σ_R (3)	$\dfrac{R_t^* - \sigma_{R*}}{R_t - \sigma_R}$ (4)	$\sigma_{R*,R}$ (5)	B_{t-1} (6)	$\bar{R}^2$ (7)	DW (8)
I.1	.031	.032	.001		.001	.001	.13	1.19
	(1.50)	(1.69)	(.23)		(.33)	(.59)	(1.41)	
I.2	.036	.033	−.0001			.001	.23	1.27
	(1.55)	(1.93)	(.04)			(.53)	(2.07)	
I.3	.029	.037	−.0003				.29	1.31
	(1.56)	(2.51)	(.08)				(3.22)	
I.4	.036	.033				.001	.31	1.25
	(1.65)	(2.07)				(.51)	(3.49)	
I.5	.029	.037					.36	1.29
	(1.66)	(2.67)					(7.15)	
I.6	.043			.026		.001	.39	1.72
	(2.71)			(2.46)		(.36)	(4.54)	
I.7	.039			.027			.44	1.76
	(3.32)			(3.13)			(9.80)	

NOTE: Columns (1) through (6), t-ratios in parentheses. Column (7), f-ratios in parentheses. Column (8) lists Durbin-Watson statistics.

since only a Koyck lag was used, the question of lagged reactions has not been satisfactorily resolved.

Equation I.1, then, is the estimate based on the previous discussion. Since the coefficient of $\sigma_{R*,R}$ is the least significant, it was dropped in equation I.2. Equations I.3 to I.5 are other combinations of these same variables. In all cases, the relative-rates-of-return variable is significant, but all risk variables fail to pass the test. Equations I.6 and I.7 approach the problem in a somewhat different way. Instead of forming separate variables for expected rate of return and risk, the investor is assumed to combine these considerations into one variable. Essentially, he makes a "conservative" estimate of the expected rate of return by taking the most likely event, R_t^*, and subtracting σ_{R*}.[16] By

---

[16] $R_t^* - \sigma_{R*}$ should not be construed as a confidence limit. It will be remembered that

TABLE 2

Optimum and Actual American Direct Investment Abroad, 1965–67 [a]

Year	$\hat{k}_t$ (1)	$\hat{D}_t$ (2)	D_t (3)	$\Delta\hat{D}_t - C_t$ (4)	$\Delta D_t - C_t$ (5)	$\Delta\hat{D}_t - C_t - S_t$ (6)	$Q_t - L_t$ (7)
1965	6.65	49.40	49.42	3.37	5.01	1.83	3.34
1966	6.29	41.91	54.71	−7.42	5.36	−9.16	2.79
1967	6.38	53.90	59.27	12.03	4.60	10.45	2.62

NOTE: Billions of dollars, except column (1) which is in percentages.

DEFINITIONS OF VARIABLES: $\hat{k}_t = \widehat{D_t/W_t}$; $\hat{D}_t = \hat{k}W_t$; L_t = direct investment by American corporations financed from foreign sources. See *Survey of Current Business*, Vol. 48, No. 3 (March, 1968), p. 20, Table D. L_t enters the balance of payments as a receipt in lines (52) and (54) and as a payment in line (33).

[a] Estimated values are based on the parameters of equation I.7 in Table 1.

making a similar calculation for domestic investment, we arrive at the single variable $(R_t^* - \sigma_{R*})/(R_t - \sigma_R)$. The use of this variable brings about results which can be adjudged superior to those of the previous equations. Equation I.7, which leaves out the external-risk variable, will be used as the final and best estimate.[17]

Having estimated the optimum stock of direct foreign-investment assets held by U.S. residents for the homogeneous period 1953–64, we are able to estimate the effects of the voluntary restraint program. It will be assumed that the introduction of VRP caused a structural shift in the holdings of American-owned direct-investment assets, and that this was the only major change that occurred during 1965–67. It is further assumed that the provisions of VRP were adhered to by all corporations. Our task, then, is to compare the actual results with those that would have obtained in the absence of VRP.

The necessary information for such a comparison is contained in Table 2. Column (1) indicates the estimated ratio of direct-investment

R_t^* is not the mean of the probability distribution from which σ_{R*} is calculated. Also, this variable implies a linear indifference curve between expected rate of return and risk.

[17] The convertibility variable was not significant in any of the equations.

assets to total corporate net worth. Column (2) then calculates the estimated optimum stock of direct-investment assets for 1965–67, which can be compared with the actual stock in column (3). In 1966 and 1967, the actual stock was higher than the optimum. However, comparing stocks may not be the relevant comparison, since VRP was concerned with reducing flows in the balance of payments. Thus, in column (4), the desired change in direct-investment assets minus C_t, assumed to have *no* balance-of-payments effects, can be compared to actual changes in column (5). In other words, columns (4) and (5) compare the desired and actual reinvested earnings and new capital flows. These figures show that VRP had the expected effect in 1967 but not in 1965 and 1966. In fact, in 1966, a negative outflow is the result predicted by equation I.7. Although reducing the stock of real assets through a method other than depreciation is difficult, in the case of direct-investment assets this reduction could be accomplished by selling off investments to foreigners and repatriating the proceeds.

However, the comparison may have to be even more refined than indicated by columns (4) and (5). Although the statements by the Secretary of Commerce are not clear on this issue, one can interpret VRP as applying to new capital outflows only.[18] In addition, VRP encouraged firms to finance their direct-investment ventures by issuing bonds in foreign markets, thus reducing the balance-of-payments effects of direct investment. Hence, we may compare the estimated capital outflow without VRP in column (6) with the actual *net* outflow, allowing for the foreign financing engendered by VRP in column (7).[19] The results are not dissimilar to the previous comparisons.

How, then, can we explain this unusual result? Essentially, our main concern is with the effect of VRP in 1966. The difference between the actual and predicted values for 1965 is too small to create firm confidence in the effect of VRP; and, in 1967, one can conclude that

[18] This is corroborated by the Department of Commerce data published on VRP. See *Survey of Current Business* (March, 1968), p. 20, Table D, although the December, 1965 statement by Secretary Connor says, "For this purpose, direct investment is defined to include the net outflow of funds from the United States plus the undistributed profits of affiliates abroad."

[19] This comparison is the most generous to VRP, since it assumes that foreign financing of direct investment occurred only because of VRP and would not have taken place in the absence of this program.

VRP appeared to be successful in achieving its aims. But, in 1966, the prediction is for a sizable inflow, when, in fact, a net outflow of $2.8 billion took place. This result can be explained by this reasoning: the introduction of VRP caused American corporations to consider the limits imposed on capital flows as minima as well as maxima, mainly because it was quite obvious from the outset that the constraints would last for some time, and would even be tightened from time to time. Given these anticipations, investors began to optimize over a longer horizon than one year. This would lead to "overinvestment" in periods where the optimum change in the stock of direct-investment assets is less than that allowed by VRP and "underinvestment" in periods where VRP was an effective constraint. The year 1966 would appear to fit into the first category. Even though, on a year-to-year basis, investors should have reduced their foreign assets in 1966, they increased them in anticipation of a higher optimum stock in future years than could be gained from the maximum allowable flows of direct investment during these later years. For the period as a whole, the "overinvestment" amounted to $5.6 billion and it may take some time and very tight constraints before firms are in a position where VRP places a burden on them.[20] By the same token, VRP cannot be said to be effective, since it has not forced firms to reduce their outflows to lower levels than would otherwise prevail.

D. FINDINGS ON FOREIGN DIRECT INVESTMENT IN THE UNITED STATES

The results for the regression equations for foreign direct investment in the United States are shown in Table 3.[21] As was the case with foreign investment by United States residents, the coefficient of the lag variable was not significant, the separate risk variable in equation II.1 does not meet a priori expectations, but $\sigma_{P,P*}$ is significant. In addition, P_t/P_t^*, B_{t-1} and the convertibility variable ($CONV$) have a

---

[20] Since this study deals with aggregate data, one can say nothing about the burden on individual firms.

[21] The equation was tested for the period 1953–64, the cutoff being dictated by the lack of data on the Canadian component of W^* and P^* after 1964 on a basis comparable to that for earlier years.

TABLE 3

Regression Results for Foreign Direct Investment in the United States, 1953–64

Coefficients and t-Ratios

Equation	Constant (1)	P_t/P_t^* (2)	σ_P/σ_{P*} (3)	$\dfrac{P_t - \sigma_P}{P_t^* - \sigma_{P*}}$ (4)	$\sigma_{P,P*}$ (5)	B_{t-1} (6)	CONV (7)	t (8)	$\bar{R}^2$ (9)	DW (10)
II.1	.334 (5.82)	-.118 (1.58)	-.022 (1.11)		.044 (5.41)	-.005 (.62)	-.083 (3.53)		.94 (35.83)	2.18
II.2	.296 (8.95)	.059 (.95)	.011 (.81)		.015 (1.69)	.019 (2.59)	.054 (1.44)	-.021 (3.87)	.98 (101.85)	1.62
II.3	.263 (8.62)	.152 (4.91)	.022 (1.59)			.026 (4.01)	.099 (3.19)	-.029 (9.15)	.98 (93.06)	2.26
II.4	.258 (7.70)	.162 (4.86)				.023 (3.35)	.078 (2.52)	-.027 (8.66)	.97 (95.01)	2.41
II.5	.291 (7.47)			.107 (3.33)		.023 (2.52)	.074 (1.81)	-.025 (6.19)	.95 (55.47)	1.89

NOTE: Columns (1) through (8), t-ratios in parentheses. Column (9), t-ratios in parentheses. Column (10) lists Durbin-Watson statistics.

sign opposite to the expected one. Because of a suspected upward bias in the time-trend of W^*, a time-variable, t, was introduced in equation II.2. This produced somewhat better results. Equations II.3 and II.4 represent other equations with the risk variables dropped one at a time. Equation II.5 combines the rate of return and risk variables, as was done in equation I.6. It is not clear, however, that equation II.5 is better than equation II.4. It may be that the risk factor enters into the decision-making process in a much more complicated fashion than is depicted here, but in the absence of more specific knowledge about the formation of risk variables, equation II.5 is put forward as the best result.

4   CONCLUSIONS

GIVEN the estimates of the holdings of direct-investment assets, what can be said about influencing these holdings through policy decisions? In the first place, one can have legitimate doubts about the effects of the voluntary restraint program. Unless VRP can be designed so that the actual flow of direct-investment funds is less than that implied by optimum portfolio decisions, it cannot be said that VRP has improved the balance of payments in relation to what it would have been in the absence of VRP. In order for VRP to improve the balance of payments in each period, it would be necessary to estimate the desired flow for each period and then constrain the actual flow to a lesser amount. In addition, a much clearer statement is required concerning the place of retained earnings in the program, since reducing re-patriated earnings (thereby increasing retained earnings) is a substitute for new flows and has the same effect on the balance of payments.

Aside from selective instruments such as the voluntary restraint program and the interest equalization tax, what effects can be expected from monetary and fiscal policy acting directly on the holdings of direct-investment assets and indirectly on the balance of payments? In a Mundellian framework [11, 12] one would rely heavily on monetary policy to influence the balance of payments, since it has a comparative advantage over fiscal policy in this respect. But Mundell's analysis has serious limitations once it is applied to a portfolio model in a static framework. In the first place, his theory is based on the assumption that an increase in the interest rate resulting from tighter monetary policy will give rise to a continuing higher inflow (or reduced outflow). However, when wealth constraints and risk considerations enter the portfolio manager's decision, this assumption can no longer be true. At best, such a policy will result in a short-term improvement in the balance of payments; once portfolios are adjusted, the higher interest rates will have no further effect.

Given that a policy change cannot have a permanent effect on the balance of payments, it can at least have a temporary effect by influencing the optimum stock of assets. For instance, assume that the United States has a short-term deficit in its balance of payments. To aid in the adjustment process, it can increase the optimum stock of foreign direct-investment assets in the United States and decrease the optimum stock of American-owned direct-investment assets abroad.[22] Both of these effects will improve the balance of payments. However, it is no longer clear that monetary policy is better suited than fiscal policy to bring about this result.

Lowering corporate taxes, for instance, increases the after-tax rate of return in the United States and thereby encourages investors to shift assets from abroad to the United States.[23] But, again, it should be emphasized that this change in the balance of payments is temporary. In this model, the tax reduction would have its effect within one year, after which the new tax structure would have no further influence on optimum stocks or the balance of payments.[24]

On the other hand, monetary policy may not have even a predictable short-run effect on the balance of payments. In a portfolio model, where a whole spectrum of rates of return enters the decision-

[22] Assume now that the adjustments to these changes in the optimum stocks are entered in the balance of payments instead of taking place through nonentries.

[23] This increase in the rate of return increases the investors' measure of risk and might offset some of the improvement in the balance of payments, but one could argue that a variation in the rate of return brought about by a tax cut would not alter the investors' appraisal of risk factors. On the other hand, this argument makes the standard deviation a less suitable measure of risk, since it cannot distinguish between predictable and unpredictable variations in the rate of return.

[24] It is also assumed that this policy does not affect any other items in the balance of payments (directly or indirectly) during the adjustment period.

TABLE 4

Simple Correlation Coefficients Among
Interest Rates and Rates of Return

	i_{us}	r_{us}	R_t
r_{us}	.96		
R_t	.54	.35	
P_t	.35	.29	.53

NOTE: i_{us} is the annual average of
Treasury bill yields; r_{us} is the annual
average of interest rates on long-term
U.S. government bonds.

making process of the investor, it is no longer acceptable to imply that a higher interest rate will attract capital from abroad. Tighter monetary policy will presumably increase the Treasury bill rate and the long-term government bond rate, but its effect on the profitability of real investment is more difficult to measure. The effect of higher interest rates on rates of return on investments, as discussed here, requires a more sophisticated analysis than is now available.[25] In addition, there is little empirical evidence that all of the relevant rates of return move together. A simple correlation matrix in Table 4 indicates this.

Even though lagged relationships may have shown higher correlation coefficients, the evidence appears to point to a much more complex determination of rates of return on direct-investment assets. Hence, higher interest rates may attract portfolio capital, both long-term and short-term, but the effect on flows of direct-investment capital is at best ambiguous.

No attempt has been made in this study to analyze the effects of direct investment on the balance of payments in a dynamic framework. It is obvious, however, that if the net worth of American corporations is growing faster than that of foreign corporations (assuming an equal base), then the outflows of direct-investment capital will be larger than

---

[25] See Harkness [3] for a discussion of the effect of monetary policy on bond prices and the supply price of capital, and of the ambiguity of the effects of monetary policy on the balance of payments.

the inflows, leading to a deficit in the balance of payments.[26] Any other dynamic changes in the independent variables will also have effects on the balance of payments. For instance, increasing the interest rate (or all relevant rates of return) can lead to higher permanent inflows of capital in the balance of payments.[27] Since elementary observation of balance-of-payments data indicates that there has been no tendency toward smaller capital flows—an indication that the system is settling down to a static equilibrium—it is these dynamic properties of portfolio models that must be investigated more fully in order to gain better insights into the balance-of-payments adjustment process over time.

To conclude this paper, a word of caution is in order. It is quite evident that the data requirements for portfolio models are often not fulfilled, and thus a number of compromises with the theory have been made. There are at least two major gaps in our data requirements: (1) While flow data for the balance of payments for the United States and other countries have improved both in extent and sophistication, much more needs to be done on stock data, such as foreign assets and liabilities of American corporations, and particularly on the components that cause a change in these stocks from one period to the next. (2) Data for rates of return on capital both in the United States and abroad, derived mainly from taxation statistics, require a firmer

[26] The same result would occur if the growth rates were equal but the U.S. net worth started from a larger base.

[27] Assume a growth path of W so that $W_t = W_{t-1} + J$ $(t = 1, \ldots, m)$ where J is a constant. This simple relation is used so that in the absence of a policy change the flow in the balance of payments as measured by ΔA_t will be constant. If the proportion of the portfolio assigned to an asset is k, then in any time period

$$\Delta A_t = k \cdot J. \tag{a}$$

Now, in the next time period, assume a policy instrument is applied so that there is a once-for-all increase in k to k'. Then,

$$\Delta A_{t+1} = k \cdot J + \Delta k \cdot W_t + \Delta k \cdot J, \tag{b}$$

where $\Delta k = k' - k > 0$. The first term is the same as in (a) and thus stems from growth in assets; the last two terms represent temporary increases in the flow brought about by the stock adjustment to a change in k. Assuming this adjustment to be completed, the flow in the next period is

$$\Delta A_{t+2} = k'J. \tag{c}$$

It can readily be seen that $\Delta A_{t+2} > \Delta A_t$. Hence an increase in interest rates (or any other policy change that influences k) can have a permanent effect on the level of capital flows in the balance of payments.

grounding in economic theory and greater comparability than is the case at present. In view of these deficiencies, the estimated equations are rather fragile and can best be described as first approximations of the intended structural model. As more and better data are accumulated, not only will these estimates become more robust and reliable, but also more elaborate models will become testable.[28]

REFERENCES

1. Branson, William H., *Financial Capital Flows in the U.S. Balance of Payments*. Amsterdam, North-Holland Publishing Co., 1968.
2. Grubel, Herbert G., "Internationally Diversified Portfolios: Welfare Gains and Capital Flows." *American Economic Review,* Vol. LVIII, No. 5 (December, 1968), pp. 1299–1314.
3. Harkness, Jon P., "Monetary and Fiscal Policy in Closed and Open Economies — The Portfolio Approach" (unpublished Ph.D. dissertation, Queen's University), 1969.
4. Kindleberger, Charles P., *International Economics*. Homewood, Richard A. Irwin, Inc., 1968.
5. Leamer, Edward E., and Stern, Robert M., *Quantitative International Economics*. Boston, Allyn and Bacon, 1970.
6. Lee, C. H., "A Stock-Adjustment Analysis of Capital Movements: The United States–Canadian Case." *Journal of Political Economy,* Vol. 77, No. 4 (July, 1969), pp. 512–523.
7. McKinnon, Ronald I., "Portfolio Balance and International Payments Adjustments" in *Monetary Problems of the International Economy,* R. A. Mundell and A. K. Swoboda, eds. Chicago, University of Chicago Press, 1969.
8. ——— and Oates, Wallace E., *The Implications of International Economic Integration for Monetary, Fiscal and Exchange-Rate Policy* (Princeton Studies in International Finance, No. 16). Princeton, 1966.

[28] For instance, Richardson [15] has argued that there is a major distinction between an initial investment abroad and continuing investments of established firms. If and when data are categorized on this basis, this interesting proposition can be tested.

9. Markowitz, Harry M., *Portfolio Selection: Efficient Diversification of Investments.* New York, John Wiley and Sons, 1959.
10. Miller, Norman C., and Whitman, Marina v. N., "A Mean-Variance Analysis of United States Long-Term Portfolio Investment." *Quarterly Journal of Economics,* Vol. LXXXIV, No. 2 (May, 1970), pp. 175–196.
11. Mundell, Robert A., "The Appropriate Use of Monetary and Fiscal Policy for Internal and External Stability." *International Monetary Fund Staff Papers* (March, 1962), pp. 70–79.
12. ———— "On the Selection of a Program of Economic Policy with an Application to the Current Situation in the United States." *Banca Nazionale Del Lavoro Quarterly Review,* Vol. 16, No. 66 (September, 1963), pp. 262–284.
13. Prachowny, Martin F. J., *A Structural Model of the U.S. Balance of Payments.* Amsterdam, North-Holland Publishing Co., 1969.
14. Review Committee for Balance of Payments Statistics, *The Balance of Payments Statistics of the United States: A Review and Appraisal.* Washington, 1965.
15. Richardson, J. David, "On 'Going Abroad': The Firm's Initial Investment Decision." University of Michigan Research Seminar in International Economics, Discussion Paper 17, 1970.
16. Tobin, James, "Liquidity Preference as Behaviour Towards Risk." *Review of Economic Studies,* Vol. 25, No. 67 (February, 1958), pp. 65–86.

INTERNATIONAL CAPITAL FLOWS AND THE TAKE-OVER OF DOMESTIC COMPANIES BY FOREIGN FIRMS: CANADA, 1945–61

GRANT L. REUBER · The University of Western Ontario

FRANK ROSEMAN · University of Alberta

1 INTRODUCTION

TRADITIONAL concerns about business mergers within countries have broadened during the past decade or two to encompass international mergers as well. This development has reflected the substantial growth since 1945 in the international flow of direct investment and the growing importance of the large, integrated international corporation. A wide range of questions have been raised in the fast-growing literature on these developments, including questions about the factors giving rise to increased direct investment, the importance and characteristics of foreign ownership and control, the benefits and costs of direct investment to the capital importing and exporting countries, and the non-economic implications for the host country of having a sizable portion of its leading industries owned and controlled abroad.

Much of this discussion has been foreshadowed by developments in Canada, which received very large flows of direct investment before these became important elsewhere, and where foreign ownership and control has long been enshrined as a major issue of public policy. At present, nonresidents control over a third of the assets in major sectors of the Canadian economy, including control over three-quarters of the assets in the oil and gas industry, and three-fifths of the assets in the mining and smelting and manufacturing industries. In 1966, direct investment by U.S. residents accounted for about 40 per cent of the *new* investment in plant and equipment in Canada, com-

465

pared with 6 per cent for Britain and the Common Market countries.[1]

Despite the attention that has recently been given to foreign take-overs in many countries, economic analysis in this area continues to be seriously hampered by a lack of reliable data susceptible to meaningful analysis. In 1969, the Government of Canada released a new and unique body of statistical information on all foreign and domestic mergers occurring in Canada from 1945 to 1961.[2] These data significantly enhance the range of information available on the subject. In the discussion in Sections 2 and 3, the relative importance and leading characteristics of foreign take-overs are examined on the basis of this information. In the remaining sections, an attempt is made to identify and assess the importance of the leading determinants of foreign take-over activity. Although the data do not extend beyond 1961, it is noteworthy that they cover the period when Canada absorbed a large share of the flows of direct investment to industrial countries and when foreign control over Canadian firms increased most rapidly — from 25 per cent of the total assets of leading sectors of the Canadian economy in 1948 to 34 per cent in 1963.[3] Since the early sixties, Canada has absorbed a much smaller share of total flows of direct investment and the rate of increase in foreign ownership and control has remained virtually unchanged.[4]

[1] Christopher Layton, *Trans-Atlantic Investments*. Boulogne-Sur-Seine, France, 1967, Table C, p. 14.

[2] Grant L. Reuber and Frank Roseman, *The Take-Over of Canadian Firms, 1945–61, An Empirical Analysis*. Economic Council of Canada, Special Study No. 10, Ottawa, 1969. The present paper summarizes some of the main findings reported in this monograph and presents the results of further analysis undertaken since this initial study was completed. Details regarding the data and definitions employed in the current paper and some of the estimates that are reported may be found in this earlier study.

In addition to the help received previously from those cited in the monograph, the authors wish to acknowledge the helpful comments and suggestions made on an earlier draft of the present paper by G. C. Eads, T. Horst, C. P. Kindleberger, and E. T. Penrose. We are also indebted to Miss P. Skene, our invaluable research assistant. Throughout this paper, the terms *mergers, acquisitions,* and *take-overs* are regarded as synonyms and are used interchangeably.

[3] These sectors include manufacturing, petroleum and natural gas, mining and smelting, railways and other utilities, and merchandising. The figures are based on the book value of capital employed in each industry. Dominion Bureau of Statistics, *The Canadian Balance of International Payments, 1963, 1964 and 1965 and International Investment Position*, Table XIV, p. 127. *Dominion Bureau of Statistics Weekly*, February 20, 1970, p. 4.

[4] From 1957 to 1960, Canada accounted for 35 per cent of gross flows of direct investment into industrial countries; the corresponding figure for 1961 to 1964 is 16

A central feature of the research strategy adopted for this analysis is the use of domestic mergers as a control group against which to assess the importance, leading characteristics, and determinants of foreign take-overs. Foreign mergers may be viewed simply as a part of the more general phenomenon of business mergers common in most countries. Accordingly, much of the theory and empirical evidence that has emerged from the study of domestic mergers may be drawn upon to illuminate foreign merger activity as well.[5] Moreover, if one wishes to understand more clearly what influence international boundaries have on the characteristics of merging firms and the factors influencing merger activity, it is helpful to compare foreign mergers with domestic mergers occurring simultaneously.

2 THE RELATIVE IMPORTANCE OF FOREIGN TAKE-OVERS

FROM 1945 to 1961, over 639 foreign mergers occurred in Canada, compared with 1,187 domestic mergers (as shown in Table 1). This 1:2 ratio for the period as a whole compares with a ratio of 1:2½ for the period prior to 1954 and roughly 1:1½ for the period after 1954. The average value of foreign take-overs (total price paid divided by number) increased over five times from 1945–49 to 1960–61, compared with a twofold increase over the same period in the average value of domestic take-overs and in the price of business investment in new plant and equipment. From 1945 to 1949 the average value of firms acquired in foreign take-overs was 29 per cent less than the average

per cent. Marcus Diamond, "Trends in the Flow of International Private Capital, 1957–65." International Monetary Fund, *Staff Papers,* March, 1967, Table 2.

[5] This approach would appear to be similar to that developed by Stephen H. Hymer, as reported by Charles P. Kindleberger in his book, *American Business Abroad.* New Haven, Yale University Press, 1969, p. 11. Hymer evidently argues that direct investment "belongs more to the theory of industrial organization than to the theory of international capital flows." For an excellent recent discussion of foreign investment, combining the approaches of international trade theory and industrial organization, see Richard E. Caves, "International Corporations: The Industrial Economics of Foreign Investment." *Economica,* Vol. XXXVIII, No. 149 (February, 1971), pp. 1–27.

TABLE 1

Number and Average Value of Firms Acquired in Foreign and Domestic
Mergers and Number of Canadian Firms, 1945–1961
(*values in thousands of dollars*)

Year	Number of Foreign Acquisitions		Number of Domestic Acquisitions	Number of Domestic Firms	Average Value of Col. (1)	Average Value of Col. (3)
	Total (1)	By U.S. Firms (2)	(3)	(4)	(5)	(6)
1945	23	20	51	27,229	755	348
1946	15	9	64	30,442	528	719
1947	13	9	32	34,087	339	276
1948	14	12	39	35,960	317	1,059
1949	11	6	27	37,467	513	1,057
1950	9	6	36	40,545	1,060	1,012
1951	19	14	61	43,365	1,977	1,192
1952	17	10	59	45,777	946	603
1953	25	14	68	49,745	1,210	744
1954	43	24	61	54,434	1,949	852
1955	56	32	78	59,773	2,631	1,270
1956	54	34	81	67,480	3,004	573
1957	35	19	68	73,823	2,697	2,438
1958	60	46	80	80,770	1,650	2,099
1959	66	46	120	88,806	1,093	1,632
1960	93	52	110	97,549	3,000	1,803
1961	86	63	148	106,309	1,981	972
Total	639	416	1,183			

SOURCE: Reuber and Roseman, *op. cit.,* Tables 3-1 and 3-2.

value of firms acquired in domestic take-overs. For the last five years
of our sample period, the average value of firms acquired in foreign
take-overs exceeded that of firms acquired in domestic take-overs by
14 per cent. In short, during this period both the number and size of
foreign take-overs increased relative to the number and size of domestic take-overs.

In the remainder of this section, attention will focus on three additional yardsticks of comparison: the number of firms in Canada and the United States; the number of employees in Canada; and the non-resident control of Canadian industry.

NUMBER OF FIRMS

About 100,000 companies filed tax returns in Canada in 1961, compared with 1,200,000 in the United States in the same year. From this perspective, the number of foreign take-overs in Canada has been small, in no year exceeding $1/10$ of 1 per cent of all companies in Canada. Moreover, it is noteworthy that although companies in the United States have outnumbered companies in Canada by a ratio of about 12:1, the ratio of foreign to domestic mergers has been 1:2. In this restricted sense, there is prima facie evidence that the international political boundary has mattered: apparently it has served to inhibit considerably the take-over of Canadian firms by firms in the United States. Otherwise, one would expect the ratio of foreign to domestic take-overs to approximate more closely the ratio of the number of firms in each country.[6]

Another basis of comparison might be the number of mergers in the United States. Unfortunately, as already noted, the data on the number of mergers in the United States are very incomplete, accounting, perhaps, for only one-third to one-half of the number of mergers that actually took place. According to data released by the Federal Trade Commission, 8,092 mergers occurred in the United States from 1945 to 1961.[7] Arbitrarily doubling this figure to allow for underreporting, one may say that during this period, take-overs in Canada by firms in the United States, numbering 416, were equal to roughly 2.6 per cent of the number of domestic mergers in the United States.

[6] If one considers only border states in the United States — in order to allow for the possible influence of distance and differences in industrial structure related to climate — the ratio of the number of United States companies to Canadian companies in 1961 was about 5:1.

[7] *Economic Concentration,* Part 2, "Mergers and Other Factors Affecting Concentration." U.S. Congress, Senate Hearings before the Sub-committee on Antitrust and Monopoly of the Committee of the Judiciary, S. Res. 40, 89th Congress, 1st Session, March 16, 17, 18, April 13, 14, 15 and 21, 1965. Washington, 1965, p. 504. Bernard A. Kemp, "Understanding Merger Activity — Assessing the Structural Effects of Mergers." *The Bulletin,* New York University, Nos. 55–56 (April, 1969), Chapter V and p. 57.

NUMBER OF EMPLOYEES

The firms acquired in foreign take-overs employed about 105,000 employees at the time of their take-over. Those acquired in domestic take-overs employed about 115,000 persons. In mid-1953 — midway between 1945 and 1961 — the labor force engaged in nonagricultural production in Canada was about four million. On this basis, one may say that 2.6 per cent of the nonagricultural labor force in Canada was affected by foreign take-overs at the time they took place, while about 2.9 per cent was affected by domestic take-overs.

BALANCE OF PAYMENTS AND NONRESIDENT
CONTROL OF CANADIAN INDUSTRY

Two main questions arise in connection with the balance of payments and the nonresident control of Canadian industry. The first is the extent to which foreign investment for take-over purposes has been accompanied by a transfer of capital to Canada, and to what extent it has represented an increase in foreign control without a transfer of capital.[8] This is essentially concerned with changes in the supply of foreign exchange associated with foreign take-overs. Unfortunately, it is not feasible to analyze this question with the available figures. Although the data on foreign take-overs indicate the amount of cash paid when firms were acquired, they do not indicate how much of this cash originated abroad, and how much domestically.[9]

The second question concerns the extent to which the postwar increase in foreign ownership and control over Canadian firms, referred to earlier, can be attributed to firms taken over by nonresidents from 1945 to 1961. It is apparent that foreign acquisitions from 1945 to 1961, valued at the time of acquisition, account for only a relatively small part of the assets controlled by nonresidents in various sectors

[8] This point is discussed briefly by Charles P. Kindleberger, *op. cit.*, pp. 2–3 and p. 23, where he claims that it is largely true that "direct investment does not represent a capital movement."

[9] Of the total price paid for acquisitions by foreigners from 1945 to 1961, at least 60 per cent was paid in cash — in comparison to the 51 per cent paid in cash by domestic acquiring firms.

of Canadian industry in 1962.[10] For manufacturing, the estimated ratio is 12 per cent; for mining and trade, 5 per cent; for transportation, 38 per cent; and for construction, 5 per cent. Within the manufacturing sector, the largest ratios occur for leather, wood, paper, and non-metallic minerals. Apparently, the level of assets controlled by non-residents in 1962 mainly reflected (a) the acquisition and growth of firms prior to 1945; (b) the growth of firms — after they were acquired by nonresidents — during the years from 1945 to 1961; and (c) the establishment and growth of new enterprises undertaken by nonresidents.

3   THE LEADING CHARACTERISTICS OF
MERGING FIRMS

SINCE a more detailed review is available elsewhere, only a few of the leading characteristics of merging firms will be discussed here.[11] These include the nationality of acquired and acquiring firms; the age, size, and industrial distribution of firms; the degree to which acquisitions were concentrated among acquiring firms; the profitability of acquired firms; and the market relationships among merging firms.

As for nationality, 82 per cent of the firms acquired by non-residents from 1945 to 1961 were Canadian, 13 per cent were controlled by Americans, and 5 per cent were controlled in Britain (omitting cases where the premerger nationality of control was not reported). Of the acquiring firms, 65 per cent were American, 27 per cent were British, and 8 per cent were established in other countries. Four-fifths of these mergers consisted of a single firm buying out a single firm, and over 73 per cent of the foreign acquisitions were made through Canadian-based subsidiaries. The median age and size characteristics of firms acquired in foreign and domestic mergers may be summarized as follows: [12]

---

[10] For further details, see Reuber and Roseman, op. cit., pp. 40–42.

[11] Ibid., Chapters 4 and 5.

[12] Because the distributions are highly skewed in the direction of the larger classes, the value of the mean is consistently greater than the value of the median.

		Foreign Mergers	Domestic Mergers
Age (years):	All Acquired Firms	14.3	13.7
	Acquired Firms of Canadian Nationality	12.9	
Size:	Sales (million dollars)	1.1	0.7
	Assets (million dollars)	0.7	0.4
	Employees (number)	54	43

One may say that on the average, firms acquired in foreign mergers were larger than those acquired in domestic mergers. Moreover, taxation data indicate that the mean size of firms acquired in both foreign and domestic mergers was considerably greater—five to eight times greater—than the mean size of all firms in existence in Canada, whether measured in terms of assets or sales. This said, it is also worth noting that about half of the firms acquired in foreign mergers had less than 50 employees, assets under $700,000, and sales less than $1 million; three-quarters had fewer than 200 employees.

Because the coverage of the questionnaire was less complete for those industrial sectors that do not come under the jurisdiction of the Combines Act, the industrial distribution of firms acquired in foreign mergers can be compared only very roughly with the industrial distribution of firms acquired in domestic mergers and the distribution of the population of firms in Canada. The main point that emerges from such a comparison is the relatively heavy concentration of foreign mergers in the manufacturing sector relative to other sectors, to domestic mergers, and to the number of firms in existence. The second most important sector is trade, though in this sector foreign mergers are relatively less numerous than domestic mergers and fewer relative to the number of firms. These same general patterns are evident when one considers the industrial distribution of acquiring firms. Within the manufacturing sector, foreign acquisitions were widely dispersed among various industries.

The evidence indicates that merger activity was less concentrated among foreign acquiring firms than among domestic acquiring firms. In both cases, a large majority of firms acquired no more than two firms each. The nine foreign acquiring firms that made ten or more acquisitions accounted for 20 per cent of all foreign acquisitions.

The aggregate picture on the profitability of acquired firms may be summarized as follows:

	Foreign Mergers	Domestic Mergers
Median Profit Rate of Acquired Firms Earning a Profit (per cent) *	17.0	18.7
Percentage of Acquired Firms Incurring Losses	19.0	22.8

* Profit Rate = reported book profit as a percentage of reported net worth.

One of the striking features of the profit picture which develops when the figures are disaggregated is the extent to which acquired firms in mining were less profitable than those acquired in other industrial sectors: more than two-fifths of the firms acquired in both foreign and domestic mergers were incurring losses, and the median rate of profit for those earning a profit was about one-quarter of that earned in other sectors. It is also noteworthy, however, that in the mining sector, firms involved in foreign acquisitions were more profitable than those involved in domestic acquisitions — in the sense of having a higher median profit rate and including a lower percentage of companies suffering losses.

Finally, there is the question of the marketing relationships prevailing among merging companies. Consideration of this issue anticipates to some extent the discussion on reasons for mergers, since, presumably, questions of market expansion and market power enter into the decision to buy out another firm. From 1945 to 1961, the relative importance of mergers in the four broad categories of merger types describing the direction of expansion of the acquiring firm was as shown on the table which follows.[13]

Unfortunately, the data are very incomplete in indicating the market orientation and market position of acquiring and acquired firms entering into mergers. Nevertheless, for what they are worth, the figures suggest that firms acquired in both foreign and domestic mergers primarily served the domestic market. In the large majority of cases,

[13] These categories, together with various subcategories, are defined in Reuber and Roseman, *op. cit.,* Chapter 5.

	Foreign Mergers (per cent)		Domestic Mergers (per cent)	
Broad Horizontal: Horizontal	27		47	
Geographic Market Extension	14		12	
Product Extension	11		9	
Other	6	58	6	74
Vertical: Forward	20		11	
Backward	11	31	7	18
Conglomerate:		11		8
		100		100

both the acquiring and acquired firms in foreign mergers held less than a quarter of the market for their particular outputs. If anything, the market share of firms entering domestic mergers was somewhat higher. At the same time, the evidence—imperfect as it is—indicates that both foreign and domestic acquiring companies tended to have a high rank in their respective industries prior to merging, and that they improved their market position as a consequence of merging.

Charles P. Kindleberger has argued that horizontal integration reflects internal economies of scale, resulting in increased monopoly power and, consequently, higher profits.[14] Vertical integration is said to reflect external economies mainly. These are alleged to arise from the improved coordination and planning made possible when industries are integrated, as well as from a reduction in risk and uncertainty. To a considerable degree, such external economies may reflect pecuniary gains due to the overcoming of market inefficiencies in coordinating activities at several stages of production, and to the inability of the market for technology to eliminate the rents from a technological monopoly.

If one accepts this line of argument, the foregoing evidence on types of mergers suggests that internal economies were an important factor in both foreign and domestic mergers, and that the pace of competition may have been impaired by these mergers. At the same time, it is important to note that this factor, as measured by the share of

[14] Kindleberger, op. cit., pp. 19–25.

horizontal mergers, was less important for foreign than for domestic mergers. On the other hand, external economies—as indicated by the share of vertical mergers—were apparently a more important consideration in foreign mergers than in domestic ones.

4 REPORTED REASONS FOR MERGING

ECONOMISTS generally tend to be skeptical about information obtained from businessmen by questionnaires aimed at reporting the reasons for their actions; and at least the usual dash of salt is justified in considering the evidence to be presented here. Respondents were asked to indicate (*a*) "the reasons which led the reporting company or firm in this instance to choose the merger route to expansion rather than to rely on internal growth," and (*b*) "details of the economies, if any, secured by the merger which were not otherwise obtainable." For various reasons that are reviewed elsewhere, not much can be made of this evidence. Nevertheless, it is worthwhile to note a few of the main impressions that it conveys.

One impression is that, in general, more of the initiative to undertake mergers came from buyers than from sellers. Separating the reasons reported into these two categories as well as one can, it appears that demand factors and initiative from the buyer were relatively more important than supply factors and initiative from the seller in about 73 per cent of foreign take-overs, and in about 65 per cent of domestic take-overs.[15]

On the demand side, two considerations stand out for both types of merger: "it was cheaper and less risky to acquire another firm than to build a new one," and "something unique was acquired through the acquisition." These are scarcely surprising responses, but the underlying rationale given for them is of some interest. For the first state-

---

[15] These percentages relate only to those firms who reported reasons. For a review of this approach, see E. T. Penrose, *The Theory of the Growth of the Firm*. Oxford, Basil Blackwell, 1959, pp. 158 ff. This author also cites conflicting evidence on the relative importance of demand and supply considerations in relation to domestic United States mergers.

ment, the response from both foreign and domestic acquiring firms indicates that considerable importance was attached to the speed with which expansion could be achieved via a take-over and also to the gaining of immediate access to an assured market. As for gaining control over certain unique assets possessed by the acquired firms, the following assets were particularly noted: management, particularly emphasized in the case of foreign acquisitions; know-how and processes; licenses or permits from regulatory authorities, given greater emphasis in domestic acquisitions; access to brands or trademarks, given particular emphasis in domestic acquisitions; trade connections, given special emphasis in foreign acquisitions.

On the sellers' side, the most frequently given reason for merging is that the firm was on the market and the "owner(s) wanted to sell." Some mention is also made of the business being "available at a bargain price." Although further details are not provided in many instances, some of the more frequently identified considerations include such factors as retirement, and financial and competitive difficulties. The importance of this latter factor tends to be supported in the case of domestic mergers when one separates out profit and loss companies. For loss companies, supply considerations are mentioned more frequently than for profit companies. For foreign acquisitions, however, losses by the acquired firm are cited much less frequently as a factor leading to take-over than they are for domestic acquisitions.

Finally, there is the interesting question of the economies made possible by expansion through merger. This question is of particular interest as far as Canada is concerned because of the claim frequently heard that Canadian plants are too small, or, where they are large, that the output mix produced in them is too diversified to reap fully the potential economies of large-scale production.[16] Again, the evidence is not reliable enough to give more than an impression. Nevertheless, it suggests that mergers did not give rise to much by way of cost reductions. Negligible or no economies were reported in 56 per cent of the foreign acquisitions reporting, and in 41 per cent of domestic acquisitions. Such economies as were reported were largely con-

[16] See, for example, D. J. Daly, B. A. Keys, and E. J. Spence, *Scale and Specialization in Canadian Manufacturing*. Staff Study No. 21, prepared for the Economic Council of Canada, Ottawa, 1968. Note also the references cited there.

centrated in head-office activities, not at the plant level. The head-office economies were reported to be largely savings in administration and improvements in management. At the plant level, a few references were made to savings in production and distribution costs. The most striking result, however, is negative; no reference whatever was made to reduced costs due to increased specialization as a reason for foreign acquisitions, and in only 1 per cent of the responses on domestic acquisitions was this factor mentioned.

5 THE INTERINDUSTRY MIX OF FOREIGN TAKE-OVER ACTIVITY

IN ORDER to explain interindustry variations in the ratio of foreign to total (foreign and domestic) mergers in each industry, it is necessary to define this ratio more precisely. Acquisitions may be defined in terms of the numbers of firms acquired *in* the ith industry or, alternatively, *by* firms in the ith industry. The latter concept allows firms in one industry to acquire firms in other industries, as in vertical and conglomerate mergers. The former concept does not allow for this possibility, and there is no particular reason why there should be a relation between the number of acquired firms in an industry and the number of acquiring firms in that industry. Since the characteristics of the acquiring firms classified on an industry basis are important from the standpoint of testing some of the explanatory variables that we introduce later, N_{ib} and M_{ib} are defined in terms of the acquisitions *made by* firms in the ith industry. A second definition, which is more restrictive, limits N_{ih} and M_{ih} to those cases where both the acquiring and acquired firms are in the same industry, i.e., horizontal mergers. Thus, the two ratios – the interindustry variation of which is to be explained – are: $N_{ib}/(N_{ib} + M_{ib})$ and $N_{ih}/(N_{ih} + M_{ih})$, or NB_i and NH_i for short.

The approach adopted to explain interindustry variations in these ratios may be characterized as a search procedure intended to track down the probable influence of various possibilities suggested by *ad hoc* theorizing rather than an empirical test of a comprehensive prespecified theory of why such variations occur. This approach has been dictated in large measure by the absence of any corpus of theory on this subject. Moreover, as will become apparent, the analysis has been further hampered by a small set of observations affording only limited degrees of freedom for testing hypotheses, as well as by a lack of satisfactory statistical data for many variables that one might wish to test in arguments explaining variations in the ratios in question.

In the series of experiments undertaken to explain variations in these ratios for manufacturing, the following explanatory variables were considered:

$FN_i =$ the ratio of the number of foreign-controlled firms in industry i (F_{in}) to the total number of firms, foreign (F_{in}) and domestically controlled (F_{im}), in industry $i = F_{in}/(F_{in} + F_{im})$

$R_{t_i} =$ the average tariff rate (duty collections $\div$ value of imports) in industry i for all imports

$R_{d_i} =$ the average tariff rate for dutiable imports

$Q_i =$ the tariff-induced differential in marginal costs in industry i

$Ly_i =$ the supply of internally generated funds (capital cost allowances + depletion allowances + profits − cash dividend payments) of profit and loss firms in industry i, relative to the size of assets in industry i, from 1948 to 1961

$S_{in}/S_{it} =$ the ratio of the average size (total assets $\div$ number) of foreign-controlled firms in Canada in industry i (S_{in}) to the average size of all firms (S_{it}) in Canada in industry i

$ES_i =$ economies of scale in industry i

$G_i =$ the average rate of growth in output in industry i from 1945 to 1961

$PR_i =$ the average rate of profit for profit and loss companies in industry i, relative to net worth in industry i, from 1948 to 1961

$T_i =$ foreign trade participation in industry i (imports + exports $\div$ value added)

$R\&D_i =$ company-sponsored research and development expenditures in the United States in industry i, as a percentage of sales in that industry in the United States

The primary question posed in these experiments has been whether there is any evidence of a statistically significant association between variations in these variables and the interindustry mix of foreign merger activity, as reflected in the two ratios defined earlier. In order to investigate this question, a series of linear equations were fitted by ordinary least squares to a panel of cross-sectional industry data, including the foregoing variables singly, and in a variety of combinations, as explanatory factors. In interpreting the results, particular attention has been given to the value of the t-ratios and to the appropriateness of the sign of the estimated coefficient for each variable, to the stability of the estimated coefficient for each variable in successive tests, and to the value of the coefficient of multiple determination adjusted for degrees of freedom, $\bar{R}^2$. For the most part, the statistical analysis has been run on an eighteen two-digit industry classification. Two-digit industry classifications are quite heterogeneous and, as a consequence, may give rise to spurious results. In order to check out this possibility, some tests, where feasible, were also run on three- and four-digit industry classifications and on subperiods.

Before considering this evidence in detail, it may be helpful to summarize briefly the principal results. The evidence indicates a highly significant association between variations in the degree of foreign control of Canadian industry, FN_i, and NB_i or NH_i. Further, after allowance has been made for a common element applying to all industries, the estimates suggest that variations in NB_i and NH_i tend to be roughly proportional to variations in FN_i. In addition, the estimates provide evidence of a fairly significant association between variations in NB_i or NH_i and in the level of tariff protection — and, also, in the supply of internally generated cash flows. On the other hand, the little evidence does not warrant much confidence in an association between variations in NB_i or NH_i and in the indexes included in the analysis relating to the size of firms, economies of scale, growth in output during the sample period, average profit rates, trade participation, and research and development expenditures.

SIGNIFICANT ASSOCIATIONS

Consider first the degree of foreign ownership, FN_i. Suppose that there are two industries, X and Y, and that nonresidents control 25 per cent of the firms in X and 75 per cent of the firms in Y. Assume, also, that foreign- and domestically controlled firms have an equal propensity to engage in merger activity, are equally well placed to buy up other firms, are equally likely to become aware of firms likely to be for sale, have equal advantages to gain from mergers, and so forth. All other things being equal, one might expect approximately 25 per cent of the mergers in industry X and 75 per cent of the mergers in industry Y to be foreign mergers, as we have defined them. In other words, one might expect the distribution of foreign and domestic takeovers to be directly proportional to the initial distribution of foreign- and domestically controlled firms. In its simplest form, this hypothesis can be written [17]

$$NB_i = \beta FN_i, \qquad \text{where } \beta = 1. \tag{1}$$

A variant of this hypothesis might allow for a constant differential, α, between these two ratios:

$$NB_i = \alpha + \beta FN_i, \qquad \text{where } \alpha \neq 0 \text{ and } \beta = 1. \tag{2}$$

The constant term, α, allows for a constant proportion of all merger activity in all industries to be foreign merger activity even if $FN_i = 0$. This common factor across industries might reflect various influences, such as a difference between tax laws in Canada and the United States, for example. As for β, if one found its value was not significantly different from unity, one might conclude that foreign ownership has little influence on the interindustry distribution of foreign merger activity in the sense that variations in NB_i are proportional to variations in FN_i. If, however, β was significantly greater than unity, one might conclude that foreign ownership enhanced foreign take-overs; and if β was significantly less than unity, one might conclude that foreign ownership served to restrict foreign take-overs.

[17] Here, and in the equations that follow, reference is made only to NB_i but the empirical estimates were based on both NB_i and NH_i.

The estimates of equation (2), based on an eighteen two-digit industry classification, are as follows:

$$NB_i = 0.191 + 0.890FN_i; \qquad \bar{R}^2 = .56 \qquad (3)$$
$$(2.41) \quad (4.79)$$

$$NH_i = 0.206 + 1.004FN_i; \qquad \bar{R}^2 = .75 \qquad (4)$$
$$(3.43) \quad (7.15)$$

where t-ratios are shown in parentheses below the associated parameters.[18]

In both equations, the estimates of β are highly significant, lending, in addition, some support to the hypothesis that β is not significantly different from unity — though, of course, the best point estimate of β is that given in each equation. For equation (3), the probability of mistakenly rejecting the hypothesis $\beta = 1$ is about 50 chances in 100, while for equation (4), it is about 97 chances in 100. Hence, using conventional confidence limits, there is more reason for accepting the hypothesis than rejecting it. Finally, the values of $\bar{R}^2$ may be considered quite high.

A number of qualifications related to the data should be noted.[19] First, the definition of foreign control underlying FB_i and FH_i differs somewhat from that underlying FN_i. It made little difference to the results when the definition of FN_i was changed and the analysis rerun. Secondly, FN_i relates to 1962 — the earliest year for which this information is available — while NB_i and NH_i reflect take-overs during the period 1945 to 1961. Acquisitions during this period presumably had some effect on the degree of foreign control at the end of the period. This difficulty is unavoidable, and one cannot check on its probable importance because of the lack of data on interindustry ownership and control patterns prior to 1962. To the extent that this effect is unevenly distributed among industries, the bias introduced may be unsystematic.

---

[18] When run on a four-digit-industry classification, equation (3) is as follows:
$$NB_i = .129 + .877FN_i.$$
$$(1.75) \quad (4.89)$$

[19] For further details, see Reuber and Roseman, *op. cit.*, pp. 116–117. The source of FN_i is: *Corporations and Labour Unions Returns Act, 1962*. Ottawa, 1965. Tables 4A–22A. The data for FN_i are given in Reuber and Roseman, *op. cit.*, p. 119.

TABLE 2

Selected Estimates of Equation (5): Seventeen Two-Digit Industries
$$(NB_i \text{ or } NH_i = \alpha + \beta FN_i + \gamma_j X_{j_i})$$

Equation Number	Dependent Variable	$\hat{\alpha}$	$\hat{\beta}$	$\hat{\gamma}$	X_j	$\bar{R}^2$
1	NB_i	8.625 (1.00)	0.846 (4.93)	0.976 (2.23)	R_{t_i}	.70
2	NB_i	−5.775 (0.44)	0.913 (5.36)	1.312 (2.26)	R_{d_i}	.70
3 [a]	NB_i	24.81 (0.91)	0.742 (3.78)	43.39 (1.79)	Q_i	.64
4	NH_i	14.60 (2.08)	0.981 (7.05)	0.567 (1.60)	R_{t_i}	.80
5	NH_i	9.144 (0.83)	1.017 (7.11)	0.608 (1.25)	R_{d_i}	.79
6 [a]	NH_i	−2.583 (0.12)	0.898 (5.93)	24.41 (1.30)	Q_i	.78
7	NB_i	32.11 (2.05)	0.915 (4.71)	−182.1 (0.99)	Ly_i	.56
8	NH_i	43.90 (4.47)	1.053 (2.79)	−323.1 (2.79)	Ly_i	.82
9	NB_i	0.153 (0.62)	0.913 (3.80)	0.018 (0.16)	S_{i_n}/S_{i_t}	.54
10	NH_i	0.062 (0.36)	1.171 (7.01)	0.126 (1.67)	S_{i_n}/S_{i_t}	.77
11 [b]	NB_i	24.49 (0.15)	0.857 (3.167)	−4.538 (0.032)	ES_i	.52
12 [b]	NH_i	125.5 (1.10)	0.919 (4.78)	−93.54 (0.92)	ES_i	.74
13	NB_i	11.85 (0.82)	0.817 (3.59)	5.263 (0.60)	G_i	.60
14	NH_i	29.40 (2.74)	1.090 (6.46)	−6.476 (1.00)	G_i	.78
15	NB_i	31.24 (1.95)	0.921 (4.68)	−91.83 (0.89)	PR_i	.55
16	NH_i	41.776 (3.95)	1.064 (8.18)	−158.626 (2.33)	PR_i	.80
17	NB_i	19.83 (2.36)	0.934 (4.56)	−0.250 (0.74)	T_i	.60

TABLE 2 (*concluded*)

Equation Number	Dependent Variable	$\hat{\alpha}$	$\hat{\beta}$	$\hat{\gamma}$	X_j	$\overline{R}^2$
18	NH_i	20.05 (3.14)	0.973 (6.25)	0.0167 (0.65)	T_i	.77
19	NB_i	19.34 (2.27)	0.832 (3.08)	176.60 (0.30)	$R\&D_i$	.59
20	NH_i	20.65 (3.19)	0.998 (4.86)	19.65 (0.043)	$R\&D_i$	.76

[a] 16 observations; food and beverages excluded.

[b] 14 observations; machinery, electrical products, petroleum and coal products excluded.

Furthermore, given that the number of firms in Canada increased substantially from 1945 to 1961, and that throughout this period both foreign and domestic acquisitions accounted for only a small proportion of the firms in the country, it is not obvious that take-overs from 1945 to 1961 particularly constrained variations in FN_i.

Equations (3) and (4) leave some 45 to 25 per cent of the variation in NB_i and NH_i to be explained in terms of factors other than foreign control. Thus, one may expand equation (2) to include X_j, representing other factors influencing NB_i and NH_i,

$$NB_i = \alpha + \beta FN_i + \gamma_j X_{j_i}. \qquad (5)$$

Selected estimates of this equation, including a number of possibilities for X_j, are presented in Table 2. It will be noted that the estimate of β remains highly significant in all of these tests, and that this coefficient is relatively stable, with a value close to unity. The estimated values of α, on the other hand, vary considerably in size and statistical significance. The two additional factors that seem to be significantly related to NB_i and NH_i, according to Table 2, are the level of Canadian tariffs and the supply of internally generated funds.

In the literature, it has long been recognized that tariffs tend to stimulate inflows of direct investment—e.g., in the discussions on tariff factors [20] — and a number of empirical studies have tended to corroborate the influence of tariffs on direct investment.[21] The higher the level of protection afforded an industry, the greater the incentive for foreigners to increase their direct investments in that country. The relevant rate for evaluating the influence on investment is the tariff-induced differential in gross marginal costs, Q (resulting from the tariff on both output and inputs), relative to the pretariff price of sales in the importing country, rather than the nominal tariff rate on final output, R.[22]

Equations (1) through (6) of Table 2 include either R or Q as explanatory variables, defining R_t as the average rate of duty collections on all imports, and R_d as the average rate of duty collections on dutiable imports.[23] The t-ratios for estimates of γ indicate a statistically significant association between NB_i and R_{t_i} and R_{d_i}, and a close-to-significant association between NH_i and these variables. On the other hand, the estimated coefficients for Q_i [24] are highly insignificant, even though, in principle, one would expect Q_i to be more closely related

[20] Charles P. Kindleberger, *International Economics*, Homewood, Ill., Richard D. Irwin, 1968, 4th edition, pp. 110–112, provides a textbook example. Thomas Horst, in an unpublished Ph.D. dissertation entitled "A Theoretical and Empirical Analysis of American Exports and Direct Investments," University of Rochester, 1969, formally derives this conclusion using a behavioral model in which international firms choose an optimal production-sales-export strategy on the basis of profit-maximization principles. Ronald J. Wonnacott and Paul Wonnacott in *Free Trade Between the United States and Canada,* Cambridge, Mass., Harvard University Press, 1967, provide an extended discussion of the relationship between tariffs and the location of industry, and empirical evidence on this relationship for Canada.

[21] E.g., Donald T. Brash, *American Investment in Australian Industry,* Cambridge, Mass., Harvard University Press, 1966, *inter alia* (particularly Chapter III); Herbert A. Marshall, Frank A. Southard, Jr., and Kenneth W. Taylor, *Canadian-American Industry: A Study in International Investment,* New Haven, Yale University Press, 1936.

[22] This conclusion is derived formally by Horst, *op. cit.*, on the conventional assumptions made in the literature concerning effective protection.

[23] R_{t_i} and R_{d_i} were estimated from detailed data provided by the Dominion Bureau of Statistics. The data relate to 1966, which is well after the end of our sample period. Unfortunately, earlier data were not available in sufficient detail. Although some tariff changes occurred after 1961, it is assumed that these were not of sufficient importance to invalidate the use of 1966 data for our purpose here.

[24] The definitions for Q_i are those derived by Horst, *op. cit.* He also kindly provided the authors with his data. These data are necessarily subject to a number of limitations. Suspicion about their quality is increased by the disparity between Horst's estimates of nominal tariff rates by industry class and those derived by the authors from detailed Dominion Bureau of Statistics data. The simple correlation coefficient between R_{t_i}, as derived here, and the corresponding figure derived by Horst is .48.

to foreign merger activity than R. The most likely explanation is the inadequacy of the statistics for Q_i, which have necessarily been put together from a number of sources and are subject to major difficulties on several grounds.

Internal cash flow, Ly_i, is the other factor that, according to Table 1, is significantly related to NH_i,[25] Ly_i is negatively related to both NB_i and NH_i; the t-ratios for the estimates of γ are highly significant in equation (8) but insignificant in (7). The rationale for this influence is explored in greater detail in the next section. Its importance, as emphasized by Kindleberger, arises from the growth of firms and from capital-market imperfections giving large foreign firms access to cheaper and more readily available funds for expansion.[26]

When all these explanatory variables are combined to explain NB_i and NH_i one obtains

$$NB_i = 17.296 + 0.866FN_i + 0.914R_{t_i} - 169.320Ly_i; \quad \bar{R}^2 = .64 \quad (6)$$
$$\quad (1.08) \quad (4.87) \quad\quad (2.00) \quad\quad\quad (1.04)$$

$$NH_i = 37.327 + 1.032FN_i + 0.406R_{t_i} - 291.690Ly_i; \quad \bar{R}^2 = .83 \quad (7)$$
$$\quad (3.46) \quad (8.60) \quad\quad (1.32) \quad\quad\quad (2.52)$$

$$NB_i = 6.825 + 0.939FN_i + 1.291R_{d_i} - 169.320Ly_i; \quad \bar{R}^2 = .66 \quad (8)$$
$$\quad (0.38) \quad (5.47) \quad\quad (2.23) \quad\quad\quad (1.04)$$

$$NH_i = 32.77 + 1.064FN_i + 0.568R_{d_i} - 317.495Ly_i; \quad \bar{R}^2 = .84 \quad (9)$$
$$\quad (2.67) \quad (9.04) \quad\quad (1.43) \quad\quad\quad (2.84)$$

All coefficients retain the same sign as in Table 2, the coefficients for FN_i remaining highly significant and approximately unity. The coefficients for R_i are generally smaller; the coefficients for R_{t_i} and R_{d_i} are insignificant when NH_i is the dependent variable, but both are fairly significant in the equations explaining NB_i. The coefficients for Ly_i also change somewhat in size; they remain significant when NH_i is the

---

[25] Ly_i = (capital cost allowances + depletion allowances + profits − cash dividend payments)/(total assets) for profit and loss firms in industry i, 1948 to 1961. These figures were derived from the Department of National Revenue, *Taxation Statistics*. In three industries the data were regrouped to approximate the classification for NH_i and NB_i. These reclassifications are as follows: primary metals (FN_i) = primary iron and steel (tax data); metal fabrication = boilers and fabricated structural steel; machinery = machinery n. e. c.

[26] Kindleberger, *American Business Abroad*, pp. 17–18 and 23–25.

dependent variable and insignificant when NB_i is the dependent variable. The values of $\bar{R}^2$ may be considered quite high for cross-sectional data. A major problem with these relationships, of course, is that there are only 14 degrees of freedom, which allows only limited scope for cross-sectional variation.

As a further check on these relationships, the estimates were rerun on data that excluded acquisitions by firms that did not have operations in Canada prior to taking over a Canadian firm. This was done on the ground that foreign firms with existing Canadian operations are likely to be more comparable to acquiring domestic firms in terms of knowledge of Canadian market conditions and access to information about purchasable firms. This refinement did not materially alter the pattern of significant associations shown in Table 2.

As a second check, the relationships were rerun on two subperiods: 1950 to 1955, and 1956 to 1961. The period 1945 to 1950 was excluded on two grounds: first, this period was marked by postwar readjustment and the heavy inflow of foreign capital to develop Canadian natural resources; and, secondly, the data for Ly_i have been published only from 1948 onward. Besides dividing the remaining period into two periods of five years each, the end of 1955 represents a peak in the number of foreign take-overs. Subsequently, the number of foreign take-overs decreased rather sharply for two years, increasing, thereafter, beyond the 1955 peak.

As is evident from the Appendix, in the estimates for these two subperiods the coefficients for FN_i are all highly significant statistically, with t-ratios ranging from 5.9 to 2.8. The coefficients for Ly_i are statistically insignificant in estimates based on the first period, but they are fairly significant for estimates based on the subsequent period — with t-ratios ranging from 1.6 to 2.2. The coefficients for the tariff variable are marginally significant for both periods when the dependent variable is NB_i, with t-ratios ranging from 1.0 to 1.3; however, the coefficients for the tariff variable for both periods are insignificant when the dependent variable is NH_i.

INSIGNIFICANT ASSOCIATIONS

Among the other variables considered is the size of firm. In the next section it is argued that take-overs are possible because of differences in the constraints impinging upon buyers and sellers.[27] If one assumes that smaller firms are subject to greater constraints than larger firms, and that international firms, F_i, are generally larger than domestic firms, S_{it}, one might expect NB_i and NH_i to be systematically related to F_i/S_{it}. In statistical terms, however, it is difficult to define F_i in a meaningful way. Defining F_i as the average size of all firms, by industry, in the United States was considered unsatisfactory, since this would include a host of firms for which the prospects of taking over a foreign firm are negligible. Instead, F_i was defined in terms of the average size of foreign-controlled firms operating in Canada, S_{in}; the size variable becoming S_{in}/S_{it}. In another set of tests, the total value of the assets of foreign-controlled firms was related to the total value of assets for all firms in the industry, $A_{in}/(A_{in} + A_{im})$.[28] It is acknowledged that neither of these variables is very satisfactory, and not much significance can be attached to the evidence shown in Table 2, indicating that variations in these size variables are not significantly related to variations in NB_i and NH_i when these variables are added to equation (2).

Economies of scale in various industries, ES, is a related and equally difficult factor to take into account. The best available measure of economies of scale at the two-digit industry level in Canada is that derived by C. J. Hodgins,[29] using a cross-sectional analysis of establishment data based on a production-function approach. As the study emphasizes, these estimates are subject to many limitations, not the least of which is the question of product mix re-

[27] This view is elaborated in Penrose, *op. cit.*, pp. 156 ff., and also in Kindleberger, *American Business Abroad,* Chapter 1. Kindleberger discusses these constraints within the context of monopolistic competition.

[28] Data for $A_{in}/(A_{in} + A_{im})$ and S_{in}/S_{it} are for 1962, and were derived from *Corporations and Labour Unions Returns Act, 1962.* Ottawa, 1962, Tables 4A–22A. See Reuber and Roseman, *op. cit.,* p. 119.

[29] C. J. Hodgins, "On Estimating the Economies of Large-Scale Production: Some Tests on Data for the Canadian Manufacturing Sector." Unpublished Ph.D. dissertation, University of Chicago, 1968.

ferred to earlier. Hence, it is uncertain whether the failure to find a significant association between ES_i and NB_i and NH_i reflects the lack of any association or the inadequacy of the information available on economies of scale.

Another variable that is given considerable prominence in theories of the firm is growth, G, here defined as growth in output from 1945 to 1961.[30] One might argue that the more rapid the rate of growth in an industry, the more apparent will become the differences in the constraints impinging upon firms; moreover, these disparities may actually widen. If because of their size and diversity, their international characteristics, and other factors, the constraints bearing on foreign firms are less stringent than those bearing on domestic firms (including domestic buyers as well as sellers), one might expect NB_i and NH_i to be positively related to growth rates across industries. When tested empirically, however, on the basis of equation (5), the coefficient of G is highly insignificant statistically.

A further possible influence on the interindustry mix of foreign merger activity might presumably be the profitability of industries, PR.[31] Although this influence could be either positive or negative, one might very well think it more likely to be positive for at least two reasons. First, profitability might reflect the growth of the industry, which, as suggested earlier, one might expect to be positively associated with NB_i and NH_i. Inclusion of a profits variable on this rationale provides an indirect test of the growth hypothesis. Secondly, one might argue that foreign firms, less constrained in a number of ways than their domestic counterparts, could out-compete domestic firms for the acquisition of firms in more profitable industries, leaving those firms in less profitable industries for domestic absorption. This rationale is doubtful on logical grounds, since, presumably, the price paid for firms reflects their profitability in different industries. Nevertheless, it conforms with the picture painted in some popular commen-

---

[30] E.g., Kindleberger, *American Business Abroad*, pp. 6 ff. G is equal to the percentage change in the index of industrial production in industry i from 1946–47 (average) to 1960–61 (average). Dominion Bureau of Statistics, *General Review of the Manufacturing Industries of Canada, 1961*, Tables 5 and 6.

[31] PR is the unweighted average profit on net worth before tax, 1948 to 1961, as reported in Department of National Revenue, *Taxation Statistics*.

taries, depicting foreigners as taking over the most profitable sectors of the Canadian economy and leaving the dregs to local residents. The estimates of equation (5) do not confirm this picture. In fact, the co-efficient for PR is consistently negative, suggesting exactly the opposite picture. In many of the tests run, the coefficient was insignificant, but in some it was significant. This result may be rationalized on the ground that profits have an effect on internal cash flows, which, in turn, according to the evidence presented earlier, influence foreign merger activity. With lower profits, cash flow is lower, thereby enhancing the probability of foreign take-overs, and vice versa.

Still another variable to be considered is trade participation, T_i.[32] This variable was included on two grounds. First, foreign-trade participation might reflect the degree of competitive pressure prevailing in an industry, which might conceivably be reflected in foreign take-over activity. Secondly, foreign-trade participation might serve as an index of import substitution and export prospects, which presumably might also influence foreign take-over activity. The estimates of γ failed, however, to suggest a significant association between T_i and either NB_i or NH_i.

The final variable to be considered is research and development expenditure, $R\&D_i$.[33] During the past decade, Raymond Vernon and others have focused considerable attention on this factor as an influence on international trade and investment.[34] The evidence adduced indicates a positive association between $R\&D$ expenditures in

[32] Based on United Nations data on sources of exports and imports, classified on a two-digit-industry basis, and on the Dominion Bureau of Statistics census of manufacturing data on value-added, also classified by two-digit industries. All data relate to 1964.

[33] Data provided by Thomas Horst, *op. cit.*, based on National Science Foundation, *Research and Development in Industry, Annual Report, 1963,* and U.S. Department of Commerce, *Census of Manufacturing, 1963.* In addition, estimates were made using (*i*) R and D expenditures in the United States, by industry, for the years 1958 to 1961 (excluding tobacco, leather, and printing); and (*ii*) R and D expenditures in Canada ÷ R and D expenditures in the United States, by industry, in 1963. These data were compiled from National Science Foundation, *Basic Research, Applied Research and Development in Industry, 1964,* and Dominion Bureau of Statistics, *Industrial Research and Development Expenditures in Canada,* 1965, p. 22, Table 3. The coefficients for $R\&D_i$ remained insignificant for both of these definitions of the variable.

[34] E.g., William Gruber, Dilup Mehta, and Raymond Vernon, "The R and D Factor in International Trade and International Investment of United States Industries." *The Journal of Political Economy,* Vol. 75, No. 1 (February, 1967), pp. 20–37, and the references cited there.

the United States and the propensity to undertake direct investments abroad. The theoretical rationale for this view is open to questions so far as trade and investment relationships between Canada and the United States are concerned, since it is not apparent why a firm with an advantage over its competitors in $R\&D$ should choose to establish subsidiary operations rather than to export its products.[35] The empirical evidence also raises some questions. For example, the information available suggests that foreign subsidiaries in Canada undertake as much $R\&D$ expenditure on the average as do domestically controlled firms.[36] If firms go abroad because of the advantage which $R\&D$ expenditure at home gives them in foreign markets, one might expect their $R\&D$ expenditures in the foreign market to be less than that of local firms. Nevertheless, leaving these and other questions aside, $R\&D_i$ was included in equation (5). As indicated in Table 2, there is no evidence of a statistically significant association between $R\&D_i$ and the relative level of foreign take-over activity.

There are a number of additional variables that one might wish to consider. Among these are the degree of concentration in various industries, the extent of merger activity in the corresponding industry in the United States — on the assumption that foreign merger activity in Canada in large part reflects a spillover of merger activity in the United States — and the incidence of commercial failures in various industries. A lack of satisfactory data precluded experiments with these and other possibilities.

[35] Two general reasons are suggested by Gruber, Mehta, and Vernon (*ibid.*, p. 21) for a relation between R and D and foreign investment: (*i*) the large-scale marketing of technically sophisticated products demands the existence of local facilities; and (*ii*) investment is necessary to protect the technology-based oligopoly of United States producers against infringement by other foreign producers and local producers. These reasons are not very persuasive as far as Canada is concerned. Not only is United States production located in close proximity to the Canadian market, but also local Canadian markets are frequently closer to United States producers than to Canadian ones. Moreover, leaving aside the tariff, it is not very convincing to suggest that any technology-based oligopoly which the United States may have in Canada is seriously threatened by competition from abroad, or by local competition — especially when this technology-based oligopoly is based on the principle of "keeping ahead of the pack" (as it appears to be in these discussions) rather than on a once-for-all differential which, over time, might become eroded as outside technology caught up with that in the United States.

[36] A. E. Safarian, *Foreign Ownership of Canadian Industry*. Toronto, McGraw-Hill, 1966, pp. 281–282.

6 MACROECONOMIC INFLUENCES AND INTERTEMPORAL VARIATIONS IN FOREIGN TAKE-OVER ACTIVITY

IN ORDER for a foreign merger to occur under competitive market conditions, the net present value of a local firm to a foreign buyer, NPV_f, must exceed its net present value to the local seller, NPV_s, and to all potential domestic buyers, NPV_b. It is apparent that a variety of differences in market circumstances and constraints impinging upon foreign buyers compared with those impinging upon domestic buyers and sellers might arise, which would result in $NPV_f > NPV_b > NPV_s$. On the demand side, there may be differences in expectations about market demand, differences in access to markets and market information, differences in access to marketing skills, differences in product range, and so forth. On the supply side, there may be differences in the price and access to factor inputs and financial resources, differences in the access to technology and managerial skills, differences in risk and attitudes toward risk-bearing, differences in the length of the planning horizon, differences in access to scale economies, as well as other factors. For the most part, smaller firms seem to be subject to more stringent constraints on both the demand and supply sides than are larger firms, reinforcing the tendency for larger firms to absorb smaller ones.

Related to this is the question of why foreign firms choose to buy existing facilities rather than to establish new facilities. Presumably this is because the NPV_s of firms taken over is less than the cost of establishing comparable new facilities — including goodwill and other intangibles — and of overcoming other barriers to entry.

In examining the influence of general economic conditions on year-to-year variations in the number of foreign mergers, one is in effect attempting to identify the particular features of the economic environment that give rise to year-to-year variations in NPV_f relative to NPV_b and NPV_s. The investigation of this question reported below is based on time-series analysis, applied by fitting a series of linear equations by ordinary least squares to annual data for the period 1945 to 1961. The first part of the analysis — like that in the previous section—is essentially a search procedure, while the second part reports on several tests performed on the relationships that emerged from this search.[37]

In the tests undertaken in the first part of the analysis, the following variables were considered:

A = the number of mergers in the United States

F = the number of commercial failures in Canada

L = the supply of funds generated internally in Canadian corporations; the level of business activity in Canada, as measured by the level of unemployment, U; the index of industrial production, I; and profits per unit of manufacturing output, π

Z = the level of stock prices in Canada

x = deviations in Canada's foreign-exchange rate from \$1.00 Canadian = \$1.00 U.S.

i = the level of short-term interest rates in Canada

i_a = the level of short-term interest rates in the United States

i' = the difference between short-term interest rates in Canada and the United States, i.e., $i - i_a$

Z' = the difference between the level of stock market prices in Canada and the United States

V = the income velocity of circulation of money, as a proxy for credit conditions (money stock $\div GNP$)

D = changes in antitrust laws and law enforcement in the United States

t = a time trend

ESTIMATED RELATIONSHIPS

The "best" estimate emerging from these experiments is

$$N = 3.32 + 0.0677A + 0.0329F - 20.46L.$$
$$(5.15) \quad\quad (3.40) \quad\quad\quad (2.17) \quad\quad\quad\quad\quad (10)$$
$$\bar{R}^2 = .92 \quad\quad DW = 2.77$$

[37] The analysis concentrates throughout on the number of mergers, rather than on the value. The value of mergers reflects not only the number of firms but their average value, which can be expected to vary widely because of the size of the firms taken over and

N is the number of foreign mergers and DW is the Durbin-Watson statistic. In effect, this relationship suggests that variations in the number of foreign take-overs in Canada can be largely explained by a spillover of merger activity in the United States, conditioned by variations in the level of business activity in Canada and the liquidity of Canadian corporations. The rationale for including these variables and details on the tests run are discussed elsewhere; only a summary is presented here.[38]

As noted at the outset, a central premise of the methodology underlying this paper is that foreign take-overs in Canada may simply be, to a considerable extent, a manifestation of the more general phenomenon of industrial mergers occurring in North America. If so, one would expect a highly significant positive association between A and N, as is, in fact, indicated by equation (10) and all other tests run. A may be viewed as an index of the propensity of firms in the United States to engage in merger activity, reflecting attitudes toward long-run economic prospects, the most efficient method of expanding output and markets, attitudes toward market strategies, views about probable future developments with respect to antitrust laws and law enforcement, and so forth. The merger literature for the United States frequently refers to the merger "waves" that have occurred in the past, and attempts have been made to explain these waves, in part, at least, in terms of underlying attitudes and motivation of businessmen toward mergers.[39] If this applies within the United States, it is equally plausible to expect the propensity of businessmen to engage in merger ac-

other factors. At the same time, the average value of the firms taken over may have little or no relation to the reasons why firms are taken over, which is our primary interest here. A number of tests were run on the value of firms, but these seemed inconclusive and unpromising.

[38] Reuber and Roseman, *op. cit.*, Chapter 7; Grant L. Reuber, "Antitrust and the Take-Over Activity of American Firms in Canada: A Further Analysis." *The Journal of Law and Economics,* Vol. XII (October, 1969), pp. 405–417.

[39] *Economic Concentration* (cited in full in footnote 7): testimony by Mueller, pp. 505–508; Ralph L. Nelson, *Merger Movements in American Industry, 1895–1956,* New York, NBER, 1959, Chapter 5; Jesse W. Markham, "Survey of the Evidence and Findings on Mergers," in *Business Concentration and Price Policy,* New York, NBER, 1955, pp. 146–154; George F. Stigler, "Monopoly and Oligopoly by Merger," in *Readings in Industrial Organization and Public Policy,* The American Economic Association, Richard B. Heflebower and George W. Stocking, eds., Homewood, Ill., Richard D. Irwin, 1958, pp. 69–80.

tivity to be a factor influencing their merger activity in Canada. In addition, variations in A may serve as an appropriate proxy variable for a variety of economic factors that directly influence the willingness of firms in the United States to undertake mergers — such factors as credit conditions in the United States and changes in the business outlook. To the extent that A reflects underlying attitudes to merger activity in the United States and the effects of contemporary economic conditions, variations in A can be expected to reflect changes in the demand for Canadian firms. By including A in the relationship, one is, in effect, directly posing the hypothesis that take-overs in Canada by firms in the United States reflect, to some extent, a spillover of merger activity in the United States.

The other explanatory variables included in equation (10) reflect variations in economic conditions in Canada, which, though similar, are not identical to variations in economic conditions in the United States. The supply of internally generated funds, L, is negatively related to N, which is consistent with the evidence presented in the previous section. As internally generated funds become less readily available among Canadian corporations, the cost of capital can be expected to rise for both potential domestic buyers and sellers of local firms.[40] Ceteris paribus, NPV_f will rise relative to NPV_b and NPV_s as a consequence. It is evident that, to some extent, the supply of internally generated funds in Canada can be expected to vary independently of the supply of such funds in the United States. Moreover, variation in the supply of internally generated funds in the United States is allowed for separately, to some degree, via variations in A. In addition, since many acquiring foreign firms are larger than domestic firms, and have much more diversified and easier access to outside funds, any general reduction in corporate liquidity and tightening of credit conditions in North America can be expected to place foreign firms at an advantage relative to domestically owned Canadian firms — in other words, NPV_f will tend to rise relative to NPV_b and NPV_s.[41]

[40] For a theoretical elaboration of this view, see James S. Duesenberry, *Business Cycles and Economic Growth.* New York, McGraw-Hill, 1958, Chapter 5.

[41] Evidence that the incidence of tighter credit conditions is greater for small firms than for large firms is available from a variety of sources, of which three may be noted: *Employment, Growth and Price Levels,* "Answers to Questions on Monetary Policy and Debt Management," *Hearings,* Joint Economic Committee, Part 6C, 86th Con-

The number of commercial failures in Canada, F, is positively related to N. This association seems plausible for at least three reasons: (a) F relates to economic conditions in Canada and, therefore, is likely to have a more direct effect on local firms than on foreign firms, which will be influenced by foreign economic conditions as well; (b) the effect of business conditions on foreign demand for Canadian firms will to some extent be reflected in A, leaving F to reflect mainly the partial effect of this factor on the supply side of the market; (c) although owners may prefer to hold on to firms for a variety of noneconomic reasons as profits decline, this preference can only be indulged up to the point where bankruptcy is imminent. At that point, the pressure to give up the business is irresistible. Consequently, one would expect an increase in bankruptcies to be associated with an increase in mergers, and vice versa.

Two further points may be noted in connection with equation (10). First, the value of $\bar{R}^2$ is quite high, indicating that the relationship explains over 92 per cent of the variation in N, while the value of DW gives no evidence of significant autocorrelation in the residuals at the 95 per cent confidence level. Secondly, F and L are highly collinear ($r = .97$), which can be expected to reduce the size of the estimated t-ratios. Because of this bias, the association between these variables and N is probably even more significant than is suggested by the estimated t-ratios for the coefficients of F and L.

In the course of developing equation (10) an alternative relationship was developed, which, on strictly statistical grounds, is as satisfactory as equation (10).

$$N = 41.95 - 2.195Z' + 0.334Z - 19.443i_a + 5.080t - 8.015U. \quad (11)$$
$$ (7.51) \quad (2.07) \quad (5.45) \quad (3.90) \quad (3.46)$$

$$\bar{R}^2 = .97 \qquad DW = 2.30$$

This relationship is consistent with equation (10) in pointing to much the same general influences on foreign mergers in Canada. At the same time, it does not lend itself as easily to sorting out the influence of

gress, 1st Session, Washington, 1959, pp. 1773–74; Bank of Canada, *Annual Report, 1959*, p. 6; John H. Young and John F. Helliwell, "The Effect of Monetary Policy on Corporations," *Report of the Royal Commission on Banking and Finance*, Appendix Volume, 1964, Ottawa, 1965, p. 387.

496 • INTERNATIONAL MOBILITY AND MOVEMENT OF CAPITAL

merger activity on the part of firms in the United States, on the one hand, and domestic influences, on the other. In addition, the tests to which each relationship was exposed indicated that equation (10) is preferable in a number of respects.

The rationale for including the explanatory variables in equation (11) will not be considered here at any length. Two of these variables (as well as some of those listed earlier) have been rationalized and pointed out as important in studies on merger activity in the United States: the current level of economic activity (as reflected by U or I or π) and the level of stock market prices.[42] Z' may be rationalized on the ground that variations in Z' reflect variations in the cost of capital between Canada and the United States, although it is conceded that it may reflect other influences as well. Variations in i_a may presumably be viewed as a proxy for variations in credit conditions in the United States. And t, as always, is included to allow for a variety of broad secular factors about which we know little or nothing.

No satisfactory and statistically significant association was established in any of the tests run between N and the other variables listed earlier—x, I, π, i', V, and D. A special word might be said about D—changes in antitrust laws and law enforcement in the United States; and x—the exchange-rate variable. It has been suggested that because of tougher antitrust laws and law enforcement during the 1950's, companies in the United States embarked on increased take-over activity in Canada.[43] As discussed elsewhere, this hypothesis does not stand up when it is examined in the light of the more comprehensive questionnaire data now available and the employment of more rigorous tests based on equation (10).[44] As for the exchange rate, one would expect this variable to be insignificant, since both the purchase price and future returns on the investment are denominated in foreign exchange from the standpoint of the foreign buyer. Moreover, since for most of the period in question, Canada had a free exchange rate, peculiarities related to the possible over- or undervaluation of the exchange rate do not enter the picture.[45]

[42] Mueller *op. cit.*, pp. 505–508; Nelson, *op. cit.*; Markham, *op. cit.*

[43] C. J. Maule, "Antitrust and the Take-Over Activity of American Firms in Canada." *The Journal of Law and Economics* (October, 1968), pp. 423–432.

[44] Reuber, *loc. cit.*

[45] Professor Kindleberger has pointed out that German authors, in particular, have sometimes ascribed U.S. investment in Germany to the overvaluation of the dollar in relation to the mark.

TESTS OF THE RELATIONSHIPS

Two relationships that seemed to explain changes in foreign mergers reasonably well having been derived; both were subjected to three tests.[46] The first test was to determine how plausible each relationship looked when fitted to data on the number of domestic take-overs. The second test was to see how well each relationship stood up to disaggregation. The third test was to assess the predictive power of each.

When M, the number of domestic mergers, was substituted for N in the initial tests of equations (10) and (11), the coefficients of all the explanatory variables except A and Z were insignificant. The "best" relationship explaining M was:

$$M = 2.44 + 1.894Z - 32.52L. \tag{12}$$
$$(6.31) \qquad (3.19)$$

$$\bar{R}^2 = .89 \qquad DW = 1.69$$

When A was added to this relationship, its coefficient was insignificant. Equation (12) is consistent with evidence for the United States cited earlier, indicating a relationship between stock-market prices and domestic mergers.[47] In addition, it reemphasizes the role of corporate liquidity.

The tests using disaggregated data were based on the following components of N: (a) acquisitions of only those firms previously controlled in Canada; (b) acquisitions in the manufacturing sector of the economy of Canadian firms and all firms; (c) acquisitions in the trade sector of Canadian firms and all firms; and (d) firms acquired in broad horizontal mergers, and in nonhorizontal mergers. Comparing the signs and t-ratios of the estimated coefficients for the explanatory variables, one may summarize the results of these disaggregative tests as follows:

(a) The signs of the coefficients of all the explanatory variables in the equations based on equation (10) are consistent and conform with the signs of the corresponding coefficients in the aggregate equa-

---

[46] These are described in detail in Reuber and Roseman, *op. cit.*, pp. 152–172.

[47] It is also consistent with econometric evidence indicating that increases in stock-market prices in Canada, presumably reflecting an anticipation of business prospects, are significantly and positively related to new investment in plant and equipment.

tions. The same is true of the constant term with one exception.

(b) The values of R^2 are consistently high, and the values of DW give no evidence of significant autocorrelation in the computed residuals at the 5 per cent confidence level.

(c) The level of significance remains fairly high for the estimated coefficients in the disaggregated equations. The coefficient for A is significant in all cases; the coefficient for F is significant in seven of the nine cases; and the coefficient for L is significant in five of the nine cases.

(d) Comparing the performance of equation (11) with that of equation (10), one finds (i) somewhat less consistency with respect to the signs of the estimated coefficients, (ii) somewhat lower $\bar{R}^2$ for the corresponding estimates based on equation (10) in six of the nine cases, and (iii) somewhat fewer—and a less consistent pattern of—significant t-ratios. These considerations, combined with the fact that equation (11) is based on 11 degrees of freedom compared with 13 for equation (10), suggest some preference for the latter.

One danger of concentrating attention on the number of mergers is that one may be unable to detect influences on merger activity that are related to the size of the acquired firm. Accordingly, it is particularly significant that relationships (10) and (11) stood up well on the foregoing basis when they were reestimated for small (less than 50 employees) acquisitions (N_s) and larger (more than 50 employees) acquisitions (N_l).[48]

The use of predictive tests was seriously impaired because the data could not be satisfactorily updated beyond 1961, as had originally been hoped. A much weaker test was devised, in which each relationship was fitted to the two subperiods 1945–59 and 1947–61. The power of each of these reestimated relationships to predict the two years preceding, or following, each of these subperiods was then com-

[48]　$N_s = -4.77 + 0.033A + 0.0084F - 4.09L;\ R^2 = .84$
　　　　(3.71)　　(1.28)　　(0.64)

$N_l = 2.90 + 0.024A + 0.015F - 9.60L;\ \bar{R}^2 = .90$
　　　　(3.84)　　(3.20)　　(2.11)

$N_s = 22.13 + 0.042Z - 1.231Z' - 6.08i_a - 2.83U + 1.76t;\ \bar{R}^2 = .96$
　　　　(5.07)　　(8.44)　　(3.36)　　(2.41)　　(2.66)

$N_l = 10.93 + 0.18Z - 0.58Z' - 6.80i - 3.52U + 2.06t;\ \bar{R}^2 = .82$
　　　　(1.20)　　(2.10)　　(1.99)　　(1.59)　　(1.65)

pared with the other relationship, and with the predictive power of three naive models defined as follows:

$$\hat{N}_t = N_{t-1}; \tag{13}$$

$$\hat{N}_t = (\bar{N}/\bar{M})M_t; \tag{14}$$

$$\hat{N}_t = (\bar{N}/\bar{A})A_t; \tag{15}$$

where $\bar{N}$ and $\bar{M}$ are the average number of foreign and domestic mergers in Canada, and A is the average number of domestic mergers in the United States. These averages are based on 1947 to 1951 when predicting 1945 and 1946, and on 1955 to 1959 when predicting 1960 and 1961. In addition, the performance of the two relationships in question was compared with these naive models for the full period, employing mean values of M, N, and A for 1945 to 1961. Predictive power in these tests is measured by the square root of the average deviation between the actual number of mergers and the number estimated from the relationship, i.e.,

$$\sqrt{\frac{\Sigma \ (actual - estimated)^2}{number \ of \ observations}}.$$

The results of this test may be summarized as follows:

(a) Equation (10) is a better predictor than equation (11) and any of the naive models of the years immediately preceding or following the subperiods specified for the tests.[49]

(b) The root mean of the squared deviations of the actual from the estimated number of mergers falls within the standard error of estimate of equation (10); it is more than twice the standard error of estimate for equation (11).

(c) The estimated coefficients for the subperiod equations are much more stable for equation (10) than for equation (11).

(d) Both estimates outperform the naive models for the full period 1945 to 1961. As one would expect from the higher value of R^2, equation (11) also outperforms equation (10) by a small margin for the full period.

---

[49] Equation (10) is slightly inferior to the predictions based on two of the naive models for 1945–46 but much superior to any of the naive models for 1960–61.

7 SUMMARY AND CONCLUSIONS

PERHAPS the most serious deficiencies that run through most of the preceding analysis are: (*a*) lack of a tightly knit, fully specified, testable theory of business behavior as it relates to merger activity, and (*b*) lack of reliable data that would make it feasible to run more rigorous empirical tests, not only on any new and better theories that might be developed but also on the *ad hoc* workaday theories that are the common currency in this area at present. Although the data on which the foregoing discussion is based represent a considerable extension in the information available on foreign take-overs in Canada, it is evident that many dark corners remain. In order to illuminate the subject more clearly, more comprehensive and up-to-date information of better quality is required on a wide range of variables for descriptive, as well as analytical, purposes.

Secondly, it is evident that only a limited range of questions have been considered in this paper and that other important aspects of the issue of foreign ownership and control have not been considered, e.g., questions relating to the policies, practices, and performance of foreign-controlled firms; the benefits of foreign investment; and so forth. Some of these questions have been explored by other authors.[50]

Subject to these caveats, what are some of the main implications and conclusions to be drawn from the analysis? One is methodological. As noted at the outset, a central feature of the approach adopted has been to evaluate foreign take-overs in relation to domestic take-overs occurring at the same time, on the ground that the approach places foreign take-overs within the appropriate framework of economic analysis, provides a clearer perspective on the phenomenon, and enhances the testing power of available analytical tools.

On the substantive side, the analysis suggests that variations in the number of take-overs are partly explained over time by the level of merger activity in the United States, and that variations across industries are roughly proportional to the existing pattern of foreign con-

---

[50] See Safarian, *op. cit.*, and the references cited there; and Rudolph G. Penner, "The Benefits of Foreign Investment in Canada, 1950 to 1956," *The Canadian Journal of Economics and Political Science* (May, 1966), pp. 172–183.

trol among industries. In addition to these "exogenous" variables, variations in the number of foreign take-overs appear to be sensitive to a number of policy variables: tariff policy; the flow of internally generated corporate funds, which is influenced by government financial policies; and the level of business activity, which is conditioned by government stabilization policies.

Viewed within the context of the literature on direct foreign investment and industrial organization, neither of the two "exogenous" variables noted above has received much, if any, attention. At one place or another, limited attention has been given to the three policy variables mentioned. The influence of tariff policy has been noted in the literature on direct investment, and the level of economic activity has been pointed to as an influence on domestic merger activity. Relatively little attention has been given to internal cash flows in either branch of the literature. At the same time, it is noteworthy that the foregoing analysis raises some doubts concerning the influence of a number of other variables that appear in the literature as factors affecting mergers and direct foreign investment – e.g., growth; economies of scale; size; research and development; and changes in United States antitrust laws and law enforcement.

Within the context of Canadian economic policy, the evidence suggests a number of general conclusions. First, only a relatively small portion of the level of foreign control of Canadian industry in 1962 is attributable to take-overs per se from 1945 to 1961. Secondly, relative to the number of firms in Canada, the number of take-overs has been small. Thirdly, though differing somewhat, the characteristics of foreign take-overs may be considered to be broadly similar to those of domestic take-overs, not exhibiting characteristics that pose obvious causes for alarm.

Finally, there is the question of what, if any, attention has been given to foreign take-overs in formulating policy, and what influence policies have had on take-over activity. In Canada, it seems fair to say that in the past, each of the policy variables noted above has been regulated largely without recognition of the relationship between these variables and take-over activity or its importance. Failure to recognize the relationships in question has frequently given rise to paradoxical situations where the strongest advocates of economic nationalism espouse, in one context, policies that, in another, have indirectly tended to increase the foreign take-overs which they oppose. Evidence of such situations may be found in the record of Canadian tariff policies,[51] as well as in the record of Canadian fiscal,[52] monetary, and debt-management policies.[53]

Aside from providing yet another illustration of the universal principle that everything is related to everything else, the record of Canadian policy during this period suggests that active concern about foreign take-overs adds still a further objective to the already overloaded objective function of government, further complicating the exercise of tariff, fiscal, monetary, and debt-management policies. For this additional objective to be allowed for rationally in formulating policies, it is evident that more must be known about foreign direct investment and take-overs than is currently the case.

[51] The authors are unaware of any suggestions that tariff reductions be implemented to reduce foreign investment and take-overs. There is some evidence of attempts to use the tariff to increase the inflow of direct investment. This usually is expressed in words to the effect that if Canada reduces its tariffs without taking additional steps, investors will locate their plants in the United States and export to Canada rather than maintaining and expanding their Canadian plants. This concern was voiced, for example, in discussions of the Canada–U.S. automotive agreement. See Wonnacott and Wonnacott, *op. cit.*, Appendices A and B.

[52] Royal Commission on Taxation, *Report*. Ottawa, 1966, Vol. VI, pp. 158–162. See also the papers by R. A. Musgrave and Arnold C. Harberger reviewing the *Report* in *The Canadian Journal of Economics* (February, 1968), pp. 178–182 and pp. 186–194.

[53] The most striking paradox is, perhaps, evident in the case of monetary and debt-management policy. In common with most countries, Canada pursued increasingly restrictive monetary and debt-management policies from 1945 to 1961. Two features, however, particularly distinguish Canadian policy during the late 1950's. One was a massive Conversion Loan in 1958, which, in the course of three months, increased the average term to maturity on the public debt from eight years to fourteen years nine months. The second was the very tight monetary policies pursued from 1958 to 1961 while the unemployment rates ranged from 5.5 to 7.8 per cent, averaging 6.8 per cent. Both measures tended to reduce corporate liquidity and raise the cost of capital. In addition, these restrictive policies tended to increase the number of commercial failures. From both standpoints, therefore, our evidence suggests that the policies in question tended to increase the number of foreign take-overs. The paradox is that all of this occurred under the aegis of a government that came to office in 1957 on a platform of reducing, or at least arresting, the growth of foreign control over Canadian industry – a policy that was actively supported by the then Governor of the Bank of Canada.

APPENDIX

Selected Estimates of Equation (5) for Two Subperiods: 1950–55, 1956–61
$$(NB_i \text{ or } NH_i = \alpha + \beta FN_i + \gamma_j X_{ji})$$

Equation Number	Dependent Variable	$\hat{\alpha}$	$\hat{\beta}$	$\hat{\gamma}$	X_j	$\bar{R}^2$
			1950–55			
1	NB_i	17.841	0.922			.55
		(1.97)	(4.27)			
2	NB_i	−6.128	1.027	1.224	R_{d_i}	.56
		(0.25)	(4.33)	(1.05)		
3	NB_i	15.001	0.911	0.367	Ly_i	.52
		(0.92)	(3.96)	(0.21)		
4	NH_i	12.811	1.282			.70
		(1.48)	(5.34)			
5	NH_i	5.218	1.301	0.406	R_{d_i}	.67
		(0.21)	(5.06)	(0.33)		
6	NH_i	22.874	1.330	−1.325	Ly_i	.69
		(1.60)	(5.36)	(0.89)		
			1956–61			
7	NB_i	24.162	0.693			.33
		(2.33)	(2.80)			
8	NB_i	−2.237	0.809	1.348	R_{d_i}	.33
		(0.08)	(2.97)	(1.00)		
9	NB_i	42.596	0.724	−2.787	Ly_i	.40
		(2.77)	(3.08)	(1.56)		
10	NH_i	25.836	0.877			.41
		(2.49)	(3.05)			
11	NH_i	22.141	0.886	0.198	R_{d_i}	.35
		(0.74)	(2.87)	(0.13)		
12	NH_i	49.299	0.870	−3.398	Ly_i	.56
		(3.49)	(3.50)	(2.15)		

NOTE: Equations explaining NB_i exclude furniture and tobacco; equations explaining NH_i exclude rubber, furniture, tobacco, and petroleum. These industries were excluded from these equations because either the numerator or the denominator of the ratio was equal to zero.

COMMENTS

ROBERT E. LIPSEY

QUEENS COLLEGE AND NATIONAL BUREAU OF ECONOMIC RESEARCH

As several papers make clear, portfolio-adjustment or stock-adjustment models are certainly "in" as a way of analyzing foreign investment. Prachowny makes a good case for concluding that this approach is logical for direct investment as well as for financial investment. In the end, however, I find the model that he produces, neat as it is, unconvincing for two reasons. First, I do not think that it catches most of the motivations for direct investment. Second, even if the model were good in theoretical terms, the data used for estimating the coefficients are so far from the variables that they are supposed to represent that I am highly skeptical regarding his interpretation of the coefficients and their use for policy recommendations.

The basis for his model is the argument that the share of its assets a firm will hold abroad depends on the relative rates of return at home and in foreign countries, adjusted for the relative risk. The model offers no theory as to why foreign investment becomes more or less profitable relative to domestic, but, rather, puts forward an explanation of the way in which corporations react to differences in the profitability of investment. As Prachowny states, it would be hard to find a theory that categorically denies the assumptions that he makes, although his contention is really true only until he defines his variables more precisely.

Even at this general level, there is an unstated assumption—not so much in the theoretical model as in the realization—which I think illegitimate. This is that the foreign and domestic operations of a company, or of all companies together, are essentially independent. The foreign investment does not affect domestic profitability, and domestic investment does not affect foreign profitability. Without this assumption, the author could not argue that the relevant return on foreign investment is the ratio of profits earned abroad to investment abroad. If the investment abroad adds to domestic profits, or domestic investment adds to foreign profits, the model is seriously undermined.

While the assumption may be valid in some cases, it must surely be invalid for others. Domestic profitability for some companies must be affected by foreign investments in, say, copper mining or petroleum, or banana production; or by foreign manufacturing which competes with exports or domestic sales, or promotes exports (an automobile assembly plant). Presumably the company will consider the impact on total profit, domestic or foreign, of any investment here or abroad. Perhaps this is what the author had in mind in his theoretical discussion, since he speaks only of the expected rate of return on each type of asset, without defining the rate.

When we come to the empirical implementation of the model, we are in a world that often I do not recognize. It is assumed that the desired stock of assets is achieved within a year, on the ground that titles to direct investment assets "can be bought and sold with not much more difficulty than other long-term portfolio assets." That seems highly unlikely if one thinks, for example, of the time required to develop new sources of minerals, or of the difficulty of selling an assembly plant geared to American cars to a European or Japanese producer. The author himself says later that direct investment assets "rarely enter the market," a fact which suggests that such assets are not readily traded.

The variable for the stock of American direct investment abroad is the estimate by the U.S. Department of Commerce of the book value of this investment, and it is compared with the market value of corporate stock outstanding in the United States to show the share of corporate assets invested abroad. As is pointed out, a book value is being compared with a market value here, but the consequences of that disparity are not noted. There is probably a serious downward bias in the estimate of direct-investment assets, since Canadian and U.K. stock prices almost tripled over the period covered, and prices of equities in other countries rose by similar amounts. In the face of this rise, the residual change in the estimated value of American direct investment—that is, the change other than that from investment flows and reinvested earnings—was negative in all but two years, a strong indication that capital gains from this source did not enter the estimates or that American firms were making very poor investments.

Not only the trend but the year-to-year fluctuations in the ratio of holdings of foreign assets to holdings of domestic assets reflect this mixture of book values and market values. The large decline from 1953 to 1955, for example, results from the rapid rise in stock prices during those years, and the major increases in the ratio reflect poor performance of the stock market in the United States, as in 1953, 1957, 1960, 1962, and 1966. Of course, these stock-price movements may reflect current or anticipated changes in profits, but I suspect that relationship is not what the author had in mind.

The earnings variables seem to have a similarly odd relationship. The foreign earnings relate to all types of direct investment, including investments in natural-resource industries such as petroleum. The domestic-earnings rate applies only to manufacturing, and the ratio between them may be as likely to reflect the relation of petroleum earnings to manufacturing earnings as the ratio of foreign to domestic earnings.

Aside from the differences in coverage between the two earnings series, I am skeptical of the earnings data in general. These are, after all, comparisons of earnings within the same companies, as shown on the books of these companies. There must be a good deal of leeway for a company in allocating profits to the affiliate or to the parent, as tax or other considerations dictate, by determining intracompany prices, charges for services, and other elements of cost. If that is the case, it is hard to be sure that the earnings comparisons we see are the ones that govern the investment policy of the companies.

These rates of return are adjusted for the risk involved in each type of investment, the risk being measured by the variability of the earnings rate in the time series. I doubt that this measures the main elements of risk involved in foreign operations, which I would take to be that of expropriation or other hostile actions by host governments; or, in some industries, of actions by other countries (including the United States) that affect the size of the market an affiliate can serve. To capture the risks facing an investor, a cross-sectional measure reflecting the range of experiences within an industry might be more appropriate than a time-series measure.

If I am correct in thinking that the variables used here — and, therefore, the coefficients obtained — do not measure what they are supposed to measure, what do they represent? The level of direct-investment assets rose very steadily throughout the period, without many changes in the rate of growth. The level of the value of stock outstanding of American companies, however, showed large changes in rates of growth and declined in several years, and the movement of this series can be traced largely, although not entirely, to changes in stock prices. Thus, the fluctuations in the ratio of foreign to domestic assets largely represent fluctuations in stock prices in the United States.

The independent variable representing the ratio of foreign to domestic earnings mainly reflects the fluctuations of domestic earnings, since direct-investment earnings abroad were comparatively stable, at least after 1958. It seems quite possible, then, that the relationship between domestic/foreign-earnings ratios and the corresponding asset-holdings ratios reflects the impact of changes in corporate earnings in the United States upon stock prices, and that no effect on direct investment is caught here at all, except to the extent that movements of stock prices might affect direct investment.

Despite these criticisms, I think that the approach to analyzing direct-investment decisions through discrepancies between desired and actual holdings of direct-investment assets is potentially a revealing one. Perhaps the variable to be explained should be, in fact, the rate of flow of new capital from the United States, as in the flow models described, or the rate of expenditure on plant and equipment, since these variables are under the control of individual companies. The ratio of foreign to total assets is only partially under the control of the parent companies, and the amount of investment required to reach an "appropriate" ratio in some sense is absurdly large at times. To keep the ratio constant between 1953 and 1954, for example, would have required an investment of over $7 billion at a time when the annual outflow was averaging something more like $700 million. A fairly long period should, therefore, be allowed in the model for adjustment to the desired investment levels.

The main problem in Prachowny's paper is one that afflicts quite a few of the other papers put forward at this conference. The authors have, for the most part, tried to follow the virtuous route of creating a theoretically sensible model and then estimating an empirical counterpart, carefully avoiding fishing expeditions that might land variables that are statistically significant but not part of the model. However, since at least some of the variables in the model have no empirical counterpart, the creators of the model must search for proxies, some of which are related to the corresponding variables in the model mainly by hope. The proxies are then renamed to present them as the proper variables. In effect, the fishing expedition has been transformed from fishing for variables to fishing for proxies, and I am not sure the degree of virtue achieved is as great as is sometimes claimed.

The paper by Reuber and Roseman is somewhat difficult to comment on in any general way, owing to the lack of a theoretical structure to explain differences in take-over rates among industries. Various attempts are made to account for the rate of merger activity, but I miss here what several of the other papers included: some definition of the goals that the firm is attempting to reach by its merger activity, and an explanation of why there should be differences among industries in either the goals or their effects on merger activity. My main comments, then, are on the specific empirical findings and on the questions which they raise.

A problem with the data in general is the reliance on numbers of mergers, rather than on the aggregate assets or employment involved, for many of the analyses. There is an advantage to this procedure, in that single large cases do not overwhelm the evidence of many smaller examples, but there is also the disadvantage that it is difficult to assay the significance of numbers for the activity of the economy without some measures of the values involved.

One finding mentioned in Section 2 is that the number of take-overs of Canadian firms by firms in the United States is small compared with the number of take-overs by Canadian firms, particularly in view of the much greater number of firms in the United States. This comparison may be affected by differences in the definition of a firm in the two countries, and by the industrial composition of each one's business population. The United States might have, for example, many more small banks, retail stores, private landlords, and others who inflate the figure for the total number of firms.

Since 73 per cent of the foreign acquisitions of Canadian firms were made by Canadian affiliates of foreign firms, it is obvious that the tendency toward such take-overs was far stronger among firms already in Canada than among the general run of firms in the United States. It might be interesting to compare take-overs by Canadian-owned firms with those by foreign-owned Canadian firms to test whether the latter show the same propensity toward growth by merger as do the domestically owned firms.

The question of industrial composition may also affect another of the results. Foreign mergers are shown to be vertical, both forward and backward, to a much greater extent than are domestic mergers, while domestic mergers are predominantly horizontal. It is not clear from the data presented here (although it may be in the original source) whether this difference between foreign and domestic firms reflected their ownership or only their industry composition, since the type of merger may be dependent on the industry to a large extent.

The main part of the paper is an analysis of the factors determining the share of foreign-owned companies in merger activity within individual industries, as represented, once again, by numbers of mergers. One of the variables used is the share of foreign ownership in the number of existing firms, but I believe that there is a misinterpretation of the coefficients of the equations in the first statement of the results. Given the relation

$$NB_i = \beta FN_i,$$

where NB_i is the share of foreign firms in mergers and FN_i is their share in ownership, $\beta = 1$ is said to imply that "foreign ownership, per se, has little influence on the interindustry distribution of foreign merger activity." On the contrary, if the $\bar{R}^2$ is high, the distribution of foreign ownership determines the distribution of foreign merger activity in this case. We can say, however, if we ignore the constant term in the equations, that a coefficient of one implies that foreign ownership does not affect the level of total merger activity in an industry, since foreign and domestic firms have the same propensity to merge. A coefficient greater than unity implies that foreign firms have a higher propensity toward mergers than domestic ones, and that foreign ownership works to increase the tendency toward mergers.

A second variable found to be significant, in general, is the nominal level of tariffs, as represented by the ratio of tariff collections to total or dutiable imports in the industry. These ratios are subject to the objections usually made to such measures of the tariff level in comparisons among countries: a tariff high enough to exclude a product does not appear in this calculation at all; and any high tariff, by reducing imports of the product subject to it, reduces the weight of that product in the tariff ratio. Thus, of two industries with the same average tariff rates on pretariff imports, the one with a mixture of very high and very low rates may appear to have a lower average tariff level after the imposition of the tariff, because its tariffs distorted the composition of trade to a greater degree, shifting it toward the low-tariff items.

In a number of cases, it would be interesting to know what the results would have been had the share in assets, rather than the share in numbers of firms, been used as the independent variable. This might be a reasonable way of estimating even the number of mergers if a firm with $100 million in assets is ten times as likely to take over another firm as one with $10 million in assets. Relating the share in the number of firms to the share in the number of mergers seems to imply that larger firms will make larger mergers — but no more mergers — than small firms.

It does not seem overly surprising that the tariff level does not have much influence on NH_i, intraindustry mergers. Since most firms in the United States involved in mergers are already established in the given industry, they have already taken advantage of the tariff, and it is not clear that a merger within the industry would add anything to that advantage. It might be more likely that the tariff level would influence the number of take-overs by firms in the United States not previously in the Canadian industry.

Another possibility for the tariff variable would be changes in the level of tariffs. One might suppose that the degree of ownership by firms in the United States at any time represents some adaptation to tariffs and other economic circumstances. A take-over implies that the adaptation was incomplete. Would it not be sensible to expect that one would find foreign take-overs more frequent at a given tariff level when that level represents a large increase over the past level than when it represents a long-standing tariff? This is particularly logical because a take-over is a way of adding capacity quickly, instead of slowly from internal growth, and might be thought of as the expected response to an unexpected change in circumstances.

Among the variables that failed to explain the distribution of mergers was the relation between the average size of foreign-owned firms and the average size of all firms in the industry, the expectation being that where foreign-owned firms are larger, they will be subject to fewer financial constraints and more able to take over Canadian firms. Probably the relevant variable here would not be the size of the Canadian affiliate of the American firm but the size of the latter, since this size would determine the ability to raise funds for take-overs. Such a variable would be fairly easy to insert in an equation, the expectation being that firms in the United States would account for a relatively high proportion of mergers in those industries in which the parent companies are particularly large relative to Canadian companies.

RONALD I. McKINNON
STANFORD UNIVERSITY

A number of logical and statistical problems in Prachowny's analysis create difficulty in interpreting his empirical results. These difficulties seem endemic in estimating flows of foreign investment in general, and direct investment in particular.

UTILITY, DEMAND, AND NET WORTH

Prachowny starts off by specifying a utility function $U(R)$, which he does not use to generate his asset-demand function (page 444) as given below; that depends on much more than R:

$$A_1 = A_1(R_1, R_2, \sigma_{R_1}, \sigma_{R_2}, \sigma_{R_{12}}, \sigma_e, W),$$

where $W = A_1 + A_2$.

Since the utility function is not spelled out, neither is the maximization process which motivates the representative corporation. Hence, the reader is given no guidance as to what a priori restriction one might impose on the form of the demand function. Specifically, given the known limitations of mean-variance analysis — not to mention mean-variance-covariance analysis — it would be nice to know what could plausibly be assumed. For example, is the corporation maximizing expected utility through time (appropriately discounted), or is it maximizing the present net worth of its outstanding common shares, or is it maximizing the market value of all its outstanding securities? Perhaps all of these maxima lead to the same estimating equation, but the reader is left in the dark as to whether this is true.

In the actual estimation procedure, Prachowny imposes the condition that the elasticity of A_1 with respect to W is unity, but there is no a priori justification provided. Intuitively, one feels that it would not be plausible for a firm in the middle of an overseas diversification program (which might take several years to complete) to keep the value of its net worth abroad proportional to domestic net worth.

Much direct investment overseas has been largely financed by overseas bond issues and bank-borrowing by the parent firm, which then uses the proceeds to set up, or invest in, a subsidiary. Again, the relationship to the net worth of the parent firm hardly seems binding in choosing the level of overseas investment. This kind of financial manipulation is important for testing the effectiveness of the U.S. voluntary restraint program, as the author does later on, because it would be a form of direct investment which complies with the program and which, indeed, was induced by the program. A well worked-out utility function or maximization procedure would be a big help in isolating these issues.

The author makes a useful point in showing that certain flow variables — such as reinvested earnings and capital outflows — cannot be used formally to predict complete changes in the balance-sheet position abroad because C, as defined below, does not enter international payments.

$$\Delta A_1 = Q + S + C$$

where
Q = capital outflow,
S = reinvested earnings, and
C = correction for windfalls, expropriations, and other unexpected events.

But, unfortunately, he includes depreciation flows in C and suggests that companies "may want to offset depreciation during the period by new capital flows." However, if overseas earnings are accounted for correctly, they are net of depreciation, and there is no need for continuously compensating capital outflows.

THE STATISTICAL TECHNIQUES

Consider the estimating equation which Prachowny used:

$$\frac{D_t}{W_t} = \alpha_0 + \alpha_1 \left(\frac{R_t^*}{R_t}\right) + \alpha_2 \left(\frac{\sigma_R^*}{\sigma_R}\right) + \alpha_3 \sigma_{RR}^* + \alpha_4 B_{t-1} + U.$$

The construction of R_t^* (per cent earnings on direct investment abroad) and R_t (per cent earnings on United States manufacturing) is not discussed in detail, but it appears as if these signify current profits divided by the market valuation of net worth. In the case of R_t^*, book value of foreign assets had to be used although the author would have preferred their market valuation. Thus, R_t cannot represent the "real" rates of return on the underlying physical assets.

For example, if profitability goes up in home investment and this increase in profitability is perceived as such, the stocks will be revalued upward, so that the apparent rate of return is unchanged. Correspondingly, swings in stock-market valuations could introduce large differences in R_t and R_t^* which are as hard to interpret as the animal spirits that guide year-to-year fluctuations in the stock market. Thus, the immediate implications of short-term variance in R_t, denoted by the truncated σ_R, are difficult to see. The use of σ_{R^*R} is a complete puzzle, not discussed anywhere by the author. Given the data and conceptual difficulties in constructing R_t^* and R_t, one might like to run each separately to see which one was providing the explanation.

The deficit of the United States in its balance of payments on a liquidity basis—lagged one period—is included as a measure of risk. There are all kinds of questions regarding the liquidity definition. Witness 1968 and 1969, when the liquidity deficit became very large even by past standards, but the official-settlements measure of the balance showed a surplus. From a purely statistical point of view, the use of B_{t-1} very likely introduces simultaneity bias into the estimation procedure as long as there is some year-to-year correlation in the B's. The author makes some additional *ad hoc* adjustments in his estimating procedures to get a "better fit," but it is beyond my capacity to judge their statistical verity.

A principal consideration in setting up stock-adjustment models has been to avoid the necessity of specifying instantaneous adjustment within the time period for which data are collected. One can look at observed flows over several periods as an adjustment to a preferred stock position. This would seem to be important here, as one would not expect firms to adjust their portfolios of direct investment within one year if there was a change in foreign relative to domestic profitability. Yet Prachowny does not make lagged adjustment a significant part of his model, as he himself notes.

In conclusion, I am quite prepared to believe, with Prachowny, that the voluntary restraint program was not effective, but I have not reached this conclusion on the basis of the analysis provided here. It is difficult to generate believable models which predict capital flows and direct investment in isolation from other international payments.

THE NORTH AMERICAN ECONOMY

The paper by Reuber and Roseman examines the merger activities of American firms in Canada. Their analysis is virtually unique in terms of the comprehensiveness of the data and the thoroughness of the statistical procedures used to test various hypotheses. Although Canada is significantly different from most other recipients of foreign direct investment, it has had long historical experience in this area, and foreign direct investment has been very large. Mergers or take-overs represent an important part of that investment. The contribution of the two authors is a significant one, both for Canada and for its implications elsewhere.

In order to project the Canadian experience for other countries, it is necessary to decide whether Canada behaves simply as part of the North American economy or has, in fact, some relevant characteristics of its own which set it apart as a distinct economy. Here the authors offer two conflicting pieces of evidence:

1. The ratio of foreign to domestic mergers in Canada has been of the order of 1:2, whereas the ratio of the numbers of firms in the United States and in Canada has been of the order of 12:1. It is, however, difficult to get an appropriate measure of geographical proximity. It could well be that, within certain regions of the United States, the ratio of "foreign" to "domestic" mergers is closer to the ratio for Canada. It also appears that take-overs in Canada by firms in the United States were only 2.6 per cent of total mergers in the United States, whereas the Canadian economy is probably about 8 per cent of the size of the American one.

2. On the other hand, waves of merger activity within the United Sates through time seem to be fairly strongly reflected in Canada, and the authors use an index of total mergers in the United States to explain a high proportion of the variance in Canadian mergers through time. Without a more fundamental explanation, this would suggest that there are similar forces operating in both economies, while Canada still maintains a distinctive economic identity for this purpose.

COMPARATIVE ADVANTAGE

One interesting aspect of the analysis is the tendency for ownership by American firms in Canada to concentrate and stabilize in particular industries, even if one disaggregates down past the two-digit industries. Those sectors of mineral extraction and manufacturing which were dominated by foreigners prior to 1945 remain dominated by subsequent merger activity and internal growth. Oil and gas exploration and automobile manufacturing are extreme examples. Correspondingly, there is only a limited tendency for foreign firms to branch out into other activities.

Foreign domination seems particularly marked in what might be called "tradable"-goods sectors, inclusive of manufacturing and mineral extraction, but it is less strong in the nontradables sector, where services are heavily represented. This tendency seems to be borne out by the positive correlation between foreign merger activity and tariff barriers, as one would predict from the old "tariff factory" argument. That is, those manufacturing industries with higher tariffs are more subject to foreign take-overs. This is welcome statistical support for a venerable hypothesis.

Within the tradable-goods sectors, it would be interesting to go further into explaining why foreigners may have competitive advantages in some areas, but not in others. I realize that this more general investigation of foreign comparative advantage may lead the authors too far afield from their announced intention of simply explaining merger activity. However, if there is a tendency for foreign control to stabilize and limit itself to particular activities, this would be valuable information for countries where foreign direct investment is as yet less pronounced than it is in Canada.

THE FINANCIAL CONSTRAINT

The impact on merger activity of an internal financial constraint within Canadian firms was particularly interesting to me. The authors show, in equations (10) and (12), that both domestic and foreign mergers are quite sensitive to the internally generated flow of funds. The fact that mergers seem to take place with the least immediately profitable, or illiquid, Canadian firms is contrary to prevailing Canadian mythology. Moreover, if we could construct proxy variables for the relative tightness of credit in the two countries, we would expect tight money-market conditions in Canada vis-à-vis the United States to be an important determinant of merger activity and new direct investment. Unfortunately, interest-rate proxies may be quite poor measures of ease or tightness. Notwithstanding this, the authors do find some statistical evidence (equation (11), page 495) that the American rate of interest is negatively correlated with foreign mergers.

If the absence of internal funds and the inadequacy of domestic money markets are important reasons for the acceptance of mergers —particularly foreign ones—on the part of Canadian firms, this would suggest that Canada might be less prone to foreign take-overs than would be a less developed economy with a more primitive banking system. Even Canada may have followed financial policies which artificially accentuated foreign mergers. In the 1945–61 period, there was a low ceiling (approximately 7 per cent) on what Canadian commercial banks could charge for loans. This, of course, led to substantial non-interest rationing, which might partially explain why the authors could not get a significant Canadian interest-rate variable. During the latter part of the period under consideration, Canada was subjected to unusually tight and disruptive monetary policies by James Coyne, Governor of the Bank of Canada. Taken together, the effects of these two factors on foreign take-overs may have been not insignificant.

To help one understand fully the importance of the financial constraint in foreign take-over activity, it would have been desirable had the authors obtained information on the net financial transfers (or balance-of-payments effect) of a given amount of foreign direct investment — since foreign direct investment could, in principle, be financed from the Canadian money market. However, they have tried, and this material was not available. One can speculate that a badly functioning domestic banking system would not only attract direct investment from abroad, but make it easier for large, well-known international corporations to get local finance by issuing bonds or commercial paper. Lesser known, but possibly quite efficient, domestic entrepreneurs may be shut out because of ceilings on bank deposit and lending rates.

In summary, Reuber and Roseman have succeeded admirably in their goal of showing how monetary and tariff policy may have accentuated merger activity in Canada. Their analysis immediately suggests how the greater distortions in foreign trade and finance in less-developed countries may — in the absence of other inhibiting controls — accentuate direct investment there far beyond the level which could be described as socially or economically optimal.

THE IMPACT OF TAXATION ON CAPITAL FLOWS AND THE BALANCE OF PAYMENTS IN CANADA

ALAN R. DOBELL · University of Toronto
THOMAS A. WILSON · University of Toronto

THIS study estimates, by analysis of an aggregate model of the Canadian economy, some possible effects on capital flows and the balance of payments of two alternative tax-reform packages. The general approach follows conventional lines, although application on the scale attempted in this paper is somewhat unusual, and the two tax-reform packages actually evaluated are both novel and interesting in themselves. The first represents the proposals set out in the *Report of the Royal Commission on Taxation* (The Carter Commission) in 1967,[1] and the second is based on the proposals for tax reform contained in a White Paper issued by the Canadian government in October 1969.[2]

We employ a consistent macroeconomic model of Canada embodying conditions of flow equilibrium customary in analysis of monetary and fiscal policy in an open economy. Within the framework of the model, we represent proposed tax reforms as changes in tax parameters or shifts in behavioral relationships. Given such a representation, we may then ask how such changes alter the equilibrium of the system and how, on balance, trade and flows of capital are affected.[3]

Thus we may think of the model as described by the system

$$H(x, z) = 0$$

$$F(x, z; \tau) = 0,$$

NOTE: Research support from an Izaak Walton Killam Award by the Canada Council is gratefully acknowledged.

[1] *Report of the Royal Commission on Taxation* (six volumes). Ottawa, Queen's Printer, 1967 (hereafter, Carter Report).

[2] Honorable E. J. Benson, *Proposals for Tax Reform*. Ottawa, Queen's Printer, 1969.

[3] J. F. Helliwell, "Simulating the Macroeconomic Effect of the Carter Proposals." *Canadian Journal of Economics*, Supp. 1 (February, 1968), pp. 233–254, describes a prior attempt to carry out a similar assessment.

519

where H is a vector-valued function of the flows z and the equilibrating variables x, representing the equilibrium conditions of the model, and F is a vector-valued function of the same variables (depending on the vector τ of tax parameters), representing the behavioral relations describing the determination of the endogenous flows.[4]

We consider a change in the tax system to be represented formally by movement to a new vector τ, and are therefore concerned with the differential system

$$\begin{bmatrix} H_x & H_z \\ F_x & F_z \end{bmatrix} \begin{bmatrix} dx \\ dz \end{bmatrix} = \begin{bmatrix} 0 \\ F_\tau d\tau \end{bmatrix}.$$

We wish to estimate the constant column, or vector of *initial shocks* (shifts in the behavioral relations), $F_\tau d\tau$, resulting from a proposed change in tax structure, and then to determine the subsequent changes, dx in equilibrating variables and dz in flows, necessary to restore equilibrium. We shall call the solution to the subset of equations arising from the condition $dF = 0$, subject to the restriction $dx = 0$, the *impact effect* of the tax change. This solution represents the changes necessary to ensure that all behavioral and accounting relationships are respected, but before any market adjustment through price or yield changes (or compensating government policies) occurs. The *final effect* is the unrestricted solution to the complete differential system. A *compensated* policy change involves imposition of some constraints $dz_i = 0$.

In order to determine these solutions, we require numerical estimates for the shocks, $F_\tau d\tau$, and the partial derivatives, F_x and F_z, of the behavioral relationships. (The coefficients H_x and H_z are nonstochastic values given directly by the form of the flow-equilibrium conditions employed.)

---

[4] Since the model incorporates sectoral sources and uses-of-funds constraints, these behavioral relations either must be determined so that all flows are automatically consistent with such constraints, in which case behavioral relations for each endogenous flow appear explicitly while the constraints are omitted, or else behavioral relations for some flows must be omitted, leaving these flows to be determined residually by the requirements of accounting balance in each sector, then appearing explicitly in the model. We have followed the latter procedure.

EQUILIBRIUM CONDITIONS

WE DEAL in this model with markets for five paper assets — domestic bonds, equity of domestic extractive industries, equity of domestic nonextractive industries, foreign securities, and money — along with markets for foreign exchange and for goods. The core of our model is a set of equilibrium conditions for these markets. Specifically, we impose a condition of equilibrium in the balance of payments, on the bond market, the two equity markets, the goods market, and the money market.

In addition, we recognize five accounting identities. These are statements of the sources and uses of corporate funds, statements describing the disposition of corporate incomes for the two sectors (extractive and nonextractive industries), and an identity describing the uses of personal saving.

These two sets of conditions yield eleven relationships. As always, one is redundant in this general-equilibrium system, and we drop the balance-of-payments equation. Moreover, we assume that monetary policy accommodates itself to money-market demands so as to maintain equilibrium in asset markets and in the balance of payments. Monetary policy, therefore, is determined endogenously in this model, and we may omit explicit representation of the money market.[5]

Thus we arrive at a system of nine equations, the first four being the clearing conditions for asset markets and goods markets, and the others being, essentially, sources-and-uses-of-funds statements for corporations and households, together with two conditions embodying our assumption that underlying real-capital structures (and therefore net before-tax operating incomes of producers) are unaltered. Let us now specify these equations more precisely.

The model is focused particularly on the balance of payments and flows of capital. Therefore, among its most important components are the items that enter the balance-of-payments statement itself.

For present purposes we shall consider only the summary variables shown in Table 1. The first equilibrium condition can then be

---

[5] The inclusion of the money market equation would merely serve to indicate the change in the money supply required to sustain the equilibrium solution.

TABLE 1

Glossary and Notation
*(in order of appearance in the rows of the coefficient matrix; all variables
are to be interpreted as differentials)*

BE	Bond issues by the extractive industry, both resident and nonresident
BN	Bond issues by the nonextractive industry, both resident and non-resident
NE	New issues of equity, extractive industry
NN	New issues of equity, nonextractive industry
RE	Corporate retentions, extractive industry
RN	Corporate retentions, nonextractive industry
DPAE	Dividends paid abroad, extractive industry
DPAN	Dividends paid abroad, nonextractive industry
FDE	Foreigners' direct investment in Canada, extractive industry
FDN	Foreigners' direct investment in Canada, nonextractive industry
CDE	Direct investment abroad by the Canadian extractive industry
CDN	Direct investment abroad by the Canadian nonextractive industry
CCAE	Capital consumption allowances, extractive industry
CCAN	Capital consumption allowances, nonextractive industry
IPA	Interest paid abroad
IFA	Interest from abroad
DFAE	Dividends received from abroad, extractive industry
DFAN	Dividends received from abroad, nonextractive industry
CSE	Canadian demand for securities, extractive industry
CSN	Canadian demand for securities, nonextractive industry
FSE	Foreign demand for securities, extractive industry
FSN	Foreign demand for securities, nonextractive industry
FB	Foreign demand for Canadian bonds in Canadian markets
CS	Canadian demand for foreign securities
TE	Taxes levied on nonresident firms, extractive industry
TER	Taxes levied on resident firms, extractive industry (in all computations, present data limitations force aggregation of TE with TER)
TN	Taxes levied on nonresident firms, nonextractive industry
TNR	Taxes levied on resident firms, nonextractive industry (in all computations, present data limitations force aggregation of TN with TNR)
TO	Other taxes
PS	Personal saving
X	Net Exports
IE	Investment, extractive industry
IN	Investment, nonextractive industry
G	Government expenditure

TABLE 1 (*concluded*)

q_e	Price of equity in the extractive industry relative to price of bonds
q_n	Price of equity in the nonextractive industry relative to price of bonds
R	Rate of interest
CB	Canadian demand for bonds
DDE	Dividends paid to domestic shareholders, extractive industry
DDN	Dividends paid to domestic shareholders, nonextractive industry
ϕ	Change in official holdings of gold and foreign exchange

derived as follows. From the balance-of-payments statement we have one relationship that determines the rate of change in official holdings of gold and foreign-exchange reserves, namely,

$$X + DFAE + DFAN + IFA - DPAE - DPAN - IPA + FDE$$
$$+ FDN - CDE - CDN + FB + FSE + FSN - CF - \phi = 0. \quad (0)$$

We shall interpret equilibrium in the balance of payments as requiring, simply, that ϕ, the change in official holdings, be zero.

Turning to the bond market, there are two categories of supplier: the government issuing debt to finance whatever portion of its deficit is not matched by an increase in the money supply, and resident or nonresident corporations in the extractive or nonextractive industries, issuing debt to meet part of their capital requirements. From the condition that the flow demand, resident and nonresident, be balanced by the debt issue of those suppliers, we obtain an equation[6]

$$FB + CB - BE - BER - BN - BNR$$
$$- [G - TE - TER - TN - TNR - TO - \dot{M}^s + \phi] = 0. \quad (1)$$

For present purposes, in order to obtain estimates of the different degrees of pressure on the prices for equities of firms in the extractive and nonextractive industries, we suppose that the markets for these securities are sufficiently segmented so that their yields need not nec-

[6] Our model assumes that full sterilization of inflows occurs directly through the money supply; although alternative procedures are conceivable, we do not wish to consider the consequences of less-than-full sterilization, or of full sterilization accomplished by other means.

essarily be forced into balance. Then we obtain two market-clearing conditions,

$$FSE + CSE - NE - NER = 0 \qquad (2)$$

and

$$FSN + CSN - NN - NNR = 0, \qquad (3)$$

for the markets for the shares of corporations in each of these two sectors.

The fundamental national-income identity, or generalized saving-investment identity, appears in this context as a single equation:

$$IE - RE - CCAE - DPAE + IER + DFAE - RER - CCAER + IN$$
$$- RN - CCAN - DPAN + INR + DFAN - RNR - CCANR + G$$
$$- TE - TER - TN - TNR - TO + X + IFA - IPA - PS = 0. \quad (4)$$

This equation has a natural interpretation in terms of the contributions of firms in extractive and nonextractive industries, the government, and households, to sources and uses of saving.

A similar condition of accounting balance must hold in the financing of investment by each firm or class of firms. If for each of the four classes of firm (extractive, nonextractive; resident, nonresident) a condition of this type is imposed, one obtains four equations to be added to the model. In fact, however, we have found it necessary to aggregate the resident and foreign-owned firms in each of the two industry classes. Thus we obtain the following two equations:

$$BE + NE + RE + CCAE + FDE - CDE - IE = 0, \qquad (5)$$

and

$$BN + NN + RN + CCAN + FDN - CDN - IN = 0. \qquad (6)$$

Since, as noted earlier, we are examining a flow equilibrium, we assume that no changes in cash balances or in the net position on short-term assets or liabilities may occur.

Since the rate of addition to domestically held financial assets is necessarily equal to personal saving, one has also

$$PS - CSE - CSN - CF - CB - \dot{M} = 0. \qquad (7)$$

We take — as a first approximation — the assumption that gross operating incomes and operating expenses remain roughly unchanged following the hypothetical implementation of the proposed reforms. In a neoclassical world, this amounts to assuming the period of analysis to be sufficiently short so that one can ignore the effects of changes in capital stocks upon marginal rates of return to capital. However, in a more eclectic (and more realistic) world, one also needs to assume that no short-run shifting of the changes in the corporate-income tax occurs. While the precise extent, if any, of such shifting in the United States remains an unresolved empirical issue, in a more open economy possible forward shifting of domestic corporate-income taxes is much more limited, because of the actual or potential competition from foreign goods as the Carter Commission indicates.[7] Backward shifting — as is implied by certain models of wage determination — remains a possibility, however.

In our analysis, we assume that there is no backward shifting onto wage changes; however, we do allow for some backward shifting of certain taxes onto the value of oil-bearing land. This has the effect of shifting the burden of any increase in taxes on the oil industry, in part, onto provincial revenues.

The model is designed to analyze the financial flow equilibrium expected to prevail before any substantial adjustment of real capital stocks has occurred. This design implies that net before-tax operating incomes of corporations are unaffected by the reforms, provided that aggregate demand is unchanged. If net operating income is unchanged, then the following two conditions describe the disposition of changes in the components of operating income in each of the producing sectors:

$$RE + DPAE + CCAE - DFAE + TE + TER + DDE = 0, \quad (8)$$

and

$$RN + DPAN + CCAN - DFAN + TN + TNR + DDN = 0. \quad (9)$$

Finally, as discussed earlier, equilibrium requires that the rate of increase in the money supply be willingly accepted, so that one has the condition

[7] Carter Report, Vol. II, pp. 144–146.

$$\dot{M} - \dot{M}^s = 0. \tag{10}$$

These eleven equations 0–10, all interpreted in terms of differentials, constitute the set of equilibrium conditions of our model.[8] Any predictions about the effects of the proposed tax reforms must, to be consistent, satisfy all the conditions. If the initial impacts of the proposed reforms are such that these conditions are not all satisfied, then interest rates, equity yields, and the level of aggregate income would be forced to adjust.

This subsequent adjustment creates one important difficulty that must be solved: any income adjustment that might be stimulated by the reforms would confound simple aggregate-demand effects with the tax-structure effects that we are trying to isolate. Therefore we specify that the process of adjustment, whatever it is, leaves the level of demand unchanged. Moreover, we specify that the adjustment be such that the new rates of interest and equity yields, whatever they are, are sustainable without further change. Finally, we examine only adjustments that are consistent with equilibrium in the balance of payments. The upshot of these restrictions is that we insist that all the above equilibrium conditions be sustained, with government fiscal policy and money supply so determined as to permit aggregate demand to be maintained unchanged while preserving balance-of-payments equilibrium.

With this understood, we may proceed to complete and simplify the system. We first add behavioral relations describing the independent determination of all flow variables entering the system. We set $\dot{M} = 0$, and drop equation (10).[9]

Summing equations 1–9 yields the balance-of-payments constraint, equation (0); we therefore drop that equation from our explicit system. Moreover, the way in which budget constraints enter the determination of the flows in equations 5–9 requires that one component of each

---

[8] The usual qualifications—that we must suppose a linearized system to yield an adequate approximation to the adjustment of the model following a substantial shock, and that the model began initially in (or sufficiently close to) flow equilibrium—of course apply.

[9] This analytical simplification could be dispensed with, in studying a growing economy, by supposing both income and money supply to grow at constant relative rates; for present purposes there is little to be gained by this analytical sophistication.

be determined residually. Hence we drop the behavioral relations for *BE*, *BN*, *CB*, *DDE*, and *DDN*.

The system thus reduces to nine explicit conditions. Three are equilibrium conditions referring to asset markets, and there are three asset-yield variables to serve as equilibrating variables. Government expenditure is determined so as to maintain aggregate demand constant; loosely, *G* may be viewed as determined by equation (4). Accounting identities and budget constraints (along with our assumption that real stocks are not altered under the new tax system) are inherent in equations 5–9; these, therefore, may be thought of as determining *BE*, *BN*, *CB*, *DDE*, and *DDN* as residuals. The remaining equations are behavioral relations, the specification of which is described in the next section.

SPECIFICATION OF BEHAVIORAL RELATIONS

THIS section outlines the equations explaining the dependent variables in our model, dealing first with the various components of the balance of payments, and then with the equations for saving, investment, and other financial flows in the economy.

In each equation, allowance is made for the shock or perturbation introduced by the tax reforms, together with feedback effects from any adjustments in interest rates, relative prices of equities in the extractive and nonextractive sectors, government expenditure, and other endogenous income or expenditure variables. The impact effects, which reflect the direct effect of proposed tax reforms on the dependent variable in each equation, naturally differ between the two tax-reform proposals and, therefore, are discussed separately below. Here we consider the form of the various behavioral relations.

A. PORTFOLIO-CAPITAL FLOWS

The situations we examine obviously involve changes in the relative attractiveness of Canadian equities to Canadians and in the relative attractiveness of some of these securities to nonresidents. It is necessary, therefore, to separate trade in Canadian equities from trade in Canadian bonds.

In addition, since the indirect effects of the reforms may affect interest rates in Canada, the relative attractiveness of Canadian bonds vis-à-vis foreign securities is likely to change. Therefore it is necessary also to distinguish net trade in foreign securities (mainly foreign equities) from net trade in Canadian bonds and stocks.

We assume that the direction and magnitude of international flows of portfolio capital are determined solely on the basis of the relative after-tax yields to nonresident and resident investors. The effects of the tax reforms are therefore felt simply through the changes in relative yields for the three types of security brought about by the changes in the tax structure, assuming that interest rates and before-tax equity yields are given.

The indirect effects of the tax reforms are likely to be very important for these flows, however. Domestic interest rates and equity prices will, in fact, change, thereby affecting further the relative yields on these securities. The over-all sensitivity of total net flows of long-term portfolio capital has been estimated within the context of three complete quarterly econometric models of the Canadian economy, and one complete annual model.[10] While the three quarterly equations yield comparable (and substantial) sensitivities to interest-rate differentials, the interest-rate sensitivity suggested by the annual model is much lower.

We have therefore carried out two sets of runs — one using an over-all yield sensitivity based on the equation of the Rhomberg quarterly model,[11] and one using the lower coefficient of the TRACE annual

[10] R. R. Rhomberg, "A Model of the Canadian Economy under Fixed and Fluctuating Exchange Rates." *Journal of Political Economy* (February, 1964), pp. 1–31; L. H. Officer, *An Econometric Model of Canada Under the Fluctuating Exchange Rate.* Cambridge, Mass., Harvard University Press, 1968; J. F. Helliwell, L. H. Officer, H. D. Shapiro, and I. A. Stewart, *The Structure of RDX1,* Bank of Canada, Staff Research Study No. 3, 1969; N. K. Choudry, Y. Kotowitz, J. A. Sawyer, and J. W. L. Winder, *TRACE, 1969: An Annual Econometric Model of the Canadian Economy.* Toronto, University of Toronto Press, 1971.

[11] As the yield sensitivity in the Rhomberg model refers only to portfolio flows from the United States to Canada, it was adjusted to be representative of all portfolio capital flows to Canada.

model.[12] Because of problems with the existing equation of the annual model, and because the three quarterly models yield roughly consistent results, we choose to emphasize the results obtained through the use of the yield sensitivity based on the Rhomberg model. Better estimates may perhaps be obtained from a complete analysis of the recently published flow-of-funds accounts.[13]

Unfortunately, none of these models examines these capital flows classified into the three types that concern us. A search of the available empirical literature in Canada and the United States did not turn up separate estimates of the yield sensitivities of these three types of capital flow. Indeed, the main thrust of the conclusions in the literature seems to be that capital flows generally are determined by factors other than relative after-tax yields.

As a result, we decided to construct estimates of the yield sensitivity for each of the subcomponents of the total inflow of portfolio capital from the above over-all yield sensitivities on the basis of the following assumptions:

1. The relative yield sensitivity (yield response/existing holdings) of American purchases of Canadian stocks is one-half of the relative yield sensitivity of American purchases of Canadian bonds. The sensitivity of our results to this strategic assumption will be examined later.
2. The relative yield sensitivity of purchases of Canadian stocks by other nonresidents and of Canadian purchases of foreign securities is the same as that of American purchases of Canadian stock.
3. The relative yield sensitivity of purchases of Canadian bonds by other nonresidents is the same as that of American purchases of Canadian bonds.

These three assumptions permit us to construct estimates of the average yield response of each of the three types of inflow of portfolio

[12] The coefficient used is the sum of the coefficients for the long-term and short-term interest-rate differentials.

[13] A preliminary report on the financial flow accounts in Canada is now available (Dominion Bureau of Statistics, *Financial Flow Accounts 1962–67*. Ottawa, Queen's Printer, 1969).

capital. The details of the calculation procedures are described in a previous paper.[14]

In order to examine the effects of changes in the tax structure and of changes in the yield of equities relative to bonds, the following two additional assumptions are necessary:

4. The response of each type of capital flow depends solely on the differentials between its after-tax yield to the relevant investor and the after-tax yield on alternative financial investments.
5. The aggregate response of Canadian investors to changes in the tax structure may be approximated by the behavior of a "typical" investor holding "typical" Canadian and foreign securities.

The resulting yield and relative price sensitivities of foreign purchases of bonds (FB), foreign purchases of stocks (FS), and Canadian purchases of foreign securities (CF) based on these assumptions and the alternative over-all yield sensitivities are presented in Table 2. Using the Rhomberg equation, for example, we obtain a yield sensitivity of $+10.15$ for foreign purchases of stocks, which implies a relative equity-price sensitivity of these purchases of $-.550$.[15] This response is then divided into the extractive and nonextractive industries in proportion to the share of resident-controlled capital in each of these sectors.

In addition to the substitution effects represented by the coefficients for interest rates and relative prices, allowance must be made for the effects of any change in the total volume of personal savings induced by the reforms. We base our estimate of the proportion of the change in personal saving that is channeled into the demand for foreign equities upon the relative importance of Canadian purchases of foreign securities to total personal saving.

[14] A. R. Dobell and T. A. Wilson, "Overall Effects of the Proposed Tax Reforms: Savings, Investment, and the Balance of Payments." Institute for the Quantitative Analysis of Social and Economic Policy, Working Paper #6806.

[15] Using as a base an average corporate bond yield of 5.2 per cent, a percentage point change in bond yields corresponds to an 18.45 per cent change in bond prices. Relative price sensitivities are therefore obtained by dividing the yield sensitivities by 0.1845 (and reversing the sign).

TABLE 2

Structural Coefficients: Interest-Rate and Relative-Price Sensitivities of Capital Flows

Capital Flows	Relative-Price Equities		Interest Rate r
	(Extractive) q_e	(Nonextractive) q_n	
A. Rhomberg			
CSE C(26)	.118	0	−0.72
CSN C(27)	0	1.06	−6.52
FSE C(28)	.065	0	−1.21
FSN C(29)	0	.485	−8.94
FB C(30)	0	0	−61.30
CF C(31)	−.047	−.345	7.24
B. TRACE			
CSE C(26)	.042	0	−0.26
CSN C(27)	0	.379	−2.34
FSE C(28)	.023	0	−0.43
FSN C(29)	0	.174	−3.21
FB C(30)	0	0	−22.00
CF C(31)	−.017	−.124	2.59

NOTE: Interest-rate sensitivities are expressed in billions of dollars per unit of yield. Relative-price sensitivities are expressed in billions of dollars. This means, for example, that one percentage point rise (a rise of .01 unit) in yields would increase the foreign demand for the equities of the nonextractive sector by .089 billion dollars; such a rise in yields would be equivalent, in effect, to a relative price increase of .185 in q_n (or 18½ per cent). Multiplying .186 by the relative-price coefficient .485 yields the same response of .089 billion dollars. For this particular capital flow, we have assumed that the effect of a change in equity yields is the same, whether or not it is accompanied by a change in interest rates.

B. DIRECT INVESTMENT

The available empirical evidence suggests that foreign direct investment in Canada is not very sensitive to changes in yields on marketable securities. Rhomberg, for example, found some response of direct investment to changes in the interest-rate differential, but this response is much lower than that of portfolio flows.

We therefore allow for only modest feedback effects of changes in interest rates upon these flows. We estimate that a one per cent increase in the interest-rate differential would increase total foreign direct investment by $80 million, a figure obtained by scaling Rhomberg's estimate [16] by the ratio of total foreign direct investment in Canada to United States direct investment in Canada. As a first approximation, we shall assume that the effect of relative changes in equity prices is commensurate with the interest-rate effect, after adjusting for the relative importance of equity issues to total funds raised in Canada.

We also make allowance for a modest yield effect on Canadian direct investment abroad, based on scaling Rhomberg's coefficient for American direct investment in Canada by the relative importance of the two capital flows. For simplicity we assume that all Canadian direct investment is channeled through the nonextractive sector.

C. DIVIDEND OUTFLOWS

An increase in corporate taxes levied upon foreign-owned firms can be accommodated by either a reduction in dividend outflows or by an increase in foreign direct investment,[17] with equivalent balance-of-payments effects. Since some minor tax advantages accrue to foreign firms when they reduce dividend outflows rather than increase foreign direct investment, we shall adopt the convention that this effect of the tax reforms bears wholly upon dividend outflows. These effects may be treated wholly as shock effects, and, therefore, are discussed in the following section.

[16] Rhomberg, *op. cit.*, p. 10.
[17] As stated, we assume that before-tax profits are not affected by the tax reforms.

D. NET EXPORTS

Net exports (excluding exports and imports of capital services) will be affected by any loss of export markets that might follow the tax reforms, and by any change in imports resulting from a change in the composition of final demand. For reasons to be discussed below, we assume that there will be no loss of export markets.

An import equation is based on the input-output equation developed by J. A. Sawyer.[18] This equation relates imports to the components of final demand as follows:

$IMP = .193CONS + .243IE$ (excluding land purchases)

$$+ .290IN + .066G + .134EXP.$$

However, as GNP is constant in the equilibrium solutions of the model, and since exports are constant by assumption, we may solve the above equation in terms of G, IE, and IN, by substituting for C from the GNP identity, thus obtaining the following equation:

$$X = .158G - .120IN - .062IE.$$

E. THE DOMESTIC DEMAND FOR DOMESTIC SECURITIES

The supply of domestic securities is composed of net sales by foreigners (the inverse of the capital inflow), net new equity issues by Canadian corporations, and new issues of bonds by Canadian corporations and by Canadian governments.

The demand is simply the financial saving of the household sector less net purchases of foreign securities by Canadians. A portion of this saving flow may, of course, be channeled through financial intermediaries, such as life insurance companies and pension plans.

The model requires specification of the effects of relative changes in yields on equities, bonds, and foreign securities upon the composi-

[18] J. A. Sawyer, "Some Effects on the Current Account of the Balance of International Payments of Implementing Recommendations of the Royal Commission on Taxation." Institute for the Quantitative Analysis of Social and Economic Policy, University of Toronto, Working Paper #6805.

tion of the flow of personal saving.[19] Unfortunately, there is as yet no evidence on the yield sensitivity of the allocation of personal saving between these assets in Canada. However, we have already constructed an estimate of the sensitivity of Canadian purchases of foreign securities to changes in Canadian equity yields. It is reasonable to suppose that the bulk of such changes in holdings represents a switch of domestic equities for foreign securities, since most foreign securities held are equities. We shall therefore assume that a rise in Canadian interest rates induces such switching from foreign to Canadian equities (when the price of equities relative to bonds is constant).

In addition, a fall in the price of equities relative to the price of bonds will induce switching from domestic bonds, as well as from foreign equities to domestic equities. While bonds are not as close substitutes for domestic equities as are foreign equities, domestic holdings of bonds are much larger than are domestic holdings of foreign securities. We therefore assume that the extent of switching from bonds to Canadian stocks is twice as important as switching from foreign securities to Canadian stocks. Using the yield sensitivities estimated by Rhomberg, this would imply that the total response of the domestic demand for equities with respect to a one percentage point rise in stock yields is $217.2 million. This implies a relative price sensitivity of −1177.

Since the tax reforms would affect the attractiveness of Canadian equities at prevailing levels of interest rates and stock prices, allowance must be made for an impact effect. The impact effects are based on estimates of the effect of the tax reforms upon after-tax rates of return to resident noninstitutional investors, given the above yield sensitivity.

In addition, one of the tax-reform proposals analyzed provides a great inducement to hold equities for pension plans and for life insurance companies that set up trusteed pension plans. The impact of the original Carter proposals upon equity holdings of pension plans and life insurance companies has been studied by Courchene and Robin-

---

[19] We ignore residential construction throughout the analysis, and assume that none of the induced changes in personal saving leads to increases in owners' equity in owner-occupied houses.

son,[20] and estimated impact effects based on their work are presented below.

However, since the size of present holdings of equities by such financial intermediaries is not large, it would not be reasonable to adjust downward the estimate of the increase in direct acquisitions of equities by households by that amount. For the analysis of the original Carter proposals, we therefore add the estimate of the increased holdings of equities by pension plans to the estimated impacts for non-institutional investors.

While the adjustments in the demands for assets following the reforms will reflect mainly the repercussions of changes in after-tax yields and resulting adjustments in relative prices, it would be unwise to neglect the effect of changes in personal saving on these demands. To ignore these would be to assume that the whole of any change in personal savings induced by the reforms is felt in the domestic demand for bonds, since the latter is determined residually from the personal saving identity. We therefore assume that any increase in personal saving is divided between purchases of domestic bonds, purchases of domestic equities, and purchases of foreign securities in proportion to the observed relative importance of these purchases.

F. PERSONAL SAVING

The estimates of the effects of tax reforms upon personal saving are obtained by combining an equation determining discretionary personal saving based on the work of Winder,[21] with an estimated shock effect on contractual savings for the original Carter reform provided in the study by Courchene and Robinson. The shock effects of the alternative tax system upon the components of personal saving are presented below.

The equation determining personal saving is based on a simple

---

[20] T. J. Courchene and T. R. Robinson, "Contractual Savings With and Without Carter." Institute for the Quantitative Analysis of Social and Economic Policy, Working Paper #6801.

[21] J. W. L. Winder, "Discretionary Personal Savings." Institute for the Quantitative Analysis of Social and Economic Policy, Working Paper #6802.

permanent-income model. Since we lock the economic system at a given level of aggregate demand via compensatory change in government expenditures or general tax levels, personal saving will be affected by changes in personal taxes resulting directly and indirectly from the reforms, as well as by changes in dividends and corporate tax rebates that vary with the level of investment. The marginal propensity to save out of changes in these tax payments is set at .10. Following Winder, the marginal propensity to save out of dividend payments is set at .30.

The only other variable allowed to affect personal saving is the rate of interest. The coefficient for this variable is taken directly from the study by Winder.

G. CORPORATE RETENTIONS

The estimated impact effects and the feedback equations for the retentions of resident-owned firms are based on a study by one of the authors.[22] The impact effects, which take the integration or partial integration of personal and corporate taxes into account along with the proposed increases in taxes at the corporate level, are discussed more fully in the next section.

Since investment is an endogenous variable in the model, allowance must be made for a feedback effect upon gross retentions via changes in capital consumption allowances. According to the estimates presented by Wilson, a unit change in capital consumption allowances (CCA) leads to an increase in gross retentions of .82, financed by a reduction in corporate taxes of .50 and a decrease in dividends of .32. Since investment in the extractive sector is assumed to be insensitive to changes in interest rates or equity prices, such a feedback need only be specified for the nonextractive sector.

However, in the impact effect for resident-owned firms in the extractive sector, allowance must be made for their estimated reduction in investment. We make implicit allowance for this by specifying that

---

[22] T. A. Wilson, "Implications of the Carter Corporate Reforms for Corporate Savings Behaviour." Institute for the Quantitative Analysis of Social and Economic Policy, Working Paper #6803.

the total reduction in the retentions of these firms equals the total increase in their corporate taxes.

The effects of the reforms upon the gross retentions of foreign-owned firms is simply the estimated reduction in dividends paid abroad, described above, less the increase in corporate taxes paid by these firms. For example, under the original Carter proposals, the dividend outflow from nonresident-owned firms in the extractive industries will fall by $19 million, but their corporate taxes are estimated to rise by $142 million. Hence their retentions must *fall* by $123 million. For nonresident firms in the nonextractive industries, on the other hand, the increase in corporate taxes of $117 million is largely offset by a reduction in the dividend outflow of $92 million. Gross retentions are therefore estimated to fall by $25 million.

The equations determining retentions used in the analyses are obtained by adding the relevant equations for resident and nonresident-owned firms.

H. INVESTMENT

The investment relation for the nonextractive sector is based on a study prepared by one of the authors for the Carter Commission.[23] The equations estimated in that study imply an interest-elasticity of investment of -0.67. Therefore, a negative interest-rate feedback effect is specified, based on this elasticity. It is assumed that there will be no feedback via adjustments of equity prices, on the grounds that any incentive or disincentive provided by the tax reforms would have already been accounted for in the calculation of the impact effects described in the next section.

The investment effects in the mineral extractive sector of the original Carter proposals are based on a study by G. D. Quirin.[24] No allowance is made for any feedback effects from either interest rates or equity prices. Since the tax reforms for the mineral industry proposed

[23] T. A. Wilson, *Capital Investment and the Cost of Capital: A Dynamic Analysis.* Study No. 30, Royal Commission on Taxation, Ottawa, Queen's Printer, 1967.

[24] G. D. Quirin, "Economic Consequences on the Primary Mineral Industries of the Adoption of the Recommendations of the Royal Commission on Taxation." Institute for the Quantitative Analysis of Social and Economic Policy, Working Paper #6804.

in the White Paper will have no effect on revenues within the period
of our analysis, we assume that they will also have no effect on investment in that sector.[25]

I. NEW EQUITY ISSUES

The integration or partial integration of the corporate and personal
income taxes could affect the volume of new issues by affecting the
relative price of equities. In the absence of empirical estimates of the
sensitivity of new issues to changes in yields, we simply assume that
the elasticity of these issues to changes in the relative price of equities
is unity for each of the two sectors.

J. GOVERNMENT REVENUES

We assume that ultimately any necessary compensatory variations
in discretionary fiscal policy will be effected by either changes in government expenditure (G), or changes in other taxes (TO); in neither
case do corporate taxes vary. However, induced changes in investment
in the nonextractive industries will have direct effects on government
revenues by changing capital consumption allowances (CCA). An increase in CCA would imply an increase in corporate taxes, offset to
some extent by a reduction in personal tax rebates under integration.[26]
Assuming that the average allowable CCA rate for the first year is
12½ per cent, this would imply a reduction in revenues from corporate
taxes of .0625 per dollar change in investment in that sector.

More important than these feedback effects are the estimated impact effects of any tax reform upon government revenues. These are
discussed in the following section, in which we turn from specifying
the behavioral relations (and thus the coefficient matrix) for our model
to representing the proposed tax reforms as a perturbation of that
system.

[25] It should be remembered that we are focusing the analysis on a Keynesian-type
intermediate run, during which financial flows may adjust to new equilibrium levels, but
within which real capital stocks are unlikely to be significantly altered.
[26] As will be explained later, integration of the corporate and personal income taxes
permits stockholders to obtain a rebate for corporate income tax paid.

ALTERNATIVE TAX SYSTEMS AND THEIR REPRESENTATION IN THE MODEL

THE MACROECONOMIC flow model described in the previous section can be used to estimate the over-all effects of changes in the tax structure upon saving, investment, the components of the balance of payments, and other endogenous variables in the model. As described earlier, what is required in addition to the matrix of coefficients linking the various variables is:

1. A vector of shock effects — measuring the partial effects of tax proposals on each endogenous variable, holding the other variables constant; and
2. The specification of the compensatory adjustments in fiscal and monetary policy designed to maintain both a given level of aggregate demand and equilibrium in the balance of payments.

Given these specifications, the model solutions provide estimates of the equilibrium effects upon the endogenous variables of changes in the tax structure; these effects take into account the specified interactions among all the variables of the model.

We shall use this model to assess the economic effects of the following three tax reform proposals:

1. That of the Carter Report on taxation [27] (also referred to below as "original Carter");
2. That put forward by the Minister of Finance in the recently published White Paper on Taxation; [28] and
3. A set of proposals based on the original Carter recommendations, but modified to be comparable with the White Paper proposal (henceforth described as "modified Carter").

Before proceeding to the specification of the vectors of initial shocks, a brief description of the relevant features of each of these tax proposals in relation to the present Canadian tax structure is in order.

[27] See note 1, above.
[28] E. J. Benson, *op. cit.*

THE ORIGINAL CARTER PROPOSALS

The Carter Royal Commission recommended the most sweeping tax-reform package since the original evolution of the income-tax system. The revenue-raising features of this package most relevant for our analysis are the following:

1. Special provisions in the existing tax law that favor the extractive sector (oil and mining) were to be abolished. These include percentage depletion and a three-year tax holiday for new mines.
2. Special provisions favoring life-insurance companies and financial institutions were to be eliminated.
3. The low 21 per cent rate on the first $35,000 of corporate income was to be eliminated—henceforth all corporate income would be taxed at a flat 50 per cent rate. The effects of this provision on existing incorporated small businesses and on new businesses would be offset, in part, by a special provision for accelerated capital-cost allowances.
4. In contrast to the existing Canadian system, where capital gains bear no tax, all capital gains were to be taxed henceforth at full personal rates upon realization. Deemed realization would occur upon the gift or bequest of an asset.
5. Gifts and bequests were to be treated as income to the recipient and to be taxed at full marginal rates. Under the present law, bequests are subject to an estate tax, and gifts are taxed to the donor. The rates of this tax are well below those of the personal income tax.

Most of the other changes in the tax law recommended by the Carter Commission involved the "spending" of much of the revenue gained by the above set of reforms. These involved lower marginal rates in the personal income tax, the treatment of the family as the basic unit of taxation, and the establishment of a separate schedule of family rates,[29] liberalized averaging and employment-expense deductions, and

[29] Unlike the American "income-splitting" provision, under Canadian law husbands and wives are taxed as individuals. This means that families in the middle- and upper-

lower revenues from federal sales taxes. For our analysis, however, the most important revenue-losing reform recommended is the full integration of the corporate and personal income taxes. Under this proposal corporate and personal income taxes were to be fully integrated for *resident stockholders of Canadian corporations.* All corporate income was to be reported as income by the shareholder, who would receive full credit for the corporate tax paid. In essence, this provision would mean that the corporate tax would be abolished for resident shareholders of Canadian corporations.

The net revenue effects of the various Carter proposals in relation to the system prevailing at the time of the Carter Report are shown in Table 3. As is apparent, reasonably large increases in taxation at the corporate level would be offset by reductions in personal-income and sales taxes. On balance the system proposed would have increased revenues by a modest amount.

During the interval between the publication of the Carter Report and the publication of the White Paper, several tax changes were made,[30] the net effects of which were to raise sales and income taxes. In the budget of 1968,[31] the government changed the treatment of life-insurance and financial institutions, largely following the recommendations of the Carter Report. Consequently a comparison of the original Carter proposals with the present (1969) tax system would show that the Carter proposals would *reduce* revenues substantially.

THE WHITE PAPER PROPOSALS

The proposals made in the White Paper differ from the Carter proposals in several ways. First, although modifications in the treatment of oil and mining were provided for, the new proposals — replacing percentage depletion and the three-year tax holiday for new mines by a

income brackets are taxed relatively more heavily than is the case in the United States. For most families, the Carter Family Rates Schedule would be virtually equivalent to American "income-splitting."

[30] The two most important changes were the imposition of the surtax on corporate and personal incomes and the imposition of the "social development tax."

[31] Budget Speech delivered by the Hon. Edgar J. Benson, Minister of Finance, House of Commons, October 22, 1968.

TABLE 3

Revenue Effects of Proposed Tax Reforms
(*millions of dollars per year*)

Tax Change	Original Carter (in relation to 1966 system)[a]	Modified Carter (in relation to 1969 system)	White Paper (in relation to 1969 system)[b]
A. Corporate income tax			
Oil & mining reforms (extractive)	+176[c]	+204[d]	22[e]
Abolition of dual rate	+258	+390[f]	390
Other corporate reforms (excluding life insurance)	+48	+30[g]	148
Subtotal (nonextractive)	+306	+420	538
Life insurance and co-operatives	+15[h]	–	–
B. Personal income tax			
Integration	−363	–	−230
Gifts and bequests[i]	+210	–	–
Other personal reforms	−38	–	+300
Total personal income tax	−191	−960[j]	+70
C. Sales tax	−125	no change	no change
D. Total revenue	+181	−336	+630

[a] Source: Tables 35–15 and 37–3 of the Carter Report (Vol. 6). Corporate revenues are as estimated in Table 37–3; personal income-tax revenues are adjusted downwards by $6 million to preserve consistency with total revenues as estimated in Table 35–15. (All estimates relative to the tax system as at 1966.)

[b] Source: The White Paper, *op. cit.*, Tables 15 and 16.

[c] Takes into account the federal tax gain as a result of reduced write-offs because investment declines, and the provincial revenue loss due to backward shifting onto land values.

[d] Carter estimates from column I were multiplied by the ratio of profits in 1969 to profits in 1964 for the mining sector.

new "incentive depletion" scheme and more rapid depreciation of mining equipment—were not to take effect for five years. Secondly, for "widely held" Canadian corporations, the corporate and personal income taxes were to be partly, rather than fully, integrated,[32] and pension funds were not to benefit from this integration. Under this proposal, cash or stock dividends would be subject to a 50 per cent gross-up, but only 50 per cent of the corporate tax paid on the income would be credited.

One-half of the capital gains on the shares of widely held Canadian companies would be subject to the capital-gains tax. In addition, there would be a deemed realization of gains on such shares every five years. Capital gains on all other assets would be subject to taxation at full rates *only* upon actual realization. Upon bequest of assets at death, capital gains would escape taxation until subsequently realized by the recipient of the asset.

[32] Income from "closely held" Canadian corporations was to be fully integrated. A corporation is defined as widely held if its stocks are listed on any exchange, or traded over the counter.

---

[e] Total revenues raised by corporate reforms other than the dual rate have been prorated between the extractive and nonextractive sectors on the basis of the division of revenues for "other corporate reforms" shown in Table 37–3 of the Carter Report, *op. cit.*

[f] Estimates are taken from the White Paper, Table 16.

[g] Carter estimates from column I were multiplied by the ratio of corporate profits in 1969 to corporate profits in 1964; estimated revenues yielded by the current corporate surtax were then deducted.

[h] Additional revenue loss due to life insurance companies and other intermediaries shifting the composition of their portfolios in favor of equities, and thereby benefiting from integration, is taken into account.

[i] Net effect of including gifts and bequests in income and abolishing existing separate taxes.

[j] Carter revenue estimates from Table 35–15 of the Carter Report, *op. cit.*, were projected to 1969 using an income elasticity estimated as follows: the measured income elasticity of the 1967 system across the 1964–69 period was adjusted upward by Bossons' estimate of the difference in the income elasticities of the two systems (John Bossons, *A General Income Tax Analyser*, Ottawa, Queen's Printer, 1967, pp. 52–54). The large revenue loss in relation to the 1969 system reflects the existence of the personal income-tax surcharge and the social development tax, neither of which was in effect in 1967.

While the top marginal rates in the personal income tax were to be lowered to 51.2 per cent under the White Paper proposals, marginal rates throughout most of the income distribution were to be raised. The generous proposals of the Carter Report regarding averaging, employment-expense deductions, and so on, were made less generous, and Carter's family-unit proposal was not recommended.[33] As the White Paper dealt only with income taxes, the sales-tax reductions proposed by Carter need not be taken into account. The main revenue-losing proposal in the White Paper was an increase in the exemptions for adults from the present level of $1000 to $1400.

The estimated revenue effects as presented in the White Paper are shown in Table 3. In contrast to the Carter proposals, the tax structure proposed by the White Paper would raise a more substantial amount of revenue at the end of five years. Moreover, there is some reason to believe that these revenue estimates may err on the conservative side.[34]

Because of the various tax changes enacted between the publications of the two reports, and because the White Paper does not deal with sales taxes, we believe that it is necessary to modify the Carter proposals for purposes of comparison with the White Paper, as well as to update the estimated revenue effects to a more current year. These modifications are as follows:

1. The sales-tax recommendations of the Carter Report are ignored.
2. The recommended reforms on life-insurance and financial institutions are ignored.
3. Credit for corporation income tax is not extended to pension plans.
4. The revenue estimates are updated to the year 1969, to make them directly comparable with those of the White Paper.

[33] The Minister of Finance did state, however, that it would be possible to consider the family unit proposal as a further installment of reform subsequently (White Paper, p. 15).

[34] According to press reports, the Ontario government has prepared estimates of the revenue effects of the White Paper proposal that are double those of the federal government.

The revenue effects of the modified Carter scheme evaluated for the year 1969 are also shown in Table 3. While this scheme would raise larger revenues at the corporate level than would the White Paper proposals, this increase is more than offset by the substantial revenue loss occurring at the personal level. The result, in contrast to the White Paper scheme, is that the modified Carter scheme would *reduce* government revenues in relation to the current tax structure.

SPECIFICATION OF IMPACT VECTORS

The three tax schemes are directly represented in our model in terms of three tax variables:

TE (corporate taxes paid by the mineral extractive sector);
TN (other corporate taxes — excluding taxes on life insurance companies);
TO (all other taxes).

However, the details of the tax structure are also taken into account in the specification of the shock effects in the equations determining investment, corporate saving, and demands for asset flows. Before proceeding to the specification of shock effects upon corporate retentions and investment, a brief description of the way in which integration of the corporate and personal taxes could affect corporate behavior is in order.

Integration or partial integration of the corporate and personal income taxes can be viewed as consisting of two steps:

1. A reduction in the rate of tax upon cash dividend distributions, and
2. A change in the effective rate of tax on corporation profits.

Algebraically the existing system and the two alternative systems for large companies can be specified as follows:

1. Current system —

$$TC = .50\pi + (m - .20)^*DC.$$

2. Carter proposals —

$$TC = .50\pi + (m - .50)^*(DC + RET) + mGW$$

or

$$TC = m(\pi + GW).$$

3. White Paper proposals (assuming retentions are declared as stock dividends) [35] —

$$TC = .50\pi + m(1.50)(DC + RET) - .25\pi + m \cdot GW/2$$

or

$$TC = (.75m + .25)\pi + m \cdot GW/2,$$

where

TC = total tax paid on corporate source income
π = before-tax corporate profits
m = marginal rate of tax on personal income
DC = cash dividends
RET = retentions
GW = "Goodwill Gains" [36] (capital gains on shares in excess of reported retentions).

It is reasonable to assume that firms will react to that portion of the tax change that bears on cash dividends in the same way as they have reacted to changes in the dividend credit under the existing system,[37] and that they would react to changes in the effective over-all rate of tax in the same way as they reacted in the past to changes in marginal corporate-tax rates. On the basis of these assumptions, we estimate the shock effects of the reforms upon corporate saving by

[35] Unlike the Carter Proposals, under the White Paper stockholders would not receive credit for corporate tax paid on retained earnings, unless they were declared as stock dividends.

[36] For a study of the relative importance of dividends, retentions, and goodwill gains in the over-all rate of return on Canadian equities, see John Bossons' *Rates of Return on Canadian Common Stocks: Dividends, Retentions, and Goodwill Gains*. Royal Commission on Taxation, Study No. 27, Ottawa, Queen's Printer, 1967.

[37] Dividends received from Canadian corporations are subject to a 20 per cent dividend credit under the present system. The dividend credit was originally introduced in 1949 at a level of 10 per cent, and was doubled to the present level four years later.

resident-owned corporations, using an empirically estimated cash-dividend function.[38] The effect on investment in the nonextractive sector is based on an aggregate-investment function,[39] on the further assumption that the elasticity of investment with respect to changes in the after-corporate-tax rate of return is the same as its (negative) interest elasticity.

The estimated negative shock effects of the Carter proposals on investment in the extractive sector are based on a study of that sector by G. D. Quirin.[40] Since the revenue impact of the mineral industry reforms proposed in the White Paper is estimated to be negligible for the first five years,[41] we shall assume that these reforms will also have no effect on investment. (A subsequent computation allowing for a significant reduction in investment in this sector revealed no drastically different results.)

The equations referred to above indicate that, for the typical stockholder in the 35–40 per cent marginal-rate bracket for personal income tax, the Carter proposals would lower the marginal tax burden on corporate-source income, whereas the White Paper proposals would increase it. Hence, the impact effect of the White Paper on investment is negative, whereas, outside the extractive sector, the Carter proposals would have a positive effect.

The impact effect on the demand for assets is based on the various yield sensitivities discussed above, together with estimates, developed by John Bossons,[42] of the impact effects of the alternative tax proposals on after-tax rates of return to shareholders. While Bossons did not consider the specific White Paper proposals, the White Paper proposals may be approximated by a linear combination of two alternatives to the Carter proposals that were explicitly studied by Bossons. As is shown in Table 4, we estimate that, whereas the Carter proposals would raise total after-tax yields to resident noninstitutional investors

---

[38] An empirical examination of the effects of changes in the dividend credit is contained in the study of corporate savings behavior by Wilson (T. A. Wilson, "Implications of the Carter Corporate Reforms for Corporate Savings Behaviour").

[39] T. A. Wilson, *Capital Investment and the Cost of Capital.*

[40] G. D. Quirin, *op. cit.;* cf. White Paper, Table 16, p. 96.

[41] E. J. Benson, *op. cit.*

[42] J. D. Bossons, "The Effect of the Carter Proposals and Alternative Proposals on Stock Prices." Canadian Tax Foundation, Annual Tax Conference, 1967, pp. 132–152.

TABLE 4

Effects of Alternative Tax Proposals on After-Tax Yields
(Nonextractive Sector)
(*per cent*)

Income Class (thousands of dollars)	Modified Carter [a]	Half-Credit, Half-Gain [b]	Cash Dividend Integration	White Paper [c]
5–6	18.9	−3.1	+2.3	+0.5
8–10	17.1	−5.2	+1.6	−0.7
15–20	11.0	−10.4	−0.6	−3.9
35–50	−0.2	−21.1	−4.8	−10.2
200–300	−8.0	−29.8	−8.0	−15.2
Over-all effect	17.5	−10.0	+1.0	−2.7

[a] Source: John Bossons, "The Effect of the Carter Proposals and of Alternative Proposals on Stock Prices," Table 5, p. 140.

[b] Source: *Ibid.,* Table 6, p. 143.

[c] Assuming marginal personal rates unchanged, the White Paper proposal may be derived by a weighted average of the two alternatives to Carter examined by Bossons; the cash dividend integration scheme has a weight of $2/3$, and the half-credit, half-gain scheme a weight of $1/3$.

by about 17 per cent, the White Paper proposals would depress after-tax yields slightly.[43]

Because these reforms will affect corporate cash flow, investment, and retentions, they must necessarily affect either the dividend outflow to nonresidents or the direct-investment component of the capital inflow. Since the balance-of-payments consequences do not depend on the mechanism of transfer, we shall adopt the convention that the

[43] This is, of course, consistent with the estimated impact effects on investment. It might, however, be inconsistent with the estimates of the revenue effects of partial integration published in the White Paper itself. Since the White Paper estimates show that integration would lose revenue, the two analyses would be consistent only if the increase in the effective tax burden on investment at the margin is more than offset by the elimination of dividend taxes and the reduction in the taxes to intramarginal stockholders, such as persons in lower income groups, and by the reduction in taxes to owners of closely held corporations (who, under the White Paper proposals, would benefit from the full integration of corporate and personal income taxes).

TABLE 5

Effects of Alternative Tax Proposals on Dividend Outflows
(*millions of dollars per year*)

Variable	Original Carter	Modified Carter	White Paper
Extractive (nonresident)			
Tax revenues [a]	+121	+143	+15
Investment [b]	−94	−94	0
Capital requirements	+27	+49	+15
Increased use of Canadian sources of funds	+7	+13	+4
Reduction in dividend outflow	+20	+36	+11
Nonextractive (nonresident)			
Tax revenues	+117	+138	+197
Investment	0	0	0
Capital requirements	+117	+138	+197
Increased use of Canadian sources of funds	+20	+22	+34
Reduction in dividend outflow	+97	+114	+163

[a] Includes changes in provincial land revenues.
[b] Excludes land costs.

corporate responses to tax changes affect the dividend outflows for the two producing sectors. Table 5 presents the relevant calculations of the effects on these flows, and demonstrates one effect of these tax changes, particularly those of the Carter proposals, which has appeared paradoxical to some observers — that the increase in the tax burden on the corporate-source income of nonresidents would have positive balance-of-payments effects via these financial flows. Given our assumptions, what is happening is that the reduction in corporate cash flow for nonresident firms is greater than the reduction in investment by these firms,[44] so that capital requirements are increased. If the nonresident

[44] Since the marginal corporate income tax rate is not changed for firms outside the extractive sector in any of the reforms, we assume that there will be no change in real domestic investment by any such firms. The estimated reduction in investment by foreign-owned firms in the extractive sector is based on the study by Quirin.

firms continue to finance their over-all capital requirements in the same proportions as between domestic and foreign sources, these firms will have to reduce their dividend outflow (or increase their direct investment into Canada), thereby giving rise to the positive balance-of-payments effects.

Under the original Carter proposals, a great incentive to invest in Canadian equities would be provided to pension funds. It is likely that this incentive would stimulate a large increase in both contractual savings and in the demand for equities. We have taken estimates of both these impact effects from a detailed study by Courchene and Robinson [45] on the likely reaction of life-insurance companies and pension plans to the reforms proposed by the Carter Commission. The estimated total shock effect of the Carter proposals upon personal saving is the sum of the shock effect on contractual saving and the shock effect on discretionary saving. Estimates of the latter, found in the study by Winder, take the former into account and are consistent with them.

The shock effects of the reforms upon foreign direct investment in Canada are zero, since, as noted above, any effects on the flow of funds from foreign firms to their Canadian subsidiaries are represented as opposite adjustments in dividend outflows. However, it is likely that there will be a small negative shock effect on Canadian direct investment abroad under the Carter proposals, since full integration of the personal and corporate income taxes would increase the attractiveness of domestic investments relative to foreign. Since partial integration would not provide nearly as great an incentive to invest in domestic real assets, we specify a zero impact effect in the analysis of the White Paper proposals. [46]

The alternative vectors of impact effects of the three tax schemes are presented here in Table 6. The detailed calculations underlying these estimates are discussed elsewhere. [47] As is apparent, the vector of impact effects differs sharply between Carter (or modified Carter) and the White Paper, indicating that these are indeed quite different tax systems when viewed in this way.

[45] Courchene and Robinson, *op. cit.*
[46] The proposed treatment of foreign-source income of Canadian corporations is discussed in sections 4.40 and 6.16 of the White Paper.
[47] Dobell and Wilson, *op. cit.*

TABLE 6

Vector of Initial Shocks for Alternative Tax Reform Proposals and Alternative Base Years

(components not shown taken to be zero throughout)

Shock in Equation for:	Carter 1966 [a]				Carter Modified 1969		White Paper 1969	
	Rhomberg			TRACE	Rhomberg	TRACE	Rhomberg	TRACE
	1:1	1:2	1:4					
RE C(12)	−.156	−.156	−.156	−.156	−.168	−.168	−.006	−.006
RN C(13)	−.003	−.003	−.003	−.003	−.027	−.027	−.102	−.102
DPAE C(14)	−.020	−.020	−.020	−.020	−.036	−.036	−.011	−.011
DPAN C(15)	−.097	−.097	−.097	−.097	−.114	−.114	−.163	−.163
CDN C(19)	−.012	−.012	−.012	−.012	−.012	−.012	0	0
CSE C(26)	0	0	0	0	0	0	−.006	−.002
CSN C(27)	.583	.413	.315	.280	.206	.074	−.026	−.009
FSE C(28)	−.039	−.022	−.011	−.008	−.022	−.008	0	0
CF C(31)	−.125	−.069	−.036	−.025	−.069	−.025	0	0
TE C(32)	.176	.176	.176	.176	.204	.204	.022	.022
TN C(34)	.306	.306	.306	.306	.420	.420	.538	.538
TO C(36)	−.301	−.301	−.301	−.301	−.960	−.960	.070	.070
PS C(37)	.120	.120	.120	.120	0	0	0	0
IE C(39)	−.115	−.115	−.115	−.115	−.115	−.115	0	0
IN C(40)	.318	.318	.318	.318	.369	.369	−.186	−.186

[a] For revised (1967) revenue estimates in the original Carter system, set $C(36) = -.582$, $C(37) = .153$.

COMPENSATORY POLICY ADJUSTMENTS

The behavior model developed earlier is designed explicitly for the purpose of examining the equilibrium effects of changes in the tax structure at a given level of national income, and the conventional multiplier-accelerator trappings of models of national-income determination are therefore absent. As noted, in order to evaluate properly the structural effects of specific proposals for tax reform, it is necessary to build in a compensatory mechanism designed to stabilize aggregate demand. Otherwise the results will reflect a mixture of the structural effects and changes in national income, making the results most difficult to interpret, particularly when, as is the case with the White Paper and Carter proposals, the recommended tax structures have opposite effects on government revenue.

In a highly open economy, such as Canada's, a system of fixed-exchange rates means that only those solutions compatible with balance-of-payments equilibrium represent viable choices open to the policymaker.[48] Therefore we further constrain the analysis by setting the rate of change of official holdings of foreign exchange equal to zero, which means that we treat the balance-of-payments equilibrium as a constraint on the solutions.

These two restrictions — balance-of-payments equilibrium and maintenance of aggregate demand at a fixed level — are, of course, not automatically satisfied in the system of equations. In general, in the absence of compensatory macroeconomic policies, a specific set of tax changes would affect aggregate demand and upset the equilibrium in the balance of payments — even if the tax changes had no net impact effect on government revenues.

Balance-of-payments equilibrium, at a given level of aggregate demand, may be ensured by allowing for compensatory variations in general fiscal and monetary policies. In all solutions of the model, the function of interest rates and equity prices is to clear the flows of demands and supplies in the relevant capital markets at yields consistent with balance-of-payments equilibrium. This means that monetary policy must act so as to accommodate the changes in yields necessary,

---

[48] Other solutions are necessarily transitory and are therefore inconsistent with the flow equilibrium model that we have constructed.

since the resulting interest rates would not automatically equate the demand for money with the existing stock of money.

In the case of general fiscal policy, two simple alternatives exist: variations in government expenditure and variations in general tax revenues. We use both mechanisms in alternative solutions, since the effects of the changes in the tax structure are not independent of the compensatory fiscal mechanism specified. The use of government expenditure, (G), as a policy instrument presents no conceptual difficulties and may indeed represent the most likely policy action that would be adopted, particularly in the case of a set of revenue-raising reforms put forward by the government itself.[49] However, the use of this variable has the drawback that it implies a contraction or expansion in the size of government expenditure in response to the tax changes, a response that would not be neutral with respect to either interest rates or the balance of trade. Hence, in a comparison of alternative tax reforms that have widely differing effects on government revenues, the comparative effects of using this particular compensatory mechanism could be distorted.

At first glance it is tempting to allow for a general scaling upward or downward of all three tax variables. This is inappropriate, however, since certain features of the recommended tax changes may be regarded as more fundamental than others. In particular, both Carter and the White Paper recommended a particular rate of tax on corporate profits, in part because of prevailing levels of corporate tax rates in the United States. Consequently, in the "general tax compensated"

---

[49] Indeed the Canadian business community has expressed the fear that the White Paper proposals are being put forward partly as a means of raising government expenditure levels in the future. However, other possible explanations should be mentioned:

1. because of the uncertainties of estimating the revenue effects of such far-reaching tax changes, the government may hesitate to commit itself to revenue-losing reforms or reductions in rates at this time;
2. since sales-tax reforms are the next item on the tax-reform agenda, the government may intend to spend the revenues gained in the income-tax reforms in sales-tax reductions;
3. the government may feel, in the light of the current economic situation, that a tightening of fiscal policy is desirable;
4. in order to ensure no reduction of revenue in the early transitional years of reform, the government may adopt rates that would ultimately yield revenue increases, intending to introduce successive future tax reductions as the transition proceeds.

solutions, we allow for only TO—general revenues from personal-income and sales taxes—to vary. Since sales taxes are presumably more neutral with respect to saving and investment decisions than are income taxes, purists may choose to regard compensatory changes in TO as resulting from changes in sales taxes alone. Needless to add, a comparison of the solutions using the alternative compensatory mechanism provides some insight into the structural effects of tax-compensated changes in government expenditure as well.

Having specified all the elements to be used in our analysis, we turn, in the next section, to a discussion of the alternative model solutions, and of the implications for capital flows and the balance of payments.

RESULTS AND CONCLUSIONS

MODEL solutions were obtained for three variations on each of the three tax proposals. Using the yield elasticities estimated by Rhomberg, we carried out the computations first with compensating fiscal policy accomplished through expenditure variations, and then through changes in taxes. The third variation involved the use of the TRACE yield sensitivities within a government-expenditure-compensated solution.

The runs analyzing the original Carter reforms are not directly comparable with the others, since the former refer to incomes as of 1964 rather than 1969. We therefore concentrate our discussion on a comparison between the White Paper and the modified Carter proposals, both of which take as their basis the income and revenue structure of the 1969 tax system. First, we shall examine the effects on the balance of payments. Second, we shall consider the implications of these for the equity and bond market. Third, we assess the effects on the sources and uses of gross saving—saving, investment, government revenues, government expenditure, and net exports. Finally, we discuss very briefly the sensitivity of our results to various changes in the underlying assumptions.

BALANCE-OF-PAYMENTS EFFECTS OF THE TAX REFORMS

The consequences of the alternative tax reforms for the components of the balance of payments are summarized in Table 7. All three tax proposals have net positive impact effects on the balance of payments, indicating that in the absence of compensatory policy adjustments and changes in the rates of interest and equity prices, these proposals would cause an increase in the accumulation of official holdings of gold and foreign exchange. This positive impact effect can be traced, in all three cases, to the increase of the tax burden on corporations owned by nonresidents, which causes a reduction in their dividend outflows.

The equilibrium solutions reveal that all the final changes in the components of the balance of payments are modest; however, the pattern of effects differs between the modified Carter and the White Paper proposals in interesting ways. The modified Carter proposals would, according to our estimates, cause a net worsening of the current account on merchandise trade, whereas the White Paper would improve the merchandise balance. This reflects the fact, discussed further below, that the modified Carter proposal would increase investment, whereas the White Paper would reduce it. Since investment has a high import content, this explains the worsening in the balance of merchandise trade that occurs under the modified Carter proposals as compared with the improvement projected under the White Paper proposals.

Of perhaps greater interest – given Canadian concern about foreign ownership and control – are the effects on the various flows of equity and direct investment. The modified Carter proposals apparently would cause a modest (but not trivial) reduction in foreign purchases of Canadian equity (including direct investment). In the tax-compensated solutions, the over-all gross swing [50] in the portfolio-equity and direct-investment flows amounts to $120 million per year

[50] The gross swing is the reduction in Canadian purchases of foreign equity (including direct investment abroad) *plus* the reduction in foreign purchases of Canadian equity (including direct investment in Canada), on the grounds that in an expanding economy both of these changes would tend to increase Canadian ownership of Canadian equity. The net balance-of-payments effect is, of course, the difference between the two equity flows.

TABLE 7

Balance-of-Payments Effects of Selected Tax Reforms [a]

(millions of dollars per year)

| | | | | Equilibrium Solutions | | | | | |
| | | | | G Compensated | | | T Compensated | | |
Flow	Carter	Modified Carter	White Paper	Carter	Modified Carter	White Paper	Carter	Modified Carter	White Paper
				Capital Account					
-CF	67	69	2	3	45	-3	3	47	-4
FSE	-22	-22	0	-17	-17	0	-17	-17	0
FSN	0	0	0	-96	-38	-8	-96	-39	-7
FB	0	0	0	31	3	-189	14	-96	-153
FDE	0	0	0	4	3	-6	0	0	-5
FDN	0	0	0	-4	-2	-14	-10	-10	-12
-CDN	12	12	0	14	12	-9	7	7	-7
				Current Account					
-DPAE	20	36	11	20	36	11	20	36	11
-DPAN	97	114	103	97	114	163	97	114	163
X	-31	-37	22	-51	-156	55	-30	-43	14
				Change in Official Reserves					
	143	172	198	0	0	0	0	0	0

[a] All of the entries in the table refer to solutions using the Rhomberg yield sensitivities.

with a net effect on the over-all balance of payments of −$12 million per year. Under the White Paper proposals, the incentive to "buy back" Canadian industry appears to be much less; the gross swing is only $13 million per year, with a slightly larger net negative balance-of-payments effect (−$35 million per year).

In the tax-compensated runs, the proposed reforms cause a reduction in foreign purchases of bonds because of the downward pressure on interest rates. Since the decrease in interest rates is larger under the White Paper, so is the reduction in foreign purchases of bonds. The expenditure-compensated runs give rise to a larger reduction in bond purchases in the White Paper solutions, and a tiny increase in bond purchases under the modified Carter proposals, reflecting the wide divergence in government expenditure necessary to compensate for the divergence in revenue effects.

It is also noteworthy, in comparing the government-expenditure-compensated runs with the tax-compensated trials, that the net balance on merchandise trade is quite sensitive to the compensatory mechanism specified. This reflects the very low import content of government expenditure. Aside from these two items, the equilibrium response of the components of the balance of payments is not much affected by the change in the compensatory mechanism.

The balance-of-payments results thus indicate that, provided appropriate compensatory macroeconomic policies are adopted, the ultimate effect of these two tax reforms upon the components of the balance of payments is quite modest. The estimated changes lie, generally, within observed year-to-year changes in these flows.

CAPITAL MARKETS EFFECTS OF THE TAX REFORMS

TURNING to the capital markets, we see a different picture of the various adjustments in capital flows and of the shifts in yields and relative prices required to achieve equilibrium. Table 8 tabulates the equilibrium effects of the various reform proposals on the bond and equity markets. Under the modified Carter proposals, positive shock effects would occur in the market for nonextractive equities, and negative shock effects in the market for extractive equities.

TABLE 8

Equilibrium Effects in Bond and Equity Markets of Selected Tax Reforms
(*millions of dollars per year*)

Market	G Compensated		T Compensated	
	Modified Carter	White Paper	Modified Carter	White Paper
A. Bond Market				
New issues:				
Extractive	56	18	62	15
Nonextractive	263	68	318	47
Government	−396	−360	−665	−261
Demands:				
Domestic	−79	−86	−189	−46
Foreign	3	−189	−96	−153
Change in interest rate				
(basis points)	0	−31	−16	−25
B. Equity Markets				
Extractive:				
New issues	−7	−5	−9	−4
Domestic demand	10	−5	8	−5
Foreign demand	−38	0	−17	0
Change in relative price				
(per cent)	−8.0	−6.3	−11.2	−5.2
Nonextractive:				
New issues	85	−29	83	−28
Domestic demand	123	−21	122	−21
Foreign demand	−38	−8	−39	−7
Change in relative price				
(per cent)	8.2	−4.1	5.2	−3.1

NOTE: All solutions based on Rhomberg yield sensitivities.

This table shows fairly large changes in flows occurring in the bond market under the modified Carter proposals, mainly as a result of the reduction in government borrowing requirements. This reduction is offset by reductions in demand by both domestic and foreign lenders, and by increases in new corporate issues in response to the rise in investment and the fall in the rate of interest.

Under the White Paper proposals, these effects, while in the same direction, are muted. This softening of response reflects the reduction in private investment that directly reduces the new issues of corporate bonds, but that indirectly creates a need for a more expansionary fiscal policy. This, in turn, causes a smaller reduction in government borrowing requirements.

Interestingly enough, the adjustments to both sets of reforms apparently require only very modest reductions in interest rates—16 basis points under the modified Carter proposals, and 25 basis points under the White Paper proposals.

In the equity markets the modified Carter proposals would cause a modest rise in the price of nonextractive equities relative to bonds, while the White Paper would cause a slight reduction. This result mainly reflects the stimulus to investment in nonextractive equities under the modified Carter proposals, and the slight initial reduction in after-tax rates of return to investors that would occur under the White Paper. Given the slight reduction in interest rates that would occur, however, the absolute price of nonextractive equities would, virtually, be unchanged under the White Paper proposals.

Equity prices in the extractive sector would experience a more substantial reduction of 11 per cent under the modified Carter proposals, reflecting the much more stringent tax changes applied to that sector. Under the White Paper proposals, there is not much difference between the two corporate sectors.

Summary sources-and-uses-of-funds statements for the four key runs involving the White Paper and modified Carter proposals are presented in Table 9.

In the tax-compensated solutions, both the White Paper and modified Carter proposals would cause a reduction in private saving and an increase in the government surplus, as well as an increase in net investment abroad. However, the modified Carter proposals would give rise to a much more substantial increase in the government surplus. This difference reflects the divergent effects of the two proposals on total domestic investment: Whereas the modified Carter proposals would give rise to an increase in investment of $299 million, the White

TABLE 9

Summary of Sources and Uses of Funds: Equilibrium Effects of Selected
Tax Reforms
(*millions of dollars per year*)

Sources and Uses [a]	G Compensated		T Compensated	
	Modified Carter	White Paper	Modified Carter	White Paper
Personal saving	8	−109	−105	−68
Corporate saving	−157	−118	−153	−120
Total private saving	−151	−227	−258	−188
Total government revenues	−359	636	665	261
Government expenditure	−755	276		
Government surplus	396	360	665	261
Domestic investment	253	−97	299	−114
Current account balance (net investment abroad)	−6	229	107	188

[a] Sources and uses do not exactly balance because of rounding.

Paper proposals would reduce investment by $114 million. Although a net swing in investment of $400 million is not large, it is also not trivial (it would amount to about five per cent of total plant and equipment expenditures for this past year). Hence we could draw the conclusion that there is a nontrivial difference between the two proposals with respect to the objective of economic growth.[51] For the modified Carter proposals, the use of expenditure changes rather than tax changes in the compensatory mechanism leads to a reduction in the government surplus, which is largely offset by effects on private saving in the current-account balance. Under the White Paper, expenditure compensa-

[51] Of course a complete assessment of the total impact of these proposals on rates of economic growth must include an analysis of the resource allocation effects and the impact of altered effective marginal tax rates on the supply of labor. On both grounds, however, the modified Carter proposals would appear to have an edge over the White Paper proposals.

tion leads to an increase in the surplus, which is ultimately offset by reductions in private saving and an increase in the current-account balance.

SENSITIVITY OF RESULTS

Before turning to our conclusions, it is worth pausing to consider the sensitivity of our results to variations in some of our basic assumptions. The model presented in this paper is designed to be an explicit general-equilibrium flow model, and many of its parameters are based on empirical estimates. However, many of these estimates have large standard errors, and others are derived on the basis of assumptions for which little evidence can be adduced in support. However, trials embodying elasticities based on the low interest-rate sensitivities from the annual econometric model TRACE show roughly the same qualitative results as those that use the Rhomberg elasticities. The same is true of two further sets of runs (not shown) in which the ratio of the yield sensitivity of bond flows to that of equity flows is allowed to vary from 1:1 to 1:4.

Furthermore, in an earlier version of this study dealing only with the original Carter proposals, we also carried out an analysis of the sensitivity of results to variations in a single element or a single column of the coefficient matrix. For coefficients within a wide interval around the estimated values we adopt here, our general conclusions appeared to hold. Thus these sensitivity experiments appear to confirm the general robustness of the over-all system when allowance is made for equilibrating adjustments in asset markets, as well as for the direct impacts of proposed tax structure changes.

CONCLUSIONS

Our purpose in carrying out this analysis has been to study not only the relations between tax changes and capital flows per se (although we find that an increasingly fascinating subject). We have also been motivated by a desire to know whether the requirement to maintain balance-of-payments equilibrium in a highly open economy seriously constrains the scope for policy choices within the general area of tax reform. Since all our experiments involve the acceptance of a system of fixed exchange rates, they can perhaps be regarded as providing a stringent test of the assumption—frequently made in Canada, both in general and with reference to the two formal tax proposals examined here—that the great degree of openness in our economy means that we cannot freely choose a tax structure radically different from that of our major trading partner.[52]

Our model does not permit us to address the question of the short-run adjustments that may follow upon fundamental changes in the tax structure. It is conceivable—if one believes in the stock-adjustment models now gaining increased currency on theoretical grounds—that very large destabilizing flows of capital could occur during the period in which portfolios are being adjusted following a change in the tax structure. Nevertheless, none of the empirical work we have seen suggests any tendency for flows of saving and wealth accumulation to become as specialized as models having rapid portfolio adjustment would require. Nor do we discount the effects of inertia and institutional rigidities in smoothing the process of stock adjustment likely to follow a major tax-reform bill.

What our results do suggest is that, in any case, once any short-run storm has been weathered, the equilibrium effects of tax changes on capital flows and yields are modest enough to be readily accommodated through the use of normal macroeconomic policies for compensatory purposes.

We have examined three tax-reform proposals, all of which can be described as more fundamental than any tax reform seriously put forward in the United States in the 1960's. Any of the three structural reforms apparently could have been implemented without devastating side effects on the balance of payments or on the flow of funds within the domestic economy. Therefore, we venture the conclusion that it is likely that the internal political constraints within a federal state, and the political pressures exerted by special-interest groups, may well set effective constraints on the choices of federal policymakers regarding the tax structure long before balance-of-payments considerations need become important.

[52] This phrase has recently been repeated *ad nauseam* in some circles despite the fact that there are already major differences between the tax structures of Canada and the United States.

CAPITAL MOVEMENTS AND ECONOMIC GROWTH IN DEVELOPED COUNTRIES

GEORGE H. BORTS · Brown University
KENNETH J. KOPECKY · Ohio State University

THE study of capital movements has occupied an anomalous position in the literature of international economics. Treated as an exogenous disturbance, it provided the occasion for early studies of balance-of-payments adjustment and early theories of the adjustment mechanism. But the early theorists assumed that capital movements, like unilateral transfers, were not a permanent part of the scene; and the early theories of adjustment did not deal satisfactorily with the concept of a permanent equilibrium with a nonzero balance on current account. For this reason little attention was given to the determination of the reverse flow of interest and dividends associated with the private financing of capital movements. For many years the last word was that of John E. Cairnes [4], who wrote about it in the nineteenth century.

The story has changed considerably in the last twenty years. The mathematical relation between capital export and the reverse flow of income payments has been explored by Evsey Domar [6], Dragoslav Avramovic [1], and Philip Neher [12]. A theory of the balance of payments that explains both the current and the capital accounts has been expounded by Lloyd Metzler [10] and Robert Mundell [11], and the relations between capital movements and economic growth have been treated by George Borts [3], James Ingram [7], Harry Johnson [8], and Jeffrey Williamson [13]. In these modern theories, equilibrium in the over-all balance of payments, in the market for commodities, and in the money market, implies that the balance on current account equals the excess of saving over domestic investment, and, in turn, equals the negative of the balance on capital account. Capital

NOTE: This study was carried out under National Science Foundation Grant No. 4554–4.

movements are therefore explained by the determinants of saving and investment.

The theories of Metzler and Mundell are static in the same sense that the Keynesian model is static: the capital stock is constant, and investment is a function of the interest rate, with the equilibrium values of the variables persisting through time. The static approach, therefore, will not explain the determination of the flow of payments of interest and dividends, because a constant rate of capital flow implies a growing, not a constant, level of income payments to foreign investment. Moreover, the static model has nothing to say about the relation between economic growth and the flow of capital.

In this paper we use a growth model to generate a country's equilibrium pattern of investment and saving, flow of capital, and the return flow of interest and dividends from overseas. Investment is explained by the long-run equilibrium conditions of the capital market — in the sense that a particular level of investment is required to maintain an equilibrum relation between the stocks of labor and capital, and the flow of output. Thus, the level of investment depends upon the interest costs of borrowing, the parameters of the production function, the relative prices of productive factors, and the growth rate of output. In general, a country will have a higher level of investment, the higher its rate of growth, the lower the interest cost of borrowing, and the greater the elasticity of output with respect to capital.

The return flow of interest and dividends depends on the past history of capital flows into or out of a country. A country that has exported capital will experience an inflow of interest and dividend payments that are, properly, part of its gross national product (GNP). Consequently, current saving, which depends in part on the level of GNP, will be influenced by the extent of capital flows in previous periods. The model must therefore contain two relations between capital flows and saving: one, the direct relation that constitutes the definition of the capital flow, and the second, the feedback from interest and dividends through GNP to the level of saving.

One important implication of our work is that all monetary magnitudes may grow at the same rate as the return flow of dividends and interest, and this will be the rate of growth of GNP. Thus, in dynamic equilibrium, a country remains a debtor or a creditor forever, and changes in this status must be explained by parameter changes in the model. This is an advance over Domar's earlier findings that the return flow of payments might grow faster than foreign investment.

A second result is that movements of capital are explained independently of interest differentials among countries, and take place in the face of the same worldwide interest rate.

A third result is that capital movements are explained independently of monetary and exchange-rate policy. Instead, they are determined by the nonmonetary characteristics of the economy. Our model indicates that, ceteris paribus, a country lends *more* abroad the lower its real-growth rate, the higher its saving (plus taxes) rate, the smaller the share of output paid to capital, the smaller the government deficit, and the higher the world interest rate.[1] These parameters are used to provide a statistical verification of the model.

1   NET FACTOR INCOME EARNED ABROAD

A. CONCEPT AND MEASUREMENT

When a country's balance of payments is in equilibrium, a surplus on current account will be offset by a deficit on capital account. Such a country is said to be transferring goods and services abroad and financing the transfer by an export of capital. The real transfer might also be financed by gifts, reparations, or flows of international money. We shall, however, assume that all real transfers are financed by securities transactions in the capital account, and we shall correct the data insofar as other methods of financing are quantitatively important.

The securities flows making up the balance on capital account generate a reverse flow of interest and dividends that we shall designate as net factor income earned abroad (NFIEA). NFIEA ap-

---

[1] Professor Lorie Tarshis correctly pointed out in his comments on this paper that this relation between lending and the world interest rate is a "partial," not an "aggregative," relation. It is clear that for the world as a whole, saving equals investment, and the observed relations between world lending and the interest rate depend on which schedules have shifted over time.

pears in the balance of payments as part of the current account, and in the national income accounts as part of a country's GNP. NFIEA makes up the difference between GNP (the total income earned by the residents of a geographic area) and gross domestic product (GDP – the total income earned by the resources employed in a given area). Thus, NFIEA is generated because of geographic differences between the site of employment and the residence of the resource owner, and it will normally consist of payments both to labor and capital. We shall assume, however, that NFIEA consists only of payments to capital, and adjust the data where there is evidence that payments to labor are significant in magnitude. In a closed economy NFIEA would, of course, be zero.

NFIEA is a measure of the net debtor or creditor status of a country, because it reflects the past history of capital flows between one country and the rest of the world. We shall, in the rest of the paper, use NFIEA as the dependent variable to be explained.

The magnitude of variations in NFIEA among developed countries may be seen in Table 1. For each of thirteen member countries of the Organization for Economic Cooperation and Development, we have computed the ratio of NFIEA to GNP in 1965.

The first column uses the data from the national income statistics of the country. The ratio varies from −1.64 per cent for Canada (a debtor position) to +1.87 per cent for Switzerland (a creditor position). These ratios are lower than one might expect from a steady history of capital flowing into Canada and out of Switzerland; and we suspect that they will approach their long-run steady-state values in a number of decades. We may illustrate the long-run steady-state value by the following hypothetical calculations for Canada, which will be followed, in a later section, by a more explicit model that may be applied to all of the countries:

The NFIEA will grow over time because of new borrowing or a change in the rate of return that foreign owners earn on old borrowing. Assume that the rate of return has remained constant, and that the current deficit was financed entirely by long-term borrowing. Then write D as NFIEA, $\dot{D}$ as its rate of change over time, r as the interest cost of borrowing, and B as the balance on current account. We have $\dot{D} = rB$. Assume that D grows at the same rate as GNP, a rate denoted as

TABLE 1

Ratios of Net Factor Income Earned Abroad to
Gross National Product for Thirteen OECD
Countries, 1965

Country	Observed Ratio	Corrected Ratio
Austria	−.0023	+.0096
Belgium	+.0007	+.0177
Canada	−.0164	−.0170
Denmark	−.0013	+.0049
France [a]	+.0069	+.0154
Germany	−.0041	+.0100
Ireland [b]	+.0138	+.0438
Japan	−.0022	−.0001
Netherlands	+.0107	+.0328
Norway	−.0100	−.0086
Sweden	+.0023	+.0107
Switzerland	+.0187	+.0673
United Kingdom	+.0112	+.0165

SOURCE: NFIEA and GNP are taken from publications of the International Monetary Fund [14, 15] and the Organization for Economic Cooperation and Development [16, 17, 18].
[a] Metropolitan France.
[b] 1964.

g. We then have $D = (r/g)B$. Write GNP as Z, and $D/Z = (r/g)B/Z$. For the sake of illustration, assume a 10 per cent cost of borrowing, and a 4 per cent growth rate. For Canada, the observed B/Z is equal to −2 per cent. That is to say, in the ten years up to 1965, Canada experienced deficits on current account that averaged 2 per cent of GNP. We would then expect the steady-state value of D/Z to equal −5 per cent, instead of the observed −1.64 per cent.

The second column in Table 1 contains a more precise measure of the ratio of NFIEA to GNP. Examination shows that the corrected ratios in this column are generally greater algebraically than the raw ratios of the first column. The corrections took three forms, and were made to obtain a measure of NFIEA that is closer to the theoretical entity than the published statistics.

1. There is an asymmetry in the way in which the national accounts treat foreign — as opposed to domestically generated — payments to capital. Capital that is domestically owned and domestically employed generates a number of types of income that are included in gross product: interest and dividends, retained earnings, depreciation, corporate income taxes, and rental income. When capital is owned abroad, however, not all the gross income imputed to it is included in the balance-of-payments or GNP accounts. Present measurement of NFIEA is consistent with the idea that the balance-of-payments accounts include only cash transactions. This treatment understates the income that capital earns abroad, because it fails to include the total cash flow of foreign investment accruing to the owner or shareholder. It is our contention that the balance of payments should include an imputed value for retained earnings. If a dollar of earnings is retained abroad, it should be recorded simultaneously as a payment to the domestic owner (appearing in the current account) and a reinvestment (appearing in the capital account). Therefore, the first correction we have made in NFIEA is an imputation to include retained earnings on the equity portion of foreign investment. (An Appendix providing details of this correction will be supplied by the authors upon request.) In general, this correction will increase the absolute magnitude of NFIEA, raising the absolute values of the ratios in the table. It is also our contention that depreciation on foreign-owned capital should be entered in the country's GNP, although it is not part of the balance of payments or of NFIEA. In that way, GNP would include both gross domestic investment (GDI) and gross foreign investment (GFI).

2. The second and third corrections are made in order to account for overseas resource transfers that do not generate a return flow of NFIEA. The model we use predicts NFIEA as if it were generated by *all* overseas transfers. If some transfers are financed by foreign-exchange reserves or constitute gifts in the form of reparations, then the observed NFIEA will fall short of what the theory predicts. We have corrected NFIEA by adding an imputation of what the interest and dividend flow would be if reparations flows yielded a return like an ordinary foreign investment. The reparations constituted a significant

item in the balance of payments of Austria, Germany, and Japan, and the correction explains, in part, why their ratios increase algebraically, as seen in the second column of Table 1.

The third item to be corrected is the flow of international reserves. Again a correction is made, imputing interest to the stock of accumulated reserves. This correction explains, in part, the increase in NFIEA for France, Germany, and Switzerland. (The Appendix to this paper also provides details of these corrections.)

B. A PRELIMINARY TEST

In the hypothetical example of the previous section, it was assumed that the change in NFIEA equaled the borrowing rate multiplied by the balance on current account. Consequently, it is assumed that no changes occur in the return on old investments. These assumptions have been tested by the use of a sign comparison: the year-to-year change in NFIEA (as corrected) should have the same sign as the balance on current account. For the thirteen countries, data are available for almost every year from 1956 through 1965, 113 observations in all.[2]

We have tabulated the simultaneous occurrence of increases or decreases in NFIEA with the sign of the balance on current account, leading to the following contingency table.

Net Factor Income Earned Abroad	Balance on Current Account	
	Positive	Negative
Rose	44	21
Fell	14	34

The probability that these observations were generated at random may be rejected by using a chi-square test at a 1 per cent level of sig-

[2] Irish data were not available for 1956, 1957, and 1965; Japanese data were unavailable for 1956. Moreover, the observations for 1960 were not included in the sample because of large speculative movements of funds.

nificance. Thus, we have some indication that NFIEA may be explained by the model presented below.

2 MODELS OF GROWTH AND CAPITAL MOVEMENTS

THE relationship between NFIEA, the balance of payments, and GNP may be explored through a simple growth model. All monetary magnitudes grow at the same rate in the steady-state solution, and the results of this solution will be presented first. We shall derive the determinants of NFIEA as a percentage of GNP. The solutions will depend upon the parameters of the growth model: the rate of growth of GNP, the rate of interest, the savings-income ratio, the share of GNP spent and taxed by government, and the share of GDP invested by private business.

NFIEA is treated as the result of all past lending,

$$D_t \equiv \sum_{\tau=1}^{t} r_\tau B_\tau, \tag{1}$$

where D_t is NFIEA in year t, the present, and r_τ is the interest-rate terms on which lending occurred in year τ. If we assume that the interest rate remains unchanged over time, or that changes in the current interest rate have no effect on past loan contracts, we may write the time derivative of (1) as

$$\dot{D}_t = r_t B_t. \tag{2}$$

Changes in NFIEA thus occur because of current lending. Assume, in addition, that all surpluses on current account are financed by deficits on capital account. B_t is therefore measured by the balance on current account or its negative, the balance on capital account. Assume that the market for goods and services is continuously in equilibrium, so that B_t equals the excess of saving over investment (these being defined, for the moment, to include taxes and government spending). We may then write

$$\dot{D}_t = r \,[\text{saving-investment}]. \tag{3}$$

Assume that saving is a fixed proportion, s, of GNP (Z_1), and investment is a fixed proportion, i, of GDP (Z_2), and that all monetary magnitudes grow at the percentage rate g. We then have

$$gD = rsZ_1 - riZ_2. \tag{4}$$

Ignoring foreign depreciation charges for the moment, we know that NFIEA, by definition, is the difference between GNP and GDP:

$$D \equiv Z_1 - Z_2. \tag{5}$$

By substitution, we then obtain

$$Z_1 = Z_2 \left[\frac{g - ri}{g - rs} \right]. \tag{6}$$

It will turn out that stability of the solution requires that both the numerator and the denominator be positive. We also obtain solutions for B_t, the level of current lending (balance of payments on current account), and D_t, NFIEA:

$$B = Z_1 \left[\frac{g(s - i)}{g - ri} \right], \tag{7}$$

and

$$D = Z_1 \left[\frac{r(s - i)}{g - ri} \right]. \tag{8}$$

Thus, the long-run steady-state debtor or creditor position of the country depends on the difference between s, the share of GNP saved and taxed, and i, the share of GDP privately invested (and spent by government). In the statistical investigations to be described in later sections, we shall concentrate on the dependent variable D/Z_1.

Equation (8) provides an explanation for the ratio of NFIEA to GNP, which is in terms of four parameters: r, the interest rate; g, the growth rate; s; and i. With the aid of a more explicit model, these parameters may be shown to depend on a larger number of behavior coefficients. The model will be presented in this section, together with detailed analyses of s and i.

THE SHARE OF GNP SAVED

Total saving in the economy includes household and business saving and government taxes. When we are dealing with gross saving, depreciation will be included. The following assumptions have been made:

1. *Net private saving* by households and business is assumed to be a function of national disposable income. Gross private saving will equal net private saving plus depreciation on all owned capital, whether employed at home or abroad. Introduce the following symbols:

S = Net private saving
DEP_N = Depreciation on all owned capital
T = Taxes collected on personal and corporate income
Q = Taxes collected from excises

We shall assume a saving function

$$S = \alpha[Z_1 - DEP_N - T - Q]. \qquad (9)$$

2. *Government saving.* Further, it will be assumed that T (income taxes) is a given fraction τ of GNP at market prices, and Q (excise taxes) a given fraction ψ of GDP at factor cost. It will turn out that τ and ψ have slightly different effects on capital movements, because excise taxes will affect the profitability and level of investment.

3. *Depreciation,* which is included in gross saving, occurs on all owned capital, whether employed at home or abroad. For a country that is a net borrower this means that some depreciation on domestically employed capital is part of some other country's gross saving and GNP. Depreciation will be treated like net profit, as part of the total return to capital. Rather than regard it as a physical phenomenon, we shall instead argue that, just as some r per cent measures the net return to capital, there is an $(r + \beta)$ per cent that measures the gross return. The percentage β is therefore the portion of the total return to capital that cannot be considered as net return. This approach permits a direct estimate of the depreciation on capital employed at home and abroad. On capital employed at home, we may define domestic depreciation as

$$DEP_d \equiv \beta \times \text{value of home-employed capital.}$$

If we think of GDP, Z_2, as produced by a Cobb-Douglas production function, with capital-coefficient b, then with a competitive capital market, the flow of gross income to home-employed capital is $(r + \beta) \times$ value of capital, which equals $bZ_2/(1 + \psi)$. The $(1 + \psi)$ term in the denominator converts Z_2 from market prices to factor prices because of excise taxation. Therefore,

$$\text{value of home-employed capital} \equiv bZ_2/(r + \beta)(1 + \psi) \quad (10)$$

and

$$\text{domestic depreciation} \equiv \beta b Z_2/(r + \beta)(1 + \psi). \quad (11)$$

Let us assume that the same depreciation factor applies on home-employed and foreign-employed capital. (This problem is less important for a net debtor.) Then the value of foreign-employed capital is the discounted value of NFIEA, D/r, and assuming that all of NFIEA is equity return, foreign depreciation $\equiv DEP_F \equiv (\beta/r) \times$ NFIEA. These two methods of estimating depreciation will be carried into the model.

THE SHARE OF GDP INVESTED

For the purpose of this paper, investment was defined to include government spending, as it appears in the national income accounts. We shall assume that the government spends a given fraction, θ, of GNP, and we shall not break this total down between consumption and investment.

Gross private investment consists of depreciation on domestically employed capital plus net increases in the stock of domestically employed capital. We have already indicated that the depreciation function may be derived from a neoclassical production function. The investment function will be treated in a symmetric fashion. Again, assume that the value of domestically employed capital is described by equation (10). Further assume that b, β, and r remain unchanged. Increases in the stock of capital can be in either physical or money units, and be related to long-run changes in Z_2. Write the net value of domestically employed capital as KP_K, where P_K is the price and K the net physical stock. P_K may bear little resemblance to the GDP deflator. Further assume that P_K has a known path through time with a given growth rate,

γ, which may be positive or negative. Then net investment may be written as $\dot{K}P_K$, where the dot denotes a time derivative. From equation (10), net investment equals

$$\frac{b\dot{Z}_2 - b\gamma Z_2}{(r + \beta)(1 + \psi)}. \tag{12}$$

Again assume that g is the growth of Z_2. Then net investment is equal to

$$\frac{bZ_2}{(1 + \psi)(r + \beta)}\,(g - \gamma) \tag{13}$$

and gross investment is equal to

$$\frac{bZ_2}{(1 + \psi)(r + \beta)}\,(g - \gamma + \beta). \tag{14}$$

It should be noted that when P_K, the price of capital goods, has the same time path as the GDP deflator, the term $g - \gamma$ becomes, simply, the growth of GDP in real terms. On the other hand, if capital goods were imported, the term $g - \gamma$ would decompose into the sum of the real rate of growth of GDP plus a term that measured changes in the terms of trade between GDP and imported capital goods.

DEFINITIONS OF NET FACTOR INCOME EARNED ABROAD

The above considerations lead to new definitions of the relation among GNP, GDP, and NFIEA. Previously NFIEA was simply GNP − GDP, or $Z_1 = Z_2 + D$. Now we have

$$Z_1 = Z_2 + D + DEP_F = Z_2 + D\left[\frac{r + \beta}{r}\right].$$

Depreciation on foreign-employed capital is added to NFIEA before adding up to GNP. The sum of NFIEA and foreign depreciation will be called gross factor income earned abroad (GFIEA). Where NFIEA was denoted as D, GFIEA is $(r + \beta/r)D$. We may then proceed, as earlier, to derive an equilibrium ratio of NFIEA to GNP. As before, we have

$$\frac{gD}{r} = B = \text{net saving} + \text{taxes} - \text{net investment} - \text{government spending.} \tag{15}$$

Substitute for the four entities in brackets

net saving $= \alpha[Z_1 - DEP_N - T - Q]$,

taxes $= T + Q = \tau Z_1 + \left[\dfrac{\psi}{1+\psi}\right]Z_2$,

net investment $= \dfrac{b(g-\gamma)}{(\beta+r)(1+\psi)}Z_2$,

government spending $= \theta Z_1$,

$DEP_N \equiv DEP_D + DEP_F$,

$DEP_D \equiv \dfrac{\beta b Z}{(\beta+r)(1+\psi)}$, and

$DEP_F \equiv \dfrac{\beta}{r}D$.

We obtain the following relation between D (NFIEA) and GNP.

$$\frac{D}{Z_1} = \frac{r}{r+\beta}\left[\frac{N_2 - (1+\psi)(g-N_1)}{N_2}\right], \qquad (16)$$

where

$N_1 \equiv (\beta + r)[\tau(1 - \alpha) + \theta] + \alpha r$, and

$N_2 \equiv (1 + \psi)g - b(g - \gamma) + \alpha\beta(1 - b) + \psi[\beta + r(1 - \alpha)]$.

Equation (16) is the predicted long-run, steady-state ratio of NFIEA to GNP. The ratio of GFIEA to GNP is obtained simply by multiplication through both sides by $(r + \beta/r)$. The ratio D/Z_1 depends on a number of parameters that have been estimated for each country. Shown next to each parameter is the sign of the partial derivative of D/Z_1 with respect to the parameter, evaluated at a zero net debtor position:

r the interest rate +

β the depreciation rate +

α the saving coefficient +

τ the income tax rate +

ψ the excise tax rate +

g the growth of GDP −

γ the growth of prices of imported capital goods +

θ the share of GNP spent by government −

b the gross share of GDP imputed to capital − .

We see that a country will lend more, the higher the world interest rate, its depreciation rate, its saving rate, its tax rates; the *faster* the increases of prices of imported capital goods; the *lower* its growth rate; the share of GDP spent by government; and the gross share of output imputed to capital.

3 BEHAVIOR ASSUMPTIONS

IN THE preceding section, we presented a growth model that yielded an equilibrium steady-state ratio of NFIEA to GNP. The underlying assumptions of this model are that it allows all domestic monetary magnitudes to grow at the same rate, g, and that the interest cost of borrowing remains unchanged. In order to show precisely how the results are derived, it is necessary to specify a model for an open, growing economy. While the following assumptions may appear un-realistic, they do have the property of yielding the solutions derived earlier. After the model is presented, we shall comment on alternative sets of assumptions that might be employed. We shall describe in detail only those behavior assumptions that are added to the ones made in the previous section.

It is assumed that the country may be characterized as producing a single commodity, which may be consumed at home by households or government, or exported abroad; all investment goods are imported. The country is at full employment and uses labor and accumulated capital to produce its one commodity. The economy is characterized by pure and perfect competition and fixed exchange rates. The demand for the export commodity is infinitely elastic at the world price, and this demand function grows over time at a rate determined in the rest of the world. Thus the price level in this country is the same as the price of exports.

The level of employment is determined by demographic conditions, and the level of output per worker is determined by the ratio of capital to labor and the technological level of the production function. It is assumed that the world capital market is perfect and the supply is of infinite elasticity to individuals in this country, so that they may borrow or lend unlimited amounts with no effect on the world interest rate. This interest rate and the terms of trade will together determine the equilibrium ratio of capital to labor in the country; and in conjunction with the technological level of the production function, determine output per worker. Thus total output and the price level are determined under this model, and they determine gross domestic product at market prices. Through time GDP will grow, because of increases in the labor supply, in export prices, and in the level of output per worker due to autonomous technological change.

The economy may be represented by a system of 21 equations having 21 variables. The methods of solution and the stability conditions are given in the Appendix at the end of this paper.

$$X \equiv X_c + X_e + X_g. \tag{17}$$

Definition of output disposal into c, consumption; e, exports; g, government.

$$Z_2 \equiv X P_x. \tag{18}$$

Definition of gross domestic product at market prices.

$$P_x = P_0 e^{\rho t}. \tag{19}$$

Infinitely elastic world demand for exports, growing at rate ρ.

$$X = A_t L^{1-b} K^b. \tag{20}$$

Cobb-Douglas production function with autonomous technological change, growing at rate μ.

$$A_t = A_0 e^{\mu t}. \tag{21}$$

$$L = L_0 e^{\lambda t}. \tag{22}$$

Full employment assumed, with labor force growing at rate λ.

$$(r + \beta) K P_K = \frac{b X P_x}{1 + \psi}. \tag{23}$$

Equilibrium in capital-goods market.

$$r = \bar{r}. \tag{24}$$

Interest rate given in world market.

$$Z_1 = Z_2 + D + DEP_F. \tag{25}$$

Definition of GNP.

$$S = \alpha[Z_1 - DEP_N - T - Q]. \tag{26}$$

Net national saving function.

$$I \equiv \dot{K}P_K + DEP_D. \tag{27}$$

Definition of gross domestic investment.

$$P_K = P_0 e^{\gamma t}. \tag{28}$$

Time path of price of imported capital goods.

$$X_g P_X = \theta Z_1. \tag{29}$$

Government demands a fixed proportion of GNP.

$$Z_1 \equiv X_c P_X + S + T + Q + DEP_N. \tag{30}$$

GNP is consumed, or saved, or taxed.

$$T = \tau Z_1. \tag{31}$$

Income tax function.

$$Q = \frac{\psi}{1 + \psi} Z_2. \tag{32}$$

Excise tax function.

$$DEP_N \equiv DEP_D + DEP_F. \tag{33}$$

$$DEP_D \equiv \beta K P_K. \tag{34}$$

$$DEP_F \equiv \frac{\beta}{r}\,D. \tag{35}$$

$$D \equiv r\Sigma B. \tag{36}$$

$$B \equiv XeP_X - I + D. \tag{37}$$

Balance on current account.

This simple model will not explain a number of relevant phenomena. First, the level of output is not responsive to changes in aggregate demand. Full employment is assumed, and output grows at a constant rate, because of the instantaneous adjustment of the capital stock, which keeps labor and capital growing at the same rate. Second, there are no monetary variables in the model. The price level is exogenously determined by the world demand for exports. It would be possible to add a function describing the demand for money, but in order to retain the original conclusions, one would have to assume that the supply of money grew at the same rate as did the rest of the system. Moreover, money would have to be fiat money, and not a commodity domestically produced or imported. Third, the explanation of investment, while dynamic, is nevertheless unsophisticated. There are no lags in the response of entrepreneurs to changes in profit, and consequently no investment cycles in the response to parametric changes. Fourth, the price level and the price of exports are identical. There is no domestic goods sector, and no mechanism by which changes in the terms of trade alter the internal allocation of productive resources. Fifth, there is no relation between the prices of exports and the volume of exports. Exports are in fact a residual, determined as the difference between domestic production and domestic uses of output. Sixth, we assume a fixed interest rate, determined in the international capital market, at which borrowing and lending freely occur. There are no constraints in the form of increasing interest costs as the volume of borrowing expands.

Some of these limitations are impossible to alter without giving up the major hypotheses that come out of the model. Others are abstractions introduced for convenience, and could be eliminated in a more detailed specification of economic relationships. A few examples will be given.

1. If the level of output were responsive to changes in aggregate demand, the system's rate of growth would be, presumably, independent of demographic and technological variables, and would depend, instead, on the growth of private and government spending and on the growth of the money supply. The present model is a conscious choice to explain flows of capital in a framework that is independent of aggregate demand variables. Nevertheless, one could, with alternative assumptions, generate a model in which unemployment existed, so that output would be responsive to aggregate demand.

2. The model could be adapted to include a monetary sector, with corresponding changes in the solution for the level of capital export that was privately financed. If a monetary sector is introduced, then behavior equations—consistent with the regimes of fixed exchange rates in the current world economy—would have to be introduced for the supply of money.

3. Some experiments were made with equations for lagged investment behavior. In the steady-state solutions, they did not increase the explanatory power of the model.

4. It is not necessary to use a one-sector model. This is done as a statistical convenience. Other models developed have included a domestic good, whose price bears an equilibrium relation to the price of exports. This relation shifts over time if there are differential rates of technological change or differences in capital intensity in the production functions for exports and domestic goods.

5. It is not necessary to assume an infinitely elastic demand for exports. Models using negatively sloped demand functions have been developed. The solutions then depend on the rate of growth of world export demand, and the price and income elasticity of export demand.

6. One assumption that cannot be sacrificed is the fixed return on investment. Balanced-growth solutions with full employment are not possible if the return on investment changes through time.

4 STATISTICAL TESTING

TWO types of test were performed on the model. In the first, the parameters of the model were used as independent variables in a multiple-regression estimation of the variable D/Z_1. In the second, a predicted level of D/Z_1 was derived for each country, and then compared with the actual level. The predicted level is a short-run value based on the steady-state value of D/Z_1.

A. MULTIPLE REGRESSION

For each country and each observation period, we can measure the values of the parameters of the model: g, α, b, r, ψ, τ, θ, and the value of the dependent variable. Methods of measurement are described in an Appendix that is available upon request. We have 39 observations, three on each country, constituting the periods 1956–59; 1960–62; 1963–65. The individual observations were considered independent of each other, and this assumption could not be contradicted by time-period effects measured through dummy variables. Moreover, no attempt was made to stratify the sample by region or country dummy variables. The regressions of D/Z_1 on these independent variables yielded the coefficients shown in Table 2, with standard errors in parentheses.

The five columns of Table 2 show estimated regression coefficients and standard errors for a selectively reduced group of independent variables. In the first column, all independent variables are used, and all but τ (the income-tax rate) have the correct signs. That is, the sign agrees with the partial derivative of the steady-state solution for D/Z_1 with respect to the independent variable. Significant coefficients are found for g, α, and b. There are a number of reasons why τ should come out with an incorrect sign. First, it is correlated with θ, the government-spending rate, and with ψ, the excise-tax rate. Elimination of τ (column 2), yields estimates of coefficients for ψ and θ that have the correct sign and exceed their standard errors.

The interest-rate variable, r, is also of small significance in explaining D/Z_1 although the sign of the coefficient is correct. We suspect two reasons. First, because of difficulties in measuring the interest cost of borrowing, there are errors in measuring r. Second, the interest rate does not vary substantially from one country to another, or from one time period to the next. In fact the theory that generates our hypothesis does not require interest differentials in order to explain flows of capital.

TABLE 2

Regression Coefficients with D/Z_1 as Dependent Variable: Thirteen
Countries, Thirty-nine Observations, 1956–65

Independent Variable	Regression Equations				
	(1)	(2)	(3)	(4)	(5)
g	−.915	−.953	−.799	−.799	−.789
	(.240) [a]	(.200)	(.170)	(.178)	(.174)
α	+.669	+.679	+.556	+.613	+.609
	(.143)	(.137)	(.108)	(.109)	(.107)
b	−.227	−.231	−.214	−.207	−.190
	(.072)	(.070)	(.060)	(.072)	(.060)
r	+.004	+.015	−	+.082	−
	(.182)	(.175)		(.179)	
ψ	+.147	+.195	−	−	−
	(.209)	(.133)			
τ	−.041	−	−	−	−
	(.138)				
θ	−.125	−.171	−.116	−	−
	(.173)	(.079)	(.067)		
Constant term	.088	.087	.101	.051	.055
R	.754	.754	.734	.708	.706

[a] Standard errors are shown in parentheses.

Column 3 of the table shows the four most significant variables:
g, α, b and θ. Column 5 shows that deletion of θ has only a minor effect
on the other coefficients. In both columns 3 and 5, the coefficients of
g, α, and b are significant at 1 per cent.

These four variables not only show the most significant coefficients, but they also carry the greatest weight, quantitatively, in explaining D/Z_1. The quantitative significance of each independent variable is shown in Table 3, where we have its sample mean and variance,
each multiplied by its regression coefficient from column 1 of Table 2.

Whether measured by the product of sample mean and regression
coefficient, or sample variance and regression coefficient, the four variables g, α, b, and θ carry the greatest quantitative importance. Thus

TABLE 3

Independent Variables in Regression

Variable	Sample Mean	Sample Variance ($\times 10^{-3}$)	Sample Mean $\times$ Regression Coefficient	Sample Variance $\times$ Regression Coefficient ($\times 10^{-3}$)
g	.064	0.44	−.058	−.40
α	.139	1.46	.093	.98
b	.381	2.83	−.087	−.64
r	.133	0.36	.001	
ψ	.126	0.99	.019	.15
τ	.178	2.04	−.007	−.08
θ	.245	2.24	−.031	−.28

the theory that identified seven independent variables is left with four survivors: the rate of growth, the saving ratio, the capital coefficient, and the rate of government spending.

Confidence in the value of these coefficients is enhanced by comparison with a study carried out by G. H. Borts on data for regions of the United States. The regression of D/Z_1 on g, α, and b was made for the forty-eight contiguous states for the year 1953. The coefficients and their standard errors are shown in the first column of Table 4. There is a remarkable similarity in these results as compared with the OECD countries shown in the columns of Table 2.

It was noted earlier that the observation sample for the present study consists of three repeated observations on 13 countries. The possibility of an unnoticed change in economic structure is therefore present. Two checks were employed: First the regressions were rerun to see if elimination of the first period (1956–59) would influence the results. The data for this period are likely to be less reliable than for later periods. Furthermore, the postwar freedom of capital movements only began at the end of the 1950's. When the regression of column 5, Table 2, is rerun without the 1956–59 data, we obtain coefficients that are still highly significant and virtually unchanged numerically. These are

TABLE 4

Table of Regression Coefficients: D/Z_1 as
Dependent Variable

Independent Variable	(1)	(2)
g	−.918	−.794
	(.511)	(.238)
α	+.677	+.641
	(.163)	(.130)
b	−.197	−.172
	(.117)	(.073)
Constant	+.056	.045
R	.705	.726
Number of observations	48	26

shown in column 2, Table 4. Thus, if a change in economic structure occurred after 1959, it does not show up in the coefficients. The second check was the use of dummy variables in the regression to determine the possible existence of structural change that influenced all countries simultaneously in a given period. None of the dummies was significant. We did not make use of regional or individual country dummies, for lack of a priori reasons for such identifications.[3] Nevertheless, calculating the residuals from the regression shown in column 1, Table 2, there are persistent overpredictions or underpredictions for the following countries, with no discernible pattern:

D/Z_1 Overpredicted	D/Z_1 Underpredicted
Canada	Austria
France	Denmark
Japan	Ireland
Norway	Switzerland
Sweden	
United Kingdom	

[3] Two fishing expeditions into the data are worth reporting on. In the first, the countries were divided by size into large (0) and small (1), and the dummy was significantly

B. PREDICTION OF STEADY-STATE RATIOS

The parameters of the model were used to estimate a steady-state value of D/Z_1 from equation (16), in the section dealing with models of growth and capital movements. This steady-state value would be approached over time if the parameters held their values throughout and there were no other disturbances to the system. Of course, such a case is unthinkable. Nevertheless, as a first step, the constructed values of D/Z_1 were correlated with the observed values; the constructed values made use of parameters for each of the three periods, 1956–59, 1960–62, and 1963–65. Thus, we had 39 constructed estimates of D/Z_1, three for each country. Each constructed estimate of D/Z_1 was compared with the observed value for the same period, and a correlation coefficient of +.39 was obtained, significant but not large. However, this is a very poor test of the empirical validity of the model, since the parameter values, and consequently the asymptotic value of D/Z_1, change from year to year. A second test is suggested by the differential equation that is solved to give a time path for NFIEA and GNP. This prediction equation may be illustrated by returning to the very simple growth model presented earlier in the paper. It will be recalled that we obtained a steady-state solution for Z_1 and Z_2 (GNP and GDP):

$$Z_1 = Z_2 \left[\frac{g - ri}{g - rs} \right].$$

The full solution contains, in addition, a transitional term that reflects the initial conditions. If we write the bracketed expression above as z, then the full solution is

$$Z_1(t) = z \times Z_2(t) + Ce^{rst},$$

where

$$C = Z_1(0) - Z_2(0) \times z.$$

positive, indicating that the small countries, on the average, lent more than the large ones. The meaning is unclear. In the second foray, the countries were divided into borrowers (0) and lenders (1). The dummy was positive, indicating that the function fitted to all observations would underestimate the volume of borrowing. This is consistent with the finding that the variance of predicted D/Z_1 is less than the variance of observed D/Z_1.

Therefore, with $Z_2(t)$ growing at the rate g, we also have

$$\frac{Z_1(t)}{Z_2(t)} = z + \frac{C}{Z_2(0)} e^{(rs-g)t},$$

an expression that will converge to z if $rs - g$ is negative.

As a consequence, the expression D/Z_1 equals

$$\frac{D(t)}{Z_1(t)} = 1 - \frac{1}{z + \dfrac{C}{Z_2(0)} e^{(rs-g)t}}.$$

This is the prediction equation for D/Z_1, which may be used once we have a value for

$$\frac{C}{Z_2(0)} = \frac{Z_1(0)}{Z_2(0)} - z.$$

$Z_1(0)/Z_2(0)$ is obtained from the observed (1956–59) values of Z_1 and Z_2. The (1960–62) value for z is derived from the steady-state equation:

$$z = \frac{g - ri}{g - rs}.$$

Thus the term $C/Z_2(0)$ is specified. The 1960–62 period is treated as occurring one period later than the 1956–59 period, and D/Z is thus estimated:

$$(D/Z)(60\text{--}62) = 1 - \frac{1}{z + \dfrac{C}{Z_2(0)} e^{(rs-g)}}.$$

This estimate is referred to as $\bar{D}/\bar{Z}$. When the actual observations are compared with the predicted values, we obtain the following regression relation:

$$D/Z = -.00018 + .981\bar{D}/\bar{Z}.$$
$$(.024)$$

$$R = .993$$

Here we have used 26 observations and predictions, 13 for the 1960–62 period and 13 for the 1962–65 period. While these results look impressive and yield a regression coefficient insignificantly different from unity, there is an alternative hypothesis against which the theoretical prediction must be judged. The alternative hypothesis is simply that the ratio D/Z_1 for one period is best predicted by the observed ratio for the preceding period. A simple way to test the alternative hypothesis is to use the lagged value as a second independent variable to determine the statistical significance of its coefficient. We then obtain a multiple regression relation

$$D/Z_1 = -.00011 + .791\bar{D}/\bar{Z} + .186[D/Z](t-1).$$
$$(.221) \qquad (.216)$$
$$R = .993$$

We see that the use of the lagged value neither adds explanatory power nor yields a statistically significant coefficient. The conclusion is that the prediction based on the theoretical model provides a good explanation of the ratio of NFIEA to GNP.

5   CONCLUSION

THE MOST impressive statistical confirmation comes from the multiple-regression tests. The agreement in sign between the estimated coefficients and the partial derivatives of D/Z_1 indicates that each parameter (but τ) affects the dependent variable as predicted. Further, there is striking agreement between the estimates of the coefficients of g, α, and b from data for OECD countries and for the 48 contiguous states of the United States.

We are less impressed with the results of the last test, because the D/Z_1 ratios for each country are reasonably stable through time. While the preceding period D/Z_1 value does not provide much additional explanation, it is, nevertheless, highly correlated with subsequent values.

Assuming that the theory provides a valid explanation of capital movements, what have we learned that we did not know before? There are three major conclusions.

First, movements of capital can be explained by the same factors that explain the growth of an economy: the growth of population and technology, the improvement in the terms of trade between exports and imported capital goods, the saving rate, and the capital-coefficient. Government policy directed toward influencing capital movements can operate on these parameters.

Second, it is not necessary to introduce monetary factors to explain why or how capital transfers occur. Monetary variables may influence capital movements, however, if the excess demand for money has an influence on the excess demand for goods. In the present model, such an influence was not assumed. Our assumptions imply that monetary and foreign-exchange policies directed toward target values of international reserves have no influence on the balance of trade, and only affect the balance on private capital account and the reported level of NFIEA. The tests on the data do not repudiate this assumption.

Third, the theory of balance-of-payments adjustment should be enlarged to take these possibilities into account.

APPENDIX: THE SOLUTION AND STABILITY OF THE MODEL

IN THE solution for Z_1 (GNP), two principal substitutions are required. These include the equilibrium condition for Z_1 and the growth rate of Z_2 (GDP).

Since the model contains physical commodities valued at a set of prices and long-term securities valued as the assets that households, firms, and the government can demand and supply, we need to specify only one condition of market equilibrium. A one-country model of this type should properly specify four markets: goods, securities, money, and foreign exchange. We have assumed that the money market and the balance of payments are in equilibrium. Thus equilibrium in the securities market implies equilibrium in the goods market. The equilibrium conditions for Z_1 can be found by equating the demand and supply functions for Z_1. From the demand side,

$$Z_1^d = C + G + I + E - MP_M + D + DEP_F, \tag{38}$$

where $E = X_e P_x$, MP_M represents the value of imports, $C = X_C P_x$, and I represents gross domestic investment (GDI). The supply equation is

$$Z_1^s = C + S + T + Q + DEP_N. \tag{39}$$

Equating the two, we have

$$E - MP_M + D = S + T + Q - G - \text{net } I. \tag{40}$$

This equation says that net foreign investment equals net national savings minus net domestic investment plus the government's surplus. We shall substitute equation (40) for B, the balance on current account, whenever B appears in the solution of Z_1.

The growth rate g of Z_2 depends only upon certain parameters and is therefore constant and independent of the other economic relationships in the model. We can derive g as follows:

Multiplying the price of output (19) and the production function (20) gives us

$$XP_x = P_x A_t L^{1-b} K^b. \tag{41}$$

Take the log derivative of XP_x with respect to time, and substitute the specified growth rates of P_x, A_t, and L. Denote the growth rate of XP_x as g.

$$g = \rho + \mu + (1 - b)\lambda + \frac{b\dot{K}}{K}. \tag{42}$$

An expression for $\dot{K}/K$ can be obtained from capital's equilibrium condition in equation (23). It equals

$$\frac{\dot{K}}{K} = g - \gamma. \tag{43}$$

Substituting (43) into (42) gives us

$$g = \frac{\rho}{1-b} + \frac{\mu}{1-b} + \lambda - \frac{b\gamma}{1-b}. \tag{44}$$

Since g is not a function of time in (44) we can write XP_x as

$$XP_x = X_0 P_{x0} e^{gt} \tag{45}$$

for a given initial condition $XP_x(0) = X_0 P_{x0}$.

We are now ready to solve the model in terms of the variable Z_1. From (25) and (35) we obtain

$$Z_1 = Z_2 + \left(\frac{\beta + r}{r}\right)D. \tag{46}$$

The time derivative of this equation is

$$\dot{Z}_1 = \dot{Z}_2 + \left(\frac{\beta + r}{r}\right)\dot{D}. \tag{47}$$

Since $D = rB$, we can substitute equation (40) for B. From (45) we know that $\dot{Z}_2 = gZ_2$. Therefore, (47) can be rewritten as

$$\dot{Z}_1 = gZ_2 + (\beta + r)[S + T + Q - G - \text{net } I]. \tag{48}$$

From the equations of the model, the values of S, T, Q, G, and net I can be described solely as functions of Z_1 and Z_2. Consequently (48) can be written as

$$\dot{Z}_1 - N_1 Z_1 = \frac{N_2}{1 + \psi} X_0 P_{x0} e^{gt}, \tag{49}$$

where
$N_1 \equiv (\beta + r)[\tau(1 - \alpha) + \theta] + r\alpha$ and
$N_2 \equiv (1 + \psi)g - b(g - \gamma) + \alpha\beta(1 - b) + \psi[\beta + r(1 - \alpha)]$.

Equation (49) is a linear nonhomogeneous differential equation that has constant coefficients. Its solution is

$$Z_1(t) = \frac{N_2 \times X_0 P_{x0} e^{gt}}{(1 + \psi)(g - N_1)} + c_1 e^{N_1 t} \tag{50}$$

where c_1 = constant of integration.

Since by inspection $N_2 > 0$, we must impose the stability condition $g - N_1 > 0$ in order to ensure that the model has a positive solution for Z_1.

The econometric tests performed on the model are concerned principally with the value of D/Z_1. This ratio can be derived in the following fashion:

Dividing equation (50) by $XP_x \equiv Z_2$ we obtain

$$\frac{Z_1}{Z_2} = \frac{N_2}{(1 + \psi)(g - N_1)} + \frac{c_1 e^{(N_1 - g)t}}{X_0 P_{x0}}. \tag{51}$$

As long as the stability condition is satisfied, Z_1/Z_2 will approach the value $N_2/(1 + \psi)(g - N_1)$ as $t \to \infty$. Assuming that the long-run steady-state solution has been attained,

$$\frac{Z_2}{Z_1} = \frac{(1 + \psi)(g - N_1)}{N_2}. \tag{52}$$

From equation (46) we can write D/Z_1 as

$$\frac{D}{Z_1} = \left[1 - \frac{Z_2}{Z_1}\right] \frac{r}{r + \beta}. \tag{53}$$

Substituting equation (52) for Z_2/Z_1 we obtain as the steady-state value of D/Z_1

$$\frac{D}{Z_1} = \frac{r}{r + \beta} \left[\frac{N_2 - (1 + \psi)(g - N_1)}{N_2}\right]. \tag{54}$$

The long-run debtor or creditor position of the nation depends on the sign of the term $N_2 - (1 + \psi)(g - N_1)$. A positive value indicates that the country is a net creditor in its long-term lending; a negative sign implies a net debtor position in relation to the rest of the world.

REFERENCES

1. Avramovic, Dragoslav, *Debt Servicing Problems of Low Income Countries*. International Bank for Reconstruction and Development. Baltimore, Johns Hopkins Press, 1960.
2. Borts, George H., "Growth and Capital Movements Among U.S. Regions in the Postwar Period." *American Economic Review, Papers and Proceedings*, 58 (May, 1968), pp. 155–161.
3. ――― "A Theory of Long-Run International Capital Movements." *Journal of Political Economy*, 72 (August, 1964), pp. 341–359.
4. Cairnes, J. E., *Some Leading Principles of Political Economy Newly Expounded*. New York, 1874.
5. Denison, Edward F., *Why Growth Rates Differ*. Washington, D.C., Brookings Institution, 1967.

6. Domar, Evsey, "The Effect of Foreign Investment on the Balance of Payments." *American Economic Review,* 40 (December, 1950), pp. 805–826.
7. Ingram, James, *Regional Payments Mechanisms: The Case of Puerto Rico.* Chapel Hill, University of North Carolina Press, 1962.
8. Johnson, Harry, "Equilibrium Growth in an International Economy." *Canadian Journal of Economics,* 19 (November, 1953), pp. 478–500.
9. Lewis, Cleona, *The United States and Foreign Investment Problems.* Washington, D.C., Brookings Institution, 1948.
10. Metzler, Lloyd, "The Process of International Adjustment Under Conditions of Full Employment: A Keynesian View," reprinted in R. E. Caves and H. G. Johnson, eds., *Readings in International Economics.* Homewood, Richard D. Irwin, Inc., 1968.
11. Mundell, Robert, "Capital Mobility and Stabilization Policy Under Fixed and Flexible Exchange Rates," reprinted in R. E. Caves and H. G. Johnson, eds., *Readings in International Economics.* Homewood, Richard D. Irwin, Inc., 1968.
12. Neher, Philip, "A Neo-Classical Theory of International Capital Movements," unpublished doctoral dissertation, Brown University, 1966.
13. Williamson, Jeffrey, "Real Growth, Monetary Disturbances, and the Transfer Process: The United States, 1879–1900." *Southern Economic Journal,* 29 (January, 1963), pp. 167–180.
14. International Monetary Fund, *Balance of Payments Yearbook, 1955–1965.* Washington, D.C.
15. ——— *International Financial Statistics, Supplement to 1966–1967 and Vol. 22, No. 6.* June, 1969, Washington, D.C.
16. Organization for Economic Cooperation and Development, *Statistics of National Accounts 1950–1961.* Paris, 1964.
17. ——— *National Accounts Statistics, 1956–1965.* Paris.
18. ——— *General Statistics, 1964.* Paris.

COMMENTS

LORIE TARSHIS
STANFORD UNIVERSITY

The two papers that have been assigned to me for comment, when read successively, will create a state of at least mild schizophrenia in most readers. The first, by Dobell and Wilson, which attempts to assess policy alternatives, relies very strongly, though by no means wholly, on the effects to be expected from changes in relative yields earned on securities issued in Canada and in the United States. Shifts in relative interest rates, or something like them, are at least partly responsible for shifts in the balance of payments and in the capital accounts, even when the initiating development is a substantial change in the Canadian tax structure. The other paper, by Borts and Kopecky, seeks to account for flows of capital without the slightest reference, so far as I can see, to yield differentials; nevertheless, the independent variables it specifies seem to explain recent experience to a surprising degree.

It is clear that each of these studies, in its own way, can contribute something to our understanding of movements of capital. It is equally clear—but rather unfortunate—that collaboration between the two pairs of authors was surprisingly—to use that term again—lacking. Indeed, it is doubtful that their work stems from the same general discipline, an observation that throws an unflattering, though not necessarily inaccurate, light upon the state of the subject.

The Borts-Kopecky study does not deal directly with capital movements; instead it focuses on the factors that determine the ratio of NFIEA to the GNP. But if we assume, as the authors do, no change over time in the rate of return on assets held abroad, then the long-run maintenance of that ratio will imply, for a country that begins life as a net creditor, a growth in its net capital exports that eventually will match the growth in its GNP; if the ratio rises, it implies an even faster growth in its net capital exports. Thus, when the authors isolate factors that would, according to them, lead to a rise in that ratio, I shall simply take it to mean that these factors would also lead to a rapid increase in — and sooner or later a high rate of net capital exports from — the country in question.

They reach their results by analyzing a model from which almost everything has been stripped away — some will feel that the simplifying has gone too far and that even some essentials have been removed.

Their model seems to consist of one very small country embedded in a very big and rather passive world that sometimes looks like outer space. The small economy's net exports are determined directly by saving minus investment, suitably defined. Its net exports, it must be emphasized, are treated as a mere residual — or a balancing item that must take whatever value is required for the maintenance of equilibrium in the goods market. Both investment and saving, in turn, are determined by such factors as the economy's rate of growth, its rate of saving, its own rate of interest (which, however, equals the rate in the rest of space), the rate of depreciation of its capital assets, its tax rate, the share of its GNP purchased by government, and capital's imputed share in its GDP. It is notable that conditions outside the economy play no role in the determination of its exports. Now, clearly, one cannot argue with an identity, although one can question the uses to which it is put. Its most dangerous feature is, of course, that by itself it can tell us nothing about what is cause and what is effect — or, more generally, about the directions in which causal influences operate. Of course, we can interpret their equations as doing no more than establishing the fact that there is a complex functional relationship involving all the variables they mention — and, in a richer (and, I would hold, more fruitful) model, many more of them. Their list of variables includes those that they regard as their primary dependent variables. But on that interpretation their work may tell us little about what determines capital movements.

There may be something to be said for assuming that an economy's net exports are determined in such a way when that country is selling in a perfectly competitive market, for then it can dispose of all its output at a price that is independent of the amount it chooses to sell. And if, at the same time, its domestic buyers have a prior claim upon that output, its net exports would be determined as is done in the authors' model. However, it is not obvious that any economy — even the smallest — begins to meet these conditions. Indeed, the only example that seems even to approach these conditions is — or rather was — South Africa in the days when it knew it could sell gold without limit at $35 an ounce.

Once we explicitly take into account a feature that is surely *central* to any problem of international economics — namely, that there must be at least two economies — we can see how misleading the authors' assumption that net exports and, subsequently, net capital movements, are a mere residual, must be. Their results presumably apply to any other country, too, and not simply to the one on which our attention was first focused. Hence, their conclusion that, to take an example, a country's *net* exports will rise in direct proportion to the level of world interest rates, would apply to the other country — assuming that there are only two — just as it does to the first. So a rise in world interest rates would lead to an increase in the *net* international lending of each country. Likewise, a rise in the tax rate of each country would lead both to expand their *net* lending simultaneously and not simply their gross lending. And so would a general decline in their rates of growth.

I admit that in stating my objection in these terms I compound the error of composition. However, it is difficult to resist the temptation to do so as a means of bringing out clearly that the authors, in their empirical tests, seem to fall into the same trap. A result in which net exports and net lending of both countries rise simultaneously is not so much paradoxical as it is surrealist. And the resolution of what I shall call the paradox must be either that a country's net exports are not residually determined, or, as an alternative, that the beginning point for one country, which must be a net debtor if the other is a net creditor, makes a real difference in the results. I do not find it in the least upsetting to be forced to conclude that the first point is correct and that all the variables — taxes, saving, investment, exports, imports, and even capital movements — are, in fact, mutually determined and, indeed, are determined by forces operating on both sides of the border; that, for example, something that induces investors in one country to buy securities from investors in another may lead (or the purchase itself will lead) to a modification of the forces that determine tax yields, domestic investment spending, net capital exports, and so on, in both countries.

When I began to work on this paper and noted the absence of differential interest rates, I felt as though I were hearing, "Look, Dad, no hands." As I thought more about it, and realized that their model makes a country's exports no more than a balancing item—an Errors and Omissions figure, if you will, in its goods-market accounts—I began to hear, "Gee whiz, Dad, no feet either!" And when I got to the end and saw that one country's capital movements were to be explained without the least reference to the situation in other countries, I couldn't help wondering whether there was even a bike on the road. Simplification seems to have gone too far.

In our earlier discussions questions were raised about the explanatory power of a model that has two countries and only one money, as a common-currency area implies; even more questionable is a model designed to explain international capital movements with only one currency and one country, or at least one currency, one country, and outer space.

I grant that my remarks might be less appreciated *if* the authors' analysis were meant to apply to, say, Luxemburg or San Marino. But their empirical tests suggest that they also had larger economies such as France, Germany, or Japan in mind.

And yet with so little at hand, they seem able to explain so much. An equation having only the single economy's rate of growth, its saving rate, and the share of its GDP imputed to capital in it, and one in which the first two are of paramount importance, gives results for these larger economies which are decidedly well correlated with the observed values for the rates mentioned earlier.

I suppose for one who makes no claim to being an econometrician, that the most congenial explanation for this can be found in the remarks Bryant and Hendershott made in their paper. In any event, I cannot take seriously the very excellent results of an empirical test of a relationship which is theoretically unpersuasive—at least to me. There appears to be less to their results than meets the eye.

The paper by Dobell and Wilson is at once more ambitious— because it does grapple with the problem of mutual interdependence— and less ambitious, because it seeks to isolate the effects of certain specific changes in Canadian taxes by holding all other factors constant.

Here, the results are, in a way, not at all surprising—even though that itself is surprising, as I shall try to show.

Most of what I shall call the temporarily final effect of what amounts to a rise in the tax on the corporate profits of Canadian firms, together with the exposure of those profits to the personal-income tax, seems to have its source in a reduction in the payments abroad of dividends by foreign-owned firms as well as in the discouragement that nonresidents would face in purchasing Canada's securities. But at least it is comforting to find that one's intuition is not completely wrong when attention is paid, as the authors do, to various indirect effects— in the money and securities markets, in the goods markets and so on.

Not that their model is altogether general, or indeed that it is even always general enough to answer the questions they place before us in a really useful way. Investment spending, for example, is permitted to respond to changes in securities markets. But the final equilibrium, in the authors' sense of the term, does not allow for changes in investment that might be induced by changes in expected yields on new projects. This limitation is not to be criticized, though taking it to suggest something about the time path of the process and implying that their answer is at least true for, say, the end of the first year, would, I think, be a mistake.

If I have any worry, then, about their procedures and their results, it comes down to what I hold to be an insufficiently careful statement of their theoretical work.

Suppose that two kinds of securities are issued, one in Canada, and the other in the United States. And suppose, to begin with, that some of each are held on both sides of the border. Now, if the Canadian government were to raise the tax on the profits of Canadian corporations—and the tax could not be "passed on"—this would result in a reduction in the yield offered by Canadian securities at their old price. But it would not necessarily lead to any movement of capital (considering, here, only the stock of securities already issued). Indeed, if all investors were affected in exactly the same way—or thought they were—there would not be even any transactions as a result of the new tax. Transactions could occur only if some investors reacted differently to this higher tax than did other investors. And their transactions would only be *international* in character—and thus comprise a capital movement—if investors on one side of the border figured that their after-tax yield was affected by more or by less than investors on the other side estimated theirs to be. That could, of course, happen. Indeed, if Canadian investors could claim some credit against their personal income tax, while investors in the United States could not (as seems likely with the proposals under study), Canada would export capital. But if the tables were turned, and American investors were allowed to claim part credit against their personal income tax for this higher tax on the profits of the Canadian firms in which they held shares, while Canadian investors were not able to do this, Canada would *import*—not export—capital as a result of such a tax rise.

Space does not permit me to develop these notions about the effects of changes in the rates of taxes, but I believe that these effects hold equally for changes in the rates of interest. And they create some doubt in my mind as to measurements of interest-rate sensitivity obtained in the usual way—including those used by Dobell and Wilson. Not every differential change in interest rates—assuming, for example, that in the absence of capital mobility rates in one country would rise and in the other decline—is bound to bring forth "normal" capital movements, or indeed *any* capital movements—even when objective restrictions on foreign investment are lacking. So much depends upon the causes of the differential shift in interest rates. And so much, too, depends upon the differences in speculative opinion among the investors of each of the countries taken separately.

For the study in question this implies that the empirically determined values for the interest-rate sensitivity of flows of capital are likely to be wide of the mark, unless the model used to determine these values is a good deal more complex than those normally used. The results are perhaps not very sensitive to the values taken, but they must be sensitive to something; and most of the other parameters look no more promising.

BELA BALASSA

JOHNS HOPKINS UNIVERSITY

We are indebted to Dobell and Wilson and to Borts and Kopecky for their interesting and provocative contributions to the conference. At the same time, one is struck by differences in the methods of analysis used in the two papers. Borts and Kopecky suggest that international capital flows are explained by differences in ex ante saving and investment and not by differences in yields. By contrast, variations in yields associated with proposed tax reforms occupy a central place in Dobell and Wilson's analysis of the possible effects of these reforms on capital movements and the balance of payments in Canada. Instead of comparing the two papers, however, I will comment on them individually. Following customary procedure, I will emphasize points of disagreement rather than agreement.

Dobell and Wilson have estimated the effects of alternative tax-reform proposals on capital flows and on the balance of payments in Canada. They also show the revenue effects of the proposed reforms and their impact on domestic capital markets, saving, and investment. A distinction is made between the "impact effect" that appears in the first round, the "final effect" that provides an unconstrained solution after all equilibrium conditions are satisfied, and the "compensated effect" that involves the imposition of balance-of-payments and aggregate-demand constraints on the solution of the model.

In the introduction to the paper, the authors note that they seek to develop "a consistent macroeconomic model of Canada" (p. 519) from which the effects of alternative tax reforms can be derived. Instead of estimating the model from time-series observations, however, they use extraneous information on various economic relationships, obtained from a variety of sources, as building blocks for the model. Several questions arise in connection with this procedure.

There is, first, the question of whether the estimates of the individual relationships are consistent with each other, since they have been derived by the use of different methods and refer to different time periods. Second, the results are affected by the lack of estimates concerning some of the relationships pertaining to international capital flows, such as the yield sensitivity of the three types of portfolio investment included in the model: foreign purchases of Canadian bonds, foreign purchases of Canadian stocks, and Canadian purchases of foreign securities. Third, the conclusion that "the available empirical evidence suggests that foreign direct investment in Canada is not very sensitive to changes in yields on marketable securities" (p. 532) may not be applicable when the effects of proposed tax reforms are evaluated, because decisions are likely to be more sensitive to once-for-all changes in yields than to changes that may be considered temporary.

According to Dobell and Wilson's estimates presented in Table 4, the "impact effect" of the proposed reforms would entail an improvement in Canada's balance of payments in the area of $140–$200 million. This result would follow largely because of the reduced outflow of dividends and, apart from the White Paper proposals, reductions in Canadian purchases of foreign securities. Accordingly, under the assumption of fixed exchange rates and an accommodating monetary policy, balance-of-payments equilibrium and the maintenance of aggregate demand would require an expansionary fiscal policy in the form of increases in government expenditure or reductions in taxes.

The estimates of the impact effect on the balance of payments are, however, sensitive to the assumptions made. Moreover, the policy recommendations are affected by the separation of the changes following the tax reform into those included under the impact effect and those subsumed under the final effect of the unconstrained solution. I will consider these questions as they pertain to foreign direct and portfolio investment in Canada.

Dobell and Wilson note: "The estimated negative shock effects of the Carter proposals on investment in the extractive sector are based on a study of that sector by G. D. Quirin. Since the revenue impact of the mineral-industry reforms proposed in the White Paper is estimated to be negligible for the first five years, we shall assume that these reforms will also have no effect on investment" (p. 547). We cannot judge the reasonableness of Quirin's estimate, since the methods used are not indicated in the paper under discussion. As to the effects under the White Paper proposals, the assumption that investors would not be affected by tax increases publicly scheduled for five years hence is open to question. Since the period of recoupment in extractive industries is rather long, anticipations tending to reduce the amount invested by both domestic and foreign firms are likely to be at work.

Questions also come to mind concerning the author's treatment of the effects of tax reform on investment which takes place outside the extractive sector. Such investment is supposed to depend on the marginal corporate-tax rate, which would not change under any of the reforms. While this may be the appropriate assumption with respect to capacity expansion by existing firms, it would not be appropriate for investment by new firms. For new firms, the average—rather than the marginal—tax rate will be relevant. The rise in the average tax rate under the three reform proposals would thus provide disincentives to investment by new firms—domestic as well as foreign—and thereby tend further to reduce foreign direct investment in Canada.

The authors' results concerning the flow of funds from—or to—existing subsidiaries of foreign companies are also open to criticism. In nonextractive industries where investment is assumed to remain unchanged, the capital requirements of these firms would go up by the full amount of the increased tax payment, while in extractive industries capital requirements would rise by the difference between the increase in tax payments and the decrease in investment by foreigners. It is further assumed that nonresident firms would continue to finance their increased capital requirements from domestic and foreign sources in the same proportions as heretofore. Correspondingly, the outflow of dividends would be reduced by 83 per cent of the increase in capital requirements in nonextractive industry and 77 per cent in extractive industry (Table 3). This decrease in the outflow of dividends accounts, in turn, for 60 to 80 per cent of the estimated improvement in the Canadian balance of payments under the three proposed tax reforms.

Dobell and Wilson thus assume a passive behavior on the part of the international corporation: increased taxes would affect neither the decision to invest nor the share of financing from Canadian sources. Rather than financing the increase in tax requirements through reduced outflow of dividends, however, the reduced availability of funds generated internally might well induce foreign companies to augment the share of borrowing in Canada or to reduce planned investment by their subsidiaries. At any rate, the relationship between the uses of financing for new investments and for increased taxes on the one hand,

and that between the sources of foreign financing from the inflow of capital and from reduction in dividends on the other, is at best tenuous. All in all, the balance-of-payments effects of the proposed tax reforms on direct investment and dividend flows might then well be unfavorable rather than favorable for Canada's balance of payments.

Further questions concerning the effects of the proposed tax reforms on portfolio investment also come to mind. The authors note that for the typical investor in the 35–40 per cent marginal bracket, the combined effect of changes in corporate and personal taxes would lower the marginal tax burden on income from corporate sources under the Carter proposals and increase it under the White Paper. The importance of the latter is said to be negligible, while the former would affect Canada's balance of payments favorably by inducing a switch from foreign to domestic securities. By contrast, the impact effect of the tax-reform proposals on investment in Canadian securities by foreigners is taken to be nil.

The asymmetrical treatment of portfolio investment by Canadians and foreigners reflects the assumption that while the former will react immediately to changes in after-tax yields resulting from the tax reform, the latter will adjust their portfolios only after a time lag. These assumptions do not appear realistic, however. As reductions in the rate of personal taxes are not applicable to them, foreign investors will tend to switch out of Canadian securities that will offer lower after-tax earnings and dividend yields at the higher corporate-tax rates. And there is no reason to assume that foreign investors would postpone making such decisions.

It should be added that adverse changes in Canada's balance of payments due to the sale (or reduced purchase) of Canadian securities by foreigners would tend to be much greater than the beneficial change that would result from switching by Canadians. On the one hand, the volume of securities in question is substantially greater in the first case than it is in the second; on the other, the absolute magnitude of the change in yields is greater for the foreign investor than it is for the Canadian, for whom there are compensating changes in personal taxes. By including transactions in Canadian securities by foreigners under the "impact effect," there is little doubt that the balance-of-payments effects of the proposed tax reforms on portfolio investments would be unfavorable.

These considerations suggest the conclusion that, in the absence of compensatory fiscal policies, the tax reforms proposed in recent years may well lead to a deterioration rather than an improvement in Canada's balance of payments. This conclusion has important implications for policy making. While, on the basis of their results, Dobell and Wilson presumably would advise the government to accompany tax reform by an expansionary fiscal policy, under the modified assumptions suggested here a deflationary policy might be in order.

In their paper, Borts and Kopecky set out to explain flows of international capital and factor payments within the framework of a growth model. In the simplest formulation of the model, net foreign lending is derived as the difference between ex ante saving and investment which, in turn, depend on the exogenously determined gross national and gross domestic products. Yield differentials do not enter into the determination of foreign investment and the rate of interest is assumed to be the same in all countries.

The model will generate a stream of international factor payments that will grow at the same rate as the economy, while the absolute amount of these payments—at any one point in time—will depend on the growth rate, the rate of interest, and the net capital flow. Apart from the special case when the rate of growth equals the interest rate, however, international factor payments will not equal the capital flow, so that indebtedness will change in absolute amounts though not as a proportion of the GDP.

The model is developed further by separating private and public savings, and including depreciation, the share of GDP imputed to capital, the increase of prices of imported capital goods, income and excise tax rates, and the share of GNP spent by government as variables. Subsequently, the model is specified in greater detail by postulating an aggregate production function of the Cobb-Douglas type with technological change, and assuming that the country produces a single commodity that is either consumed domestically or exported and faces infinitely elastic demand abroad. Investment goods are imported in the amount necessary to provide for the country's investment needs, which are determined by the condition that the capital stock must grow at the same rate as does the supply of labor. The amount exported is a residual sufficient to cover the capital outflow net of international factor payments as well as the value of imports.

These modifications do not alter the basic character of the model. Economic growth is taken to be exogenous, depending only on the growth of the labor supply and the rate of autonomous technical change. In turn, domestic saving and investment will depend on the GNP and the GDP, respectively; and, for given depreciation rates, the rate of interest, tax rates, and prices of capital goods, both will grow at the same rate of equilibrium as the GDP (and GNP). Now, as foreign investment is taken as a residual – the difference between domestic saving and investment – it, too, will grow at this rate and so will foreign factor payments.

The determination of capital flows is thus mechanistic in the model; these flows are assumed to equal the difference between domestically determined saving and investment. No inquiry is made, however, regarding the way in which decisions on foreign investment are arrived at. Should one wish to specify the behavior assumptions concerning the determination of foreign investment, these would have to involve international differences in the rates of return. But once rates of return are introduced, these may also affect domestic saving and investment, which is not allowed in the model.

The absence of behavior assumptions concerning the determination of foreign investment, coupled with the lack of a feedback from rates of return to investment and saving, makes the model appear unrealistic as a description of the real world. A further deficiency is the lack of feedback from foreign investment to economic growth; it is assumed that the latter affects the former but not vice versa.

These weaknesses of the model may be illuminated by a historical example: the flow of capital from Britain to the so-called regions of recent settlement in the early part of the century. At that time, an increasing proportion of British savings were invested abroad. With the share of saving in national income remaining at 10–15 per cent a year, foreign investment came to surpass one-half of domestic saving in Britain.[1] These flows cannot be explained by reference to saving

[1] Cf. A. K. Cairncross, *Home and Foreign Investment, 1870–1913,* Cambridge, Cambridge University Press, 1953.

propensities and the investment needs of exogenously determined economic growth in the capital exporting and importing areas. Rather, capital movement between the two areas responded to investment opportunities, as they were perceived by lenders and borrowers. The flow of capital, in turn, importantly affected the rate of economic growth in Britain as well as in the regions of recent settlement — reducing the rate of growth in the former and increasing it in the latter. Thus, rather than being exogenous, growth has been a *result* of capital flows.

These considerations focus attention on weaknesses in the logical structure of the model. Instead of the causation going from economic growth to investment and saving, and then again to capital flows, one may wish to explain capital flows by international differences in the rates of return, which will affect investment and saving and, ultimately, the rate of growth of the economy. In a more sophisticated model, the two explanations may be combined, that is, one may take account of interactions and feedbacks among the relevant variables.

But how about the statistical results obtained with the model? Due to its year-to-year volatility, the authors do not take capital flows as the dependent variable but use, instead, the amount of foreign factor payments (NFIEA) or, more precisely, the ratio of these factor payments to GNP. Combining data of thirteen industrial countries, excluding the United States, for three subperiods after World War II, they regress this ratio on the variables referred to earlier. The ratio of foreign factor payments to GNP appears to be positively correlated with the saving coefficient, and negatively correlated with the rate of economic growth, the share of GDP imputed to capital, and, in one of the regressions, the share of GNP spent by the government. The coefficient of determination is approximately .5.

While these results are consistent with the hypotheses advanced by the authors, they are consistent with other hypotheses as well. As noted above, the outflow of capital associated with receipts on the factor-payments account will tend to reduce the rate of economic growth. Moreover, to the extent that a high share of capital corresponds to a high rate of return, the situation will attract foreign investment and thus give rise to factor payments abroad. In permitting a larger amount of private and public investment, the inflow of capital will also tend to be associated with a relatively high share of government spending in

GNP. Finally, the possibilities of investment abroad may encourage saving by providing a higher rate of return than would be obtainable otherwise. This might have happened in France around the turn of the century, when it appeared that the high rates of interest paid on Russian bonds induced saving, even on the part of low-income classes.

The statistical results are thus consistent with alternative hypotheses and further testing would be necessary to choose among them, or, rather, efforts would need to be made to test a more sophisticated model that specified interactions among the relevant variables as suggested above. Similar considerations apply to the close correspondence of the regression results obtained from the model at hand and from Borts' earlier work on the (then) 48 states of the United States. This correspondence indicates the similarity of the factors affecting international and interregional capital flows but is consistent with hypotheses other than those advanced by the authors.

I come, finally, to the relationship between observed and steady-state values of the ratio of foreign factor payments (NFIEA) to GNP. Having obtained a low correlation between the two, the authors construct predicted values by utilizing the simplest form of the model and compare these with observed values for the previous period. The correlation coefficient between "constructed" and observed values is .99. But, as the authors also note, the results are hardly impressive considering the stability of the ratio of NFIEA to GNP.

FINANCIAL INTERMEDIATION AS AN EXPLANATION OF ENDURING "DEFICITS" IN THE BALANCE OF PAYMENTS

WALTER S. SALANT · The Brookings Institution

INTRODUCTION

IN THIS paper, I consider the subject described in its title mainly by reviewing and appraising the criticisms that have been made of the hypothesis of international financial intermediation, which, for brevity, I shall call IFI. This hypothesis, first set forth by Professor Kindleberger's essay of 1965 [16], and further expounded and developed by him, Professor Despres, and myself,[1] has elicited both criticism and support. I shall seek to state it, to compare it with other explanations of enduring deficits, and then to discuss the criticisms it has evoked.

Since my title contains words that are more than normally unfamiliar or ambiguous, it is more necessary than usual to begin by defining terms. I shall begin at the end of the title and work forward toward its beginning.

By "balance-of-payments deficit," I shall not mean the deficit on goods and services, or on current account (which also includes unilateral transfers), or the "basic" deficit (which is the deficit on current account and long-term capital transactions combined). I shall confine my meaning to the two concepts of accounting deficits called the "liquidity" deficit and the "official settlements" deficit. Since the problem posed in the title appears to refer to an accounting balance, which records what has actually occurred, I shall use these concepts

---

[1] See [4]. This article and Kindleberger's Princeton essay are not the only, or even the first, papers to have advanced arguments based on the IFI hypothesis, although they may have put the argument most explicitly and the Despres-Kindleberger-Salant article has been the main focus of the criticisms. Among earlier writings are those of James Ingram [14] and Tibor Scitovsky [40, Chapter II].

in that ex post sense. However, since the concern with deficits arises largely because of the widespread belief that they reflect an ex ante disequilibrium in the foreign-exchange market, I shall sometimes refer to that concept as well, making it clear that I then refer to an excess of demand for foreign exchange over supply at the existing exchange rate, and not to an excess of purchases over nonofficial sales.[2]

By "enduring," I shall mean an ex post deficit that has continued for, say, five or more years, an ex ante deficit that can be considered a disequilibrium in the sense that it is inherently incapable of continuing indefinitely, and one that is consistent with equilibrium in that sense.

I forgo defining "explanation," not because it is too simple to need definition but because defining it is too difficult and, I trust, unnecessary for our purposes. It may well be the word in the title that most needs explanation.

The term "international financial intermediation" poses problems for me. Financial intermediation in general consists of the acquisition of a financial asset, accompanied by the simultaneous creation of a financial liability, which may include an equity security (or equity in the form of undistributed net income, provided shareholders are regarded as separate entities from the corporations in which they hold shares). It is represented by the intermediary's increase in financial assets or in financial liabilities, whichever is smaller. Any excess of the increase in its financial assets over the increase in its financial liabilities, insofar as it is not accompanied by decreases of nonfinancial assets, represents saving; insofar as it is matched by decreases of nonfinancial assets, it is disinvestment. That much appears clear. Application of this definition to the international transactions of a country suggests that the measure of IFI should be the increase in a country's foreign financial assets, or the increase in its liabilities to foreigners, whichever is smaller. The excess of increase in assets over increase in liabilities, then, would be foreign investment that is transferred in the form of a

---

[2] The distinction between ex post and ex ante concepts of the balance of payments is discussed in Machlup's essay "Three Concepts of the Balance of Payments and the So-Called Dollar Shortage" [27]. The concept of an "exchange market" balance is equivalent to what that article calls the "market" balance. It is discussed in Gardner [7] and criticized in Machlup's "The Mysterious Numbers Game of Balance-of-Payments Statistics" [27]. See also Lary [23].

current-account surplus (and, perhaps, gold), rather than by inter-mediation.

Arthur Laffer has raised the question of whether that measure is sufficiently comprehensive. I understand that he would include in IFI the entire amount of increase in international financial assets or, at least, the entire amount of increases held by financial intermediary firms, and not merely the amount that is matched by an increase in liabilities to foreigners. His rationale appears to be that a country may intermediate not only between foreign lenders and foreign borrowers, but also between its own lenders and foreign borrowers. One reason that I resist this view is that when we talk about the role of a country as a whole, we, in effect, treat the various entities within it as though they were consolidated. From this aggregative point of view, the excess of an increase in a country's financial assets over an increase in its liabilities to foreigners represents foreign lending but not international financial intermediation.

Another criterion for determining whether an intermediary firm that borrows from a compatriot and lends to a foreigner is engaging in intermediation that can be called international, is whether the inter-mediary service that it provides is being exported or sold to a domestic resident. This presents a more difficult problem. The test might be whether the service that the intermediary renders is paid for by the compatriot of the intermediary or by the foreigner. Analysis of this question might take us far afield and it is not necessary for dealing with the questions I wish to consider here. I shall, therefore, regard IFI as excluding the excess of the increase in a country's foreign finan-cial assets over the increase in its liabilities to foreigners.

The fact that these questions of definition center around capital flows prompts me to observe that most of the conventional theory of international payments equilibrium is irrelevant to the problem that it claims to analyze. This problem is the identification of the conditions of equilibrium in the foreign-exchange market and the process by which equilibrium, once disturbed, is restored—if it is restored. Most analy-ses, however, are concerned only with current-account transactions, which are responsible for only a portion of the bids, offers, and trans-actions in the foreign-exchange market when capital is mobile (i.e., when would-be demanders and suppliers of international financial assets may freely offer, and bid for, foreign exchange, regardless of whether any capital actually moves). To the extent that such analyses exclude the capital account, they do not address the problem. If one defines the issue as one of explaining the causes, effects, and processes of eliminating deficits and surpluses in the total balance of payments, instead of defining it in terms of the foreign-exchange market, the conclusion is the same: until the past few years, most of the literature has been irrelevant, except insofar as the current account does not feed back to the capital account at all.[3]

THE HYPOTHESIS OF INTERNATIONAL FINANCIAL INTERMEDIATION

THE hypothesis of international financial intermediation grew out of a combination of the general theory of financial intermediation pioneered by Gurley and Shaw [9] and the observation that, beginning in 1950, the United States had persistent "liquidity deficits," accompanied for some years by great strength of the dollar in the foreign-

[3] The survey by Anne Krueger [18] supports the conclusion that most of the literature is irrelevant. Early in her article, she says that the first problem of balance-of-payments theory is to formulate the nature of the external constraint. Two paragraphs later, she points out that "the question of the nature of the external constraint is bypassed." She observes that "the analysis of capital flows between countries as an integrated part of payments models has only begun to receive attention. Indeed, . . . there is no widely accepted theory incorporating both current and capital account items. The most thoroughly explored models in payments theory are those which consider only current account transactions and a means of payment" (pp. 2–3). Even Harry Johnson's well-known article, "Towards a General Theory of the Balance of Payments" [15], which sets out to analyze the total balance of payments and makes a valuable contribution toward doing so by distinguishing between stock and flow disequilibria, concentrates on the distinction between expenditure-switching and expenditure-changing, which is a relapse into analysis of the current account. The first word in the title of Johnson's essay suggests that he was well aware that he had taken only some steps in the necessary direction. Further progress has been made by Mundell [32], McKinnon [29, 30], Floyd [6], Laffer [19], Scitovsky [41], and others.

It may be noted that Krueger, after observing that "a deficit only implies a net change in a country's asset position," remarks that "it is obvious that none of these asset reductions could continue indefinitely" (p. 2, col. 2), and later questions the possibility that deficits and net capital inflows can continue indefinitely (pp. 22–23). The conclusion that deficits on current account cannot continue indefinitely is incorrect when applied to growing economies, as I stated [35] and Domar [5] elaborated twenty years ago.

exchange market. This strength reflected a demand for dollar assets by both private foreigners and foreign monetary authorities, who, on balance, preferred dollars to gold for at least most of the 1950's. Even after 1957, when liquidity deficits grew to a size that caused alarm, private holders continued to accumulate liquid dollar assets. In the ten years beginning in 1960, when the data first permit separating increases in holdings of liquid dollar assets by monetary authorities from increases in holdings by other foreigners, the recorded holdings of others have risen in every year; in six of these ten years they rose by more than $1 billion a year. At the same time, outflows of American private capital, mainly long term, increased. Thus, the United States was increasing its foreign financial assets and its liquid financial liabilities to foreigners at the same time. The simultaneous strength of the dollar and the accumulation of dollar assets by foreign monetary authorities during the 1950's showed that the increase in the liquid liabilities of the United States was a response to an increasing total "stock demand." It appeared, therefore, that the United States was performing the role of a financial intermediary.

Three different phenomena could explain this role. The first, put forward by Kindleberger in 1965 [16], is that foreign asset-holders have a higher demand for liquidity, in relation to the supply of such assets made available by foreign borrowers, than American asset-holders have in relation to American supply — with demand and supply in both areas measured at the level and structure of interest rates that would prevail in both areas if capital could not flow between them. In other words, the hypothesis is that foreign asset-holders want short-term or liquid assets in larger quantities than foreign borrowers are willing to supply at the interest rates that would prevail if capital could not move into and out of the United States, with the opposite relationship prevailing in the United States. Although the Kindleberger statement does not say so, financial intermediaries in the two areas must be included among the suppliers and demanders, for the hypothesis requires that foreign financial intermediaries do not fully bridge the gap, and that the United States as a nation is (or American intermediaries are) willing to do so.[4] Americans issue liquid liabilities against them-

[4] The reason financial intermediaries must be included in the model is explained in Salant [37, p. 182].

selves that foreign asset-holders are willing to hold, and they buy the long-term obligations that foreign borrowers want to sell, but cannot sell at equally low yields abroad. This hypothesis of a difference in liquidity preference between the United States and foreign countries can give rise to an exchange of long-term assets for liquid assets.

Such a difference in liquidity preference, however, is not the sole, or even a necessary, explanation of international financial intermediation. Differences in the degree of competitiveness of the financial intermediary industries of the two areas can also account for it; so can differences in their costs of intermediating. That there is either a higher degree of oligopoly or higher costs in the financial-intermediary industries of other countries is indicated by the fact that spreads between the rates banks pay on short-term deposits and the rates that they charge, even to short-term borrowers, are wider abroad than in the United States. These spreads provide an opportunity for financial intermediation by American banks, which are content to accept narrower spreads. Both of these reasons for intermediation could give rise to foreign acquisitions of dollar deposits and American acquisition of short-term claims against (i.e., bank loans to) foreigners.

That these three explanations are distinct and independent becomes clear when one considers that, on the one hand, a pure difference in liquidity preference could give rise to short-term loans by foreigners directly to American industry. In that case, no intermediaries would be involved. On the other hand, if foreign intermediation is more oligopolistic, or is conducted at higher cost than American intermediation, American intermediaries have incentives to operate abroad, even if the liquidity-preference patterns of asset-holders and borrowers abroad are identical with those in the United States.

The fact that foreigners had (and have) a positive demand for increments of liquid dollar assets makes it clear that the amount of the net balance of payments on the liquidity definition is not determined only by influences operating on the transactions placed "above the line" in that definition, with the liquidity balance being a mere residual. Sound theory supports the idea that, even under a monetary system of fixed exchange rates with reserves held in gold and dollars, none of the elements in the account should be assumed to be free to take on any value whatsoever. All, including gold holdings, should be treated as variables, since assets and liabilities must be willingly held. Willingness to purchase and to sell the existing flow of goods and services, and to hold the existing stock of assets at existing prices, is implied in the definition of equilibrium in other parts of economic theory; it should be employed in explanations of the balance of payments as well. The existence of a positive foreign "net-flow demand" for liquid dollar assets and gold combined which exceeds the increase in world monetary gold stocks implies that a deficit of the United States on the liquidity definition is not only consistent with equilibrium in the foreign-exchange market but is a necessary condition of it, inasmuch as it can be met only from a decrease in American gold holdings, an increase in liquid liabilities to foreigners, or some combination of the two. Or, to put it differently, in the absence of a deficit, there would be foreign excess demand for gold cum dollars.

I have said that financial intermediation is performed when, and to the degree that, financial assets and liabilities increase simultaneously. The omission of any reference to the relative liquidity of these assets and liabilities implies that countries acquiring liquid assets and less-liquid liabilities, as well as those acquiring liquid liabilities and less-liquid assets, act as international financial intermediaries. The domestic correlative of this implied proposition is that when an individual borrows from his bank mainly to buy a house, but also uses some of the proceeds to maintain a higher cash balance, he — and not only his bank — is acting as a financial intermediary. Such a definition appears too broad, but narrowing it also raises difficult questions. I shall simply avoid the problem of whether, when financial aggregates are rising, practically everyone is to be regarded as a financial intermediary, treating that question, for present purposes, as unimportant to the general thrust of the IFI hypothesis.

The functions of financial intermediation have been identified by Arthur Laffer (in an unpublished paper dated March, 1968) as gathering information about rates of return (presumably those obtainable on primary loans) and the bringing together of lenders and borrowers,[5]

---

[5] Logically, the brokerage function does not require financial intermediation, since brokers can bring buyers and sellers of financial assets together without owning such assets or issuing financial liabilities against themselves. Presumably, however, a broker can perform this function more efficiently if he holds some inventory of financial assets for his own account so that he may provide them to prospective buyers (lenders) who

thereby reducing the margin between lending and borrowing rates; pooling assets with "somewhat independent" risks and thereby reducing the risks of portfolios; and lengthening the investment-planning period, thereby lowering the relative weight of the risk factor.

Because economies of scale are important in gathering information relevant to primary securities, performing brokerage functions, and pooling assets of varying risks, a large economy like that of the United States is likely to develop the financial-intermediary function most effectively. Its size also plays a role by making it important in world trade, and therefore making its currency more needed for foreign trade transactions to which it is a party; this, in turn, promotes its use in transactions to which it is not a party.

It may help to clarify the concept of IFI further, and at the same time pave the way for discussion of some criticisms of it in the next section of this paper, if I set forth some explanations of enduring deficits that do not, I think, involve international financial intermediation.

ALTERNATIVE THEORIES OF ENDURING DEFICITS

THERE now seems to be widespread, perhaps even general, agreement that when international trade is growing, equilibrium is consistent with liquidity deficits in the balances of payments of vehicle-currency countries, i.e., countries whose currencies are used to make settlements in private foreign trade (Lederer [24], Chittenden [3], Bernstein [2], Mundell [32], Machlup [26, pp. 303 ff.]). Before publication of the first Kindleberger article in 1965, this conclusion was not widely accepted and was certainly rarely stated, although I had suggested that flows of foreign liquid capital to the United States are probably related positively to its bank loans to foreigners, the growth of its exports, and the growth of total world trade [36, pp. 18–19].

Some economists who do not, at least explicitly, embrace the IFI hypothesis appear to agree that a deficit, even on the official-settle-

appear when sellers of suitable primary securities (borrowers) are not at hand. If a broker finances such inventories entirely with his own capital, he is presumably still not a financial intermediary, but to the extent that he issues liabilities against himself, he is one.

ments definition, is consistent with equilibrium for a reserve-currency country under certain conditions. This agreement is based on recognition that under conditions of growth, foreign monetary authorities, as well as private foreigners, may have a growing stock demand (and therefore a positive flow demand) for a reserve currency that would cause the reserve-currency country to have an official-settlements deficit, and that these deficits can be sustained, given either of two conditions. One is that the monetary system provides sufficient growth of net reserves to enable a reserve-currency country, if it manages its affairs reasonably well, to maintain reserve assets in a relation to its liabilities to foreign monetary authorities that will not give rise to self-justifying speculation against the reserve currency. The other is that the monetary system provides no alternative reserve asset to foreign monetary authorities.

The argument that an official-settlements deficit is inconsistent with equilibrium is based on the fact, or assumption, that neither of these conditions is fulfilled. The proponents of the IFI hypothesis neither dispute that one of these conditions must be fulfilled if an official-settlements deficit is to be sustainable nor assert that either is currently fulfilled.[6] They argue, rather, that the provision by the financial center of liquidity to private and official foreigners — and especially to private foreigners — is a useful function, and that the monetary system ought to be adapted to permit its continuation. But this is a normative point. From the point of view of positive analysis, their main difference with others appears to concern the question of what gives rise to enduring deficits. One way of posing the question is to ask, What has caused the deficits actually experienced since World War II by the United States, the country whose deficits the IFI seeks to explain? Have these deficits been accompanied by an equilibrium in the foreign-exchange market (apart from speculation) not calling for adjustment, or do they reflect a disequilibrium to which adjustment has not been made?

[6] When neither condition is fulfilled, and official holders of the reserve currency are known to have access to an alternative form of reserve, liquidity deficits of the reserve-currency country give rise to speculation against that currency. This speculation increases the rate at which reserve-currency balances accrue to foreign monetary authorities and may increase them above the levels that these authorities are willing to hold when they have the alternative of converting such balances into gold. The result is that on this definition, a deficit cannot be sustained indefinitely.

Even "equilibrium deficits," however, may have various causes under conditions of growth. Some economists who do not associate themselves with the IFI hypothesis nevertheless agree that world economic growth may give rise to deficits of the United States that are consistent with equilibrium, and offer explanations based on the concept of portfolio balance. If their view is taken into account, the question becomes whether all deficits based on balanced expansions of asset portfolios in two or more countries reflect something that can be called "international financial intermediation," or whether the concept of such intermediation is more limited, describing only one kind of balanced expansion of portfolios.

Most theories that offer explanations of enduring deficits explain them as a condition of equilibrium. One that does not is Machlup's theory of the "Transfer Gap" in the United States balance of payments, which offers an explanation of persistent *dis*equilibrium [28]. Machlup, after adjusting United States current and capital account data, calculates two series for the period 1950–67, Net Real Transfers and Net Financial Transfers (hereafter referred to as NRT and NFT, respectively). The difference between them, which he calls the Transfer Gap,[7] is intended to be an approximate ex post measure of the failure of adjustment, i.e., the extent to which capital movements that are presumed to be autonomous exceed net exports of nonmilitary goods and services other than the services attributed to American-owned capital abroad.

Machlup finds that, despite substantial annual changes in NFT, NRT tends to change in the same direction, and that the Transfer Gap shows strikingly little variation. Although this Gap had a range of $4.1 billion (between $.7 and $4.8 billion) in the period 1950–67, it lay

[7] Machlup defines Net Real Transfers as the net current-account balance, modified to exclude unilateral transfers, exports of goods and services under military grants, imports of foreign services by the military, and investment income. He defines Net Financial Transfers as the net capital account, excluding changes in reserve assets, in liabilities to foreign official agencies, and in liabilities of the U.S. government or of American banks to others, plus unilateral transfers, military expenditures abroad, and investment income. Thus, the Transfer Gap, being the difference between them, consists of the liquidity deficit plus the increase in nonliquid liabilities of the U.S. government and banks, the net short-term borrowing reported by American residents other than banks, and net errors and omissions [28, pp. 202–207]. See Addendum of this paper for comments on Machlup's treatment of some components of the balance of payments, as well as a confirmation of his broad statistical results based on later figures.

within a range of only $1.4 billion (between $1.5 and $2.9 billion) in eleven of the eighteen years. Moreover, he found that in most years the annual changes in NFT and in NRT were in the same direction. Apparently, changes in NFT were accompanied by changes in NRT that kept the Transfer Gap within a relatively restricted range, suggesting that an adjustment process was at work.

The question that Machlup poses is, Why does this process keep the Transfer Gap within a limited range centering on $2.3 billion instead of on zero? His hunch is that "monetary and fiscal policies became circumspect and restrictive whenever the deficit increased beyond the accustomed level, and became more relaxed and more liberal whenever the payments position showed signs of improvement."

I see nothing in the Machlup hypothesis that makes it implausible on the face of it although I have some reservations about statistical matters. (See Addendum.) Other hypotheses, however, are equally plausible.

One significant question is whether all of the Transfer Gap, as measured by Machlup, represents a disequilibrium in the American payments position. Machlup recognizes that "it is surely incorrect to regard all changes in the size of liquid, near-liquid, and pseudo-liquid dollar assets as accommodating capital movements" (i.e., those induced by conditions in the foreign-exchange market). He cites four reasons why private foreign holders may want to increase their dollar balances and recognizes that two, which are associated with a rise of transactions demand under conditions of growth, are sustainable. (He would include them in his estimate of autonomous financial transfers if they could be identified.)

This demand is the main element of Machlup's Transfer Gap that I regard as sustainable under conditions of growth. I would add only that foreign monetary authorities are affected by similar considerations and, therefore, also have a growing transactions demand for dollar holdings. Thus, I do not have any major difference of opinion with Machlup on the theoretical issue. Note, however, that until the sustainable element of foreign-capital inflow can be identified and shifted from the Transfer Gap to Net Financial Transfers, we cannot know whether the relation between them, so revised, yields incremental relationships as stable as he found or, if it does, whether the

Gap tends to be substantially above zero.[8] As Machlup observed, econometric techniques might make it possible to separate changes in foreign dollar holdings "explained" by growth in world trade from other changes. To me, such tests do not appear needed in order to make it clear that the Transfer Gap can reflect a foreign demand to acquire dollar assets and, therefore, can be consistent with equilibrium.[9] What was pointed out in 1963 in *The United States Balance of Payments in 1968* [38, p. 1] — that "the dollar could be strong in the foreign-exchange markets when the United States had a deficit in its balance of payments" — and agreed to by Machlup [26, p. 303] is now increasingly recognized.[10]

The underlying unanswered question in the Machlup hypothesis is why the American authorities relax their efforts to reduce the Transfer Gap (or the deficit on which their attention is concentrated) before it reaches zero. Lack of an answer to that further question does not

[8] If it were possible to include all accommodating finance in the Gap and get it out of NFT, what should we expect the regression of this Gap on NFT, thus revised, to look like? If the Gap reflected random deviations from an equilibrium level, one should expect that its average value would be zero, and that it would have no significant relation to Net Financial Transfers. These results imply that the constant would not differ significantly from zero. If NFT has a rising trend and there is a lag in adjustment of NRT, one should expect a positive relation between the Gap and first-differences in Net Financial Transfers, with a constant not significantly different from zero.

[9] Arthur Laffer [19] sought to find a statistical "explanation" of monthly flows of private, foreign short-term capital into the United States during the period 1959–64 and concluded that growth in the value of world trade was an important determinant of such inflows. Whether the Machlup Transfer Gap represents a disequilibrium in the payments position might also be tested by seeing how, if at all, the Gap is associated with the position of the dollar in the foreign-exchange market. Such a test, however, would require taking into account complications created by official interventions in the foreign-exchange market and the difficulties of comparing yields on "similar" assets in different countries.

[10] Houthakker, who was led by deficits and purchasing-power calculations to believe that the dollar was overvalued by as much as 15 or 20 per cent in relation to most European currencies even in 1963, after prices in the United States had for several years risen less than European prices, and the mark and guilder had been revalued in 1961 [12, p. 217], conceded in late 1969 that neither the liquidity nor the official-settlements definitions of the net balance "gives an adequate picture of our current international transactions." He observed that during 1969 "in the face of the huge liquidity deficit, the dollar has remained strong in the foreign-exchange market" and that in the third quarter of 1969, the dollar remained strong despite an official-settlements deficit. "If we want to analyze the strength or weakness of the dollar," he said, "these two concepts are of very limited usefulness" [13]. I suspect that similar difficulties would be found with Machlup's version of the Transfer Gap because, as he recognizes, it includes inflows that are not merely accommodating.

mean, of course, that Machlup's hypothesis is incorrect. One explanation might be that the authorities are unwilling to accept the domestic effects of the measures needed to eliminate the assumed international disequilibrium completely, while being willing to accept such a disequilibrium if it is of limited size. One might also explain it through some neurotic characteristic analogous to that which makes some people invariably late for appointments by an almost invariant interval. When pressed, they hurry enough to limit their tardiness to approximately that interval; when they have time to spare, they manage to waste just enough of it to be equally tardy.

But it is also possible that some of the persistent "gap," or "deficit," reflects a foreign demand for increments of liquid dollar assets. It is to be noted that Machlup's empirical analysis takes account, at least explicitly, only of data for the United States. If a reduction of the gap, or deficit, to less than the persistent amount would cause an undue starvation of foreign demand for dollar assets, market forces might be set in motion abroad that would increase the resistance to its further reduction. In that case, the enduring gap, or deficit, would turn out to be the result of foreign demand for more dollars, and would reflect the requirements of portfolio equilibrium, rather than the persistence of disequilibrium.

While Machlup offers an explanation of what he believes to be persistent disequilibrium, others offer theories to explain equilibrium deficits. These theories may be regarded as a subclass of a larger class of theories that explain gross flows of capital in opposite directions. The effects of such gross flows on net balances depend on the types of assets that each area purchases from the other, and on how net balances are defined. If, for example, the flows in both directions are equal and consist of long-term assets other than marketable United States government bonds and notes, they do not affect the basic balance, the liquidity balance, or the official-settlements balance.

One possibility is that ultimate savers resident in an area lend directly to foreign spenders on goods and services, while foreign ultimate savers lend directly to domestic spenders on goods and services. In such a case, there would be no indirect securities (that is, securities issued by intermediaries to finance the purchase of financial assets) and no financial intermediation. Even if the United States borrowed short and lent equal amounts long, it would not have a liquidity deficit in its balance of payments, since in the liquidity definition increases in short-term liabilities to foreigners reported by American nonbanking concerns (other than the U.S. Treasury) are not regarded as liquid liabilities. In this case, there would be gross flows of financial assets in opposite directions that would not involve financial intermediaries and would not cause a deficit either on a liquidity or on an official-settlements basis, but could be enduring. However, if some of the American borrowing from foreigners was done by the U.S. government, financial assets would flow in opposite directions without involving financial intermediary firms, but there would be a liquidity deficit, and it could be enduring. Neither of these possible cases explains the past liquidity deficits of the United States. The second case, involving U.S. government borrowing abroad without the use of financial intermediary firms, can, at least, be imagined as a future possibility; but the first case, in which other American residents do the borrowing, could hardly occur on a scale large enough to be of practical importance on the world scene. Ultimate borrowers and ultimate lenders in different countries do not know enough about each other and cannot get enough information about each other at costs less than would be incurred either by financial intermediaries or by ultimate lenders and ultimate borrowers residing in the same country. Such transactions appear likely to occur, if at all, only in special cases where communication of information is close—for example, between small neighboring countries; between relatives and friends in different countries; where highly sophisticated savers in less-developed countries prefer to lend directly to business firms in a developed country, rather than to any borrowers in their own; or where some sophisticated savers (nonprofit foundations, for example) in a developed country lend directly to finance purchases of goods and services by a borrower in another country.

It would appear—at first sight, at least—that such transactions would always be small, unless brokers came into existence who found ultimate borrowers and ultimate lenders in different countries without being intermediaries themselves. One might suppose that, even then, such a brokerage enterprise would probably use the information for its own benefit, borrowing and lending on its own account, and thereby becoming an intermediary. However, the existence of organized security exchanges and of an industry of more-or-less pure securities brokers suggests that cross-flows of financial assets might be, or become, substantial without intermediaries. A basis for portfolio diversification is provided in the models of portfolio balance described by Markowitz and Tobin. Grubel [8] shows that there is an empirical basis for diversification across national boundaries. It is clear from these models that enduring growth in two areas can give rise to enduring cross-flows of financial assets. Moreover, if there are securities markets in both areas which perform the brokerage function, these flows can be large, even without the direct participation of intermediaries. As the wealth of asset-holders in both areas grows, they may increase their holdings of assets in the other area as well as in their own, so that capital may flow in both directions merely as a result of international diversification of growing portfolios. Grubel's measurements of the benefits to investors of such diversification are confined to investments in common stocks—equal cross-flows of which do not affect deficits or surpluses—but such diversification need not be confined to long-term securities. As Grubel observes, the same motives can also explain flows of short-term securities. Cross-flows of assets that involve foreign investment in liquid claims against the United States contribute to a liquidity deficit in the balance of payments of the United States, irrespective of the amount, or maturity, of the foreign assets bought by Americans.

[While this statement was correct when the paper was given, the concept of the "liquidity balance" to which it refers has since been replaced in U.S. official statistics by that of a "net liquidity balance," which treats changes in liquid foreign assets owned by Americans as offsetting changes in U.S. liquid liabilities to foreigners. This statement, therefore, does not apply to the "liquidity balance" as it is defined at the time of publication.]

These considerations suggest that with growth and efficient brokerage in several areas, there could be an enduring liquidity deficit of the United States without the direct participation of financial intermediary firms. Corresponding diversification of assets by foreign monetary authorities could also give rise to an official-settlements deficit.

Another theory of enduring deficits consistent with equilibrium under conditions of economic growth rests on the assumption that growth of real income, and the increasing wealth that may be presumed to accompany it, give rise to an increased demand for holdings of money. Mundell [32] shows that insofar as a country's money supply bears a fixed relation to its holdings of international reserves, growth in the demand of its residents for domestic money will set in motion forces that produce an over-all surplus in the balance of payments — this surplus being equal to the reserve increase commensurate with the additional supply of domestic money needed to satisfy the increased demand. Thus, according to Mundell, when a country's domestic stock of money bears a fixed relation to its international reserves, the monetary implication of growth is a surplus in its balance of payments. This conclusion, sketched briefly by Scitovsky as early as 1957 [40, pp. 89–90], is contrary to the widely held theory that growth, because of its income effect on the current account, tends to make for a deficit.

Mundell does not explain how his model could lead to enduring deficits for a country with positive growth, but equilibrium deficits for a reserve-currency country that is growing can be derived from his model and some other conditions. If the world economy is growing, the growth in demand for domestic money requires a growth in international reserves, unless countries are satisfied to reduce the ratio of their international reserves to their holdings of domestic money. If *net* international reserves (which, before the advent of Special Drawing Rights, meant world stocks of monetary gold) grow fast enough to satisfy the demand, everyone can have surpluses; then the growth of demand for domestic money does not require any country to have deficits. However, if international monetary reserves consist partly of national currencies, as they do in the present system, growth in the demand for international reserves can be satisfied by growth in the supply of reserve currency as well as of net monetary reserves; and the demand of growing countries will be forced in this direction if the world supply of net monetary reserves grows by less than the growth in demand for total international reserves on the part of non-reserve-currency countries. If the reserve-currency countries allow the supplies of their money to grow enough to meet growing foreign demand for reserves, they will have a growth in liabilities and, since these will be liabilities to foreign monetary authorities, they will have deficits on the official-settlements definition.[11]

Mundell considered the implications of growth for the balance of payments from the point of view of only one country, saying nothing explicit about what was happening in the rest of the world. A positive relationship between the rate of growth and the sign of the net balance of payments of the United States was also found by Williamson in his study of the United States in the century before World War I [45]. Arthur Laffer, in [20] and in his paper for this conference, has developed the monetary implications of growth for the balance of payments in a world model. His hypothesis is that while a positive rate in a country's growth does not necessarily make for a surplus in its balance of payments, a more rapid rate of growth than that of the rest of the world does so, unless the growth of its money stock relative to that of the rest of the world is sufficient to offset this effect; it has an adverse effect on the country's current-account balance but a larger favorable effect on its capital account. (The model in [20] abstracts from government activities, including open-market operations, which modify the results.) Laffer tests his hypothesis empirically by regressing, first, changes in the ratios of current-account balances to GNP's of twenty-two countries on changes in their percentage rates of income growth and, then, changes in the ratios of their total net balances of payments to their GNP's on the same variable.[12] He finds that both regressions are consistent with his hypothesis; net balances on goods and services (measured relative to GNP) are negatively related to rates of growth, as conventional theory suggests, but *total* net balances (also measured relative to GNP) have a positive relation to growth. Laffer finds that the latter, as well as the former, result is statistically highly significant.

---

[11] Mundell's simple model, in depicting this argument, employs an assumption that the demand for money by the residents of a country is only for domestic money. This assumption leaves no room for changes in monetary liabilities to foreign private holders. The distinction between domestic holdings of domestic money, domestic holdings of foreign money, and foreign holdings of domestic money is also absent in Harry Johnson's earlier article [15].

[12] The changes measured take place between the periods 1951–55 and 1956–60, and between 1956–60 and 1961–65, for twenty-two countries. The data for the two time periods are pooled, so that the number of observations is twice the number of countries. Current account and total net balances are measured as ratios to gross national expenditure.

If a rate of growth faster than that of the rest of the world gives rise to an excess demand for both goods and money, and an excess supply of nonmonetary financial assets (i.e., to a balance-of-payments surplus), a relatively slow one gives rise to a deficit. Thus, we have here another theory of enduring deficits.

This theory, too, can account for equilibrium deficits without invoking the operation of financial intermediary enterprises. It posits a growth in the transactions demand for money associated with economic growth that could be fully satisfied by an increase in the stock of what, for the world, is "outside money," i.e., net world monetary reserves. However, if that demand is not satisfied by this means, it can be satisfied only by an expansion of what, for the world, is "inside money." This implies that a portion of the increase in reserves of surplus countries is matched by an increase in the liquid liabilities to foreigners of a reserve-currency country, which—being liquid—must be liabilities of a financial intermediary. Under the conditions posited by the theory, as implied by Mundell and explicitly developed by Laffer, the relatively fast-growing world outside the reserve-currency country has an excess of net capital imports over current-account deficit, i.e., a surplus. If the differential in growth generates a surplus large enough to exceed the growth in the world's net monetary reserves, the theory implies that the reserve-currency countries, in the aggregate, have capital exports along with growth of liquid liabilities, and are thereby providing international financial intermediation. Thus, the Mundell-Laffer theory implies that growth in the world outside the reserve-currency countries, if sufficiently faster than the growth in those countries, creates a demand for international reserves that is satisfied by more rapid growth in gross than in net international reserves. This theory need not imply a higher *level* of preference for liquid assets in the non-reserve-currency countries, but it does imply a more rapid *growth* in their demand for liquid assets, attributing that to greater rapidity of economic growth and a resulting greater increase in transactions demand.[13]

[13] See the Addendum for additional comments on Laffer's model and for suggestions for further research relating to it.

CRITICISMS OF THE HYPOTHESIS

THIS section of the paper reviews some of the criticisms that have been made of the IFI hypothesis. In doing so, it distinguishes between criticisms of the hypothesis as positive economic analysis of the function performed by the United States in the world economy, and criticisms of the normative or policy propositions espoused by proponents of the hypothesis, i.e., criticisms which assert that continued intermediation by the United States is undesirable because it is incompatible with the existing international monetary system or with related institutions. I make this distinction because, as I have stated earlier, I do not regard the hypothesis as saying that the international monetary system, especially as it existed until March, 1968 (which, be it noted, is not at all the same as the present system), was perfectly compatible with the continued performance of IFI by the United States or by any other country—particularly if one includes, along with the international monetary system, the prevailing ideas about how it should work. It is no criticism of a theory about what is occurring in the world to say that it should not be occurring, or that its continuation is inconsistent with existing institutions. Economists can and do analyze the causes—and, however ineffectually, the effects—of inflation without making recommendations for or against it. Similarly, they can logically find a prevailing practice economically beneficial but inconsistent with existing institutions, as one might do in the case of banking without a central bank and deposit insurance. If their analysis is correct, perhaps the institutions should be made compatible with performance of the function, rather than terminating the performance of that function.

Because I am here chiefly interested in the positive analysis, first I shall deal quickly with the criticisms of the normative and policy aspects of the hypothesis.

CRITICISMS OF POLICY IMPLICATIONS

1. One criticism of the IFI hypothesis is that the mere explanation or interpretation of the role of the United States in the world as the performance of financial intermediation is not enough to sustain

confidence in the dollar (Halm [10]). This observation may be correct, but it seems to me relevant only to whether the United States could continue to perform the role of the financial intermediary under the gold-dollar monetary system as it existed before March, 1968.

Moreover, I doubt that this criticism is, in fact, correct. The confidence that the system requires is in the foreign-exchange value of the currency, and the degree of that confidence cannot be inferred from the ex post balance-of-payments position, especially if and when that position shows a deficit only on the liquidity definition. A deficit on that definition is compatible with an excess demand for dollars in the foreign-exchange market at the existing price, and a surplus is compatible with an excess supply of dollars.

2. It is also argued that the high volatility of short-term capital impedes the operation of national monetary policy and that — since performance of the intermediary function implies that the intermediary receives continuing inflows of foreign short-term capital — the performance of intermediation itself is incompatible with the operation of national monetary policy. This argument assumes that any interference with the operation of monetary policy on a national basis is bad, which one might question. Perhaps more important from an analytical point of view is the fact that the volatility of foreign-owned short-term capital would create problems, irrespective of whether one interprets the presence of such capital as evidence of financial intermediation or in some other way. The issue of volatility has little to do with the IFI hypothesis; it has to do, rather, with the compatibility of a fixed-rate monetary system and national stabilization. Although the encouragement of IFI certainly increases the amount of international short-term-asset holding, any financial center, if faced with a liquidity crisis, must either have very large reserves or credit facilities or be forced to adopt direct controls or internal policies that it may regard as undesirable on domestic grounds. Whatever the relation between IFI and the volatility problem, I see nothing wrong with solving it by having a lender of last resort that has, or can create, resources large enough to handle crisis situations.

3. Also dependent on the existing monetary system is the criticism that short-term capital flows cannot permanently and increasingly finance the deficits of the intermediating country in the face of a deteri-

oration of its net reserve position. It is not necessary, however, that the increase of liquid liabilities of a financial center, which is inherent in its performance of the intermediary function, should cause deterioration of the relation of its liquid assets to its liquid liabilities. A monetary system designed to permit performance of this function should also provide for adequate increases in its reserve assets.

4. It is also true, as some critics point out, that the system of adjustable pegs accentuates the problem created by volatile short-term capital movements. But this fact alone does not imply that IFI is undesirable. It simply raises the question of whether the advantages of international integration of capital markets outweigh the disadvantages of fixity of rates, or of their discontinuous adjustment. Indeed, the implication that the discrete adjustability of exchange-rate pegs is upsetting could well lead to the conclusion that rates should be fixed absolutely and forever. That might make short-term capital less volatile. In any case, a world monetary system comparable to the national monetary system of a large country like the United States would make the volatility of capital harmless; reserves would be adequate to take care of such movements, while the fixity of exchange rates, if it could be made credible, would drastically reduce the incentives for such capital to move in large quantities at one time.

All of the above arguments concern the incompatibility of international financial intermediation with a particular system of international monetary institutions. Analytically—and also in practice, given a long enough period of time—that incompatibility, if it exists, does not refute the proposition that IFI accounts for deficits. At most, it implies that the continued performance of this function and the continuation of the existing monetary system are incompatible. That incompatibility no more implies that the function should not be performed than it implies that the system should be changed and the performance of the function be continued.

CRITICISMS OF POSITIVE ANALYSIS

To turn now to the criticisms of the hypothesis as positive economic analysis, a number of these criticisms appear to me to be based upon misunderstanding of the hypothesis.

1. The first criticism is that the theory conflicts with the fact that American financial investment in Europe—more precisely, the cumulative flow of capital since 1955—has fallen short of the flow of capital from Europe to the United States if one excludes movements of European official funds. One element of this argument, as stated by Triffin [43, pp. 9–15], is the assumption that the hypothesis claims to explain only the cross-flows of financial assets between Europe and the United States, i.e., that it relates only to regional bilateral movements of capital. It is true that the article in the *Economist* and Kindleberger's first article did focus attention on asset preferences and capital markets in Europe. Nevertheless, a bilateral interpretation is not implied by the hypothesis. For the United States to provide financial intermediary services to the rest of the world, it is no more necessary that it lend to the same country or area from which it borrows than it is necessary for a domestic financial intermediary to lend to someone doing business on the same street as the depositor from which it borrows. Financial intermediation is being performed if the United States borrows from Europe and lends to other areas just as much as if it borrows from, and lends to, Europe. Thus, the hypothesis cannot be refuted by an appeal to bilateral statistics.

2. A second criticism by Triffin, which also seems to me invalid as a refutation, is that a substantial portion of the assets acquired by the United States takes the form of direct investment. The criticism asserts that these investments should be excluded because "the initiative certainly lies far more with the American investor than with any autonomous desire of Europeans to raise long-term funds in the United States, as is assumed by our three authors" [43, p. 11]. As I have explained elsewhere [37, pp. 186–187], if such investment increases, it makes no difference to the validity of the analysis whether the buyers or the sellers of the equity take the initiative. When American investors buy equity interests from European investors, the sellers receive liquid funds. They may have no demand for them at the existing interest rates yielded by liquid funds, but they must do something with the proceeds. They can hold them in liquid form or they can buy securities of intermediate or long term, thereby reducing interest rates for those maturities and transferring the liquid assets to someone else who, at the lowered interest rates, is willing to have more liquid assets. It is

obvious, therefore, that even direct investment by the United States increases European private holdings of liquid assets in the form either of dollars or of the national currencies of the holders. Whatever sellers of the equities do, American direct investment contributes to easing the credit or capital markets, or both, in the foreign country; correspondingly, any restrictions on such investment will tighten those markets. Thus, the analysis applies to direct investment as much as to other forms of capital flow.

3. A third objection is that a substantial part of the foreign holdings of liquid dollar assets in the United States is held by official, not private, holders. Triffin, after appearing to regard this fact as a valid objection, then recognizes that the intermediation thesis takes into account the possibility that the demands of private foreigners for liquid assets may be for assets denominated in their national currencies, rather than in dollars. It asserts that this demand is satisfied by the acquisition of balances in national currencies from the foreign resident's central bank, which accepts the excess dollars supplied in the private market.[14]

4. Another criticism is that foreigners make some long-term investments in the United States and that these capital flows do not reflect a desire for liquid assets. This objection ignores the postulate that the basis for IFI is not confined to differences in liquidity preference between the United States and other countries. As I have already observed, that difference was the sole basis for it in Kindleberger's

---

[14] See [43, pp. 12–13]. In a footnote, Triffin says that this extension of the intermediation thesis to the dollars accumulated by foreign monetary authorities seems to be defended mostly by Kindleberger, and that I express considerable doubts about it. My doubts extended only to the portion of dollars accumulated by foreign monetary authorities unwillingly; I had, and have, no doubt that the portion held willingly should be regarded as part of the intermediation process. I even questioned the proposition that the "involuntary" changes in official holdings of dollars should be excluded, because no holdings are "involuntary" in relation to the alternatives that confront the holder. If the alternative of gold were not available to the monetary authorities, there would be no question that the entire increase of holdings should be included, and little question that they would have been as large as, or larger than, when the gold alternative was available. In other words, I see no reason to suppose that without the gold alternative, foreign monetary authorities would have increased their total reserves by smaller amounts. (See [37, p. 186n].) The question of whether "involuntary" foreign official holdings are to be excluded from intermediation is analogous to the question of whether the amount of intermediation performed by a bank is diminished when a portion of the liquid assets held by depositors is withdrawn in the form of currency.

original article [16], but I expanded his model and pointed out two other possible bases for it. I introduced into the model a financial-intermediary industry, which was not explicitly present in his model, and pointed out that IFI could arise both from differences between the market structures of the American and foreign financial-intermediary industries, and from differences in their economic efficiency and consequently their costs of doing business. In this expanded model, the maturities of financial assets flowing to the United States need not differ from the maturities of those flowing from the United States.

Moreover, the conventional criterion for judging the liquidity of financial assets does not coincide fully with that implied even by the original Kindleberger model. The conventional criterion is that an asset is liquid if its original maturity is less than a year or if it is a U.S. government security (other than a Roosa bond). However, a more satisfactory economic criterion would take into account the incremental costs and benefits of early, as contrasted with later, liquidation of an asset, including in these benefits the imputed values of convenience and anxiety avoided. The difference in costs between liquidating a given asset at different periods of time affects its liquidity. Comparing the liquidity of different assets requires a comparison of the costs of liquidating them in the same periods of time. On this economic criterion, shares in American Telephone and Telegraph Corporation are a more liquid asset than, say, a nine-month loan to a borrower known only to the residents of a small country with a limited capital market. Even shares in a New York-based real-estate investment trust may be more liquid than such a loan. It follows that even a model in which IFI is based entirely on differences in liquidity preference would not be upset by a demonstration that foreign holdings of American assets were predominantly in long-term assets other than U.S. government securities or that American holdings of foreign assets were of short-term character. American assets held by foreigners, despite being long-term and nongovernmental, may still be liquid, while foreign assets held by Americans may be short-term but relatively illiquid. For this reason, as well as for reasons I have mentioned in the second section of this paper, IFI can take place without giving rise to a deficit on either the liquidity or official-settlements definition. It seems clear, however, that the cross-flows of financial assets could take a form that would give rise to deficits on either definition. How enduring these deficits would be is discussed below.

5. Another objection to the IFI hypothesis is based on the view that such intermediation constitutes a monetary veil behind which nothing "real" occurs. I confess to finding this objection a bit confusing. It appears to involve two different points, but they were put forward together and seem to depend on the same allegation of fact. One such argument is that, since the long-term funds that have been lent remain in the lending country as short-term balances, nothing happens in international trade. Real resources stay where they are; the long-term lender does not have to produce an export surplus and the short-term lender does not add, via imports, to his productive capacity. The second and logically separable part of the argument is that if such intermediation has no trade effects, "the European countries ought to be able to mobilize their own productive resources through their credit systems and their monetary and fiscal policies. The roundabout way of an international financial circuit . . . is basically unnecessary" (Halm [10, p. 5]).

In my view, this argument errs on several grounds. First, the context makes it clear that the statement "real resources stay where they are" means that long-term lending does not produce an export surplus and that short-term lending does not produce an import surplus. (In both cases "surplus" is to be interpreted as a larger surplus or smaller deficit than the country would otherwise have had.) The mere absence of effects on export or import surpluses, however, does not imply that the allocation of resources *within* each country is the same as it would have been in the absence of intermediation. Thus, the fact alleged does not imply that there is no effect at all on international trade, for the composition of trade may be affected. Similarly, it does not imply that the short-term lender has not added to his productive capacity. Moreover, he may add to his real income or welfare without adding to his productive capacity by getting more liquidity or a higher interest rate for a given liquidity. This criticism implies that financial intermediation, whether domestic or international, has no real effects if it does not alter the relation between the aggregate income and the spending on goods and services of any economic unit. It entirely ignores the possibility that intermediation may alter the composition of spending between consumption and capital formation or affect the allocation of resources in other ways. It is inconsistent with the concession, made in the same criticism a few sentences later, that IFI may have lowered European interest rates and thereby stimulated investment. If an effect on real resources required an effect upon trade surpluses or deficits, changes in tariffs would also be of no significance because, like IFI, they would have no effect on the equilibrium levels of trade surpluses or deficits but would "merely" affect the allocation of resources within the partner countries.

Moreover, even if the trade effect of IFI were nil, which we have no reason to suppose is the case, it would not follow that foreign countries "ought to be able to mobilize their own productive resources through their credit systems and their monetary and fiscal policies," if "ought to be able" means that they would do so, given their preferences as to assets and liabilities and their existing financial-intermediary institutions. The question, "Why should not the same effect be achieved through domestic monetary policies, since no real resources are transferred?" is asked but not answered. That the same effect is, in fact, not achieved in this way indicates that there must be some reason.[15]

Although it may be true that "we cannot see" any real changes in current accounts in the raw statistics, this does not mean that the cross-flows of assets have no effect upon them, any more than our inability to "see" (in the same sense) the gains from international trade means that they do not occur. To the extent that the United States lends long and borrows short, and lends at higher rates than it pays for what it borrows, it earns an interest differential which shows up in the current account. If foreigners find it profitable both to lend to the United States and to borrow from it, the United States is apparently providing some financial services to foreigners. The provision of these services can be

[15] In Halm's essay, the theme of the section entitled "The Transfer Problem" appears to be that the dollar glut existing at the time he wrote was a side effect of a massive transfer problem, made inevitable by the failure of the United States to develop export surpluses large enough to transfer economic and military-aid expenditures, and that this dollar glut gave Europe excessive liquidity and threatened it with "imported inflation." I assume that this is intended to be a summary of his views and not an independent argument, because in the latter case, the reasoning would be circular. Thus, the statement that "only when the trade balance cannot be adjusted will it be necessary to match, to that extent, foreign long-term borrowing or foreign short-term lending in the form of privately or officially held dollar balances" assumes the points at issue.

explained by the theory of international trade in the same way that the provision of any service to foreigners is explained: the country providing the services apparently has a comparative advantage in supplying them and earns a return in doing so. The return appears as a difference in interest rates and financial commissions, but from the point of view of economic analysis, it can be imputed to payment for resources of labor and capital invested in intermediation, just as payment for any current export may be so analyzed. Viewed in this light, the long-run growth of the intermediary country's liquid liabilities to foreigners does not represent an excess supply of its money or near-money but a growth in foreign stock demand for financial assets denominated in its currency. A growth in that stock demand is consistent with portfolio balance when the foreign economy is growing.

The real gain to foreigners from the importation of financial intermediary services may take several forms. First, the availability of a foreign financial asset that provides the lender or borrower with a larger bundle of utilities in the form of interest, safety, and liquidity than he could have obtained at home increases his real income directly. Second, it may cause lenders to increase saving out of given incomes, as compared with what such saving would have been if the only intermediation available were provided domestically, and thereby make possible a higher level of investment. Third, the better access of borrowers to capital is likely to result in a better allocation of a given amount of investment outlays than would otherwise occur. Fourth, beside increasing investment by increasing saving at given levels of income, an increase in efficiency of intermediation reduces the amount of capital and labor absorbed in the process of transforming saving into investment, and thereby makes more resources available for investment or consumption.

DIFFERENCES IN LIQUIDITY PREFERENCE?

Let us consider criticisms of some of the specific reasons given by proponents of IFI for the role that they attribute to the United States. The original and best-known reason is the hypothesis, first put forward by Kindleberger, that the preference for liquidity abroad is higher than that in the United States, with the result that foreign borrowers are less willing to supply short-term financial obligations and foreign lenders prefer financial assets in liquid form—these preferences, in both cases, being interpreted as relative to those of American borrowers and lenders. As a result, foreign long-term assets can be more readily sold in the United States and liquid financial assets more readily supplied by the United States than abroad.

6. One criticism of this view has been made by Lamfalussy, first in a book [21] and more recently in a paper [22]. As I understand Lamfalussy's argument, it denies that European households shun medium- and long-term financial assets and that European corporations have difficulty in selling them. He says "the new issue market in common stock has been much stronger in Europe than in the United States" and cites figures showing that in the years 1960–65 four EEC countries, Germany, France, Italy, Belgium, . . . issued about two and a half times as many new equities as the United States, i.e., an annual average of $3.4 billion compared to $1.0 billion in the United States. Moreover, he says that, in 1964, German and French corporations issued long-term and medium-term debt equivalent to $8.4 billion, compared with only $4.9 billion in the United States, and that the proportions for the period 1960–65 as a whole were "not basically dissimilar" from these. He argues that both common stocks and bonds issued in Europe by corporations and various government agencies are sold to a large extent directly to households on a retail basis, with intermediaries playing a relatively small role in the new issues market. As a result, direct security purchases form a substantial proportion of the acquisition of financial assets by European households. These households direct only a relatively small proportion of their financial investments toward those institutional investors (insurance companies and pension trusts) which in the United States and the United Kingdom are the main purchasers of securities.

Lamfalussy says nothing, however, about the yields required to induce households to purchase these securities. That they purchase a substantial proportion directly and relatively little through intermediaries, and that the proportion purchased by intermediaries for their own accounts is small in comparison with the corresponding proportion in the United States, tells us nothing about the relative liquidity preferences of households in Europe and the United States but only something about the *relation* between preferences of households and intermediary institutions in Europe compared with the corresponding relation within the United States. The facts he cites are consistent with European households having liquidity preferences that exceed those of American households if that excess is less than the excess of European intermediaries' liquidity preferences over those of American intermediaries. In other words, European households may buy a larger proportion of medium- and long-term securities directly and a smaller proportion indirectly than do American households, not because their liquidity preference is lower than that of American households, but because the liquidity preference of European intermediaries is greater than that of American intermediaries. Lamfalussy is observing single points on curves relating price and quantity, whereas the hypothesis concerning relative liquidity preferences has to do with the relative positions of the curves. One can deduce nothing about that by observing differences in actual quantity without reference to price.

Lamfalussy also points out that the total of direct securities purchases and investments with institutional investors forms approximately the same proportion of the gross acquisition of financial assets by households in Europe as in the United States or in the United Kingdom, except in France, where the proportion is lower. Or, to put it the other way around, the accumulation of currency, bank deposits, and saving deposits forms the same proportion in all countries considered, except in France, where that proportion is higher. This fact does not have the implications that Lamfalussy sees in it. If, in continental Europe, accumulations of liquid assets are as high as they are in the United States or the United Kingdom but yield much less, that fact supports, rather than conflicts with, the thesis that liquidity preference is higher in Europe.

Lamfalussy also points out that a high proportion of bonds taken up by households in Europe is issued by financial intermediaries, which finance themselves by issuing bonds and which, in turn, grant long-term or medium-term loans to corporations. He refers here to nationalized or seminationalized intermediaries of a specialized kind, which he says scarcely exist in the United States and are much weaker in the United Kingdom. These intermediaries and the commercial banking system lend long-term and medium-term funds to corporations in proportions unknown in either the United States or the United Kingdom. He says that ten-year loans have become a common feature in continental banking, with the result that the dominant types of financial intermediary in Europe are the commercial banks and the specialized lending institutions, just as the dominant types in the United Kingdom and the United States for long-term finance are the insurance companies and the pension-trust funds. The European commercial-banking system also sells securities directly to households in the manner of retail stores. He recognizes that this is not intermediation but retail distribution and says it explains the well-known weakness of the secondary markets. He then adds, somewhat mysteriously, that "it must be clearly understood that the weakness of the secondary market is not [the] equivalent of a weakness in the primary market. Indeed, the opposite is true." I should suppose that weakness of the secondary market must be important in reducing the demand for such financial assets and a major factor making for high yields. That primary markets in Europe "have been able to accommodate substantially larger equity and debt issues than the U.S. market" implies nothing about comparative liquidity preference among European households. We can infer nothing about demand curves for these assets merely from the volume of transactions; we must know the yields at which transactions occur.[16]

As Lamfalussy makes clear, there are very serious and perhaps insuperable difficulties in making valid comparisons of interest rates on various financial assets in the United States and in continental Europe. (He does not, however, relate his discussion of interest rates to his discussion of asset acquisitions and so does not appear to recognize my first criticism.) He points out that taxation and a number of other

[16] Lamfalussy says that the belief that liquidity preference is higher in Europe than in the United States grew from the observation that per capita currency circulation is higher in countries like Belgium, Switzerland, France, Italy, Germany, and the Netherlands than in the United States or in the United Kingdom. He points out that both the EEC and the OECD reports on capital markets reaffirm the belief that this is a sign of a higher liquidity preference and quote more extensive statistics than the partial figures of currency holdings alone. This fact played no part in my participation in the IFI hypothesis, since, in my view, differences in liquidity preference are only one possible explanation of international financial intermediation. Kindleberger assures me that his views about national differences in liquidity preference were not based on the relative quantities of holdings of one asset, unrelated to asset prices.

related facts make it difficult to find out what interest rates really are. For example, European households keep a very high proportion of their semiliquid assets in savings deposits, but the liquidity of these deposits varies considerably from one country to another and, indeed, from one financial institution to another. Moreover, the tax advantages attached to these deposits are so complicated that it is impossible to separate the interest differential from the tax differential; the latter may vary even among different deposits in a given financial institution, depending on the size of the holder's family. Because of these and other complications, a 3½ per cent rate on savings deposits can be as high as 6 or 7 per cent in terms of pretax interest income in some cases and only 4 per cent, or even less, in others.

Lamfalussy further argues that if one tries to bypass these difficulties by measuring the cost of financial intermediation directly, one may encounter even more formidable difficulties. It is difficult to compare costs and returns of various categories of liabilities and assets, and if we give up the effort to measure the yields on categories of assets, "the comparison of the over-all yield gap would be only marginally more significant, for banks earn more and more income from fees, underwriting and selling commissions which have nothing to do with their borrowing and lending activity" [22, p. 6]. This fact may make it difficult to use the difference between the total revenues and the costs of intermediaries to test the hypothesis that international financial intermediation arises from differences in liquidity preference; but I doubt that it rules out the possibility of testing the more general hypothesis, in which such differences are only one of several possible explanations. The fees and the underwriting and selling commissions to which he refers are largely returns earned by supplying services that, in my view, are very much a part of the provision of financial intermediation, whether one chooses (as I do) to regard them as part of borrowing and lending activity or not. Surely the underwriting and selling commissions that a borrowing firm pays are part of the net cost of the capital that it thereby obtains. It is hard to see what fees, underwriting and selling commissions Lamfalussy refers to as "having nothing to do" with borrowing and lending activity.

A second kind of evidence relevant to the intermediation hypothesis, as applied internationally, centers on interest-rate relationships.

Any research workers ambitious enough to try to put interest-rate statistics on a comparable basis, despite the difficulties pointed out by Lamfalussy, should be aware of exactly what interest-rate relationships the IFI hypothesis implies. It is sometimes said that the hypothesis implies that the gap between the yields of liquid and illiquid financial assets should be greater in Europe than in the United States. I would make two observations about that statement. First, differences in liquidity preference would cause the spreads between liquid and illiquid assets to differ in the two areas when international intermediation does not take place; but when it does take place, it may be expected to reduce, if not eliminate, the difference in spreads, just as trade reduces or eliminates differences in spreads among prices of traded commodities. Consequently, what the researcher should look for is a difference between areas in the spreads between yields of liquid and illiquid assets when international intermediation is impeded, a reduction in that difference when the impediments are reduced, and an increase in it when they are increased. He should not expect to find great differences in spreads between the major markets in Europe and the United States while such intermediation is occurring.

For this reason, I suggest that it might be worthwhile to see how the difference in spreads between liquid and illiquid assets in the United States and in Europe changed between the years before 1958 and the period from 1959 to approximately the middle of 1963. (The end of 1958 was the time when European currencies took the largest jump toward convertibility, and the middle of 1963 marks the period when obstacles were first imposed on the export of American capital in the form of the Interest Equalization Tax.) One might also compare the difference in spreads in the second of these periods with the difference in the period beginning in, say, 1965, when the United States imposed substantial barriers to the outflow of American capital. I do not know if detailed research would show that these are the best terminal points for the relevant periods or whether some technique other than the use of discrete periods would be better. The essential point is that one must not merely compare European and American spreads but must see whether any difference between them is affected by the possibilities, or actual occurrence, of financial intermediation across national boundaries.

My second observation is that a difference between areas in their spreads between yields on liquid and illiquid assets is relevant only to that strand of the IFI hypothesis attributing intermediation to differences in liquidity preferences. It is not relevant to the hypothesis that such intermediation can also result from differences in efficiency between European and American intermediaries, or from differences in the market structure of the financial industries in the two areas, which might make the American industry more competitive and willing to accept lower rates of return. To test this hypothesis, one would need data on the gross margins of financial intermediaries in the two areas when international intermediation does not take place, and when it does, in order to see how the relation between the gross margins is affected by it. These gross margins would be reflected in spreads of interest rates, but not necessarily in spreads between rates on liquid and illiquid assets. Indeed, if this explanation is to be distinguished from the explanation based on liquidity preference, the effects of differences in liquidity should be eliminated, the relevant spreads becoming those between the interest rates that intermediaries pay to lenders and those that they charge to borrowers.

Then, in order to make a further distinction between the explanations based on differences in efficiency and those based on differences in market structure or competitiveness, one must break the spread between the rates that intermediaries pay and those that they charge into its two components — costs of inputs (other than funds borrowed) and profits — and one must examine how that breakdown is affected by the absence, or presence, of international intermediation.

Thus, at least two kinds of difference in spread have to be taken into account: those between yields on liquid and illiquid assets, and those between borrowers and lenders. It is obvious that even if we make a crude dichotomy of financial assets (merely between liquid and illiquid assets) and forget that the degree of liquidity is a continuum, we have four categories — liquid assets, illiquid assets, borrowers, and lenders — so that we have to consider four interest rates both in the United States and abroad.[17]

[17] A test of the liquidity-preference explanation requires an examination of the effects of international capital flows on the differences between rates charged to borrowers on more and less liquid funds in the two areas, and also on the differences between the rates

7. Another criticism of the hypothesis of differences in liquidity preference is that the evidence shows that Europeans actually are willing to acquire long-term securities. Thus, E. M. Bernstein, in private conversation during 1967, expressed the opinion that among several attributes of financial assets, the one most important to European lenders is the currency in which the security is denominated. The next most important, he thought, is the nationality of the obligor, which affects the laws governing the transaction, the rights of ownership, and other considerations. He ranked the maturity of the asset last among these three attributes, characterizing it as unimportant. As evidence that currency of denomination has primary importance, Bernstein cited the large volume of long-term Eurodollar bonds that Europeans buy.

Aliber [1] also appears to conclude that maturity is not important. He states that the curve relating yield to maturity on the dollar liabilities of the French government is less steep than that depicting its franc liabilities, and argues that since the risk of default is the same on both, the difference reflects exchange risk. I agree that such a difference in slopes seems to show that the market takes account of exchange risk and regards it as correlated with the maturity of the securities, but this does not imply that maturity (or, better, liquidity) is *not* a factor. Aliber also finds that the yield curve on the dollar liabilities of the French government is steeper than that on the dollar liabilities of the United States government, the difference largely reflecting the risk of default, there being no difference in exchange risk. (He notes that it may also reflect differences in marketability in the two countries.) Aliber reports only the difference in steepness of the yield curves; he does not tell us anything about the relationship of one curve to the other at either end of the maturity scale. Since the difference in steepness of these curves for securities of the same obligor reflects a correlation between assessment of exchange risks and maturity, it cannot tell us anything about the relative importance of exchange risk and

paid to lenders on more and less liquid fund in the two areas. A test of the other two explanations, considered together, requires a comparison of the differences between borrowing and lending rates in the two areas. Furthermore, a test that distinguishes between the efficiency and competitiveness hypotheses requires a breaking down of the differences between borrowing and lending rates into their cost and profit components, as already indicated.

maturity. To appraise the role of exchange risk alone, we need to know whether the dollar obligations of the French government bear a higher yield than its franc obligations at the short end of the maturity scale. If they do not, I would infer that exchange risk is not rated very high. It is true that the slope of the yield curve for franc obligations is a purer measure of preferences for short over long maturities (i.e., it is a measure free of exchange risk), and that the greater steepness of the curve for dollar obligations, which reflects both maturity and exchange risk, establishes the presence of exchange risk. It does not, however, establish the absence of a preference for liquidity; nor does it establish whether that preference is higher, lower, or equal to the corresponding preference in the United States.

Considering all of the points discussed in this section, I conclude that no valid empirical evidence has been produced that damages the hypothesis that preference for liquidity is lower in the United States than abroad. I think it also true, however, that no empirical evidence has been adduced that gives stronger support to that hypothesis than to alternative hypotheses. If these conclusions are correct, the hypothesis retains the same status that it had when first put forward; no additional relevant evidence has been adduced on either side.

GREATER COMPETITIVENESS OF AMERICAN INTERMEDIARIES?

8. The only reference that I have seen to my own suggestion that the United States may export financial intermediary services because American intermediaries are more competitive than those in Europe is Halm's observation that "an explanation of high interest rates by monopolistic features of the European credit market is difficult to maintain in view of the extreme fungibility of the market object" [10, p. 4]. Citing the statement of Despres, Kindleberger, and myself [4] that money is "costless to store and to transport" and "the easiest commodity to arbitrage in time and in space," he says that these reasons not only prevent government control of international capital flows from working well but make ineffective private attempts to compartmentalize the domestic credit market and to raise interest rates by monopolistic devices.

It appears to me that "attempts" are not necessary to compartmentalize the domestic credit market. In the absence of intermediaries, the domestic credit market would be compartmentalized with no effort on the part of anyone; positive attempts are needed to break down the compartments, and this is what financial intermediaries do. How effectively a domestic intermediary industry does that job depends, of course, upon its degree of competitiveness, which is influenced by both the aggressiveness of the members of the industry and the ease of entering it. The same comment may be made about raising interest rates by "monopolistic devices." Interest rates to borrowers will exceed those paid to lenders by more, the less competitive the intermediaries are. They need not resort to devices specifically designed to widen those margins if they are not aggressively competitive or if there are institutional barriers to entry. Neither of these aspects of competitiveness of the European industry relative to that of the United States (aggressiveness and ease of entry) can be appraised on the basis of a priori assumptions or inferences from the ineffectiveness of government controls over capital flows — especially when the ineffectiveness of controls results partly from the very competitiveness of American intermediaries, which the hypothesis asserts to be superior.

Students of European capital markets appear to support the view that competition among intermediaries is restricted in Europe, and have suggested that it is more so than in the United States. Unfortunately, their testimony consists of expressions of judgment rather than statistical information. The study by Sidney Rolfe says the following:

> Whereas in the U.S. there exists intense competition among several types of lenders for long-term business . . . these tasks tend to be more neatly parcelled into noncompetitive sectors in Europe. Thus, long-term lending is largely left to special credit institutions that refinance themselves by bond sales and to savings banks using a certain ratio of deposits. This imparts a degree of rigidity to lending markets, although changing conditions make this rigidity less warranted. Thus, while the liabilities of commercial banks have increasingly changed from demand to savings deposits, requiring less liquidity, the structure of assets has in most countries not followed suit [34, p. 49].

Rolfe goes on to say that while statistical evidence is sparse and "probably not too meaningful," so that qualitative judgment must be relied upon, some evidence does exist. In his judgment, what forces borrowers to go directly to the public is the inability of financial intermediaries to supply long-term credit through the bond market. Since retail sales of bonds to households are more expensive than bulk sales to institutions, and since "households have a high liquidity preference" (his words), such borrowing will cost more. It requires a greater spread of rates. He then cites data to show that the spread of interest rates in Europe is higher than that in the United States, measuring these spreads by the difference between interest rates paid on short-term savings deposits and those paid by borrowers for long-term or bond loans. He presents data showing that during 1964, in virtually every European country, that difference exceeded 3 per cent, while in the United States it was about half of one per cent.[18]

The group of experts appointed by the EEC, in their report *The Development of the European Capital Market,* noted that the scope of operations of European financial intermediaries was limited by exchange control, fiscal laws, and exchange risks, but was also impeded by other restrictions deriving from operating rules imposed on the financial institutions by law or by administrative regulation [42, Chapter 12]. While the experts made these observations in connection with the participation of intermediaries in the European capital market and their operation across national boundaries, it is clear that the impediments they refer to operate domestically as well. They point out, for example, that banks (except in the Netherlands, and in Germany in the case of very large sums) are restricted in the interest rates that they may pay on deposits, and that these restrictions limit the extent to which the banks may bid against each other for deposits. One reason for these maximum limits was the prevention of competition likely to endanger the security of deposits. A second reason was to allow the banks to lend at reasonable rates. Surely a limitation on the price of inputs is not an effective way to limit the price of the output;

[18] The text of Rolfe's study refers to Table 10 but clearly should refer to Table 11. His data come from the OECD's *Study on Improvement of Capital Markets,* Annex V, C(66)78.

indeed, it is more likely to limit the number of suppliers and expand the gross margins of those already in the industry.

The EEC experts found that the problem of supplying capital to enterprises and public authorities is not attributable to any general lack of saving but to the way in which saving is channeled to would-be users. The experts note that there is an "excessive bias toward liquidity" and a "reluctance to engage in risk investment and contractual saving." They express the view that these features may not reflect the preferences of transactors as much as the nature of present financial structures (p. 77), which results from factors that emerged after two periods of "fundamental imbalance." The first, in the 1930's, led to restriction of competition in the field of credit and to rigid compartmentalization of various national markets. The second was the reconstruction period after World War II, when "the dearth of savings in relation to the swollen requirements led the authorities to introduce measures for compulsory direction of available resources" (p. 78).

GREATER EFFICIENCY OF AMERICAN INTERMEDIARIES

9. The view that the comparative inefficiency of European capital markets has been an important cause of capital movements between the United States and Europe, in the sense of cross-flows of capital, has not, to my knowledge, been criticized. Donald Heckerman [11], while agreeing that such inefficiency has probably caused European interest rates—especially long-term rates—to be high, questions whether it can explain capital movements "between the United States and Europe." The argument makes clear, however, that he refers to *net* capital flows from the United States to Europe, which are not at issue in the IFI hypothesis.

CHANGES IN THE BALANCE OF PAYMENTS OF
THE UNITED STATES SINCE 1968

10. Lamfalussy, in his 1969 paper [22], writes that serious doubts are also cast on the Despres-Kindleberger-Salant thesis by changes in the balance of payments of the United States in 1968. In that year "the

United States has ceased to acquire long-term private assets; in fact, there has been a *decline* in the net long-term private claims of the U.S. economy over the rest of the world." He recognized that this decline had been going on for only eighteen months when he wrote, and that it would be unwise to regard these changes as a reversal of trends; nonetheless he thought that the mere emergence of the decline cast serious doubts on the theory.

I agree that what happens in so short a period has little significance for our theory. For that very reason, I do not understand how the new development can cast doubt on it. Nothing in the IFI hypothesis denies the possibility of short-period movements counter to the general trend that it envisages.

Moreover, the hypothesis does not deny that foreign reluctance to hold long-term securities can be overcome by high expected rates of return. A large element — $1.3 billion — in the change to which Lamfalussy refers was an increase in foreign purchases of American common stocks. Expected rates of return on common stocks include both the dividend yield and the expected capital gain. When the American stock market is booming, this expected rate of return may be high indeed and may attract foreign long-term capital. But such a flow is also likely to be short-lived — and it turned out to be short-lived in this instance. Foreign purchases of American common stocks, which had risen in the last quarter of 1968 and the first quarter of 1969 to $792 million and $752 million, respectively, fell to $152 million and $169 million, respectively, in the second and third quarters of 1969. The decline in net purchases began after January, 1969, when they totaled $360 million, and was still in progress in June, when foreigners sold $105 million of American stocks, on balance. This decline coincided with a reversal of the rise in American stock prices. (A chart showing quarterly data on foreign purchases of U.S. stocks, U.S. stock prices, and European stock prices appears on page 33 of the September, 1969, *Survey of Current Business.*)

As Kindleberger observed in discussing Lamfalussy's paper, the fact of disintermediation in 1968 — if it was a fact — does not imply that intermediation had not occurred before. I doubt, moreover, that the changes of capital flows in 1968, which provided the occasion for Lamfalussy's argument, constituted disintermediation. Disintermediation is the reversal, although perhaps only a partial reversal, of prior intermediation. One would expect it to take the form of repatriation of American capital from abroad, accompanied by repatriation of foreign capital invested in the United States, i.e., disinvestment by each area in the other. Even reductions in investment abroad by both areas would be only a reduction of intermediation if such investment remained positive. Apparently neither of these matching movements occurred in 1968.

I noted earlier that holdings of publicly issued American common stocks were so readily marketable that they could be regarded as liquid assets; their purchase by foreigners conforms to the IFI hypothesis very well. I concede that even if we regard the increase of such holdings as the acquisition of liquid assets by foreigners and deduct them from the inflow of foreign long-term capital to the United States, the remaining increase in foreign long-term capital flows into the United States in 1968 would still be $2.3 billion. If we also deduct the nearly $500 million representing the United Kingdom's liquidation in 1967 of American securities other than U.S. Treasury issues, an increase of $1.8 billion in foreign long-term investment in the United States between the two years remains to be explained. Of this $1.8 billion, nearly $1.7 billion consisted of an increase in new issues of securities sold abroad by American corporations. This rise of American borrowing abroad does not appear to be inconsistent with the intermediation hypothesis when one considers that it was forced by governmental barriers to capital flows. In any event, this increase was very short-lived; the annual rate of such sales relapsed in the second and third quarters of 1969 to $730 million, little more than one-third of the 1968 level.[19]

The theory of financial intermediation suggests that disintermediation or reductions in intermediation, whether domestic or international, could result from one of three causes. One of them is that the asset preferences of ultimate lenders and the liability preferences of ultimate borrowers might become more similar, so that purchases of primary

[19] See Table D-2 of December, 1969, *Survey of Current Business*. New issues of securities sold abroad by American corporations exclude both securities issued by subsidiaries incorporated abroad and funds obtained abroad by American corporations through bank loans and other credits.

securities by ultimate lenders would increase relative to financing as a whole, and the use of intermediaries would become less necessary. A second possible cause is a decline in foreign capital formation that reduces the demand for the services of intermediaries, given the proportion of foreign capital formation financed through intermediaries. A third possibility is an increase in the demand for capital in the intermediary country itself, which would cause the rate of return on domestic capital formation to rise relative to the rate its citizens could earn by buying financial assets of other long-term borrowers. (An illustration of this cause of disintermediation in the case of a single financial intermediary firm would be an insurance company's liquidation of some of its security holdings to purchase housing, because the return on housing has improved relative to that on securities.) Any of these changes would cause total financial disintermediation or reduce total intermediation. They could also have the same effect on the portion of total intermediation that is international.

In addition, international financial disintermediation could also be caused—or international intermediation reduced—by a shift within a given total of intermediation from international to domestic intermediation. Such a shift would occur, for example, if the comparative efficiency (or competitiveness) of intermediaries increased in the area in which it was relatively less. Such an improvement in European intermediation may, in fact, have been occurring in the past few years, as the growth of mutual funds in Europe suggests.[20] Such a development might reduce American financial intermediation in Europe in the future, but it probably does not explain the large changes in the capital account of the United States between 1967 and 1968. Neither does the second of the possible causes mentioned above. A decline in capital formation abroad does not appear to have occurred.

[20] Since these mutual funds seem to have been promoted mainly by Americans, it is a fine question whether their growth should be considered part of American financial intermediation. If an American starts a mutual fund in Europe, selling its shares to Europeans and investing only in European securities, is it American or European intermediation? Technically, if the company is American, the intermediation is international. This is one illustration of the difficulty of attaching much importance to the concept of nationality in an increasingly integrated world. The anomaly of calling this intermediation international is no greater than that of calling the sale of a commodity by an American in Europe to a European embassy located in Washington an American export and a European import, which is what balance-of-payments rules call for.

The third possible cause is a more plausible explanation of the changes in the capital account in 1968; capital formation in the United States rose steadily through 1968 and 1969. Assuming, however, that the rate of expected increase in American prices will be reduced in 1970 or 1971, and taking into account the declining percentage of capacity utilized, the present high rate of capital formation in the United States relative to that abroad (and measured in dollars) appears likely to be temporary.

From these considerations, I am unable to find anything that casts doubt on the international financial intermediation hypothesis, either in the evidence adduced by Lamfalussy, or in any other facts that I have observed about recent changes in the balance of payments of the United States.

CONCLUDING OBSERVATIONS

AFTER looking over the recent developments in the theory of international payments, I conclude that the compatibility of payments deficits with equilibrium under conditions of growth is now accepted so widely among leading students that it can be regarded as an established theorem. The major development of the past few years appears to me to be the introduction of the portfolio approach. In fact, the general acceptance of that approach may be the most notable feature of this conference. Continuing portfolio balance combined with continuing world economic growth can account for cross-flows of financial assets, with or without deficits, on any definition. The explanation of deficits as the consequence of international financial intermediation is one member of the larger class of portfolio theories, both because portfolio theories can account for cross-flows of financial assets that do not imply deficits or surpluses, and because they can account for cross-flows that do not logically require financial intermediaries. A question which remains is whether all theories of equilibrium deficits invoke international financial intermediation in some form; some of them may be independent of it.

Restoration of a disturbance in portfolio balance, or lagged adjustment to a change in desired portfolios, involves a stock adjustment that is transitory. Continuous maintenance of balance in growth of portfolios such as accompanies world economic growth can account for continuous cross-flows of financial assets consistent with equilibrium. Continuing cross-flows of financial assets can account for, but do not necessarily imply, enduring deficits in balances of payments on both the liquidity and official-settlements definitions. Whether they imply liquidity deficits depends on whether or not a net transfer of assets officially labeled "liquid" occurs. Whether they imply official-settlements deficits depends on whether a net transfer of officially held assets occurs.

Present theories of balance in growing portfolios include growth in demand for the stock of money or near-money. Some explain it as necessary for transactions purposes, and associate the growth in demand with growth in income. Others associate it with precautionary balances and the growth of wealth. A theory that excluded growth in both transactions and precautionary demand for money or near-money would be extremely unrealistic; realism probably requires us to include the growth of both types of demand. International financial intermediation comes into this picture when one country can supply assets other than outside money in excess of the demand of its own residents at a particular price, while others can supply them at that price (plus the price-equivalent of barriers to their international flow) only in amounts that fall short of their domestic demand. These excess supplies and demands may reflect differences in tastes (e.g., Kindleberger's difference in national liquidity preference), including the tastes of the intermediaries themselves; they may reflect differences in the costs of providing the intermediary services (including variations in the profits demanded, which, of course, are part of supply price); or they may reflect differences in the competitiveness of intermediaries.

I think we are far from able to estimate how much of the liquidity deficit of the United States can be accounted for by a comparative advantage in the provision of financial-intermediary services. An estimate really calls for an econometric model covering most of the world and designed to explain the demand and supply conditions for liquid assets of residents in different areas. It should distinguish between official and nonofficial suppliers and demanders in the markets for financial assets; between interest rates on assets representing different degrees of liquidity, or perhaps risk (defined as variance of price); and also between the rates charged by financial intermediaries to borrowers and the rates paid by them to lenders. It must also take into account levels of world trade (with which Laffer found foreign private demand for dollars to be associated) and many other variables. Without such a model, we can only make guesses. My own guess would be, on the one hand, that financial intermediation by the United States does not account for all of the liquidity deficit of the past two decades, but, on the other hand, that the increase of liquid liabilities of the United States willingly held by nonofficial foreigners—$11.6 billion in the period 1960 to 1968, or 58 per cent of the total liquidity deficit of $20.0 billion—implies that it does account for much of that deficit.

ADDENDUM

MACHLUP'S "TRANSFER GAP OF THE UNITED STATES"

The following comments on Machlup's results and treatment of various components of the balance of payments of the United States may be of interest for their own sake although they deviate from the main track of this paper.

First, Machlup's broad statistical conclusions are reinforced by revised data for 1964–67, new data for 1968, and preliminary estimates for 1969. From 1966 to 1967, NRT and NFT (as he defines them) changed in the same direction, whereas the figures available when he wrote showed them as changing in opposite directions. In 1968 and 1969, they also changed in the same direction. Therefore, the number of years in which annual changes were in the same direction becomes 16 out of 19, instead of being 13 out of 17. The revised figures reduce the Transfer Gap in 1966 and 1967, but only by $0.2 to $0.3 billion, on the basis of rounded figures. For 1968 and 1969, it was $2.6 billion and $3.9 billion, respectively, compared with the (revised) average of $2.5 billion for the period 1950–67.

Machlup's calculation of the regression of NRT on NFT for the period 1950 to 1966 (omitting 1967 because it lay well off the regression line of the other observations) gave the equation

$$NRT = -1.74 + 0.92NFT,$$
$$(1.8) \quad (6.0)$$

with $R^2 = 0.71$ and the t-statistics indicated by the numbers in parentheses under the parameters. Using the figures now available for years since 1964 and fitting the regression to data for 1950 to 1969, the equation becomes

$$NRT_{rev} = -1.50 + 0.85NFT_{rev}.$$
$$(1.6) \quad (5.9)$$

The $\bar{R}^2$ is 0.64, the coefficient of NFT remains significant at a 99 per cent level of confidence, and the constant term remains not significantly different from zero at a 95 per cent level of confidence. These equations imply the following relationships of transfer gaps (TG) to NFT:

$$TG = \$1.74 \text{ billion} + 0.08NFT$$

$$TG_{rev} = \$1.49 \text{ billion} + 0.15NFT_{rev}.$$

The relationship between changes in NRT and NFT, which is reflected in these derived equations as a relationship between changes in NFT and TG, appears to imply that an adjustment process is at work, but the nonsignificance of the constant's difference from zero appears to throw doubt on the finding that the adjustment process tends to stop when the transfer gap is still substantially larger than zero. Nevertheless, I refrain from concluding that this makes Machlup's hypothesis implausible, partly because the t-values in both equations are very close to being statistically significant, and partly because untutored instinct tells me that, judging from the figures for the Transfer Gap, it would be foolish to bet that for any year in the near future that gap would be as low as 8 or even 15 per cent of Net Financial Transfers, as an equation with a zero constant and the same coefficients for Net Financial Transfers would imply.

The foregoing calculations accept Machlup's allocations of the detailed categories of the international transactions of the United States. Some of the transactions that Machlup treated as autonomous and included in Net Financial Transfers might as plausibly be treated as accommodating and placed in the Transfer Gap, while the increase in long-term liabilities of American banks might reasonably be treated as Net Financial Transfers, rather than as part of the Transfer Gap. One may also question his treatment of dividend income as a Net Financial Transfer, rather than as a Net Real Transfer (of which it would be a negative component), since it presumably responds partly to changes of income abroad and thus contains a large nonautonomous factor. American receipts of income on direct investments abroad have risen steadily from $1.3 billion in 1950 to $5.6 billion in 1969, and their excess over American payments of both private interest and dividends to foreigners has risen from nearly $1.0 billion in 1950 to nearly $2.0 billion in 1969. Shifting these transactions would not affect the Transfer Gap, since it would affect NFT and NRT by equal amounts, but it might affect the stability of the relationship between them. Any further experimentation with the Machlup idea might include an investigation of the behavior of some of these components of the balance of payments, reallocating them and revising the estimates of the Transfer Gap on the basis of the results, and then going on to examine the relationship of the revised Transfer Gap to Net Financial Transfers.

LAFFER'S "ANTI-TRADITIONAL THEORY"

The Laffer model [20] appears to me a promising extension and test of ideas suggested or formulated by Scitovsky and Mundell concerning the effects of growth on the balance of payments, therefore justifying some further comments and suggestions.

It is clear that Laffer's model can account for enduring deficits of the United States when its economy is growing more slowly than the weighted world average. However, the model also implies that the United States would have a surplus when it grows more rapidly than other countries but other countries are, nevertheless, growing. The question then arises, How can the increasing transactions demand of other countries for their domestic money be satisfied when the world's net monetary reserves grow by less than is required to support a supply of their domestic money that satisfies the growth in foreigners' demand?

One answer may be that the assumption in Laffer's model of a fixed relation between a country's domestic money and its international reserves breaks down; i.e., that this ratio must be reduced. There is another possible answer, however. Laffer defines the net balance of payments as the change in *gross* international reserves and applies this definition to the United States as well as to other countries. Consequently, the increase in American liabilities to foreign monetary authorities does not affect his measure of the balance of payments, but it still provides foreign monetary authorities with the reserve basis for increasing their domestic money supplies. Thus, when the world outside the United States grows absolutely, but less rapidly than the United States, its need for a growth of reserves (a balance-of-payments surplus) can be reconciled with a surplus of the United States on Laffer's definition, assuming that the United States has an increase in reserve assets and, at the same time, a larger increase in liabilities to foreign monetary authorities. In that way, the Laffer model is consistent with a deficit of the United States, defined as a decrease of *net* reserves, that can endure not only while American growth is slower than that of the rest of the world but when it is faster, too.

It is true that in such a situation, other countries in the aggregate would have a surplus or zero net balance, which result appears inconsistent with Laffer's theoretical hypothesis. While it would not necessarily cause failure to meet his empirical test, which relates *changes* in the ratio of net balances to GNP to *changes* in rates of growth relative to the world's average rate of growth, this inconsistency shows that the model tested does not represent the theoretical hypothesis precisely. To pass Laffer's empirical test, it is sufficient for deterioration in a country's rate of growth relative to the world's growth rate to cause a deterioration in the ratio of its net balance to its GNP. To conform to the theoretical hypothesis, however, a rate of growth lower than the world average should produce a negative ratio of net balance to GNP. Thus, the behavior of a country's balance of payments could pass the empirical test without conforming to the theoretical hypothesis.

I have mentioned above that Laffer applies his measurement of net balances as changes in gross reserves to the reserve-currency countries (the United States and the United Kingdom), as well as to other countries. His theoretical hypothesis, however, appears to call for the application of a net-reserve concept to these countries, since increases in the demand of their residents for money can be satisfied not only by increases in the total amount of the domestic money stock, which require increases in reserve assets, but also by the transfer of foreign-owned portions of an unchanged money stock to domestic ownership. Such transfers reduce liquid liabilities to foreigners and thereby make for a surplus—at least on the liquidity definition; and if the reduction is in liabilities to foreign official holders, on the official-settlements definition, too. Laffer has informed me that his empirical results would not be much affected by exclusion of the United States and the United Kingdom from his test. It would be of interest to know how his results would be affected if the net balances of these two countries were included but were defined as changes in net, rather than gross, reserves.

The Laffer model in [20] abstracts from governmental creation of nominal money. Laffer, like Mundell before him, recognized that the creation of such money by governments may contribute to explaining actual events. As Mundell noted [32, pp. 137–38], while growth—or, in Laffer's model, relative growth—*per se* tends to induce a balance-of-payments surplus, "credit creation" by the monetary authority of the growing—or relatively growing—country can reduce or eliminate that surplus. In his paper in the present volume, Laffer has developed and tested an expanded model that allows for the creation of nominal money, thereby overcoming that limitation of his earlier one.

REFERENCES

1. Aliber, Robert V., "Exchange Risk, Yield Curves, and the Pattern of Capital Flows." *Journal of Finance,* May, 1969, pp. 361–370.
2. Bernstein, Edward M., Statement in *Contingency Planning for U.S. International Monetary Policy.* Joint Economic Committee, 89th U.S. Congress, 2nd Session, Washington, 1966.
3. Chittenden, George, Statement in *The Balance of Payments Sta-*

tistics. Hearings before the Subcommittee on Economic Statistics of the Joint Economic Committee, Part 2, 89th U.S. Congress, 1st Session, Washington, 1965. Relevant excerpts printed in *Morgan Guaranty Survey,* June, 1965.

4. Despres, Emile, Kindleberger, Charles P., and Salant, Walter S., "The Dollar and World Liquidity: A Minority View." *Economist,* February 5, 1966, pp. 526–529. Republished with minor additions as Brookings Reprint No. 115, April, 1966. Latter version reprinted in L. H. Officer and T. D. Willett, eds., *The International Monetary System: Problems and Proposals.* Englewood Cliffs, New Jersey, Prentice-Hall, Inc., 1969.

5. Domar, Evsey D., "The Effects of Foreign Investment on the Balance of Payments." *American Economic Review,* December, 1950; reprinted in Domar, *Essays in the Theory of Economic Growth.* New York, Oxford University Press, 1957.

6. Floyd, John E., "International Capital Movements and Monetary Equilibrium." *American Economic Review,* September, 1969, pp. 472–492.

7. Gardner, Walter R., "An Exchange-Market Analysis of the U.S. Balance of Payments." *International Monetary Fund Staff Papers,* Vol. VIII, May, 1961.

8. Grubel, Herbert, "Internationally Diversified Portfolios: Welfare Gains and Capital Flows." *American Economic Review,* December, 1968.

9. Gurley, John G., and Shaw, Edward S., *Money in a Theory of Finance.* Washington, The Brookings Institution, 1961.

10. Halm, George, "International Financial Intermediation: Deficits Benign and Malignant," in *Essays in International Finance,* No. 68. Princeton, International Finance Section, June, 1968.

11. Heckerman, Donald G., " 'Inefficient' European Capital Markets as an Explanation of International Capital Movements." *Journal of Money, Credit and Banking,* February, 1969, pp. 121–123.

12. Houthakker, Hendrik S., Statement in *The United States Balance of Payments — Statements by Economists, Bankers, and Others on The Brookings Institution Study,* "*The United States Balance of Payments in 1968.*" Submitted to the Joint Economic Committee, 88th Congress, 1st Session, Washington, 1963.

13. —— "The Public Interest in the Balance of Payments." Speech at the Conference of the Financial Analysts Federation, Baltimore, November 20, 1969. Multilithed. Washington, Council of Economic Advisers.

14. Ingram, James C., "A Proposal for Financial Integration in the Atlantic Community," in *Factors Affecting the United States Balance of Payments*. A compilation of studies prepared for the Subcommittee on International Exchange and Payments of the Joint Economic Committee. Washington, 87th Congress, 2nd Session, 1962.

15. Johnson, Harry G., "Towards a General Theory of the Balance of Payments," in *International Trade and Economic Growth: Studies in Pure Theory*. London, George Allen and Unwin, Ltd., 1958. Reprinted in R. E. Caves and H. G. Johnson, eds., *A. E. A. Readings in International Economics*. Homewood, Illinois, Richard D. Irwin, Inc., 1968.

16. Kindleberger, Charles P., "Balance-of-Payments Deficits and the International Market for Liquidity," in *Essays in International Finance,* No. 46. Princeton, International Finance Section, May, 1965.

17. Kolm, Serge-Christophe, "La Monetisation Americaine du Capital Français." Mimeographed. Undated (available in November, 1967).

18. Krueger, Anne O., "Balance-of-Payments Theory." *Journal of Economic Literature,* March, 1969, pp. 1–26.

19. Laffer, Arthur B., "Short-Term Capital and the Voluntary Credit Restraint Program." Multilithed. September, 1968.

20. —— "An Anti-Traditional Theory of the Balance-of-Payments." Unpublished paper.

21. Lamfalussy, Alexandre, *Les Marchés Financiers en Europe*. Paris, Presses Universitaires de France, 1968.

22. —— "European Capital Markets and Financial Intermediation by the United States." A paper given at the International Economic Association's Conference on the Mutual Repercussions of North American and Western European Economic Policies, Alvor Praia Hotel, Algarve, Portugal (August 24 to September 4, 1969).

23. Lary, Hal B., *Problems of the United States as World Trader and*

Banker. New York, National Bureau of Economic Research, 1963.

24. Lederer, Walther, Statement in *The Balance of Payments Statistics.* Hearings before the Subcommittee on Economic Statistics of the Joint Economic Committee, Part 2, 89th Congress, 1st Session. Washington, 1965, pp. 166 ff.

25. Lindert, Peter H., "Key Currencies and Gold, 1900–13." *Princeton Studies in International Finance,* No. 24. Princeton, International Finance Section, 1969.

26. Machlup, Fritz, Statement in *The United States Balance of Payments—Statements by Economists, Bankers, and Others on The Brookings Institution Study, "The United States Balance of Payments in 1968."* Joint Economic Committee, 88th Congress, 1st Session. Washington, 1963.

27. ――― *International Payments, Debts and Gold.* New York, Charles Scribner's Sons, 1964.

28. ――― "The Transfer Gap of the United States." *Banca Nazionale del Lavoro Quarterly Review,* No. 86, September, 1968. Reprinted as No. 11 in *Reprints in International Finance.* Princeton, International Finance Section, 1968.

29. McKinnon, Ronald I., "Portfolio Balance and International Payments Adjustment," in Robert A. Mundell and Alexander K. Swoboda, eds., *Monetary Problems of the International Economy.* Chicago, University of Chicago Press, 1969.

30. ――― "Private and Official International Money: The Case for the Dollar," in *Essays in International Finance,* No. 74. Princeton, International Finance Section, April, 1969.

31. ――― and Oates, Wallace E., "The Implications of International Economic Integration for Monetary, Fiscal, and Exchange-Rate Policy." *Princeton Studies in International Finance,* No. 16. Princeton, International Finance Section, 1966.

32. Mundell, Robert A., "Growth and the Balance of Payments," in *Monetary Problems of the International Economy.* Chicago, University of Chicago Press, 1968.

33. ――― Statement to Republican Seminar on Balance-of-Payments, Planning and Research Committee, The Republican Conference. House of Representatives, Washington, January 24, 1968; re-

printed in Congressional Record, 90th Congress, 2nd Session, February 5, 1968, pp. 2133–2163. Washington, 1968.

34. Rolfe, Sidney, *Capital Markets in Atlantic Economic Relationships*. Paris, The Atlantic Institute, 1968.

35. Salant, Walter S., "The Domestic Effects of Capital Export Under the Point Four Program." *American Economic Review, Papers and Proceedings,* May, 1950, pp. 495–510.

36. —— "A New Look at the U.S. Balance of Payments." Statement before the International Finance Subcommittee of the Senate Banking and Currency Committee, March 18, 1965, printed in *Continuing Deficits in Our Balance of Payments and the Resulting Outflow of Gold: Part I,* 89th Congress, 1st Session; and (with revised figures) as Reprint 92 by The Brookings Institution, May, 1965.

37. —— "Capital Markets and the Balance of Payments of a Financial Center," in William J. Fellner, Fritz Machlup, and Robert Triffin, eds., *Maintaining and Restoring Balance in International Payments.* Princeton, The Princeton University Press, 1966. Reprinted as Brookings Reprint No. 23, December, 1966.

38. —— Despres, Emile, Krause, Lawrence K., Rivlin, Alice M., and Tarshis, Lorie, *The United States Balance of Payments in 1968.* Washington, The Brookings Institution, 1963.

39. Salin, Pascal, "Macroeconomic Equilibrium in International Relations." A paper prepared for the Congress of the International Economic Association, Montreal, 1968. Multilithed.

40. Scitovsky, Tibor, *Economic Theory and Western European Integration.* London, George Allen and Unwin, Ltd., 1958.

41. —— *Money and the Balance of Payments.* Chicago, Rand McNally & Co., 1969.

42. Segré, Claudio, et al. *The Development of a European Capital Market* (Report of a Group of Experts). Brussels, European Economic Community Commission, November, 1966.

43. Triffin, Robert, "The Balance of Payments and the Foreign Investment Position of the United States," in *Essays in International Finance,* No. 55. Princeton, International Finance Section, September, 1966.

44. Whitman, Marina von N., *International and Interregional Pay-*

ments Adjustment: A Synthetic View. Princeton Studies in International Finance, No. 19. Princeton, International Finance Section, 1967.
45. Williamson, Jeffrey G., *American Growth and the Balance of Payments 1820--1913.* Chapel Hill, University of North Carolina Press, 1964.

INTERNATIONAL FINANCIAL INTERMEDIATION: INTERPRETATION AND EMPIRICAL ANALYSIS

ARTHUR B. LAFFER · University of Chicago

IN THEIR now classic article, Despres, Kindleberger, and Salant [2] set forth a novel framework for analyzing the balance of payments of the United States. If correct, their analysis, which is referred to as the hypothesis of International Financial Intermediation (IFI), leads to the following conclusions: (*a*) Persistent deficits, within some limits, may not be an indication of a disequilibrium position in the sense that the dollar is overvalued relative to other currencies. Instead, these deficits may actually be necessary for a healthy world economy. (*b*) Lack of confidence in the dollar is brought about by a failure to understand the international role of the dollar. (*c*) Unless controls are exceptionally pervasive, the normal tools of macroeconomic policy are likely to fail in controlling the deficit. A fourth point derived from the Despres-Kindleberger-Salant analysis is that most interpretations of the deficit of the United States incorrectly emphasize a need for additional external liquidity, when instead, the private capital market can, and should, provide this external liquidity in addition to internal liquidity.

The purpose of this paper is twofold. First, a formal model will be developed that is consistent with my conception of the IFI hypothesis. The model will be formalized in such a manner that its implications can be systematically derived. Secondly, the hypothesis itself will be tested with quarterly data covering ten years of balance-of-payments experience of the United States.

In general, one can visualize equilibrium analyses of the balance of payments in three broad classes of models. The first class, which is

NOTE: Comments and discussions with R. Coates, E. Fama, and R. Mundell proved very helpful to me. I also want to thank R. Cocks and R. Winter for helping in the statistical work.

661

currently accepted orthodoxy, assumes that, both conceptually and empirically, the monetary movements, i.e., appr ximately the below-the-line account of the "official settlements" balance, is the residual. The second class of models assumes that the bond market, i.e., an approximate equivalent to the capital accounts of the balance of payments, is the residual. The IFI hypothesis fits into this second class of models. The third class which, to my knowledge, has never been seriously advanced, assumes that the residual is the current account of the balance of payments. Naturally, in a fully specified complete system, it should make little difference which account is the residual. (In the traditional literature on the balance of payments, the residual account is often referred to as being induced.) Given the progress of general-equilibrium theory to date, such consistency among the three broad categories does not exist. In general, the empirical results tend not to reject the IFI hypothesis. It is, however, impossible with our data to distinguish this hypothesis from one that postulates a world in which the bond market is the residual.

At the outset, it must be emphasized that any attempt to formalize the IFI hypothesis must discard many of the caveats and qualifications which appeared in the original article. This simplification is not done to ridicule the model or to expose it to the maximum risk of rejection. The purpose is merely to present the essential features of the model in as simple a manner as possible. One major strand of the Despres-Kindleberger-Salant paper is omitted entirely from the present analysis — the trade in longer-term financial assets. Although admittedly important from many points of view, trade in such financial assets does not materially affect the over-all balance-of-payments figures. In addition, from an empirical viewpoint, data on gross long-term flows would be difficult to obtain.

1 INTERNATIONAL FINANCIAL INTERMEDIATION: INTERPRETATION

THE IFI hypothesis begins by postulating a demand for money on the part of private sectors in the individual countries. In general, three arguments enter this demand function: the over-all price level, real income, and a price term for money. Both the over-all price level and real income affect the demand for money positively and with roughly the same magnitude. The demand for money, however, is negatively related to the price term for money. Thus, the higher the price of money, the lower the demand. The "price of money" should be thought of as an interest rate which includes implicit price factors – the availability of money and so on.[1] Let us describe country i's demand function for money as follows:

$$L_i = kY_iP + l_ir, \text{ where } i = 1, n \tag{1}$$

and

$$k > 0, l_i < 0,$$

and where L_i is the demand for nominal money on the part of country i; k is the nominal income coefficient of the demand for money – assumed to be the same for all countries; and Y_i is the level of real income prevailing in country i. P is the world's price level – assumed to be the same in all countries. The interest-rate coefficient of the demand for money in country i is l_i, where $l_i/Y_i = w_i$, and where w_i is assumed to be constant. Finally, r is the world's interest rate – assumed to be the same in all countries.[2]

Starting from equation (1), country i's demand function for money, the amount of additional nominal money demanded between two points in time, $\dot{L}_i$, by country i is as follows:[3]

$$\dot{L}_i = kP\dot{Y}_i + kY_i\dot{P} + l_i\dot{r} + r\dot{l}_i, \tag{2}$$

where a dot over a variable represents the change in that variable over the time period. Thus, the increase in the demand for money depends crucially upon the change in the level of real income, the change in the

---

[1] For several reasons an interest rate is not the price of money. In the first place, money often has an explicit yield in the form of lower service charges or preferential borrowing rates. Secondly, holding short-term bonds is only one alternative to holding money, and for this reason, some average of the price of money in terms of other alternatives must also be included in its price. Finally, the rate of interest refers only to the price one must pay to hold money for one period, whereas the price of money includes its price in perpetuity.

[2] See [2, p. 47].

[3] The interaction term, $k\dot{Y}_i\dot{P}$, is assumed to be so small that it can be neglected without affecting the argument.

world's price level, and the change in the level of the world's price term for money.

At this stage of the development of the model, we can bring in the unique aspects of the IFI hypothesis. According to Despres, Kindleberger, and Salant, "Banks and other financial intermediaries, unlike traders, are paid to give up liquidity. The United States is no more in deficit when it lends long and borrows short than is a bank when it makes a loan and enters a deposit on its books" [2, p. 44]. Thus, the unique role of the United States is that of major supplier of money to the rest of the world. In an extreme form, in order to simplify the analysis without loss of generality, we can consider the United States as the sole supplier of money to the world. Thus, from one equilibrium position to the next, the increase in the world's supply of money, $\dot{M}S$, originates in the United States. In order to maintain equilibrium, the world's increase in the demand for money must equal the world's increase in the supply of money. Thus,

$$\sum_i \dot{L}_i = \dot{M}S. \tag{3}$$

Substituting equation (2) into equation (3) and transposing terms, we obtain the following relationship:

$$\dot{M}S = \dot{P}k\sum_i \dot{Y}_i + k\dot{P}\sum_i Y_i + \dot{r}\sum_i l_i + r\sum_i \dot{l}_i. \tag{4}$$

We are now able to solve for the change in the equilibrium of the world's price level over the time period under consideration:

$$\dot{P} = \frac{\dot{M}S - Pk\sum \dot{Y}_i - \dot{r}\sum l_i - r\sum \dot{l}_i}{k\sum Y_i}. \tag{5}$$

As stated earlier, l_i/Y_i equals w_i, where w_i is a constant for each country i, and therefore $\dot{l}_i = w_i \dot{Y}_i$. Substituting again, we obtain the somewhat more familiar relationship of

$$\dot{P} = \frac{\dot{M}S}{k\sum Y_i} - P\bar{g} - \frac{\dot{r}\bar{w}}{k} - \frac{r\bar{w}\bar{g}}{k}, \quad^4 \tag{6}$$

where $\bar{g} = \dfrac{\sum \dot{Y}_i}{\sum Y_i}$, and $\bar{w} = \dfrac{\sum l_i}{\sum Y_i}$.

[4] Growth in real output, Y_i, and the proportional interest-rate coefficient of the demand for money, w_i, are assumed to be independent such that $\sum w_i \dot{Y}_i = \bar{w}\sum \dot{Y}_i$.

Here the absolute change in the equilibrium price level is functionally related to the increase in the money supply of the United States, the real rate of growth of the world economy, and the change in the world's price term for money. Equation (6) represents the equilibrium change in the price level of the world. We are now able to go back to the increase in the demand for money by each country i, because we have ensured the completeness of the system insofar as the increase in the supply of money is equal to the increase in the demand for money. Hence from equations (2) and (6) we obtain

$$\dot{L}_i = kP\dot{Y}_i + l_i\dot{r} + r\dot{l}_i + kY_i \left(\frac{\dot{M}S}{k\Sigma Y_i} - P\bar{g} - \frac{\dot{r}\bar{w}}{k} - \frac{r\bar{w}\bar{g}}{k} \right). \qquad (7)$$

Cancelling terms, we obtain the following:

$$\dot{L}_i = p_i\dot{M}S + (kP + rw_i)(\dot{Y}_i - \bar{g}Y_i) + (w_i - \bar{w})Y_i\dot{r},^5 \qquad (8)$$

where $p_i = Y_i/\Sigma Y_i$.

This then represents the equilibrium increase in money—both demand and supply—for each and every country i.

Now, for any country i other than the United States, insofar as we have assumed that all the increase in the supply of money comes about via the monetary authorities of the United States, the increase in money must reveal itself in the balance of payments.[6] Thus the increase in the stock of money is equal to the over-all surplus in the balance of payments or, in other words, exports less imports plus net capital inflows. Hence,

$$\dot{L}_i = X_i - M_i + K_i, \qquad (9)$$

where X_i is country i's export of goods and services, M_i is country i's import of goods and services, and K_i is this country's net international capital inflow. Transposing the terms, we obtain an expression for country i's net capital inflows:

$$K_i = -(X_i - M_i) + \dot{L}_i, \qquad (10)$$

and substituting equation (8) into equation (10) we get

---

[5] This assumes that $r\bar{g}$ is sufficiently small so that it can safely be ignored.

[6] Credit creation is ignored in this paper but may, in fact, be very important. A good analysis of credit creation can be found in Mundell [5].

$$K_i = -(X_i - M_i) + (kP + rw_i)(\dot{Y}_i - Y_i\bar{g}) + p_i\dot{M}S + Y_i\dot{r}(w_i - \bar{w}). \quad (11)$$

For the United States, the financial intermediary nation, the increase in domestically held money does not come solely from balance-of-payments surpluses. Being the intermediary nation, the United States is the world's producer of money and, therefore, the increase in domestically held money equals the amount of domestically produced money less the over-all payments deficit. Hence,

$$\dot{L}_{US} = X_{US} - M_{US} + K_{US} + \dot{M}S. \quad (9')$$

Solving for net capital inflows into the United States, we get

$$K_{US} = -(X_{US} - M_{US}) + \dot{L}_{US} - \dot{M}S. \quad (10')$$

Substituting equation (8) into equation (10') and combining terms, we obtain

$$K_{US} = -(X_{US} - M_{US}) - (1 - p_{US})\dot{M}S$$
$$+ (kP + rw_{US})(\dot{Y}_{US} - Y_{US}\bar{g}) + Y_{US}\dot{r}(w_{US} - \bar{w}). \quad (11')$$

With this formulation for net capital inflows into the United States, we have most of the essence of the IFI hypothesis. Despres, Kindleberger, and Salant argue that, unless pushed to extremes, the change in the interest-rate coefficient, $w_{US} - \bar{w}$, is, in fact, very small. This can be seen from their statement that "an attempt to halt the capital outflow by raising rates in the United States either would have little effect over any prolonged period or else would cripple European growth" [2, pp. 46–47]. Needless to say, the size of $w_{US} - \bar{w}$ is an empirical question.

From the equation determining the capital flows we can also understand how the authors can conclude:

> With capital markets unrestricted, attempts to correct the "deficit" by ordinary macro-economic weapons are likely to fail. It may be possible to expand the current account surplus at first by deflation of United States income and prices relative to those of Europe; but gross financial capital flows will still exceed real transfers of goods and services so long as capital formation remains high in Europe [2, p. 43].

This is most easily seen if we solve for the over-all balance of payments of the United States. Analytically this is nothing more than adding exports and subtracting imports from the net-capital-inflow equation—equation (11′). This is shown as equation (12):

$$B_{US} = -(1 - p_{US})\dot{M}S + (kP + rw_{US})(\dot{Y}_{US} - Y_{US}\bar{g}) + Y_{US}\dot{r}(w_{US} - \bar{w}), \quad (12)$$

where B_{US} is the over-all balance of payments of the United States.

From this relationship, the current account does not enter into the determination of the over-all balance of payments. In fact, any increase or decrease in the current-account surplus of the United States will be matched *pari passu* by an increase or decrease in the deficit on capital account. Furthermore, the only factors that will affect the over-all balance of payments of the United States are the absolute increase in the supply of money in the United States, the relative rate of income growth between the United States and Europe (or—in the authors' own phrase—"capital formation"), and finally, the diminutive effect (according to Despres, Kindleberger, and Salant) of changes in the price term for money. In one sense, the authors err when they imply that monetary policy, one of the "ordinary macro-economic weapons," will not succeed. This, however, may be explained by their implicit assumption (found also in their description of the goods market) that Europe is a "small country," i.e., $p_{US} = 1$. In this sense, $1 - p_{US}$ would equal zero.

So far we have implicitly been referring to the liquidity definition of the United States balance of payments and its implied definition of net capital inflows as excluding increases in American liquid liabilities to foreigners. When we move to the official-settlements definition of the balance of payments—which appears to be far preferable—we have to include an analysis of changes in American liquid liabilities to private foreigners. Despres, Kindleberger, and Salant [2, p. 49] argue that foreigners, in general, will wish to accumulate liquid dollar assets for dollar-transactions purposes and possibly as compensating balances for dollar debts. Thus, net private capital inflows into the United States additionally will be a function of changes in the level of foreign dollar transactions, ΔXSA. Adding this to the net-capital-inflows equation (11′), we obtain the following over-all equation for private and net capital flows of the United States:

$$K_{US} = -(X_{US} - M_{US}) - (1 - p_{US})\dot{M}S + (kP + rw_{US})(\dot{Y}_{US} - Y_{US}\bar{g})$$
$$+ Y_{US}\dot{r}(w_{US} - \bar{w}) + a\Delta XSA, \quad (13)$$

where $a > 0$.

Equation (13), with a minor adaptation, is the equation which will be used to test the IFI hypothesis in the next section.

2 INTERNATIONAL FINANCIAL INTERMEDIATION: EMPIRICAL ANALYSIS

IN THE first section of this paper, I formally developed the equation for the equilibrium net capital inflow of the international financial intermediary, the United States. In this section, I plan to test that model as simply and as thoroughly as the existing data and theory permit. In general, my results support this version of the IFI hypothesis although they do not enable one to distinguish the IFI hypothesis from models such as those found in the work of Mundell [6] or Laffer [4].

The data (see the Appendix) are on a quarterly basis and go from the first quarter of 1958 through the last quarter of 1967. Thus, there are forty observations of the balance-of-payments data for the United States and of other variables.

Prior to the actual testing of the model, I want to make one modest adjustment. The average rate of growth in the world, $\bar{g}$, can be decomposed into two separate factors: the growth rates of the United States and the rest of the world. Thus, $\dot{Y}_{US} - Y_{US}\bar{g}$ becomes $(1 - p_{US})\dot{Y}_{US} - p_{US}\dot{Y}_F$. The equation for the net capital inflow of the United States now reads as follows:

$$K_{US} = -(X_{US} - M_{US}) - (1 - p_{US})\dot{M}S - (kP + rw_{US})p_{US}\dot{Y}_F$$
$$+ (kP + rw_{US})(1 - p_{US})\dot{Y}_{US} + Y_{US}\dot{r}(w_{US} - \bar{w}) + a\Delta XSA. \quad (14)$$

The empirical counterparts to the above theoretical variables are as follows: [7]

---

[7] The actual data and their sources are in the Appendix.

K_{US} is the net private capital flow of the United States (both foreign and domestic) plus errors and omissions;

$X_{US} - M_{US}$ is the total current-account balance of the United States;

$\dot{M}S$ is the change in the money supply of the United States;

$\dot{Y}_F$ is the change in a weighted average of foreign industrial production indices;

$\dot{Y}_{US}$ is the change in the industrial production index of the United States;

ΔXSA is the monthly change in the seasonally adjusted monthly exports of the United States; and

$Y_{US}\dot{r}$ is the change in velocity—the industrial production index of the United States divided by the money supply—standardized by the level of the industrial production index.[8]

The results of the first regression are as follows: [9]

$$K = -39.7 - 1.04(X - M) - .419\dot{M}S + 580\dot{Y}_{US}$$
$$\quad (.33) \quad (8.89) \qquad (2.22) \qquad (2.31)$$

$$+ 4.58\dot{Y}_F + .452\Delta XSA + 429Y_{US}\dot{r}.$$
$$(0.11) \qquad (2.08) \qquad (2.28)$$

$$\overline{R}^2 = .724 \qquad F = 14.4 \qquad SEE = 425 \qquad DW = 1.82$$

After eliminating the statistically insignificant variable from the regression we obtain [10]

---

[8] Our theory to date deals with the world's price term for money, which should represent some composite average of alternative assets' nominal yields less the nominal yield on money itself. Estimation of either the composite average or the nominal yield on money is subject to sufficient error virtually to guarantee spurious results. We, therefore, went directly to a measure of velocity, which is the variable the price of money should, in fact, affect.

[9] The numbers in parentheses below the coefficients are the t-tests, e.g., the coefficients divided by their respective standard errors.

[10] Putting this equation in its balance-of-payments form (e.g., $K - X + M$), as was done in Laffer [4], has virtually no effect on either the coefficients or their t-tests. The $\overline{R}^2$ and F are .293 and 3.63, respectively.

$$K = -30.3 \quad - 1.04(X - M) - \quad .425\dot{M}S + 590\dot{Y}_{US}$$
$$(0.33) \ (9.23) \qquad\qquad (2.40) \qquad\qquad (2.53)$$

$$+ \ .456\Delta XSA + 436Y_{US}\dot{r}.$$
$$(2.24) \qquad\qquad (2.48)$$

$$\bar{R}^2 = .724 \qquad F = 17.8 \qquad SEE = 418 \qquad DW = 1.80$$

Increases and decreases in foreign income are found not to have a statistically significant effect on net capital inflows of the United States. This is the lone piece of evidence that mars the otherwise confirming results for this version of the IFI hypothesis.

The IFI hypothesis postulates that the partial derivative of the net private capital movements with respect to the current account should, in fact, be minus one. The net regression coefficient was -1.04, which is less than one-half of one standard error away from minus one. The change in the money-supply variable presents the strongest evidence in support of this version of the IFI hypothesis, even though it is tacitly rejected by the authors of the IFI hypothesis. An increase in the money supply of the United States of one billion dollars during a quarter is associated with an additional net capital outflow of 425 million dollars.[11] This relationship (425:1000) approximates the proportion of world income earned by countries with convertible currencies other than the United States, $1 - p_{US}$.[12] If the United States were not a producer of the international money, we should expect to find a positive relationship between net capital inflows and changes in the money supply. To the extent that the United States is not the sole producer of money in the world, the coefficient of the change in the money-supply variable is biased upward, i.e., the true coefficient should be more negative.

Increases in the industrial production index of the United States also fit neatly into this version of the IFI hypothesis. When the index is converted to roughly equivalent GNP terms, this relationship between the industrial production index and the balance of payments can be interpreted as stating that a one billion dollar increase in GNP will lead to a net inflow of approximately one hundred million dollars,

[11] In terms of proportions, this would be roughly 30 per cent.
[12] John Exter of First National City Bank has been perhaps the major proponent of this view.

ceteris paribus. This coefficient is almost identical with the coefficient found in Laffer [4]. It also strikes at the very heart of traditional policy and theory, insofar as an increase in domestic income improves the country's balance of payments. Also, in the earlier study it was found that an increase in domestic income causes a deterioration in the current account and an improvement in the capital account that more than compensates for the deterioration of the current account. These results are found here too.

Changes in the seasonally adjusted level of exports from the United States—changes in the level of foreign dollar transactions—are also found to be empirically relevant. Their relationship to net capital inflows approximates what might be expected. Foreigners hold approximately one-half a quarter's transactions in dollar balances. Naturally, increases in foreign dollar transactions are, on the average, greater than increases in American exports; but, similarly, increases in foreign dollar balances are, on the average, greater than the increases in their deposits in the United States.

The final variable, $Y_{US}r$, is also statistically significant. The principal policy conclusion coming from this variable, as Despres, Kindleberger, and Salant state, is that one cannot really hope to use interest-rate policy as a tool for correcting the balance of payments.

All in all, it does not appear that this version of the IFI hypothesis is to be rejected as statistically insignificant, or as unimportant. The actual data and the theory mesh quite nicely, even without any lags.

To summarize, it is somewhat overwhelming, even to a fervent adherent of the classical theory of balance-of-payments adjustment, to see just how closely the hypothesis fits the actual data on a quarterly basis. During the period from the first quarter of 1958 through the fourth quarter of 1967, many environmental factors changed substantially, and these changes could conceivably have had a major influence on the balance of payments of the United States. Yet, one can scarcely find a ripple of their transitory effects, let alone any lasting ones.[13] These results were obtained without an intricate and complex econometric or theoretical structure. The model assumes that adjustment is instantaneous and that coefficients are linear as well as identical across nations, and it includes a mere handful of variables. None-

[13] See Cooper [1] and Laffer [3].

theless, the hypothesis it represents appears to be relevant from an empirical point of view.

The conclusions from a classical analysis of the balance of payments warrant far more attention than they have been getting. Deficits need not imply disequilibrium in any meaningful sense of the word, and there is no evidence that they do. Lack of confidence in the dollar does, perhaps, represent a misunderstanding of the world economy and not any true weakness of the dollar. Policy, unless extreme, appears to have had little, if any, effect on the balance of payments. Finally, supplying external as well as internal liquidity is well within the powers of a private capital market.

APPENDIX: THE DATA

Date	K_{US} (1)	$X - M$ (2)	$\dot{M}S$ (3)	ΔXSA (4)	$\dot{Y}_{US}$ (5)	$\dot{Y}_F$ (6)	$Y_{US}\dot{r}$ (7)
58-I	−232	107	−6.50	−532	−4.5	−.4	.347
58-II	−934	89	1.90	57	3.8	−.4	−3.897
58-III	175	−325	2.10	32	3.9	1.1	−3.684
58-IV	−243	63	7.10	−46	4.2	1.0	1.031
59-I	546	−559	−4.80	−142	4.4	3.1	−11.200
59-II	600	−697	.60	32	5.1	2.7	−6.276
59-III	878	−825	.80	438	−5.9	3.2	8.418
59-IV	−144	−171	2.90	−3	5.5	5.6	−4.647
60-I	31	41	−5.90	382	1.0	−1.3	−7.230
60-II	−77	292	−1.10	258	−.9	4.5	.038
60-III	−609	14	1.90	198	−1.8	.9	4.176
60-IV	−1998	1260	4.20	22	−4.2	2.1	9.674
61-I	−958	971	−3.90	139	.2	1.6	−4.179
61-II	−845	746	.50	−250	7.1	2.1	−9.131
61-III	600	79	1.80	285	1.1	1.1	.398
61-IV	−1358	1080	6.30	187	3.6	3.2	1.700
62-I	−491	462	−4.60	−76	1.4	.7	−6.409
62-II	−256	866	−.40	435	1.6	.9	−2.380
62-III	−948	41	.60	−40	1.2	2.5	−.861
62-IV	−1030	918	6.60	−75	−.7	−.2	7.447
63-I	−241	670	−4.00	−62	2.2	1.0	−6.800
63-II	−351	953	.70	567	4.2	4.7	−4.411
63-III	−64	−110	2.30	58	−.1	2.8	2.418
63-IV	−1082	1490	6.70	397	1.4	4.1	5.019
64-I	−1382	1700	−4.40	554	2.2	4.1	−7.129
64-II	−1166	1330	.50	−96	2.6	.3	−2.582
64-III	−330	653	3.70	338	2.4	1.7	.902
64-IV	−1239	1940	6.90	186	4.1	3.3	2.093
65-I	−1583	1080	−5.10	−765	2.6	1.3	−8.188
65-II	−818	1340	.60	1400	2.0	3.1	−1.659
65-III	−64	249	3.60	−115	.8	1.8	2.706
65-IV	−1260	1390	8.90	36	5.2	2.0	2.990
66-I	−945	825	−4.20	408	5.0	5.6	−9.983
66-II	−173	699	.80	117	2.8	.4	−2.257
66-III	668	−449	1.10	267	1.2	2.5	−.193
66-IV	−739	1080	6.10	147	1.8	1.5	4.163
67-I	−1096	721	−3.90	312	−3.1	.4	−.483
67-II	508	564	2.40	6	−.8	1.7	3.279
67-III	1313	−425	4.10	136	1.2	3.9	2.756
67-IV	−63	831	8.80	−17	5.2	8.0	2.884

(*continued*)

SOURCES:

Column 1. Net capital flows in millions of dollars is the sum of (a) "Transactions in U.S. Private Assets (net)," line 32 of "U.S. International Transactions," table 1, page 31 of the *Survey of Current Business,* September, 1968; (b) "Transactions in Foreign Assets in the U.S.," line 50 of the above table; and (c) "Errors and Omissions," line 60 of the above table, and previous issues of the *Survey of Current Business.*

Column 2. Current account in millions of dollars is the balance on goods, services, and unilateral transfers (net), line 31 of "U.S. International Transactions," table 1, page 31 of the *Survey of Current Business,* September, 1968, and previous issues. This account may also be obtained by the summation of the balance on goods and services, line 23, and unilateral transfers (net), line 25 of the above table.

Column 3. Money supply, defined as the total of demand deposits and currency, is from "Money Supply and Related Data," page A-16 of the *Federal Reserve Bulletin,* February, 1968, and previous issues. Quarterly changes were calculated from "not seasonally adjusted" end-of-quarter figures. These data are in billions of dollars.

Column 4. Seasonally adjusted exports of goods and services (excluding transfers under military grants) in millions of dollars is line 2 of "U.S. International Transactions – Seasonally Adjusted," table 2, page 32 of the *Survey of Current Business,* September, 1968, and previous issues. Quarterly changes were based on these end-of-quarter figures.

Column 5. Index of Industrial Production (U.S., 1957–59 = 100) is from the *Federal Reserve Bulletin,* Industrial Production S.A., February, 1968, page A-52, and previous issues. Quarterly changes were based on these end-of-quarter figures.

Column 6. Index of Industrial Production (Foreign, 1957–59 = 100) is a composite index with a weighting based on dollar GNP of the included countries for the period 1957–59. The data for the individual indices are from Appendix Section C: "Historical Data for Selected Series," *Business Conditions Digest* (previously *Business Cycle Developments*), Department of Commerce, Bureau of the Census, December, 1969. OECD, Europe, and Canada are on page 105; and Japan is on page 107. The composite index was calculated on a quarterly basis and quarterly changes were derived from these figures for ends of quarters.

Column 7. Quarterly change in velocity, standardized for income, is identical to the quarterly change in the ratio of Index of Industrial Production (U.S.) to the level of money supply, multiplied by the Index of Industrial Production. See above, paragraphs 3 and 5, for the sources.

REFERENCES

1. Cooper, Richard, "The Interest Equalization Tax: An Experiment in the Separation of Capital Markets." Paper No. 78, Economic Growth Center, Yale University.
2. Despres, Emile, Kindleberger, Charles P., and Salant, Walter S., "The Dollar and World Liquidity—A Minority View." *Economist,* February 5, 1966. Reprinted in Thomas D. Willett and Lawrence H. Officer, eds., *The International Monetary System—Problems and Proposals.* Englewood Cliffs, N.J., Prentice-Hall, Inc., 1969.
3. Laffer, Arthur B., "Short-Term Capital Movements and the Voluntary Foreign Credit Restraint Program." Unpublished paper.
4. ——— "An Antitraditional Theory of the Balance of Payments." Unpublished paper.
5. Mundell, Robert A., "Growth and the Balance of Payments," in *Monetary Problems of the International Economy.* Chicago, University of Chicago Press, 1968.
6. ——— "The International Distribution of Money in a Growing World Economy." Unpublished manuscript.

COMMENTS

JOSEPH M. BURNS

RICE UNIVERSITY

The papers by Salant and Laffer on international financial intermediation (IFI) are of current interest. Balance-of-payments statistics reveal this country to have been in an almost continuous deficit position for the past two decades. In the first part of this period, the deficits were welcomed by most economists, owing to the "dollar shortage" in foreign countries. More recently, the deficits have been viewed with great concern by most economists, owing to the "dollar glut" abroad.

The examination of IFI may well be the most important recent development in the field of international economics. The examination was first carried out by Kindleberger in his pioneering article of 1965.[1] It was expanded and refined by Despres, Kindleberger, and Salant in their 1966 article.[2] Since that time, there has been much discussion of IFI.[3] In their papers, both Salant and Laffer continue this timely discussion.

Salant's paper examines the IFI hypothesis, pointing out that much of the criticism advanced against it is invalid. In addition, he argues that other parts of the criticism do not necessarily disprove this theorem.

Laffer, in his paper, seeks to formalize the hypothesis so that its implications can be systematically derived. In addition, he seeks to

NOTE: I was at the University of California, Los Angeles, when this material was prepared. My thanks go to Benjamin Klein for many helpful discussions on the subject.

[1] Charles P. Kindleberger, "Balance-of-Payments Deficits and the International Market for Liquidity." *Essays in International Finance*, No. 46. Princeton, International Finance Section, 1965.

[2] Emile Despres, Charles P. Kindleberger, Walter S. Salant, "The Dollar and World Liquidity—A Minority View." *Economist*, February 5, 1966, pp. 526–529. Reprinted by The Brookings Institution, Washington, April, 1966.

[3] See, for example, Lawrence H. Officer and Thomas D. Willett, eds., *The International Monetary System*. Englewood Cliffs, N.J., Prentice-Hall, Inc., 1969, Part II, Section A; and George N. Halm, "International Financial Intermediation: Deficits Benign and Malignant." *Essays in International Finance*, No. 68. Princeton, International Finance Section, 1968.

test it. Laffer points out that his results tend to support the IFI hypothesis, while not necessarily disproving alternative hypotheses.

The inconclusive nature of the results of the empirical studies would appear to be, in part at least, attributable to the imprecise nature of what, in fact, the IFI hypothesis is. From Section 2 of Salant's paper, I would guess that what Salant has in mind are, among other things, the possible explanations of why IFI occurs. An examination of Laffer's introductory comments on what the hypothesis points out also raises some question as to what it is. Each of the statements is in a sense correct, but also in a sense incorrect, or at least, imprecise.

Salant's discussion of both what is entailed by IFI, and what its effects are, is very interesting and potentially very useful. If the nature and effects of IFI could be clarified, empirical implications could probably be more easily obtained. At that point, empirical studies would probably be more productive than they appear to be at present. In contrast to the 1966 article, the policy implications of Salant's paper appear to be well stated. In the earlier article, the alleged compatibility of IFI with the existing international monetary system was unwarranted.

IFI differs from domestic financial intermediation in the entity taking part in the intermediation: domestically, the entity is a financial intermediary institution—a commercial bank, a savings and loan association, a mutual savings bank, a credit union; internationally, it is the United States as a whole. Thus, the United States may be engaged in IFI with, or without, the participation of what we consider a domestic financial intermediary institution.

IFI also differs from domestic financial intermediation in the nature of the assets purchased and issued: domestically, the assets purchased and issued are financial securities—equities or debt;[4] internationally, the assets may be real on one side of the transaction.[5] Thus,

---

[4] See, for example, John G. Gurley and E. S. Shaw, *Money in a Theory of Finance.* Washington, The Brookings Institution, 1960, pp. 94 and 192; and Joseph M. Burns, "The Relative Decline of Commercial Banks: A Note." *Journal of Political Economy,* Vol. 77, No. 1 (January/February, 1969), pp. 122–129.

[5] The broader definition of intermediation has interesting implications for the domestic economy. In particular, it would suggest that corporations may be regarded as intermediaries between real assets and financial assets. I am indebted to Raymond Goldsmith for helpful discussions on this point.

there would appear to be no reason why the financial outflows and inflows associated with IFI would have to be equal. To simplify the analysis, I shall assume that such financial flows are equal. This assumption is implicit in much of the discussion about IFI.

Financial intermediation is a type of financial innovation. Such innovations may be in direct, as well as indirect, finance. Necessary conditions giving rise to domestic financial innovations include the existence of finance costs facing borrowers and lenders. The finance costs are essentially twofold in nature: both transaction costs and uncertainty facing savers and investors (together with the assumption of risk aversion).

Financial innovations—direct or indirect—serve to reduce the finance costs of savers and investors, thereby bringing about a greater volume of saving and investment (on the assumption that both saving and investment are interest-elastic to some extent). Financial intermediaries are in a unique position to reduce these finance costs. The large size and diversity of their assets enables them to pool the real risk of savers; and the large size and diversity of the securities they issue enables them to pool the risk of illiquidity facing the savers.[6]

For IFI to take place, an additional factor must be added to the conditions stated above: differences in spreads as between liquid and illiquid assets in two countries or regions. Needless to say, there are infinite degrees of liquidity or illiquidity of an asset. Thus, the difference in spreads would have to refer to those found between assets of comparable liquidity.[7]

One important qualification of this point regarding the difference in interest-rate spreads should be mentioned—namely, that the costs entailed in IFI by the United States would have to be as great as they are domestically within the United States. If this were not the case, then IFI could take place even if spreads were identical. There does not appear to be any a priori reason why such a difference in costs would exist. It is, however, possible that differences in governmental

---

[6] These points are covered more fully in Joseph M. Burns, "On the Effects of Financial Innovations," *Quarterly Review of Economics and Business,* Vol. 11, No. 2 (Summer, 1971), pp. 83–95.

[7] If both the long-term and short-term assets in one country differed in liquidity from their counterparts in another country, the yield curves would not necessarily intersect.

regulations might enable financial intermediation to be carried out in a more efficient manner internationally by the United States than within our own country. If this were the case, then the qualification raised would be relevant.

The differences in spreads, as Salant suggests, may be attributed to a difference in either liquidity preference or the efficiency of finance — direct or indirect — between the two countries or regions. The difference in the efficiency of finance may, in turn, be attributed to a difference in either the market structure of the finance industry in the two countries (regions) or the efficiency of a given market structure. The empirical distinction between these latter cases is extremely difficult, owing to the problem entailed in separating the operating costs from the profits of a financial institution.[8]

There does not appear to be any a priori reason for the existence of such differences in liquidity preference. In addition, some empirical evidence appears to cast serious doubt on this explanation of the existence of IFI.[9] This is not to say that such differences may not exist. In this connection, it is of interest to note that Kindleberger, in his 1965 article, makes no mention as to why such differences should occur. Yet, these differences were the *raison d'être*, according to Kindleberger, of IFI. In the Despres-Kindleberger-Salant article of 1966, the only reference to why such a difference might exist is a statement that Europeans have had half a century of wars, inflations, and capital levies. Of course, in the 1966 article, the authors present two other explanations of why IFI might take place. In Salant's present article, again no mention is made of why such differences might exist.

As to differences in financial efficiency — both direct and indirect — there are strong reasons for believing the American financial structure to be more efficient than the European one. An appropriate explanation of this difference in financial efficiency would have to go into the factors affecting financial developments within a country. Suffice it to say here that financial developments in a country are affected,

[8] Cf. Joseph M. Burns, "An Examination of the Operating Efficiency of Three Financial Intermediaries." *Journal of Financial and Quantitative Analysis,* Vol. IV, No. 5 (January, 1970), pp. 541–558.

[9] See Salant's references to Lamfalussy's writings. Also cf. Richard N. Cooper, *The Economics of Interdependence: Economic Policy in the Atlantic Community.* New York, McGraw-Hill, 1968, Chap. V.

among other things, by the nature and level of a country's real development.[10]

In any event, if a difference in interest-rate spreads did exist, there would be an incentive for IFI to take place. As Salant points out, once IFI takes place, the difference in interest-rate spreads, when comparing the two countries, is likely to be reduced—and, in the extreme case, eliminated.

As suggested earlier, foreigners will benefit by the IFI of the United States via the reduction in the finance costs of both its savers and investors. In this way, the level of saving and of investment will be enhanced (on the assumption made earlier about the interest-elasticity of these two schedules). For this reason, as Salant points out, the criticism advanced by Halm that IFI is a "monetary veil" is invalid.

As for the United States, we will benefit by earning a return in our role as international financial intermediator. Costs, however, are also likely to be present. They will, in fact, be present if the United States desires to retain its present rate of exchange, and if an increase in the volume of IFI serves to diminish foreigners' confidence in the ability of the United States to retain that rate, thereby putting pressure on it. A corollary of the above point is that costs may well be present if the United States wishes to retain an independent monetary policy. In addition, it is interesting to note that if benefits and costs exist for the United States, a particular amount of IFI will be optimal.

In closing, let me comment very briefly about some implications of IFI carried out by the United States. First of all, as Salant and Kindleberger, among others, have suggested, existing definitions of the balance-of-payments position of a country—including the "liquidity" and "official-transactions" ones—do not necessarily indicate whether or not the country is in international-payments equilibrium.[11] A mean-

[10] See, for example, John G. Gurley and E. S. Shaw, "The Growth of Debt and Money in the United States, 1800–1950: A Suggested Interpretation." *Review of Economics and Statistics,* XXXIX (August, 1957), pp. 250–262; John G. Gurley, "Financial Structures in Developing Economies," in D. Krivine, ed., *Fiscal and Monetary Problems in Developing States.* New York, Praeger, 1967; and Richard N. Cooper, *The Economics of Interdependence: Economic Policy in the Atlantic Community.* The Atlantic Policy Studies. New York, McGraw-Hill, Inc., 1968, Chap. V.

[11] Cf. C. P. Kindleberger, "Measuring Equilibrium in the Balance of Payments." *Journal of Political Economy,* Vol. 77, No. 6 (November/December, 1969), pp. 873–891.

ingful criterion of the international-payments position of the United States would appear to be the existence and magnitude of pressure on the exchange rate of the United States dollar.

Secondly, the degree of confidence in the dollar would not necessarily be related solely to the ratio of international reserves of the United States to its liquid liabilities to all foreigners or to official foreigners.[12] Indeed, for a given degree of confidence, this ratio might be expected to diminish, the larger the size of the liquid liabilities – as well as the longer the time period in which the United States maintains the international value of its currency. The first expectation is based on an application of the law of large numbers (as well as an implicit assumption regarding the average size of liability); the second expectation, on the assumption that a learning process about the liquidity of the dollar would enhance foreigners' confidence in it.

FRANCO MODIGLIANI

MASSACHUSETTS INSTITUTE OF TECHNOLOGY

Walter Salant has provided us with a useful and stimulating review of the controversy that has been generated by certain views advocated by Despres, Kindleberger, and himself, which he labels the hypothesis of International Financial Intermediation (IFI). This hypothesis has been given a variety of interpretations, and Salant himself is concerned with several, though it is not always altogether clear which particular interpretation is being defended at any one point.

One interpretation suggested by the title is that the IFI hypothesis consists of the proposition that "IFI behavior" by a country can explain its exhibiting an enduring deficit in its balance of payments. In this connection, "IFI behavior" is defined in Section 1 as the simultaneous expansion of a country's foreign assets and of its liabilities to foreigners. Initially, only financial assets are explicitly included in this definition, but, at a later point, it is suggested that tangible assets (direct investment) should be included too. Furthermore, a balance-of-payments deficit is defined as either a "liquidity" or an "official-settlement" deficit. As long as we confine ourselves to the liquidity definition, I cannot see how anyone could seriously argue against this very broad interpretation of the IFI hypothesis, for it strikes me as little more than a tautology. Clearly, the simultaneous expansions of assets and liabilities will account for an expansion of liabilities and can account, in particular, for an expansion of liquid liabilities, or a liquidity deficit. Since it is an undisputed fact that the United States did exhibit IFI behavior in the relevant period, it is hardly surprising that Salant should conclude again and again that no argument set forth by the critics could reject this interpretation of the IFI hypothesis as applied to the United States. However, the criticism was actually concerned with other interpretations, some of which are reviewed below.

One such interpretation construes the essence of the IFI hypothesis as postulating that the IFI behavior of the United States reflects intermediation, in the narrower sense of intervening between primary lender and final borrowers of foreign countries, either directly through specialized institutions or indirectly through the operation of markets. This is a substantive hypothesis, for the observed IFI behavior could have occurred without strict intermediation, as Salant acknowledges at the beginning of his discussion of "Alternative Theories of Enduring Deficits" in Section 2. Indeed, with the dollar used both as a measure and a medium of exchange in international transactions, one might expect that an expansion of trade would lead foreign transactors to increase the stock of short-term dollar claims. Since the United States was also a net exporter of capital, it follows that both its assets and liabilities might have been expected to rise in any event. In fact, one might expect that many other developed countries would, on balance, also exhibit IFI behavior. Hence, whether the IFI behavior of the United States reflected to a significant extent strict intermediations, because of differences in liquidity preferences or because of the greater efficiency of its financial institutions, is an interesting empirical question. Unfortunately, after an extensive examination of the arguments and the available facts, Salant has to admit that the evidence is so far inadequate for a reliable answer, and I can only associate myself with this conclusion.

A third and much bolder interpretation, which the authors themselves have felt it appropriate to qualify, is that for an IFI country, and for the United States in particular, an enduring deficit does not imply any real imbalance but is instead a healthy symptom of growth and hence should not be a source of concern. In my view, while this position is substantially valid—at least as a first approximation—in the case of a conventional financial intermediary, there are some real pitfalls in extending it by analogy to an IFI country and to the United States in particular. The point is that a conventional financial intermediary (with appropriate qualification for the central bank and, to some extent, the banking system) can expand its assets only within limits set by the need of finding willing holders of its liabilities. As long as it can find such holders, there may well be little ground for concern regarding the rate at which its liabilities expand. But these limits do not apply to the United States, since an increase in its liabilities to foreigners in excess of what the foreign private sector would wish to hold must, at least in the first instance, be absorbed by the central bank in order to maintain the fixed parity. Accordingly, the analogy with financial intermediaries and the implication that one need not be concerned with the rate of increase in liabilities has some validity as long as the increased liabilities are *willingly* held by private foreign holders, i.e., as long as there is *no deficit on the official-settlements basis.* It follows that the size of the deficit on the liquidity basis may not per se be worthy of much attention. This is an implication of the IFI hypothesis on which Despres-Kindleberger-Salant have justifiably laid great stress, though it must be recognized that many others reached the same conclusion without recourse to the IFI hypothesis. This view is, by now, largely accepted for the United States, while other countries have long relied on a different definition of deficit—typically, the basic balance, which involves the increase in net rather than gross, short-term liabilities.

But, for the reasons put forward above, the conclusion that in employing an analogy with conventional financial intermediation, one need not be concerned with the rate of growth of liabilities or the size of the deficit, loses much of its validity when it comes to the official-settlements deficit. This does not mean that any continuing deficit on official settlements is *ipso facto* an indication of balance-of-payments disturbances that need to be corrected. Such a deficit does mean that the strength of the dollar on foreign-exchange markets is being maintained through central-bank intervention, and in this sense, it might be taken as prima facie indication of difficulties; however, for a variety of reasons, it is not conclusive evidence.

On the one hand, some expansion of dollar reserves by foreign central banks may be appropriate, depending on the nature of prevailing arrangements with respect to reserve assets and their growth. On the other hand, one cannot safely infer that the deficit is of a bearable size from the mere fact that the foreign central banks are absorbing these deficits in their dollar reserves, when this result is achieved through the exercise of a variety of pressures (so-called unwilling holding). Again, the official-settlements deficit may hide the extent to which the dollar is being supported by central-bank operations, owing to the practice of some foreign central banks of reducing their direct holdings of dollar assets reserves by lending them to their commercial banks, which, in turn, hold dollar assets. Since these are recorded as private holdings, they do not appear in the official-settlements deficit. Last but not least, a strong current showing on an official-settlements basis, while it is an indication of current strength, may not necessarily imply a healthy state of affairs if, as in recent times, it results from a large volume of short-term borrowing and volatile foreign financial investments, accompanied by a weak current account.

Nonetheless, all of the above qualifications do not change the basic conclusion that, beyond some point, a deficit on an official-settlements basis will become excessive, a conclusion with which Salant would presumably not disagree, as is apparent from his final remarks. Unfortunately, it also is clear from these remarks that the IFI hypothesis, however interpreted, cannot be of much help in identifying just where that border line lies.

AUTHOR INDEX

SUBJECT INDEX

Accelerators, in international firms, investment behavior model, 368
Accounting policies, *see* National accounts
Acquisitions, *see* British investment policy; Direct investment and balance-of-payments model; French investment policy; German investment policy; Take-over of Canadian firms study
Activities model, 10
  capital flow view of, 173–175
  compared with transactor models, 246–249
  difficulties with, 175–176
  portfolio view of, 174–175
Adjustable pegs system, 627
Adjustment mechanism deficiencies, 288
Aggregate time-series model, asset equations, 329–330
  compared with Commerce Department model, 330–332, 338–339
  data for, 332
  financial equations for, 327–328
  financial equations results, 335–338
  investment in current assets, 334–335
  minimization of exchange-rate losses, 328–329
  and mobility associated with international firms, 326–327
  and Modigliani-Miller theorem, 327–328
  plant and equipment expenditures, 332–334
  results for, 345–346
  symbols used, 346*t*
Aggregation, and capital movements, 317
  in foreign-investment studies, 366
American Economic Association, 246
American Ford Company, 400
Annual Report of the Council of Economic Advisers, 5
"Anti-traditional" theory, and international financial intermediation hypothesis, 652–654
Antitrust laws, and foreign take-overs, 496
Asset-demand equation, 174

Asset equations, in aggregative time-series model, 329–330
Asset preference theory, in closed economy, 93–96
  in two-country model, 96–102
  See also Asset preferences
Asset preferences, and activity models compared with transactor models, 247
  and international financial intermediation hypothesis, 646–647
Assets, annual changes in, 359
  of Canadian-based subsidiaries, 472
  in Canadian taxation-effects model, 521–527
  data sources for total changes in, 350–351
  long-term, and financial intermediation, 634
  purchased abroad, 10
  in two-equation model, 255, 270–271
  See also Current assets; Stock of assets
Australia, British capital outflows to, 41
  and British direct investments, 38

Balance on capital account, and balance on current account, 15
Balance of current transactions, 30–32
Balance of indebtedness, in portfolio-balance theory, 100
Balance of monetary movements, 30–32
Balance of payments, in activity models, 173
  British, 80–81, 85–87
  and British exchange-control regulations, 40–41
  and capital exports, 83
  and capital mobility of international firms models, 325–326
  and capital movements, 6–7
  and capital restriction, 43
  and direct foreign investment, 85, 324, 371, 432–435
  and domestic price levels, 122
  in EEC financial markets, 58
  and EEC integration, 84
  effects of shifts in exogenous variables, 105–106, 108

689

Forward rates, 188t, 190t–192t
France, capital inflows and outflows, 64, 67t
  economic policies of 1968, 158–159
  long-term interest rates, 74–75, 75t
  private long-term capital flows, 65t
  short-term interest rate movements, 76, 76t
  See also French investment policy
Free-trade output, 48–49
French investment policy, 13–14, 62t, 429–430
  and balance-of-payments problems, 422
  and ban on take-overs, 409–410
  and Community Competition Policy, 406–411
  compared with British and German policies, 416–417, 418t, 419t, 420–421
  and economic planning, 423–425
  and EEC regulations, 413
  and government restrictions, 435–436, 439–441
  and international agreements, 403–404
  and technology gap, 426–427
  under Finance Minister G.-d'Estaing, 1962–1965, 404–411
  under Finance Minister M. Debré, 1966–1968, 411–414
Full-capacity output, in difference-equation model, 162
  ratio to capital, in balance-of-payments model, 133
Fully employed economy model, findings of, 121–123
  and foreign inflation, 118–121
  and impact of commercial policy on domestic prices, 115–116
  and impact of fiscal policy on domestic prices, 116–118
  and impact of monetary policy on domestic prices, 110–115
  portfolio-balance theory of capital movements in, 102–110

"Gambler's winning" hypothesis, 384
Gaps in Technology, 426–427, 427n
GDP, in economic-growth model, 573–576, 594, 604–605
  and net factor income earned abroad, 566
  and trade restrictions, 48–49
Gelsenkirchner Bergewerk, 415
General Electric Co., 407
Geographic patterns of British long-term inflows and outflows, 32–34
German investment policy, 13–14, 62t, 429–430
  and balance-of-payments problems, 422
  compared with French and British policies, 416–417, 418t, 419t, 420–421
  and government restrictions, 435–436, 439–441
  liberalness of, 414–415
  and oil industry, 415–416
Germany, capital flows and growth rates, 84
  capital inflows and outflows, 67t
  private long-term capital flows, 65t
  short-term interest rate movements, 76, 76t
  See also German investment policy
GM-Frigidaire Co., 404
GNP, deviations from time trend of, 12
  in economic-growth model, 564, 572–573, 578, 604–605
  government demand as fixed proportion of, 578
  and net factor income earned abroad, 566–571, 593–694, 605–606
  and short-term foreign assets, 274–275
  and two-equation model, 280–281
Gold-dollar monetary system, and international financial intermediation hypothesis, 626
Government lending and borrowing, among EEC countries, 69–70
Government restrictions, and capital flow, 12
  and EEC integration, 77
  on foreign investment, 397n, 435–436
  in Great Britain, 399–403
  in Japanese bank-borrowing study, 211
  and mobility of capital, 2–3, 4–5
  and short-term capital movements in EEC countries, 70
  on trade and capital exports compared, 86
  See also Balance-of-payments policies; Capital controls
Government revenues, in Canadian taxation-effects model, 538
Government saving, in GNP-saved estimates, 572
Government spending, and demand-to-capital ratio, 155
  and foreign inflation, 120
Grants, and British official capital movements, 34–36
Great Britain, balance-of-payments stabilization in, 85–87
  control of capital exports by, 88–89
  direct-investment holdings in U.S., 448, 448n
  as financial middleman, 27, 78–80

699

Interest rates (cont.)
    and direct foreign investment, 461–462
    domestic, and capital flow, 12
    in economic-growth model, 564, 565, 577, 578, 581, 596
    in EEC countries, 61, 82–83
    and EEC integration, 56–57, 72–77
    and financial intermediation, 637–638, 678–679
    and flow of short-term funds, 12
    and international capital movements, 121
    in international firms investment-behavior model, 369
    in Japanese bank-borrowing study, 208–209
    and measurement of capital, 93n
    and misspecification of desired stock, 231–233
    in portfolio-adjustment model, 242–243
    and portfolio-balance model, 292–296
    sensitivity of financial capital to, 163
    and short-term capital movements, 289–290, 319–322
    in two-equation model, 267, 275n
Interindustry mix in foreign take-over activity, 477–479, 515–516
    and insignificant associations, 487–496
    and significant associations, 480–481, 482t, 483–486
Internal cash flow, and foreign take-overs, 485
    and interindustry mix in foreign take-overs, 489
Internal funds, and foreign take-overs, 494, 516–517
    in international firms investment-behavior model, 369
International-agency long-term capital flows, and EEC integration, 69–70
International capital movements, *see* Capital movements
International financial intermediation, *see* Financial intermediation and enduring balance-of-payments "deficits" study; Financial intermediation hypothesis; Financial intermediation model
International Financial Statistics, 284
International firms capital-mobility study, aggregative time-series model for, 326–330
    and aggregative time-series model compared with Commerce Department model, 330–332, 338–339
    capital flows covered by, 324
    data sources for, 332, 350–352

and determination of desired levels of current and fixed assets, 347–348
and determination of level of borrowing of foreign currencies, 348–349
evaluation of, 354–355, 365–366
findings of, 345–346, 364–365
goals of, 323
homogeneity of sample for, 362–364
impact of accounting policies on, 361–362, 363t
impact of balance-of-payments programs on, 340–345, 346
and implications of Modigliani-Miller theorem, 355–356
and minimization of exchange-rate losses, 356–359
and minimization of risk of devaluation losses, 348–349
plant and equipment expenditures in, 360–361
and prediction of direct-investment flows, 359–360
and prior models, 325–326
and results with Department of Commerce model, 338–339
and results with proposed model, 332–338
sales and depreciation estimates for, 352–353
International firms investment- and financial-behavior model, and balance-of-payments policy, 391–394
empirical results with, 380–381, 382t–383t, 384–385, 386t, 387–390
equations and variables used for, 368–380
evaluation of, 432–435, 437–439
findings of, 394–396
and movements of capital, 12–13
International Monetary Fund, 73–74, 73n, 86, 268
International monetary system, and adjustment-mechanism deficiencies, 288
International reserves, ratio to domestic money, 653–654
    in two-equation model, 276–277
Interregional commerce, in balance-of-payments model, 133
Intra-EEC capital mobility, changes in, 77–78
    EEC integration and, 51–52, 82–83
    and Eurodollar and Eurobond markets, 71
    and private long-term investments, 61–69
    and public and international agency long-term capital flows, 69–70

Leverage (cont.)
  in international firms investment- and
    financial-behavior model, 370, 380
Liabilities, of EEC countries, 69
  and international financial intermedia-
    tion, 646–647, 683–684
Life-insurance companies, and transactor
  models, 178
Linear homogeneity assumption, 210,
    223–225
Liquidity, and balance-of-payments defi-
    cits, 615, 619
  and capital mobility, 127, 129
  of European household savings, 637
  and fiscal policy, 156–159
  and international financial intermedia-
    tion, 611–612, 621, 628–629, 633–
    641, 649–650, 667, 679
  in portfolio-adjustment model, 240
  reasons for imposing constraints on,
    125, 127

McGraw-Hill, 332, 332n
Machines Bull, 407
Macroeconomic factors, and foreign take-
  over activity, 491–499, 516–517
Manufacturing industries, Canadian, 465,
  478
Marginal efficiency of investment, com-
    pared with cost of funds, 437–438
  in international firms investment- and
    financial-behavior model, 368
  proxy variable for, 433–434
Market values, in foreign direct-invest-
  ment model, 452–453
Markowitz-Tobin theory, 210
Mathematical models, and economic
  planning, 170
Mean-variance approach, 255
Merchandise trade, and capital movements
  model, 203, 204t, 204–205
Mergers, in U.S., 469
    See also Direct foreign investment;
    Take-over of Canadian firms study
Mining and smelting, Canadian, 465
Misallocation of resources, and trade re-
  striction, 47
Misspecification, of desired-stock equa-
    tions, 250–251
  impact on analysis of capital flows, 230–
    236
Mobile labor, 152, 163
Mobility of capital, see Capital mobility
Modigliani-Miller theorem, 370n
  for aggregative time-series model, 327–
    328

and implications for international area,
    355–356
Monetary expansion rates, and price
    levels, 110–115, 122
Monetary factors, in economic-growth
    model, 579, 580, 588
Monetary policy, and international finan-
    cial intermediation hypothesis, 626–
    627
  in portfolio-adjustment model, 242
  and price levels, 110–115, 121
  and short-term capital movements, 287
  and sliding parity, 304–307
Monetary union, for EEC countries, 78
Money supply, and balance-of-payments
    deficits, 622
  and prices, 110–115, 164–165
  in small, fully employed economy, 9–10
Monopolies Commission (Great Britain),
    402
Monopolies and Mergers Act (Great
    Britain), 402
Movements of capital, see Capital move-
    ments
Multicollinearity, 194
  in portfolio-adjustment model, 241
Multinational enterprises, see Interna-
    tional firms
Multiple regression tests, of economic-
    growth model, 581–584

National accounts, impact on international
    firms, and capital-mobility study,
    361–362, 363t
  and net factor income earned abroad,
    568–569
  payments to capital in, 568
National Bureau of Economic Research,
    87
National interest, and English investment
    policy, 403
National Plan (France), 407
Net balances to GNP ratio, 653
Net capital inflows, in financial intermedia-
    tion model, 665–666
Net creditor status, and net factor income
    earned abroad, 566–567
Net debtor status, and net factor income
    earned abroad, 566–567
Net factor income earned abroad, concept
    and measurement of, 565–569
  in economic-growth model, 570–571
  as percentage of GNP, 570–571, 593–
    594, 605–606
  test of assumptions about, 569–570
Net Financial Transfers, 650–652

702

and balance-of-payments deficits, 616–619

Net fixed assets, accounting methods for, 362, 363t

Net national saving function, in economic-growth model, 578

Net outflows, impact of investment on, 390
in international firms investment-behavior model, 369–370
and recessions, 392
See also Net outflows equations

Net-outflows equation, 374
of international firms investment-behavior model, 371, 378, 388
regression coefficients for, 386t

Net private saving by households and business, in GNP-saved estimates, 572

Net Real Transfers, 650–652
and balance-of-payments deficits, 616–619
definition of, 616n

Net worth, in foreign direct-investment model, 511–513
in portfolio-adjustment model, 240

Netherlands, capital inflows and outflows, 64, 67t
direct-investment holdings in U.S., 448, 448n
and foreign investment, 62t
long-term interest rates, 74–75, 75t
private long-term capital flows, 65t
short-term interest rate movements, 76, 76t

New issues, in Canadian taxation-effects model, 538
of EEC countries, 67–68, 68t

New sterling issue, in London capital markets, 39

New Zealand, British capital outflows to, 41
and British exchange-control regulation, 42

Nonfinancial corporations, in transaction models, 176–177

Nonmonetary characteristics, in economic-growth model, 565

Nonprofit foundations, and transactor models, 178

Nonsterling securities, British purchases of, 40n–41n

OECD, Code of Liberalization of Capital Movements of the, 403–404
and technological gaps, 426–427

OECD countries, ratios of net factor in-

come earned abroad to GNP, 566, 567t, 568–570

Oil industry, British, 36
Canadian, 465
and German investment policy, 415–416

One-country models, *see* Capital movements and economic-growth study

Optimum stock determinants, in foreign direct-investment model, 444–447

Organization for Economic Cooperation and Development, *see* OECD

Outflows, *see* Capital movements; Net outflow; Net-outflow equation

Output, and interindustry mix in foreign take-overs, 488
ratio of capital to, 161
relationship between unemployment and, 45–46
See also Full-capacity output; Output per worker

Output per worker, in economic-growth model, 576, 577

Partial-adjustment equations, 219, 221
in international firms investment-behavior model, 371
misspecification of, 233, 234t–235t, 236

Partial-adjustment models, 262

Payments to capital, in national accounts, 568

Pension funds, and transactor models, 178

Perfect competition, 129n–130n

Perfect markets assumption, 355–356

Perfect monopoly, 129n–130n

Perfectly mobile labor, and balance-of-payments model, 132–142

Perpetual income-stream, and measure of physical capital goods, 92–93, 98–99, 98n, 99n

Personal saving, in Canadian taxation-effects study, 530, 535–536

Phillips Curve, 143, 146, 162

Plant and equipment expenditures, in aggregate time-series model, 332–334
estimation of, 365–366
impact of balance-of-payments of 1965–1968 on, 341–343
in international firms and capital-mobility study, 360–361

Policy, of international firms, 364
See also Balance-of-payments policy; Commercial policy; Domestic policy; Fiscal policy; Monetary policy

Polynomial approximation, and estimation of lagged responses, 218–219

Portfolio-adjustment models, 10